Copyright in the Age of Online Access

Information Law Series (INFO)

VOLUME 40

Editor

Prof. P. Bernt Hugenholtz, Institute for Information Law, University of Amsterdam.

Objective & Readership

Publications in the Information Law Series focus on current legal issues of information law and are aimed at scholars, practitioners, and policy makers who are active in the rapidly expanding area of information law and policy.

Introduction & Contents

The advent of the information society has put the field of information law squarely on the map. Information law is the law relating to the production, marketing, distribution, and use of information goods and services. The field of information law therefore cuts across traditional legal boundaries, and encompasses a wide set of legal issues at the crossroads of intellectual property, media law, telecommunications law, freedom of expression, and right to privacy. Recent volumes in the Information Law Series deal with copyright enforcement on the Internet, interoperability among computer programs, harmonization of copyright at the European level, intellectual property and human rights, public broadcasting in Europe, the future of the public domain, conditional access in digital broadcasting, and the 'three-step test' in copyright.

The titles published in this series are listed at the end of this volume.

Copyright in the Age of Online Access

Alternative Compensation Systems in EU Law

João Pedro Quintais

Wolters Kluwer

Published by:
Kluwer Law International B.V.
PO Box 316
2400 AH Alphen aan den Rijn
The Netherlands
Website: www.wolterskluwerlr.com

Sold and distributed in North, Central and South America by:
Wolters Kluwer Legal & Regulatory U.S.
7201 McKinney Circle
Frederick, MD 21704
United States of America
Email: customer.service@wolterskluwer.com

Sold and distributed in all other countries by:
Quadrant
Rockwood House
Haywards Heath
West Sussex
RH16 3DH
United Kingdom
Email: international-customerservice@wolterskluwer.com

Printed on acid-free paper.

ISBN 978-90-411-8667-6

e-book: ISBN 978-90-411-8679-9
web-PDF: ISBN 978-90-411-8680-5

Printed and bound by CPI Group (UK) Ltd, Croydon, CR0 4YY

Table of Contents

Abbreviations

ACS	Alternative Compensation System(s)
ACTA	Anti-Counterfeiting Trade Agreement
AG	Advocate General
ALAI	*Association Littéraire et Artistique Internationale* (International Literary and Artistic Association)
BC	Berne Convention for the Protection of Artistic and Literary Works
BGH	*Bundesgerichtshof* (the German Federal Court of Justice)
BIRPI	*Bureaux Internationaux Reunis pour la Protection de la Propiete Intellectuelle* (United International Bureaux for the Protection of Intellectual Property)
Charter	Charter of Fundamental Rights of the EU
CISAC	*Confédération Internationale des Sociétés d'Auteurs et Compositeurs* (International Confederation of Authors and Composers Societies)
CJEU	Court of Justice of the European Union (former European Court of Justice (ECJ))
CMO(s)	Collective Rights Management Organisation(s)
DRM	Digital Rights Management
ECHR	European Convention on Human Rights
ECL	Extended Collective Licence (or Licensing)
ECtHR	European Court of Human Rights
EP	European Parliament
EU	European Union

GEMA	*Gesellschaft für musikalische Aufführungs- und mechanische Vervielfältigungsrechte* (German society for musical performing and mechanical reproduction rights)
HADOPI	*Haute Autorité pour la Diffusion des œuvres et la Protection des droits d'auteur sur Internet*. Also refers to the law that set up this authority, the Law No. 2009-669 of June 12, 2009, promoting the Dissemination and Protection of Creation on the Internet
ICESCR	International Covenant on Economic, Social and Cultural Rights
ISP	Internet Service Provider(s)
P2P	Peer-to-Peer
RC	Rome Convention for the Protection of Performers, Producers of Phonograms and Broadcasting Organizations
TEU	Treaty on European Union
TFEU	Treaty on the Functioning of the European Union
TPM(s)	Technological Protection Measure(s)
TRIPS	Agreement on Trade-Related Aspects of Intellectual Property Law
UGC	User Created/Generated Content
UDHR	Universal Declaration of Human Rights
VCLT	Vienna Convention on the Law of Treaties
WCT	WIPO Copyright Treaty
WIPO	World Intellectual Property Organization
WIPO Treaties	The WCT and WPPT
WPPT	WIPO Performances and Phonograms Treaty
WTO	World Trade Organization

Figures and Tables

Figures

Tables

Acknowledgements

This book is a slightly revised and updated version of my doctoral dissertation, defended at the University of Amsterdam on 12 January 2017. Writing a doctoral dissertation is as much an academic journey as it is one of personal discovery. It would not have been possible without the support and encouragement of many people, who contributed not only to my research, but also to my academic and personal development during this period. It is not possible to mention them all, but I would like to single out a few.

First, I would like to thank my supervisor Bernt Hugenholtz and co-supervisor Lucie Guibault. Their supervision was outstanding, as was their availability, patience, constructive criticism, and friendship. I am particularly indebted to Bernt for turning my career path away from law practice and towards academic research, which I am passionate about. As a master's student in Munich, in the now distant years of 2010/2011, I was fortunate to have him as a professor and thesis supervisor. It was also Bernt who invited me to join the Institute for Information Law (IViR) in 2012 to do research in such an exciting project. I would also like to thank the remaining members of my Doctorate Committee, Prof. Dr Mireille van Eechoud, Prof. Dr Christophe Geiger, Prof. Dr Daniel Gervais, Prof. Dr Natali Helberger, and Dr Joost Poort. I was likewise honoured to have sitting in the committee during the defence ceremony Prof. Dr Nico van Eijk, Prof. Dr Egbert Dommering, and Prof. Dr Thomas Hoeren.

I was lucky to conduct most of my doctoral research at IViR, an institute with an exceptional intellectual and social ambiance. I am grateful to all past and current researchers and staff I have crossed paths with. I would like to thank in particular the following colleagues for their generosity and availability in helping me think through my research ideas, concerns, and doubts: Christina Angelopoulos, Balázs Bodó, Kelly Breemen, Vicky Breemen, Annabel Brody, Marco Caspers, Christian Handke, Joris van Hoboken, Catherine Jasserand, Tarlach McGonagle, Gerard Mom, Manon Oostveen, Christiaan Alberdingk Thijm, Stef van Gompel, Joan-Josep Vallbé, and Frederik Borgesius. I also wish to leave particular thanks for the outstanding staff support provided by Anja Dobbelsteen and Rosanne van der Waal, without whom I would either be lost in a bureaucratic maze, or still in search of an obscure publication.

Part of my dissertation was written during a research stay in UC Berkeley, School of Law. In this inspiring academic environment I had the privilege to discuss my research with Pamela Samuelson, to whom I am thankful for the time and guidance provided. I also want to especially mention the following academics who manifested interest in my research and kindly shared some of their time, insights, and patience to my great benefit: Philippe Aigrain, Volker Grassmuck, Séverine Dusollier, Neil Netanel, Alexander Peukert, Martin Senftleben, and Jacqueline Seignette.

This research would not have been possible without the financial assistance from the *Nederlandse Organisatie voor Wetenschappelijk Onderzoek* – The Netherlands Organisation for Scientific Research (Project number 407-11-050). My research stay in Berkeley was made possible by a grant from the *Prof. Mr E.A. van Nieuwenhoven Helbach Stichting*.

To my friends (in Portugal, Amsterdam, and all over the world) and my family, I am thankful for all the support, encouragement, and patience, especially during those times where you deserved more attention and presence than I was able to give. A special thanks to my parents Fernanda e João, my younger brother Miguel, and my grandmother Gabriela; the distance that separates us is great, but you are always with me. Finally, I would like to express my appreciation and love to Melanie, my partner in life, crime, and academic research.

João Pedro Quintais
Amsterdam, January 2017

Note to the Readers

The research for this book was completed on 30 June 2016. Subsequent developments in the relevant law are therefore not reflected in this study, with the exception of updates relating to judgments of the CJEU and AG Opinions cited in the text and published until 31 December 2016. The book therefore does not examine in detail, and only makes cursory reference to, the European Commission's proposals on copyright reform released on 14 September 2016, most notably the proposed Copyright in the Digital Single Market Directive (COM(2016)593).

Chapter 1

Introduction: Challenges for Copyright in the Online Environment

1.1 BACKGROUND AND PROBLEM DEFINITION

In the European Union (EU), more than 80% of households now have an Internet connection.[1] Most individuals aged between 16 and 74 years use the Internet, a number that will only rise over time.[2] As Internet penetration and the number of connected consumers increase, so does the importance of copyright law to the regulation of their everyday online lives. When individuals stream music, download a film, access an e-book, create a mash-up, share a video online, or (in some cases) post hyperlinks to protected content, they are usually carrying out copyright relevant acts.[3]

Copyright is a type of intellectual property right and, in EU law, enjoys fundamental rights protection as property. This status derives from the statement in Article 17(2) of the Charter of Fundamental Rights (Charter)

---

1. Eurostat, 2015, with 'information society statistics' on households and individuals (Data extracted in June 2015).
2. *Ibid.*, referring to numbers as from the beginning of 2014 and noting that the proportion of non-users was down to 18% in 2014 (Data extracted in June 2015).
3. Unless specified, 'copyright' and its variations refer to copyright and related rights. Likewise, 'work' and its variations refer to subject matter protected under copyright and related rights.

that 'intellectual property shall be protected', as well as from multiple references in other legislative acts.[4]

In essence, copyright is a bundle of separate and distinct rights that apply to certain uses of protected works, such as literary works, sound recordings, films, and paintings. The principle of exclusivity is central to this form of protection.[5] According to this principle, the use of works is subject to a default prohibition and authorisation rule that allows right holders to individually manage and enforce their rights.[6] The owner of the copyright, or person to whom the owner grants the exclusive benefit of one or more rights comprising the copyright, has in general the *exclusive* right to reproduce, adapt, communicate or make the work available to the public, or to authorise others to do so. These rights apply in the digital environment.

For a good part of its early history, copyright was aimed at regulating the use of works in tangible media between professionals and for commercial purposes.[7] In that realm, the legal mechanism of the exclusive right was adequate, and its place at the centre of the legal framework justified.

Technological development and evolving social norms slowly changed this landscape. A legislative trend surfaced whereby the emergence of new technologies enabling the exploitation and, later, the mere use or enjoyment of works, was met by a corresponding extension of the law to that use. As a rule, each such extension generally followed the legal template of exclusivity, placing increasing emphasis on strict enforcement of rights.[8]

And so it is that the remit of copyright grew to include the printing press, piano rolls, photography, cinematography, sound recordings, broadcast by satellite and cable, reprography, analogue tape recording, digital technology, and the Internet.[9]

It is possible to trace this evolution in international copyright law by following the different revisions of the Berne Convention for the Protection of Literary and Artistic Works (BC), the 1994 Agreement on Trade-Related Aspects of Intellectual Property Law (TRIPS) and, in relation to use over digital networks, the 1996 WIPO Copyright Treaty (WCT), and the 1996 WIPO Performances and Phonograms Treaty (WPPT).

4. On the qualification of copyright as property, see: Art. 1 Protocol No. 1 ECHR; Art. 17(2) Charter; recital 9 InfoSoc Directive; recital 32 Enforcement Directive; Follow-Up Green Paper 1996, p. 8.
5. Kur & Schovsbo, 2011, p. 9., noting that, in continental Europe, exclusivity 'is an essential feature firmly anchored in the 'natural right' character of an author's claim to her work'.
6. Rahmatian, 2011, p. 371, qualifying copyright as both a negative and positive right, noting its internal dimension as 'the right to use, especially in the form of the right to assign or license'.
7. Gervais, 2009, pp. 845–848, 851, 869–870.
8. Pereira, 2008, p. 8.
9. Liu, 2001, p. 1255.

When the latter treaties came along, the EU was already in the middle of a legislative programme to tackle the challenges of territoriality. This on-going effort of upward harmonisation has so far resulted in ten directives on copyright and related rights.[10] These instruments have often surpassed international minimum standards of protection, on the pretext of *inter alia* removing disparities amounting to barriers to the free movement of goods and services.[11] The centrepiece of the copyright *acquis* is the InfoSoc Directive, which implements the WCT and WPPT into EU law and adapts it to the information society.

As technology evolved, it increasingly allowed individuals to use works in a low-cost and ubiquitous manner for private and non-commercial purposes. Internet users read, view, display, copy, rip, cut, paste, remix, mash-up, edit, link, and appropriate works. They do this through different devices and for varied purposes, including leisure, entertainment, communication, artistic expression, parody, and critique. Borrowing and recreating have always been a part of our cultural practices, but the Internet enables users to do so from a wider pool of works, with greater ease, while disseminating the results widely at low cost.[12]

By extending the scope of copyright protection and exclusivity to these uses, the law shifted from primarily applying to professional relationships, to also regulating acts of enjoyment and expression in the online environment.[13] One consequence was the reduction of space for otherwise lawful non-market activities and the cultural production and expression that goes with them.[14]

The application of this legal regime to 'mass' online use by individuals created a mismatch between the law and technology-influenced social norms.[15] On the one hand, online sharing is low cost and ubiquitous; on the other, copyright relies on exclusivity and enforcement. The result is an increase in unauthorised production and dissemination of works, with a corresponding decrease in the public legitimacy of the law.[16] This disconnect

10. The relevant directives are: the Software Directive (1991, amended and codified 2009); the SatCab Directive (1993); the Term Directive (1993, amended 2011); the Database Directive (1996); the Rental Right Directive (1996, amended and codified 2006); the InfoSoc Directive (2001); the Resale Right Directive (2001), Enforcement Directive (2004); the Orphan Works Directive (2012); the CRM Directive (2014).
11. Hugenholtz, 2009a, p. 17. On the process of harmonisation in EU copyright law, *see* Eechoud et al., 2009; Hugenholtz, 2009a, 2013a.
12. *See* Lessig, 2008, describing the shift from a 'Read/Only' to a 'Read/Write' culture. In this article, 'digital content' refers to data produced and supplied in digital form. Cf. Art. 2(11) Consumer Rights Directive.
13. Gervais, 2009, pp. 845–857, 869–870.
14. Benkler, 2006, p. 385–ff, Boyle, 2003; Lessig, 2001, 2004; Palfrey, 2010.
15. Hugenholtz, 2013b, p. 26.
16. Lessig, 2008, p. 253ff, arguing for a legal reform that deregulates amateur creativity (i.e., transformative uses), 'decriminalizes copies' (and instead focuses on 'uses'), and

raises the need to rethink the law in light of its lack of social acceptance and technological adequacy.

The problem is amplified by the ineffectiveness and costs of copyright enforcement. Online enforcement against mass unauthorised use or file sharing is difficult due to the challenges posed by technology and high transaction costs associated with pursuing thousands (if not millions) of infringers.[17] The persistence of this unauthorised use despite the ratcheting of enforcement measures and litigation in the past decade is illustrative of this.

Since the advent of the first Peer-to-Peer (P2P) networks, rights holders have sought to prevent large-scale infringement through litigation. The targets of lawsuits have included the demand-side of the unauthorised market (the individual file-sharers), and the supply-side, i.e., the platforms that accommodate and enable unauthorised use.[18] The latter include P2P software providers and Internet Service Providers (ISPs) supplying the infrastructure for data flows.[19]

Taking advantage of the available space in EU law, including the liability rules in the E-Commerce Directive, rights holders concentrated their efforts on obtaining injunctions for filtering,[20] blocking,[21] and disclosure of information in relation to allegedly infringing subscribers.[22] There have also been notable efforts made towards the adoption of so-called 'graduated response systems'. These are systems where ISPs monitor subscribers' potential illegal actions or act upon notification of the same by rights holders, serving notices and warnings to cease infringement. If users continue their practices after a number of warnings, sanctions are applied, including

decriminalises file sharing via compulsory/statutory licensing or voluntary collective licensing. *See also*: Benkler, 2006, p. 278, 383ff; Zittrain, 2008, pp. 192–193.

17. The term 'file sharing' is used in this study to mean the online exchange of copyright-protected material without the authorisation rights holder, also referred to as 'unauthorised file sharing,' 'illegal file sharing,' and 'online piracy'. Cf. Poort & Weda, 2015, p. 63 (n. 1).
18. The demand/supply-side description is taken from Poort et al., 2014.
19. Giblin, 2014b. On the fundamental rights-based restrictions on the implementation of said systems in Europe, *see infra* 5.3.3.6. On their general ineffectiveness, *see* Geiger, 2014a; HADOPI DREV – Départment Recherche Etudes et Veille, 2013.
20. In simple terms, filtering consists of 'content-control software applications designed to automatically block the display or downloading of selected material on a web browser or other Internet application'. *See* Angelopoulos, 2009, p. 2, citing Council of Europe Recommendation CM/Rec(2008) 6. A similar broad definition is used by Palfrey, 2010, pp. 10–11.
21. 'Blocking' refers to the prevention of access to websites, P2P networks, or accounts of infringing users. For example, website blocking injunctions can take the form of DNS and IP address blocking or deep packet inspection. *See* DLA Piper, 2009, p. 22.
22. *See* DLA Piper, 2009, p. 22, providing examples of national case law. Website blocking injunctions, in particular, became a widely used enforcement measure in many EU jurisdictions. *See* Angelopoulos, 2014; Husovec, 2013; Husovec & Peguera, 2015. Reporting on the increase in use of website blocking injunctions in Europe, *see* Meale, 2013; E. Rosati, 2015.

'suspension and termination of service, capping of bandwidth, and blocking of sites, portals and protocols'.[23]

The current trend is to increase the role and responsibility of Internet intermediaries in online enforcement. This entails targeting online gatekeepers like ISPs, advertisers, search engines, mobile operators, and payment providers.[24] This trend fits into a broader tactic by rights holders to remedy a perceived 'value gap' between intermediaries' digital revenues, generated by the online dissemination of content, and the lack of fair remuneration for rights holders for that use.[25] The tactic has materialised in the so-called 'value gap' proposal in the draft Copyright in the Digital Single Market Directive, which proposal aims at regulating the use of protected content by information society providers giving access to large amounts of works and other subject-matter uploaded by their users.[26]

Despite this multi-layered strategy, there is little causal evidence that enforcement is effective in significantly reducing online infringement.[27] It is true that rights holders have had success in shutting down numerous unauthorised platforms. However, both file sharing and the numbers of available P2P applications have continued to rise.[28] Empirical evidence suggests that litigation has at best a short-term deterrent effect before demand and supply relapse into infringing practices through alternative channels.[29] Furthermore, complex enforcement approaches, like graduated-response systems, are costly and inefficient.[30]

But strict enforcement is not only ineffective; it may also be *undesirable*. On the one hand, it is now apparent that these measures alienate consumers and erode the respect for and public legitimacy of copyright law. On the other hand, they risk disrespecting fundamental rights and freedoms of individuals and intermediaries.

In EU law, fundamental rights have emerged as an external constraint on copyright enforcement online. In several cases before the Court of Justice

---

23. Yu, 2010, p. 1374.
24. Geiger, 2014a; Giblin, 2012, pp. 58–59, 115; IFPI, 2013, 2015.
25. *See* e.g. IFPI, 2015, p. 22; International Confederation of Music Publishers, 2015.
26. *See* Art. 13 and recital 38 of the Proposal for a Directive of the European Parliament and of the Council on copyright in the Digital Single Market, COM(2016)593. For criticism, *see* Stalla-Bourdillon et al., 2016.
27. *See* Giblin, 2014b; Handke, Bodó & Vallbé, 2015; Lunney, 2014; Poort et al., 2014; Poort & Weda, 2015.
28. See: Gervais, 2010, p. 16, arguing that mass-scale use has brought about a reshaping of the copyright landscape, making it apparent that, short of expelling users from the Internet there is no effective way to prevent these practices; Bridy, 2009, p. 604, noting that '[a]s an empirical matter, the mass lawsuits appear to have had only a transitory deterrent effect'. *See also* Cammaerts & Meng, 2011; Eijk, Poort & Rutten, 2010, p. 53; Gervais, 2004; Giblin, 2012, pp. 58–59, Harris, 2012, Huygen et al., 2009.
29. *See* Poort et al., 2014, pp. 2–4, with further references.
30. *See* Geiger, 2014a, pp. 5–11, 2014c, pp. 134–138, Giblin, 2014a, 2014b; HADOPI DREV – Département Recherche Etudes et Veille, 2013; Lescure, 2013.

of the European Union (CJEU), measures such as filtering, blocking, and disclosing ISP subscribers' information have been limited by the application of freedom of expression and information online, privacy in telecommunications, respect for personal data, and freedom to conduct a business.[31] The Court's jurisprudence requires that a 'fair balance' is reached between the protection of the right of property in copyright and competing fundamental rights, sometimes giving primacy to the latter.[32] At the legislative level, similar considerations have led to the rejection of graduated-response systems.[33]

In contrast to enforcement, the market is more efficient at addressing infringement. Research shows that authorised services with an attractive price and catalogue can decrease demand for unauthorised websites and develop new markets.[34] Thus, private ordering can address to some extent unmet demand as one of the causes of online infringement.[35] The spectacular rise of authorised film and music streaming services like Netflix and Spotify is a testament to this development.

Nevertheless, legal channels appear insufficient to cater in full to consumers' demands and habits.[36] Users aspire to a new pattern of cultural consumption characterised by multi-device and multi-screen availability, and the opportunity to reproduce, share and modify cultural works. The market will not entirely solve this problem, due in no small part to the complexities inherent in the territorial and substantive fragmentation of exclusive rights. These factors suggest that the gap between consumer demands and market offerings will persist.[37]

Finally, the current system fails to adequately remunerate individual authors and performers for their creative efforts. In a content market transitioning from ownership to access-based models, global digital rights revenues for the entertainment industry have steadily increased.[38] Individual

31. *See infra* 4.4.1.4 and 5.3.3.6.
32. *See infra* 4.4.1.4 and 5.3.3. In Europe, the legal basis for the cited fundamental freedoms and rights is found in Arts 8 and 10 ECHR, and Arts 7, 8, 11 and 16 Charter.
33. *See* Art. 1(3)(a) Framework Directive. On fundamental rights concerns with graduated response systems, *see infra* 5.3.3.6.
34. Vallbé et al., 2015, p. 2 with references to empirical studies, including Poort & Weda, 2015. *See also* Giblin, 2014a, 2014b, p. 210.
35. Vallbé et al., 2015, pp. 2–4, noting that the success of early P2P networks and growth of cultural black markets in the absence of lawful offers were indicative of consumers' willingness to adopt online distribution of cultural works before rights holders.
36. Kantar Media, 2012; Poort & Leenheer, 2012; Vallbé et al., 2015.
37. *See* Ricolfi, 2007, p. 300, making a similar argument. *See also* Grece et al., 2015, pp. 132–133, and Communication on Modern European Copyright Framework 2015, p. 4 (noting the problems caused by territoriality).
38. IFPI, 2015, p. 6 (for number and trends in the recording industry; See, e.g., Grece et al., 2015, p. 14: 'From 2009 to 2013, the audiovisual turnover from the audiovisual activities of the 50 major worldwide groups rose from USD 361.5 billion to USD 425 billion'.) Motion Picture Association of America, 2015, pp. 2, 4–7. *See also* the positive data

creators' shares, however, have not risen accordingly in the digital environment. In fact, creators often transfer their rights for little consideration to other rights holders (e.g., phonogram or film producers) as a result of their weakened bargaining position.[39]

A copyright policy that emphasises repression over monetisation of use fails to address the issue of fair remuneration for creators and pre-empts the exploration of alternatives for remunerated access. Of course, contractual imbalances can be tackled by EU-level regulation of contractual practices between creators and exploiters.[40] Still, collective rights management schemes and legal licences, coupled with unwaivable remuneration rights, have historically been adequate solutions to challenges of enforcement and fair compensation.[41] (As we shall see, these legal schemes play a central role in the present book.)

Against this background, there is an urgent need to find a lawful way for online users to access, use and share digitised works in a manner that not only promotes the development of the information society but also fairly compensates creators and other right holders. From a policy perspective, copyright should harness and stimulate the democratic and social welfare benefits from developments in communications networks and social norms.[42] The challenge is to do so in compliance with EU copyright law and the related *acquis communautaire*.

This book examines the issue and explores a possible solution for modernising the EU copyright framework, in the form of a model of access and remuneration.[43] The analysis is concerned with 'legalisation' proposals for unauthorised non-commercial online use by individuals.

These proposals advance legal mechanisms that restrict the exercise or scope of exclusive rights applicable to online acts by Internet users. The acts in question are typically those of downloading, streaming, uploading, sharing or modifying copyright works. The scope of proposals frequently includes the online rights of reproduction and communication to the public (and only seldom adaptation), and traditional categories of works, like music and film (often excluding software and databases). The restriction to exclusive rights

---

reported in Giblin, 2014b, p. 210. 'The movie industry has broken its record for worldwide box office receipts for the last *seven* years straight.'. Grece et al., 2015, pp. 75–77, 132–133 (growth of European consumer spending and of the number of customers for online subscription video-on-demand; this trend will continue in the future).

39. Flowers, 2015; Vallbé et al., 2015, pp. 1–4.
40. Communication on Modern European Copyright Framework 2015, p. 10.
41. *See infra* 2.3, 2.5, 3.3.5, and 5.3.3.3. *See also* Communication on Modern European Copyright Framework 2015, p. 10.
42. *See* Benkler, 2006, p. 276; Lessig, 2008. 'Policy' is defined here as 'a course of action adopted or proposed by an organisation or person, more specifically an action which implies a choice of one action among others'. Cf. Gerven, 2008, p. 14.
43. Mention efforts to modernise copyright through increased enforcement by the Commission.

is accompanied by rules ensuring remuneration for rights holders (or solely creators) of works included in the scheme. As a result, a previously unauthorised use becomes 'permitted-but-paid'.[44]

In short, legalisation proposals aim to regulate mass use of works through licensing schemes, subject to payment of compensation. Among the schemes studied throughout this book are different models of collective rights management (voluntary, extended, and mandatory), statutory and compulsory licences, and state-funded systems.

Legalisation proposals come with different labels. Among the most influential discussed throughout this book are proposals for a 'tax-and-royalty system', '*licence globale*', 'content' or 'culture flat-rate', 'creative contribution', 'file sharing' or 'broadband levy', 'sharing licence', or an 'alternative reward system'.[45] For convenience, these proposals are referred to under the umbrella term 'Alternative Compensation Systems' (ACS). The models are 'alternative' insofar as they favour remunerated access over exclusivity and enforcement for large-scale online use by individuals.

Since the early 2000s, ACS have been proposed by legal and economics scholars, advocacy groups, and political parties. Legislative proposals were presented in the national parliaments of Portugal, France, Germany, Belgium, and Italy.[46] Discussion on the topic also surfaced in debates on EU copyright reform, especially in the context of efforts by the Commission and Parliament to update the private copying system.[47]

In 2011, the European Parliament commissioned a study on 'content flat-rates'.[48] In 2014, it adopted a resolution recommending the examination of the possibility of levying cloud services, a development that would approximate private copying to an ACS for certain digital reproductions.[49] The draft version of the resolution went further. It mentioned the need to 'examine the possibility of legalizing works sharing for non-commercial purposes so as to guarantee consumers access to a wide variety of content and real choice in terms of cultural diversity'.[50]

In addition, empirical research encourages the study of legalisation models. First, because it suggests the existence of public support for ACS,

44. On the notion of 'permitted-but-paid', *see* Ginsburg, 2014b. There is significant research on schemes external to copyright but with similar effects, such as Aigrain, 2008, 2012; La Quadrature du Net & Aigrain, 2013.
45. *See* Chapter 3 for discussion and categorisation of these proposals.
46. *Ibid.*, for further analysis of these proposals.
47. *See* Report Public Consultation on the Review of the EU Copyright Rules 2014, pp. 72–77, where ACS are mentioned as a regulation model favoured by certain end-user/consumer respondents. *See also* Vitorino, 2013.
48. Modot et al., 2011.
49. *See* EP Resolution Private Copying Levies 2014, and Castex Report 2013, para. 30.
50. *See* Castex Report 2013, para. 27. The suggestion was dropped in the final version of the document.

despite the reputational damage caused to rights holders by strict enforcement strategies. Second, because it highlights the economic promise of these models.

There is evidence of public support for ACS. This is especially true among users already consuming culture online, including high-intensity file-sharers. For instance, a recent study in the Netherlands suggests that increased usage of legal channels indicates greater inclination to support ACS, as well as greater willingness to pay. The same study shows that support is strongest for legalisation schemes that provide holistic access to works, with few usage restrictions, and at a reasonable price (e.g., a surcharge on the monthly rate of Internet access, within the price range of existing premium streaming services like Netflix and Spotify).[51]

Furthermore, there is also research suggesting that ACS may be welfare increasing, despite the scepticism of some economists.[52] For example, a recent study in the Netherlands assessed the economic viability of a statutory licence ACS for recorded music. It concluded that a well-designed system makes users and rights holders better off as a whole by increasing their total welfare compared to the status quo.[53] If nothing else, this research highlights the likely cost of exclusivity over a model of remunerated access.

The potential benefits of a welfare-increasing ACS are significant. Rights holders would see increased revenues and savings in enforcement costs. Creators could benefit too if the system includes a mandatory requirement for fair compensation, thereby mitigating problems with fair remuneration in digital exploitation channels. End-users would face a lower risk of infringement, increased legal certainty for their online activities, and experience better online access to works. In the long term, an ACS could promote the circulation of culture, technological development, and fair competition between online service providers of works. These are all good arguments for a legal exploration of these systems in EU copyright law.

1.2 RESEARCH QUESTIONS

This book aims to answer the following research questions:

> Are Alternative Compensation Systems for non-commercial online use of works by individuals admissible under EU copyright law and consistent with its objectives and, if so, to what extent? How can and should EU copyright law incorporate an Alternative Compensation System?

51. Vallbé et al., 2015. For other studies with similar results, *see* Collopy & Bahanovich, 2012; Karaganis & Renkema, 2013; SPEDIDAM, 2006; Swedish Performing Rights Society (STIM), 2009; Wiggin & Entertainment Media Research, 2011.
52. Handke et al., 2015; Vallbé et al., 2015.
53. Handke et al., 2015.

Before addressing methodology, some remarks about the research questions and terminology are necessary. The concept of 'ACS' was explained in the previous section. It is an umbrella term for different proposals promoting the legalisation of large-scale non-commercial online use of works between individuals. These proposals seek to restrict the exercise or scope of the exclusive right, including the possibility of individual management and enforcement, promoting in its stead legal models that enable works to be accessed and used in return for remuneration.

The 'individuals' mentioned in the research questions are natural persons. They may be consumers of digital works or services acting outside their trade or business (benefiting from consumer law protection), users of works outside a consumer-trader relationship, or follow-on creators that build on pre-existing materials – and are thus potential authors of transformative works.[54]

This book is concerned with Internet users that engage in 'non-commercial' online use of works.[55] The term 'non-commercial' is challenging to define in the online environment. Historically, copyright regulated commercial use in the public sphere. In Europe, as Chapter 2 explains, this changed with the emergence of the German private copying model in the 1950s–1960s. Decisions by the German Federal Court of Justice (BGH) extended the scope of the reproduction right to the private sphere and imposed contributory liability on manufacturers, whilst balancing the need for technological innovation and respect for the constitutional right of privacy.[56]

Fast-forward to the present-day information society and the role of end-users has changed drastically, as illustrated by the rich and diverse ways in which they use digital content. In this context, drawing distinctions between amateur/non-commercial and professional/commercial use for analytical purposes is difficult and, some argue, undesirable.[57]

Still, there are good reasons to rely on this distinction as an analytical tool, insofar as we perceive it to be closer to a *standard* than a *rule*.[58] Here,

54. Mazziotti, 2008, pp. 4–5, referring to the concept of 'end-user'. *See also* Benkler et al., 2013; Hilty & Nérisson, 2012, pp. 89–90, noting that these new users, because they are more socio-culturally and politically engaged through the use of technology, are increasingly perceived as 'citizens' instead of mere customers, and even play a significant role in shaping copyright debates.
55. A 'commercial user' can be defined as a person or entity involved in the provision of goods or services that for their business activities requires a licence from right holders of copyright and/or related rights. *See* SWD CRM Directive 2012, p. 195. N.B. some follow-on creators may likewise qualify as commercial users if they market their transformative works.
56. *See* Collová, 1991, pp. 35–149; Hugenholtz, 2012a, pp. 180–191; Reinbothe, 1981, pp. 36–49.
57. Fisher, 2010, pp. 1433–1436 & n. 97. *See also* Lohmann, 2014.
58. See, generally, Schlag, 1985.

a rule is a detailed statutory provision, akin to a list, spelling out the cases in which a use of a work qualifies as non-commercial. Uses outside that list would not be included in the ACS. A standard, in contrast, constitutes 'a more flexible framework designed to give courts both guidance and significant leeway in determining the uses' susceptible of qualification as non-commercial, 'while keeping in mind the interests of rights holders'.[59]

Many consumptive and creative acts by Internet users take place in the private sphere or are clearly not for direct commercial purpose or with a profit-making aim. Thus, the challenges of defining commerciality are circumscribed. Whether a use is non-commercial could be defined by case law pursuant to a reasonable standard.

Several *acquis* provisions use the 'non-commercial' concept in connection with copyright limitations and collective rights management. On the one hand, limitations variously privilege acts that are 'neither directly nor indirectly commercial', for a 'direct or indirect commercial ... advantage', of non-commercial 'nature', 'purpose' or for a non-commercial 'advantage'.[60] On the other hand, the CRM Directive states that CMOs must ensure rights holders have the right to grant licences for non-commercial use of any rights, categories of rights or types of works and other subject matter that they may choose.[61]

The legislative recognition of the 'non-commercial' notion in the *acquis* should lead to its qualification as an autonomous concept of EU law, subject to uniform interpretation by the CJEU.[62]

This basic understanding of the concept as an EU copyright law standard that includes non-market and non-profit acts by individuals is an analytical starting point, to be given meaning and effect throughout this book.[63]

1.3 METHODOLOGY

This is a study in copyright law, within the broader area of information law. Information law relates to 'the production, marketing, distribution and use of information goods and services', and comprises 'a wide set of legal issues at the crossroads of intellectual property, media law, telecommunications law, freedom of expression and right to privacy'.[64] As a normative concept,

59. *See* Perzanowski & Schultz, 2014, p. 1545, making a similar distinction in relation to prospective legislation of digital exhaustion.
60. *See* Art. 5(2)(b) (for 'ends that are neither directly or indirectly commercial'), 5(2)(e), 5(3)(a), 5(3)(b) InfoSoc Directive. *See also* Art. 6(5) Orphan Works Directive.
61. *See* Art. 5(3) and recital 19 CRM Directive.
62. Metzger & Heinemann, 2015.
63. *See infra* 3.3.1, 3.4.2, 4.4.3.2, 5.1, 5.3.2.3, and 6.2.3.
64. Institute for Information Law, 2012, pp. 1, 3.

information law aims to 'contribute to a legal framework that best serves the information society while respecting fundamental rights and freedoms'.[65]

Here, these aims are applied to the field of digital copyright by answering questions of law through normative legal research, i.e., 'normative assertions, views and concepts' with regard to a specific legal system.[66] The book asks *what the law is* in order to assess *what the law ought to be*,[67] using doctrinal analysis to develop theoretical and prescriptive arguments for reform of EU copyright law.

The objective of the analysis is not an 'ideal' normative theory, but rather one that assumes a variety of constraints on the choice of legal rules, namely their legal and political feasibility.[68] The analysis aspires to be pragmatic and relevant for EU copyright policy. Hence, it does not consider proposals that require a complete overhaul of existing law, the abrogation of international treaties, or the abolishment of copyright protection for non-commercial use. For instance, the book looks at legalisation schemes external to copyright (e.g., based on taxation) to examine their characteristics, some of which are susceptible of transplant to copyright systems; however, it does not examine their legal feasibility.[69]

The investigation is carried out through the internal legal perspective of the copyright *acquis communautaire*. The *acquis* includes primary legislation, secondary legislation, and case law from the Court that form part of the EU legal order in the area of copyright.[70] It is in relation to this legal framework and its objectives that the book assesses the admissibility, normative consistency and desirability of ACS. The sources used in the analysis include legislation, case law and doctrine (predominantly legal literature in the field of copyright), gathered through desk research.[71]

'Primary' law consists of the Treaties (Treaty on European Union (TEU) and Treaty on the Functioning of the European Union (TFEU) and the Charter – which has 'the same legal value as the Treaties'[72] – together with fundamental or general principles of EU law developed by the Court, 'including the requirement to protect fundamental rights'.[73] The EU fundamental rights framework includes principles derived from the European Convention on Human Rights (ECHR) and national constitutional traditions,

65. *Ibid.*, p. 3.
66. Van Gestel, Micklitz & Maduro, 2012, p. 2.
67. *Ibid.*, p. 4, using this expression to define the essence of normative legal research.
68. On positive theory as constraint, *see* Vermeule, 2007, pp. 394–395.
69. *See* the analysis of 'State Systems' *infra* at 3.3.6.
70. Eurofund, *Industrial Relations Dictionary*, *Acquis Communautaire*, http://www.eurofound.europa.eu/observatories/eurwork/industrial-relations-dictionary/acquis-communautaire (accessed 31.01.2017).
71. The vast majority of sources referred to are in English. Where a choice existed between an English language source and an alternative in another language, the English language was preferred.
72. Art. 6(1) first subpara TEU.
73. Bradley, 2014, p. 103.

some of which are codified in the Charter,[74] thereby justifying the occasional reference to these sources. This includes decisions on the interpretation of these instruments by competent bodies, such as the European Court of Human Rights (ECtHR) and national constitutional courts.

'Secondary' law includes unilateral acts based directly on the Treaties, which must comply with primary law.[75] The most relevant acts for this book are the multiple directives on copyright and related rights.[76] Because the research questions focus on non-commercial online use by individuals, the InfoSoc Directive and its interpretation by the CJEU will take centre stage in the analysis. Furthermore, as the book is concerned with copyright, references to related or neighbouring rights are limited. Beyond the directives, the research considers other relevant 'unilateral acts' in the field of copyright, such as decisions, opinions, recommendations, communications, white papers, and green papers.[77]

Within EU copyright law, several topics are outside the scope of the research. They include rules on the protection of software, databases, videogames, orphan works, the non-harmonised right of adaptation, and moral rights.[78] The study also excludes areas of EU law outside copyright that may indirectly influence the legal study of ACS, such as competition law, conditional access, consumer law, and electronic commerce law.[79]

EU law is an autonomous body of law largely independent from national law.[80] It is the exclusive jurisdiction of the CJEU, which has the power to provide authoritative interpretation on its rules, largely dependent

74. Griffiths, 2013.
75. Bradley, 2014, pp. 103–104; Ramalho, 2014, pp. 21–22. Art. 288 TFEU contains a list of unilateral acts that are secondary sources of law, such as regulations, directives, decisions, opinions, and recommendations.
76. The relevant directives are: Software Directive (1991, amended and codified 2009); SatCab Directive (1993); Term Directive (1993, amended 2011); Database Directive (1996); Rental Right Directive (1996, amended and codified 2006); InfoSoc Directive (2001); Resale Right Directive (2001); Enforcement Directive (2004); Orphan Works Directive (2012); CRM Directive (2014). N.B. that the Enforcement Directive applies also to other intellectual property rights.
77. 'Unilateral acts' include those typified in Art. 288 TFEU (decisions, opinions and recommendations) and those considered 'atypical', exemplified in the text. *See* EUR-Lex, *Sources of European Law*, http://eur-lex.europa.eu/legal-content/EN/TXT/?uri=uriserv:l14534 (accessed 31.01.2017).
78. N.B. that Chapter 4 contains a brief reference to the right of adaption when discussing the issue of digital adaptations (4.2.7) and limitations applicable thereto (4.4.4).
79. The regulation of the topics mentioned is found for example in Arts 101 and 102 TFEU (on the constraints posed by competition law on CMOs), the Consumer Rights Directive, the Conditional Access Directive (containing rules that articulate with those on TPMs in the InfoSoc Directive), the AVMS Directive, and the E-Commerce Directive. Despite this exclusion, due to the blurring of the lines between primary and secondary liability in EU copyright law, Chapters 5 and 6 make brief references the E-Commerce Directive's liability exemptions for online intermediaries.
80. Rösler, 2012, p. 979.

on the obligation by national courts to refer cases under Article 267 TFEU.[81] Since 2009, there have been frequent references for a preliminary ruling on the interpretation of open concepts in the *acquis*, namely in the InfoSoc Directive. Due to doubts as to its competence basis and normative admissibility, some authors label this practice as 'harmonization by stealth' or 'judicial activism'.[82]

Regardless, the CJEU's case law plays a vital role in shaping the law applicable to mass online use. It also contains key normative considerations regarding how far the law can and should be reformed to accommodate this use. As such, understanding the Court's case law and method of interpretation is essential to examine ACS and answer the book's research questions.

Interpretation of EU copyright law follows the traditional literal (semantic or semiotic), systematic (or contextual) and purposive (or teleological) methods. These are frequently used together and combined with the 'peculiar canons' of EU law, such as the principles of effectiveness, proportionality, and uniform application.[83]

The teleological method is prevalent in the CJEU's copyright jurisprudence. This prevalence is based on the application of the principles of effectiveness and autonomous interpretation, as well as a range of arguments linked to the objectives of EU copyright, found in the preambles of directives. A notable example is the interpretation of notions in directives as autonomous concepts of EU law, requiring uniform interpretation.[84] The InfoSoc Directive, in particular, is used as a horizontal harmonisation instrument, with its recitals playing the role of veritable harmonisation guides.[85]

The objectives of the copyright *acquis*, as viewed by the Court, have been identified through empirical analysis by Favale, Kretschmer and Torremans. These objectives are: a 'high level of protection for copyright

81. Art. 19 TEU. *See* Rösler, 2012, pp. 979–980. Art. 267 TFEU gives the CJEU jurisdiction to give preliminary rulings concerning both the interpretation of primary law and the 'the validity and interpretation of acts of the institutions, bodies, offices or agencies of the Union'.
82. *See* Eechoud, 2012; Favale, Kretschmer & Torremans, 2015, pp. 31–32; Hugenholtz, 2013a, pp. 513–521; Leistner, 2014, pp. 560–561. This practice does not seem common in other areas of EU secondary law. *See* Rösler, 2012, p. 979.
83. Favale et al., 2015, pp. 37, 53–55. In its copyright jurisprudence, it is notable that the Court often refers back to its previous case law in support of its legal reasoning, but never explicitly reverses previous judgments. *Ibid.*, pp. 56–57. *See also* Rösler, 2012, p. 979, noting that the common objective of interpretation is its effectiveness (*effet utile*).
84. *See* Geiger & Schönherr, 2014b, pp. 554–556.
85. In general, *see* Rösler, 2012, p. 979. The author argues that this method is consistent with the EU's functional perspective, and highlights the difficulty in using it when the interpreter identifies conflicting purposes underlying the same provision. For the copyright *acquis*, *see* Geiger & Schönherr, 2014b, pp. 449–500; Leistner, 2014, pp. 560, 599.

holders', 'fair competition', 'circulation of culture', 'fair balance between the rights and interests of authors and the rights of users', 'harmonisation', 'adequate compensation', 'resolving legal uncertainty', and 'technological development'.[86] It is in light of such objectives that proposals for EU copyright law reform ought to be evaluated. Therefore, they are used throughout the book not only to understand the Court's teleological arguments in adjudicating the law, but also in the normative assessment of ACS.[87]

In the process of analysing EU copyright law, it is important to recognise that this legal regime operates in a multi-level system. The directives are interpreted in respect of primary law *and* in light of international copyright agreements. The main agreements considered here are the BC, TRIPS and the WCT, to which all EU Member States are parties. The EU as an organisation is a member of TRIPS and the World Intellectual Property Organization (WIPO) Treaties, making them binding on its institutions and Member States.[88] In addition, TRIPS and the WCT incorporate by reference the most relevant substantive provisions of the BC.[89] The InfoSoc Directive, furthermore, implements the WCT in the *acquis*.

This framework imposes two important obligations. The first is the obligation to comply with international treaties, including the incorporated provisions of the BC.[90] The second, and related, obligation is to interpret EU law in light of international law, 'in particular where its provisions are intended specifically to give effect to an international agreement concluded by the Community'.[91]

Finally, to determine the meaning of international law, the aforementioned treaties must be interpreted according to the principles of the Vienna

86. Favale et al., 2015, pp. 33, 66–67. The authors note also the Court's preference for the teleological method and that these arguments, while possibly rhetorical, may provide an indication of whether the outcome of a case is favourable to rights holders or to users.
87. *See infra* 4.4.1 and 5.5.
88. Cf. Art. 216 TFEU. *See* Geiger & Schönherr, 2014a, p. 135 & n. 102, 2014b, p. 443, citing CJEU jurisprudence in support of this principle regarding 'mixed agreements', such as TRIPS and the WCT. N.B. the WIPO Treaties were approved on behalf of the European Community by Council Decision 2000/278/EC.
89. Arts 9(1) TRIPS and 1(4) WCT incorporate by reference Arts 1–21 and the Appendix BC. N.B. Art. 1 WPPT states that the treaty shall not derogate from existing obligations that Contracting Parties have to each other under the RC.
90. CJEU, *Laserdisken II*, para. 39; CJEU, *Luksan*, para. 59; CJEU, *DR and TV2 Danmark*, para. 29.
91. CJEU, *Peek & Cloppenburg*, paras 29–33; CJEU, *SGAE*, para. 35; CJEU, *Murphy*, para. 189; CJEU, *Infopaq I*, para. 32; CJEU, *Painer*, para. 126; CJEU, *UsedSoft*, para. 42; CJEU, *Donner*, para. 23. An interpretation in light of international treaties can be understood as part of the Court's systematic or contextual method of interpretation, as well as an express objective of the InfoSoc Directive. *See* Favale et al., 2015, pp. 37, 52, 72. The objective of consistency with international obligation is expressed in recitals 15 and 44 InfoSoc Directive.

Convention on the Law Treaties of 1969 (VCLT).[92] In simple terms, the VCLT rules on treaty interpretation favour a literal approach to determine the ordinary meaning of a treaty provision in good faith, combined with systematic analysis ('context') and teleological elements ('object and purpose'). In addition, these rules allow, at a subordinate level, recourse to extrinsic elements (e.g., preparatory works) that demonstrate the intentions of the parties to the treaty. As we shall see, in this book, these rules have most significance for the analysis of the three-step test in Chapter 5.

1.4 SCIENTIFIC AND SOCIETAL RELEVANCE

This study aims to contribute to the body of knowledge in the area of EU copyright law. The problem of large-scale unauthorised online use and the preservation of a sphere of enjoyment and expression online have inspired some academic literature on ACS.[93] But this literature has limitations.

First, most studies pay little attention to normative legal research. Second, many are restricted to specific modes of dissemination – commonly P2P – or subject matter, usually music.[94] In a rapidly evolving technological landscape, such analyses risk obsolescence and are of limited value vis-à-vis other uses or protected subject matter. Third, many studies focus on the applicable international copyright treaties, United States (US) law or specific national laws. Hence, they are of less relevance to the copyright *acquis*, where rules on copyright limitations and collective rights management are different, especially relative to the US.[95] Finally, many authors refrain from designing potentially viable legal models.[96] When they do, some of the proposals are purely theoretical, or wholly unrealistic.[97]

This book addresses these lacunae by undertaking in-depth research on ACS under EU copyright law.[98] The study aims to be pragmatic; the aim is reinforced by the development of the study in the context of an interdisciplinary research project on the legal, social and economic feasibility of

92. *See* s. 3, Part III ('observance, application and interpretation of treaties'), Arts 31–33 VCLT. It is generally considered that Arts 31–33 VCLT 'codify customary public international law on the matters covered' and that international treaties on copyright should be interpreted in its light. *See* Kur, 2008, p. 22; Ricketson, 2003, p. 5; Ricketson & Ginsburg, 2006, pp. 181–182, 189; Senftleben, 2004, p. 99.
93. Chapter 3 contains a systematic analysis of the literature and proposals on ACS.
94. See, e.g., Fisher, 2004; Litman, 2004; Lohmann, 2004, 2008; Netanel, 2003.
95. See, e.g., Goldstein & Hugenholtz, 2013, pp. 275–281, 371–376.
96. Among these exceptions, *see* Fisher, 2004; Netanel, 2003.
97. Eckersley, 2004, 2012.
98. Some existing literature partially analyses ACS against the background of the EU copyright Directives. *See* Bernault & Lebois, 2005; Colin, 2011a, 2011b; Séverine Dusollier & Colin, 2011; Frosio, 2011; Quintais, 2012; von Lewinski, 2005.

ACS.[99] The findings of that project provide empirical justifications for the legal inquiry into ACS, and are embedded into key parts of the analysis.[100]

The societal relevance of this book was illustrated in section 1.1. The large majority of the EU population uses the Internet.[101] For a significant number of individuals, their online acts of enjoyment and expression are restricted by copyright, and the existing model of exclusivity with enforcement is problematic for all parties involved. This problem should be addressed by EU policy makers. Online enforcement is either impossible (de facto or due to high transaction costs) or undesirable, as it risks encroaching upon fundamental rights and freedoms of individuals and intermediaries. Criminalisation and strict enforcement alienate end-users – with file-sharers being among the best clients of the content industries – and diminish the respect for, and legitimacy of, copyright law. Furthermore, emerging online business models, like streaming platforms, despite generating significant rights revenue, fail to provide fair remuneration to creators or capture the market for mass-scale non-commercial use.

These challenges suggest an urgent need to study pragmatic legal solutions that enable end-users access to works in the digital environment, while assuring remuneration to creators or all rights holders, and promoting the development of the information society. The book addresses that need by exploring flexibilities in EU copyright law in search of a consistent regulation of non-commercial online use. In doing so, the study offers policy makers a blueprint for reform of the *acquis* through ACS.

1.5 OUTLINE

The main research questions are restated here:

> Are Alternative Compensation Systems for non-commercial online use of works by individuals admissible under EU copyright law and consistent with its objectives and, if so, to what extent? How can and should EU copyright law incorporate an Alternative Compensation System?

The questions aim at studying the legal admissibility and normative consistency of an ACS with the EU copyright *acquis*. The different components of the questions are recast as sub-research questions, answered sequentially in each chapter.

---

99. Institute for Information Law (IViR), *Research, Copyright in an Age of Access: Alternatives to Copyright Enforcement*, https://www.ivir.nl/projects/copyright-in-an-age-of-access-alternatives-to-copyright-enforcement/ (accessed 31.01.2017).

100. *See supra* 1.1, and *infra* 5.3.2.3.3, and 5.3.3.3. On the relationship between empirical research and normative questions, especially the challenge of 'incorporating results from empirical studies into normative scholarship and practice', *see* Leeuw, 2015.

101. Eurostat, 2015.

History is a good teacher. This is especially true for copyright law, a field that has evolved in a dialectic relationship with technology. Chapter 2 seeks to understand whether ACS are a wholly new phenomenon or have instructive precedents in the history of copyright. To do so, it asks the following questions: What influential historical examples of copyright rules qualify as precedents to ACS? What is their legal design? What justifications underlie their adoption? The objective is to draw lessons from the past for the examination of similar models in the online environment. The chapter examines two influential copyright rules that qualify as precedents to ACS: private copying and broadcasting compulsory licences. The objective is to uncover their legal characteristics and justifications for implementation.

Chapter 3 investigates how best to conceptualise legalisation proposals and their attributes in light of EU copyright law. In other words, how to understand these proposals in a legally coherent way that enables the study of their nature, characteristics and effects as compared to each other and EU law. The questions this chapter examines are: What legal models are most commonly used for legalisation proposals? How can these models be qualified in light of EU copyright law? What is their nature and effect on the exclusive right? What are their main attributes? The chapter designs a conceptual framework that systemises different types of ACS and their attributes, while connecting these to the *acquis*. The analysis focuses on different models of collective rights management – voluntary, extended, and mandatory –, on legal licences, and on state-funded systems. The chapter clarifies the scope and effects of legalisation proposals, as well as the central role of CMOs in their design. This research is primarily conceptual, setting the stage for the subsequent compliance and normative analysis of legalisation proposals in light of EU law.

Chapter 4 then maps the space available in the *acquis* for non-commercial online use by individuals, which is instrumental in evaluating the potential scope of an ACS. The main question addressed here is: how does the bundle of exclusive rights and corresponding limitations in the *acquis* apply to non-commercial online use by individuals? The analysis provides a snapshot of *what the law is* in light of CJEU interpretation. It first proposes a typology of online use by individuals, including browsing, downloading, streaming, stream capture, uploading, hyperlinking, and digital adaptations. This typology is then examined against the exclusive rights of reproduction and communication to the public in the *acquis*. Where a use triggers the application of an exclusive right, the chapter assesses whether it may nonetheless be authorised by an exception or limitation, namely for temporary and transient use, private copying, quotation, incidental inclusion, and caricature, parody, or pastiche. Because the Court often follows a teleological method of interpretation, and sometimes relies on fundamental rights to define the scope of exclusive rights and limitations, the legal research in this chapter is both descriptive and normative. The chapter elucidates the legal status of mass online use and the extent to which the types of ACS identified in Chapter 3 would necessitate legislative reforms in the *acquis*.

Chapter 5 is the heart of the book. It is divided in two main parts, which analyse the doctrinal and normative aspects of the book's main research questions. The first part of the chapter builds on the previous analysis which determined that a statutory licence ACS offers the greatest promise for regulation of non-commercial use, while dealing with complex issues of substantive and territorial fragmentation of copyright in the EU. However, such a licence entails the adoption of one or more limitations to the exclusive rights of reproduction and communication to the public. Therefore, it must pass the three-step test. In this light, the chapter inquires whether and to what extent is a statutory licence ACS for non-commercial online use by individuals admissible under EU copyright law, namely the three-step test. Answering this question helps to elucidate the space available in the *acquis* for the adoption of a limitation-based ACS. It also clarifies important normative issues, as the test is used to conduct a fair balancing exercise between the interests of creators, rights holders and the public, including the interest in the respect of users and intermediaries' fundamental rights.

The second part of the chapter turns to the key normative question of this book: to what extent is a model of access and remuneration, such as an ACS, consistent with the general aims of copyright and the particular objectives of EU copyright law? This inquiry is made in light of the prevailing rationales of copyright and the objectives of the *acquis*, recasting the normative insights gained throughout the book. In light of these elements, it is argued that EU copyright law can and should regulate non-commercial individual online use through a right of access and remuneration.

Chapter 6 offers conclusions and a proposal on how EU copyright law ought to incorporate an ACS. The first part of the chapter summarises the main findings of the study and teases out its descriptive and normative conclusions. The second part advances a reform proposal for the regulation of non-commercial online acts by end-users through a model of remunerated access. It advances a blueprint for a compensated limitation for non-commercial individual use that is consistent with EU copyright law. Following the pragmatic approach of the study, that blueprint is susceptible of adaptation to less stringent collective rights management models, supplemented by a soft law approach, which may be politically more feasible in the short to medium-term.

Chapter 2

Copyright Rewind: Precedents for Compensation Systems

2.1 INTRODUCTION

This chapter examines precedents to ACS. Precedents are current or previous legal rules adopted to address similar problems to those associated with large-scale online infringement: market failure due to excessive transaction costs, difficult or undesirable enforcement of exclusive rights, and the regulation by copyright of disruptive technological developments.

The focus of the analysis is on the justifications, development and design of alternative legal models (to exclusive rights) for the regulation of mass use that ensure remuneration to creators or exploiters. The chapter explores copyright history to understand how certain precedents balance competing interests within copyright through regimes that share core attributes with ACS.

The chapter asks the following research questions.

What historical examples of copyright rules qualify as influential precedents to ACS?
What is their legal design?
What justifications underlie their adoption?

Answers to these questions enable a better understanding of the ACS taxonomy in Chapter 3, and provide background and texture to the normative legal research of the book. The analysis is descriptive in that it analyses and interprets legal rules and principles, and normative to the extent it looks at justifications for their introduction and design.[1]

To answer the research questions, two representative precedents are selected and their legal development traced through time. The focus is on primary legal sources, playing particular attention to their context, object and purpose.

A historical approach assists in understanding current rules, shedding light on legal developments, providing insights into dynamics of legal change, and explaining its underlying causes.[2] It informs the opinions of authorities and, as a result, impacts legal interpretation.[3]

The discussion on online infringement recasts previous debates on adequate copyright responses to new technologies and changing market or consumer practices. Reactions to mass use often trigger re-assessment of the concepts of exclusivity and enforcement, weighed against efforts to balance the interests of rights holders and the public.[4] The analysis intends to harness the lessons of copyright past with the expectation that these are useful for its future.

The chapter proceeds as follows. Section 2.2 explains the process of precedent selection. Section 2.3 examines the mechanics and justifications for the first precedent: statutory licensing for private copying. Section 2.4 does the same for the second precedent: the compulsory licence for broadcasting and communication to the public. Section 2.5 presents the conclusions of the analysis.

2.2 PRECEDENT SELECTION

Many ACS proposals are extensions or adaptations of copyright schemes that emerged in response to disruptive technologies, market failure in the licensing and enforcement of copyright, or the undesirability of such enforcement in certain circumstances (e.g., against individuals in their private sphere). ACS precedents have been selected from that pool of schemes.

Precedents should assist in the subsequent examination of ACS against the EU copyright *acquis*. Hence, only rules that have a connection with this legal framework qualify. The aim is not to offer a detailed examination of *acquis* provisions that implement precedents, but instead to look at the legal

1. This internal/external distinction is a theoretical explanatory device; it mirrors the similar distinction made in legal history scholarship, on which see, e.g., Handler, 2013; Ibbetson, 2005.
2. *See* Handler, 2013, p. 95; Ibbetson, 2005, p. 878; Rose, 2010, pp. 14, 38. For copyright and technology, *see* Brad Sherman & Wiseman, 2012, pp. 2, 6.
3. *See supra* 1.3.
4. Taking an historical approach does not make this chapter an exercise in legal history research. On the latter, *see* Boorstin, 1941; Handler, 2013; Ibbetson, 2005; Rose, 2010.

history and the rules (some of which are still in force) that helped shape them.

In addition, precedents ought to have explanatory power vis-à-vis legalisation proposals, sharing core characteristics. Building on the preliminary characterisation of ACS in Chapter 1, it is possible to advance four attributes for precedents. They should:

- Constitute a copyright rule or scheme.
- Regulate large-scale or mass use of works.
- Provide a non-voluntary licence that aggregates works and types of use, as an alternative to exclusive rights.
- Ensure remuneration or compensation to creators or all rights holders.

These attributes – *copyright rule*, *mass use regulation*, *non-voluntary licence* and *compensation* – encapsulate the essential trade-off between remunerated access to works (for users) and control of use (by rights holders) that is the touchstone of ACS.

There are numerous candidates for precedents in international and European copyright law. They include statutory licences for private copying and reprography, 'residual' remuneration rights,[5] the compulsory licence for mechanical reproduction of phonograms,[6] the compulsory licences for broadcasting and cable retransmission, and the public lending right.

As several candidates possess the required attributes, it is necessary to filter the selection. This is done by introducing a criterion of diversity. An ACS regulates multiple exclusive rights, namely reproduction and communication to the public, including the right of making available. Thus, it is justifiable to select an influential precedent for each of those rights, as opposed to choosing regimes that apply to the same right. The remainder of this section looks at each attribute and the diversity criterion for selection of precedents.

2.2.1 Copyright Rule or Scheme

This attribute excludes rules outside the field of copyright, such as taxation or public grants. There are some ACS proposals of this type. According to them, non-commercial online use of works would not be subject to copyright protection, but creators would receive compensation through a tax paid out of the state budget, *ex ante/post* grants, or rewards. Chapter 3 explains these

5. These are typically unalienable non-exclusive remuneration rights granted mostly to authors and performers by operation of law after transfer or assignment of exclusive rights. *See* Ficsor, 2003b, p. 308. Examples are Arts 14*ter* BC, 7(3) WCT, 9(2) WPPT, 14(4) TRIPS, 5 Rental Right Directive, and 1 Resale Right Directive.
6. Art. 13 BC. On the history of this provision, *see* Okpaluba, 2012, pp. 96–100.

proposals, as some of their features are susceptible of transplant to copyright schemes.[7]

Yet, most ACS are internal to copyright law and proposals to move regulation of non-commercial use completely outside the field are politically unrealistic, as they would require abrogation of international treaties and an overhaul of the *acquis*. Hence, a precedent that is external to copyright law has low explanatory power.

This view makes historical examination of public lending right systems less appealing due to their origins outside copyright regulation, despite later integration in national copyright laws and the Rental Right Directive.[8]

2.2.2 Regulation of Large-Scale or Mass Use

The terms 'large-scale' or 'mass' refer to a large number of copyright-relevant acts in relation to a significant number of works. They are abstractions to describe the online activities of end-users giving rise to infringement on a wide-scale, enabled by technologies for reproduction and dissemination of near perfect copies of works. Although this book focuses on the regulation of non-commercial use, this particular attribute does not intend to qualify the use in question as 'commercial' or 'non-commercial'.[9]

P2P file sharing is a good example of a mass use. It involves up- and downloading of works by thousands or millions of Internet users. These activities are typically restricted under the exclusive rights of reproduction and communication to the public.

A clear case of a copyright rule regulating mass use is the private copying limitation and accompanying statutory licence. The limitation privileges reproductions made by end-users for non-commercial purposes in the private sphere, while guaranteeing fair compensation to rights holders. This model is often cited as inspiration for ACS and has the potential to apply to acts of downloading. It is therefore the most suitable precedent for the right of reproduction.

Following the diversity criterion, the choice of private copying would imply the exclusion of other rules applying to the reproduction right, such as the compulsory licence for mechanical reproduction of phonograms in the BC, and the reprography statutory license, which allows commercial and institutional users to make mass reproductions of works on paper or any similar medium through photographic techniques against the payment of fair

7. *See infra* 3.3.6.
8. For analysis of the public lending right before the rental Right Directive, *see* ALAI, 1983, and Explanatory Memorandum Rental Right Directive, pp. 12–18.
9. *See* Geller, 1991, pp. 23–25, for a different definition of mass use as an antonym to 'market use'. Some ACS proposals cover commercial and non-commercial use (*see infra* 3.4.2). However, the focus of this study is on the latter, ACS for non-commercial use. Cf. *supra* 1.2.

compensation to rights holders, but without their authorisation.[10] Because the origins and development of reprography and private copying are intertwined, examining reprography in addition to private copying would add little value to the analysis.

Conversely, the compulsory licence for broadcasting appears a good choice. Like reprography, the licence regulates large-scale use due to the high aggregate number of copyright acts and works involved, even if the number of commercial users (e.g., copy shops or broadcasters) included is low. In contrast to reprography, the compulsory licence for broadcasting applies to the right of communication to the public. It allows broadcasting organisations to transmit by wireless means for public reception (meaning an indefinite number of end-users) vast quantities of works, against payment of equitable remuneration but without a requirement for authorisation. Moreover, the licence has the potential to cover online use such as webcasting of musical works and phonograms.[11]

Other schemes, like those applying to residual remuneration rights (rental and *droit de suite*) are inadequate for precedents. They primarily regulate the legal effects of the transfer or assignment of exclusive rights and cover a relatively small number of uses.[12]

2.2.3 Non-voluntary Licences

'Non-voluntary licences' are legal mechanisms that enable mass use of works absent authorisation and subject to the payment of remuneration or compensation. In international copyright law, the meaning of the term is sometimes unclear and usually tied to the expressions 'exercise' and 'conditions on exercise' of rights. The expressions refer to the option for domestic laws to regulate certain copyright use through legal licences or mandatory collective management.[13] These mechanisms have different effects on the nature and exercise of the exclusive right. Figure 2.1 contains a simplified conceptual map of non-voluntary licences.

10. *See* Dreier, 2006, p. 57, on the potential conflict between Art. 13 BC and Art. 2(a) InfoSoc Directive. Dreier admits the possibility of compulsory licences and exemplifies with the existing German scheme under Art. 13 BC. On reprography, *see* Art. 5(2)(a) InfoSoc Directive.
11. *See infra* 2.4.
12. Geller, 1991, p. 23 & n. 7, not qualifying the commercial rental of copies as a mass use but rather a market use. However, Geller recognises its 'appearance of a mass use, at least when the chain of privity from the author to the renting end-users is broken by the first sale or exhaustion doctrine.'
13. *See infra* 3.2 and 3.3.4.2.

Figure 2.1 Non-voluntary Licences

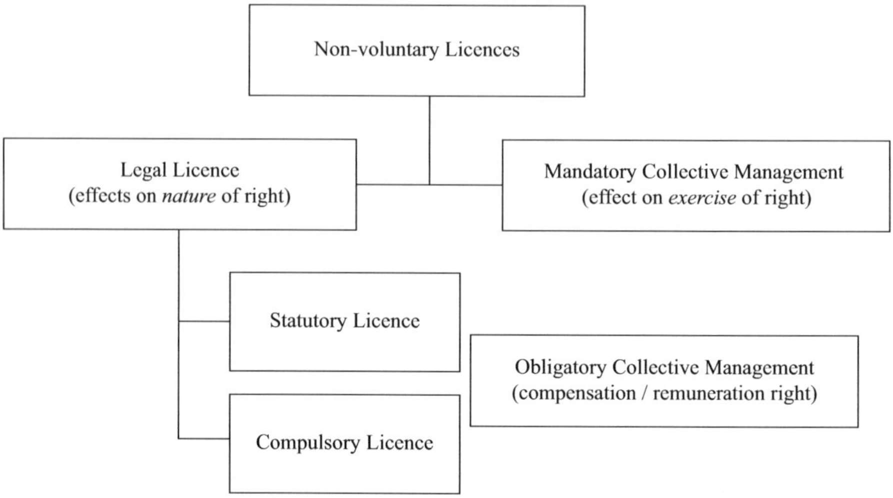

'Legal licences' include statutory and compulsory licences. Statutory licences restrict the nature of a pre-existing exclusive right through the application of a compensated limitation. The term 'compulsory licence' is used both as a synonym for statutory licence and with different meanings. In the context of this chapter, it is sufficient to note that compulsory licences do not usually regulate a pre-existing exclusive right; rather, they are imposed *ab initio* to govern a new type of use through a 'self-standing' remuneration right.[14] (The possible meanings of the term 'compulsory licence' are detailed in the ACS taxonomy in Chapter 3.)

Private copying and compulsory licensing for broadcasting provide examples of the different types of licence with a link to the *acquis*. The first is based on a statutory licence tied to a compensated limitation, and is recognised in Article 5(2)(b) InfoSoc Directive. The second relates to a remunerated non-exclusive right tied to a compulsory licence, traces of which are found in the SatCab and Rental Right Directives. Both licences are typically administered through obligatory collective management.[15]

In this book, a distinction is made between two schemes where collective rights management is imposed for administration of copyright. 'Mandatory' collective management is the term used to refer to schemes imposed by legislators in order to regulate *exclusive* rights through the intervention of a CMO. In contrast, the term 'obligatory' collective management is used for cases where collective administration accompanies legal

14. von Lewinski, 2008, pp. 55–56.
15. *See* Art. 4 SatCab Directive and Arts 8 and 10 Rental Right Directive.

licences as the model for administration of remuneration or compensation rights. As explained in Chapter 3, many ACS proposals rely on both schemes.[16]

Mandatory collective management is distinguishable from legal licences in that it does not impose restrictions on the nature of the exclusive right per se. It is not a copyright limitation but instead a restriction on the exercise of copyright (*see* Figure 2.1).[17] Therefore, this model of collective management can theoretically apply to exclusive rights, as exemplified by the special regime for the cable retransmission right in the SatCab Directive.[18] (Chapter 3 explores the rationale for this distinction and its implications. Importantly, not all authors categorise mandatory collective management as a non-voluntary licence.[19])

2.2.4 Equitable Remuneration or Fair Compensation

To qualify as precedent, the non-voluntary licence selected must ensure compensation for rights holders or at least creators. Outside remuneration through royalties for the use of exclusive rights, EU copyright law recognises two categories of compensation element – equitable remuneration and fair compensation – that reflect different non-voluntary licences.

The concept of equitable remuneration attaches to self-standing remuneration rights or rights of remuneration per se. These are rights designed from origin not as restrictions to exclusivity, but as non-exclusive rights vested in rights holders (typically creators) to obtain monetary consideration from the use of their works or related subject matter by third parties.[20] Equitable remuneration rights are directly provided in 'international copyright and related rights norms, and in national copyright laws, as a right to such remuneration'.[21]

Equitable remuneration rights are commonly tied to compulsory licences for uses or forms of exploitation of works not previously covered by an exclusive right. Examples at the international level are the equitable remuneration rights for broadcasting of works and for 'secondary uses' of phonograms.[22] In the *acquis*, it is possible to find a right for an unwaivable and equitable remuneration for rental, an optional right of remuneration for

16. *See infra* 3.3.4. On the conceptual distinction between mandatory and obligatory collective management, *see also infra* 3.2.
17. *See infra* 3.3.4.2, for discussion on the legal nature and effects of mandatory collective management.
18. Arts 8–12 SatCab Directive. *See infra* 2.4.4 and 3.3.4.
19. See, e.g., Depreeuw, 2014, p. 297.
20. Ficsor, 2010, pp. 44–46; von Lewinski, 2008, p. 55.
21. Ficsor, 2003b, p. 307.
22. Arts 11*bis* BC and 12 RC. *See infra* 2.4.2 and 2.4.3.

public lending, and rights for a single equitable remuneration for broadcasting and communication to the public.[23]

In international treaties, the concept of 'equitable' remuneration is often undefined and domestic laws have leeway to shape it beyond the ordinary meaning of a fair and just remuneration. Most commentators understand the term to signify that use of the work under the compulsory licence entitles authors to receive compensation equal or similar to that which would be obtained following negotiations in the absence of the licence. The resulting remuneration could be similar to the market value of the use, but could also be lower, depending on the factors considered (e.g., frequency of use), the balance of negotiations between stakeholders, and the position of the national (executive, legislative or judicial) body competent to set the final rates, absent agreement.[24]

In the *acquis*, although similar considerations are valid, the CJEU interprets the concept of equitable remuneration as based on the 'value of the use in trade' and following a logic of balance between competing interests.[25] Regarding calculation of the right of equitable remuneration for broadcasting (Article 8(2) Rental Right Directive), the Court allows the same to operate:

> by reference to variable and fixed factors, such as the number of hours of phonograms broadcast, the viewing and listening densities achieved by the radio and television broadcasters represented by the broadcast organisation, the tariffs fixed by agreement in the field of performance rights and broadcast rights in respect of musical works protected by copyright, the tariffs set by the public broadcast organisations in the Member States bordering on the Member State concerned, and the amounts paid by commercial stations, provided that that model is such as to enable a proper balance to be achieved between the interests of performing artists and producers in obtaining remuneration for the broadcast of a particular phonogram, and the interests of third parties in being able to broadcast the phonogram on terms that are reasonable, and that it does not contravene any principle of Community law.[26]

'Fair compensation' has different contours. This concept accompanies certain limitation-based statutory licences. Before the InfoSoc Directive, most European systems would subject compensated limitations to the payment of equitable remuneration, following the blueprint of other non-exclusive rights in the *acquis*. After the directive, that concept was replaced by 'fair compensation'. Rights of fair compensation are now recognised for

23. Respectively, Arts 5, 6 and 8(2) Rental Right Directive.
24. See, e.g., Arts 11*bis*(2) BC and 12 RC, analysed *infra* at 2.4.2 and 2.4.3, respectively.
25. See, concerning Art.8(2) Rental Right Directive: CJEU, *Sena*, paras 36–37; CJEU, *Lagardère*, para. 50.
26. CJEU, *Sena*, para. 46. *See also* CJEU, *Kanal 5 and TV4*, paras 37, 41.

reprographic reproductions, private copying, reproductions of broadcasts by non-commercial social institutions, and for use of orphan works by specific organisations.[27] Furthermore, recital 36 InfoSoc Directive suggests a preference of the EU legislator for the concept of fair compensation in connection with future compensated limitations on the directive's exclusive rights of reproduction, communication to the public, and distribution.[28]

Recital 35 InfoSoc Directive clarifies that the 'form, detailed arrangements and possible level' of fair compensation should take into consideration the particular circumstances of the use, and that the potential harm caused by such use to rights holders provides a 'valuable criterion' to evaluate those circumstances. Therefore, the notion of 'harm' is the basis of fair compensation.[29] If the harm is reduced or non-existent, it is possible that the payment of fair compensation is reduced or eliminated accordingly. This reduction or elimination is possible where other payments for the same use have been made (e.g., as part of a licence fee) or the use in question causes minimal harm (*de minimis*). Finally, the level of fair compensation should take into consideration the degree of use of technological protection measures (TPMs).[30]

Although the directive is silent on the topic, the CJEU has interpreted fair compensation as an autonomous concept of EU law[31] and, after weighing different objectives of the InfoSoc Directive – establishing a high level of protection, safeguarding internal market competition and striking a 'fair balance' – qualified the right as unwaivable.[32]

---

27. See, respectively, Arts 5(2)(a), (b) and (e) InfoSoc Directive, and 6(5) Orphan Works Directive.
28. Recital 36 reads: 'The Member States may provide for fair compensation for rightholders also when applying the optional provisions on exceptions or limitations which do not require such compensation.' Following the objective of harmonious interpretation of limitations in recital 31, it would make sense to adopt the concept of fair compensation to *new* compensated limitations on the exclusive rights in the InfoSoc Directive.
29. *See* Art. 5(2) and recital 35 InfoSoc Directive. *See infra* 2.3.3 and 4.4.3.3. Beyond the legal bases referenced, the concept of 'fair compensation' in the *acquis* is developed in the following CJEU judgments: *Padawan*, *Stichting de Thuiskopie*, *VG Wort*, *Amazon.com*, *Luksan*, *ACI Adam*; *Copydan*, and *Reprobel*. For analysis, *see* Poort & Quintais, 2013; Quintais, 2015b.
30. Recital 35 and Art. 5(2)(b) InfoSoc Directive.
31. *See* CJEU, *Padawan*, paras 32, 37, applying by analogy to the concept of 'equitable remuneration' in Art. 8(2) Rental Right Directive. *See also* CJEU, *Sena*, para 24.
32. *See* Art. 5(2)(b) and recitals 31 and 32 InfoSoc Directive. On the unwaivable character of fair compensation *see* CJEU, *Luksan*, paras 100, 102, 104–106. *See also*: CJEU, *Padawan*, paras 34–35; CJEU, *Stichting de Thuiskopie*, para 34; CJEU, *Murphy*, para. 186, identifying as the principal objective of the InfoSoc Directive the establishment of a 'high level of protection of authors, allowing them to obtain an appropriate reward for the use of their works'; CJEU, *DR and TV2 Danmark*, para. 35. For the use of the fair balance criteria in recital 31 within the context of the Court's systematic interpretation of provisions in the directive, *see infra* 4.4.1.4 and 5.3.3.

2.2.5 Selection of Precedents

In conclusion, precedents are copyright rules that regulate mass use of works through non-voluntary licences and subject to compensation. They address challenges resulting from technological disruption, market failure related to difficulties in licensing or enforcement of copyright, and undesirable enforceability of copyright. Under the criteria adopted here, the legal regimes most suited to serve as precedents are statutory licences for private copying and compulsory licences for broadcasting and communication to the public. Both schemes are frequently exercised through collective management, and have influenced multiple ACS proposals.[33]

2.3 STATUTORY LICENSING FOR PRIVATE COPYING

The origin of the private copying levy system can be traced back to landmark decisions of the *Bundesgerichtshof* (BGH) between 1955 and 1964, namely in the *Grundig Reporter* and *Personalausweise* cases, which influenced the draft of the 1965 German Copyright Act.[34]

The invention, in the 1930s, and market introduction in Germany, in the 1950s, of magnetic tape recording, followed by massive consumer uptake, allowed end-users for the first time to mechanically copy or 'home tape' works, especially sound recordings. The litigation that ensued led to the introduction of a non-voluntary licensing scheme for private copying in the 1965 Act.[35]

The initial scope of the German levy system covered tape recording equipment, but was extended to tape media in 1985. Technological developments, a drop in equipment prices, and the high degree of penetration of consumer recording devices in Germany all contributed to the steady expansion of levy targets to encompass multiple reproduction technologies and related supports.[36]

German levy schemes were influential in other European countries' laws and throughout the world.[37] They likewise impacted international copyright law, with private copying featuring in UNESCO and WIPO

33. *See infra* 3.3.4 and 3.3.5.
34. See: BGH, 18.05.1955, I ZR 8/54 ('Grundig Reporter I'); BGH, 18.05.1955, I ZR 10/54 ('Grundig Reporter II'); BGH, 22.01.1960, I ZR 41/58 ('GEMA-Hinweis'); BGH, 29.05.1964, I ZR 4/63 ('Personalausweise').
35. Hugenholtz, 2012a, p. 179; Reinbothe, 1981, p. 36.
36. Reporting figures for the German market and that of other Member States *see* Green Paper on Copyright and the Challenge of Technology 1988, pp. 110–113.
37. On the general significance of the German Act as a model of international copyright law, *see* Cornish, 1995, p. 804.

agendas, as well as in the preparatory works of the 1967 Stockholm act of the BC – playing a role in shaping the three-step test – and the 1996 WIPO Treaties. Finally, the German scheme provided the blueprint for the private copying limitation in the InfoSoc Directive.

Because it involves acts of reproduction, private copying calls into play Article 2 InfoSoc Directive. That provision contemplates a broad exclusive right, covering all digital acts of reproduction over the Internet, except transient copies.[38] Article 5(2)(b) InfoSoc Directive allows Member States to provide limitations to the Article 2 reproduction right:

> in respect of reproductions on any medium made by a natural person for private use and for ends that are neither directly nor indirectly commercial, on condition that the rightholders receive fair compensation which takes account of the application or non-application of technological measures referred to in Article 6 to the work or subject-matter concerned.

This constitutes the so-called private copying limitation. Its implementation is conditional upon the grant of fair compensation, calculated with reference to the criteria mentioned above in 2.2.4. The directive does not mention levies, but the recognition of a fair compensation right is a tacit endorsement of levy systems existing in national legislatures.[39] This section examines the development of the private copying limitation from its inception to its inclusion in the InfoSoc Directive.

2.3.1 A German Legal Creation

The years of 1927 (in the USA) and 1928 (in Germany) saw the issue of the first patents for inventions of sound carrying magnetic tapes.[40] Following the early development of tape recording technology and its adoption by commercial users in Germany in the 1930s, notably the widespread use of the 'Magnetophon' by the German public radio service, the 1950s saw the gradual transition of tape recorders into the consumer market.[41]

Interoperability was a design feature of such devices, including a function for recording radio broadcasts and phonograms – for which they were duly advertised – allowing home taping of works.[42] Consumer adoption

38. Arts 2 and 5(1) InfoSoc Directive. Note also that recitals 9 and 11 seem to favour an '*in dubio pro autore*' interpretation of this right. *See* Ohly, 2009, p. 217.
39. Hugenholtz, 2012a, pp. 192–193.
40. Boytha, 1993, pp. 295–296.
41. Hugenholtz, 2012a, p. 181. *See also* Green Paper on Copyright and the Challenge of Technology 1988, p. 101.
42. BGH, 18.05.1955, I ZR 8/54 ('Grundig Reporter I'), 493 *apud*. Hugenholtz, 2012a, p. 181.

of the technology was exponential, and the same was used to record both protected content and that not protected by copyright (e.g., dictation).[43]

The German author's CMO for musical performing and mechanical reproduction rights – the *Gesellschaft für musikalische Aufführungs- und mechanische Vervielfältigungsrechte* (GEMA) – was quick to recognise and label the phenomenon a 'large-scale infringement of the musical works it represented'.[44] Its reaction was to propose that every device owner pay a monthly amount as consideration for the authorisation for home taping.[45] This proposal for a 'personal possession' licence was met with widespread criticism.

The objections to the proposal were many and varied: the reproduction devices were similar to other licence-free objects (like musical instruments) allowing infringing use; the licensing requirement conflicted with the constitutional right of privacy; and unauthorised use resulted more from the industry's inability to meet consumer demand than from home taping activities.[46] (It is remarkable that near identical arguments are central to today's online infringement debate.)

The GEMA proposal never made it to law. Instead, some manufacturers and producers entered into a voluntary licensing scheme with the organisation, agreeing to pay a one-off amount of '1% of the production value of each manufactured tape recorder', as consideration for an authorisation to sell consumers 'GEMA free machines'.[47] As Hugenholtz points out, this scheme is at the inception of the 1965 statutory levy system.[48]

Nevertheless, other manufacturers refused the 'voluntary levy' on the grounds of non-liability for private acts of end-users and relying on the express authorisation for personal use copies in the 1901 German Copyright Act.[49] In response, GEMA sued.

2.3.1.1 Pre-1965: The GEMA Litigation that Shaped the Act

In 1952, GEMA and multiple record companies sued several tape recorder manufacturers.[50] Besides asking for damages, the plaintiffs sought two injunctions against manufacturers, aimed at preventing both the sale of tape recorders without their authorisation and related advertising that did not include a notice on the GEMA licence requirement.[51]

43. Hugenholtz, 2012a, p. 181.
44. *Ibid.*, p. 182 citing the reaction in 1950 from Dr Eric Schulze, General Director of GEMA.
45. *Ibid.*, p. 182.
46. *Ibid.*
47. *Ibid.*, pp. 182, 189.
48. *Ibid.*, p. 189.
49. *Ibid.*, p. 183. On the rules in the 1901 Act, *see* Collová, 1966, p. 100–ff.
50. Hugenholtz, 2012a, p. 183; Mac, 1973, p. 107.
51. Hugenholtz, 2012a, p. 183; Reinbothe, 1981, p. 38.

To some surprise, the Berlin Court of First Instance awarded the injunctions in 1953, stating that not only were end-users infringing authors' exclusive rights, but that 'dealers' of recording devices and tapes were likewise infringing because they participated in 'the illicit utilization for putting the devices at the public's disposal without informing the purchasers of their liability'.[52]

As a result, two identical cases – *Grundig Reporter I* and *II* – made it to the BGH. The first focused on copyright managed by GEMA, whilst the second addressed related rights in sound recordings held by plaintiff record companies.[53] The cases were decided in 1955.

The legal bases for the lawsuit were Articles 11(1) and 15 of the 1901 German Copyright Act. The first provision gave copyright owners an exclusive right of reproduction, while Article 15(2) exempted copying for non-commercial private purposes.[54] In essence, the *Grundig Reporter* cases examined, first, whether private non-commercial home taping triggered the exclusive reproduction right and, second, whether the private use exception exempted home taping.[55]

The issue 'sharply divided' German legal doctrine. One school of thought relied on literal statutory interpretation and the principle that copyright did not extend to the private sphere. That line of thinking echoed Kohler's proposition to exclude consumptive uses from copyright protection. Another school of thought, including the likes of Ulmer, understood home recording technology as fundamentally transforming the role of users within the copyright ecosystem, justifying their analogy to commercial users for liability purposes.[56]

In its *Grundig Reporter* decisions, the BGH sided with the latter, in what can be viewed as a watershed moment for copyright regulation – a shift from focusing primarily on market use to regulating large-scale non-profit individual use as well.[57] For the Court, private use was an exception to the general exclusive right, and thus subject to strict interpretation. The legislative history of the 1901 Act made clear that this exception was not meant to cover home taping of musical works, a possibility 'beyond the imagination of the legislator'.[58]

Home recording technology thus posed a conflict unforeseen by the legislator, leaving the BGH with a margin of discretion to develop the law

52. Collová, 1966, p. 106.
53. Hugenholtz, 2012a, p. 183; Reinbothe, 1981, p. 37.
54. Reinbothe, 1981, p. 37.
55. *Ibid.*, p. 38.
56. *See* Hugenholtz, 2012a, p. 184, providing a summary of the debate. *See also* Ulmer, 1986, pp. 711–712, expounding similar arguments vis-a-vis reprography.
57. Geller, 1991, p. 13.
58. Reinbothe, 1981, p. 38.

through interpretation. In doing so, the Court favoured teleological and purposive interpretation of the law over its literal element.[59] Established case law on conflicts of interest of this nature was to the effect that the 'creative sphere of the authors' prevailed over the 'private sphere of the user'.[60]

In light of this, the BGH was of the opinion that authors enjoyed a right to a 'just pecuniary reward' for all use of works, irrespective of technical means. Although reflected in Article 27(2) of the Universal Declaration of Human Rights (UDHR), the right did not require statutory recognition, as it derived from natural law and found its justification in the fact that individuals 'enjoyed' the work.[61] The nature of the right was such that it applied even for use that 'did not show any direct economic profit'.[62] Thus framed, the scope of the exclusive reproduction right included home taping acts and left no freedom to make private copies under German law.[63]

The BGH further justified the strict reading of the exception on its limited rationale under the 1901 Act, which was 'to allow financially weak musicians to make hand-written copies of copyright protected sheet music'.[64] From that perspective, it made little sense to extend the exception to all consumers.

That was especially true, the BGH added, because the quality of home taped copies posed a risk of subsequent commercial piracy, and would negatively influence record sales, likely harming authors' economic interests.[65] Pursuant to these justifications, the enforceability of the right was immaterial to the recognition of its existence.[66]

However, because consumers made the copies, application of the exclusive right to home taping did not imply direct liability for manufacturers. The BGH cleared this liability hurdle through the application by analogy of the indirect liability concept developed under German patent case law. The court justified the analogy on the basis of recording devices' susceptibility to use for copyright infringement, and manufacturers' express advertisement of such use.[67] As a result, manufacturers and producers in both *Grundig*

---

59. Hugenholtz, 2012a, p. 185; Reinbothe, 1981, p. 39.
60. BGH, 18.05.1955, I ZR 8/54 ('Grundig Reporter I'), 497, *apud.* Hugenholtz, 2012a, p. 185; Reinbothe, 1981, p. 39.
61. *See* Hugenholtz, 2012a, p. 185, citing BGH, 18.05.1955, I ZR 8/54 ('Grundig Reporter I'), 496.
62. Reinbothe, 1981, p. 39.
63. Hugenholtz, 2012a, p. 185 citing BGH, 18.05.1955, I ZR 8/54 ('Grundig Reporter I'), 496.
64. BGH, 18.05.1955, I ZR 8/54 ('Grundig Reporter I'), 498, *apud.* Hugenholtz, 2012a, p. 186.
65. *See* Reinbothe, 1981, p. 39; Senftleben, 2004, p. 54. *See also* BGH, 18.05.1955, I ZR 8/54 ('Grundig Reporter I'), 498–499, *apud.* Hugenholtz, 2012a, p. 186.
66. Reinbothe, 1981, p. 39. *See also* BGH, 18.05.1955, I ZR 8/54 ('Grundig Reporter I'), 499, *apud.* Hugenholtz, 2012a, p. 186.
67. Hugenholtz, 2012a, p. 186.

Reporter cases were subject to injunctions and ordered to only sell their devices with 'GEMA-notices'. Despite this, no damages were awarded.[68]

Predictably, the reaction of device manufacturers was to cease advertising infringing uses, in an effort to escape liability and the GEMA-notice requirement.[69] True to form, GEMA filed new lawsuits against Grundig and retailers, which caused the BGH to extend the obligation to include GEMA-notices in all advertisements for reproduction devices, irrespective of the reference to infringing uses.[70]

GEMA continued to pursue the litigation route against manufacturers/producers, retailers and, on occasion, private owners of devices. However, despite legal successes, the litigation did not yield the desired results.[71] This was for two main reasons. First, the monitoring and enforceability of the exclusivity claim on the ground was difficult. Second, the legal barriers erected by the right of privacy under Article 13 of the German Constitution hampered enforcement attempts.[72] To make things worse, consumer uptake of GEMA user licences was negligible when compared to the number of devices sold.[73]

In the midst of this climate, the German Government submitted a new draft copyright law to Parliament in 1962. The draft included a remuneration right for private use but failed to impose liability for payment of the remuneration on manufacturers/producers, considering they 'did not undertake an exploitation of works in the sense of copyright'; instead, liability for payment resided with equipment owners, i.e., consumers.[74]

In a parallel track, GEMA stepped up efforts to force producers into its licensing programme. It asked a Berlin court to order device manufacturers to request information from wholesalers and retailers on the identity of consumers purchasing equipment. The objective was to subsequently approach consumers and either monitor the lawfulness of their use or propose a licence.[75] That litigation led to the BGH's landmark 1964 *Personalausweise* decision.

In *Personalausweise*, the BGH restated its earlier case law and ruled that the mere placement of 'equipment on the market could of itself be held as aiding and abetting innumerable violations of copyright'. However, the

68. *See* Collová, 1966, p. 108; Reinbothe, 1981, p. 39; Hugenholtz, 2012a, p. 186.
69. Hugenholtz, 2012a, pp. 186–187.
70. Collová, 1966, p. 110; Hugenholtz, 2012a, p. 187 & nn. 35 & 36. The case against Grundig was BGH, 22.01.1960, I ZR 41/58 ('GEMA-Hinweis').
71. Hugenholtz, 2012a, p. 187. *See also* Collová, 1966, p. 111 with references to cases against individuals.
72. Reinbothe, 1981, p. 39; Senftleben, 2004, p. 54.
73. Hugenholtz, 2012a, p. 187.
74. Collová, 1966, pp. 116–117; Hugenholtz, 2012a, p. 189; Reinbothe, 1981, p. 39; Mac, 1973, pp. 109–111.
75. Collová, 1966, pp. 108–110; Hugenholtz, 2012a, p. 187.

court refused to impose a general prohibition on the sale of recording devices, essentially on two grounds. The first was the susceptibility of the devices to use for non-infringing purposes. The second was the lack of proportionality of such a ban vis-à-vis the constitutional right of privacy (or inviolability of a citizen's home).[76] In addition, the judgment nudged the parties towards a licensing scheme where intermediaries could pass on the royalty or fee to end-users in the retail price, which the court considered the best way for GEMA to collect equitable remuneration for authors.[77]

2.3.1.2 The 1965 German Copyright Act and Its 1985 Amendment

Personalausweise had a decisive influence on the legislative process of the 1965 German Copyright Act.[78] The Judiciary Committee of the German Parliament cited the judgment to emphasise that producers 'took express advantage of the popularity of private home taping', and justify a proposal for a levy whereby the liability for payment resided with manufacturers/producers, under what became Article 53(5) of the new Act.[79]

On the rationale and design for the system, the committee opined that the exclusive reproduction right did extend to home taping acts, but enforcing the same was not feasible.[80] It did not view the use of devices for non-infringing purposes as an obstacle to levies, due to the likely use of those devices for recording works.[81] Furthermore, the committee expected producers to pass on the levy to consumers in the retail price of tape recorders, a well-known practice in the analogous case of 'publishing licenses or the production of records'.[82]

In advancing its arguments, the committee was concerned with finding a balanced solution – one which respected the fact that limitations in the 1965 Act were 'imposed in the public interest' – but was mindful of not leading 'to unjustified advancement of private commercial interests of users'.[83]

76. Hugenholtz, 2012a, p. 189; Reinbothe, 1981, p. 39; Senftleben, 2004, pp. 54–55.
77. Hugenholtz, 2012a, p. 188 noting that the Court suggests a 'one-time lump sum payment'. *See also* Mac, 1973, p. 109.
78. Collová, 1966, pp. 116–118; Mac, 1973, pp. 109–111; Senftleben, 2004, p. 55.
79. Collová, 1966, p. 119; Reinbothe, 1981, p. 40; Mac, 1973, pp. 111–113.
80. Mac, 1973, p. 111.
81. Reinbothe, 1981, p. 40; Mac, 1973, p. 113. According to Reinbothe, 1981, p. 40, the Committee had doubts on a similar probability regarding blank tapes, which led to their exclusion as levy targets. For a different opinion, *see* Nordemann, 1980, p. 51, noting limitations in recording devices at the time, which caused copying to remain 'in reasonable frames' and reduced the need to also levy recording tapes.
82. Collová, 1966, pp. 118–120; Reinbothe, 1981, p. 40.
83. Nordemann, 1980, p. 54.

Article 53 (and in particular its paragraph 5) of the Act granted authors a remuneration right for acts of private use by means of sound or video recording; the right was further extended to performers, producers of phonograms and films.[84] The provision imposed liability on producers and importers of recording devices to pay remuneration to rights holders for the possibility of making copies of works that their devices offered.[85]

Because only producers/importers of tape recorders 'suitable' for private recordings were liable for payment, liability was excluded in relation to 'professional purpose' or 'dictation' recording apparatus.[86] The law brought importers of devices into the scheme to make effective payment claims otherwise directed at foreign producers of devices, which risked being unenforceable; devices intended for export were not subject to levies.[87]

The aim was to circumscribe levy targets to devices used within the German territory, mirroring the jurisdiction of the German Copyright Act. Reinbothe argues that such a feature made the levy a 'copyright remuneration' instead of a tax, precisely because it provided 'for the opportunity … to make such reproductions' within the Act's jurisdiction.[88]

Calculation of remuneration was based on a percentage (5%) of the devices' manufacture or factory price.[89] Due to transaction costs related to the enforcement of the remuneration claim, Article 53(5) imposed a system of obligatory collective management. The model, known at the time for management of other equitable remuneration rights,[90] was to be carried out by a sole CMO.[91]

Different organisations – including GEMA (for musical authors), VG Wort (for literary authors), and GVL (for performing artists and producers of phonograms) – set up the *Zentralstelle für private Überspielungsrechte* to function as a central agency for collection of the levy and its distribution to

84. *See* Reinbothe, 1981, p. 41; Mac, 1973, p. 107; Nordemann, 1980, p. 50. Related rights owners were beneficiaries by virtue of Arts 84, 85(3) and 94(4) of the Act. *See* Collová, 1991, p. 44. However, broadcasting organisations were excluded, an exclusion that was kept in subsequent amendments of the law. See: Art. 87(3) 1985 German Copyright Act; Green Paper on Copyright and the Challenge of Technology 1988, p. 105.
85. Collová, 1966, p. 114; Dietz, 1986; Senftleben, 2004, p. 55.
86. Collová, 1966, pp. 114–115, 119–120, 1991, p. 42; Reinbothe, 1981, p. 41.
87. Collová, 1966, pp. 114–115, 120–121, 1991, pp. 42–44; Reinbothe, 1981, p. 41.
88. Reinbothe, 1981, pp. 41–42.
89. Collová, 1991, p. 44; Reinbothe, 1981, p. 42. In practice and until 1980, German CMOs only managed to negotiate percentages between 2.2% and 'slightly over' 4%, and had difficulties monitoring the accuracy of the data disclosed by debtors. *See* Nordemann, 1980, p. 52, arguing that the remuneration right left authors' CMOs in a weaker bargaining position as compared to the exclusive right.
90. *See* Reinbothe, 2010, p. 220, identifying the artists' resale right (s. 26), rental and lending rights (s. 27), and mechanical licensing (s. 61).
91. Collová, 1991, p. 43; Reinbothe, 1981, p. 42 & n. 22.

member CMOs, as well as negotiation broker between rights holders and levy debtors.[92]

The levy system's final judicial hurdle was cleared following enactment of the 1965 Act. In 1971, in an action brought by the recording equipment producer Uhe, the German Federal Constitutional Court assessed the compatibility of Article 53(5) with multiple constitutional rights and duties: freedom of action, equal protection, freedom of profession, and protection of property.[93] The court considered the levy scheme to be in line with the German Constitution. The judgment relied on the likelihood that devices would be used for infringing purposes, and the possibility that levies would be passed on to purchasers, thus preventing unequal treatment of certain levied manufacturers.[94]

Twenty years after its implementation, in 1985, the private copying levy system was amended. The German legislator extended the levy to blank tapes, and implemented a model for the fixation of amounts through periodically revised tariffs, instead of on a percentage basis.[95] The change was an attempt to curtail problems in enforcing the limitation, and aimed primarily at popular lower fidelity cassette recorders and millions of blank tapes sold annually in Germany.[96]

Due to the technology-neutral legal formula of the provision – 'equipment suitable for making such reproductions' – and the rapid development of consumer-ready copying technology, the scope of the levy gradually expanded and developed to encompass a plethora of analogue, and later digital, devices and media, ranging from cassette recorders and VCRs, to CDs, USB sticks, external discs and so forth.[97]

In 1986, the fifty-sixth Congress of the International Literary and Artistic Association (ALAI) in Berne discussed copyright levies and the 1985 German Copyright Act. Professor Françon broached the topic in the general report on 'the future of copyright', as did Dr Adolf Dietz in a complementary report on private copying and reprography.[98] The reports and ensuing discussions reflected two main criticisms of levies. The first was that levies represented a 'dangerous' trend towards non-voluntary copyright

92. See: Mac, 1973, p. 117; Reinbothe, 1981, pp. 42–43, explaining the functioning of the collection and distribution system in detail. *See also* Dietz, 1986, pp. 255–256, identifying other CMOs involved, and Hugenholtz, 2012a, p. 190.
93. Respectively, Arts 2, 3, 12, and 14 of the then German Constitution. Reinbothe, 1981, p. 40. BVerfG (German Federal Constitutional Court), 07.07.1971 – 1 BvR 775/66 ('Private Tonbandvervielfältigungen').
94. Hugenholtz, 2012a, p. 190; Reinbothe, 1981, p. 47.
95. Collová, 1991, p. 48; Dietz, 1986, p. 254-; Senftleben, 2004, p. 55 & n. 280. *See also* Hugenholtz, 2012a, pp. 190–191 & n. 190; Reinbothe, 1981, pp. 46–47, relating this extension to the decrease in price of recording equipment.
96. *See* Nordemann, 1980, p. 51 describing the types of devices and tapes massively used in Germany and excluded from the 1965 Act. *See also* Collová, 1991, p. 48.
97. Hugenholtz, 2012a, pp. 190–191.
98. ALAI, 1987, pp. 199–235, 254–258.

licensing, which challenged the principle of exclusivity and left authors in a weaker bargaining position. The second was that the workings of levy systems through CMOs were not efficient or transparent.[99]

For the participants, including leading scholars of the time, statutory licensing for private copying was justified on a pragmatic basis, as the best available solution for the exercise of rights, the exploitation of which involves unenforceable mass use.[100]

Despite criticism on certain aspects of the system, the amounts collected under it increased gradually since its inception and the model became widely accepted in Germany.[101] It was only a matter of time until improvements in consumer reproduction technology made other countries feel the need to implement levy systems based on the German model.

2.3.2 A Legal Chronology of International Developments

2.3.2.1 Berne Convention: The 1967 Stockholm Revision Conference

Prior to 1965, private copying was present but not prominent in international copyright debates. From the rights holders' standpoint, the push for a statutory licensing solution was advocated in various resolutions and recommendations of the International Confederation of Authors and Composers Societies (CISAC).

As early as 1949, the issue of reproduction for private use and the possibility of a 'statutory grant of remuneration calculated on equipment and/or blank tapes' were discussed in a CISAC assembly meeting. There, the need was expressed to reach a 'new solution capable of protecting the legitimate interests of authors without impairing the dissemination of science and culture that is made possible by such new inventions'.[102] Following that initial pronouncement, it is possible to find other mentions of the topic up until the confederation's Rome congress in 1962. These, however, had little to no follow-up.

Such apathy can be partially justified by the fact that, although popular, the technologies of tape recorders, reel-to-reel tapes, and audio cassettes

99. *See* Dietz, 1986; Françon, 1986, pp. 213–217, 221–222. *See also* ALAI, 1987, pp. 261–283 (interventions of Ziegler, Freegard, Moller, Kerever, Uchtenhagen, Stewart, Clark and Françon).
100. See, e.g., ALAI, 1987, pp. 265, 274–275, 280–281 (interventions of Moller, Uchtenhagen and Françon).
101. See: Mac, 1973, p. 99 reporting increases between 1965 and 1970; Dietz, 1986, p. 257, reporting numbers for the second semester of 1985; Reinbothe, 1981, p. 46; Hugenholtz, 2012a, p. 190. *Contra*, Nordemann, 1980, p. 51ff., arguing that they 1965 system was not 'elastic enough' to adjust to technical developments, worked against authors, and that an exclusive right would provide a better solution.
102. Collová, 1991, pp. 36–38.

were in their infancy, with the respective industries 'experiencing production and marketing difficulties'.[103] Private copying and the legal developments in Germany, however, would end up having significant influence on the design of the three-step test at the 1967 Stockholm revision conference of the BC.[104] (The test, currently set forth in Article 9(2) BC, states: 'It shall be a matter for legislation in the countries of the Union to permit the reproduction of such works in certain special cases, provided that such reproduction does not conflict with a normal exploitation of the work and does not unreasonably prejudice the legitimate interests of the author')

The conference was preceded in 1965 by a report from a committee of governmental experts from the *Bureaux Internationaux Reunis pour la Protection de la Propiete Intellectuelle* (BIRPI).[105] The report advanced two main proposals on this topic. First, introducing a 'general provision establishing the right of reproduction jure conventionis', i.e., as a minimum of protection. Second, recognising a formula allowing national legislation to 'provide for exceptions' in favour of cultural and public interests, thus limiting the 'recognition and exercise' of the reproduction right. The latter point, in particular, gave rise to much debate in the committee of experts.[106]

The main argument for introducing the right was the 'obvious' principle that 'all the forms of exploiting a work which have, or are likely to acquire, considerable economic or practical importance must in principle be reserved to the authors'. Exceptions to this principle, the report stated, were 'unacceptable'.[107]

Nevertheless, national laws contained an array of exceptions 'in various public and cultural interests', including for private use.[108] In that light, the report proposed that Article 9 BC include a three-part formula for introducing 'exceptions of lesser importance': (1) respect for other Berne provisions; (2) definition of 'clearly specified purposes', e.g., private use; and (3) that exceptions 'not enter into economic competition with the work'.[109]

The BIRPI report considered a provision of this type a superior option to an exhaustive list of exceptions.[110] The report further admits that exceptions are valid absent a 'right to claim remuneration'. Still, it goes on, if a remuneration right is granted, 'the scope of the power to make exceptions widens to some extent'.[111]

103. *Ibid.*
104. Senftleben, 2004, p. 53. For an overview of the conference, *see* Masouyé, 1967.
105. BIRPI, 1965. For context and details, *see* Van Nus, 1967. N.B. in Stockholm BIRPI became WIPO.
106. BIRPI, 1965, pp. 8, 46–52; Van Nus, 1967, pp. 153–155.
107. BIRPI, 1965, p. 47.
108. *Ibid.*, p. 47 & n. 23.
109. *Ibid.*, pp. 48–49.
110. *Ibid.*, p. 49 & n. 24.
111. *Ibid.*, p. 49.

At the Stockholm conference, the Main Committee I discussed the right of reproduction in Articles 9, 10 and 10*bis* BC.[112] The conference introduced for the first time a general reproduction right applying to all literary and artistic works 'in any manner or form' in Article 9(1).[113] Concerns with private copying shaped the right.

For instance, Germany proposed that the provision include a reference to recording of protected works 'by instruments capable of reproducing them mechanically'. Other proposals were broader in scope, but the consensus was that a general reproduction right would encompass such recordings, including for private use.[114]

The programme's draft paragraph (2) set out the general exceptions to the reproduction right, enabling national legislation to permit them in three cases, divided into items *(a)*, *(b)* and *(c)*. *Item (a)* referred to 'private use', *item (b)* to 'judicial or administrative purposes', and *item (c)* included the future second and third conditions of the three-step test.[115] *Item (a)* and its influence on *item (c)* are of interest here.

A reading of the committee's debates clarifies the relevant opposing interests. On one level, there were proposals to prevent exceptions to a general reproduction right.[116] Countries like France, the Netherlands and Italy wished to replace 'private use' with the narrower 'individual or family use', while including a more general formula in *item (c)*. Germany, for its part, wished to make the private use exception subject to a third condition in *item (c)*: that reproduction should not conflict with the 'author's right to obtain equitable remuneration', to be fixed by a competent authority, absent agreement between the interested parties.[117]

In Germany's view, it was not possible in Stockholm to reach international consensus on a private copying exception. Regardless, further study on the rapid phenomenon of home taping was needed, as it threatened the 'substance' of the reproduction right itself.[118]

An opposing scheme to extend exceptions was advocated by developing countries. They argued for applying general or territorially limited compulsory licensing for reproduction – by regulating the 'conditions of exercise' of the right – coupled with a remuneration right for authors.[119]

A third proposition, embodied in a proposal by the UK delegate, was to eliminate *items (a)* and *(b)* and introduce a single formula, to be merged with

112. Records BC Stockholm 1967, pp. 851–862, 1142–1150.
113. *Ibid.*, pp. 851–856, 1142–1144.
114. *Ibid.*, p. 1143–1144.
115. *Ibid.*, p. 1144.
116. *Ibid.*
117. Records BC Stockholm 1967, pp. 624–625, 629, 634, 682, 704–705, 1144 (docs. S/13, S/18, S67, S/70, S/81, and S/67). *See also* Collová, 1991, p. 86.
118. Records BC Stockholm 1967, pp. 624–625 (doc. S/13).
119. *Ibid.*, pp. 621, 705–706, 820–821 (docs. S/13, S/75 and S/86).

item (c): 'in certain special cases where the reproduction does not unreasonably prejudice the legitimate interests of the authors.'[120]

After re-ordering the conditions and adjusting the text, the committee adopted that proposal. In this drafting exercise, it appears that the conditions (steps) of the test are intended as cumulative and subject to sequential analysis. To that effect, only if reproduction acts (1) do not conflict with the normal exploitation of the work, *and* (2) do not unreasonably prejudice the legitimate interests of the author, then (3) 'would it be possible in certain special cases to introduce a compulsory license, or to provide for use without payment'.[121]

The three-step test, as a rule directed at national legislators, was born. Equitable remuneration was a constituent part of its conditions, concretely its third step, essential for the validity of certain exceptions.[122] The Committee went so far as to illustrate its application:

> A practical example might be photocopying for various purposes. If it consists of producing a very large number of copies, it may not be permitted, as it conflicts with a normal exploitation of the work. If it implies a rather large number of copies for use in industrial undertakings, it may not unreasonably prejudice the legitimate interests of the author, provided that, according to national legislation, an equitable remuneration is paid. If a small number of copies is made, photocopying may be permitted without payment, particularly for individual or scientific use.[123]

For the purpose of clarification and following the above-mentioned German proposal, Article 9(3) of the Stockholm Act stated that 'any sound or visual recording' was to qualify as a reproduction.[124] Hence, private use exceptions for recordings of those materials were subject to the three-step test.

In the end, the discussion on private copying and the national (German) legislative private copying experience were instrumental in shaping the three-step test, especially in relation to the element of remuneration.[125] Private use linked to a remuneration right was apparently within the confines of the test, as would be certain reprography levy systems. For some authors, like Collovà, private copying *without remuneration* was in general not

120. *Ibid.*, pp. 640 (doc. S/13), 710 (doc. S/81), 737 (doc. S/238).
121. *Ibid.*, pp. 757–762, 771–772, 1145–1146. For an early criticism of the vagueness of the formula, *see* Rouart, 1967, p. 299–ff.
122. Collová, 1991, p. 84; Senftleben, 2004, pp. 55–56.
123. Records Stockholm 1967, p. 758 (doc. S/721).
124. *Ibid.*, p. 624, 704, 1146 (docs S/13, S/67).
125. Senftleben, 2004, pp. 55–58. *See* Records Stockholm 1967, pp. 624–625, 682, 705 (docs. S/13, S/18, S/75).

acceptable under the test, as it could lead to 'the massive use of protected material without payment'.[126]

That view was to some extent echoed by Ulmer. The influential author argued 'the aim should be, insofar as exceptions are made in certain cases to the prohibition of reproduction, that a royalty should be paid to the author'.[127] To be sure, that was the understanding of Germany, which in 1974 adhered to 1971 Paris Act of the BC, maintaining Articles 53 and 54 of the German Copyright Act. Therefore, it is possible to view those provisions as examples of permissible limitations under the three-step test.[128]

In fact, it seems uncontroversial that the compromise wording of the three-step test left room for diverse national designs for remunerated private use limitations.[129] These, together with other limitations to the exclusive reproduction right considered admissible by Union countries in the Stockholm debates, find their justification in different manifestations of the public interest.[130] (Chapter 5 returns to this point in detail in when examining whether an ACS is consistent with the three-step test.)

2.3.2.2 Post-Stockholm: From 1967 to the 1990s

The national debate on levies initially evolved at a slow pace.[131] That changed once tape recording technology matured and became consumer-ready. The technological evolution led to a viral spread of the German blueprint through continental Europe in the 1980s and early 1990s. National private copying levy systems were adopted in Austria (1980), Norway (1981), Sweden (1982), Hungary (1982), Finland (1984/1985), France (1985), Portugal (1985), Spain (1987), the Netherlands (1989/1991), Switzerland (1992), Denmark (1992), Italy (1992), Belgium (1994), and Greece (1994).[132]

As noted by the EU Commission, 'the compact cassette marked a revolution the in popular music field', replacing vinyl discs and affording

126. Collová, 1991, p. 88.
127. Ulmer, 1986, p. 712.
128. Senftleben, 2004, p. 58.
129. Green Paper on Copyright and the Challenge of Technology 1988, pp. 102–103.
130. See, e.g., Records BC Stockholm 1967, pp. 627 (Belgium, S/18), 629 (Denmark, S/13). *See also* Collová, 1991, p. 86.
131. *See* Collová, 1966, for a comparative analysis of the application of copyright to acts of home-taping before Stockholm.
132. See: Green Paper on Copyright and the Challenge of Technology 1988, pp. 102–103, 103ff.; Collová, 1991, pp. 46–52, 106–107, stressing that Austria was the first country to target reproduction media; Hugenholtz, 2012a, pp. 191–192. On the French model, levy implementation followed the abandonment of a 'parafiscal' tax approach. *See* Astier, 1986.

consumers with a portable and durable recording media, which proved increasingly popular. VCRs and (later) compact discs followed.[133]

During the same period, European common law countries, such as the UK and Ireland, devoted 'much discussion' to copyright levies but ultimately rejected their implementation, in part due to 'effective lobbying by blank tape manufacturers'.[134]

In the majority of cases after 1985 (the date of the amended German Copyright Act), European levy systems had a dual basis, targeting recording devices and media.[135] At the same time, several countries outside Europe were seriously considering the implementation of similar systems.[136] In some cases and with varying scopes of implementation – like in the US, Japan and Russia – those intentions materialised in the 1990s.[137]

Similarly to the German model, the vast majority of emerging levy systems defined the remuneration right for private copying as internal to copyright, instead of a tax. This qualification, Collovà argues, results from the rationale, functions and beneficiaries of the levy.[138] The consequence of accepting the remuneration right as internal to copyright is that both the right and the levy system are subject to international copyright law, namely the national treatment and three-step test provisions of the BC.[139] The presence of copyright levies in the WIPO agenda, notably in the preparatory works for the 1996 WIPO treaties, illustrates the universal acceptance of this legal qualification.

2.3.2.3 Preparatory Works for the 1996 WIPO Treaties

In 1989, the Berne Union assembly and conference of representatives adopted the WIPO programme. The programme included a provision for convening a committee of experts on a possible protocol to the BC. WIPO's programme for the 1990–1991 biennium stated that the 'protocol would be mainly destined to clarify the existing, or establish new, international norms

133. Green Paper on Copyright and the Challenge of Technology 1988, p. 101, noting that re-usable optical discs were not yet marketed for consumers, but were on their way.
134. Cornish, 1993, p. 312.
135. The conclusion reflects the data reported in Collová, 1991, pp. 46–52.
136. Burger, 1988a, p. 321 & n. 6.
137. See: Audio Home Recording Act of 1992, Pub. L. No. 102–563, 106 Stat. 4237 (1992) (codified in ss 1001–1010 US Copyright Act); Australian Copyright Council, 2001, pp. 7–17; Hugenholtz, 2012a, p. 192. For a comparative analysis of the legal challenges and treatment of home taping in US and German laws, *see* Mac, 1973.
138. Collová, 1991, p. 52ff. Finland, Norway, and Spain are exceptions, funding their levy through the General State Budget. On this topic, *see* CJEU, *EGEDA II*, and *infra* 3.3.6.
139. See: Burger, 1988a, 1988b; Collová, 1991, p. 52ff., 104; Goldstein & Hugenholtz, 2013, pp. 110–111. *See also* Geller, 1991, p. 53–ff, explaining the challenges arising from the application of the national treatment principle.

where, under the present text of the Berne Convention, doubts may exist as to the extent to which that Convention applies'.[140]

After convening in 1991 and 1992, the Committee divided into two groups: one focusing on a possible protocol to Berne (the 'Berne Protocol Committee') and another on the preparation of a new instrument on the protection of related rights holders (the 'New Instrument Committee').[141] The work of both committees led to the so-called 'basic proposals' for the 1996 Geneva diplomatic conference. Private copying was on the agenda of both committees.

The Berne Protocol Committee was of the opinion that, before the introduction of digital recording, home taping only infringed the third condition of the three-step test, as it unreasonably prejudiced the interests of authors. To overcome or reduce such prejudice to reasonable levels, some form of payment was warranted, e.g., via levies on recording equipment or media.[142]

Nevertheless, the advent of optical and digital recording meant that serial reproduction – 'reproduction of more than one generation' of perfect copies – was now possible, even for private purposes. If unrestricted, digital private copying would also pose a conflict with the normal exploitation of works, and with step two of the test. Therefore, such acts should be restricted unless it was possible to eliminate the conflict and reduce the prejudice to reasonable levels.[143]

In that light, the committee proposed that a future Berne Protocol include a broad exclusive reproduction right, covering copying for personal purposes. Limitations to that right were possible if they did not exempt serial digital reproductions but only acts of copying for personal purposes of sound recordings and audio-visual works, and certain reprographic uses. Permitted limitations were subject to remuneration through levies on equipment (used for personal purposes) or blank supports, paid by the respective manufacturers or importers.[144]

The proposal was favourably received but raised doubts on the 'nature and extent of possible provisions'.[145] Different views were expressed on the feasibility of a private copying prohibition, its applicability to software, the impact of copy-protection mechanisms, and the implementation of a remuneration right. In view of these challenges and the need to streamline the agenda, the committee's mandate was reduced in September 1992, and private copying was dropped from the agenda as a result.[146]

140. Records WIPO Treaties 1996, p. 161.
141. *Ibid.*, pp. 161–162.
142. Ficsor, 2002c, pp. 390–391.
143. WIPO Document BCP/CE/I/3, p. 13 (paras 97–98).
144. *Ibid.*, pp. 13–15.
145. Ficsor, 2002c, p. 392.
146. *Ibid.*

The New Instrument Committee, for its part, suggested that private copying of performances and phonograms be subject to the three-step test, by aligning Article 15(1)(a) RC with the requirements of Article 9(2) BC.[147] Echoing the debates of the Berne Protocol Committee, the proposal was justified by developments in reproduction technology and the conflicts it posed to rights holders' normal exploitation of works, as well as their legitimate interests. In a similar fashion, the New Instrument Committee endorsed the implementation of a levy system based on a right to remuneration for performers and phonogram producers to compensate them for private copying of sound recordings, underscoring that such remuneration would comply with the third prong of the three-step test.[148]

This proposal was subject to 'extensive and animated debate', including discussions on the necessity of remuneration, its nature – with consensus on its qualification as a non-exclusive right, instead of a tax – its copyright relevancy, and its possible extension to audio-visual records.[149] However, as with the Berne Protocol Committee, and probably 'due to the perceived absence of agreement' on the issue, the topic did not make it to the fourth session of the agenda and, consequently, to the basic proposals discussed at the 1996 Geneva diplomatic conference.[150]

Most of the themes animating the international levies debate, already present at the inception of copyright levies in Germany, featured prominently in EU-level discussions in the lead up to the InfoSoc Directive.

2.3.3 Manifestations in the *Acquis*

Copyright levies have historically been controversial in EU copyright law and policy, sparking stakeholder and institutional debate. Following a Recommendation of the Council of Europe favouring the introduction of a remuneration right for private copying of sound and audio-visual recordings, levies made it to the harmonisation agenda in 1988.[151]

Chapter 3 of the 1998 Green Paper on Copyright and the Challenge of Technology addressed home taping of sound and visual recordings, which it defines as unauthorised reproductions by consumers for personal needs.[152] The Green Paper reported on claims from rights holders on the economic harm caused by home taping, the technological developments increasing its ease and attractiveness, together with divergent national responses in the

147. *Ibid.*
148. *See* WIPO Document BCP/CE/II/1, pp. 11–12, and Ficsor, 2002c, p. 392.
149. Ficsor, 2002c, p. 393 (citing Document INR/CE/II/1).
150. *Ibid.*, p. 394.
151. Council of Europe Recommendation No. R (88) 2. *See also* Collová, 1991, p. 56, and Green Paper on Copyright and the Challenge of Technology 1988, pp. 99–142.
152. Green Paper on Copyright and the Challenge of Technology 1988, p. 99.

form of 'taxes or levies'. The latter, it stated, could have negative effects on incentives to creation of works and the functioning of the internal market.[153]

The Commission recognised that 'a clear picture is difficult to draw' as to the effect of home copying on the market for audio-visual recordings or even its impact on the exploitation of works.[154] Nonetheless, private copying was already a 'common practice', which digital technological developments would further facilitate. Therefore, it was important to allow 'these dynamic technologies to evolve in a way that is most beneficial to the producer and consumer'.[155]

On one side of the spectrum, rights holders demanded greater protection through levies or technical measures, because mass use conflicted with the normal exploitation of copied works and unreasonably prejudiced their interests. The technical measures approach in particular gained favour vis-à-vis digital use as rights holders considered levy schemes 'inadequate to deal with the allegedly greater economic harm which DAT [digital audio tape recording] could imply.'[156]

Opposing this view were the hardware industry and (some) consumer representatives, who challenged claims of economic harm to rights holders. They argued that such harm was either insubstantial, not caused by private copying, or was actually priced into the purchase of content items. They further claimed home copying had the benefits of stimulating content demand and creating additional markets (e.g., for sale or rental of pre-recorded items).[157]

These interest groups also objected to levy systems on different grounds: that they did not reflect actual usage, were difficult to apply to multipurpose devices/media, and misallocated revenues. However, they showed openness to a 'compromise technical solution' for the technical measures approach.[158]

In its assessment, the Commission stated that home copying had 'negative but unquantifiable effects on the legitimate exploitation of recorded works', however these would tend to increase significantly for digital use. In relation to private copying, it considered there to be no negative effect from the first copy made from lawful sources, only from subsequent reproductions. Rights holders risked losses where home copying was a substitute for sales of pre-recorded material.[159]

Therefore, the Commission suggested the adoption of measures to curb these acts and indirectly stimulate lawful content sales. Such measures did not include Community-wide legislation for home copying, but rather the

153. *Ibid.*, pp. 100–117.
154. *Ibid.*, pp. 113–117.
155. *Ibid.*, pp. 110–113, 118–119.
156. *Ibid.*, 120–122.
157. *Ibid.*, pp. 122–124.
158. *Ibid.*
159. *Ibid.*, pp. 126–128, 136.

fostering of device-level 'technical solutions' to prevent private copying, if feasible and adequately balancing opposing interests. Levies should be retained only where Member States felt they were the 'best way to remunerate rights holders'; digital private copying in particular was considered a challenge better addressed by technological – rather than levy-based – solutions.[160]

Not satisfied with this policy orientation, CMOs pursued the matter in 1989 and 1990 through joint declarations requesting specific legislation for a remuneration right coupled with a levy targeting equipment/media; for digital audio tape recording, they pushed for an approach combining levies with 'compulsory' copy control mechanisms.[161]

In its 1990 Follow-up to the Green Paper, the Commission set up its working programme for copyright up until the date of establishment of the internal market (31 December 1992).[162] A 'large majority' of stakeholders manifested themselves to be against the prohibition on home copying, with most rights holders supporting levy systems, while hardware companies and consumer representatives opposed them. All parties supported the adoption of a 'Serial Copy Management System', a copy restriction system for devices that only permitted copies from the 'original work'. Rights holders, however, demanded a remuneration right for copies authorised in this manner as well.[163]

Given these developments, the Commission endorsed the general use of the Serial Copy Management System and stated its intention to propose a draft 'directive on home copying of sound and audiovisual recordings' to the Council in 1991.[164] That proposal never officially materialised and rules on private copying only made it to the *acquis* in a limited form much later in the 2001 InfoSoc Directive.[165]

Following the adoption of TRIPS and the 1994 Bangemman Report's recommendation for the creation of a community framework for intellectual property in the digital environment, the year 1995 saw the arrival of a new Green Paper on Copyright and Related Rights in the Information Society, setting out the Commission's harmonisation agenda.[166]

The Green Paper described the challenges technological developments pose to the criterion of private use and the risk they turn 'home copying into a fully-fledged form of exploitation'. It argued that the possibility of perfect copies raises the risks of piracy and non-remunerated use, simultaneously

160. *Ibid.*, pp. 129–143.
161. Collová, 1991, pp. 64–66.
162. Follow-up Green Paper 1990, pp. 11–13.
163. *Ibid.*, p. 12.
164. *Ibid.*, pp. 13, 39.
165. Eechoud et al., 2009, p. 7; Poort & Quintais, 2013.
166. Green Paper on Copyright and Related Rights in the Information Society 1995.

creating a need for community-wide remuneration arrangements and copy restriction 'techniques'.[167]

Private copying levies were at this stage a reality in most Member States. While the Green Paper recognised that analogue private copying is 'impossible to control', it considered that digitisation opens up the possibility of strict control of reproductions and, as such, the need to re-examine exceptions.[168]

In that context, the 'permissible' nature of private copying depended on whether the control of reproductions is possible. Where technical means can limit or prevent such use, 'there is no further justification for what amounts to a system of statutory licensing and equitable remuneration'.[169] The Commission further criticised the BC three-step test for its uncertainty, illustrated by the different approaches taken by Member States to the regulation of private copying. Where the limitation existed, it was noted that technical restriction measures could not be made compulsory; however, the legality of digital private copying should be reassessed in light of technological possibilities for monitoring, preventing or limiting it.[170]

In 1996, one month before the Geneva diplomatic conference preceding the WIPO Treaties, the Commission published its Follow-Up to the Green Paper.[171] It emerged from the intervening consultations that rights holders now opposed any limitations, believing these would conflict with the normal exploitation of work. They contended that technology would soon enable 'effective control of private copying'. User groups, contrariwise, contested an unfettered exclusive right.[172]

The Commission prioritised the adoption of a broad reproduction right and limitations thereto, stressing the need to harmonise different national regimes regulating private copying, especially in the 'new electronic environment'. It further proposed harmonisation of 'legal protection of the integrity of technical identification and protection schemes'.[173]

For the Commission, a statutory licence with a remuneration right to regulate private copying was admissible only where the use does not conflict with the normal exploitation of works *and* the 'exclusive right is not enforceable for whatever reason'. Outside those boundaries, it was only possible to exempt activities from the exclusive right through future EU legislation setting out defined limitations in the 'interests of users or the public at large', subject to the three-step test.[174]

167. *Ibid.*, pp. 26, 28.
168. *Ibid.*, p. 49.
169. *Ibid.*, p. 50.
170. *Ibid.*, pp. 52, 75, 79 83, exemplifying with a technology called Serial Copy Management System.
171. Follow-up Green Paper 1996.
172. *Ibid.*, p. 11.
173. *Ibid.*, pp. 11–12, 15–17, 22.
174. *Ibid.*, pp. 11–12.

Under the test's tutelage, even with absolute control of digital use, it was still possible for the private copying limitation to apply. That was because, the Commission claimed, 'situations will continue to exist in which an unlimited exclusive right would not appear appropriate or enforceable, notably due to privacy reasons.' If the limitation was allowed, the expected economic impact of private use requires certain acts to 'be subject to a legal license and equitable remuneration.'[175] It is worth noting that this is one of the few instances where the Commission expressly recognised – following the example of the German model – an overriding fundamental rights-based justification for the private copying limitation, beyond market failure.

In 1997, the Commission presented its proposal for the InfoSoc Directive, accompanied by an explanatory memorandum. The memorandum essentially restated the main points of the communications preceding it.[176] It stated that most Member States' laws contain a private copying limitation, motivated by two main factors: the non-enforceability of exclusive rights for such use, and the non-desirability of enforcement for privacy reasons. The document added that in eleven of fifteen cases the limitation was compensated through a levy system. The scope and functioning of levy systems is diverse; however, most systems do not distinguish between analogue and digital devices or media. Furthermore, the economic significance of private copying revenues was considerable, with the expectation that analogue and digital private copying would remain relevant for the next 15 years.[177]

In this light, the Commission proposed a rule allowing Member States to implement private copying limitations for reproductions 'on audio, visual or audio-visual recording media', without the requirement of fair compensation.[178] The concept of 'private copying' included analogue and digital reproductions made for private use (understood in a 'narrow sense') and non-commercial aims, meaning it had to be 'confined to a private context'.[179]

The Commission's expectation was that developments in digital reproduction, allowing users to make unlimited perfect copies, would be counteracted by improvements enabling 'effective control' thereof, potentially leading to the phasing-out of levies and their replacement by 'individual licensing solutions ... at least in the on-line environment.' Consequently, the expectation was for Member States to eventually abolish or limit the exception's scope in the digital realm.[180]

For the time being, however, due to uncertainties with enforcement and consumer behaviour, it was preferable to allow Member States the flexibility

175. *Ibid.*, p. 12.
176. Proposal InfoSoc Directive 1997.
177. *Ibid.*, p. 13.
178. *Ibid.*, pp. 29–30, 45.
179. *Ibid.*, p. 30.
180. *Ibid.*

of maintaining or introducing exceptions for analogue and digital private copying, subject to the three-step test and the Commission's watchful eye.[181]

The proposal was subject to numerous amendments by the European Parliament on first reading,[182] some of which were accepted by the Commission in its amended proposal, namely the condition of fair compensation, and the recognition of a link between private copying and 'the existence of operational, reliable and effective' TPMs.[183]

When, in September 2000, the Council adopted its Common Position, Article 5(2)(b) was adjusted so that the limitation now covered 'any medium' (not just audio-visual), did not distinguish between analogue and digital copying, and took into account the application or non-application of TPMs.[184]

The European Parliament adopted the provision on second reading and, in March 2001, the Commission joined it in a Common Position. The latter clarified that the limitation allowed copies to be made 'for and on behalf of a natural person for private use', and would cover acts for 'ends that are neither directly or indirectly commercial'.[185] The final version of the InfoSoc Directive, which contains the private copying limitation in Article 5(2)(b), was adopted on 9 April 2001 by the Council of Ministers, and published on 22 June 2001.

Most EU Member States have implemented this optional limitation and the accompanying levy system, with the exception of Cyprus, Ireland, Luxembourg and Malta. The UK introduced the limitation in 2014, but the same was overturned during the course of 2015 due to issues with the lack of a fair compensation requirement in the national implementing regulations.[186]

The limitation has generated abundant and on-going case law from the CJEU; these judgments and their implications, insofar as they are relevant for the study of an ACS in the *acquis*, are examined in the subsequent chapters.[187] Nevertheless, a few additional words are warranted on the institutional developments in this field, as the uncertainty surrounding the limitation has also given rise to multiple institutional responses.

181. *Ibid.*, pp. 30–31, noting that analogue private copying was less significant. *See also* recital 26 InfoSoc Directive.
182. *See* EP Resolution Proposal InfoSoc Directive (1st reading) 1999. *See also* von Lewinski & Walter, 2010, p. 1010.
183. Amended Proposal InfoSoc Directive 1999, paras 2(1), 2(2) and III.(Comment to Art. 5(2)(ba)).
184. Common Position (EC) No 48/2000.
185. Proposal InfoSoc Directive – Adoption by Commission of opinion on EP amendments on 2nd reading, COM/2001/0170 final, p. 3.
186. *See* WIPO & Stichting de Thuiskopie, 2016, pp. 3, 6. On the UK provision, *see* High Court of Justice of England and Wales, 17.07. 2015, Case No. CO/5444/2014, [2015] EWHC 2041 (Admin).
187. *See infra* 4.4.3, 5.3.2.1, 5.3.2.3 and 5.3.3.2.

Among these were stakeholder consultations in 2006 and 2008, as well as a 2011 communication from the Commission referring to comprehensive action in the field.[188] In 2013, Commission-appointed mediator António Vitorino presented his recommendations on private copying and reprography levies.[189] Between January and March 2014 the Commission launched a public consultation to review and modernise EU copyright rules, including a section on private copying and reprography, reflecting insights from the Vitorino recommendations and recent CJEU judgments. The subsequent Commission report summarising the results of the consultation identifies this as a topic of concern to end-users/consumers, intermediaries, distributors and other service providers.[190]

Furthermore, in February 2014, the European Parliament passed a resolution on private copying levies where it considers it a 'virtuous system in need of modernization and harmonization' and identifies a set of challenges that need to be addressed, including the possibility of levying cloud services.[191] The following year, a European Parliament Resolution returned to the topic, albeit without adding much in the way of detail.[192] Private copying levies remain on the Commission's agenda to this very day as an 'on-going initiative'.[193]

2.3.4 Conclusions on Statutory Licensing for Private Copying

The private copying limitation and levy aim at solving the problem of mass home copying of works by consumers for personal non-commercial purposes. The model emerged in Germany in the 1950s–1960s in the wake of the

188. The documents relating to stakeholder consultations available at European Commission, *The EU Single Market, Copyright and Neighbouring Rights, Private copying levies*, http://ec.europa.eu/internal_market/copyright/levy_reform/index_en.htm (accessed 31.01.2017). *See also* Communication IPR Strategy 2011, pp. 12–13, 23, and Communication on Content in the Digital Single Market 2012, p. 4, for a subsequent, less comprehensive, approach to copyright levies.
189. Vitorino, 2013.
190. Public Consultation on the review of the EU copyright rules, launched 5 December 2013, available at http://ec.europa.eu/internal_market/consultations/2013/copyright-rules/ (accessed 31.01.2017), pp. 31–33 (Questions 64–71), Report Public Consultation on the Review of the EU Copyright Rules 2014, pp. 72–77.
191. EP Resolution Private Copying Levies 2014. On the private copying issues of cloud-based services, *see* Senftleben, 2013a, pp. 91–93. On stakeholders' concerns surrounding the interaction between cloud services and private copying, *see* Report Public Consultation on the Review of the EU Copyright Rules 2014, pp. 72–77.
192. *See* EP Resolution Implementation InfoSoc Directive 2015, paras 57–60.
193. Eechoud et al., 2009, p. 7; Poort & Quintais, 2013. *See also* European Commission, *The EU Single Market, Copyright and Neighbouring Rights, Private copying levies*, http://ec.europa.eu/internal_market/copyright/levy_reform/index_en.htm (accessed 31.01.2017).

commercial success of recording devices and the ensuing litigation by GEMA against manufacturers.

From a policy standpoint, private copying touches upon different legitimate interests: fair remuneration of authors for potentially harmful home taping activities, the public interest in dissemination of knowledge and information, technological development (of recording technology), consumer protection, and privacy. The German model uses the limitation and the levy system as means to solve the conflict between the creative sphere of authors and the private sphere of users.

In a sequence of landmark decisions, the BGH first extended the scope of the reproduction right to the private sphere, and imposed liability on manufacturers indirectly contributing to the infringing use. Authors initially prevailed due to the recognition of a natural right to a 'just pecuniary reward' for mass home taping of works. This inaugurated the intrusion of copyright regulation in the private sphere.

However, the BGH refused to impose a general ban on the sale of recording devices due to their susceptibility to use for non infringing purposes, and the lack of proportionality of the ban in light of the fundamental right of privacy. Furthermore, the court steered the German legislator towards a statutory licensing system, based on an equitable remuneration right and managed by CMOs.

The German model was built on a remunerated limitation and statutory licensing, allowing users to reproduce sound and visual recordings. Remuneration was collected through levies, targeting first devices and later media 'suitable' for private (not professional) copying purposes, within the law's jurisdiction.

The expansion of levy targets was a result of developments in recording technology and the neutral statutory formula, which extended to equipment or media 'susceptible of' use for private copying. That combination enabled application by analogy of pre-existing rationales to new technologies, a process that remains to this day. It also enabled technological development by preventing intermediaries from being subject to liability for copyright infringement.

Manufacturers and importers paid the levy in respect of the opportunity to make private copies offered by their devices or media. Yet, they could pass on the levy to consumers within the retail price, as these were the only direct beneficiaries of the legal 'permission'. This design is privacy respecting, as it ensures a link to the actual user is maintained, and is equitable, insofar as it causes intermediary debtors to share the burden of activities from which they benefit.[194]

194. Geller, 1991, pp. 33–35. *See also* Hilty & Nérisson, 2012, p. 62, noting that '[c]onsideration of privacy and the weak feasibility of any control in such an area explains the fact why lawmakers authorized the private copy'.

Calculation of the levy was on a percentage basis or via statutory tariffs, with the remuneration intended to reflect the use of works authorised by the limitation. In this way, the remuneration right is internal to copyright – rather than a tax – and subject to rules in international copyright treaties, like national treatment and the three-step test.

The high transaction costs associated with enforcement of the remuneration claim justify the coupling of the statutory licence with obligatory collective management. CMOs thus intermediate between rights holders and debtors for the definition, collection and distribution of the levy.

Ultimately, the German private copying model was the result of balancing the principle of exclusivity against economic and non-economic motivations: market failure in the regulation of mass home taping activities, and inadequacy of enforcement in the private sphere linked to users' fundamental right of privacy.

The German model was disseminated throughout Europe and is currently a staple of most Member States' national copyright laws. At international level, the topic was discussed in the 1967 Stockholm revision of Berne and in the preparatory works for the 1996 WIPO Treaties.

In Stockholm, the German model shaped the debate on the three-step test. It influenced the consideration of equitable remuneration as a tool to reduce rights holder's prejudice to reasonable levels (step three of the test) and, thus, as a condition for the admissibility – and broadening – of copyright limitations. Remuneration may act as a public interest component for restrictions on exclusivity, leading to a normative equilibrium between authors and users.

In Geneva, the possibility of perfect copies offered by digital technology led to arguments that private copying would also conflict with the normal exploitation of works (step two of the test). A feature of this debate, which would be present at EU level, was the promise of control of digital use through technological measures and the subsequent possibility of phasing out levies.

In the EU, debate on harmonisation of private copying started in 1988 and included promises of a specific directive. Emerging from the discussions was the growing belief by the Commission and rights holders in the possibility of technological control of use, strengthening arguments that digital limitations would run counter to the three-step test and even facilitate commercial piracy.

Still, the elimination of the levy on this basis was never consensual, leaving as an intermediate solution its co-existence with TPMs. The Commission first suggested this combined approach in 1990, and built upon it in subsequent communications, emphasising that compensated limitations should respect the three-step test and apply where enforcement would not be possible or desirable due to privacy concerns.

The result was the modest framework of the optional limitation in Article 5(2)(b) InfoSoc Directive (and related recitals), aimed at providing

Member States with the flexibility to implement 'TPM-compliant' statutory licences, subject to the test. This provision follows the blueprint of the German model and expands upon it, by allowing digital reproductions and additional subject matter, and regulating the legal interface with TPMs.[195]

A significant departure from the German tradition seems to be that the remuneration claim is not rooted in a natural right of the author to a just pecuniary reward. Instead, it is based on a fair compensation right linked to a notion of harm, said link reflecting the market failure rationale.

However, it is arguable that the 'harm' in question relates to the impossibility of monetising private use, which in turn is caused either by the impossibility of licencing and enforcement (market failure) or the inadequacy of mechanisms to do so (privacy rationale). From that standpoint, it is possible to retain a fundamental rights justification for this model of restrictions to exclusivity, which subsists even where market failures are curable (which is still not the case, as full digital control of copyright use and the phasing-out of levies have not come to fruition). To be sure, privacy concerns are at the root of the InfoSoc Directive's provision, as explicitly stated in its 1997 explanatory memorandum.[196]

2.4 COMPULSORY LICENSING FOR BROADCASTING AND COMMUNICATION TO THE PUBLIC

The regulation of broadcasting in international and EU copyright law is an entangled web of provisions crafted in response to a technology that revolutionised the communication of works to the public and its economic exploitation across national borders.

From the early days of amateur experimentalism with the transmission of radio waves at the beginning of the twentieth century, to the development of radio, television, and satellite broadcasting, the law has struggled to incorporate the technology. The profound impact of broadcasting on the dissemination of knowledge and culture, as well as on the democratic process, was also visible in the copyright field.

This section first examines the early days of broadcasting as a means to provide background to the technology, its impact on society and the copyright issues it raises. The analysis then proceeds to study how and why international copyright law, after subsuming broadcasting within the concept of communication to the public, allows for compulsory licensing of the right. As we shall see, international rules play a greater role in shaping this precedent then they do with private copying.

195. *See infra* 4.4.1.2 and 4.4.3.5.

196. Proposal InfoSoc Directive 1997, pp. 13, 19–20, 43 (proposed recital 34). On the privacy justification of private copying, *see also* Helberger & Hugenholtz, 2007, pp. 1068–1069.

The focus is on the compulsory licence of Article 11*bis*(2) BC. However, other provisions on related rights in the RC, TRIPS, and WPPT allow for the implementation of such licences for acts of broadcasting and communication to the public against the payment of equitable remuneration. Although the BC licence was not implemented in the *acquis*, it helped shape compulsory licensing of several related rights that influence broadcasting and the communication to the public rights in the Rental Right and SatCab Directives.[197] As explained below, due to the lack of harmonisation of the right of communication to the public for related rights holders in Article 3(2) InfoSoc Directive, the Rental Right and SatCab Directives allow certain compulsory licences where these are admissible under the RC.[198]

2.4.1 The Early Days of Broadcasting

Broadcasting is the transmission of sounds and/or images for reception by a dispersed audience using electromagnetic radiation or waves, without the assistance of 'artificial means of guidance or support', like wire or cable.[199] Most broadcasting occurs over the electromagnetic spectrum, a natural and common resource the regulation and allocation of which is subject to national and international communications policy.[200]

Discussion on the technology dates as far back as the 1880s, and the first experiences with radio-communications systems, by Marconi and Tesla, from 1896 and 1897.[201] In the early 1890s, the German scientist Heinrich Hertz discovered electromagnetic or 'Hertzian' waves, initially used to 'communicate the telegraphs dots and dashes'; around that period, the first reports surface of use of radio signals by the US Navy.[202]

As early as 1905–1906 it is possible to identify the amateur pioneers of broadcasting in the US, who operated rudimentary radio stations, talked with each other, and listened to 'radio signals from ships at sea'.[203] These experimental amateur activities significantly preceded the first commercial

197. *See* Arts 8 and 10 Rental Right Directive, and Art. 4 SatCab Directive.
198. *See* Dreier, 2010, p. 434 referring to Art. 15(2) RC. *See also* Art. 1(2) InfoSoc Directive. *See infra* 2.4.4.
199. *See* Ricketson, 1987, p. 435. When such artificial means are used, the transmission in question can be called a 'cable retransmission'.
200. Pool, 2009, pp. 2, 8–9, 113–116. *See also* Benkler, 2012, on issues of spectrum regulation.
201. *See* G. Austin, 2012, noting that both men held patents on the technology in the US and UK.
202. Austin, 2012; Wu, 2011, p. 34.
203. Wu, 2011 noting that, in their contemporary dictionaries, 'broadcast' was a seeding technique meaning '[c]ast or dispersed in all directions, as seed from the hand in sowing, widely diffused'.

radio transmissions in 1919–1920, distributed through radio waves from transmitters to receiving devices with antennas.[204]

The early days of radio broadcasting in the US were characterised by the co-existence of different models, from amateur radio clubs, to radio stations of universities, churches, hotels, newspapers, the US military, and a few commercial stations. Radio was mostly local, partly due to limitations in the range of transmissions, and the content transmitted was irregular.[205] Between 1912 and 1922, the combination of 'massive amateur and commercial exploitation' with war production led to a boom in radio innovation in the US.[206] By 1924, more than a thousand broadcast stations existed and over 2 million broadcast-ready radio sets had been sold.[207]

Across the Atlantic, the development of broadcasting suffered an interruption during World War I (1914–1918).[208] There is evidence that the first broadcast programmes on a fixed schedule were made in the Netherlands in late 1919, by an early Dutch radio pioneer, Mr Hanso Schotanus à Steringa Idzerda.[209] It was only in 1922 that a UK consortium of radio manufacturers formed the BBC, which came into existence as a public 'crown' corporation in 1927, one year before the Rome Act of the BC.[210] In Germany, the first radio stations went on air in Berlin in 1932.[211] By the 1930s, however, radio challenged the influence of film and had become the 'dominant form of entertainment'.[212]

The major technology shift produced by broadcasting, when compared with the previous telegraph technology, was an evolution from one-to-one to one-to-many communication of messages to multiple devices. Broadcasting, as a medium of mass communication, allowed all within reach of the broadcast to 'see or hear the same program at the same time' without requiring 'that the public is assembled in one location'.[213] Radio, in these early days, became 'the technological vehicle that allowed synchronized communication to a new audience'.[214]

---

204. See, generally, Austin, 2012; Pool, 2009; Wu, 2011
205. Wu, 2011.
206. Benkler, 2012.
207. Pool, 2009; Wu, 2011. On the development of the US radio industry and its regulation in this period, *see* Austin, 2012, Benkler, 2012, Wu, 2011.
208. Wikipedia, *History of Broadcasting*, https://en.wikipedia.org/wiki/History_of_broadcasting (accessed 31.01.2017).
209. van de Donk et al., 2005, p. 29.
210. Lord Windlesham, 1980, pp. 18–23; Wu, 2011.
211. Wikipedia, *History of Broadcasting*, https://en.wikipedia.org/wiki/History_of_broadcasting (accessed 31.01.2017).
212. Austin, 2012; Wu, 2011.
213. Depreeuw, 2014, pp. 268–269.
214. Austin, 2012.

The rise of radio broadcasting saw three general regulatory and funding models emerge. Whereas the US favoured a commercial model,[215] the UK followed a public service model, largely justified on the assertion that 'a politically independent system of broadcasting is an essential element in a free society'.[216] A similar model was in place in pre-Nazi Germany.[217] Conversely, some countries, during specific periods of their history – Nazi Germany (post-1933) and New Zealand (1930–1960) – favoured a model of government control.[218]

For Ithiel de Sola Pool, the propensity for national control of radio broadcast in Europe was motivated by the rise of social democratic parties and a socialist ideology favouring nationalisation of a new and invaluable resource. In the US, these factors were viewed sceptically because of censorship and free speech concerns, leading the country's regulators to follow a market-based approach.[219] It is fair to say that the public information and propaganda potential of broadcasting meant that radio played an important role during the 1930s, both in democratic and totalitarian governments.[220]

Broadcasting also had a profound effect on copyright, mainly because protected works constituted a significant portion of the content transmitted.[221] The programming of radio broadcasting, for example, primarily consisted of phonograph musical recordings.[222] Broadcast music became part of social interactions and firms' business practices, a tool to promote musical works and artists, the technology itself, and other types of content (e.g., newspapers, films).[223] Advertising grew into the standard business model for radio, proving in time 'almost a license to print money' and, together with sponsorship, 'gave radio stations a sustainable financial basis'.[224]

The question facing copyright policy makers in the early days of broadcasting was how to balance 'the traditional view of authors' rights with these new modes of communication: are new formulations of rights required, or do old formulations still hold good, necessitating only a flexible

215. On the development of US federal regulation of radio, *see* Austin, 2012; Benkler, 2012; Pool, 2009.
216. Lord Windlesham, 1980 noting that the BBC was accountable to parliament and its net revenue depended on the issue of broadcast receiving licences and, initially, on 'a royalty fee added to the price of radio sets'. *See also* Wu, 2011.
217. Wikipedia, *History of Broadcasting*, https://en.wikipedia.org/wiki/History_of_broadcasting (accessed 31.01.2017). Pre-Nazi Germany had a radio broadcasting system supervised by the Post Office, which charged a listening fee of two *reichmark* per receiver, and limited radio frequencies.
218. Austin, 2012. On the German model, *see* Wu, 2011.
219. Pool, 2009.
220. Ricketson, 1987, p. 435.
221. *Ibid.*, pp. 436–437.
222. Austin, 2012, p. 121.
223. *Ibid.*, pp. 122–123.
224. Wu, 2011.

interpretation to apply to these changed conditions?'[225] (This question could easily apply to the Internet as a means of disseminating works, and to the regulation of non-commercial online use.)

In the US, court battles in the 1920s 'established that radio broadcasting implicated public performance rights of copyright owners'.[226] Ginsburg speculates that this was due to economic reasons and fears that unlicensed and free broadcasting would undercut rights holders' revenues.[227] The move allowed US performing rights organisations to access the operation of radio broadcasters, setting the stage for a blanket voluntary collective licensing system under which the organisation provides access to its repertoire against a percentage of the radio station's revenues. The system survives to this day[228] and, in the context of the ACS debate, was proposed as the legal framework for a P2P blanket licence.[229]

In Europe, the potential for exploitation of works through broadcasting became apparent only after World War I, namely through the transmission of musical compositions and plays to individual receivers in people's homes, a 'far wider audience than possible at one specific location'.[230] For the most part, domestic legislators grappled with the new reality by interpreting existing law to protect authors against unauthorised exploitation of works through the new technology.[231]

In a 1925 resolution, the ALAI urged that 'radio electric transmission' of literary and artistic works be treated as a public performance.[232] This was in the middle of the period of consolidation of broadcasting, but almost a decade before the advent of FM radio transmission.[233]

The ALAI resolution eventually led to the discussion of a broadcasting right in the 1928 Rome revision conference of the BC.[234] The programme proposal initially referred to a right of communication to the public by 'telegraphy', 'telephony' or 'other analogous means serving to transmit the sounds or images'.[235] The reference to 'artistic works' and 'images' seems to

225. Ricketson, 1987, pp. 436–437.
226. Austin, 2012, pp. 123–128.
227. Ginsburg, 2001, pp. 1620–1621.
228. Austin, 2012, pp. 127–128.
229. See, e.g., Lohmann, 2004, 2008; Quintais, 2012. *See infra* 3.3.2.2.
230. Ricketson, 1987, pp. 434–435.
231. Depreeuw, 2014, p. 267 & n. 65; Ricketson, 1987, p. 437.
232. Records Rome 1928, p. 59, referring to the ALAI conference of 1925.
233. On the development of FM radio transmission as from 1934, *see* Wu, 2011.
234. N.B. that the term 'broadcasting' was only adopted in the 1971 Stockholm revision as the English translation of the French 'radiodiffusion'. Until then, both English and French texts used 'radiodiffusion'. This terminology choice, however, does not imply the exclusion of broadcasting of visual content from the scope of the provision. *See* Depreeuw, 2014, pp. 268–270; Ricketson, 1987, pp. 438–439. *See also* Records BC Rome 1928, p. 76.
235. Records BC Rome 1928, p. 76.

indicate the 'possibilities posed by the imminent advent of television'.[236] However, television was still in its infancy, explaining why specific discussions regarding television broadcasting are found only in the preparatory works of the 1948 Brussels Act of the BC.[237]

In fact, it was necessary to wait until 1928 for the first experimental demonstrations of electronic televisions (by Farnsworth and Baird), the introduction of the first mechanical televisions on the market (by General Electric), and for the beginning of television broadcasts in the US. In Europe, following the first experimental broadcasts in 1929, the BBC only started its regular television broadcasting in 1936; one year earlier, in 1935, television broadcasts started in Nazi Germany.[238] However, this development was put on hold due to World War II.

After the War, in 1948, the Brussels Act amended the BC regulation of broadcasting in an attempt to capture the developments of radio broadcasting and the relatively new invention of television. The convention did not yield a definition of broadcasting. According to Ricketson, the likely reason was the existence of a general international understanding of the term as an act of communication to the public. This understanding was embodied in the radio regulations of the International Telecommunications Union, which in that same year of 1948 defined broadcasting as a 'radiocommunications [*sic*] service of transmissions to be received directly by the general public'.[239] The consensus as to the meaning of the term is also apparent from the preparatory documents of the Brussels Act.[240]

The impact of broadcasting was magnified by the advent of satellites (and later cable), which expanded its scope 'enormously', making possible 'the diffusion of programmes from one continent to another, and even to most of the world at one time'. The result was an erosion of the relevance of national boundaries in the realm of communications technology, and 'profound effects' on fields like 'popular education and entertainment, the conduct of international trade and business, diplomacy and defense'.[241]

This more versatile use of wireless technologies, as well as technical solutions for rebroadcasting and communication by wire, complicated the task of copyright. In particular, the introduction of separate technical steps in the process of disseminating the signals to the public (e.g., intermediary transmissions between providers before reaching the public), meant that copyright law struggled to qualify these technical acts.[242]

As shown below, the BC does not deal expressly with satellite broadcasting, although its Article 11*bis*(1) applies to territorial broadcasting

236. Ricketson, 1987, p. 437.
237. *See infra* 2.4.2.
238. Wu, 2011.
239. Ricketson, 1987, p. 440.
240. Records BC Brussels 1948, p. 265.
241. Ricketson, 1987, pp. 436–437. *See also* Austin, 2012.
242. Depreeuw, 2014, pp. 264–265, 273, 280–282.

and most acts of satellite broadcasting, as well as to acts of retransmission via wire or cable.[243] In the EU, the issue was only settled in the 1993 SatCab Directive. The directive draws a legal distinction between acts of cable retransmission and satellite broadcasting, applying to all types of satellite transmissions, whether the signal is received directly, or after decoding by an intermediary.[244]

Against this background, the remainder of this section explains the mechanics and justifications for the legal regulation of broadcasting of works (in the BC) and related subject matter (in the RC, TRIPS and WPPT) under a compulsory licensing system, as well as their manifestations in the *acquis*.

2.4.2 Compulsory Licensing for Broadcasting and Communication to the Public in the Berne Convention

2.4.2.1 Analysis

The BC does not provide for a general right of communication to the public. Instead, it includes different rights spanning different subject matter for separate types of communication to the public: Articles 11, 11*bis*, 11*ter* and 14(1)(ii).

Article 11*bis*(1) BC regulates a set of these rights that apply to all subject matter in the BC and includes broadcasting, rebroadcasting, communication by wire of broadcast works, and communication by loudspeaker.

The provision includes both so-called 'primary uses' – to authorise broadcasting and other wireless communications of works – and 'secondary uses' of broadcast works, namely their rebroadcast or public communication by wire. With the exception of communication by loudspeaker, Article 11*bis*(1) only covers acts of communication to a public at a distance.[245]

The BC does not define 'broadcasting' but the term applies solely to acts of *wireless diffusion*. The provision is technology neutral and can thus apply to new means of wireless transmission. Originally, the right applied to transmissions through Hertzian waves, known as 'terrestrial broadcasting'. As the technology developed, the right extended to certain types of satellite broadcasting, covering a far wider public, potentially across different

243. Explanatory Memorandum SatCab Directive, pp. 9–13, describing the application of Art. 11*bis* BC to different acts of satellite broadcasting.
244. Art. 1(2)(c) and recital 6 SatCab Directive.
245. The exception is Art. 11*bis*(1)(iii) BC: 'public communication by loudspeaker or any other analogous instrument transmitting, by signs, sounds or images, the broadcast of the work'. *See* Dreier, 2006, pp. 51–52; Ficsor, 2003b, p. 77; von Lewinski, 2008, p. 151. A violation of the exclusive right provided in para. (iii) by US law originated the WTO dispute in *US–Copyright*, discussed in Chapter 5.

countries.[246] The limitation to wireless acts means that broadcasting does not include original cable transmissions, which are covered by separate provisions of the BC.[247]

Secondary uses of the original broadcast also require authorisation if the user is different from the original broadcaster. These uses include cable retransmission, wired digital retransmission – including streaming of radio or television broadcasts, and webcasting – or *wireless rebroadcasts* of the original broadcast.[248]

This piecemeal approach created gaps in the legal protection for acts of communication to the public, such as primary wire transmissions of non-broadcast works, including Internet transmissions of 'literary and photographic works and other visual creations'.[249] These gaps were later filled at international and EU levels by the general rights of communication to the public in Article 8 WCT and Article 3(1) InfoSoc Directive.[250]

Article 11*bis*(2) BC addresses 'compulsory licenses', although it only mentions the term in its heading:

> It shall be a matter for legislation in the countries of the Union to determine the conditions under which the rights mentioned in the preceding paragraph may be exercised, but these conditions shall apply only in the countries where they have been prescribed. They shall not in any circumstances be prejudicial to the moral rights of the author, nor to his right to obtain equitable remuneration which, in the absence of agreement, shall be fixed by competent authority.

There is debate on the meaning of the term 'conditions', as it relates to the exercise of the right. The term is typically understood as *allowing*, but not requiring, domestic legislators to subject the exclusive acts listed in Article 11*bis*(1) to non-voluntary licences. Hence, national laws may subject broadcasting to either mandatory exercise via collective rights management

---

246. Depreeuw, 2014, pp. 273–274. For issues with the application of the BC provision to intermediate satellite transmissions, *see* Depreeuw, 2014, pp. 284, 318–321.
247. Dreier, 2006, p. 52; von Lewinski, 2008, p. 149 at 149. *See also* Ficsor, 2003b, p. 74–ff; Ricketson, 1987, p. 439–ff; Ricketson & Ginsburg, 2006, pp. 717, 741–742, discussing the evolution of the interpretation of the concept of broadcast under different communication and emission theories.
248. Ricketson & Ginsburg, 2006, pp. 732, 734–738. N.B. that the original broadcaster's authorisation covers rebroadcasting.
249. Depreeuw, 2014, p. 301. *See* Ficsor, 2003b, p. 77–ff; Ricketson, 1987, p. 449; Ricketson & Ginsburg, 2006, pp. 733, 735, 740–742; von Lewinski, 2008, p. 150, noting that this provision does not cover cable originated programmes or original wired webcast transmissions (included in Arts 11(1)(ii), 11*ter*(1)(ii), 14(1)(ii) and 14*bis*(1) BC).
250. *See* Arts 11, 11*bis*, 11*ter*, 14(1)(ii) and 14*bis* BC. *See* Ricketson & Ginsburg, 2006, pp. 741–743 discussing whether the BC rights of communication to the public include not only 'push' but also 'pull' (on-demand) technologies, as well as hybrid cases like pay-per-view broadcast and cable services.

(maintaining unchanged the exclusive nature of the right) or to compulsory licensing, which causes the right to become non-exclusive.[251]

Ricketson and Ginsburg list four kinds of admissible compulsory licences under this provision, some of which apply in the online environment:

(i) broadcasting of sounds and images, including by satellite;
(ii) rebroadcasting of broadcasts of works where this is done by an organization other than the original one, including by satellite;
(iii) wired rediffusion of broadcasts of works, where this is done by an organization other than the original one, including by cable and digital dissemination (for example, by the 'streaming' of radio or television broadcasts);
(iv) public communication by loudspeaker or any other similar instrument of the broadcast of the work.[252]

The licence is limited to the territory of the state for which it is granted, and thus cannot legitimise the broadcast of works elsewhere. The territorial limitation can have an impact due to diverse interpretations of the meaning of broadcasting, for example in the case of certain types of satellite transmissions.[253]

Beyond the respect of moral rights, the main condition for the admissibility of compulsory licences is that authors receive 'equitable remuneration'.[254] The remuneration is fixed by agreement between authors and commercial users (typically broadcasting organisations) or, where that fails, by the competent national authority.[255] All remaining aspects of the system are subject to domestic law, including the definition of the remuneration and the role of CMOs.

The ordinary meaning of 'equitable' suggests that the remuneration should be fair and just. Some scholars submit that authors are entitled to an amount similar to what they would potentially receive in the market absent the compulsory licence. However, that quantum is difficult to calculate in

---

251. Ficsor, 2002c, pp. 272, 275, 2003b, p. 79. *See also* Explanatory Memorandum SatCab Directive, p. 16. Similarly, although not mentioning collective rights management, *see* Ricketson, 1987, p. 525; Ricketson & Ginsburg, 2006, pp. 822–823; von Lewinski, 2008, p. 166. On the concept of non-voluntary licences, *see supra* 2.2.3. On the doctrinal discussion surrounding the legal qualification and effects of mandatory collective management, *see infra* 3.3.4.2.
252. Ricketson & Ginsburg, 2006, pp. 822–823, noting that the article does not cover original wired transmissions (e.g., via the Internet) and retransmissions of the same.
253. *See* Ricketson, 1987, p. 526, Ricketson & Ginsburg, 2006, pp. 823–824; von Lewinski, 2008, p. 166.
254. Ricketson, 2003, p. 31 & n. 75 suggests, based on the Records of the 1948 Brussels revision conference, that it is possible the word 'conditions' also extends to free use, subject to payment of equitable remuneration.
255. Ricketson, 1987, pp. 521, 527.

light of the impact of the licence on the authors' bargaining position.[256] Hence, equitable remuneration is not necessarily 'the market value of the use in question', a realisation that gives importance to the role of the executive, legislative or judicial authority competent to fix the amount.[257]

Furthermore, equitable remuneration does not include amounts for 'ephemeral recordings' made by a broadcasting organisation 'by means of its own facilities and used for its own broadcasts' pursuant to Article 11*bis*(3) BC.[258] Broadcasting acts are distinct from those of recording; the first are acts of communication to the public, and the second are acts of reproduction.

Article 11*bis*(3) BC recognises this by requiring express authorisation for ephemeral recording, but allowing countries to exempt from authorisation acts of archival preservation of those recordings, if they have exceptional documentary character.[259] This exemption *may* be subject to equitable remuneration.[260]

Finally, Article 8 WCT mandates a gap-filling right of communication to the public. The right is granted 'without prejudice' to BC provisions on broadcasting and communication to the public or its limitations, such as Article 11*bis*(2) BC.[261] Consequently, as a matter of international law, it is arguable that compulsory licences granted under Article 11*bis*(2) BC are admissible even where a country has joined the WCT and recognised its general exclusive right of communication to the public.[262]

Following Ricketson and Ginsburg, if a BC member has 'previously treated *wireless on-demand communications* as coming within the local equivalent of the broadcasting and diffusion rights', it is possible to apply

256. *See* Dreier, 2006, p. 53; Ficsor, 2002c, p. 275; Ricketson, 1987, pp. 521, 527. *See also* Françon, 1986, pp. 213–215, with an early criticism of non-voluntary licences, arguing that they result in a weaker bargaining position and lower remuneration for authors.

257. Ricketson & Ginsburg, 2006, pp. 816, 824, further mentioning and seemingly endorsing a German proposal (modelled on the German patent law of that time) presented (and rejected) during the Berlin revision conference. In said proposal, the licence would be set in the interval between a 'reasonable compensation' and an amount sufficient to 'enable the licen*see* to sustain the operation of his business'.

258. For an analysis of this provision, *see* Ficsor, 2002c, pp. 275–278. Art. 5(2)(d) InfoSoc Directive allows ephemeral recording exceptions under similar wording to Art. 11*bis*(3) BC. In the field of neighbouring rights, Art. 15(1)(c) RC allows exceptions for ephemeral fixations by a broadcasting organisation 'by means of its own facilities and for its own broadcasts'.

259. Ficsor, 2002c, p. 277; Ricketson & Ginsburg, 2006, pp. 827–830; von Lewinski, 2008, pp. 164–165.

260. Ficsor, 2002c, p. 277, 2003b, p. 80; Ricketson, 1987, p. 537; Ricketson & Ginsburg, 2006, p. 829, arguing that the same may be warranted for compliance with the three-step test. *See also*: Goldstein & Hugenholtz, 2013, pp. 372–373; Ricketson, 2003 (calling this an 'uncompensated exception); and International Bureau of WIPO, 2000, pp. 4–5 (referring to it as 'free uses of protected works').

261. *See* Agreed Statement to Art. 8 WCT, which reads: ' … nothing in Art. 8 precludes a Contracting Party from applying Art. 11*bis*(2)'.

262. *See* von Lewinski & Walter, 2010, p. 979.

compulsory licensing to those transmissions.[263] Similarly, Ricolfi argues that international law leaves space for compulsory licensing of interactive on-demand (point-to-point) communication to the public, such as uploads in P2P networks. This derives from the joint reading of Article 8 WCT and its Agreed Statement, which would permit application of the BC compulsory licensing regime online, and its extension to interactive uses of making available.[264]

Regardless of their appeal and consistency with international law, these interpretations are difficult to apply to the *acquis*, as Article 3(1) InfoSoc Directive implemented Article 8 WCT through an exclusive right that includes broadcasting by any means, as well as a broad right of making available.[265] Therefore, it seems that no compulsory licence of these rights is admissible under EU law, unless compliant with the three-step test. (Chapter 5 examines whether and how a legal licence ACS fares under the test.)

2.4.2.2 Justifications

Article 11*bis*(2) BC was introduced by the 1928 Rome Act and slightly amended in the 1948 Brussels Act to the version that is currently in force. At its inception, Article 11*bis* was a reaction to the 'new discovery of broadcasting', an innovative medium for dissemination of works that introduced 'a dramatically different vehicle of thought'.[266]

Its regulation, through the 'application of the principle of the exclusive privilege to radio broadcasting ... whatever may be the conditions governing the exercise of the privilege that national legislation adopts', was classified by Mr Caselli (Rapporteur-General to the 1928 Rome revision conference) as a 'victory for copyright of considerable importance'.[267]

The introduction of compulsory licensing was justified by a combination of public interest associated with the educational and informative role of broadcasting – as 'in many countries this function was carried out by, or under the close supervision of, governmental or public authorities' – with the specific group interest of broadcasters.[268]

In particular, broadcasting organisations were concerned that CMOs representing the broadcasting rights of authors – usually monopolies on national markets – would abuse their dominant positions in negotiations with

263. Ricketson & Ginsburg, 2006, pp. 748–749 (emphasis added).
264. Ricolfi, 2007, pp. 303–304. *See also* Mazziotti, 2008, pp. 266–267. In the relevant part, the statement reads: 'It is further understood that nothing in Art. 8 precludes a Contracting Party from applying Art. 11bis(2).'
265. On the unequivocal inclusion of broadcasting in the scope of the right, *see* recital 23 InfoSoc Directive. *See also infra* 4.3.2.1.
266. Records BC Rome 1928, p. 255 (General Report).
267. *Ibid.*
268. Ricketson & Ginsburg, 2006, p. 819.

commercial users.[269] The records of the 1928 Rome conference reflect the compromise nature of the text, with discussions on the article lasting the entire proceedings. When all was said and done, this article was considered one of the most important achievements of the conference.[270]

The general report denotes a tension between two opposing approaches to regulating a radio broadcasting right. On the one hand, the British and French delegations supported its assimilation by an exclusive right. On the other hand, the Australian and New Zealand delegations recognised the cultural and social interests of this new and popular form of dissemination, particularly of musical works.[271] The debate echoed the characteristic tension between exclusivity and access when copyright faces a new technology, also central to ACS discussion.

The records of the Sub-committee on Broadcasting provide additional detail. From their reading it is clear that national laws had 'given broadcasting services a markedly social character', with delegations proving 'ill-inclined to make undertakings that might hamper the development of broadcasting as a social service.'[272] Therefore, it was 'essential to adopt principles that both safeguard the rights of authors and also reconcile than [sic] harmoniously with the social purposes of broadcasting'.[273]

Compulsory licensing is further justified on the basis that, 'in light of the general interest of the State, limitations may be imposed on copyright' where 'the need for them has been shown by that country's own experience'.[274] Thus, 'while reconciling the general public interest of the State with the interests of authors, [these rules] give useful guidance for the international protection of the author's rights regarding broadcasting'.[275]

In other words, compulsory licensing provides a model for regulating copyright use that strikes a fair balance between the interests of authors in exclusivity and remuneration, and the public interest in the access to works and development of a socially valuable technology.

Depreeuw notes accurately that broadcasting 'enabled a previously unimaginable access to (cultural) creations', and 'could be used to spread 'spiritual food' to a public on a massive scale, at high speed, which made it more efficient than the reproduction and publication or the public performance of works.'[276] In her view, this aspect, together with the concern that

269. Ricketson & Ginsburg, 2006, p. 819 & n. 283, citing the comments of the national delegations (of Australia, New Zealand, Scandinavia, and Netherlands) in the records of the 1928 Rome revision conference.
270. Records BC Rome 1928, p. 248 (General Report). The other main achievement was the recognition of the protection of moral rights in Art. 6*bis* BC.
271. *Ibid.*, p. 248 (General Report).
272. *Ibid.*, p. 230 (Sub-committee on Broadcasting).
273. *Ibid.*
274. *Ibid.*, p. 231.
275. *Ibid.*
276. Depreeuw, 2014, p. 296.

exclusivity 'could hamper the development of this economic and technical model of exploitation', justifies 'the desire of state authorities to regulate 'in the public interest''.[277] In sum, the purpose of the provision 'was to enable the contracting states to balance the author's exclusive rights with other policy considerations in other domains (e.g., education and culture).'[278]

The 1948 Brussels Act extended the scope of the exclusive right in Article 11*bis*(1) BC by introducing new items (ii) on communication to the public by wire or by rebroadcasting by a different organisation, and (iii) on communication by loudspeaker. From this moment onwards, the provision also covered acts of rebroadcasting, such as cable retransmission. Retransmission acts were necessary to respond to certain technical limitations of territorial broadcasting at that time, largely concerning the reach and quality of the signal.[279] These new means of exploitation were therefore included in the scope of the author's exclusive right.

The Brussels conference also incorporated a corresponding scope extension in paragraph (2) through some minor drafting changes and, more substantially, replacing 'right' with 'rights', thus covering all the new entitlements in paragraph (1), including cable retransmission.[280] This simple solution hides the 'impassionate debate' behind the adoption of paragraphs (2) and (3), which saw the opposing tendencies manifested in 1928 resurface with vigour.[281]

In the general report, Marcel Plaisant notes that the programme proposed took due account of the 'prodigious development of radio' since the time of the Rome conference, where that invention was in its early days.[282] He called this the '[c]onference of broadcasting, discs, cinema and artificial or natural screens', which 'reconciled copyright, a spiritual concept, to these at once so powerful and so changeable material realities'.[283]

The expansion of Article 11*bis*(1) was an attempt to trace technological developments by covering new forms of exploitation, including television and its potential future improvements.[284] That provision was considered 'inseparable from paragraph (2)', which places possible conditions for exercise 'within a fairly broad framework' and, as per the Rapporteur-General, would allow, 'in general terms, that each country may take whatever action it considers appropriate for the avoidance of all possible abuses'.[285] He concludes with the ideas of balance and fairness, stating that 'the relations

277. *Ibid.*
278. *Ibid.*, p. 297.
279. *Ibid.*, pp. 278, 280.
280. *See* Explanatory Memorandum SatCab Directive, p. 16.
281. Records BC Brussels 1948, pp. 263–264 (General Report).
282. *Ibid.*, p. 263.
283. *Ibid.*, p. 270.
284. *Ibid.*, p. 263.
285. *Ibid.*, pp. 263–264.

of authors and composers with the broadcasting … industries are laid down in equitable terms'.[286]

The heated nature of the debate emerges clearly from the Report by the Subcommittee on Broadcasting and Mechanical Instruments, where the French delegation proposed replacing the right of remuneration with an exclusive right.[287] The proposal was rejected and a decision to extend the compulsory licence to all uses covered by paragraph (1) carried the day. It was stated that 'Governments wish to retain some freedom of action' regarding the then-new field of television broadcasting.[288] The discussions suggest that the allowance of compulsory licensing was viewed as a flexible middle ground to regulate an evolving technology.

In 1967, during the Stockholm revision conference, there was an unsuccessful proposal to exclude from the scope of the compulsory licence certain uses of cinematographic works.[289] However, the licence remained unchanged as it 'provided an acceptable compromise between opposing interests'.[290]

Outside the BC, the compulsory licence in Article 11*bis*(2) was a topic of debate during the preparation of the WIPO Treaties in the Geneva Diplomatic Conference, and is mentioned in the Agreed Statement to Article 8 WCT. The statement originates in a basic proposal for the substantive provisions of the WCT prepared during the 1996 Geneva diplomatic conference.

That proposal included an Article 6 – suggested by a group of countries that included the EU and its Member States – on 'abolition of certain non-voluntary licenses', designed to obligate parties to 'no longer provide for' or 'apply' the BC licence within three years of ratification.[291] That draft provision did not contain a note on its rationale, but only a generic encouragement of collective rights management.[292]

The relevant records state solely that Article 6 'related to a bedrock principle … that copyright is a bunch of exclusive rights'.[293] Most countries opposed the provision with concerns that abolishing non-voluntary licences would require them to have in place a developed system of collective rights

286. *Ibid.*, p. 269.
287. *Ibid.*, p. 274 (Report by the Subcommittee on Broadcasting and Mechanical Instruments).
288. *Ibid. See also* Ficsor, 2002c, pp. 273–274 at 273–274.
289. Records Stockholm 1967, pp. 710, 1168, making reference to the proposal from Working Group on the regime of cinematographic works proposed (Doc. S/195). *See also* Ficsor, 2002c, p. 273.
290. Records BC Stockholm 1967, pp. 1168, 1181–1182. *See also* Van Nus, 1967, p. 163 on the preparatory works for this provision. The 1971 Paris revision Act of Berne adopted in block Arts 1–20 as amended by the Stockholm Act. On the Paris Act, *see* Ulmer, 1970, 1971.
291. Records WIPO Treaties 1996, p. 187.
292. *Ibid.*, p. 186.
293. *Ibid.*, p. 650.

management, with no further explanation on the matter.[294] After multiple amendments, the article was rejected.[295]

During the debates, some countries noted that existing BC provisions on non-voluntary licences 'were preferable and fair'.[296] The main driving force behind the deletion of the provision was strong opposition from China and other delegations, summarised as follows:[297]

> broadcasting was, in many developing countries, a popular and important form of dissemination of information and means of enjoyment of literature and art, and that non voluntary licenses for broadcasting, as established in his country [China], were helpful in that respect and even beneficial to the fair remuneration of authors and other concerned parties. He stated that strong policy reasons in the respective countries commanded that they be free to maintain such non-voluntary licenses, and that, therefore his Delegation requested the deletion of Article 6.

It is worth noting the link between the social value of the technology and the possibility it affords for the promotion of access to and enjoyment of works and therefore knowledge and culture – and fair remuneration for authors (and rights holders). These are the core justifications for compulsory licensing when contrasted with a model relying on exclusive rights. The same arguments are used to justify the adoption of ACS for non-commercial online use.[298]

In Geneva, other delegations emphasised the importance of compulsory licences to regulate competition. For example, the Portuguese delegate stated that abolishing these licences would 'cause prejudice to the just balance between authors and broadcasters' reached in 1948. 'Now that situations of monopoly occurred frequently', he added, these licences were 'needed more than ever', as they permitted 'dissemination of works and consequently culture as well as the use of archives of broadcasters which were mankind patrimony'.[299]

Concerns with competition were also pivotal to the inclusion of the final sentence of the statement, to the effect that nothing in Article 8 WCT precludes a Contracting Party from applying Article 11*bis*(2) BC. The sentence was added following an intervention from the Australian delegate, who initially sought a declaration 'that the right of communication would

294. *Ibid.*, p. 647–650.
295. *Ibid.*, p. 506 (CRNR/DC/82, 20 December 1996). After the deletion of Art. 6, the Main Committee I submitted its 'Draft Agreed Statements Concerning Treaty No. 1' to the plenary meeting of the conference, including an agreed statement on Art. 8 WCT identical to its eventually adopted version. *Ibid.*, pp. 546 (CRNR/DC/92 Corr., 20 December 1996), 548 (CRNR/DC/96, 23 December 1996).
296. *Ibid.*, p. 647 (Israel).
297. *Ibid.*, p. 756.
298. *See supra* 1.1 and *infra* 5.3.3 (on the three-step test's balancing exercise).
299. Records WIPO Treaties 1996, p. 763 (Delegation of Portugal).

have no application to the possibility of making statutory licenses with regard to retransmission'.[300] The declaration was a trade-off for waiving a proposed statement to the previous Article 6, aimed at allowing Contracting Parties to introduce legislation 'in the public interest in order to prevent or remedy any abuse of rights that may restrict or prevent competition'.[301]

2.4.3 Compulsory Licensing for Related Rights: Brief Reference

Compulsory licensing rules in the field of related rights follow the blueprint of Article 11*bis* BC and are found in the RC, WPPT and TRIPS.[302] Article 12 RC provides a compulsory licence for secondary uses of commercially published phonograms.[303] Its main justifications were fairness and the regulation of competition. It was felt that, 'as a matter of common justice', performers deserved to share profits from such use, thus correcting a form of 'unfair competition' by broadcasters.[304]

In addition, the licence aimed at striking a balance between rights holders and users (especially broadcasting organisations) due to concerns with refusals to license.[305] This aim is reflected in the imposition of a 'single' remuneration mechanism to streamline negotiations.[306]

Article 15(2) RC permits compulsory licences analogous to copyright, if compatible with the RC. Compatibility is limited to the cases covered by Articles 7(2) and 13(d) RC. The first relates to instances where performers have consented to broadcasting of their performances, and the second grants broadcasting organisations an optional right to authorise or prohibit the public communication of their television broadcasts.[307]

In relation to these provisions, it is clear from the records of the RC that 'determining the conditions' for the exercise of a right 'is a euphemism for

300. *Ibid.*, p. 779.
301. *Ibid.*
302. *See* Arts 7(2), (13(d) and 15(2) RC; Art. 14(6) TRIPS. *See also* Ricketson & Ginsburg, 2006, p. 1215.
303. *See* Records RC 1961, p. 47, clarifying the meaning of the term. *See also* Ficsor, 2003b, pp. 151–152; C. Masouyé, 1981, p. 46.
304. Records RC 1961, pp. 162, 265.
305. *Ibid.*, pp. 158ff. See: C. Masouyé, 1981, p. 46ff.; von Lewinski, 2008, p. 212.
306. By defining the remuneration as 'single', debtors (broadcasting organisations) need only satisfy one claim. Records RC 1961, pp. 49, 163 See: C. Masouyé, 1981, p. 48; von Lewinski, 2008, p. 214. As a counterpoint, the RC accommodates divergent national traditions and economic situations by allowing broad reservations. *See* Records RC 1961, pp. 48–49 (General Report), 113–114, 129–131 (Summary of Proceedings), 158ff (Working Party No. II), 266.
307. See: Ricketson, 2003, pp. 44–45; Ricketson & Ginsburg, 2006, p. 1218; von Lewinski, 2008, pp. 220–221. Noting that this would exclude analogous compulsory licences to those provided for in Arts 11*bis*(2) and 13 BC, *see* Ficsor, 2003b, p. 155; Nordemann, Vinck, Hertin & Meyer, 1990, p. 441; Ricketson & Ginsburg, 2006, p. 1218; von Lewinski, 2008, p. 220.

compulsory licenses'.[308] Article 15 RC was justified by the desire for legal consistency in allowing limitations analogous to copyright, and to avoid preferential treatment for related rights holders vis-à-vis copyright owners.[309]

Article 15 WPPT grants performers and phonogram producers a remuneration right for broadcasting and communication to the public of phonograms. It extends the scope of Article 12 RC by including indirect broadcasting, a broader concept of communication to the public – extending to webcasting and possibly near-on-demand transmissions – and additional subject matter in digital form.[310]

With the exception of live performances, the WPPT provision should allow a compulsory licence for non-interactive digital broadcasting under Articles 4 SatCab Directive, 8 Rental Right Directive and 3(2) InfoSoc Directive.[311] The last-mentioned provision includes a far-reaching exclusive right of making available, which causes any compulsory licence touching upon interactive uses, possibly including near-on-demand transmissions, to qualify as a copyright limitation.

On the table during treaty negotiations was not only the adoption of an exclusive right for online commercial subscription services[312] – broadly rejected, including by the EU delegation[313] – but also an ACS-type proposal. The latter consisted of a mandatory remuneration right for types of use where the communication could only be received 'on the basis of subscription and against payment of a fee', i.e., to certain types of near-on-demand transmission.[314]

In the end, however, the parties did not reach a consensus and drafted an Agreed Statement on subscription-based transmissions, which addresses

---

308. Records RC 1961, p. 46. *See also* Ficsor, 2003b, p. 153; Ricketson, 2003, p. 45; Ricketson & Ginsburg, 2006, p. 1218.
309. *See* Ficsor, 2002c, p. 298; C. Masouyé, 1981, p. 59; Ricketson, 2003, p. 45; von Lewinski, 2008, p. 220. N.B. the provision preceded the Berne three-step test by six years. *See also* Records RC 1961, pp. 144–145, for a surfacing of this concern in the discussion of Art. 7(2) (Working Party No. II).
310. Arts 2(f) and (g) WPPT contain definitions of 'broadcasting' and 'communication to the public'. *See* Brison, 2006, p. 171, noting that under the WPPT broadcasting follows a special regime vis-à-vis communication to the public. N.B. the RC did not define 'communication to the public', a right construed with a broader meaning in the WPPT. *See* Ficsor, 2003b, p. 252.
311. N.B. Art. 8(1) Rental Rights Directive provides an exclusive right regarding the broadcasting of live performances (for the first fixation); where that use refers to a former broadcast or fixation, Art. 8 provides only a remuneration right. *See* Nérisson, 2014, pp. 186–187.
312. *See* Records WIPO Treaties 1996, pp. 290–291, 312–315 (referring to the draft Art. 19 on the remuneration right of phonogram producers; draft Arts 12 and 19 were later merged into an Art. 20a and originated the current Art. 15 WPPT), 428–429, 459, 684–691, 769.
313. *Ibid.*, p. 685.
314. See: Ficsor, 2002c, pp. 638–640, 2003b, pp. 252–254, 297. *See also* Records WIPO Treaties 1996, pp. 429, 760–770.

the lack of certainty regarding online acts such as 'digital broadcasting, webcasting and near-on-demand-services', especially in light of the exclusive right of making available, leaving the matter for 'future resolution'.[315]

Finally, Article 14(6) TRIPS incorporates in the treaty (vis-à-vis the related rights it grants) the exceptions and reservations permitted in the RC.[316] This arguably opens the door for RC-compatible compulsory licences regarding TRIPS-related rights,[317] which would not be subject to the three-step test.[318] Therefore, it is 'an effort to align exceptions to copyright and related rights',[319] and consolidate the level of compromise achieved in the RC, with nothing in its drafting or negotiating history providing additional normative content to the rule.[320]

2.4.4 Manifestations in the *Acquis*

The final version of Article 11*bis* BC covers different acts of communication to the public of works, including broadcasting and cable retransmission. These acts are subject to different regimes in the *acquis*, which does not contain a rule equivalent to the BC compulsory licence.

The 1993 SatCab Directive – rooted in the 1984 Green Paper 'Television Without Frontiers' – regulates two rights of communication to the public relating to two forms of transmission of works: satellite broadcasting, viewed as a form of primary exploitation, and cable retransmission of broadcasts, seen as a form of secondary exploitation.[321]

First, the directive states that Member States shall provide an exclusive right for the author to authorise the communication to the public by satellite of copyright works.[322] By combining the exclusive right with a localisation criterion – a 'country-of-origin' rule – the directive sought to solve the issues of legal uncertainty on the treatment of satellite broadcasts in the EU. This solution was justified by the cross-border nature of satellite broadcasting, the inadequate national copyright protection afforded to this new technology, and

315. *See* first Agreed Statement to Art. 15 WPPT. *See also*: Brison, 2006, p. 187; Ficsor, 2003b, pp. 253–254. On the exclusive right of making available, *see* Arts 10 and 14 WPPT.
316. Contrary to the BC, the RC is not integrated in TRIPS and only specific provisions are mentioned therein, in connection to the related rights covered by the Agreement. *See* Carlos María Correa, 2007, p. 166 & n. 242; Morgan, 2010, p. 390.
317. See: Dreier & Hugenholtz, 2006, p. 208; Kamina, 2015, pp. 52–53. *Contra*: Ficsor, 2002c, p. 634–ff, who seems to disagree by stating that Art. 15 TRIPS does not contain the same type of rights as Arts 12 RC and 15 WPPT.
318. In this sense, *see* Carlos María Correa, 2007, p. 167; Morgan, 2010, pp. 390–391 (noting the unsettled nature of this assertion in legal scholarship); Proposal InfoSoc Directive 1997, p. 15. *Contra* Basso, 2000, pp. 196–197; Watal, 2001, p. 225.
319. Gervais, 2008, p. 206 (n. 296).
320. *Ibid.*; UNCTAD-ICTSD, 2005, pp. 208–212.
321. Depreeuw, 2014, p. 366.
322. Art. 2 SatCab Directive.

pragmatic commercial reasons.[323] In particular, this design addressed the fear that refusals to license in one territory would obstruct satellite transmission, harming both the public interest and the interests of authors in the exploitation of their works.[324]

In the explanatory memorandum, the Commission states the rationale for the *exclusive* nature of the right, while allowing the possibility of extended collective licensing:

> If the law of the broadcasting country does confer protection in principle, but makes a primary broadcast via direct satellite subject to a statutory license, rights owners in the entire footprint are prevented from deciding how their works will be exploited and simply receive remuneration that has been fixed by the competent authority in the broadcasting country …
>
> For this reason the proposal for a Directive rules out the introduction of statutory licenses for satellite broadcasts. If on the date of the proposal the legislation of a Member State allows agreements between an entitled organization of rights owners and a broadcaster to be declared generally binding, this possibility may be maintained subject to certain conditions.[325]

The directive's rejection of compulsory licensing is understandable in light of the choice of an exclusive right combined with a localisation criterion to regulate satellite broadcasting. If the country of origin allowed a legal licensing system, the work would be available throughout the EU without the possibility of the respective author(s) first authorising its exploitation. Hence, the prohibition was necessary to prevent differences in the level of protection within the common market from causing distortions to competition.[326]

Second, the possibility of applying the BC compulsory licence to cable retransmission acts included in Article 11*bis*(1)(ii) BC is restricted by the SatCab Directive. In strict terms, the directive does not mandate an exclusive right for these acts, merely requiring that the same are restricted under copyright.[327] However, as Depreeuw notes, several elements in the directive confirm the exclusive nature of the retransmission right, and exclude the possibility of subjecting it to statutory licensing.[328]

323. *See* Explanatory Memorandum SatCab Directive, pp. 3–4, 9–15, 21–22.
324. *Ibid.*, pp. 30–31. This issue had already been addressed in the proposal for the Rental Rights Directive, and was the topic of a Common Statement by the Council and the Commission. *See* Reinbothe & von Lewinski, 1993, p. 93 & n. 72.
325. Explanatory Memorandum SatCab Directive, pp. 22–23 (paras 35, 36). On ECL, *see infra* 3.3.3.
326. *See* recital 21 SatCab Directive. *See also* Depreeuw, 2014, p. 387.
327. Depreeuw, 2014, p. 393; Hugenholtz, 2006, p. 279.
328. Depreeuw, 2014, p. 402, referring to recital 27 and the wording of Art. 8 SatCab Directive, which mentions individual or collective contractual agreements.

The right applies only to simultaneous, unaltered and unabridged retransmissions by cable of television or radio programmes originating in another Member State – thus excluding purely national retransmissions – following an initial broadcast over the air or (unlike the BC) by wire.[329] The definition of the right thus requires a primary transmission and the use of the specific technology of cable as the means for the secondary transmission.[330]

It is noteworthy that the exercise of the right is subject to a special regime of mandatory collective management in Articles 9–12 SatCab Directive, from which only broadcasting organisations are exempted. Still, despite this special regime, the exclusive nature of the right is left intact.[331]

In essence, the directive opted for a less stringent non-voluntary licence to determine the conditions of exercise of the right, rather than affecting its exclusive nature. This solution, consistent with Article 11*bis*(2) BC, enhances the bargaining position of authors, who retain the (collective) right to prohibit the exploitation of their works.[332]

The main rationale for this option was not so much the protection of authors' interests but the facilitation of 'the practicable exploitation of programmes'.[333] The objective was to put in place a system (already used in some Member States) that ensured cable operators could acquire cable retransmission rights in a timely manner and in their entirety.[334] Mandatory collective management would shield cable operators from refusals to license by individual rights holders not represented by CMOs in relation to their rights in retransmitted programmes (the so-called 'outsider' problem).[335] The system would likewise provide that rights holders interested in cable retransmission 'would not be prevented from exploiting their rights'.[336] In the Commission's view, this solution was superior to the compulsory licensing of cable retransmission rights.[337]

Chapter 3 discusses mandatory collective management, which provides inspiration for some ACS proposals that consider it a viable model to regulate online use in EU copyright law.[338] On this point, it is unclear whether the right of cable retransmission in the SatCab Directive includes Internet retransmission. The definition of the right is specific to the technology of 'cable or microwave system', and the Commission does not

329. Arts 1(3) and 8 SatCab Directive.
330. On the requirements of initial transmission and retransmission by cable, *see* Depreeuw, 2014, pp. 393–400.
331. Hugenholtz, 2006, p. 280. Art. 10 SatCab Directive contains the exemption for broadcasting organisations.
332. Depreeuw, 2014, pp. 403–404.
333. *Ibid.*, p. 406.
334. Explanatory Memorandum SatCab Directive, p. 32.
335. Depreeuw, 2014, pp. 402–403; Rósen, 2014, pp. 234–235. *See also* Explanatory Memorandum SatCab Directive, p. 20, 24, 32.
336. Explanatory Memorandum SatCab Directive, p. 32.
337. *Ibid.*, p. 43. *See also* Hugenholtz, 2006, pp. 278–279; Rósen, 2014, p. 231.
338. *See infra* 3.3.4.

appear to have considered cable as including Internet retransmission, making it difficult to argue that these acts are subject to mandatory collective management.[339]

In its 2002 report on the directive, the Commission rejected the extension of the mandatory collective management regime to online retransmission. It considered this extension premature in light of the early stage of development of the Internet, as well as the recent InfoSoc and E-Commerce Directives, which applied to some of these acts and had not yet been transposed into national laws.[340]

Finally, regarding copyright, the 2001 InfoSoc Directive *supplements* the area-specific directives discussed above, by granting authors a broad exclusive right of communication to the public in Article 3(1). This right includes satellite broadcasting and cable retransmission.[341]

Despite the non-implementation in EU copyright law of the compulsory licensing model of Article 11*bis*(2) BC, this provision contains the blueprint for such a model in the field of related rights at international level, making it part of the *acquis* in a limited fashion.

Article 8 Rental Right Directive is based on Articles 7(1), 12 and 13(1)(a) and (d) RC. It aims at harmonising certain rights in relation to wireless (including satellite) broadcasting and communication to the public of performers, phonogram producers and broadcasting organisations.[342] Its paragraph (2), similar to Article 12 RC, states:

> Member States shall provide a right in order to ensure that a single equitable remuneration is paid by the user, if a phonogram published for commercial purposes, or a reproduction of such phonogram, is used for broadcasting by wireless means or for any communication to the public, and to ensure that this remuneration is shared between the relevant performers and phonogram producers. Member States may, in the absence of agreement between the performers and phonogram producers, lay down the conditions as to the sharing of this remuneration between them.[343]

With the exception of live performances, the right of broadcasting granted to performers and phonogram producers is not exclusive and gives

339. Depreeuw, 2014, pp. 396, 406; Hugenholtz, 2009b, p. 13.
340. Report SatCab Directive 2002, pp. 14–15.
341. Recital 23 InfoSoc Directive. *See infra* 4.3.2.
342. The definition of 'communication to the public by satellite' is included in Art. 1(2)(a) SatCab Directive. *See* Common Statement by the Council and Commission at the internal market Council meeting of 18 June 1992. Art. 4 SatCab Directive clarifies that the concept of 'broadcasting by wireless means' under Arts 8 and 10 Rental Right Directive encompasses also 'communication to the public by satellite'.
343. The provision is distinct from Art. 12 RC insofar as it does not allow reservations, applies to performers *and* producers, and covers indirect means of broadcasting.

rise to equitable remuneration under Article 8(2) Rental Right Directive. (In addition and as noted before, the exercise of the separate right of cable retransmission of broadcasts is subject to mandatory collective management in Articles 9–12 SatCab Directive.)

This provision was not contained in the original Commission proposal of 1990, but only in the amended proposal of 1992, following an Opinion of the Economic and Social Committee and discussion in the European Parliament.[344] Its introduction corresponded with the protection provided to related rights holders in the RC and, together with other rights granted to these rights holders and harmonised in the directive, intended to solve the problems caused by 'piracy connected with non-material exploitation'.[345] Regarding the right of remuneration in Article 8(2), the amended proposal merely states that this was a minimum rights provision already part of most Member States' laws.[346]

Article 10 Rental Right Directive follows Article 15 RC. It allows Member States to impose the same limitations for related rights as exist for author's rights (e.g., in Article 5 InfoSoc Directive), and permits compulsory licences if the same are compatible with the RC and the three-step test.[347] In the explanatory memorandum, the Commission expressed the need to provide compensation for limitations allowed under this provision, especially for private use, due to the 'high intensity of this kind of use'.[348] (Naturally, the private use limitation would not apply to acts of broadcasting, understood as *communication to the public*.[349])

The aforementioned chain of provisions means that compulsory licences for broadcasting of subject matter protected by related rights admissible under Article 15(2) RC are allowed by the Rental Right and SatCab Directives.[350] This is possible due to the lack of harmonisation of the right of communication to the public of related rights holders in Article 3(2) InfoSoc Directive, which only deals with the making available right.

344. On the legislative process, *see* Reinbothe & von Lewinski, 1993, pp. 19–29, 92–93, noting that the Economic and Social Committee suggested the harmonisation of broadcasting rights, and the Parliament proposed the introduction of a new Art. 6 on this topic.
345. Amended proposal Rental Right Directive 1992, pp. 3, 12, discussing the insertion of a new Art. 6*bis*, which would become Art. 8 of the directive. *See* Reinbothe & von Lewinski, 1993, pp. 17–18, noting the disappointment of performers and broadcasters with the proposal's silence on the rights broadcasting communication to the public.
346. Amended Proposal Rental Right Directive 1992, p. 13.
347. *See* Art. 10(2) RC. The three-step test in Art. 10(3) Rental Rights Directive was included by virtue of an amendment introduced by Art. 11(1)(b) InfoSoc Directive.
348. Explanatory Memorandum Rental Right Directive, pp. 58–59, discussing Art. 8 of the proposal. Private use is mentioned in Art. 10(1)(a) Rental Rights Directive.
349. CJEU, *PPI*, paras 70–77.
350. Dreier, 2010, p. 434.

Therefore, the RC rules on limitations to the exercise of rights of broadcasting and communication to the public remain in force in the *acquis*.[351]

This set-up insulates a portion of non-interactive acts of communication to the public in EU law from the umbrella of full exclusivity. These alternatives to exclusivity, as applied to large-scale acts of communication to the public in the context of new technologies, are explored in the ACS debate.

2.4.5 Conclusions on Compulsory Licensing for Broadcasting and Communication to the Public

Broadcasting introduced a communications medium allowing one-to-many simultaneous transmission of signals to a dispersed public. During the early days of the technology and well into the twentieth century, broadcasting through radio, television, and satellite influenced the dissemination of information, education, culture, and the development of the democratic process.

Broadcasting also had a profound effect on copyright and its exploitation, as the content transmitted consisted largely of protected works. The essential policy question that emerged was how to balance this new model of mass communication and exploitation with the protection of authors' rights.

Internationally, the BC answered this question in its 1928 Rome revision by balancing opposing views. One view, echoing existing national laws, supported the regulation of radio broadcasting by an exclusive right of communication to the public. Another view cautioned against extending exclusivity to these uses in light of the cultural and social interests of this new and popular form of dissemination of works. Furthermore, there were concerns that authors' CMOs, typically natural monopolies, would leverage the exclusive right and refuse to license broadcasting organisations.

In essence, it was feared that an exclusive right would hinder the development of a new economic and technical model of exploitation, and prevent public interest considerations. The interests of rights holders had to be contrasted with the public and users' interests in the promotion and development of a new and important technology – including related concerns with access to information and knowledge – and the interests of commercial users, linked to the regulation of competition and industry practice.[352] Many of the same tensions and considerations are central to the debate on how to regulate the mass communication of works to the public over the Internet.

351. Art. 1(2) InfoSoc Directive. N.B. Art. 3(2) InfoSoc Directive implements Arts 10 and 14 WPPT.
352. *See* Guibault, 2002, pp. 56–68, identifying 'regulation of industry practice and competition' as a justification behind copyright limitations. Guibault exemplifies with compulsory licences for the broadcasting and recording of musical works.

The result of the BC debate was a flexible model of remunerated access through compulsory licensing in Article 11*bis*(2). The licence strikes a fair balance between the interests of authors in exclusivity and remuneration, and the public interest in the access to works and development of a socially valuable technology.

Through a technology-neutral formula and a legislative update in 1948 (Brussels Act), the scope of the provision and the licence extended to different types of broadcasting (including through television and satellite), rebroadcasting, communication by wire of broadcast works (applicable to Internet retransmissions), and communication by loudspeaker.

Article 11*bis*(2) BC allows national laws to regulate the 'conditions of exercise' of the exclusive right. This formula, also used in the RC, enables adoption of non-voluntary licensing – compulsory licensing or mandatory collective management – subject to the respect of moral rights and payment of 'equitable remuneration'. The definition of this last concept is left to national legislators. Beyond the notion that the remuneration is fair and just, it seems that it should relate solely to the permitted use (and not to related uses governed by other rights), while bearing some connection to the market value of the use.

The BC compulsory licensing model has survived to this day in international law, despite multiple challenges in the context of BC revisions and the WIPO Treaties. The same policy arguments advanced in Rome (1928) and Brussels (1948), together with the importance of the model for the fair remuneration of creators, secured the preservation of the compulsory licence in the Agreed Statement to Article 8 WCT. This very statement, some argue, allows for the compulsory licensing of interactive acts of communication to the public, including uploads in P2P networks. (In the *acquis*, Article 3 InfoSoc Directive appears to restrict this possibility and subject such a licence to the three-step test.)

The BC provision further served as a blueprint for compulsory licensing of related rights in the RC, TRIPS and WPPT. Article 12 RC regulates secondary uses of commercially published phonograms, and Article 15 WPPT extends its scope to include certain types of non-interactive online use. Other compulsory licences applying to rebroadcasting and some forms of public communication of television broadcasts are permitted in the RC and TRIPS.[353]

The licence in Article 12 RC is also a child of compromise, between performers and producers, as licensors, and broadcasting organisations, as licensees. Authors opposed the model out of concern it would undercut their revenues. Broadcasters opposed it out of fear of refusals to license, and

353. Arts 7(2), (13(d) and 15(2) RC, and Art. 14(6) TRIPS.

because they rejected the notion that their 'secondary uses' of phonograms would have adverse economic effects.[354]

In the end, the main justifications for the compulsory licence were justice and fairness – performers and producers were entitled to a share of the profits reaped from these acts of exploitation of their protected subject matter[355] – and the desire to avoid refusals to license. Furthermore, the model was designed to prevent double payments (by attributing a 'single' remuneration) and streamline negotiations.[356] Finally, the possibility of subjecting the licensed uses to collective management was justified by the high transaction costs of individually managing and enforcing these.

As with the BC licence, there is little guidance in the RC preparatory works on the concept of equitable remuneration. The issue is mostly left to contracting states. However, commentators argue that calculation of the remuneration should refer to criteria like frequency and market value of the licensed uses.[357] Also similarly to the BC, the RC allows broad reservations as a counterpoint to the principle of equitable remuneration.

The remaining RC compulsory licences were adopted to avoid preferential treatment of related rights holders vis-à-vis authors; the same rationale holds true for the subsequent inclusion of these provisions in TRIPS.[358] The rebroadcasting licence in Article 7(2) RC was a concession to broadcasters for purposes of rights clearance.[359] Underlying this and the compulsory licence for public communications of television broadcasts in Article 13 (d) RC was also a desire to enable dissemination of content while ensuring remuneration for affected rights holders.[360] Finally, Article 15 WPPT crystallises the RC balancing of interests, without meaningfully advancing it.[361]

---

354. For discussions on the article, *see* Records RC, pp. 48–49 (General Report), 113–114, 118–121, 158 ff., 161, 165, 222–224, 265 ff. *See also* C. Masouyé, 1981, p. 46ff.; W. Nordemann et al., 1990, p. 349; von Lewinski, 2008, p. 212.
355. *See* Records RC, pp. 159 ('performers should not be excluded from sharing in the immense profits made be phonogram, producers and broadcasters through the exploitation of their performances. Such exclusion was completely unjust'), 162 ('equitable remuneration for performers, phonogram producers or both, should be adopted as a matter of common justice'), 265.
356. *Ibid.*, pp. 49, 163. *See also* C. Masouyé, 1981, p. 48; von Lewinski, 2008, p. 214.
357. See, e.g., Masouyé, 1981, p. 48; von Lewinski, 2008, p. 26.
358. On Art. 15 RC, *see* Masouyé, 1981, p. 59; Ricketson, 2003, p. 45; von Lewinski, 2008, p. 220. *See also* Records RC, pp. 144 – 145, for an expression of this concern in the discussion of Art. 7(2) RC. Regarding Art. 14(6) TRIPS and its aim to align limitations to copyright and related rights, *see* Ficsor, 2002c, p. 642; UNCTAD-ICTSD, 2005, pp. 208–212; WIPO, 1996.
359. Records RC, pp. 142–144, 173–175.
360. *Ibid.*, pp. 167–168. *See also* C. Masouyé, 1981, p. 54.
361. *See* Reinbothe & von Lewinski, 2002, pp. 375–380; Ricketson & Ginsburg, 2006, p. 1267. For discussions of the provision in the preparatory works, *see* Records WCT/WPPT (1996), pp. 288–291, 312–315, 526–527, 684–691, 769–776, 781.

In the *acquis*, broadcasting and communication to the public of works were subject to exclusive rights, but with restrictions on their exercise. The SatCab Directive first recognised distinct rights for communication to the public by satellite and cable retransmission of broadcasts. Importantly, the first right allows extended collective licensing, while the second is subject to a special regime of mandatory collective management; this regime also applies to related rights holders, except broadcasting organisations. Due to the technology-specific nature of the cable retransmission right, the latter regime probably does not apply to Internet retransmission.

For satellite broadcasting, the combination of the right with a country-of-origin rule made compulsory licensing difficult, as it could lead to forum shopping and distortions in competition. For cable retransmission, mandatory collective management was motivated by the regulation of industry practice and competition (preventing refusals to license), the protection of rights holders that wished to use the means of exploitation, and the enhancement of the fair remuneration and bargaining position of authors, who retained a collectively exercised exclusive right.

A subsequent wave of legislative action saw the recognition of a general exclusive right in Article 3 InfoSoc Directive. As noted, this right seems to block the availability of the BC compulsory licence in the EU – including its application to online use – and subject it to the three-step test.

In the field of related rights, the RC rules on limitations to the exercise of rights of broadcasting and communication to the public remain in force in the EU legal order, in part due to the limited harmonisation effected by Article 3(2) InfoSoc Directive.

The international rules described, as implemented in the Rental Right and SatCab Directives, allow compulsory licensing of the right of broadcasting (except for live performances) granted to performers and phonogram producers, subject to equitable remuneration.[362] In conformity with international law, this licence can extend to non-interactive digital broadcasting.[363] Nothing in the preparatory works of the directives suggests a shift in the rationales for these provisions, as compared to their counterparts in international treaties.

2.5 CONCLUSIONS

This chapter set out to identify historical examples of legal schemes qualifying as precedents to ACS, and understand their legal mechanics and

362. On which, *see supra* 2.2.4.

363. Although Art. 3(2) InfoSoc Directive likely blocks licensing of interactive uses. The conclusion seems admissible in light of the Agreed Statement to Art. 15 WPPT. This statement leaves open the 'complete resolution of the level of rights of broadcasting and communication to the public that should be enjoyed by performers and phonogram producers in the digital age.'

the justifications for their adoption. Precedents are copyright rules that regulate the mass use of works, by reproduction or communication to the public, through non-voluntary licences, subject to payment of compensation. They impose remunerated access over exclusivity in order to address challenges arising from technological disruption, market failure, and difficult or undesirable enforceability.

Two legal regimes are selected as precedents: statutory licences for private copying, and compulsory licences for broadcasting and communication to the public; these regimes usually rely on obligatory collective management of the underlying remuneration or compensation right. It is notable that these regimes, alone or in combination with mandatory collective management (with each model applying to different rights), serve as inspiration for multiple ACS proposals.[364]

The analysis of precedents illustrates how copyright evolves in response to technologies that enable the large-scale use and exploitation of works outside the control of rights holders. Both home taping by individuals and radio transmission to a dispersed audience were clear uses of protected works; however, it was contentious whether copyright protection applied or should apply to those uses.

The response of courts and lawmakers was to extend the exclusive right to both types of use. For private copying, the extension was justified by the right of the author to a just pecuniary reward; for broadcasting, it was rooted in reasons of fairness, as most content transmitted via the ether consisted of protected works. In the two examples, the move was influenced by concerns that failure to secure copyright protection would result in the loss of novel exploitation markets or economic harm to existing markets.

But extending exclusivity to these fields also clashed with the public interest. Regulating private copying through an exclusive right signified the first intrusion of copyright in the private sphere, and presented a conflict with consumer rights and the fundamental right of privacy. It also meant imposing secondary liability on technology providers, ultimately judged disproportionate due to the susceptibility of the technology to non-infringing use.

For broadcasting, the implication was control of a new technology with profound social value, which allowed the dissemination of culture and education, and played a key role in the democratic process. Simultaneously, there were fears that exclusivity would lead to refusal by CMOs to license broadcasting organisations, an issue of regulation of competition and industry practice.

The precedents share public interest justifications. Underlying both regimes are policy concerns related to curing market failures, securing the development of socially valuable technologies, dissemination of knowledge and culture – including access to and enjoyment of works –, fair remuneration of creators and, as regards the endorsement of obligatory collective

364. *See infra* 3.3.4 and 3.3.5.

management, a reduction of contractual imbalances for creators. The same issues are staple items of the ACS debate.

This constellation of public interest concerns forced lawmakers into balancing the interests of rights holders, the public interest, and specific group interests (of commercial users and technology providers). The result in both cases was to restrict the nature or exercise of the exclusive right in favour of non-voluntary licensing regimes. Remuneration replaced exclusivity at the centre of copyright law.

Furthermore, the technology-neutral formulation of the right and accompanying licence allowed both precedents to track technological disruption and accommodate future uses and modes of exploitation.

Against this background, the private copying model emerged in Germany in the 1950s–1960s. Following a series of landmark judicial decisions extending the right of reproduction to private copying activities – and contributory liability to technology providers –, the German legislator imposed a statutory licence model based on a limitation with equitable remuneration. End-users had legal permission to make private reproductions in return for payment of a levy.

Initially, the statutory licence was aimed at forms of tangible exploitation of some categories of works, namely home taping of sound recordings and audio-visual works. However, due to the technology-neutral formula of the law, the licence extended to incorporate mass intangible use, such as digital private copying, and a growing array of devices and media as levy targets. Providers of these devices and media were debtors of the levy, but had the right to pass it on to consumers. This design was privacy-respecting, ensured a link to the actual use, freed providers from liability for infringement, and was deemed a fair way to burden intermediaries for activities from which they profited. Due to the transaction costs of managing the system, the licence was subject to collective management.

Prior to its *acquis* recognition, private copying was discussed in the preparatory works of the BC and the WIPO Treaties. In the Stockholm revision conference, the German model was pivotal in the introduction of equitable remuneration as a public interest component of the three-step test, making remuneration a flexible tool for the admissibility and broadening of copyright limitations.

The private copying statutory licensing model has since proliferated to most EU Member States, making its way to Article 5(2)(b) InfoSoc Directive as an optional limitation. This version of the limitation, however, is combined with a fair compensation right, based on harm, indicative of a market failure rational. The debate at EU level featured some of the topics discussed at the WIPO conferences, in conjunction with the possibility of curing that market failure through technological control of digital use. The result would be a phasing-out of levies. Although enmeshed with the legal protection of TPMs in the *acquis*, the private copying limitation survived, not only due to the lack of evidence on the effectiveness of technological controls, but also due to the privacy right that underpinned it. This seems to imply that the limitation retains a fundamental rights rationale.

The BC compulsory licence for broadcasting and communication to the public followed a different path from private copying. The licence exempts broadcasters from authorisation for acts of communication to the public of works, subject to remuneration.

Its introduction in the Rome Act of 1928 was a response to the growing importance of radio broadcasting, a then-new mode of immaterial transmission and exploitation of works. The amendments promoted in the Brussels Act of 1948, together with the technology neutral definition of the right (initially referring to 'wireless diffusion'), allowed its extension to television broadcasting, some forms of satellite broadcasting, rebroadcasting, and at a later stage communication to the public 'by wire' (a concept that includes Internet retransmission).

Admissibility of compulsory licensing hinged on the treaty formula 'conditions of the exercise' of the right, a legal synonym for non-voluntary licensing, and on the payment of equitable remuneration. Determination of the remuneration was left to the discretion of national laws. Neither the convention nor commentators provide much guidance on its contents, other than it should be fair, just, reflect the use licensed, and present a link to its market value.

The balance of interests reflected by the licence allowed it to survive multiple proposals for abolishment. It is currently enshrined in the Agreed Statement to Article 8 WCT, a provision which some scholars view as allowing compulsory licensing of the right of communication to the public online in international law. In the *acquis*, however, Article 3 InfoSoc Directive apparently blocks this avenue for ACS, subjecting it to the three-step test.

The BC provision is also a valuable study subject in that it has inspired similar compulsory licences in the field of related rights, namely in the RC, TRIPS, and WPPT. To a limited extent, remnants of these are present in the *acquis*, despite the general exclusive right of communication to the public in Article 3 InfoSoc Directive, which for authors includes *inter alia* broadcasting and cable retransmission, and for related rights holders a broad right of making available to the public.

One example of non-voluntary licensing, motivated by the regulation of competition and industry practice, is the special regime of mandatory collective management of the cable retransmission right in the SatCab Directive, from which only broadcasters are exempt. Another example is specific to related rights. Consistent with international law and in light of the limited scope of Article 3(2) InfoSoc Directive, the SatCab and Rental Right Directives allow compulsory licensing of the right of broadcasting of performers and phonogram producers, including non-interactive digital broadcasting. The right is subject to equitable remuneration, on which the CJEU has provided some guidance.[365]

A striking lesson from this chapter is how much remains unchanged in copyright debates. It is difficult not to come away from studying the historical debates on both precedents with the impression that we are repeating yesterday's discussions, with slight updates, for the regulation of the use of copyright works over the Internet.

For instance, the private copying debate is riddled with alarming claims on the negative effects of home taping on rights holders' revenues, promises of technological control of copyright use, and willingness to enforce copyright at intrusive levels. Some texts could be used today merely by replacing the reference to the recording technology of the past with 'P2P' or 'file sharing'. The private copying statutory licence provided an adequate counterpoint to the extension of the exclusive reproduction right to the personal sphere. However, as we will see in Chapter 4, whilst the right tends to expand in the digital age, the limitation is narrowing. Put differently, the current system is losing the balance achieved in the German model.

All in all, perhaps the most important lesson is that the principle of exclusivity is not totemic. Rather, it is a tool to ensure copyright protection, subject to the public interest. This fundamental aspect is as old as copyright itself, as attested by the famous statement by Numa Droz in the closing speech to the 1884 Berne Conference, to the effect that 'limits to absolute protection are rightly set by the public interest.'[366]

Where the exclusive right poses a conflict with the public interest or specific group interests, remuneration and access emerge as the central concepts of copyright protection. This chapter shows that remunerated access through a model of non-voluntary licensing allows policy makers to reconcile copyright protection with the public interest in the face of technological and market disruption. For both private copying and the broadcasting licence, this model secured a fair balance across a range of competing interests that exclusivity could not.

365. *See supra* 2.2.4 and, in particular, CJEU, *Sena*, para. 46.
366. Records BC 1884, p. 67.

Chapter 3
Alternative Compensation Systems: Taxonomy of Legalisation Proposals

3.1 INTRODUCTION

The study of the admissibility and consistency of ACS with EU copyright law requires a clear understanding of their legal characteristics. To do so, it is necessary to define their nature, scope, and effects. This can be achieved through the identification, systematisation, and conceptualisation of proposals for legalisation of large-scale individual online use. This chapter sets about that task by developing a taxonomy of ACS from the perspective of EU copyright law, which can subsequently be tested against the relevant provisions of the *acquis*.

The chapter asks the following research questions:

What legal models are most commonly used for legalisation proposals?
How can these models be qualified in light of EU copyright law?
What is the nature and effect of these models on the exclusive right?
What are the main attributes of these models?

The departure point for analysis is the preliminary definition of ACS in Chapter 1. As noted, ACS is a shorthand for legal schemes, often combined with elements of collective rights management, that allow individuals to make online use of works without the direct authorisation of rights holders, subject to the payment of remuneration.[1]

The kinds of use in question are technology neutral. They can be of different types and carried out in different contexts over the Internet, such as through P2P networks, user groups, social media, streaming sites, or other web 2.0 platforms. (Chapter 4 develops a typology of online uses which it then links to exclusive rights and limitations in the *acquis*.)

The 'alternative' refers to a deviation from the application of an exclusive right and individual management to large-scale online use for personal enjoyment and expression. The former restricted use becomes permitted-but-paid through a system of 'compensation without control'.[2] Hence, an ACS implies a shift from exclusivity to remunerated access and use.

It was also noted in Chapter 1 that legalisation proposals bear different labels, beyond the overarching term ACS. These include, to name a few representative examples, Fisher's 'tax-and-royalty system', Netanel's 'non-commercial use levy', the French L'ALLIANCE Public Artistes' 'licence globale', the German Green Party's proposals for a 'content' or 'culture flat-rate', Aigrain's 'creative contribution' model, Blázquez's 'file sharing levy', Grassmuck's 'sharing license', and COMMUNIA's 'alternative reward systems'.[3]

Most proposals share the core characteristics of the precedents identified in Chapter 2. They are copyright rules that regulate mass use of works through non-voluntary licences, subject to compensation.[4] However, in order to offer a complete systematisation, this chapter also examines proposals external to copyright or that rely on voluntary licensing through collective rights management.

1. There is a vast literature in this field, covering contributions beyond legal scholarship. Among the most influential sources see: Bernault & Lebois, 2005; Dusollier & Colin, 2011; Grassmuck, 2009; Litman, 2004; Lohmann, 2004, 2008; Lunney, 2001; Netanel, 2003; Peukert, 2005. N.B. probably the first high level ACS proposal is Stallman, 1993, proposing a system for taxing digital copying through a levy on devices and media.
2. *See supra* 1.1. *See* Ginsburg, 2014b (on the notion of 'permitted-but-paid') and Wizards of OS, 2004 (with the 'Berlin Declaration on Collectively Managed Online Rights: Compensation without Control', a jointly issued declaration urging the European Commission to consider content flat-rate proposals).
3. See: Eckersley, 2004; Fisher, 2004 ('alternative compensation systems'); Fisher, 2004 ('tax-and-royalty systems'); Netanel, 2003 ('Noncommercial Use Levy')'; L'ALLIANCE public.artistes, 2005, 2006b, 2006c (using 'licence globale', a concept initially developed in 2001 by the French CMO ADAMI and officially presented in 2004; in 2005, L'ALLIANCE Public. Artistes was created with the purpose of providing institutional backing to the same); Grassmuck, 2008 ('content' and 'culture flat-rate'); Aigrain, 2008, 2012 ('creative contribution'); Blázquez, 2011, pp. 16–17 ('file sharing levy'); Grassmuck, 2013 ('sharing license'); and Frosio, 2011, p. 166 ('alternative reward systems').
4. *See supra* 2.2.

The analysis focuses on a list of texts, along with commentary and critique that can be understood as a 'canon' of the theory of ACS.[5] These materials include a selection of legalisation proposals ranging from the purely theoretical to concrete implementation legislation. From the perspective of comparative legal analysis, the selection of sources is a combination of 'typical', 'most similar', and 'influential'.[6] The selected literature is authored by academics, stakeholders, and political parties. With few exceptions (mainly in Brazil and Canada[7]), most proposals originate from the US and EU,[8] and are post-2000.[9] Due to the high level of international harmonisation in copyright and the fact that many proposals are anchored in models of collective rights management (on which the EU has a longstanding tradition in law and practice), even ACS designed for non-EU jurisdictions are considered here.[10]

The ACS definition requires access to works through blanket licensing subject to payment of compensation. These features exclude as viable legalisation options pure private ordering schemes, like those based solely on open access. Also excluded are systems built on uncompensated limitations for online use, sometimes labelled as 'digital abandon' or 'information anarchy'.[11] Proposals of this type are therefore not examined here.

5. To this effect, *see* Duncan Kennedy's parallel comments when describing the several facets of critical legal studies. *See* Kennedy, 1997, p. 10.
6. Seawright & Gerring, 2008, discussing several cross-case selection methods in scholarly research.
7. For Brazil, see: Grassmuck, 2010a; Machado & Ortellado, 2013; Souza, Machado, Mendonça, Ortellado & Schmidt, 2013. For Canada, *see* Songwriters Association of Canada, 2011.
8. In Europe, several minority political parties in different countries (Italy, Belgium, and Portugal) have advanced legislative proposals for ACS. See: Beltrandi et al., 2008; Beltrandi et al., 2007 (Italy); Hellings & Piryns, 2010; Morael & Piryns, 2010 (Belgium); and Partido Comunista Português (Grupo Parlamentar), 2012 (Portugal). In France, during the adoption process of Law No. 2006-961 of 1 August 2006 concerning Copyright and Neighbouring Rights in the Information Society (*Loi relative aux droit d'auteur et aux droits voisins dans la société de l'information*, also known as 'DADVSI'), the Parliament adopted an amendment on 21 December 2005 that regulated the act of downloading a file. This amendment was said by some to legalise P2P file sharing. This decision was subsequently reversed. *See* Geiger, 2008b, pp. 1–2.
9. N.B. some authors advance general recommendations in the sense of adopting ACS but offer little detail, preventing their qualification as full-fledged ACS proposals. See, e.g., Patry, 2011, pp. 177–189, advocating the need to implement 'a right to be paid through statutory licensing, collective management of rights, and levies'. For criticism, *see* Samuelson, 2012. *See also* Slater et al., 2005, with a comparative analysis of different proposals.
10. Momirov & Naude Fourie, 2009, discussing the application of comparative law methods and advancing a typology of modes of vertical and horizontal legal comparison.
11. Netanel, 2003, pp. 74–77, labelling the positions of Ku, Litman, Lunney and Nadel as 'digital abandon'. However, the label may not adequately reflect all cited authors' proposals, namely in the cases of Lunney, Ku & Litman, which all advance alternatives in the form of atypical legal licences. *See also* Eckersley, 2012, p. 85, defining

The design of the taxonomy is predicated on existing law. Despite their different origins, the selected proposals are qualified and systematised with reference to the copyright *acquis*. This predominantly conceptual analysis provides a building block for the subsequent study of the admissibility of an ACS in EU copyright law. However, the definition of the scope and effects of legalisation models in light of this legal framework necessarily entails some compliance analysis. For example, the examination of schemes based on collective rights management models (voluntary, extended, mandatory) requires an assessment of their scope in the *acquis*, together with consideration of the legal hurdles they may face. Nevertheless, beyond what is necessary to develop this taxonomy, the analysis of whether an ACS is admissible in EU copyright law takes place in the following chapters.

The inquiry proceeds as follows. Section 3.2 sets out a conceptual design for ACS. It identifies classification criteria for legalisation models and proposes a method to understand them through a gradual approach to exclusivity. Section 3.3 then defines the scope of ACS. The analysis delves into the legal schemes fitting the ACS definition and examines them as 'vertical' regimes susceptible of application to large-scale online use. It relates the schemes to the *acquis* and takes a position on their legal nature.[12] Section 3.4 furthers the taxonomy of legalisation proposals by looking at the characteristics of ACS, conceptualised as 'horizontal' attributes. Section 3.5 concludes.

3.2 CONCEPTUAL DESIGN

Legalisation proposals vary widely and tend to be depicted as radical departures from current law. However, a systematic and careful study of the literature tells a different story. It reveals a body of work that explores copyright law's flexibility. This section develops a conceptual design for the selection and characterisation of ACS. If first advances classification criteria to distinguish a set of legalisation models that impose restrictions to exclusivity. It then explores these models by explaining their relationship to exclusivity, leading to the selection of five types of ACS theoretically applicable to all types of works.

To design a conceptual framework, we need to identify an organising principle reflecting the aim of the subject of systematisation. The aim of ACS is the establishment of a model of remunerated access for the copyright regulation of online use of works, as an alternative to the status quo of exclusivity, individual management, and the possibility of strict enforcement against individuals. In economic terms, ACS aim to substitute a 'property

'information anarchy' as a regulatory regime where non-commercial copying is freely permitted or copyright is abolished altogether.

12. A similar approach in the literature in this field is used in Slater et al., 2005, p. 5.

rule' – imposing a default prohibition on use – with a 'liability rule' for online use by individuals.[13]

Therefore, we should classify legalisation schemes according to their effects on the application of the exclusive right to online use. This requires us to take the perspective of the rights holder, as the party affected in her pre-existing juridical entitlement. In this light, a sound organising criterion is that of the *restrictions operated by an ACS on the exclusive right.*[14]

ACS can then be classified according to the gradual level of the restrictions to the exclusive right resulting from different statutory or contractual mechanisms. The approach reflects different ways in which rights can be acquired (in a broad sense) so as to enable use absent *direct* authorisation from rights holders. This allows the division of ACS into voluntary and mandatory legal mechanisms imposing gradually higher restrictions on the nature and exercise of exclusive rights. Table 3.1 provides a representation of the classification.[15]

Table 3.1 Restrictions to Exclusivity

Level / Impact	*Nature of Right*	*Rights Acquisition Scheme or Type of Restriction*
0 / -	Exclusive	Status quo: full individual exercise of right (Private Ordering)
1 / +	Exclusive	Voluntary Collective Licensing
2 / ++	Exclusive	Extended Collective Licensing (ECL)
3/ +++	Exclusive (*debated*)	Mandatory Collective Management
4/++++	Remuneration or compensation	Compulsory or statutory licences with compensated or remunerated copyright limitations ('Legal licences'), typically exercised through collective rights management

13. *See* Kur & Schovsbo, 2011, on the reception of these terms in the field of intellectual property rights, while discussing the gradual loss of relevance of the exclusivity paradigm. *See also*: Merges, 1996, 2004a (arguing for the superiority of property rules due to the fact that parties contract around the same to avoid holdup problems); Oliar, 2012 (discussing property and liability rules in the context of the conflict on the legal protection of new technological uses of content between copyright owners and technological innovators); and Lemley, 2012 (arguing that parties not only contract around property rules, as suggested by Merges, but also around inefficient liability rules). For the original use of the term in law and economics scholarship, *see* Calabresi & Melamed, 1972.
14. Implicitly or explicitly, most scholarship adopts this basic criterion. For explicit adoption, *see* Dusollier & Colin, 2011; Gervais, 2010, von Lewinski, 2005. *See also* Kur & Schovsbo, 2011, using the 'exclusivity' characteristic of intellectual property rights as the pivotal point of the analysis of liability rules.
15. Table 1 is inspired by Gervais, 2010, p. 26.

Level / Impact	Nature of Right	Rights Acquisition Scheme or Type of Restriction
5/ +++++	No economic substantive rights	Uncompensated limitation
6/ ++++++	Remuneration claim (external to copyright)	State remuneration, compensation or reward systems; Cultural subsidies ('State Systems')

The departure point is full individual exercise of an exclusive right, absent restrictions (Level 0). This represents the status quo for most online use of works and includes *inter alia* private ordering models, such as creative commons. It can be understood as one end of the spectrum. At the other end are uncompensated limitations (Level 5), which fail to qualify as ACS due to their lack of a remuneration element. Between these extremes are the five legal schemes that satisfy a broad ACS definition. These are, from least to most restrictive:

- Voluntary collective licensing.
- Extended Collective Licensing (ECL).
- Mandatory collective management.
- Compulsory or statutory licences (jointly referred to as 'legal licences'), and
- State remuneration, compensation or reward systems, and cultural subsidies (hereinafter jointly referred to as 'State Systems').

These models constitute stand-alone legal schemes to cover all relevant mass use. Levels 1 through 4 correspond to legal and legally enabled contractual mechanisms, namely regulated forms of collective rights management. They range from the most restrictive legal licences (Level 4), a term discussed in the previous chapter, to the least restrictive voluntary collective licensing (Level 1).[16] All these schemes are internal to copyright and identified as preferred regulation models by ACS proponents.

State Systems (Level 6) differ from the previous schemes insofar as they are external to copyright. This label applies to proposals that eliminate copyright protection for (mostly non-commercial) online forms of use of works, placing the same (for the types of use in question) in the public domain. In these systems, creators are compensated not through a right of remuneration but rather through an array of tax or financing schemes to subsidise or reward creators. State Systems therefore shift the burden of incentivising the creation and dissemination of works from the copyright system to the State. As argued below, these characteristics make State Systems arguably more restrictive to the exclusive right than uncompensated limitations (Level 5).

16. Gervais, 2010, p. 26.

This classificatory method also reinforces one of the conclusions of Chapter 2, to the effect that copyright law's approach to exclusivity is not absolute but nuanced.[17] It is possible to represent the gradual approach in an axis or continuum (Figure 3.1).[18]

Figure 3.1 Alternative Compensation Systems: Axis of Gradual Restrictions on the Exclusive Right

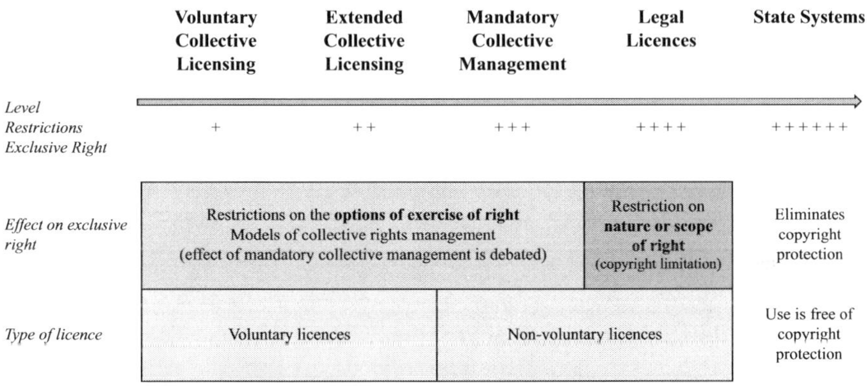

When gliding through the axis from least through increasingly more restrictive rights acquisition schemes, both the nature of substantive rights and the type of licence are affected. For instance, voluntary and ECL are typical models within which exclusive rights are managed. Their designation as 'alternatives', especially for voluntary collective licensing, should be broadly construed as relating to their opposition to full individual management *in lieu* of regulated forms of collective rights management.

Conversely, mandatory collective management, due to the restrictions imposed on the options of exercise of the right, has been subject to much scholarly debate regarding its impact on the exclusive nature of the right.[19] This issue, anticipated in Chapter 2, is examined *infra* in 3.3.4.2.

At this stage, it is sufficient to state that mandatory forms of collective rights management can apply both to exclusive and remuneration rights. As noted in the previous chapter, these two cases are distinguished by using the term 'mandatory' to refer to the application of the scheme to *exclusive rights*, and 'obligatory' to refer to its application to *remuneration or compensation rights*, typically as an adjunct to a statutory licence.[20] An example of mandatory collective management, provided in Chapter 2, is the special

17. Kur & Schovsbo, 2011, noting that although copyright is the richest example of this gradual approach in the field of intellectual property rights, the same point holds true at differing degrees to other such rights, with the notable exception of trademarks.
18. Figure 2 draws inspiration from Dusollier & Colin, 2011, pp. 817–820.
19. See: Bernault & Lebois, 2005; Colin, 2011a; Dusollier & Colin, 2011; Ficsor, 2010; Roßnagel, Jandt, Schnabel & Yliniva-Hoffman, 2009; von Lewinski, 2004, 2005.
20. *See* Guibault, 2002, pp. 26–27, with a similar distinction. *See also supra* 2.2.3.

regime applicable to the exclusive right of cable retransmission in Articles 9–12 SatCab Directive.[21] It is submitted that the legal imposition of collective management of an exclusive right does not per se affect its nature and transform it into a remuneration right. Instead, each collective rights management model – voluntary, extended, mandatory – imposes increasing restrictions on the options of exercise of the right.

Why does this distinction matter?

First, it matters because the legal qualification affects the scope of the right.[22] An exclusive right allows the application of injunctions, making effective the prohibition of use through judicially backed enforcement mechanisms. Contrariwise, remuneration or compensation rights reduce the entitlement to remuneration claims (and enforcement of the same).[23] Thus, the loss of ability to restrict access to the right and to *ex post* enforcement implies the shift from a property rule to a liability rule-based copyright regulation.[24]

Second, the distinction matters because the effect of a model on the exercise and nature of the right has consequences for its compliance with international law and the *acquis*, its legal feasibility and even normative adequacy. Furthermore, the distinction helps to clarify legal concepts that are often used with overlapping meanings in legislative texts and academic writings.

A good example, with relevance here, is that of 'non-voluntary' licences. As noted in the previous chapter, the term applies to two different models: legal licences and mandatory collective management. The first model clearly implies that the underlying right is not exclusive, but subject to remuneration or compensation. Thus, if an ACS is adopted on the basis of such a legal licence and there is no rule in the *acquis* that provides for its application to non-commercial online acts of reproduction and communication to the public, the validity of the licence depends on meeting the conditions of the three-step test in Article 5(5) InfoSoc Directive. However, if it is accepted that mandatory collective management does not constitute a copyright limitation, it will not have to meet the conditions of the test.

Of importance in drawing these distinctions is the term 'exercise'. The term has multiple possible meanings, so it is important to be clear on its connotation here.[25] A crucial use of the term is found in Article 5(2) BC,

21. *See supra* 2.4.4.
22. Kur & Schovsbo, 2011, pp. 1–16, discussing the implications of the different legal qualification of exclusive and remuneration rights.
23. *Ibid.*
24. *Ibid.*, p. 21, concluding this in connection with limits to exclusivity in patent rights, but using identical reasoning for copyright. *See also* Oliar, 2012, on the conflict between property and liability rules and the trade-offs between authorship and innovation as the 'copyright-innovation conflict'.
25. For example, the expression 'conditions on the exercise' in Art. 11*bis*(2) BC is a euphemism for compulsory licensing. *See supra* 2.4.2.

which bans formalities for the 'enjoyment' and 'exercise' of copyright. In that context, 'enjoyment' refers to author's rights coming into existence and being recognised absent any formality, whereas 'exercise' relates to formal requirements on the initiation of enforcement of copyright.[26]

Together with other copyright scholars, 'exercise' of copyright is understood here to cover a range of acts that do not touch upon the enjoyment or existence of the right. That meaning is broader but consistent with the use of the term in Article 5(2) BC. Exercise thus includes 'performing, authorising or prohibiting rights under copyright and related rights and/or claiming remuneration for acts, or taking the necessary steps to have moral rights respected'; the main modalities of exercise are individual exercise – including direct licensing, agency or representation – and collective rights management.[27]

Restrictions on the exercise of copyright are conditions imposed by law or contract that affect its transfer, management and enforcement, but not its nature or existence. Only where a legally imposed restriction affects that nature or existence does it cause a transformation from an exclusive to a remuneration or compensation right, and therefore qualifies as a copyright limitation. This understanding of exercise leads to the observation that the exclusive right has significant *elasticity*. It can stretch from individual management to the gradually more limiting collective rights management schemes, without losing its exclusive nature.

Hence, there is no complete overlap between the effect on the exclusive right of a legal model and the voluntary or non-voluntary type of licensing that underlies each scheme (*see* Figure 3.1). On the one hand, voluntary collective licensing and ECL are models to which rights holders choose to adhere or can generally opt out of, retaining the possibility of unencumbered exercise of their copyright. (Where ECL does not allow opt-out, section 3.3.3 below contends that the model is equivalent to mandatory collective management, and therefore a non-voluntary licence.)

On the other hand, although the term non-voluntary licence appears to originate in the ambiguous terminology of international treaties on compulsory licences, the label also fits well for mandatory collective management and legal licences: for neither scheme does the rights holder have the initial choice to participate or the subsequent possibility of opting out. What differs here is that mandatory collective management technically translates into a statutory restriction on the options for exercise of a right, but not on its existence as an exclusive right, as is the case with legal licences.[28]

26. van Gompel, 2011, pp. 179–193, 212. *See also*: Bernault & Lebois, 2005, pp. 55–56; Gervais, 2010, pp. 24–25, 2016, pp. 27–28; Senftleben, 2014, p. 15. On formalities, *see infra* 5.4.2.2, with further references.
27. Ficsor, 2003b, p. 288.
28. In this sense, *see* Colin, 2011a; Dusollier & Colin, 2011; von Lewinski, 2004, 2005. *See infra* 3.3.4.2.

Finally, 'State Systems' (Level 6) place the regulation of online use outside the realm of copyright protection. This makes their impact on the exercise and nature of exclusive rights the highest among all the rights acquisition schemes considered. From a conceptual standpoint, it is arguable that these systems are more restrictive than uncompensated exceptions (Level 5), commonly qualified as user *privileges* or *defences* – not rights – subject to the fulfilment of certain conditions.[29] If such conditions are not met, the use in question triggers the exclusive copyright.

The same does not hold true for State Systems. Here, because no copyright protection is afforded to the use in the first place, failure to comply with a condition of use does not imply the default application of copyright. As noted in Chapter 1, this book takes a pragmatic approach to legal reform and examines models to adapt and improve EU copyright law, rather than abolish copyright protection.[30] Adoption of State Systems would require abrogation or profound change in international treaties, which makes them legally and politically unrealistic.[31] Thus, they are only analysed in this chapter due to their influential nature in the ACS debate and the fact many of their attributes are susceptible of application to schemes internal to copyright, namely legal licences.[32]

3.3 TYPES OF ALTERNATIVE COMPENSATION SYSTEM

This section builds on the previous conceptual design by delimiting the scope of ACS in light of the *acquis*. The rights acquisition schemes identified above reflect the legal and contractual mechanisms under which ACS proposals authorise large-scale online use.

Authorisation can be direct or indirect. Authorisation is *direct* if the end-user enjoys a legal or contractual entitlement to engage in the online use without intermediation. Authorisation is *indirect* when granted to commercial users or intermediaries, even if for the ultimate benefit of end-users.[33] An intermediate case is that of authorisation with 'minimal' intermediation. This refers to contractual mechanisms between users and rights holders' representatives (such as CMOs) authorising individual online use via

29. On the discussion of exceptions or limitations as restrictions to exclusive rights (perceived as user defences) versus their consideration as affirmative user rights *see* e.g. Geiger, 2010; Guibault, 2002; Karapapa, 2012, pp. 79–98.
30. Cf. *supra* 1.2.
31. Noting the political challenge of such changes, *see* Gervais, 2005, p. 30; Griffiths, 2009, p. 11; Koelman, 2006, p. 411; Peukert, 2005, p. 52.
32. Cf. *supra* 1.2.
33. *See* Gervais, 2001, using a comparable terminology when discussing models for the acquisition of rights.

intermediaries (commonly ISPs) that are instrumental to the contractual relationship, but not parties thereto.[34]

This section analyses each rights acquisition scheme against the legal framework of the *acquis*, and describes how different legalisation proposals apply to large-scale online use. The examination begins with a background summary of collective rights management, as most legalisation models are of this type (3.3.1). This section then examines in turn each type of ACS, from least to most restrictive: voluntary collective licensing (3.3.2), ECL (3.3.3), mandatory collective management (3.3.4), legal licences (3.3.5), and State Systems (3.3.6).

3.3.1 Some Basics on Collective Rights Management

Collective rights management is both a deviation from and an alternative to the general principle of exclusivity and individual exercise of copyright. The objective of collective management is to achieve an efficient exploitation of works.[35] The price of a CMO's efficiency is 'the limitation of the freedom of contract of right holders and users'.[36]

Collective management addresses the problem of transaction costs associated with establishing, managing and enforcing copyright, inherent to its informal, fragmented, transferable and territorial nature.[37] In offering a solution to this problem, collective management emerges as an answer to the so-called 'copyright paradox', as it reconciles the exclusive nature of the right – and its default prohibition on use – with the goals of access and dissemination of works.[38] It is therefore unsurprising that legalisation proposals often rely on collective licensing.

CMOs are mostly private entities providing services that include licensing users, auditing and monitoring rights, enforcing copyright, and collecting and distributing royalties to rights holders.[39] They also develop social and cultural functions, a role recognised in the CRM Directive.[40]

Although the directive does not require CMOs established in the EU to adopt a specific legal form, it subjects them to a variety of rules on representation, membership, organisation, management of rights revenue,

34. Colin, 2011a.
35. Dusollier & Colin, 2011, p. 827.
36. Hilty & Nérisson, 2013, p. 4.
37. *See* Eckersley, 2012, pp. 230–231, for a discussion of the concept of transaction costs in ACS. The author focuses on the reduction of transaction costs in connection with collective rights management. *See also* Allen, 2000, for a broader law and economics discussion.
38. Gervais, 2010, p. 1, 2016, pp. 3–5, 15–16.
39. SWD CRM Directive 2012, p. 195.
40. Gervais, 2010, pp. 3–5, 2016, pp. 17–20. *See* recital 3 CRM Directive.

m*anagement of rights on behalf of other CMOs, relationships with users, transparency, reporting, and enforcement measures.*[41] In addition, the directive contains a special regime for CMOs established in the EU that manage authors' rights in musical works for online use on a multi-territorial basis (more on that later).[42]

In the EU, an organisation qualifies as a CMO only if its *sole or main purpose* is to act for the collective benefit of its members. Furthermore, it must fulfil at least one of the following requirements: be owned or controlled by its members; or be organised on a not-for-profit basis.[43] These organisations must act in the best interests of their members and may not impose on them obligations that are 'not objectively necessary for the protection of their rights and interests or for the effective management of their rights.'[44]

The CRM Directive distinguishes CMOs from 'independent management entities', to which it applies a more limited set of rules.[45] This new concept in the *acquis* refers to organisations authorised to manage rights on behalf of *several* rights holders for their collective benefit, as their sole or main purpose. In contrast to CMOs, these entities are *commercial* and *not owned* by rightholders.[46]

Recital 16 clarifies that independent management entities do not include audio-visual producers, record producers, broadcasters, and publishers (of books, music or newspapers), who license rights in their own interest. Managers and agents of creators do not qualify either because 'they do not manage rights in the sense of setting tariffs, granting licences or collecting money from users'.

In some countries, establishment of CMOs may depend on government authorisation. In all cases, the organisation requires acquisition of authority to license works, collect royalties, and create a repertoire of works. Such authority stems from legal provisions, contracts with rights holders, or representation agreements between CMOs, whereby one organisation mandates another to manage the rights it represents.[47] The organisation is then

41. Art. 2(1) CRM Directive.
42. Art. 2(2) CRM Directive, referring to Title III. It is noteworthy that the relevant provisions of the directive apply to entities directly or indirectly owned or controlled (wholly or in part) by a CMO, if such entities carry out an activity which, if carried out by the CMO, would be subject to the provisions of the directive. Cf. Art. 2(3) CRM Directive. On the issue of legal form, *see* recital 14.
43. Art. 3(a) CRM Directive. A 'member' is a rights holder or an entity representing rights holders, including other CMOs and associations of rights holders, fulfilling the membership requirements of the CMO and admitted by it. Cf. Art. 3(d) CRM Directive.
44. Art. 4 CRM Directive.
45. Art. 2(3) CRM Directive. *See* Guibault & Gompel, 2016, pp. 143–144.
46. Art. 3(b) CRM Directive.
47. Gervais, 2010, pp. 6–7, 2016, pp. 8–9. For a definition of representation agreement *see* Art. 3(j) CRM Directive.

authorised to grant licences on the works in respect of which it manages rights for a given territory, i.e., its 'repertoire'.[48]

The authority to license on behalf of rights holders can be granted to CMOs on an exclusive or non-exclusive basis. If granted on an exclusive basis, it will result on the organisations having a monopoly for their field and territory of operation. Indeed, most CMOs are de facto, and sometimes *de iure*, monopolies.[49] In the EU and for the online exploitation of musical works, the CRM Directive attempts to counteract this by fostering a competitive regime of multi-territorial licensing.[50]

A CMO grants licenses to users based on agreed prices or fees, also called 'tariffs', and rights holders are paid by the organisation after usage data is collected and processed.[51] In the CRM Directive, a 'user' means any person or entity carrying out acts subject to authorisation by rightholders, or the requirement to pay remuneration or compensation to rightholders, which is not acting in the capacity of a consumer.[52] A consumer, in turn, is a natural person acting for purposes outside his trade, business, craft or profession.[53] In essence, CMOs operate as intermediaries in a two-sided market between rights holders and users (Figure 3.2).

48. *See* Art. 3(l) CRM Directive. *See also* Gervais, 2016, p. 9.
49. Gervais, 2010, pp. 6–9, 2016, p. 9.
50. *See infra* 3.3.2.
51. Gervais, 2010, pp. 7–9.
52. Art. 3(k) CRM Directive.
53. Art. 2(1) Consumer Rights Directive. *See also* recital 33 CRM Directive, and Guibault & Gompel, 2016, p. 144.

Figure 3.2 CMOs as Intermediaries in a Two-Sided Market

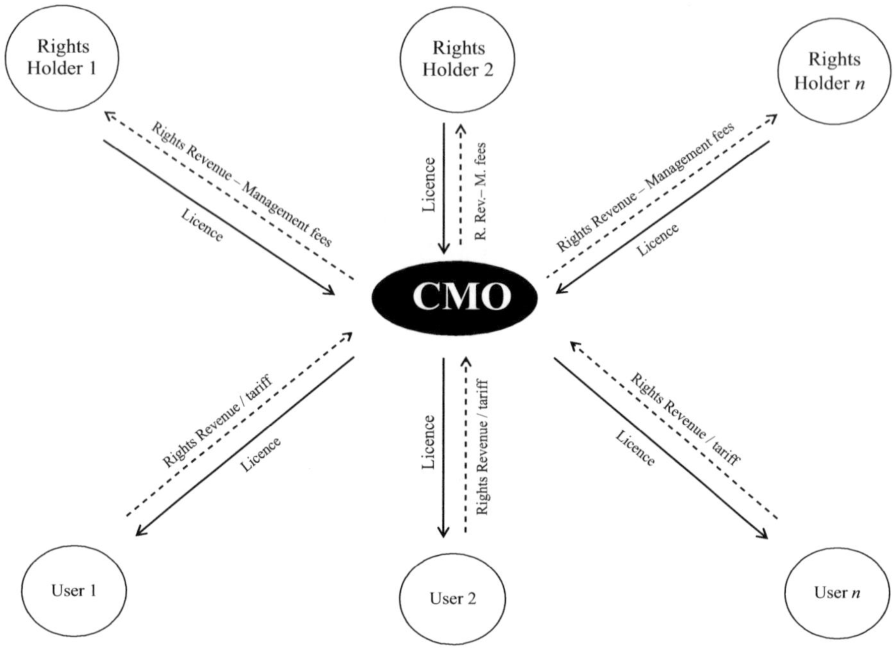

The licensing terms and tariffs are set in accordance with a combination of state intervention and CMO regulation, the level of which varies per territory.[54] The CRM Directive mandates that negotiations with users for the purposes of licensing are carried out in good faith, in a timely manner, with disclosure of the necessary information, and that licensing terms are subject to objective and non-discriminatory criteria. Furthermore, refusals to license a particular service must be presented to users in a reasoned statement.[55]

The directive further requires that rights holders receive 'appropriate remuneration' for the use of their rights. This means that tariffs for exclusive or remuneration rights must be:

> reasonable in relation to, inter alia, the economic value of the use of the rights in trade, taking into account the nature and scope of the use of the work and other subject-matter, as well as in relation to the economic value of the service provided by the collective management organisation.[56]

54. Gervais, 2010, pp. 7–9.
55. Art. 16(1)–(3) and recital 32 CRM Directive.
56. Art. 16(3) CRM Directive.

The notion of 'economic value in trade' as an objective criterion to set tariffs is used by the CJEU in *Kanal 5 and TV4*. The case involved determining whether tariffs applied by the Swedish CMO STIM for use of its music repertoire by a broadcasting organisation in television broadcasts were reasonable. The Court stated that 'in so far as such royalties are calculated on the basis of the revenue of the television broadcasting societies, they are, in principle, reasonable in relation to the economic value of the service provided by STIM.'[57] It concluded that a CMO does not abuse its dominant position by applying this tariff model, provided the same is proportionate to the actual or potential usage of the repertoire and the audience cannot be measured by a more accurate and cost-efficient method.[58]

On this point, it is worth noting the challenges of reconciling this view of 'appropriate remuneration', linked to the standard of 'economic value in trade', with the concept of fair compensation in the InfoSoc and Orphan Works Directive, based on the notion of harm. As such, appropriate remuneration should be viewed flexibly so as to accommodate the conceptual nuances of the different remuneration entitlements inherent in voluntary royalties, remuneration rights, and fair compensation rights.[59]

The income collected by a CMO on behalf of rights holders, whether deriving from an exclusive right, a right to remuneration, or a right to compensation is called 'rights revenue'.[60] The amounts charged, deducted, or offset by a CMO from rights revenue or from any income arising from the investment of rights revenue in order to cover the costs of its management services are the 'management fees' (*see* Figure 3.2).[61]

Finally, Article 5(3) CRM Directive provides rights holders a right to grant licences for 'non-commercial uses of any rights, categories of rights or types of works and other subject-matter that they may choose'. CMOs must ensure that rights holders can exercise the right, *inter alia* by deciding on the 'conditions attached to the exercise of that right' and informing their members of those conditions.[62] Importantly, there is no right to non-commercially license *individual works*.[63]

---

57. CJEU, *Kanal 5 and TV4*, para. 37. On this case, *see* Guibault & Gompel, 2016, pp. 154–155.
58. CJEU, *Kanal 5 and TV4*, para. 41.
59. Cf. Guibault, 2014, p. 750; Quintais, 2013, p. 69. On the concepts of equitable remuneration and fair compensation, *see supra* 2.2.4, 2.3.3, and *infra* 4.1.3.3.
60. Art. 3(h) CRM Directive. *See also* Arts 11–13 CRM Directive with rules on the management of rights revenue.
61. Art. 3(i) CRM Directive.
62. Recital 19 CRM Directive.
63. Guibault & Gompel, 2016, p. 151.

3.3.2 Voluntary Collective Licensing

3.3.2.1 Characterisation and Legal Framework

Voluntary collective licensing is the least restrictive form of collective rights management.[64] In this system, a CMO enters into a contract with users for the rights it represents. The licensees are typically users not acting in the capacity of consumers, as envisaged in the CRM Directive, but certain ACS proposals refer to the possibility of a CMO directly licensing end-users.[65]

Depending on how the system is set up, a commercial user (e.g., an ISP) may contract directly with a CMO and obtain the right to sublicense its customers, or act as a mere intermediary obtaining licences for the benefit of clients or subscribers, i.e., the actual users of works.[66]

The system is voluntary for rights holders and users.[67] The former are free to join a CMO and decide which works the organisation will manage. CMOs may partially curtail that freedom through contractual terms in membership requirements. Before the CRM Directive, requirements of this type might go so far as to make membership dependent on rights holders entrusting all rights to the organisation on an exclusive basis or preventing them from individual management. Since the directive, this possibility is more limited.[68] Where membership agreements are non-exclusive, rights holders retain the possibility of licensing users directly or through representatives.[69]

Voluntary licensing is a typical rights management model in the EU, increasingly used for optimising licensing activities, especially for particular rights in online music.[70] The CRM Directive prescribes a special regime for multi-territorial licensing of author's online rights in musical works, which can be viewed as a model of reinforced voluntary collective licensing.[71] This regime is the most innovative part of the directive and constitutes a regulatory novelty in European copyright law. For this reason, and because

64. Gervais, 2010, p. 26.
65. Art. 3(k) CRM Directive. *See also* SWD CRM Directive 2012, p. 195, defining 'commercial user' as 'any person or entity involved in the provision of goods or services who for its activities needs a licence from rightholders of copyrights and/or related rights'.
66. Colin, 2011a, pp. 64–77. *See also* Dusollier & Colin, 2011, pp. 823–824, arguing that the later use is known in civil law jurisdictions as a 'stipulation for another person'. It is also conceivable that certain licence agreements qualify ISP's as sub-licensors with the authority to licence end-users.
67. Lohmann, 2008, p. 2.
68. Arts 5–6 and recital 9 CRM Directive. *See also* Guibault & Gompel, 2016, pp. 151–152.
69. Art. 3(b) and recital 15 CRM Directive.
70. von Lewinski, 2005, p. 15, indicating that '[t]his model is already practiced to some extent, in particular European countries'. *See also* SWD CRM Directive 2012, pp. 5–7.
71. Arts 23–32 CRM Directive.

it illustrates the complexity of copyright fragmentation in EU law, it is important to provide an overview of its mechanics.

The multi-territorial licensing system is a development of the regulatory framework advanced in the unsuccessful 2005 Online Music Recommendation, and aims at replacing the current predominantly territorial model of online music licensing by CMOs.[72] The system aims to facilitate repertoire aggregation for online use of musical works at EU level, to develop common standards on multi-territorial licensing, and to foster efficient licensing practices.[73] Through it, the Commission hopes to reduce the complexity caused by the fragmentation of the EU digital market for online music services, approximating it to consumer expectations.[74]

In the EU, online service providers interested in music licensing need to license three sets of rights involved in the online exploitation of musical works: author's rights (from composers and lyricists), phonogram or record producer's rights, and performer's rights.[75] For online providers to offer consumers download or streaming music services, or access to films and videogames where 'music is an important element', they are required to obtain a licence for each of these rights.[76]

The record producer usually aggregates the related rights of producers and performers; conversely, rights of authors are managed by CMOs. The CRM Directive's special regime only regulates the online rights of authors. The regime does not apply to related rights of performers or producers, or to *non-online rights* in musical works, like those in relation to cable retransmission or communication to the public by satellite (*see* Figure 3.3).[77]

72. Recitals 6, 39, and 40 CRM Directive.
73. Proposal CRM Directive, pp. 6–7. *See also* Memo CRM Directive FAQ 2014, para. 15.
74. Recital 38 CRM Directive.
75. Memo CRM Directive FAQ 2014, para. 14; recitals 37 and 38 CRM Directive.
76. Recital 37 CRM Directive.
77. This is consistent with the understanding that the acts of cable retransmission do not include online use. Cf. *supra* 2.4.4. Figure 4 is inspired in the 'example of licensing for music rights in online uses' in Memo CRM Directive FAQ 2014, para. 14.

Figure 3.3 Scope of Multi-Territorial Licensing Regime in the CRM Directive

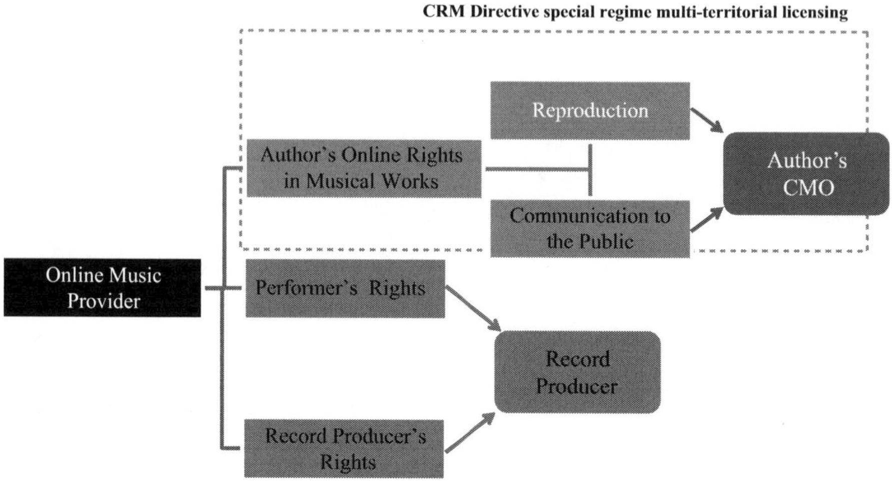

Multi-territorial licensing refers to any licence granted by a CMO covering the territory of more than one Member State, and relates to author's 'online rights in musical works' required for the provision of an online service: the rights of reproduction and communication to the public in Articles 2 and 3 InfoSoc Directive.[78] Musical works include both stand-alone works and those incorporated in audio-visual works.[79]

These exclusive rights can be managed individually by the rights holder (author or assignee, e.g., music publisher) or by CMOs. Different CMOs may manage each of the rights for the same author and further complications might arise from joint ownership of rights.[80] Therefore, in order to provide online music services, online providers must aggregate all the necessary rights from different rights holders and CMOs, and clear all of the applicable related rights (*see* Figure 3.3).[81]

CMOs established in the EU that wish to provide multi-territorial licensing for online rights in musical works must comply with a number of requirements and obligations set out in the CRM Directive.[82] These include having the capacity to process these licences electronically in an efficient and transparent manner, the provision of information on the repertoire they represent, invoicing, and payment. Only CMOs meeting these requirements are authorised to offer multi-territorial licences.[83]

78. Art. 3(m) and (n) CRM Directive. *See also* recital 37.
79. Recital 40 CRM Directive. Musical works include lyrics but exclude sheet music.
80. Recital 37 CRM Directive.
81. Recital 37 CRM Directive.
82. Art. 23 CRM Directive.
83. Arts 24–28 CRM Directive. *See* Guibault & Gompel, 2016, pp. 168–169.

The CRM Directive's special regime does not mandate multi-territorial licensing. Instead, it aims to foster and enable it by facilitating repertoire aggregation for the benefit of online service providers wishing to offer cross-border pan-EU services, while safeguarding cultural diversity and the position of consumers.[84]

In other words, the regime does not prevent CMOs from concluding reciprocal representation agreements to grant mono- or multi-territorial licences covering both their and foreign CMOs' repertoires to online service providers. Hence, two regimes that enable multi-territorial licensing of works co-exist in the framework of the CRM Directive: that of reciprocal representation agreements and the special regime described.[85]

Multi-territorial licensing is allowed in different scenarios.[86] In the first and simplest scenario, the authorised CMO can license its own repertoire to online service providers for two or more Member States.[87] In a variation of this option, a CMO that does not meet the requirements to offer multi-territorial licences may outsource the functions that it is lacking to a third party.[88]

A more complex scenario incorporates the so-called 'passport' system.[89] A CMO failing the directive's requirements can enter into a *non-exclusive* representation agreement with another CMO that meets them, who then grants multi-territorial licences for the repertoire of the first.[90] In the terminology of the *travaux préparatoires*, the authorised CMO is the 'passport entity', to which the mandating CMOs would have a 'right to tag on repertoire'.[91]

Under certain circumstances, the agreement is mandatory. If the authorised CMO is already granting or offering multi-territorial licences for the 'same category of online rights in musical works' in the repertoire of at least one other CMO, it will have an obligation to conclude the representation agreement if so requested.[92] The expression 'categories of rights' refers

84. *See* Proposal CRM Directive, p. 10. For a description of the expected impact of the directive on cultural diversity, *see* Memo CRM Directive FAQ 2014, para. 7.
85. Guibault & Gompel, 2016, pp. 158–164, explaining the system of reciprocal representation agreements in the EU, which co-exists with the special regime of multi-territorial licensing. *See also* recitals 11 and 30 CRM Directive.
86. These scenarios mirror those presented as examples in Memo CRM Directive FAQ 2014, para. 15.
87. *Ibid.*
88. *Ibid.*, paras 15, 23 (mentioning 'quality standards'). Outsourcing of this type seems to be within the spirit of recital 43 CRM Directive.
89. On the proposal, *see* Quintais, 2013.
90. Art. 29(1) and 30 CRM Directive. *See also*: Recital 44 CRM Directive: 'all multi territorial licensing should be concluded on a non-exclusive basis'; Memo CRM Directive FAQ 2014, para. 15.
91. See: SWD CRM Directive – Executive Summary 2012, pp. 5–6; SWD CRM Directive 2012, pp. 42–44, 162–165.
92. Art. 30(1) and recital 46 CRM Directive.

to forms of exploitation of the rights of reproduction and communication to the public; examples are 'broadcasting, theatrical exhibition or reproduction for online distribution'.[93]

The final scenario is that in which one or several CMOs create a subsidiary CMO to aggregate repertoire and provide multi-territorial licences.[94] This subsidiary is also subject to the obligation to conclude representation agreements as a 'passport entity'.

Importantly, whenever an authorised CMO represents another organisation for multi-territorial licensing, it has the obligation to manage the latter's repertoire on a non-discriminatory basis and subject to the same conditions applied to its own repertoire.[95] The main derogation from the special regime of the directive applies to multi-territorial licences granted by CMOs for the online right of communication to the public of musical works required by a broadcaster for use in its radio and television programmes. The exemption covers the broadcaster's use of musical works with or after the initial broadcast of programmes, including simulcasting and catch-up TV, and ancillary online materials.[96]

3.3.2.2 Legalisation Proposals

Legalisation proponents sometimes rely on voluntary collective licensing schemes, based on agreements between CMOs and commercial users, ISPs or both.[97] In an influential example, the Electronic Frontier Foundation proposes that industry-created performance rights organisations (the US equivalent to a CMO for the right of public performance) offer non-exclusive blanket licences to end-users against payment of a flat fee. The fee would be paid through dedicated websites or intermediary 'resellers', such as ISPs, Universities, P2P software vendors, and employers.[98] The direct or indirect licence granted to individuals using P2P subscriptions is designed not as a grant of rights but as a 'covenant not to sue' by the representatives of rights

93. Recital 19 CRM Directive.
94. *See* Art. 2(3), recital 17 and the relevant provisions in Title III CRM Directive, which apply to entities directly or indirectly owned or controlled, wholly or in part' by one or more CMOs.
95. Arts 29(1), 30(4)–(6) CRM Directive.
96. Art. 32 and recital 48 CRM Directive. The exemption is subject to the external control of EU competition law. Simulcasting is the 'simultaneous transmission by radio and TV stations via the Internet of sound recordings included in their single channel and free-to-air broadcasts of radio and/or TV signals, in compliance with the respective regulations on provision of broadcasting services'. Cf. Commission Decision, *IFPI Simulcasting*, p. 2 & n. 6. On the rationales and implications of the provision, *see* Guibault & Gompel, 2016, pp. 172–173.
97. See, e.g., Lohmann, 2008; Merges, 1996, 2004b, Fisher, 2004 (discussing his voluntary option), and Lincoff, 2008, reviewing and extending his 2002 proposal, making it voluntary. *See also* Lincoff, 2002.
98. Lohmann, 2008, emphasising that intermediaries are allowed to advertise such services.

holders. The covenant would immunise file-sharers from future civil (but not criminal) infringement suits.[99]

Other proposals exist. Earp and McDiarmid, for example, suggest a limited model adapted to University campus settings.[100] Fisher, in a variation from his 'tax-and-royalty' system, envisions an atypical non-profit corporation that celebrates partnership agreements with ISPs that offer end-users regular and premium subscriptions.[101]

A more ambitious proposal belongs to Sterling, who suggests a system for the worldwide licensing of a new exclusive 'internet right' through a 'Global Internet Licensing Agency'. This would be an umbrella organisation mandated by local CMOs to whom rights fragments have been granted, assigned or transferred.[102] In a similar vein, Lincoff devises a complex collective rights management system for a new 'digital transmission right' for online music, which co-exists with direct licensing practices and individual management. Lincoff's system features one CMO per territory with quasi-universal repertoires and worldwide licensing mandates for transmissions originating in its territory.[103] End-users, especially those using P2P platforms, would require licences only when playing an active role in the dissemination of works, i.e., in their communication to the public.[104]

While this is certainly the most legally feasible type of ACS, voluntary collective licensing is not without its challenges. One risk is that of free riding by certain users. This may occur where multiple users share one P2P licence, thereby reducing royalties and removing incentives to membership.[105] Another problem relates to cross-subsidisation, meaning low-volume users subsidising high volume users, motivating the first to opt out, thereby reducing the attractiveness of the licence.[106] Yet another concern is voiced in relation to the prohibitive costs associated with the logistics and implementation of the system.[107]

While these are valid concerns, perhaps the main issue with voluntary collective licences relates to the risk of insufficient participation and the model's lack of suitability to provide an overarching blanket licence for mass non-commercial online use by individuals. Quite simply, the level of territorial and substantive fragmentation of copyright at EU level may prove an insurmountable obstacle to the voluntary aggregation of sufficient

99. *Ibid.*
100. Earp & McDiarmid, 2008.
101. Fisher, 2004, pp. 252–257.
102. *See* Sterling, 2008, 2009. N.B. Sterling's system seems to have provided the blueprint for Dimita's global dissemination right.
103. Lincoff, 2008, p. 42.
104. *Ibid.*, p. 34.
105. Quintais, 2012, pp. 72–73; Yu, 2005, p. 715.
106. Dougherty, 2006, pp. 431–432; Quintais, 2012, p. 74; Yu, 2005, p. 715.
107. Dougherty, 2006, p. 429; Quintais, 2012, p. 73.

different rights in different territories to provide users with an all-encompassing repertoire.[108] The current state of the online management of music rights in the EU, described above, is a good example, showing that for certain rights, rights holders (in this case phonogram producers) are unwilling to entrust CMOs with their rights, preferring to manage them directly or through other vehicles, including independent management entities.

The participation problem is compounded for sectors of the content industry where – unlike the music, visual arts and photography sectors – collective management of online rights is not common practice.[109] Examples include 'film producers, book publishers, journal and magazine publishers or games publishers', who typically handle mono and multi-territorial licensing of online rights in Europe without the intervention of CMOs.[110] In the audio-visual sector, for instance, collective management is typical only for cable retransmission of audio-visual works.[111] It is therefore unlikely that a sufficiently high number of copyright owners entrusts the management of their online rights in audio-visual works to CMOs. As a result, the repertoire available for licensing in an ACS would be unattractive to users.

In sum, a voluntary collective management ACS requires a high level of consensus from all categories of rights holders across the EU landscape in order to achieve a workable system and licence.[112] In light of the above, that consensus appears unlikely.

3.3.3 Extended Collective Licensing

3.3.3.1 Characterisation and Legal Framework

ECL is a type of collective management that allows the offering of blanket licences for the entire repertoire represented by a CMO.[113] In this system, a CMO first enters into voluntary agreements with rights holders. When the

108. See, e.g., von Lewinski, 2005, p. 15, noting that voluntary collective licensing is most useful if CMOs manage significant parts of the available repertoire.
109. SWD CRM Directive 2012, p. 12.
110. *Ibid.*, p. 12 (& n. 50).
111. *See* Agicoa: Association of International Collective Management of Audiovisual Works, *Frequently asked questions*, http://www.agicoa.org/english/toolsandhelp/faq.html (accessed 31.01.2017). *See also* SWD CRM Directive 2012, p. 57 ('Collective licensing of film is essentially limited to cable retransmissions. These are licensed for each territory in which a cable network operates.')
112. See, making a similar point, Dusollier & Colin, 2011, pp. 833–834. *See also* Quintais, 2012, pp. 71–72.
113. SWD CRM Directive 2012, p. 197, defining 'blanket licence'. *See also* Riis & Jens Schovsbo, 2010, p. 473 & n. 4, noting that the first proposal for an ECL model is attributed to the Swedish law professor Svante Bergström.

organisation meets a representativeness criterion – meaning that it is authorised to manage a category of rights by a substantial number of domestic and foreign rights holders – a statutory presumption extends its representation powers to non-member rights holders. This extension effect by operation of law increases the organisation's repertoire and simplifies acquisition of rights.[114] In this way, ECL aims to solve the problem of providing 'fully covering licenses in cases of mass uses'.[115]

In general, a CMO meets the representativeness criterion if it represents a statutorily defined 'substantial amount of rights holders',[116] which can be of national or foreign nationality.[117] In simple terms, the organisation must be mandated, directly by rights holders and indirectly through representation agreements, to represent a relevant share of substantive rights in works used in the national market.[118]

This principle of 'indirect representation' allows for the fulfilment of the legal requirement by allowing rights aggregation in *primary* and *secondary* CMOs. The former are umbrella organisations. The latter are small and medium-sized CMOs covering specific categories of rights holders, members of a larger primary organisation qualifying to manage an ECL.[119]

Importantly, a 'substantial amount' does not necessarily mean a majority of rights holders, as such requirement might prove impractical.[120] As Gervais notes, 'substantiality is contextual': a new CMO organising rights holders in a certain area for the first time 'should have a much lower substantiality threshold to pass than a well-established collective trying to obtain an extension of the repertoire for a new licensing scheme.'[121]

ECL is a 'mixture of autonomy with state intervention': a combination of legal rules enabling and giving effect to it with agreements based on those rules, together forming a 'unique kind of collective rights administration that operates as a hybrid between compulsory licenses and traditional collective agreements'.[122]

---

114. SWD CRM Directive 2012, p. 45. *See also* Gervais, 2016, p. 24; Riis & Schovsbo, 2012, pp. 935–939.
115. Koskinen Olsson & Sigurdardottir, 2016, p. 250.
116. *See* Riis & Jens Schovsbo, 2010, p. 472 & n. 1, citing s. 50(1) of the Danish Copyright Act.
117. Riis & Jens Schovsbo, 2010, pp. 490–491. *See also* Art. 18 TFEU.
118. For a similar definition, *see* SWD CRM Directive 2012, p. 45 & n. 160. *See also* Ficsor, 2016, pp. 67–68; Koskinen-Olsson & Sigurdardottir, 2016, pp. 253–254. For an explanation of how 'indirect representation' works in Denmark using the example of umbrella organisation COPYDAN, *see* Riis & Schovsbo, 2012, pp. 935–937.
119. Riis & Schovsbo, 2012, p. 939.
120. *Ibid.*, p. 937.
121. Gervais, 2016, p. 24 & n. 64.
122. Riis & Jens Schovsbo, 2010, p. 472.

ECL has been characteristic of the Nordic countries (Denmark, Finland, Iceland, Norway and Sweden) since the 1960s.[123] It has also been deemed worthy of consideration in Central and Eastern Europe, Africa, Canada, and the US (for the licensing of orphan works), and is growing in popularity in other countries.[124] In 1984, the application of ECL provisions to cable distribution was acknowledged by WIPO. The organisation defined 'ECL-rule' as a form of collective rights management subject to the fulfilment of the following conditions: an express legal basis for representation of non-members, an indemnification covenant from CMOs to cable distributors for claims by rights holders, and equal treatment of represented and unrepresented rights holders.[125]

In the Nordic countries, ECL presents similarities and idiosyncrasies for each country. Common features are that all systems are based on the existence of functioning and transparent representative CMOs, the extension effect applies to unrepresented rights holders for the same category of works, agreements between CMOs and users are based on free negotiations, and unrepresented rights holders are guaranteed equal treatment and a right to claim individual remuneration.[126]

Another important feature of *some* ECL systems is the possibility afforded to rights holders to *opt out* of collective management and restore full individual exercise of their exclusive right, also called a 'veto right'.[127] The opt-out consists of a declaration from rights holders to the CMO managing the ECL to the effect that they do not wish the organisation to represent them. The declaration will come into effect after a reasonable deadline, following which the CMO will exclude the represented works or subject matter from its repertoire. As a whole, the procedure should be simple and not burdensome.[128]

The opt-out mechanism is often described as an essential requirement of ECL models, which seems inaccurate. If we take the Danish Copyright Act as a blueprint, the right to opt out does not assist rights holders in most types

123. *Ibid.*, pp. 472–474, noting that ECL was initially developed to respond to administration of broadcasting rights in 1961 and in 1974 begun to be used in a co-ordinated way for the management of copyright.
124. Gervais, 2010, p. 21, 2016, pp. 23–24. On the proposed application of ECL in the US, *see* Samuelson, 2016. For central and Eastern Europe, *see* Ficsor & Chatalbashev, 2016, pp. 130–133. Remarkably, a new copyright act of 2015 in Slovakia contains an ECL mechanism that applies *inter alia* to the making available right. Cf. Gera, 2016; Husovec & Gera, 2016. For a comparative study analysing the advantages and disadvantages of the introduction of a statutory system of ECL, examining the jurisdictions of Denmark, Norway, Germany and the Netherlands. *See* Hugenholtz, Gompel, Guibault & Obradović, 2014.
125. *See* Riis & Jens Schovsbo, 2010, p. 476.
126. Axhamn & Guibault, 2012, pp. 41–42.
127. Koskinen-Olsson & Sigurdardottir, 2016, p. 251; Riis & Jens Schovsbo, 2010, p. 476.
128. Ficsor, 2016, p. 68.

of ECL after operation of the extension effect.[129] In fact, once there is a legal extension of the repertoire of the CMO, unsatisfied rights holders can only challenge the calculated and distributed fees with the appropriate appellate body.[130] This non-opt-out variant of the model has been termed as 'compulsory ECL'.[131] It is not a Danish idiosyncrasy. In fact, it is characteristic of the many approved ECLs in Denmark and Norway, as well as specific categories of licence in Finland and Sweden.[132]

Whether the opt-out is a 'feature' or mere 'add-on' to the ECL model in international law or the *acquis* is uncertain as a matter of law and in academic writings.[133] Ficsor, for example, considers the presence of this option an 'indispensable condition' for the compatibility of ECL with international norms.[134] Of course, that would mean that at least some of the aforementioned compulsory ECLs in the Nordic countries would be in violation of international treaties. However, it is difficult to so conclude, not only in light of their longstanding existence, but also by references made to the model in the SatCab, InfoSoc and CRM Directives.

The SatCab Directive contains the outline of an ECL between CMOs and broadcasting organisations for the exclusive right of communication to the public by satellite concerning a given category of works. The regime is subject to two conditions, and one derogation. The first condition is that the act of communication simulcasts a terrestrial broadcast by the same broadcaster. The second condition is that the unrepresented rights holder may opt out of the system. The derogation is that the ECL does not cover cinematographic works. Furthermore, where an ECL is applied, Member States must inform the Commission of the identity of the beneficiary broadcasters, which will be publicised at EU level.[135]

Some construe this provision as implying a restricted possibility for Member States to introduce ECL, limited to situations where the model 'is indispensable or at least highly desirable for effective exercise of the given rights'.[136] Still, even if the opt-out right is an indispensable requirement for ECL under the SatCab Directive, it is difficult to generalise this rule for all other hypothetical ECL systems outside communication to the public by satellite.

Indeed, such generalisation may be inconsistent with Recitals 18 InfoSoc Directive, 24 Orphan Works Directive, and 12 CRM Directive,

---

129. Riis & Jens Schovsbo, 2010, p. 476.
130. *Ibid.*
131. Gervais, 2003, p. 40.
132. Axhamn & Guibault, 2012, pp. 30–44.
133. *See* Ficsor, 2010, pp. 63–64. *Contra* Koskinen-Olsson, 2010, pp. 290–292, not identifying opt-out as a basic element of an ECL. *See also* Riis & Jens Schovsbo, 2010, pp. 478–479, engaging in the debate without taking a position.
134. Ficsor, 2016, p. 68.
135. Art. 3(2)–(4) SatCab Directive.
136. Ficsor, 2016, p. 69.

which offer grounds to argue for the admissibility of ECL for other uses. The recitals clarify that the respective directives are without prejudice to the arrangements in Member States concerning the management of rights such as ECL. At the very least, this wording puts to rest the argument that compulsory ECLs at national level are incompatible with the *acquis*.[137] It also opens the door for application of the system to the digital networked environment.[138]

Regardless, the recognition of an opt-out right may influence the legal qualification of ECL. If the right of opt-out is retained, ECL remains voluntary and should be qualified as a restriction on the exercise of the right, but not its existence or nature. Consequently, it is not a copyright limitation.[139]

This conclusion is less clear for compulsory ECLs. In these systems, rights holders may no longer opt out and there is a statutorily imposed loss of individual exercise of rights.[140] In other words, after operation of the extension effect, the model is akin to mandatory collective management, and may therefore qualify as a non-voluntary licence. This has led some authors to consider that the model 'affects the exclusive character of copyright' and constitutes a copyright limitation.[141] Because compulsory ECL is functionally similar to mandatory collective management, the possibility that either rights management scheme constitutes a copyright limitation is analysed below in 3.3.4.2.

Finally, there is no specific *acquis* rule applying ECL to online use, although the possibility was discussed for projects involving mass use (such as EUROPEANA) and in the preparatory works of the Orphan Works Directive.[142] ECL was also viewed as a potential solution for the multi-territorial licensing of musical works in the preparatory works of the CRM Directive. The rejected proposal combined an ECL legal presumption for the

137. Koskinen-Olsson & Sigurdardottir, 2016, p. 252. *Contra*, Ficsor, 2016, pp. 70–74; Ficsor, 2010, pp. 63–64.
138. Koskinen-Olsson, 2010, p. 303; Koskinen-Olsson & Sigurdardottir, 2016, p. 252, noting that implementation of the InfoSoc Directive in the Nordic countries widened the scope of ECL in the areas of digital copying in education and library use.
139. Cf. Colin, 2011a, pp. 41, 44; Ficsor, 2016, pp. 74–75; Rosén, 2011, p. 187. *See also* Westkamp, 2007, pp. 160–161, 185–186, 192–193, reaching a similar conclusion for ECL with opt-out in several Nordic countries. *Contra*, Rydning, 2010, pp. 22–25, concluding that the extension to non-represented 'outsider authors' is a derogation to the exclusive right, at least from a functional perspective.
140. See Colin, 2011a, p. 41; Riis & Jens Schovsbo, 2010, p. 482, reaching a similar conclusion.
141. Cf. Riis & Jens Schovsbo, 2010, pp. 482–490, 497–498; Riis & Schovsbo, 2012, p. 933. *See also* Riis & Jens Schovsbo, 2010, p. 476, referring to the fact that the normal 'effect of ECL rules in the DCA [*Danish Copyright Act*] has been to turn copyright's exclusivity-based regime into a remuneration-based regime'. *See also* Gervais, 2003, p. 40: 'A compulsory extended collective licence can exist only in situations in which a non-voluntary licence can be used (for example, cable retransmission).'
142. Riis & Jens Schovsbo, 2010, pp. 472, 478.

aggregation of rights within each representative CMO, a right to opt out, and a country of origin rule for the substantive rights covered by the online use of musical works. The resulting system would allow licensing of the works through the clearing of a single pan-European licence by online music providers in their country of origin.[143]

Rejection of this option was justified primarily by fears of large-scale opt-outs leading to the need for commercial users to obtain a number of licences from rights holders and CMOs, in addition to the ECL in their country of origin. Other justifications advanced were the cumbersome requirement for rights holders to opt out in (then) twenty-seven Member States, the compliance costs associated with the legislative amendments and supervision of the system, as well as doubts as to its effectiveness.[144]

3.3.3.2 Legalisation Proposals

In light of the above, ECL appears to be an efficient licensing system for mass use online. Through the extension mechanism, it addresses two significant problems of standard voluntary collective licensing as an ACS proposition. First, the potential unwillingness of some rights holders to join the system and the resulting unrepresentative repertoire of works available for licensing to end-users. Second, it brings into the license the works of unknown rights holders.

Several ACS proposals rely on this model, but most bypass the legal risks inherent in compulsory ECLs by introducing an opt-out right.[145] The notable exceptions, which do not allow opt-out by rights holders (or only do so in a very limited fashion), are the legislative proposals advanced in Italy by Beltrandi and others (in 2007 and 2008), and in Belgium by Green Party Members of Parliament Benoit Hellings, Freya Piryns, and Jacky Morael (at different times in 2010).[146]

All ECL legalisation proposals require an *ex lege* extension of the system to unrepresented national and foreign rights holders. Aigrain goes further by proposing that, where the representativeness requirement is not

143. SWD CRM Directive 2012, pp. 45–46, identifying this as 'Option B4 – Extended collective licensing combined with a country of origin principle'. On the use of the localisation criterion for acts of satellite transmission in the SatCab Directive, *see supra* 2.4.4.

144. SWD CRM Directive 2012, pp. 172–175.

145. See, e.g., Aigrain, 2008; Ciurcina, Martin, Margoni, Morando & Ricolfi, 2009; Gervais, 2004. When discussing the application of ECL to mass online use, Gervais mentions the possibility of the opt-out constituting a simple email notice. Cf. Gervais, 2016, p. 29.

146. *See* Beltrandi et al., 2008, 2007 (Italy), Hellings & Piryns, 2010; Morael & Piryns, 2010 (Belgium), not including an opt-out feature for rights holders. However, at least the Italian proposals seem to allow a limited opt-out for copyright owners of works that have not exhausted their 'commercial cycle' ('ciclo commerciale').

met, a back-up legal licence ACS would kick in to regulate mass-scale non-commercial use by individuals.[147]

Other models apply solely to the right of making available, and operate in combination with a statutory remuneration right for the act of reproduction (e.g., the download), which is qualified as a private copy. The law would entitle CMOs and consumer organisations to conclude contracts on ECL, subject to the payment of a statutory remuneration for user downloads. That remuneration would be incorporated in the ISP subscription fee and fixed by the existing CMO for private copying in the respective country.[148]

All proposals prescribe that CMOs authorise ISPs to allow their clients to exchange files containing licensed works.[149] In the study by Modot and others for the European Parliament, the contractual role of ISPs was designed to be that of mere intermediaries offering a voluntary, value-added, private use standardised licence and collecting flat-rate amounts on behalf of CMOs.[150] This design is aimed at creating a content flat-rate 'ring-fenced from any commercial networks', but which allows all-inclusive ISP offers beneficial to consumers.[151] In this way, the system attempts to preserve the commercial exploitation of works outside the sphere of ACS, aimed at non-commercial use by private subscribers.

Assuming an ECL model contains an opt-out rule, there are two main objections to its adoption as an ACS. The first objection relates to the need to effect legal changes to the *acquis*. Indeed, it would probably be necessary to adopt secondary EU law imposing an ECL framework for non-commercial acts of reproduction and communication to the public online, perhaps including a country of origin rule to enable cross-border effect to the national licences.[152] In the particular case of ECL, the costs of supervising and managing the system, especially its opt-out mechanism in the digital environment, should also be carefully considered.

The second objection is perhaps the most relevant. For the system to work, rights holders would have to, in the first place, adhere to collective management in large enough numbers to meet a representativeness threshold sufficient to trigger the extension effect. As noted above for voluntary

147. Aigrain, 2008, discussing possible regulations for non-commercial online use and manifesting a preference for ECL with specific provisions securing net neutrality. In a later work, the author favours a legal licensing approach as a default. *See* Aigrain, 2012.
148. Gervais, 2003; Quintais, 2012, p. 63; von Lewinski, 2005, p. 15 & n. 93.
149. See, e.g., Hellings & Piryns, 2010, proposed Art. 78 quarter(1).
150. Modot et al., 2011, p. 14.
151. *Ibid.*
152. Quintais, 2012, p. 65. *See also* Guibault, 2015, proposing the 'establishment of ECL systems as a solution for the clearance of rights for the digitisation and making available of works contained in the collection of a cultural heritage institution'. In this context, Guibault argues 'that the only workable solution to the problem of extra-territorial application of ECL schemes would be to formally establish a 'country of origin' principle.' But *see infra* 6.2.7, where it is argued that it may be possible to adopt an ECL without legislative changes beyond a Commission recommendation.

collective licensing, the challenge is particularly great in sectors (such as the audio-visual) that do not have an established practice in collective rights management of online rights.[153] Even if the challenge is met, the possibility of opting out is a constant threat to the viability of the system. This is especially true as the value of the licence to end-users is linked to the breadth of the repertoire and consequent licence, especially regarding the most popular works. If major rights holders decide to withhold or hoard these works systematically, the ACS is of little value to end-users.[154]

3.3.4 Mandatory Collective Management

3.3.4.1 Characterisation and Legal Framework

Mandatory collective management is the most restrictive model of collective licensing. It prevents rights holders from directly exploiting their works, imposing by law the transfer or assignment of the exercise of rights to a CMO, which will act on their behalf.[155]

Mandatory collective management aims 'to ease copyright clearance, to reduce transaction costs for users and to limit fragmentation of copyrights'.[156] Due to the restrictions it imposes, application of mandatory collective management to exclusive rights is subject to strict requirements and should be considered only when voluntary models prove unsuitable to exercise the right.[157]

For example, the model requires specific regulation, together with a system for authorisation, accreditation or registration of the relevant CMOs at national level.[158] Also, it should be justified by market failure and high transaction costs thwarting the efficiency of individual licensing, taking into account the social or philosophical underpinnings of a particular copyright system.[159]

As noted above, collective management can be imposed in order to regulate exclusive rights or rights of remuneration/fair compensation. In the most common scenario, which is labelled here as 'obligatory' collective management, the regulation of a right of remuneration or compensation through a legal licence will imply that rights holders have a de facto or *de iure* obligation to administer the right through CMOs. More rarely, in what

153. *See supra* 3.3.2.2 and references cited.
154. Quintais, 2012, pp. 65–66.
155. Guibault, 2002, p. 26.
156. Dusollier & Colin, 2011, p. 819.
157. *See* Gervais, 2001, pp. 37–38; Sinacore-Guinn, 1993, p. 379.
158. *See* Ficsor, 2016, p. 49, applying the same requirements to ECL.
159. Guibault, 2002, pp. 26–27. *See also* Geiger & Schönherr, 2014a, p. 139, citing the CRM Directive proposal and stating that collective rights management is the preferred model of regulation for EU institutions where it 'is justified by the practical impossibility of individual management of rights'.

is called in this book 'mandatory' collective management proper, the law will require the collective administration of exclusive rights; it is this possibility in particular that makes it attractive to ACS proponents, and controversial among legal scholars.[160]

It is sometimes argued that mandatory collective management can be more beneficial to creators than an unrestricted exclusive right.[161] The model would afford them protection against the traditionally stronger bargaining position of industry stakeholders – due to the prominent role of CMOs in negotiating licensing terms with users – and avoid alienation of their exclusive rights to exploiters on imbalanced contractual terms and without appropriate remuneration.[162]

From the perspective of rights holders, mandatory collective management is functionally similar to a legal licence: both constitute externally mandated restrictions on their ability to exercise rights without the possibility of opting out. (The same is true for compulsory ECL in relation to non-members.) The similarities extend to procedural aspects, such as the determination of remuneration.[163]

In this sense, and from the viewpoint of rights holders, mandatory collective management is a non-voluntary licence. However, this similar classification as a *type of licence* (explained in Chapter 2 and adopted in Figure 3.1 above) does not necessarily result in a similar legal qualification or identical effects on the exclusive right. The question that then arises is whether mandatory collective management or compulsory ECL of *exclusive rights* affects the nature of exclusive rights.

If the answer is affirmative, mandatory collective management qualifies as a copyright limitation, whose admissibility – and that of any ACS relying on it – hinges on meeting the requirements of international law, in particular the three-step test. Should the answer be negative, the right remains exclusive and the model can form the backbone of a policy option for mass online use, subject to specific requirements applicable to collective management of rights, but not to international rules on the admissibility of compulsory licences or copyright limitations.

Academic discussion on this topic with reference to international law revolves around the wording of Article 11*bis*(2) BC, on broadcasting and communication to the public, and Article 13 BC, on mechanical recording of musical works. These articles allow countries to decide which 'conditions' to

160. *See supra* 3.2. *See also* Guibault, 2002, pp. 26–27.
161. Geiger & Schönherr, 2014a, p. 141; Kur, 2008, p. 12.
162. Colin, 2011a, pp. 39–40; Geiger & Schonherr, 2012, pp. 182–183; Gervais, 2011, p. 430; von Lewinski, 2004, pp. 8–9. *See also* Geiger, 2007b, p. 11, 2014a, p. 21, 2014b, p. 183, exemplifying with the French reprography system.
163. Guibault, 2002, p. 26, noting that the process is analogous in mandatory collective management and compulsory licences, insofar as it relies on negotiation between all stakeholders involved and, failing an agreement, is subject to fixation by an administrative or judicial body.

'determine' or 'impose' for the exercise of certain exclusive rights, subject to a set of requirements: respect of moral rights, express imposition, and equitable remuneration.[164] In both cases, the provisions' headings and preparatory works clarify that these terms refer to compulsory licensing (*see* Chapter 2).

A maiore ad minus, if these rules allow compulsory licensing, they should also permit less restrictive models, such as mandatory, extended or voluntary collective management. However, part of the academic literature takes the interpretation further and considers that, because mandatory collective management determines or imposes conditions on the exercise of copyright, it is subject to the same constraints as compulsory licences.[165] The implication is that admissibility of mandatory collective management is restricted to the scope of Articles 11*bis*(2) and 13(1) BC. These provisions, it is noted, only partially cover mass online use. For use outside that scope, an ACS based on mandatory collective management would constitute a copyright limitation.[166]

Before addressing this legal quandary, it is useful to have a complete picture of the legal framework. Mandatory collective management is common in Europe, largely for the management of certain categories of rights, such as the artist's resale right, public lending, and cable retransmission.[167] The model is used in some cases to regulate exclusive rights, such as in France and Austria, in the fields of reprography (outside a statutory licence) and communication of broadcasts to the public.[168]

In the *acquis*, regimes of mandatory collective management exist in relation to the exclusive right of cable retransmission, the equitable remuneration right for rental of a work or related subject matter, and the artist's resale right.[169]

The special regime for cable retransmission in Articles 9–12 SatCab Directive is explained in Chapter 2. As noted, the regime is unique in EU law, insofar as it is the only case of mandatory collective management of an

---

164. These provisions are incorporated by reference in the TRIPS and WCT. *See* Arts 9(1) TRIPS and 1(4) WCT.
165. See, for all, Ficsor, 2016, p. 51. *See also* Mazziotti, 2008, p. 267 calling this 'prevailing doctrine of international copyright law regarding the mandatory collective management of copyrights'.
166. Ficsor, 2016, pp. 51–52.
167. Gervais, 2001, pp. 37–38.
168. Dreier, 2010, p. 451 & n. 149, citing Arts L122-10 through L122-12 French Intellectual Property Code, and the 'similar provision … already contained in Art. 59 of the Austrian Copyright Act of 1936 … '. *See also* Guibault, 2002, pp. 26–27, noting that France chose to regulate reprography through this model instead of a statutory licence, unlike other EU Member States; and Geiger, 2014a, p. 21, 2014b, p. 182, 2014c, p. 140. Colin, 2011a, p. 25, calls the French reprography system a type of *cessio legis* with similar effects to mandatory collective management.
169. See, respectively, Art. 5 Rental Right Directive, Art. 9 SatCab Directive, and Art. 6(2) Resale Right Directive.

exclusive right. Article 9 elucidates that CMOs manage the right to refuse or grant authorisation to a cable operator for cable retransmission, even if rights holders have not transferred the management of their rights to a CMO. In this case, the CMO managing rights in the same category is deemed mandated to manage the rights of non-members. If more than one such CMO exists, rights holders may freely choose between the authorised CMOs.[170]

The remaining regimes in the *acquis* apply to remuneration rights and could therefore be qualified as instances of *obligatory* collective management. Article 5 Rental Right Directive provides for an unwaivable right to equitable remuneration, and allows for the possibility – through the use of the word 'may' in paragraphs (3) and (4) – of Member States imposing mandatory collective management of the exercise of this residual right. The paragraphs read:

> 3. The administration of this right to obtain an equitable remuneration may be entrusted to collecting societies representing authors or performers.
>
> 4. Member States may regulate whether and to what extent administration by collecting societies of the right to obtain an equitable remuneration may be imposed, as well as the question from whom this remuneration may be claimed or collected.

Member States are therefore entitled to impose collective rights management, preventing authors and performers from individual management of the right. Instead, the same is administered by a CMO, who will claim and collect the remuneration from parties to be identified by law, typically producers and rental shops (*see* Figure 3.4).

170. Art. 9(1)–(2) SatCab Directive. Art. 10 SatCab Directive exempts broadcasting organisations from this regime. For further detail, *see supra* 2.4.4.

Figure 3.4 Mandatory Collective Management Rental Right Directive

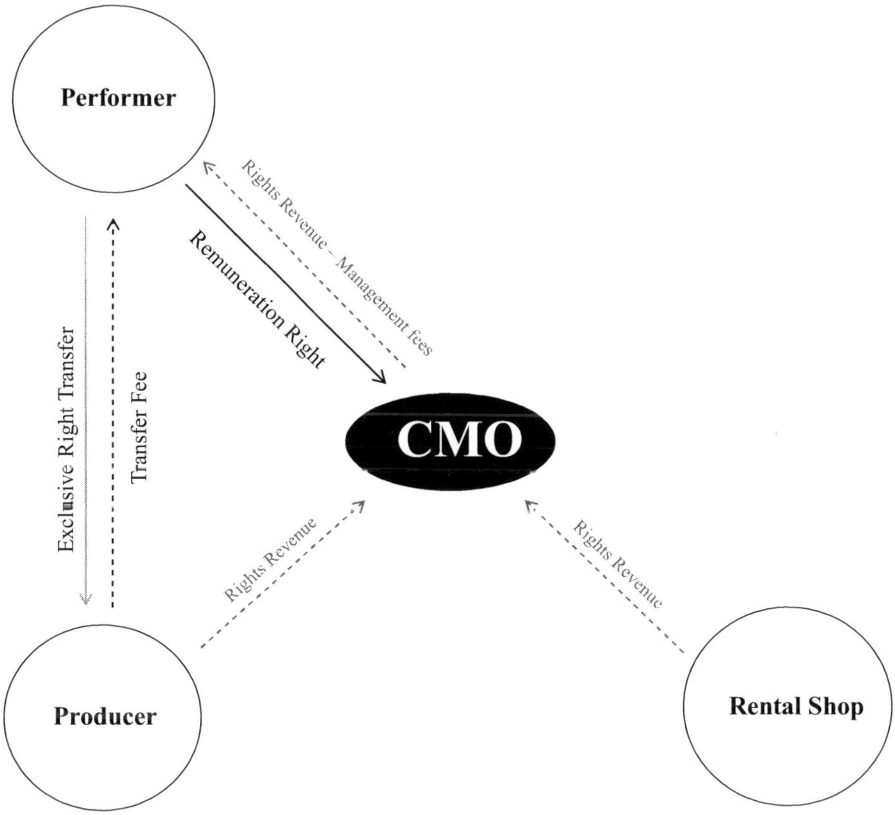

Finally, the Resale Right Directive establishes a right of remuneration. Article 6(2) thereof allows Member States to provide for 'compulsory or optional' collective management of the resulting royalty.

There are no specific rules in the *acquis* applying this model to online use of works. In fact, even in the context of the special regime of the SatCab Directive, there is little room to argue that the right of cable retransmission applies to Internet retransmissions.[171] However, as explored below, it is common for ACS proponents to advance models based on collective rights management, either as a stand-alone solution or in combination with voluntary or legal licences.[172] From the viewpoint of consistency with international and EU law, the question that lingers is how to qualify the effect of this model when applied to the exclusive right.

171. Cf. *supra* 2.4.4.
172. See *infra* 3.4.1.

3.3.4.2 Theories on Mandatory Collective Management

In essence, the controversial question in copyright scholarship relates to the legal nature of mandatory collective management, and its effect on exclusive rights. This subsection explores the different theories on the limited or broader application of mandatory collective management to exclusive rights. It is submitted that, for the reasons above, the same theories are valid *mutatis mutandis* for compulsory ECL.

3.3.4.2.1 Limited Applicability to Exclusive Rights

One school of thought limits the admissibility of mandatory collective management to remuneration or compensation rights, or when exceptionally allowed in international and EU law. International law contains such a permission in Articles 11*bis*(2) and 13(1) BC.[173] In the *acquis*, mandatory collective management is allowed when the law expressly prescribes it 'because the right in question is too specific to be found in these international rules' (e.g., the rental right).[174]

The position has undeniable pedigree. It is reflected in the WIPO Guide and Glossary and in a 2006 ALAI resolution, adopted in response to a legislative proposal for a 'licence globale' in France.[175] In both cases, it seems to mirror the view of its main proponent, Mihály Ficsor, who authored the WIPO publication and was a member of the Executive Committee of the ALAI at the time of the resolution.[176]

The ALAI Resolution states that the ordinary meaning, object and purpose of the BC provisions is clear in that 'determination or imposition of conditions' includes compulsory licences *and* mandatory collective management; the latter, furthermore, should be broadly construed as a copyright limitation.[177]

173. Sinacore-Guinn, 1993, pp. 298–299, theorises that 'mandatory affiliation' is adequate only if predicated on economic necessity or the nature of the affected rights (i.e., of remuneration). In other cases, it should be 'subjected to strict scrutiny as to whether a less intrusive option exists'. However, the author argues for the distinction of collective rights management from non-voluntary licences. *See* Sinacore-Guinn, 1993, pp. 370–378. *See also* Ficsor, 2016, pp. 51–52; Ficsor, 2010, pp. 53–59.

174. Bernault & Lebois, 2005, p. 53. Cf. Ficsor, 2016, p. 54.

175. ALAI, 2006; Ficsor, 2003a, 2012b; Gervais, 2003, p. 40; Mazziotti, 2008; Ficsor, 2010. The 2003 version of the WIPO Guide and Glossary qualifies obligatory collective management as a limitation because owners' rights 'are 'limited' … to a share from the *remuneration* collected by a *collective management organization*'. *See* Ficsor, 2003b, pp. 286–287. On the context of the resolution as a response to French legislation implementing a mandatory collective management system, *see* Mazziotti, 2008, p. 266 (& 879).

176. *See* Ficsor, 2016, pp. 49–66, for the most recent elaboration of this view.

177. Ficsor, 2016, pp. 57–66; Ficsor, 2010, pp. 49–51. In this respect, Ficsor states that mandatory collective management 'is a limitation (not an exception since the rights is

The BC only allows imposition or determination of conditions in three cases.[178] The first includes remuneration rights not based on limitations.[179] The second refers to compensated limitations, like private copying.[180] The third covers 'residual rights' of remuneration that survive transfer of some exclusive rights and are applicable thereinafter as remuneration claims; these typically benefit authors/performers and are qualified as unwaivable or non-assignable.[181] None of these cases involves collective management of exclusive rights.

To bolster this position, Ficsor points to the preparatory works of the 1928 Rome Conference of the BC, and notes the absence of clear indications that the term 'conditions' excluded obligatory collective management. Instead, the debates between national delegations demonstrate that different types of mechanism could be included in this terminology. This, he believes, places the model squarely within the scope, and therefore the requirements, of Articles 11*bis*(2) and 13 BC.[182]

This position would also find support in *acquis* regimes of mandatory (and obligatory) collective management. On the one hand, both the Rental Rights and Resale Right Directives state that Member States 'may' impose or provide for the scheme.[183] This wording is a mere permission, not an obligation, to implement the model. Where such an obligation does exist, in the SatCab Directive (which omits the auxiliary verb 'may'), a derogation is made for broadcasting organisations.[184]

From here, Ficsor argues *a contrario* that mandatory collective management can only be implemented exceptionally, when in line with international treaty provisions and expressly recognised in the *acquis*.[185] In sum, the scheme is only admissible for 'an exhaustively determined scope of exclusive rights'.[186]

The consequence of this interpretation is that mandatory collective administration (or compulsory ECL) of mass online use covered by the exclusive rights of reproduction and communication to the public would

still applicable although in a limited form; an exclusive right is limited by the condition that it may only be exercised through collective management'. *See also* Sinacore-Guinn, 1993, pp. 300–303.

178. Ficsor, 2002a, pp. 137–139, 2016, pp. 52–53; Ficsor, 2010, pp. 44–46.
179. *See* Arts 14*ter* BC. On a similar allowance for related rights of performers and phonogram producers, *see* Arts 12 RC (and the similar provision in Art. 15 WPPT). On the conceptual distinction between self standing and limitation based remuneration rights *see* von Lewinski, 2008.
180. *See* Art. 9(2) BC for the reproduction right.
181. Ficsor, 2010, pp. 44–46.
182. Ficsor, 2016, pp. 57–61.
183. Arts 5(3) and (4) Rental Directive and 6(2) Resale Right Directive.
184. Arts 9(1) and 10 SatCab Directive.
185. Ficsor, 2016, pp. 54–56; Ficsor, 2010, pp. 45–48. *But see* Colin, 2011b, pp. 37–38, classifying the *a contrario* reasoning of Ficsor as 'illogical'.
186. Ficsor, 2016, p. 61; Ficsor, 2010, pp. 50–53, 59–60.

likely constitute a copyright limitation, subject to the three-step test.[187] The only types of ACS escaping that qualification are voluntary collective licences and (arguably) ECL with the possibility to opt-out.[188]

3.3.4.2.2 Broader Applicability to Exclusive Rights

In contrast, another school of thought views mandatory collective management as consistent with minimum rights and limitations at international and EU level, and not bound by the compulsory licensing provisions of the BC. Despite the functional similarity, it is argued, mandatory collective management is not technically a copyright limitation but rather an option to regulate the exercise of exclusive rights.[189]

Proponents of this view argue that the regime of the BC compulsory licences should not determine the future scope of mandatory collective management schemes. Study of the respective preparatory works shows that Articles 11*bis*(2) and 13(1) BC have specific justifications. They are 'permitted restrictions in favor of particular groups of users', namely broadcasters and record companies, based largely on the fear of refusal to license by CMOs.[190] The purpose of the licences is to benefit those users by pre-empting negotiating conflicts with CMOs, while ensuring that rights holders receive fair remuneration for the permitted uses.[191]

In that light, von Lewinski interprets the BC reference to 'conditions' as meaning not 'any conditions' on the exercise of rights but only 'certain conditions' favouring some types of user (broadcasters and record producers) whose interests justify the compulsory licences.[192] Consequently, only those limited conditions fall within the scope of Articles 11*bis*(2) and 13(1) BC. In other words, we should not generalise the requirements of the BC compulsory licences to other schemes designed to regulate the exercise of copyright, such as mandatory collective management.

---

187. *See* Dusollier & Colin, 2011, p. 827, concluding that 'mechanisms authorizing P2P file sharing, although not explicitly provided for by the Berne Convention under a compulsory licensing or other scheme, could still be enacted if they pass the three-step test...'.
188. Ficsor, 2010, pp. 54–59.
189. See, *inter alia*: von Lewinski, 2004, p. 4 ff., discussing this issue in relation to several exclusive rights in light of Hungarian law (and compatibility with international and EU law), including the making available right but not the online reproduction right; Bernault & Lebois, 2005, p. 46ff., discussing this matter in light of French Law and its compatibility with EU and international law; Geiger, 2007b, pp. 9–12, arguing that mandatory collective management cannot be qualified as a limitation of exclusive rights as no provision in international treaties restricts national legislators in this field; Colin, 2011a, pp. 37–46, 2011b, p. 3; Dusollier & Colin, 2011, pp. 819–827; Geiger, 2014a, pp. 19–21, 2014b, pp. 180–183, 2014c, pp. 139–140; Geiger & Schönherr, 2014a.
190. Ricketson, 1987, pp. 513–527; von Lewinski, 2004, p. 5.
191. *See supra* 2.4. *See also* von Lewinski, 2004, pp. 5–6.
192. von Lewinski, 2004, pp. 5–6.

In support of this point, it is noted that the only international or EU copyright regime for mandatory collective management of exclusive rights is in the SatCab Directive.[193] This is relevant because collective rights management has existed in Europe since the mid-eighteenth century, and from an early stage copyright treaties recognised compulsory licences and copyright limitations.[194] Therefore, the argument goes, the absence of a reference in the text of the BC favours the view that mandatory collective management was not considered to affect the nucleus of exclusivity.

A more persuasive argument draws a conceptual and legal-technical distinction between legal licences and mandatory collective management. Whereas the first restrict the nature or existence of copyright, mandatory collective management restricts the 'options of exercise'.[195] The effect of legal licences is to place copyright uses 'outside the field of exclusiveness',[196] meaning that the permission to use a work does not flow directly (individual licensing) or indirectly (through a CMO) from the rights holder. Rather, the authorisation flows from the law.

In mandatory collective management, the powers to *authorise and enforce* copyright shift from the authors to their representative, the CMO, whose sole and main purpose is to act for the collective benefit of its members. As members, authors have an indirect path to influence the terms and conditions of licensing and distribution.[197] In this way, although the options for exercise of copyright are modulated, the right remains exclusive.[198]

Article 9(1) SatCab Directive is a case in point, as the positive dimension of the right (to grant an authorisation) remains intact, but there is some regulation of its exercise.[199] While moral rights are left untouched, the economic right remains transferable by contract or legal presumption. This can happen for example in the case of a 'broadcasting organization initially transmitting the subject matter', provided no prior transfer of the right was made to a CMO. Where the transfer to the broadcaster occurs, the right cannot be subject to collective exercise.[200]

193. *Ibid.*, pp. 3, 5; Geiger, 2007b, p. 9.
194. For a brief historical account, *see* Schierholz, 2010, pp. 1151–1153.
195. *See* Geiger, 2007b, p. 10, citing *IFPI Simulcast* (Commission Decision 2003/300/EC) and *Uradex* (CJEU), where in relation to Art. 9(2) SatCab Directive the CJEU 'reaffirms that the Directive has, for legal certainty and simplification of procedures, implemented a mandatory collective management of the exclusive right of cable retransmission'. *See also* Dreier, 2010, pp. 451–452; Hugenholtz, 2006, pp. 280–281.
196. Geiger, 2007b, p. 10.
197. Geiger, 2007b; von Lewinski, 2004.
198. Dusollier & Colin, 2011, p. 827.
199. Dreier, 2010, p. 451. *See also* Hugenholtz, 2006, pp. 280–281.
200. Dreier, 2010, pp. 451–452; Hugenholtz, 2006, pp. 280–281. This interpretation is confirmed by recital 28 SatCab Directive.

This view would be consistent with recital 12 CRM Directive, which lists mandatory collective management as a type of arrangement 'concerning the management of rights', along with individual management or ECL.[201]

From the conceptual and legal standpoints, then, a legal licence effects a much deeper transformation in the relationship between author and user, effectively severing the tie between them.[202] This tie, while eroded and intermediated, is retained in mandatory collective management.

The distinction can be questioned where CMOs have an obligation to license users.[203] Peukert, for example, argues that if the law imposes an unqualified legal obligation to grant licences 'to any person so requesting … exclusive rights are in fact reduced to a mere right to remuneration administered by a collecting society.'[204] Kur and Schovsbo express a similar concern that obligations to license, coupled with the monopoly position of CMOs, might lead exclusivity to 'become illusionary, at least in practice'.[205]

Although the argument is valid, it must be contextualised in the *acquis*. The CRM Directive does not impose a default obligation to license users. Rather, it imposes an obligation to negotiate in good faith with users, allowing justified refusals to license by CMOs.[206] A similar rule is contained in Article 12 SatCab Directive. At best, these are mitigated and qualified obligations to license. Even then, their objective is to prevent abuse of a dominant position by CMOs, pursuant to Article 102 TFEU. Hence, the obligation to license finds its legal justification in competition law. In its interaction with copyright, competition law functions as an external limit on the exercise of rights, but not their existence.[207]

In addition, a qualified obligation to license in mandatory collective management will not translate into significantly different practices from those occurring in voluntary collective licensing. CMOs are in the 'business of yes'; even when managing exclusive rights under a voluntary licence, a CMO 'would think twice before saying no to a willing licensee'.[208]

Finally, from the viewpoint of a systematic interpretation of the *acquis*, it is difficult to qualify mandatory collective management as a limitation.

201. *Contra* Ficsor, 2016, pp. 56–57.
202. Colin, 2011a, pp. 38–39; Geiger, 2007b, p. 10; von Lewinski, 2004, p. 5.
203. *See* Sinacore-Guinn, 1993, pp. 400–402, for an early critique.
204. Peukert, 2005, pp. 66–67.
205. Kur & Schovsbo, 2011, p. 14. The authors concede however that the case might be different if CMOs 'were forced to enter in more efficient competition with each other', as required in OMR Recommendation 2005. Cf. Kur & Schovsbo, 2011, p. 14 (& 79).
206. Art. 16, recital 31 and Annex–1(c) CRM Directive. *See supra* 3.3.1.
207. Colin, 2011a, pp. 24–25, 40, 2011b, p. 3; Dusollier & Colin, 2011, pp. 818–820; Geiger, 2007b, pp. 10–11; Hilty & Nérisson, 2012; Schierholz, 2010, p. 1152; von Lewinski, 2004, pp. 7–8. For a detailed examination of the application of EU competition law in the field of collective rights management, *see* Daum, 2010, pp. 50–70; Guibault & van Gompel, 2010; Schierholz, 2010, pp. 1157–1164, 1187–1188. N.B. the need for CMOs to comply with competition law rules is recognised in recital 17 InfoSoc Directive.
208. Gervais, 2011, p. 429.

While this model is mentioned in the recitals of other directives, it was left out of the exhaustive menu of limitations and exceptions in Article 5 InfoSoc Directive.[209] Thus, to qualify it as a limitation appears inconsistent with the *acquis* from a legal-technical standpoint.[210]

On balance, these conceptual and legal-technical arguments make the theory for a broader application of mandatory collective management more persuasive. However, they do not give *carte blanche* to the application of this regime to exclusive rights. In fact, they simply set aside the requirement of compliance with the three-step test, but not the strict requirements for application of this regime to a category of online use. Where those requirements are met, the application of mandatory collective management should be considered a valid policy option for an ACS to 'grant licences for non-commercial uses of any rights, categories of rights or types of works and other subject-matter' on behalf of rights holders, in line with Article 5(3) CRM Directive.

3.3.4.2.3 The Impact of Soulier and Doke

Although the above interpretation is preferred, the CJEU judgment in *Soulier and Doke* raises doubts on its validity. The case relates to legislation established by Articles L. 134-1 to L. 134-9 of the French Intellectual Property Code, which impose a hybrid model of collective management for certain acts of digital exploitation of out-of-print books.[211]

In this model, an approved CMO is given the right to authorise the reproduction and performance in digital form of 'out-of-print books'.[212] Subject to certain conditions, the authors of these books can either oppose to, or opt-out of, the collective exercise of their rights. For the purposes of this section, the opposition mechanism is the most relevant. According to the law, the opposition can be exercised by authors within six months after registration of a book in a specific public database indexing out-of-print books.

In the dispute at the origin of the case, the claimants put forth the argument that the French legislation established an inadmissible exception or limitation to the exclusive reproduction right in Article 2(a) InfoSoc

209. von Lewinski, 2004, pp. 13–14; Mazziotti, 2008, p. 265 (& 872).
210. See: Bernault & Lebois, 2003, p. 67, Colin, 2011a, p. 44, Geiger, 2014a, p. 19 (& 81), 2014b, pp. 182–184, 2014c, p. 139; Geiger & Schönherr, 2014a, pp. 140–141; Guibault, 2002, pp. 26–27; Hugenholtz & Okediji, 2008, p. 19; von Lewinski, 2004, p. 6. Concluding similarly in regards to the SatCab Directive, *see* Modot et al., 2011, p. 121.
211. *See* CJEU, *Soulier and Doke*, paras 14–16.
212. Art. L. 134-1 of the French Intellectual Property Code states that 'an out-of-print book means a book published in France before 1 January 2001 which is no longer commercially distributed by a publisher and is not currently published in print or in a digital format'. The competent CMO in this system is the *Société Française des Intérêts des Auteurs de l'écrit* (SOFIA).

Directive, as the same was not included among those listed exhaustively in Article 5 thereof.[213]

According to the Court, authors have an exclusive right to authorise or prohibit the use of their works, subject to the exhaustively listed limitations in the InfoSoc Directive. This exclusive right is preventive in nature, and therefore implies prior consent for the use of works.[214] Under certain conditions, that consent may be expressed implicitly.[215] For the implicit consent to be valid 'every author must actually be informed of the future use of his work by a third party and the means at his disposal to prohibit it if he so wishes'.[216] Otherwise, the Court reasons, the existence of his implicit consent appears purely hypothetical.[217]

Regarding the *ex-ante* mechanism of opposition, the CJEU considered that the French legislation failed to ensure that 'authors are actually and individually informed'. This raises the possibility that authors are unaware of the envisaged use of their works, making it impossible to regard their 'mere lack of opposition … as the expression of their implicit consent to that use'.[218] In reaching this conclusion, the Court notes that although the InfoSoc Directive allows national legislation to pursue an objective 'in the cultural interest of consumers and of society as a whole', this objective and public interest 'cannot justify a derogation not provided for by the EU legislature to the protection that authors are ensured by that directive.'[219]

On its face, this judgment appears to restrict the space available for national laws of Member States to impose mandatory collective management of the exclusive rights of reproduction and communication to the public. However, the case does not discuss non-commercial use and does not clearly qualify such model of collective rights management as a per se exception or limitation to the exclusive rights at issue. Despite that, at the very least, *Soulier and Doke* appears to reduce the legal space available in the *acquis* for mandatory collective management schemes without enabling legislation at EU level.

3.3.4.3 Legalisation Proposals

Mandatory collective management is an enticing option for regulation of large-scale individual use in digital networks. The sheer number of end-users, conditions of use, territorial and substantive fragmentation of rights, and diversity of works make individual management too cumbersome or

213. CJEU, *Soulier and Doke*, paras 19–20.
214. *Ibid.*, paras 33–34.
215. *Ibid.*, para. 35.
216. *Ibid.*, para. 38.
217. *Ibid.*, para. 39.
218. *Ibid.*, para. 43.
219. *Ibid.*, para. 45.

undesirable in the online environment, providing a good case for collective exercise of the exclusive rights involved.[220]

In addition, the model is well suited to overcoming the challenges faced by voluntary collective licensing. First, it targets the problem of rights holders' lack of willingness to rely on CMOs to administer their rights.[221] Second, it safeguards the integrity and value of the licence by avoiding the withdrawal of works through opt-out which is possible in voluntary ECL.

These challenges are addressed by making it mandatory for online exclusive rights to be managed by CMOs, reducing the possible opposition from rights holders. End-users are able to lawfully use works merely by obtaining a licence from CMOs or an intermediary licensee. In the context of an ACS, CMOs would likely negotiate with intermediaries – like ISPs or online service providers – to operationalise the end-user licence.

Among the ACS proposals studied, it is possible to find two modalities of mandatory collective management. In the first modality, the scheme applies to regulate two online rights (reproduction and communication to the public) and regulates the whole ACS.[222] In the second modality, mandatory collective management applies to the right of making available, whilst the right of reproduction is regulated through a legal licence, usually an extension of the private copying limitation. A prominent example is the French 'licence globale', which proposes that the right of making available is transferred by operation of law to a CMO approved by the government.[223] A similar design has been suggested for the German content or culture flat-rate models, and Dimita's global dissemination right.[224]

In all instances, end-users can choose to opt-in to the system through agreements with ISPs, subject to the provision of adequate pre-contractual information.[225] In effect, this makes the ACS voluntary for end-users. Finally, one French proposal uses mandatory collective management as a fall-back regulation model in case stakeholder negotiations for voluntary collective licensing are unsuccessful within a specified time period.[226]

As noted in the previous paragraph, the main challenge to an ACS of this type relates to its functional similarity with compulsory licensing. Due to the contentious nature of the issue, even scholars that do not qualify mandatory collective management as a copyright limitation suggest, for reasons of legitimacy, subjecting this legalisation option to the three-step

220. Mazziotti, 2008, p. 264; Quintais, 2012.
221. von Lewinski, 2005, discussing P2P.
222. Bernault & Lebois, 2005, noting that this variation would be based on stakeholder agreements.
223. L'ALLIANCE public.artistes, 2005, 2006b, 2006c.
224. *See* Roßnagel et al., 2009, and Dimita, 2010, designing a complex international multi-layered CMO system.
225. L'ALLIANCE public.artistes, 2005, 2006b, 2006c.
226. *See* Zelnik, Toubon & Cerutti, 2010, discussing an ACS for on-demand music download services.

test.[227] This seems an advisable approach when considering reform of EU copyright law, especially after *Soulier and Doke*.

3.3.5 Legal Licences: Statutory and Compulsory

3.3.5.1 Characterisation and Legal Framework

The terms 'statutory' and 'compulsory' licences are commonly used as synonyms.[228] They generally refer to licences imposed by law to regulate certain copyright use against the payment of compensation, remuneration, tariffs, contributions, or levies. But use of the terms is not uniform in legal and academic texts, which often denote diverse but partially overlapping schemes.[229] To grasp the scope of ACS proposals based on these models, it is important to explore the possible meanings of statutory and compulsory licences.

In Chapter 2, while recognising the interchangeable use of 'compulsory' and 'statutory', a preliminary distinction was made with reference to international and EU law.[230] It was stated that statutory licences restrict the nature of a pre-existing exclusive right by the application of a compensated limitation, whereas compulsory licences apply to self-standing remuneration rights.[231]

Another distinction can be drawn on the basis of the procedure used to determine the compensation or remuneration. Thus, Colin defines a licence as 'statutory' where the executive branch, via delegation of its legislative counterpart, is unilaterally entitled to fix the amount of compensation without prior stakeholder consultation.[232] In this context, the compensation paid is often qualified as a 'levy'.[233] Conversely, a licence is 'compulsory' if the remuneration is fixed through a bilateral or multilateral negotiation between the parties involved in the use of works.[234]

The term compulsory licence typically applies where there is a legally predetermined obligation to contract, i.e., 'where the right holder is obliged to grant a license according to a specific procedure'.[235] In this scenario, the

227. Colin, 2011a, pp. 45–46; Dusollier & Colin, 2011, pp. 819–827.
228. Peukert, 2005, p. 18, exemplifying with US law and academic writings.
229. The interchangeable use of these terms is typical in copyright scholarship. *See* Guibault, 2002, p. 25.
230. Compulsory licensing is mentioned in Arts 11*bis*(2) and 13(1) BC, Art. 15(2) *in fine* RC, and Art. 10(2) Rental Right Directive. (On the BC compulsory licence, *see supra* 2.4). Art. 8(2) and recital 21 SatCab Directive mention statutory licensing in the negative.
231. Cf. *supra* 2.2.3.
232. Colin, 2011a, p. 21.
233. Peukert, 2005, pp. 18–19.
234. Colin, 2011a, p. 21.
235. Peukert, 2005, p. 18.

legislator forces upon rights holders the basic terms of the license in the law. If no agreement is reached pursuant to those terms, users can appeal to administrative or judicial authorities, who can unilaterally fix the compensation or remuneration amount.[236] The law thus incentivises licensees and licensors to negotiate under the shadow of the licence. An example of such a provision is the 'cover' licence under the compulsory mechanical licensing scheme in the US Copyright Act.[237]

In the field of competition law, a compulsory licence means a remedy for actual or potential anti-competitive behaviour.[238] The licence is construed as an *inter partes* obligation between rights holders and users to contract on reasonable terms, pursuant to a judicial or administrative ruling.[239] Here, the licence operates more as a direct restriction to freedom of contract than to exclusivity.

In this book, 'legal licence' is the shorthand for the entire gamut of statutory or compulsory licences discussed above, *excluding those imposed as remedies for competition law violations*. For a legal licence, the law defines the scope and subject matter of the scheme, designates the CMO responsible for its management, and identifies the intermediary debtors of the remuneration. The law can establish the tariff paid under the licence directly or indirectly, through delegation to a governmental, administrative, judicial, or even an independent authority. Within those modalities, the law may subject the determination of tariffs to stakeholder negotiations, which can involve CMOs, intermediaries, consumer representatives, and experts.[240]

From a normative standpoint, a legal licence – like a copyright limitation – can have economic and/or non-economic motivations. The first relate to technology-based market failures that make effective individual management impractical or too cumbersome. The second relate to significant public interests requiring unrestricted (but remunerated) use, for example relating to the promotion of access and dissemination of works, fair remuneration to creators, or the respect of fundamental rights.[241]

A potential ACS will apply to use covered by the existing exclusive rights of reproduction and communication to the public.[242] As noted in Chapter 2, international law leaves little space for a broad legalisation

236. Guibault, 2002, p. 25; Karapapa, 2012, p. 11.
237. Section 115 US Copyright Act. Cf. Loren, 2014, p. 549; Menell, 2015, p. 494.
238. Guibault, 2002, p. 25.
239. *Ibid.*
240. Hugenholtz & Quintais, 2017 (forthcoming). *See also* SWD CRM Directive 2012, p. 197, with a definition of 'compulsory licence' that includes many of these elements.
241. See, identifying some of these motivations, Ginsburg, 2014b; Guibault, 2002, p. 22. On the respect of fundamental rights as an emerging justification for limitation in the case law of the CJEU, *see infra* 4.4.1.4, 4.4.4.1, 4.4.4.3, and 5.3.3.6.
242. *See* the detailed analysis in Chapter 4.

scheme applying to these rights under the compulsory licences for broadcasting and communication to the public in Article 11*bis*(2) BC.[243] The same conclusion is valid for the compulsory licence in Article 13 BC. This licence is limited to the recording of musical works and accompanying words (provided the authors consented to a first recording) and to the country where it is imposed (i.e., it does not automatically 'carry its lawful character' outside that territory). It is therefore unsuitable for the types of content and use covered by a broad ACS.[244]

In light of the limited scope of compulsory licences in international law, a legal licence ACS will likely affect the nature of the exclusive rights of reproduction and communication to the public, transforming them (for the licensed uses) into non-exclusive rights of remuneration or compensation.[245] In the *acquis*, it is possible to identify a myriad of such rights, traditionally recognised as benefiting creators in relation to exploiters.[246] Table 3.2 provides an overview of these rights.

Table 3.2 Acquis Remuneration and Compensation Rights

Right / Rights Holders	*Type and Nature*	*Legal Basis*
Rental of films and phonograms / author and performer	Equitable Remuneration (unwaivable)	Article 5 Rental Right Directive
Public lending of works and related subject matter / at least authors	Remuneration (optional)	Article 6 Rental Right Directive
Broadcasting (wireless) of phonograms / performers and phonogram producers	Single Equitable Remuneration	Article 8(2) Rental Right Directive
Annual supplementary remuneration (during term extension) for transfer or assignment of exclusive rights in exchange for a non-recurring payment / performer	Annual Supplementary Remuneration (unwaivable)	Article 3(2a)-(2e) Term Directive (2011)

243. Cf. *supra* 2.4.
244. Historically, Art. 13 BC reconciled the rights of authors and music publishers with those of record producers in relation to the mechanical reproduction of musical works. Cf. Ricketson & Ginsburg, 2006, pp. 809–814. N.B. Art. 14(3) BC expressly excludes audio-visual works from this regime.
245. von Lewinski, 2008, pp. 55–56.
246. *Ibid.*

Right / Rights Holders	*Type and Nature*	*Legal Basis*
Resale of art works / author of an original work of art	Remuneration (inalienable, unwaivable)	Arts 1 and 2 Resale Right Directive
Reprographic reproductions / holders of reproduction right in Article 2 InfoSoc Directive	Fair compensation (unwaivable)	Article 5(2)(a) InfoSoc Directive
Private copying (reproduction) / holders of reproduction right in Article 2 InfoSoc Directive	Fair Compensation (unwaivable)	Article 5(2)(b) InfoSoc Directive
Reproductions of broadcasts by non-commercial social institutions / holders of reproduction right in Article 2 InfoSoc Directive	Fair Compensation (unwaivable)	Article 5(2)(e) InfoSoc Directive
Use of orphan works by specific organisations / holders of right of reproduction and the right of making available to the public provided in Articles 2 and 3 InfoSoc Directive	Fair Compensation (unwaivable)	Article 6(5) Orphan Works Directive

The contours of equitable remuneration and fair compensation are explained in Chapter 2. As noted there, the main distinction between the concepts is that equitable remuneration is based on the notion of 'economic value of the use', whilst fair compensation is based on the notion of 'harm'. Furthermore, while the CRM Directive relies on an umbrella concept of 'appropriate remuneration' based on the 'economic value of the use', a systematic interpretation of the InfoSoc Directive suggests that future compensated limitations to its exclusive rights should probably be subject to fair compensation.[247]

These distinctions matter because they will shape the nature and method of calculation of the remuneration or compensation of any legal licence ACS under EU law, especially as both fair compensation and equitable remuneration are autonomous concepts of EU law.[248]

247. This view relies on recital 36 InfoSoc Directive. *See supra* 3.3.2.1. The fact that the limitation to these rights in the Orphan Works Directive in linked to a right of fair compensation seems to confirm this interpretation.

248. *See supra* 2.2.4 and, regarding fair compensation, *infra* 4.4.3.3. On the shape of the compensation element in a future legal licence ACS, *see infra* 5.3.3.3, 5.3.3.4, and 6.2.

3.3.5.2 Legalisation Proposals

The most common ACS proposals are for stand-alone or combined legal licences.[249] The majority of those refer to limitation-based licensing schemes for online use that expand existing systems, commonly private copying. Only in rare cases do authors suggest legal licences for newly created self-standing remuneration rights, such as Dimita's 'global dissemination right' or Lincoff's 'online transmission right' for music.[250]

In many cases, it is unclear whether the legal licence provides direct authorisation to consumers or to commercial users acquiring them for the benefit of the former.[251] However, the bulk of sources can be read as providing the legal authorisation directly to end-users,[252] with few instances of explicit licensing of commercial intermediaries.[253] As the proposals are diverse, it is important to explore some representative examples.

One of the most influential and developed proposals is Netanel's non-commercial use levy. This model aims to enable unhindered non-commercial P2P file sharing for most protected works, excluding software and unpublished works.[254] The proposal, in many respects, approximates European private copying systems, which are usually coupled with obligatory collective management of the respective fair compensation right.[255]

Netanel's model would impose a levy on the sale of products/services whose value is substantially enhanced by P2P, and distribute the resulting proceeds to rights holders in proportion to the volume of downloads and use of works, as measured by digital tracking and statistical sampling. It would cover acts of uploading, downloading, streaming, and digital adaptations (including remixes). Users would have either a right or a protected legal privilege to engage in these acts and rights holders would be barred from using technological measures to prevent such acts.[256] The non-commercial

---

249. The list of proposals is extensive. Among those not cited previously, see e.g. Attali, 2008; Creation-public-internet, 2011; Hayward, 2008; Love, 2003; Mehra, 2008; Oksanen & Valimaki, 2005; Schulman, 1999; Seay, 2010; Sobel, 2003.
250. Dimita, 2010; Lincoff, 2002. These rights are explained in more detail *infra* in 3.4.2.
251. See, e.g., Schulman, 1999.
252. See, e.g., Aigrain, 2012; Fisher, 2004; Love, 2003; Netanel, 2003; Peukert, 2005.
253. For such rare cases, see: Lincoff, 2002 (proposing a one-stop-shop for music where licences are granted to 'service operators' or end-user members of P2P networks and similar online communities); Sobel, 2003 (advancing a digital retailer model where ISPs act as first level licensees of digital works by paying a wholesale price to rights holders and then 'reselling' such works to subscribers at market-based retail prices); and Seay, 2010 (suggesting a model for commercial use similar to broadcasting licences).
254. Netanel, 2003. An updated version of Netanel's proposal is reported in Quintais, 2014, pp. 4–6. The original 2003 proposal excluded books because there were no established practices or markets for e-lending of digital books at the time.
255. Dusollier & Colin, 2011, p. 814.
256. Netanel, 2003; Quintais, 2014, pp. 4–6. Because of the proposed payment structure, product and service suppliers would likely not support the levy. Therefore, from a feasibility perspective, Netanel argues that the best option is to spread the payment

nature of the uses would eliminate secondary liability for the provision of related products/services, which would however subsist for commercial uses, considered to be excluded from the levy's scope.[257]

In its initial five years of existence, the levy amount would be based on the adjusted *net* revenues displaced by P2P. The rate would be set through negotiation by interested stakeholders under the threat of mandatory arbitration and pursuant to a 'fair income/return' standard set forth in the US Copyright Act for compulsory licences. The latter would not only recognise the contribution of P2P devices/services but also of authors to the creative sphere, while maximising public access to works and securing a 'reasonable remuneration' for rights holders.[258]

In contrast to Netanel, Litman advances a proposal for a hybrid legal licence ACS, combining statutory and voluntary licences for online music sharing. The system would operate on a 'presumption of shareability', meaning that unless digital copies of works indicate otherwise through a specific format (a '*.drm' file) containing electronic rights management information, the work can be freely shared. By using such a format, subject to specific requirements and a pre-determined grace period, rights holders could opt out of the system and make their works ineligible for sharing under the legal licence. The system would preferably be managed through a regulated government agency, and the compensation paid solely to creators via a mechanism designed to 'bypass unnecessary intermediaries'.[259]

In a more recent work, Depreeuw and Hubin explore – and ultimately disavow – the possibility of a limited ACS based on the application of the compulsory licence of Article 13 BC. This licence would apply to the first downstream reproduction of musical works by end-users, meaning the download or streaming of works following their lawful online availability. To avoid territorial fragmentation and be consistent with the requirements of the BC, the authors propose that the licence is implemented in the *acquis*, that the authority competent to determine the remuneration is set up at EU level, and that the debtor of the remuneration is the person or entity making the

obligation among a wide pool of debtors and targets, subject to the 'substantially enhanced value' criterion. Potential candidates include Internet access subscriptions, P2P platform providers, personal computers, tablets, CD burners, MP3 players, blank CDs, mobile phones, and mobile phone data plans.

257. Quintais, 2014, p. 5. The exclusion is justified by the political challenges in restricting exclusivity for such uses.

258. Netanel, 2003; Quintais, 2014, p. 5. According to Netanel, the criterion suggested takes into consideration: that not all P2P displaces copyright revenues, that the system should not finance pre-digital models or ensure oligopoly profits, and that consumers should be empowered in digital markets.

259. Litman, 2004.

work available (i.e., the content provider). The latter could then pass on the amount to end-users, as occurs in private copying systems.[260]

The main benefit of a legal licence ACS is that it would efficiently solve most challenges associated with territorial and substantive fragmentation, representing a comparative advantage in relation to pure collective management systems. However, to the extent a legal licence covers use within the scope of the exclusive online rights of reproduction and communication to the public in the InfoSoc Directive, it entails expansion of existing limitations to those rights. The licence must therefore pass the three-step test, which looms as a significant legal obstacle. (Chapter 4 maps the potential scope of a legal licence ACS, and Chapter 5 assesses its admissibility under the three-step test.)

3.3.6 State Systems

3.3.6.1 Characterisation and Legal Framework

State Systems are legal regimes external to copyright that allow unfettered online use while guaranteeing some level of remuneration for creators. For the most part, they are theoretical constructs presented as alternatives to the recognition of intellectual property rights.[261]

Economics scholars suggest that grants or subsidies awarded by the State may sometimes be more efficient in fostering and rewarding creative endeavour than intellectual property rights.[262] The earliest literature on this topic focuses on alternative regulation of patents, as viewed from the perspectives of economics and *law and economics*.[263] This literature challenges the economic justification for patent systems and argues for more

260. Depreeuw & Hubin, 2014, pp. 96–98, drawing a parallel with the American tradition, where compulsory licences of different types exist in relation to online use of musical works and sound recordings. The authors are sceptical of the benefits of imposing such a solution in the EU and call for empirical research on the matter (especially as they consider the market to be functioning in respect to these uses). *See also* Bernault & Lebois, 2005, pp. 44–45, arguing that a licence based on Art. 13 BC would be compatible with international law.
261. See: Shavell & Ypersele, 2001, Baker, 2003 (with a proposal for an 'artistic freedom voucher'), Fisher, 2004 (in the author's preferred option), Eckersley, 2004 (in the author's first option), Eckersley, 2012; Nadel, 2004, and La Quadrature du Net & Aigrain, 2013 (insofar as the system establishes remuneration for exchange acts post-online exhaustion of the exclusive right).
262. Shavell & Ypersele, 2001. For a literature review, *see* Eckersley, 2012, pp. 97–104.
263. For an historic analysis of such proposals in England, prior to 1800, *see* MacLeod, 1988. On the topic, *see also* Arrow, 1962; Machlup & Penrose, 1950; Polanyi, 1944; B.D. Wright, 1983.

efficient alternatives, ranging from publicly funded research and development frameworks, taxation-based funding through *ex post* rewards or prizes for inventors.[264]

In this context, Shavell and Van Ypersele propose reward systems where innovators are paid directly by the government and innovations pass directly into the public domain, thus implementing an incentive without monopoly.[265] The problem, common to industrial reward systems, is the information required for determination of reward systems or, put differently, the need to index rewards to the value of inventions.[266] Still, the authors conclude that intellectual property rights do not possess fundamental social advantages over reward systems; furthermore, an optional reward system, where innovators can choose between such legal protection and a reward system, is superior to an intellectual property regime.[267] The conclusion seems to be that for most alternative systems based on patent rewards or prizes, the success of their implementation depends on the definition of 'appropriate conditions … carefully selected for the particular economic environments in which they are to operate'.[268]

Beyond *ex post* reward proposals for patents, it is possible to find precedents for State Systems in the inception of public lending rights and, to a more limited extent, in publicly funded private copying systems.

Public lending right systems are 'government schemes to pay writers for their public good authorship, without interfering with users' ability to access large bodies of works through free public libraries.'[269] Such schemes predate current EU legal systems for public library lending, which rely on a harmonised exclusive or (optional) self-standing remuneration right for acts of lending. In the *acquis*, 'lending' is defined as 'making available for use, for a limited period of time and not for direct or indirect economic or commercial advantage, when it is made through establishments which are accessible to the public'.[270]

This harmonisation was the end result of an increase in lending activities by public libraries, which caused several European countries to introduce a public lending right for authors over the course of the twentieth century.[271] Although in some instances this right was internal to copyright,

264. *See* the sources listed in the preceding footnote. For all, see Eckersley, 2012, pp. 95–98.
265. Shavell & Ypersele, 2001.
266. Eckersley, 2012, p. 97; Shavell & Ypersele, 2001.
267. Shavell & Ypersele, 2001.
268. Eckersley, 2012, p. 98. *See also* Abramowicz, 2003.
269. Eckersley, 2012, p. 99, noting that historically, the application of public funds to copyright was viewed with scepticism, as the subsidising entities' preferences could lead to lack of losses in cultural diversity and raised concerns of censorship.
270. Arts 2(1)(b) and 6 Rental Right Directive. For an analysis of the public lending right in several countries prior to the implementation of the Rental Right Directive, *see* ALAI, 1983.
271. Report on the Public Lending Right in the EU 2002, p. 3.

the majority of European countries initially dealt with public non-commercial lending outside the copyright system.[272]

This was done in a plethora of ways. These included national funds constituted by library subscription taxes,[273] direct budget allocation,[274] government attribution/distribution of amounts per author/volume represented in public libraries,[275] or through grants and assistance on the basis of works made available without charge in public libraries (proportional to their annual budget).[276]

In the field of private copying, the situation is different. Most Member States implemented Article 5(2)(b) InfoSoc Directive with device or media based levy systems. However, at least three countries – Norway (since 1995), Spain (between 2012 and 2016), and Finland (since 2015) – adopted systems where fair compensation is paid out of the State budget, a model that resembles State Systems.[277]

The Norwegian Copyright Act states that authors shall receive fair compensation through annual grants via the State budget.[278] The fair compensation is 'funded by the Norwegian Government, as a post on the national budget', and subsequently collected by an umbrella CMO (Norwaco), which then distributes it to member (secondary) organisations representing national and foreign rights holders categories.[279] In Finland, as of 2015, an amendment to the copyright law 'introduced a new financing

272. *Ibid.*, pp. 3–4. *See also* ALAI, 1983: 'it is possible to distinguish two main groups: countries that do not recognize and those that apply the public lending right. Among the latter, some have sought a solution outside the province of copyright, and in fact only one, the Federal Republic of Germany, has accepted public lending right as an integral part of its copyright law'. Countries that did not recognise any public lending right were Italy, France and Belgium (to the extent that the existing law was considered 'dead letter'). For a description of the UK example of the 1979 Public Lending Right Act, *see* ALAI, 1983.
273. ALAI, 1983, for Belgium.
274. *Ibid.*, for the Netherlands and Sweden.
275. *Ibid.*, for Denmark, noting that works of multiple authorship were outside the system and translators had a special regime. N.B. the distribution of amounts could be done on a simple pro rata basis (e.g., as in the Dutch 'Fund for Literature' system) or pursuant to complex distribution mechanisms and detailed payment matrices (e.g., the system implemented via the Swedish Author's Fund, an apparent precursor of modern private copying levy systems).
276. *Ibid.*, for Finland.
277. WIPO & Stichting de Thuiskopie, 2016, p. 8. On the history and development of private copying systems, *see supra* 2.3. *See also Opinion AG in EGEDA II*, para. 16, mentioning in addition Estonia as a country that finances the compensation for private copying from the General State Budget.
278. *See* Art. 12 Norwegian Copyright Act.
279. WIPO, 2012, pp. 102–103. The most recent WIPO survey on private copying confirms that the '[t]he remuneration is funded by the Norwegian government as an item on the national budget' and 'The rate is set unilaterally in the national budget each year.' Cf. WIPO & Stichting de Thuiskopie, 2016, p. 123.

system for fair compensation', which replaced the previous device-based levy system with 'financing from the annual state budget.'[280]

Spain had a similar regime since December 2012. The Ministry of Culture determined the amount of compensation, which was paid once a year to competent CMOs from the State budget.[281] According to the law, the amount in question should reflect 'the damage actually caused to the rightholders as a result of reproduction of works which have been accessed legally', calculated on the basis of various criteria. However, since its inception, the total yearly amount distributed to CMOs was exactly EUR 5 million. Furthermore, payment of the amount to rights holders was made on the basis of pre-defined distribution keys.[282]

It is doubtful whether the indirect market proxy systems implemented by either legal regime for determination of compensation adequately preserves a link – as required by Article 5(2)(b) InfoSoc Directive – between the act of reproduction causing the harm to rights holders and the amount of fair compensation. If they do not, a significant part of these systems is functionally similar to State Systems for the private copying activities covered.

At least in relation to the Spanish system, some doubts were clarified by the CJEU in *EGEDA II*. The Spanish Supreme Court asked whether the Spanish scheme is compatible with Article 5(2)(b) of the InfoSoc Directive, taking into account that it is based on an estimate of the harm actually caused but cannot 'ensure that the cost of that compensation is borne by the users of private copies'. Should this be answered in the affirmative, the Spanish court further asked whether that scheme remains compatible if the total amount allocated by the budget for these purposes must be 'set within the budgetary limits established for each financial year.'[283]

In its judgment, the CJEU noted that under Spanish law the revenue allocated to the payment of fair compensation is financed from the general budget resources, i.e., by all taxpayers, *including legal persons*.[284] Furthermore, the law does not contemplate exemptions for legal persons in this respect, or allow for their reimbursement.[285] Therefore, because it fails to 'guarantee that the cost of compensation is ultimately borne solely by the users of private copies', the Spanish scheme is incompatible with Article 5(2)(b) of the InfoSoc Directive.[286] As a result of this judgment, the Spanish

280. WIPO & Stichting de Thuiskopie, 2016, p. 68.
281. *See* Art. 31 Spanish Intellectual Property Law, and, for the implementing legislation, the Royal Decree No. 1657/2012 of 7 December 2012. Cf. WIPO & Stichting de Thuiskopie, 2016, pp. 150–151.
282. WIPO & Stichting de Thuiskopie, 2016, pp. 14, 150–151.
283. CJEU, *EGEDA II*, para. 16.
284. *Ibid.*, para. 39.
285. *Ibid.*, para. 40.
286. *Ibid.*, paras 41–42. On this point the CJEU strays from the AG's Opinion, according to which financing the compensation from the General State Budget is consistent with the

Supreme Court annulled some of the controversial provisions of the Spanish law at issue.[287]

Despite this outcome, *EGEDA II* does not preclude a system that finances fair compensation for private copying through the State Budget. Rather, it opens the door for such a system provided it ensures payment of fair compensation to rights holders and guarantees its actual recovery.[288] In disavowing the specific set-up of Spanish law, the CJEU clarified that any such alternative to the traditional levy scheme must ensure that the cost of compensation is ultimately borne solely by the final user. This goal can, in theory, be achieved by allocating the revenue for private copying compensation to a budgetary item that excludes taxes imposed on legal persons.[289] Whether any implementation of this model is practical or cost-effective is, of course, a separate empirical question. Looking forward, it remains unclear what the impact of this judgment will be on those Member States (currently: Finland and Norway) that, like Spain did, finance the private copying compensation through the State Budget.

3.3.6.2 Legalisation Proposals

Pure State Systems are external to copyright. A good early example is provided by Shavell and Van Ypersele's 2001 proposal for a mandatory or optional reward system. The *mandatory* system provides that works enter the public domain upon release or publication, entitling creators to a mere claim to government rewards.[290] In the *optional* variant, authors have the choice whether to join the system. In neither model, however, are authors allowed to opt out.[291]

Another early proposal, dating from 2003, is Baker's 'artistic freedom voucher' (or 'AFV') system. The AFV, presented as 'an Internet Age alternative to copyrights', was meant to function as a different mechanism to incentivise the creation and supply of works. In this system, individuals

---

InfoSoc Directive, 'since this is not a matter of extending the scope of a levy to all taxpayers, but of a system of financing based on a different rationale.' *See Opinion AG in EGEDA II*, para. 52. The CJEU's judgement on this point made it unnecessary to examine the second question referred by the Spanish court. Cf. CJEU, *EGEDA II*, para. 43. For an analysis of the second question, *see Opinion AG in EGEDA*, paras 54–70.

287. Supreme Court Spain, 10.11.2016, Case No. 4832/2016, ECLI:ES:TS:2016:4832.
288. CJEU, *EGEDA II*, para. 37.
289. For example, national laws could provide for a scheme for exempting legal persons' taxes from inclusion in this budgetary item or, alternatively, allow legal persons to seek reimbursement of their taxes used for this purpose. Another possibility, briefly addressed by the AG, would be to introduce a specific tax or duty on natural persons to finance fair compensation. *See Opinion AG in EGEDA*, para. 51. Whether any of these variants is practical or cost-effective is, of course, a separate empirical question.
290. *See* Shavell & Ypersele, 2001, noting that the *ex post* calculation can be based on sales or other more sophisticated methods.
291. Shavell & Ypersele, 2001.

would be given refundable tax credits of about USD 100, which they would allocate to specific 'creative workers' or intermediaries (similar to CMOs) set up to pass the collected funds to creators. Both creators and intermediaries could only benefit from the voucher if registered in the system. Once registered, the recipients of the vouchers would be ineligible for copyright protection of their works for a period of time (e.g., five years). All works created by individuals within the AFV system would automatically enter the public domain. Creators would be allowed to opt out of the system at a later stage, subject to certain conditions, namely a grace period from the date a creator last received public funds.[292]

In 2004, Fisher published his influential monograph on legalisation models, in which he proposes the adoption of a 'tax-and-royalty' system. Although the author advances different ACS designs (e.g., based on legal licences and voluntary collective licensing), his preferred option appears to be for a 'governmentally administered reward system'.[293] The system would apply to commercial and non-commercial use for 'entertainment' works (mostly audio and video recordings). For a work to deserve consideration, a rights holder would have to opt in to the system and register it with a government agency (the Copyright Office). This agency would attribute a unique filename to the work, later used to track all transmissions of digital copies thereof and estimate its usage. The money to compensate rights holders for use of their works would be raised through taxes. Periodic payments amounting to a share of the tax revenue would be made to registrants by the competent agency, based on the relative usage and popularity of works. Once in place, this system would lead to the amendment of copyright law so as to eliminate most exclusive rights for online use.[294] As result, music and films would be 'readily available, legally, for free'.[295]

Conversely, Eckersley sets forth a 'virtual market reward/remuneration system' that provides blanket licensing for online use.[296] The system relies on a government-run administrative structure. It includes a tripartite compensation structure, comprising (1) progressive income taxation, (2) levies on goods, and (3) levies on Internet access services. An original feature of this proposal is that the distribution of the sums collected is determined based on end-user voting mechanisms. As described by Eckersley, this system

292. Baker, 2003.
293. Fisher, 2004, pp. 202–203.
294. Fisher, 2004, pp. 199–258. In his preferred model, Fisher proposes financing the ACS through an income tax; however, the possibility of taxing devices, media and services (e.g., Internet subscription) are also analysed. Cf. Fisher, 2004, pp. 249–251.
295. Fisher, 2004, p. 202.
296. *See* Eckersley, 2004, expanded by the author in Eckersley, 2012. In the latter version, the underlying legal mechanism lacks detail but the author expressly promotes a public funding approach, based on precedents external to copyright, such as public lending rights and government reward systems. Only the 2004 version entertains the notion of an opt-in right. Cf. Eckersley, 2004, p. 165.

approximates a state-run model with little reliance on copyright protection for the digital works and use covered.[297]

Finally, French scholar Philippe Aigrain and the advocacy group Quadrature du Net advance a high level proposal for the application of the doctrine of exhaustion to online acts of 'non-market sharing of digital works between individuals', namely those involving the rights of reproduction and communication to the public. The objectives of this proposal are twofold. First, to place online acts of non-market sharing between individuals outside the scope of copyright protection. Second, to enable 'the recognition of new social rights to remuneration and access to financing for contributors.'[298]

To achieve this second aim the proponents discuss different models for the remuneration of creators affected by the exhaustion of rights for digital works, but indicate a preference for the 'Creative Contribution scheme'. This scheme would be implemented through a legally organised resource pooling system, including a statutory contribution. Creators would be entitled to a 'remuneration/reward' funded through a monthly 'flat-rate contribution' on Internet household connections, distributed 'on the basis of data stored by voluntary users about their non-market use in the public sphere (P2P sharing, recommendation, posting on blogs, etc.)'.[299]

3.4 ATTRIBUTES OF ALTERNATIVE COMPENSATION SYSTEMS

The preceding sections provide a typology of models for copyright reform. It is now clear that most ACS are not radical departures from past and existing copyright laws, but rather adaptations of the same to regulate mass online use. This section furthers the taxonomy of ACS by looking into their constituent parts. It categorises a set of attributes that assist in defining the scope and characteristics of these systems and provides a snapshot of how they are addressed across different proposals.

The attributes analysed are the following: *subject matter scope*, *substantive rights scope*, *compensation type*, *management system*, *compensation target*, and *burden of compensation*. Depending on the type of ACS or specific legalisation proposal, the composition of each attribute may vary. By breaking proposals down into these components, it is possible to identify elements susceptible of transplant across ACS. These transplants may in turn

297. Eckersley, 2004, pp. 100–116, 152–163, 2012, p. 105–139, 141ff.
298. La Quadrature du Net & Aigrain, 2013, pp. 5–6.
299. La Quadrature du Net & Aigrain, 2013, pp. 5–6, 11–14. On the design of the creative contribution system, *see* Aigrain, 2012. *See also* Patry, 2011, p. 182, proposing a 'worldwide exhaustion of digital rights once a work has been licensed in one country' as '[n]ational or regional exhaustion is a relic of the analog world'.

improve the legal feasibility or normative desirability of the 'recipient' system.

The results of this analysis are twofold. First, it allows a better understanding of legalisation proposals, enabling comparison of benefits and costs between proposals and against the status quo, as well as their impact on rights holders and users.[300] Second, it identifies discrete attributes that can be selected from different models to devise a more flexible ACS.

3.4.1 Subject Matter Scope

In theory, an ACS can cover any type of digital content used online that is susceptible of copyright and related rights protection. This includes music, video, text, e-books, photos and other visual works, databases, software and videogames. Some of these categories can be aggregated into different classifications reflecting the nature of the work (e.g., 'multimedia works') or specific content valuations (e.g., 'entertainment works' or 'pornography').

Legalisation can therefore fluctuate between universal and restricted approaches regarding subject matter scope. A universal approach, applying to all types of subject matter, is consistent with the objective of wholesale legalisation professed by many ACS proponents. On the other hand, a vertical or sectorial approach is legally more feasible and susceptible of customisation to areas with higher levels of unauthorised file sharing – audio-visual content and, to a lesser extent, music and e-books – while not applying to areas where infringement by end-users is less problematic, like videogames, software and databases.[301]

From a different perspective, because most types of ACS rely on collective rights management, pragmatism favours applying an ACS to the categories of content traditionally managed by CMOs: music, text, visual and audio-visual. This would operate to the exclusion of subject matter such as videogames, software and databases.[302]

These considerations are not lost on legalisation proponents, whose models vary in the subject matter covered, ranging from ACS covering online music, through online music and audio-visual works, to all types of content.[303] Even in models that are universal by default, it is possible to find

300. Heijden, 2014, discussing case selection and the importance of comparative research by design.

301. See, e.g., Kantar Media, 2015, showing a low level and volume of online infringement of videogames and software in the UK for the period between March and May 2015.

302. Hugenholtz & Quintais, 2017 (forthcoming).

303. Applying to music, see, e.g., Lincoff, 2002; Litman, 2004; Love, 2003. Applying to music and audio-visual works, see, e.g., Beltrandi et al., 2007; Fisher, 2004. Applying to all types of content, see, e.g., Grassmuck & Stalder, 2003; Peukert, 2005; Sterling, 2008, 2009.

proposals that carve out certain categories of works, such as software (possibly including videogames), software *and* databases, and periodic publications.[304]

Another variation of note are proposals that subject the inclusion of works in the system to certain requirements, such as prior publication or making available (either offline or online),[305] absence of restrictions through TPMs,[306] lawfulness of source of the digital copy of the work,[307] and embargo periods in the context of media chronology systems.[308] Beyond these conditions, subject matter exclusions are either unjustified or grounded in particular market failures, technological limitations (e.g., of tracking and measurement systems), the non-expressive nature of certain works (e.g., software and databases), or legal compliance concerns.[309]

3.4.2 Substantive Rights Scope: Authorised Use

In general, an ACS authorises use protected by copyright that takes place in the digital network environment, meaning use over the Internet, either through wired or wireless means. Because an ACS aims at solving a problem situated in the digital realm, it does not usually apply to analogue use of works. Beyond that common core, there is a significant diversity of legalisation proposals.

A common approach is to identify the types of online act authorised in the system. Thus, while some proposals target discrete acts like downloading, uploading, or webcasting, others legalise bundles of online acts involved in specific technologies, such as P2P.[310]

---

304. Excluding software, see, e.g., Netanel, 2003 (discussing previously publicly released expressive subject matter), and Roßnagel et al., 2009 (describing the proposal by the German Green Party). Excluding software and databases, see, e.g., Aigrain, 2012; Bernault & Lebois, 2005. Excluding periodic publications, see, e.g., Partido Comunista Português (Grupo Parlamentar), 2012.
305. See, e.g., Netanel, 2003, and Aigrain, 2012, pp. 84, 102, 116, 158 (requiring the first publication to be online).
306. See, e.g., Eckersley, 2012; Fisher, 2004; Grassmuck & Stalder, 2003, pp. 4–5.
307. *See* Beltrandi et al., 2007 (covering file sharing reproductions from legal sources), and Creation-public-internet, 2011.
308. This is of particular relevance in the exploitation of audio-visual works. See, e.g., Creation-public-internet, 2011; L'ALLIANCE public.artistes, 2006b, 2006c.
309. See, e.g., Fisher, 2004, Netanel, 2003, pp. 41–42, and Eckersley, 2012, pp. 135–139 (considering 'non-monolithic' works to be the best fit for his virtual market, and excluding DRM-ed subject matter). Pornography is a special case, as it is implicitly or explicitly excluded from analysis in most ACS proposals. See, e.g., Eckersley, 2004, p. 163 & n. 266; Gratz, 2004, pp. 428–429. For the example of an author whose proposal includes pornography, *see* Aigrain, 2012, p. 164.
310. See, e.g., Colin, 2011a; Lohmann, 2008; von Lewinski, 2005.

These acts or bundles are then subject to legal qualification as substantive rights according to the law applicable to the proposal. In general, the rights include reproduction, communication to the public, making available, online distribution, and adaptation (or the right to prepare derivative works). The identification of such types of right is either express or derives from the reference to a category of rights.

For instance, proposals for online music may refer to 'mechanical rights' and 'performing' or 'performance' rights, terms whose meaning evolved over time. In EU law, 'mechanical rights' traditionally meant rights 'to reproduce musical works in a physical music carrier such as a record or a CD', but the term currently refers to rights 'to reproduce a musical work for online uses'; i.e., online reproductions.[311] 'Performing rights', on the other hand, generally refer to rights in the communication of works through acts like 'broadcasting on TV or radio, playing of music in places such as bars or concert halls'; the term is nowadays used with reference 'to the making available of work or other protected subject matter in the Internet'.[312]

The legal qualification also depends on the technical characterisation of acts. For instance, whether an act is on-demand (an upload in a P2P network) or linear (the transmission of a webcast) may lead to different qualifications as, respectively, an act of making available online, or a wireless communication to the public. In international copyright law, the former act triggers an exclusive right while the latter allows for compulsory licensing.[313]

The qualification may also vary depending on the applicable law. For example, in EU law, acts of download and upload in a P2P network qualify as a reproduction and communication to the public respectively (Articles 2 and 3 InfoSoc Directive). However, in the US, there are conflicting views on the application of the distribution right in section 106(3) US Copyright Act to this type of interactive dissemination of works.[314]

Furthermore, it is not always clear what right applies to certain online activities. A case in point is that of remixes, mash-ups and user-generated content. These activities involve different exclusive rights, some harmonised at international level and the *acquis* – reproduction and communication to the public – and others not, like the right of adaptation.[315] (It is also worth noting

---

311. SWD CRM Directive 2012, p. 197.
312. *Ibid.*, p. 197.
313. *See supra* 2.4.2.1.
314. *See* Depreeuw & Hubin, 2014, pp. 58–63, 75; U.S. Copyright Office, 2014, p. 10572. For criticism, *see* Ginsburg, 2014a.
315. *See* Quintais, 2012, p. 75. On the right of adaptation in the *acquis*, *see* Fechond et al., 2009, pp. 83–84, noting that the only explicit reference to this right in the *acquis* is found in Art. 4(b) Software Directive, despite general recognition of the right at national level. *See also* Hugenholtz & Senftleben, 2011. At international level, a general adaptation right and specific provisions for translations and cinematographic adaptations are found, respectively, in Arts 12, 8 and 14 BC.

that the vast majority of ACS deal only with economic rights, to the exclusion of moral rights.[316])

To address these substantive fragmentation challenges, some reform proposals suggest the creation of new rights that encapsulate the relevant acts authorised by the ACS, typically applying to online acts of communication to the public and functionally dependent acts of digital reproduction. Illustrations are Lincoff's 'online transmission right',[317] Sterling's 'Internet right',[318] Dimita's 'global dissemination right',[319] and Aigrain's 'positive social right of sharing'.[320] It is noteworthy that few proposals address the right of adaptation and, those that do, allow its withdrawal from the ACS.[321]

Beyond the online character and type of authorised use, a major distinction in legalisation proposals relates to the purpose or nature of use, namely whether the same is 'commercial' or 'non-commercial'. Most proposals target non-commercial, not-for-profit or 'non-market' activities over the Internet, as their ultimate aim is to enable large-scale online use by individuals.[322]

As noted in Chapter 1, this book also focuses on copyright reform for non-commercial online use. Based on its use in the *acquis* – in relation to compensated limitations and collective rights management – 'non-commercial' should probably be qualified as an autonomous concept of EU law.[323] The concept, however, has nebulous contours.

The term 'commercial' can encompass several meanings, including 'economic', 'for profit', 'business' and the like. Yet, the scope of non-commerciality is difficult to define, especially in the online environment.[324] At the very least, commercial should not be a synonym for economic. In private copying, for example, a limitation the scope of which excludes all

---

316. In this respect, an ACS could raise concerns in its articulation with the moral rights of disclosure and integrity (where transformative uses are authorised in the system). *See* Quintais, 2012, pp. 75–76. *See also* Goldstein & Hugenholtz, 2013, pp. 363–365, discussing the moral right of integrity under international copyright law and several national laws.
317. Lincoff, 2002, 2008. The new online transmission right would replace the rights of reproduction, performance and distribution for online purposes.
318. Sterling, 2008, 2009. The new internet right would cover the substantive rights of reproduction, communication to the public and making available when involved in the same transmission and for global purposes.
319. Dimita, 2010, pp. 210–218.
320. Aigrain, 2012, pp. 65–72.
321. Fisher, 2004, pp. 234–236; La Quadrature du Net & Aigrain, 2013.
322. While the terms 'non-commercial' and 'not-for-profit' are of common usage, the term 'non-market' is mostly used by Aigrain in works on this topic, most notably in Aigrain, 2012, pp. 15, 84, 207 & n. 5. The author borrows the term from Benkler, 2006.
323. Cf. *supra* 1.2.
324. Karapapa, 2012, p. 82.

economically significant use would be devoid of meaning and application, as many copying acts bear that significance.[325]

The challenges inherent in defining the concept could explain why ACS proponents often shy away from drawing hard and fast lines as to its meaning, beyond linking the use to online acts of natural persons.[326] For Netanel, for instance, non-commercial means that individuals 'cannot be selling copies of, access to, or advertising in connection with the protected work'.[327] Grassmuck adds that users cannot earn revenue nor solicit donations from the public, while a French law proposal requires use not be directly or indirectly commercial, a terminology borrowed from the private copying limitation in Article 5(2)(b) InfoSoc Directive.[328]

Some ACS designs authorise only online use for 'personal enjoyment', excluding economic benefits. In one case, this entails a prohibition that 'a site or a community makes available entire collections or provides its sharing services for any commercial purpose'.[329] Others, however, permit the use of intermediary 'sharing platforms', enabling the operation of centralised and decentralised systems, while exonerating a broad swath of intermediaries (caching, browsing, hosting or others) from liability, irrespective of physical location.[330]

3.4.3 Compensation Type

The type of compensation is the economic claim of copyright owners linked to the permission to use their works. This claim comes with different labels: payment, tariff, royalty, licence fee, remuneration, compensation, levy, contribution or tax.[331] The compensation is influenced by the nature of the right subject to authorisation. Some terms, like 'rights revenue' or 'tariff' apply to different types of system irrespective of whether they involve exclusive or remuneration rights. Other terms are specific to the scheme they apply to. For example, the term 'levy' is overwhelmingly used for the payment of compensation in a statutory licence, 'licence fee' or 'royalty' are more common in voluntary collective licensing,[332] and 'taxes' and 'rewards' are the province of State System proposals.[333]

325. Poort & Quintais, 2013.
326. See, e.g., Dimita, 2010, p. 212 & nn. 1513, 218, for whom non-commercial means use not made in the course of business and should be better defined at international level.
327. Netanel, 2003, p. 43.
328. See, e.g., Geiger, 2011, pp. 459–462 & n. 7, describing a French legislative proposal from 2005.
329. *See* Rocha, 2010, with a translation and explanatory comments to Art. 88(B) of the Brazilian 'Compartilhamento Legal' proposal.
330. See Partido Comunista Português (Grupo Parlamentar), 2012, proposed Arts 3 and 4.
331. *See* Geiger, 2010, p. 528, criticising the use of the term 'levy' in this context.
332. Cf. *supra* 3.3.2.
333. See, e.g., Baker, 2003; Fisher, 2004.

3.4.4 Management System

The management system refers to the 'nuts-and-bolts' of an ACS, namely the calculation, collection and distribution of the compensation. For the most part, legalisation proposals take inspiration from and extend upon existing models of collective management and statutory licensing.

The determination of the amount of compensation has two aspects: the total amount of compensation generated by an ACS, and the specific amount paid by the users for the authorised use. The latter amount relates to the burden of compensation, and is dealt with below under that heading (3.4.6).

As regards the total amount generated by the system, in collective rights management models that quantum is determined through contractual negotiation and tariff setting by CMOs, and is usually not problematic. In legal licence and State System ACS, this determination is imposed by law, with the intervention of a government agency and/or stakeholder negotiations, subject to judicial or administrative review.[334] The calculation of the amount is a complex and debated aspect of the system, mainly because it is one of the main elements in assessing its feasibility.[335]

It is possible to calculate the overall amount of compensation in an ACS using different ranges and reference points, depending on the policy objective of the system. These objectives include compensating revenue losses from piracy, curing a market failure, providing fair remuneration, or incentivising creation and access to works.

Some proposals set as a lower threshold the status quo rights revenues for comparable authorised use; if this threshold is met, the ACS is welfare increasing. Other proposals target the lost profits from unauthorised use; if the ACS covers these losses, it cures the market failure that motivated its adoption.[336] A third approach establishes a welfare increasing compensation range, using current rights revenue levels as a floor, and the value attributed by consumers to an ACS as a ceiling, for example by measuring their willingness to pay through contingent valuation methods.[337]

Whatever the model, there seems to be agreement that the total amount of compensation requires periodic adjustment after adoption of the ACS, as

---

334. There are also hybrid systems containing newly created entities for this purpose. See, e.g., Mehra, 2008 (proposing a digital clearinghouse), and Dimita, 2010 (proposing a specific WIPO agency).

335. See, e.g., Aigrain, 2012; Fisher, 2004; Netanel, 2003.

336. See, e.g., Fisher, 2004, suggesting diverse criteria, including actual or potential losses. Critics argue that this last amount is difficult to establish due to the lack of information on production costs and the potential profits of rights holders absent infringement. *See* Stan J. Liebowitz, 2003; Stanley J Liebowitz, 2005.

337. Handke et al., 2015; Handke, Quintais & Bodó, 2013. This seems to be the approach followed in Eckersley, 2004, 2012. *See also* Baker, 2003 using a contingent valuation method in his proposal for an artistic freedom voucher.

the baseline values become gradually less representative of changing market conditions over time.[338]

Except for tax-based State Systems, collection of compensation is usually the competence of a CMO designated in the ACS. Most proposals include a variation of the following set-up. The law mandates an umbrella CMO to administer the system, including collection and subsequent distribution to second-level organisations, which represent different categories of rights holders. For reasons of efficiency, the CMO will collect the amount from an intermediary debtor, like an ISP or online service provider, who may then have the right to pass it on to the final user. Some proposals devise specific government agencies for purposes of collection and distribution.[339]

The distribution of the compensation involves numerous considerations, many of which are well known to collective rights management. First, it is necessary to define the beneficiaries of the compensation, namely the categories of rights holders entitled to it. Here, there is a binary choice between proposals that benefit creators – often because of the unwaivable nature of their remuneration rights – or all rights holders.[340] The allocation of the amounts to each category is determined by law or stakeholder negotiation, and often creators are allocated a fixed share due to the unwaivable nature of their remuneration rights under the ACS.[341] Some proposals reserve a portion of the amounts collected for social and cultural purposes.[342]

The subsequent issue is how to divide the compensation among individual rights holders within a category. Individual distribution is typically the competence of second-level CMOs representing each category and only seldom of an umbrella organisation or central agency. Most proposals suggest distributing the compensation based on the measurement of online use – including relative and actual use of works online –, contingent valuation methods, or negotiated distribution keys.[343] In one notable exception, Eckersley proposes a progressive distribution system, where the

338. Referencing the necessity for periodic adjustments in light of different methods for measuring the use of works in an ACS, *see* Eckersley, 2004, 2012; Netanel, 2003.
339. See, e.g., Dimita, 2010; Eckersley, 2004, 2012; Mehra, 2008.
340. For proposals benefiting solely creators, see, e.g., Attali, 2008; Ku, 2002; Litman, 2004 For an atypical proposal benefiting creators and intermediaries under different schemes, *see* Aigrain, 2012.
341. See, e.g., Eckersley, 2012, p. 289, Introducing a mechanism similar to an unwaivable remuneration right for creators, by requiring the ACS to distribute a 'fair minimum portion of … royalties' to creators, even if these are not the current rights holders.
342. See, e.g., Aigrain, 2008.
343. *See* McDaniel, 2007, for a critical analysis of issues related to certain non-voluntary ACS proposals (limited to online music) for division and distribution of levied amounts, either through measurement of usage or contingent valuation methodologies. McDaniel ultimately denotes a preference for voluntary industry-led changes to the copyright system. Cf. McDaniel, 2007, p. 312. For an example of a specific method, *see* Lincoff, 2008, referring to benefits realised by online service providers.

compensation for lower income creators is proportionally higher than for those with higher income.[344]

Methods for measurement of online use include anonymous monitoring, sampling, tracking, census, or a combination thereof. Proposals that rely on monitoring online use typically require some type of registration of works or rights management information in a central registry to enable the measurement. More sophisticated ACS consider the length of works and trace units of consumption (e.g., download counts), or use decentralised metrics or contingent valuation surveys (e.g., by having end-users assume a role in distribution through voting mechanisms or user sampling).[345] It is worth noting that a significant number of proposals stress the need for these methods to respect the privacy of end-users.[346]

Regarding distribution, some authors note the need to define a distribution threshold, meaning that amounts collected are only distributed to rights holders if the administrative costs are covered (including management fees), and the rights holder has a minimum audience.[347]

Finally, the implementation of an ACS would require the implementation of an operational infrastructure enabling the features described above. Although built on existing collective management infrastructures and expertise, most ACS proposals would require additional capabilities, namely related to the technical systems and databases for registration of works, and measurement of online use.[348]

3.4.5 Compensation Targets

The compensation target is the good or service selected as the aim of the payment obligation. This attribute is less relevant for voluntary licences, where the payment is predominantly negotiated between CMOs and commercial users. These then have a right to offer file sharing licences to end-users, either as a stand-alone or bundled with other goods or services, such as Internet access. In these models, users have the choice of participating in the ACS by acquiring a licence in addition to their normal service.[349]

---

344. Eckersley, 2012.
345. For an example of the first, *see* Fisher, 2004. For examples of the second, *see* Aigrain, 2008; Baker, 2003; Eckersley, 2012.
346. See, e.g., Aigrain, 2008; Hellings & Piryns, 2010; Morael & Piryns, 2010.
347. Eckersley, 2012; Fisher, 2004. For an example of the second, *see* Eckersley, 2012 and Baker, 2003 (relying on a selection by tax payers on their tax form of a beneficiary creators or intermediary, or alternatively on direct payments of the tax refund).
348. Proposals vary in this respect, but for examples of elaborate new systems with numerous implementation requirements, spanning from certification requirements for intermediaries, to specific administrative resolution procedures, *see* Baker, 2003; Eckersley, 2012; Fisher, 2004.
349. See, e.g., Beltrandi et al., 2008, 2007; Lohmann, 2004.

In non-voluntary ACS, this attribute is more complex, involving a higher level of legislative intervention. For efficiency reasons, the majority of proposals target internet access services, imposing the compensation as a surcharge on the monthly household subscription paid by users to ISPs. In some cases, albeit rare, mobile connections are also targeted.[350]

The payment obligation is either fixed (a 'flat rate') or varies according to type of connection, speed of access, income of the household, or other factors, which may influence the decision to exempt certain targets or users from payment (e.g., based on age, income, or low speed of connection).[351] A few proposals view Internet access as a utility, and therefore suggest regulatory determination of minimum and maximum price bands for access.[352]

In addition to services, a number of ACS target goods, like devices, equipment, media or supports selected on the basis of their susceptibility for use in unauthorised file sharing. In these models, the compensation amounts to a percentage of the wholesale or retail price of the good.[353]

In legal licences and State Systems, user participation in the ACS is usually mandatory for those acquiring the relevant good or service. If the system targets ISP subscriptions, for instance, it is compulsory for all non-exempt connected households. Finally, it is noted that State Systems use direct or indirect taxation to generate compensation. The incidence of the taxes used to fund the ACS includes personal income and connected residential properties (e.g., proportional to the value of a household with Internet connection).[354]

3.4.6 Burden of Compensation

This final attribute identifies the party bearing the direct and indirect burden of liability for payment. Such party will be the user or an intermediary. In voluntary collective licensing, the burden of compensation lies directly with the licensee, typically a commercial user, who then offers his services to end-users on market-based prices.[355]

In other types of ACS, where the target of compensation is a good or service, the provider of the same is typically the debtor of the compensation, which is owed to the CMO with competence for collection. However, in an

350. See, e.g., Dimita, 2010, p. 212; Grassmuck, 2010a; Partido Comunista Português (Grupo Parlamentar), 2012.
351. See, in this respect, the considerations in Vallbé et al., 2015.
352. See, e.g., Hellings & Piryns, 2010; Morael & Piryns, 2010.
353. See, e.g., Netanel, 2003, targeting goods the value of which is substantially enhanced by P2P. *See also* Fisher, 2004, pp. 222–223, defining different goods as potential targets.
354. Discussing some of these options in depth, *see* Eckersley, 2012; Fisher, 2004, pp. 216–223. *See also* Baker, 2003; Eckersley, 2012, suggesting exemptions for individuals or households without Internet connection.
355. See, e.g., L'ALLIANCE public.artistes, 2006b, 2006c; Lincoff, 2008.

arrangement similar to private copying systems, most proposals allow that intermediary to pass on the amount of the payment or levy to the end-users. The result is that consumers effectively bear the burden of compensation, unless the intermediary chooses to absorb it or the consumer is exempt from payment. This approach is justified to the extent the beneficiary of the authorisation to use works in the ACS is the end-user.[356]

Whichever the model, from the perspective of end-users, an ACS is a single-interface black box through which they either choose or are obliged to pay money in return for the authorisation to use works online, which money is distributed to rights holders.[357] In this respect, most proposals are silent on whether the ACS 'levy' should be visible for end-users acquiring it, allowing it to be incorporated in the price of the Internet subscription without discrimination.[358]

3.5 CONCLUSIONS

This chapter aims at an in-depth conceptual and legal understanding of the nature, scope and effects of ACS. Based on existing legalisation proposals, it advances a taxonomy of legal schemes that qualify as ACS, their attributes, and possible combinations, against the background of international and EU copyright law.

The taxonomy categorises five types of ACS or rights acquisition schemes for the wholesale legalisation of online use. These are, from least to most restrictive of the exclusive right: voluntary collective licensing, ECL, mandatory collective management, legal licences, and State Systems. Outside the classification are private ordering models that do not involve collective rights management, and proposals relying on uncompensated limitations, which lack the essential remuneration element.

The first three models are based on collective rights management. Both voluntary collective licensing and ECL (with opt-out) are restrictions on the exercise of the exclusive right, but not on its nature. They may apply as legal mechanisms for ACS with legislative amendments that, although challenging, would retain the exclusive nature of the licensed rights.

However, issues with territorial and substantive fragmentation of copyright, costs of management and supervision, and the reliance on the continued participation of rights holders – including, in ECL, not exercising

356. For examples of proposals allowing the payment to be passed on to end-users, see: Aigrain, 2008; Attali, 2008; Baker, 2003; Beltrandi et al., 2007; Bernault & Lebois, 2005; L'ALLIANCE public.artistes, 2006a; Lincoff, 2002; Love, 2003; Netanel, 2003; Zelnik et al., 2010.

357. The remaining attributes constitute a hidden complexity for end-users and are usually defined and managed by legislators, rights holders and intermediaries.

358. Exceptionally requiring visibility of the levy, *see* Creation-public-internet, 2011; Modot et al., 2011; Songwriters Association of Canada, 2011.

large-scale opt-outs – raise serious doubts that systems of voluntary licensing can provide the type of all-encompassing multi-territorial and multi-repertoire blanket authorisation for mass non-commercial use required by an ACS.

In this respect, the remaining types of ACS, classified as 'non-voluntary' licences, are more promising. As noted, the term in quotations is used ambiguously in law and commentary. Here, it means that the exercise of copyright is imposed prima facie on the rights holder, but does not require a transformation from exclusive to remuneration right. While it is not contentious that such a transformation results from the application of limitation-based statutory licences (it is less clear whether that is the case for mandatory collective management, or for compulsory ECL (without opt-out).

To solve this conundrum, the analysis contrasts the opposing theories on the application of mandatory collective management to exclusive rights. Although this regime has functional similarities with compulsory licences, it does not seem possible to qualify it as a copyright limitation from the conceptual or legal-technical perspectives.

The consequence is that the adoption of a mandatory collective management ACS for online exclusive rights for non-commercial purposes is not subject to the three-step test. Instead, it must respect the stringent requirements for the imposition of collective management as the sole mode of exercising those rights. However, this issue is unsettled in scholarship and not formally recognised in international treaties, meaning that such a proposal is contentious both as a matter of law and as a legitimate policy option. This is all the more so in EU law following the CJEU's judgment in *Soulier and Doke*. Therefore, it is advisable to explore whether an ACS following this regime would pass the three-step test.[359]

Legal licences, which can be statutory and compulsory, require the adoption of a compensated limitation to the acts authorised by an ACS (where the same are covered by an exclusive right), accompanied by a remuneration or compensation right. As noted in Chapter 2 and further explored in the present chapter, international copyright law leaves limited space for EU-wide compulsory licensing of mass use, and certainly not for a broad blanket non-commercial licence for the rights of online reproduction and communication to the public. Where these rights are exclusive and not covered by a copyright limitation at EU level (a topic explored in Chapter 4) a legal licence ACS is subject to the three-step test.

Yet, aside from this legal challenge, a legal licence combined with collective management of underlying remuneration or compensation right(s)

359. See, following a similar logic, Colin, 2011a, pp. 45–46; Dusollier & Colin, 2011, pp. 819–827. *See also* Geiger, 2015b, p. 19: '... a less 'intrusive' alternative would be subordinating creative uses to the mandatory collective administration of works, as this would not be a limitation but a way of exercise of the exclusive right, which would therefore be more likely to be compatible with the three step-test'.

is conceptually the best solution to achieve wholesale legalisation of non-commercial use with fair remuneration. The main reason is that it adequately addresses the territorial and substantive fragmentation challenges of EU copyright law, while leveraging the infrastructure and expertise of CMOs.

State Systems, for their part, are proposals based on tax or rewards models external to copyright. Their adoption would require the replacement of copyright protection for the authorised use by a publicly funded system. Thus, even for non-commercial mass use, they constitute an unrealistic path for reform.

Further to the identification and characterisation of the above types of ACS, this chapter categorises and provides a snapshot of a set of attributes of legalisation schemes: subject matter scope, substantive rights scope, compensation type, management system, compensation target and burden of compensation. The analysis of attributes assists in defining the scope and characteristics of legalisation schemes.

The examination of carefully selected models and attributes reveals a complete picture of the scope and effects of legalisation schemes. The analysis confirms what the previous chapter hinted at, namely that most ACS types and attributes are not radically different from existing copyright mechanisms.

Rather, they are extensions and adaptations of existing regimes – namely of collective rights management and legal licences – with the objective of enabling a model of fairly remunerated access to (predominantly) mass non-commercial use online. The point is important as it is often obscured by the presentation of these models as holistic, and therefore impractical, alternatives to the status quo. Instead, by looking at ACS as a matrix of interoperable models and attributes, the taxonomy offers not only an exploration of flexibility in copyright law, but also a toolbox for policy makers to select the most legally consistent and adequate ACS blend of copyright reform.

Chapter 4

Between Rights and Limitations: Mapping the Space for the Legalisation of the Online Use of Copyright Works

4.1 INTRODUCTION

Legal reform is a normative proposition. In this book, the proposition is to improve the *acquis* and define what the law should be for the regulation of mass online use of copyright-protected works. The assessment requires clarification of *what the law is* in this respect. That is the task of the present chapter, which examines the following research question:

> How does the bundle of exclusive rights and corresponding copyright limitations in the *acquis* apply to mass online use of works by individuals?

The question aims to be technology neutral, meaning that the online use of works it refers to includes all modes and acts of dissemination, transmission, communication or making available of works online. To prevent technological obsolescence of the analysis, these acts are categorised in a typology of online uses that attempts to trace CJEU case law on application of exclusive rights and limitations to digital networks. The legal analysis refers to this typology.

The aim of the question is not only to define the baseline legal status for these non-commercial online uses of works, but also to clarify whether the current framework can accommodate an ACS and, if not, what the future scope of legalisation should be. The chapter examines rules that apply to online uses, with an emphasis on the InfoSoc Directive's exclusive rights and limitations (Articles 2–5) and their interpretation by the CJEU. The directive implements the WIPO Treaties, which include by reference multiple provisions of the BC; hence, these international treaties are briefly mentioned in order to shed light on the origin, context, meaning, and purpose of some provisions in the *acquis*.

Orbiting around the issue of the legal qualification of online uses are several elements central to the overall theme of this book. Chief among those are considerations on possible flexibilities in the interpretation of exclusive rights and limitations, as well as the autonomous concept of fair compensation. Doctrinal discussion of these topics is infused with normative considerations on the desirable scope of rights and breathing space provided by limitations in the *acquis*. Where relevant to the study of ACS, such arguments are highlighted and woven into the examination of the legal provisions, making this chapter partly normative.

The analysis proceeds as follows. After this introduction, section 4.2 advances a typology of forms of online use by individuals. This typology is then subject to legal analysis against the regimes of the harmonised rights of reproduction (4.3.1) and communication to the public (4.3.2). The analysis demonstrates that the majority of online acts by end-users, even if non-commercial, trigger the application of one or more overlapping exclusive rights and that many of the uses are subject to legal uncertainty. Section 4.4 then examines the limitations that might exempt some of the acts covered by exclusive rights. After providing background and context to the framework of limitations in the *acquis* (4.4.1), it tests the application of several limitations to previously identified uses, namely: the mandatory limitation for transient copying (4.4.2); the optional limitation for private copying (4.4.3); and the optional limitations susceptible of application to digital adaptations, namely quotations, incidental inclusion and parodies (4.4.4). The analysis shows that, despite the existence of relevant breathing spaces, a plethora of restricted acts by Internet users are not privileged by limitations. Therefore, it is in respect of such uses that the need for an ACS-type of copyright reform is more pressing. Section 4.5 summarises the chapter's findings and offers conclusions.

4.2 TYPOLOGY OF ONLINE USES

ACS proponents traditionally focus either on discrete acts (e.g., downloading, uploading, webcasting, sharing), or on bundles of acts triggered by specific technologies.[1] The acts are then abstracted into substantive rights

1. Cf. *supra* 3.4.2.

under the relevant applicable law. The present chapter uses a similar method, but first clusters different acts into a typology of online uses.

This section selects and categorises the types of use carried out by end-users in the online environment, and flags the corresponding legal issues, providing a basis for subsequent legal analysis. The selection takes into account CJEU case law on the application of the InfoSoc Directive's exclusive rights and limitations in the digital environment, thus aligning the typology with existing law at EU level. From the perspective of Internet users, the types of use involved in digital content sharing are the following: browsing, downloading, streaming, stream capture, uploading, and digital adaptations. The following paragraphs analyse each of these in turn.

4.2.1 Browsing

Web browsers are software applications whose function is to retrieve, present and traverse information resources (such as Uniform Resource Identifiers or Uniform Resource Locators Identifiers) on the Internet.[2] End-users resort to these applications to navigate the web.

The mere action of viewing a website does not cause Internet users to download content. However, the technical process of browsing requires the automatic making of on-screen and cached copies. The copies are made without human intervention beyond that of accessing the website. Moreover, the copies are retained solely for the normal duration of the user's session and deleted automatically after a certain period of time. That period varies according to the 'capacity of the cache and the extent and frequency of internet usage by the internet user concerned'.[3]

Both on-screen and cache copies are essential and universal technical features of browsing technology, necessary for the proper and efficient functioning of the Internet.[4] Therefore, unless a user sets out to download or print a protected work he is viewing, the copies in question are 'merely the incidental consequence of the use of his computer to view a website'.[5]

The legal question raised by browsing is whether on-screen and cache copies qualify as copyright reproductions by the end-user.

4.2.2 Downloading

Downloading involves the initiation, reception and saving of data – for more than transitory duration – transferred from a remote system or server

2. Wikipedia, *Web browser*, http://en.wikipedia.org/wiki/Web_browser (accessed 31.01.2017).
3. CJEU, *Meltwater*, para. 15.
4. *Ibid.*, para. 16.
5. *Ibid.*, para. 17.

(whether web, File Transfer Protocol, email or other).[6] In the context of mass online use of works, the data in question would correspond to a file that includes a protected work. Examples of relevant acts are downloading and storing films, e-books, and sound recordings from authorised and unauthorised sources on the Internet (e.g., websites, cyberlockers or P2P systems), and making subsequent copies thereof. The result of downloading is that the end-user makes a permanent downstream copy of the work.

Online service providers usually allow their subscribers to make downstream reproductions in a 'mixed form', between streaming and downloading. This model is characterised by the potential to access works offline during the period of subscription (e.g., as happens with Spotify premium playlists) for longer than a short period of time, typically subject to access and use restrictions through TPMs. Such a hybrid model – sometimes presented as an offer of 'lending' services – is more akin to (temporary) downloading than streaming, even where the user does not, strictly speaking, make a 'permanent' copy.[7]

The legal issue at stake with downloading is when and to what extent it is covered by an exclusive right and, if so, whether it is privileged by the private copying limitation.

4.2.3 Streaming

Streaming can be defined as 'a method of transmitting data packets so that the earlier packets can be reassembled and processed before the entire file is downloaded, allowing for immediate display or playback'.[8] In essence, streaming involves downloading a file and subsequently causing the downloaded data to become inaccessible. This feature has caused some technologists to define streaming as a subset of downloading that is 'an implausible and inefficient use of wireless bandwidth'.[9]

It is possible to divide streams into non-interactive/linear and interactive/on-demand. Non-interactive streams are comparable to broadcasts, as they are only available and accessible at a specified time. They include simulcasting, understood as the 'unaltered and simultaneous online retransmission of a TV or radio broadcast', and certain types of linear online streaming in webcasting.[10] For end-users receiving a live stream, the same will be 'split (copied) and sent to multiple consumers through a multicast system'.[11] In contrast, interactive streams are available on demand at a time

6. Wikipedia, *Download*, http://en.wikipedia.org/wiki/Download#cite_note-main-1 (accessed 31.01.2017).
7. Discussing these mixed forms, *see* Depreeuw & Hubin, 2014, pp. 70, 77; Jutte, 2015.
8. Anderson, 2011, p. 168.
9. Doctorow, 2009.
10. SWD CRM Directive 2012, p. 12 (fn. 51), using this terminology.
11. Anderson, 2011, p. 166.

and place chosen by the end-user; they include, for example, certain forms of on demand streaming of films and phonograms (e.g., Netflix and Spotify).[12]

In either case, the streamed copy/performance received is transient and unique to the final user; its later use is dependent upon the availability of the work at the transmitting party or uploader's end.[13] It disappears after the transmission and is retained in a memory medium only as long as required for enjoyment or, depending on the software set-up and the temporary memory capacity of the receiving device, it may be retained for longer than the user's specific 'session'.[14] The legal issue here is whether in these cases a copyright-significant reproduction has occurred.

The implications are different for the individual or service *providing* or *transmitting* the stream. Depending on the technical set-up, linear streams may or may not produce more than transient copies of the content transmitted. In contrast, interactive streams likely require permanent copies in cloud storage, from which content is 'recalled' by end-users, whereupon a unique stream/copy is produced.[15] The legal issues are twofold and relate to whether there are independent copyright-significant (1) reproductions and (2) transmissions in connection to the provision of the stream.

4.2.4 Stream Capture or Ripping

Stream capture or ripping technology works by using a software tool to 'capture, aggregate, and save all streaming data'; it is the 'Internet audio analog of VCR and DVR technology'.[16] Users employing this technology will retain a permanent copy of the protected content streamed. In this way, a stream is turned into a download, giving rise to similar legal issues plus a further issue: the extent to which this technology conflicts with legally protected forms of copy control TPMs.

4.2.5 Uploading

In contrast to downloading, uploading refers to the process of sending or transferring data from a local to a remote system – either a server or a different client – for the purpose of storage of that data.[17] Uploading involves making an upstream permanent reproduction of a work on a remote storage medium, which may be accessible only to the user or a close circle of family

12. *Ibid. See also* SWD CRM Directive 2012, p. 12 (fn. 51).
13. Depreeuw & Hubin, 2014, p. 43 (and fn. 116), defining 'uploader' as the 'person performing the acts of upload that leads to the work being accessible to a public.'
14. Anderson, 2011, p. 166.
15. *Ibid.*
16. Anderson, 2011, pp. 167–168, providing examples of stream capture services and products. *See also* Jutte, 2015, pp. 2–3, discussing 'stream ripping'.
17. Wikipedia, *Upload*, http://en.wikipedia.org/wiki/Upload (accessed 31.01.2017).

and friends (e.g., a cloud locker such as Dropbox), or to the public, as happens with YouTube or most P2P systems. The latter enable technologically sophisticated forms of uploading. For instance, the popular file sharing protocol BitTorrent used by The Pirate Bay platform functions in such a way that a final downloaded version of a file constitutes a combination of contributions from different versions of an identical file uploaded by different users.[18]

The main legal issue with uploading is the legal qualification of the acts of (1) making a copy on the server and (2) subsequent provision of access to protected works, bearing in mind that the purpose of the first is usually to enable the second.

4.2.6 Hyperlinking

Hyperlinking is an umbrella term encompassing similar types of references and means of access to other sources on the web. Hyperlinking can be characterised according to the different techniques employed and includes modalities such as 'deep-linking, framing, inline linking and embedded linking'.[19]

'Standard' hyperlinks are clickable pointers, like text, a thumbnail or other format. Once clicked, the pointers cause the web browser to redirect or 'push' the user to a different 'target' or 'destination' page. A link to a main or homepage is called 'surface' linking, while a link to a sub-page or resource is referred to as 'deep' linking.[20]

'Inline' or 'embedded' links are links where the 'browser transparently fetches material (e.g., image or another web page) and displays it as part of the current page'. In other words, the link does not push the user from the source to the target page. Instead, the content stored in another website is 'pulled' and embedded in the source website, where it appears to users.[21]

In 'framing' links, the original web page address is preserved even when linking to external pages. The content is displayed in such a way as to appear part of the linking site, within a 'frame' (e.g., a pop-up window) and without the need to open a new browser window.

Standard hyperlinks are therefore 'push' links, while the remaining techniques (inline, embedded and framing) are 'pull' links. Because all hyperlinks operate as means to refer to and access other sources online, they

18. See: Rodrigues & Druschel, 2010, for a technical description of P2P systems; Quintais, 2012 (Annex I), for a description of P2P copyright issues; Giblin, 2011, for an analysis of a decade of P2P copyright litigation; and Edstrom & Nilsson, 2009, pp. 483–484, for a description of The Pirate Bay service.
19. Headdon, 2014, pp. 662–668, 662. *See also*: Arezzo, 2014, pp. 526–527; Savola, 2014, p. 280 & n. 10; Tsoutsanis, 2014, pp. 495–509, 496–497.
20. Such links are addressed by the CJEU in *Svensson*.
21. This type of linking to a YouTube video is at stake in CJEU, *BestWater*.

constitute essential reference tools for programmers, online service providers and end-users. These tools are central to the functioning of the Internet.

At the same time, hyperlinks provide an indirect means to make works available online, meaning that they may qualify as a communication to the public under copyright law. The legal status of hyperlinks and the desirability of subjecting them to the copyright regime are debated topics in academia, having given rise to several CJEU judgments and preliminary references.[22]

4.2.7 Digital Adaptations

The making and sharing of adapted versions of works is a daily part of the online practices of end-users.[23] The results of these activities receive different and partially overlapping labels, such as derivative works, 'mash-ups', 'remixes', or 'User Created/Generated Content' (UGC).[24]

UGC is a controversial concept to define and regulate in EU copyright law.[25] It can be defined as content 'published in a specific context that required a certain creative effort and was produced outside of the professional routines and practices'[26] in which 'a pre-existing work is taken by a user as a starting point for his/her own expression … [and is] modified in one way or another to then be made available online'.[27]

There are different types of UGC, across a variety of platforms and distribution models, such as social network sites, wikis, blogs, P2P systems, music and video sharing sites, etc.[28] Among the types of UGC are remixes

22. *See infra* 4.3.2. For discussions in academia, see, e.g., ALAI, 2014, 2015a; Arezzo, 2014; European Copyright Society, 2013; Ginsburg, 2014c; Koolen, 2016; Mezei, 2016; Savola, 2014; Tsoutsanis, 2014.
23. Dougherty, 2006, pp. 430–432; Netanel, 2003, p. 3.
24. On UGC, the 'remix' culture, and their legal, social, and cultural implications, *see* Borgne-Bachschmidt et al., 2008; Lessig, 2008; McLeod & DiCola, 2011; Sinnreich, 2010. *See also*: Gervais, 2009 attempting a taxonomy of UGC divided into user-authored content, user-derived content, and user-copied content; and Triaille et al., 2013, pp. 447–545, for an in depth study of UGC against the EU legal framework.
25. European Commission, 2013, pp. 28–29, describing the setting up of a specific Working Group on this issue in the framework of the 'Licences for Europe' stakeholder dialogue, on which '[n]o consensus was reached among participating stakeholders on either the problems to be addressed or the results or even the definition of UGC … In any event, practical solutions to ease user-generated content and facilitate micro-licensing for small users were pledged by rightholders across different sectors as a result of the 'Licences for Europe' discussions'. *See also* European Commission, 2014, pp. 67–71, on the responses to the public consultation regarding UGC.
26. OECD, Vickery & Wunsch-Vincent, 2007. Wider definitions encompass smaller contributions which require less creative effort, such as 'posting to a blog or uploading a self-made photo to a website'. *See* Esmeijer, Nieuwenhuis, Mijs & Versloot, 2012.
27. Triaille et al., 2013, p. 452, excluding from the definition works created without basis on a pre-existing work ('creation from scratch') and the mere online dissemination of pre-existing works ('mere upload case').
28. Triaille et al., 2013, pp. 453–454.

or mash-ups, terms that usually refer to creative new works produced 'through changing and combining portions of existing works'.[29]

In this chapter, all these terms are included under the shorthand 'digital adaptations'. The concept includes the use of pre-existing works and their manipulation – modification, changing and combination – through software editing tools, leading to the creation of a new and distinguishable digital object (which may qualify as a protected derivative work or adaptation), and its subsequent making available over the Internet. Furthermore, only digital adaptations made by individuals for non-commercial purposes are considered in this context.

The degree of distinction or transformation of the pre-existing work in an adaptation varies. As used herein, the concept requires a low threshold of creativity and includes 'merely adding, subtracting or associating some pre-existing content with other pre-existing content'.[30] Furthermore, while in some adaptations the pre-existing work (or part thereof) is easily recognisable, in others the copyright inputs are difficult to discern.

The purpose of the adaptation may also vary, including personal enjoyment, caricature, parody, pastiche, criticism, commentary, creative expression, quotation, etc.[31] Mere technical adaptations, such as 'format-shifting' are outside the concept and fall squarely within the scope of the right of reproduction.[32]

The issues that arise regarding this type of use relate to the legal qualification of the acts involved in digital adaptations: the reproduction of the borrowed pre-existing works; the adaptation and preparation of derivatives from those works; and the follow-on making available of the works to the public via online platforms (e.g., YouTube or Vimeo).

4.3 HOW DOES THE BUNDLE OF EXCLUSIVE RIGHTS IN THE *ACQUIS* APPLY TO MASS ONLINE USE OF WORKS BY INDIVIDUALS?

International and EU law define broad exclusive rights that extend to online use. The BC sets forth minimum standards for the economic rights of translation, reproduction, public performance, broadcasting, public recitation, and adaptation.[33] Online acts by end-users might call into question the application of the BC rights of reproduction, communication to the public

29. The Department of Commerce and Internet Policy Task Force, 2013, p. 28.
30. Triaille et al., 2013, p. 455, making this clarification in order to draw a distinction with other UGC definitions which require a high degree of creativity.
31. For an in depth analysis of the music UGC, remix and mash-up genre, see: Borgne-Bachschmidt et al., 2008; Menell, 2015.
32. Triaille et al., 2013, p. 453.
33. See, respectively, Arts 8, 9, 11, 11*bis*, 11*ter* and 12 BC.

(i.e., public performance and recitation), and adaptation, as incorporated or adapted to the digital age by the WCT and WPPT.

The latter treaties include, under the purview of the public communication right, the so-called making available right, which applies in the context of interactive, on demand situations.[34] In what has been termed the 'umbrella solution', treaty members have flexibility as to the manner of implementation of this right.[35]

The WIPO Treaties were implemented in the EU by the InfoSoc Directive, which harmonised several economic rights and adapted them to the digital age.[36] The harmonised rights are reproduction, communication to the public, making available to the public, and distribution.[37] The most significant right not harmonised at EU level is the right of adaptation, although different manifestations of the same can be found in the BC and national laws.[38]

In EU law, and with the exception of distribution, these rights are susceptible of application to mass online use of copyright-protected works by individuals. The distribution right solely controls 'distribution of the work incorporated in a tangible article' and is subject to exhaustion under Article 4(2) InfoSoc Directive.[39] Hence, as a rule, this right does not apply online.

There is at least one derogation to this general rule. In its landmark *UsedSoft* judgment, the CJEU recognised the possibility of exhaustion in relation to computer programs in specific circumstances.[40] The Court ruled that the right of distribution of a copy of a software program is exhausted if the copyright holder who authorised the downloading of that copy from the Internet onto a data carrier also conferred a licence to use that copy for an unlimited period. The first lawful acquirer can rely on that exhaustion to resell their copy and unlimited licence to a subsequent acquirer. However, each reseller must make their own copy unusable at the time of its resale. Maintaining the copy would constitute an unauthorised reproduction.[41]

34. Arts 8 WCT, 10 and 14 WPPT.
35. Ficsor, 2003b, p. 209, P. Masouyé, 2009, pp. 217–221. For the situation in the US, see, e.g., U.S. Copyright Office, 2014.
36. Recital 15 InfoSoc Directive.
37. Arts 2, 3, and 4 InfoSoc Directive.
38. Hugenholtz & Senftleben, 2011, pp. 26–27. Manifestations of the right of adaptation can be found in Arts 8, 12 and 14 BC. In US law, this right is equivalent to the right to prepare derivative works (a work based on or derived from one or more pre-existing works), protected under ss 101 and 106(2) US Copyright Act. On which, *see* Menell, 2011; Samuelson, 2013.
39. *See* recitals 28 and 29, Art. 3(3) InfoSoc Directive, barring exhaustion of the right of communication to the public of works and right of making available to the public other subject-matter.
40. *See* CJEU, *UsedSoft*.
41. CJEU, *UsedSoft*, paras 70–72, 88.

There has been much academic debate on the potential extension of *UsedSoft* to other subject matter, in particular e-books.[42] In his opinion in the *VOB* case, Advocate General (AG) Szpunar contributed to the debate by stating that the public lending right 'includes the making available to the public of electronic books by libraries for a limited period of time.'[43] In the AG's view, online lending of books by libraries should be allowed, provided the making available of the e-book was first authorised by the rights holder and the book was obtained from lawful sources.[44]

The CJEU largely followed this view, but clearly delimited the scope of application of the concept of lending. According to the Court, the concept 'covers the lending of a digital copy of a book, where that lending is carried out by placing that copy on the server of a public library and allowing a user to reproduce that copy by downloading it onto his own computer, bearing in mind that only one copy may be downloaded during the lending period and that, after that period has expired, the downloaded copy can no longer be used by that user.'[45] The Court further noted that Member States can restrict this possibility to situations where the digital copy in question was first sold or distributed by or with the consent of the rights holder.[46] Furthermore, it added, the public lending limitation does not apply 'to the making available by a public library of a digital copy of a book in the case where that copy was obtained from an unlawful source.'[47]

On this basis, it is doubtful that digital exhaustion is possible outside the realm of the specific subject matter of software or the lending of electronic books, with the restrictions set out by the Court. To this point, the judgment in *Art & Allposters* clarified that the right of distribution in Article 4 InfoSoc Directive can only be exhausted in relation to the tangible support of a work, and is not subject to digital exhaustion.[48] This conclusion is supported by the AG and the Court in *VOB*, who interpret the concept of public lending as separate from the right of distribution and the commercial rental of subject matter other than books.[49] This reading is also consistent with the judgment in *Ranks/Vasiļevičs*, where despite its previous ruling in *UseSoft*, the Court found that lawful acquirers of computer programs are not allowed to resell

42. See, e.g., Leistner, 2014, pp. 574–585; Linklater, 2014; Rubí Puig, 2013.
43. *Opinion AG in VOB*, para. 80. Art. 2(1)(b) Rental Right Directive defines 'lending' as the 'making available for use, for a limited period of time and not for direct or indirect economic or commercial advantage, when it is made through establishments which are accessible to the public.'
44. *Opinion AG in VOB*, para. 88.
45. CJEU, *VOB*, para. 54.
46. *Ibid.*, para. 65.
47. *Ibid.*, para. 72.
48. CJEU, *Art & Allposters*, paras 34–40.
49. *Opinion AG in VOB*, paras 74–78; CJEU, *VOB*, paras 27–65.

back-up copies of such programs without the authorisation of the copyright owner.[50] In this light, the present chapter does not further examine the right of distribution.[51]

Having identified the relevant harmonised rights, the next step is to apply them to the typology of online uses developed in the previous section. The analysis focuses first on the right of reproduction (4.3.1) and then on the right of communication to the public (4.3.2).

4.3.1 Uses Covered by the Right of Reproduction

4.3.1.1 Legal Framework

International copyright law provides for an exclusive reproduction right with broad application in the digital environment. The right arguably includes all forms of incidental, transient or technical copies.[52] Article 9(1) BC grants authors the exclusive right of authorising the reproduction of works 'in any matter or form'.[53] Article 1(4) WCT stipulates that the 'Contracting Parties shall comply with Articles 1–21 and the Appendix of the Berne Convention', and the corresponding Agreed Statement qualifies 'the storage of a protected work in digital form in an electronic medium' as a reproduction within the meaning of Article 9 BC.[54]

This represents a paradigm shift for Internet users as compared to the physical world. Because the nature of communication networks and devices technically requires acts of reproduction and transmission, most consumptive uses of works – like acts of personal enjoyment – are now potentially subject to copyright, unless privileged by a limitation. The same conclusion applies to acts of online service providers.

In the EU, the InfoSoc Directive has implemented the WIPO Treaties as part of the so-called 'Digital Agenda', with the express aim of horizontally harmonising several economic rights and adjusting them to the digital age, thus improving 'the means to fight piracy worldwide'.[55] The implementation,

---

50. CJEU, *Ranks/Vasiļevičs*, para. 57.
51. N.B. this exclusion is applicable to EU law. The matter may be different under other national laws, such as in the US, where the WCT/WPPT umbrella solution enabled the application of distribution to on-demand downloads. *See* U.S. Copyright Office, 2014
52. von Lewinski, 2005, p. 5.
53. In the context of related rights, the reproduction right is provided for in Arts 7, 10 and 13 RC.
54. The Agreed Statements to Arts 7 and 11 WPPT contain similar provisions for performances and phonograms.
55. Recital 15 InfoSoc Directive. *See* Ohly, 2009, pp. 212, 214, noting that 'vertical harmonization' of the reproduction right had occurred for specific subject matter in the context of Arts 4(a) Software Directive, 5(a) Database Directive, and Art. 7 of the repealed 1992 version of the Rental Right Directive (in respect of related rights).

consistent with an international trend, contemplates in Article 2 a broad reproduction right for authors and related rights owners: performers, phonogram producers, film producers, and broadcasting organisations.[56]

Performers and broadcasters have a specific right of first fixation, meaning that the general reproduction right applies only to the reproductions of those fixations.[57] This distinction should not affect the assessment of the activities of Internet users, as they generally relate to digital copies of first fixations.

The scope of the right is comprehensive. It includes the prohibition of any direct or indirect, temporary or permanent reproduction by any means and in any form, in the whole or in part, of the works or subject matter of rights holders, with the exception of software and databases.[58] This generous scope results in part from the letter of the provision and the related recitals, which require a broad definition of the acts covered by the right. It also results from the CJEU's expansive reading of Article 2 – in cases like *Infopaq I*, *Infopaq II*, *Murphy*, and *SAS* – and strict reading of exceptions (more on which below).[59]

As a result, the right increasingly applies to online dissemination of content, of which reproduction is an essential constituent. In fact, the current understanding of the right is technical, meaning 'in practice … a reproduction in the technical sense, a 'copy', is equated to a reproduction in the legal sense',[60] irrespective 'of the function or the economic value of the copy'.[61] Importantly, some of the activities that trigger the exclusive right may be covered by a limitation to that right under Article 5 InfoSoc Directive.

56. Art. 2 InfoSoc Directive. *See* Ohly, 2009, p. 217, noting that recitals 9 and 11 InfoSoc Directive seem to favour a 'in dubio pro autore' interpretation of the right.
57. Under Art. 7 Rental Right Directive ('fixation right'). *See* Ohly, 2009, pp. 214–215, raising formal and substantive objections to this legislative technique.
58. *See* Art. 1(a) and (e) InfoSoc Directive. Arts 2–5 of this directive do not apply to software and databases, which are subject to special provisions in Arts 4–6 Software Directive and 5–6 Database Directive.
59. *See* recital 21 InfoSoc Directive and Leistner, 2014. For examples of CJEU interpretation, *see* e.g.: CJEU, *Infopaq I*, applying such a broad interpretation; CJEU, *Infopaq II*, narrowly interpreting exemptions for temporary acts of reproduction; CJEU, *Murphy*, interpreting the reproduction right in Art. 2(a) InfoSoc Directive as extending to transient fragments of the works within the memory of a satellite decoder and on a television screen, although exempting such acts under Art. 5(1); CJEU, *SAS*, interpreting Art. 2(a) 'as meaning that the reproduction, in a computer program or a user manual for that program, of certain elements described in the user manual for another computer program protected by copyright is capable of constituting an infringement of the copyright in the latter manual if … that reproduction constitutes the expression of the intellectual creation of the author of the user manual for the computer program protected by copyright'.
60. Triaille et al., 2013, p. 120.
61. Depreeuw & Hubin, 2014, p. 41.

4.3.1.2 Application to Activities of Internet Users

In light of this broad scope, the question is what types of use trigger the reproduction right? It is possible to divide these into uses clearly covered by the right and uses for which there is no legal certainty.

In the first group – clear cases – are all those that involve a permanent copy: downloading, stream capture, permanent copies made for the provision of interactive streams, uploading to the cloud, and uploading to a publicly accessible server. As noted in Table 4.1 below, some of these reproductions may be covered by a limitation, namely private copying in Article 5(2)(b) InfoSoc Directive.

The second group refers to legal uncertainty cases. These cases include, first, online activities of end-users that involve the making of temporary copies, such as browsing and copies made during the reception of linear or on-demand streams. These activities, as we shall see later in this chapter, may be covered by the mandatory limitation for temporary and transient copying in Article 5(1) InfoSoc Directive (*see* Table 4.1)

A second set of unclear cases involves online activities of end-users that may trigger not only the right of reproduction, but also other exclusive rights, giving rise to issues of *overlap* between different rights. These overlaps raise the question of which right or rights apply to the individual use at stake. One such issue relates to the overlap between the rights of reproduction and making available, and is visible in activities such as uploading of a file containing a work to a publicly accessible server.[62] Another issue relates to overlaps between the right of reproduction and the non-harmonised right of adaptation, and comes into play when assessing the legal status of digital adaptations, such as UGC. In the latter cases, it is possible that the use in question is privileged by copyright limitations to the reproduction right susceptible of application to certain types of adaptations, namely quotation, incidental use, or parody, in Article 5(2)(d), (i) or (k) InfoSoc Directive.

Table 4.1 provides a summary of the acts of Internet users covered by the exclusive right of reproduction pursuant to this categorisation. Section 4.4 below analyses which of these uses may be covered by exceptions and limitations to the exclusive right, such as those for temporary and transient copying (4.4.2) and private copying (4.4.3), and those applicable to reproductions made during the course of preparation or dissemination of digital adaptations (4.4.4).

62. For a study on the relationship between these exclusive rights, *see* Depreeuw & Hubin, 2014, pp. 40–106. This dissertation does not deal with issues of overlap between exclusive rights.

Table 4.1 Scope of Online Reproduction Right and Legal Certainty Issues

Type of Online Use	*Reproduction Right*	*Legal Certainty Issues*
Downloading	Yes	Application of limitation in Article 5(2)(b) InfoSoc Directive
Stream capture	Yes	Application of limitation in Article 5(2)(b) InfoSoc Directive
Copying for provision of interactive streams	Yes	Overlap with making available right
Uploading file to Cloud locker or server not accessible to the public	Yes	Application of limitation in Article 5(2)(b) InfoSoc Directive
Browsing	?	Application of limitation in Article 5(1) InfoSoc Directive
Reception of linear or on-demand stream	?	Application of limitation in Article 5(1) InfoSoc Directive
Uploading to a publicly accessible server	Yes	Overlap with making available right
Copies made in the preparation or making available of a digital adaptation	Yes	Overlap with making available right. Application of limitations in Article 5(2)(d), (i) or (k) InfoSoc Directive

4.3.2 Uses Covered by the Right of Communication to the Public

4.3.2.1 Legal Framework

At the international level, the BC divides the right of communication to the public into specific rights to perform, broadcast and recite.[63] Article 8 WCT extends the BC's subject matter and scope to the right of making works available to the public 'in such a way that members of the public may access these works from a place and at a time individually chosen by them', thus effectively including interactive and on-demand transmissions under copyright's umbrella.[64]

Article 3(1) InfoSoc Directive implements the WCT by granting authors a broad exclusive right to:

63. Goldstein & Hugenholtz, 2013, pp. 317–318.

64. *Ibid.*, p. 318. Arts 10 and 14 WPPT respectively contain identical provisions for performers and phonogram producers.

authorise or prohibit any communication to the public of their works, by wire or wireless means, including the making available to the public of their works in such a way that members of the public may access them from a place and at a time individually chosen by them.

The right, which must be interpreted broadly, covers online and offline acts.[65] According to recital 23 InfoSoc Directive, it includes the 'transmission or retransmission of a work to the public by wire or wireless means, including broadcasting', but 'should not cover any other acts'. To this effect, the CJEU has clarified that the provision cannot be construed as allowing Member States to give 'wider protection to copyright holders by laying down that the concept of communication to the public includes a wider range of activities than those referred to in that provision'.[66]

Article 3(2) InfoSoc Directive gives related rights holders a narrower right of 'making available'. This is because the InfoSoc Directive's right does not affect categories of communication to the public regulated elsewhere in the *acquis*, such as broadcasting of programmes by satellite, and cable retransmission.[67] However, the provision does not prevent national legislation from extending the exclusive right as regards (linear) acts of communication to the public online, 'provided that such an extension does not undermine the protection of copyright'.[68]

As a whole, Article 3 InfoSoc Directive covers communication at a distance, thus excluding from the scope of the right direct representation or performance.[69] The 'making available' prong refers to interactive 'on-demand' services. It does not require simultaneous reception of the work by the public and is independent of whether, where and how often the work is accessed. Hence, the right applies to access by users to a website, even if at a different time and place from the original communication.[70] Importantly, neither the right of communication nor making available is subject to exhaustion.[71]

---

65. *See* recital 23 InfoSoc Directive. See: CJEU, *ITV Broadcasting*, para. 20 (and case law cited therein); CJEU, *OSA*, para. 23; CJEU, *SBS*, para. 14; CJEU, *Reha Training*, para. 36.
66. CJEU, *Svensson*, paras 37, 41. To go above this ceiling would undermine the directive's objectives of remedying legislative differences and legal uncertainty vis-à-vis copyright protection, in a way that adversely affects the functioning of the internal market.
67. *See* Art. 4 SatCab Directive and Art. 8 Rental Right Directive, which remain applicable by virtue of Art. 1(2)(b) and (c) InfoSoc Directive.
68. *See* CJEU, *C More Entertainment*, paras 22–37, referring to broadcasts of sporting fixtures made live on the Internet under Art. 3(2)(d) InfoSoc Directive.
69. *See* recital 23 InfoSoc Directive and Common Position (EC) No. 48/2000. *See also* Ohly, 2009, p. 225.
70. Recital 25 InfoSoc Directive. *See* e.g. CJEU, *SCF*, para. 59; *C More Entertainment*, para. 26.
71. Art. 3(3) and recital 29 InfoSoc Directive. N.B. since the judgements in *Coditel I* and *II*, the CJEU has considered communication to the public to be a service and, therefore, not subject to exhaustion.

There is a vast CJEU case law on the right of communication to the public in the InfoSoc, SatCab and Rental Right Directives.[72] From these judgments it has emerged that 'communication to the public' is an autonomous concept of EU law.[73] Consequently the concept should be given the same meaning and interpreted according to the same criteria whether it is used in the context of the InfoSoc Directive (in connection to an exclusive right) or the Rental Right Directive (in connection to a remuneration right).[74] The concept of communication to the public involves a wide array of activities. These include the transmission of broadcasts in hotel rooms, spas, circuses, public places, and dental practices, as well as different aspects of communication to the public by satellite.[75]

Several recent judgments elucidate the scope of the right in the online environment. They refer to activities such as the 'live streaming' or broadcasting by a third party over the Internet of signals from commercial television broadcasters (*ITV Broadcasting*), the provision of 'clickable links' giving access to protected works (*Svensson*), the provision of framing links to protected works (*BestWater*), the direct broadcast of a sporting fixture on an Internet site (*C More Entertainment*), and the provision of hyperlinks giving access to protected works accessible on another website without the rightholder's consent (*GS Media*). In addition, a number of preliminary references address the application of Article 3(1) InfoSoc Directive to different hyperlinking scenarios (*Filmspeler and Stichting Brein v. Ziggo*).[76]

Taken together, these judgments and references illustrate how the concept of communication to the public follows the evolution of modes of exploitation of works and subject matter, and grows ever more intricate.[77] They also allow the identification of the three main criteria used to assess the

72. These cases are, in chronological order: *EGEDA I*, *Lagardère*, *SGAE*, *Airfield*, *Organismos Sillogikis*, *Murphy*, *Circul Globus*, *PPI*, *ITV Broadcasting*, *Svensson*, *OSA*, *BestWater* (Order), *Sociedade Portuguesa de Autores* (Order), *C More Entertainment*, *SBS*, *Reha Training*, and *GS Media*. Regarding the admissibility of Orders in the context of references for preliminary ruling, *see* Art. 99 of the Rules of Procedure of the Court of Justice.
73. CJEU, *SGAE*, para. 31.
74. CJEU, *Reha Training*, paras 27–34.
75. On transmissions in hotels, see: CJEU, *EGEDA I*: CJEU, *SGAE*; CJEU, *Organismos Sillogikis*; CJEU, *PPI*; CJEU, *Sociedade Portuguesa de Autores*. On transmissions in a circus, *see* CJEU, *Circul Globus*. On transmissions in a spa establishment, *see* CJEU, *OSA*. On transmissions in the premises of a rehabilitation centre, *see Reha Training*. On transmissions in a public place (a pub), *see* CJEU, *Murphy*. On transmissions in a dental practice, *see* CJEU, *SCF*. Judgments involving different aspects of communication to the public by satellite include: CJEU, *Lagardère*; CJEU, *Airfield*; CJEU, *SBS*.
76. *See* CJEU, Reference for Preliminary Ruling, Case C-160/15, *GS Media*, and *Opinion AG GS Media*; CJEU, Reference for Preliminary Ruling, Case C-527/15, *Filmspeler*, and CJEU, Reference for Preliminary Ruling, Case C-610/15, *Stichting Brein v. Ziggo*. On the first case, *see Opinion AG in Filmspeler*.
77. *See* Lucie Guibault & Quintais, 2014.

concept in EU law.[78] First, the existence of an act of communication. This criterion includes the sub-criteria of the *intervention of the user* – which the Court sometimes refers to as 'the indispensable role of the user and the deliberate nature of its intervention'[79] –, and the *sufficiency of transmission or availability*. Second, whether the communication is made to the public, including the assessment of the concepts of *new public* and *separate or specific technical means*.[80] Third, the profit-making nature of the communication. The first two criteria are essential and cumulative.[81] The third criterion, as well as some of the sub-criteria discussed, does not appear to be determinative in the eyes of the Court. Despite their different relative weight, these criteria have been classified as 'complementary'; 'not autonomous' but 'interdependent'.[82] As the Court puts it, 'those criteria may, in different situations, be present to widely varying degrees, [*and*] they must be applied both individually and in their interaction with one another'.[83]

The following paragraphs explain each criterion to the extent required to understand the scope of the right in the online environment. The focus is on the InfoSoc Directive and the authors' right of communication to the public. As a preliminary remark, it is noted that the CJEU sometimes relies on international treaties for the interpretation of different communication to the public rights in the *acquis*. Illustrations of this method are patent in *SGAE* (interpreting Article 3(1) InfoSoc Directive in light of Article 11*bis*(1)(ii) BC), *Murphy* (relying on Article 11*bis* BC), *Circul Globus* (explaining the concept of communication at a distance through Article 11(1) BC) and *SCF* (excluding direct effect of international treaties due to their lack of precision).[84]

4.3.2.1.1 An 'Act of Communication'

The InfoSoc Directive does not define the notion of 'communication', but some CJEU cases help to clarify its meaning. The Court's view largely relies

78. On the need for an 'individual assessment' of the concept in Art. 8(2) Rental Rights Directive *see* CJEU, *PPI*, para. 29 (and case law cited). On the notion that the concept has the same scope in the InfoSoc Directive, *see* CJEU, *Reha Training*, para. 33.
79. CJEU, *GS Media*, para. 35 and case law cited therein.
80. N.B. AG Bot identifies four criteria as he considers the 'new' character of the public and an independent third criterion. *See Opinion AG Reha Training*, para 44.
81. *See* e.g. CJEU, *Svensson*, para. 16; CJEU *ITV Broadcasting*, paras 21, 31; CJEU, *SBS*, para. 15. See, by analogy regarding Art. 3(2) InfoSoc Directive, CJEU, *C More Entertainment*, para. 25; CJEU, *Reha Training*, para. 37; CJEU, *GS Media*, para. 32.
82. CJEU, *SCF*, para. 79; CJEU, *Reha Training*, para. 35; *Opinion AG Reha Training*, paras. 29–35; CJEU, *GS Media*, paras. 33–34.
83. CJEU, *GS Media*, para. 31 and case law cited therein.
84. See, respectively, *SGAE*, para. 35, *Murphy*, paras 200–203, *Circul Globus*, paras 35–36, and *SCF*, paras 46, 48. For an early reference to the principles of the BC in the interpretation of this exclusive right in the *acquis*, *see Opinion AG in EGEDA I*, paras 5–7, 15.

on a broad interpretation of the exclusive right in light of the objective of a 'high level of protection'. The result is the inclusion of a comprehensive variety of acts within the notion of communication.[85]

In essence, a communication occurs when a work is transmitted or made available in such a way that members of the public may access it. This seems to imply two elements: first, an intentional or deliberate intervention by the user to make the communication and, second, the sufficiency of transmitting or making the work available, as opposed to requiring its actual and subsequent reception or access.

The first aspect – *intentional or deliberate intervention* – means that a user (the person or entity using a means of communication) will carry out an act of communication when they knowingly intervene to provide their customers access to a work, for example through a broadcast. Without that intervention, the customers, although physically within the area covered by the broadcast, would not otherwise be able to enjoy the broadcast work.[86] In other words, to qualify as a 'communication' the intervention must be more than a mere technical means that ensures or improves the communication.[87] The focus is therefore on the indispensable role of the user and deliberate nature of its intervention.[88]

The Court uses this notion of intervention in a flexible and far-reaching manner, applying it to the activities of users in diverse settings. These include the transmission of football matches in a pub on a television screen (*Murphy*), and the broadcasting of films or music in hotel rooms (*SGAE*, *PPI*), in a circus (*Circul Globus*), or in the waiting room of a dental practice (*SCF*).

An example of the Court's extensive approach is evident in *ITV Broadcasting*. The case analysed whether an Internet retransmission qualifies as a 'communication'. The Court considered that the service provided by TV Catch-up amounts to a separate act of transmission or retransmission of a work through a specific technical means. In supporting this conclusion, the Court argued that TV Catch-up's 'intervention' goes beyond the provision of a mere technical means to ensure or improve reception of the original transmission in its catchment area.[89]

On the other hand, a communication occurs independently of whether the public actually receives or accesses the work. In *SGAE*, for example, this meant that a communication to the public occurred even if customers did not

---

85. Recitals 9, 10, and 23 InfoSoc Directive. Confirming this broad interpretation of the concept of 'communication to the public', see: CJEU, *SGAE*, para. 36; CJEU, *Murphy*, para 186; CJEU, *Circul Globus*, para. 33; CJEU, *ITV Broadcasting*, para. 20; CJEU, *Svensson*, para. 17; CJEU, *OSA*, para. 23; CJEU, *SBS*, para. 14.
86. CJEU, *SGAE*, para. 42; CJEU, *Organismos Sillogikis*, para. 38, CJEU, *Murphy*, para. 195; CJEU, *SCF*, para. 82; CJEU, *PPI*, para. 31.
87. CJEU, *SGAE*, para. 42, CJEU, *Murphy*, para. 194.
88. CJEU, *GS Media*, para. 34 and case law cited therein.
89. CJEU, *ITV Broadcasting*, paras 28–30.

switch on the television and had not actually accessed the works.[90] In *Svensson*, the Court considered that the provision of direct access to the work via a link from one website to another constitutes an act of 'making available' and, therefore, a 'communication to the public'.[91]

On this point, the AG in *GS Media* disagreed with *Svensson*. He argued that where a link points to a freely accessible work it is merely facilitating the access thereto; the 'actual 'making available' was the action by the person who effected the initial communication'.[92] The key to establishing an act of communication, he continued, is whether the intervention of the linker is 'vital or indispensable in order to benefit from or enjoy works'.[93] Because the work is already freely accessible, the link does not constitute an indispensable intervention and is therefore not an act of communication to the public.[94]

Whether an act of 'transmission' of the work is required for there to be a communication seems to hinge on the interactive or linear nature of the act. Thus, *Svensson* does not require that a transmission occurs for there to be an act of communication, which is consistent as a matter of law with the making available prong of the right of communication to the public.[95] It has been argued that such a view is also consistent with a broad interpretation of the right, aimed at providing a high level of protection to rights holders and ensuring that the concept of 'act of communication' retains sufficient flexibility to survive technological obsolescence.[96]

However, this approach is not followed by the CJEU in relation to non-interactive/linear acts of communication, whether or not over the Internet. In fact, judgments involving these types of communication appear to require a 'transmission' of the protected works, irrespective of the technical means or process used.[97]

---

90. See, e.g., CJEU, *SGAE*, para. 43.
91. CJEU *Svensson*, paras 19-20.
92. *Opinion AG in GS Media*, para. 54.
93. *Ibid.*, paras 55–57 (cit. para. 57). On this point, the AG relied on CJEU, *Murphy*, paras 195–196.
94. *Opinion AG in GS Media*, paras 58–62, noting that this interpretation makes the analysis of the new public criterion unnecessary.
95. *See* Leistner, 2015, pp. 632–633: 'the mere possibility of access for members of the public will suffice even if they do not specifically make use of that opportunity'. *See also* Mezei, 2016, p. 788: ' … it is irrelevant [*for the right of making available*] whether or not access has actually been obtained.' *But see* Computer & Communications Industry Association, 2016; European Copyright Society, 2013, arguing on the basis of the *travaux préparatoires* of the InfoSoc Directive for the necessity of an act of 'transmission' for the copyright qualification of the use.
96. *Opinion AG in GS Media*, paras 48–52.
97. CJEU, *Murphy*, para 193, CJEU, *ITV Broadcasting*, paras 28–30; CJEU, *OSA*, para. 25, CJEU, *SBS*, para. 16; CJEU, *Reha Training*, paras 37–39. N.B. that no reception of the transmission is required.

4.3.2.1.2 Communication to the 'Public'

The second cumulative criterion is that an act of communication is made to the 'public'. The CJEU considers that this concept must be construed similarly across the InfoSoc, SatCab and Rental Right Directives.[98]

The Court interprets 'public' as including an 'indeterminate' and 'fairly large number' of recipients as potential beneficiaries of the communication.[99] The concept further contains a *de minimis* threshold, which rules out groups of persons that are too small or insignificant.[100] To determine that threshold, it is necessary to consider the 'cumulative effects of making works available to potential audiences', taking into consideration the number of persons having access to the same work at the same time and in succession.[101] Clearly, this threshold filters out communications of a work or subject matter that are 'private', in the sense that they occur within a delimited circle of family or friends.[102] Whether the concept of private encompasses all non-public acts is unclear.

As noted, the exclusive right only includes communications to a public at a distance, i.e., not present at the place of origin of the act.[103] Beyond that distance element, the Court sometimes requires that the public must be 'targeted by the user and receptive, in one way or another, to that communication, and not merely 'caught' by chance'.[104]

Finally, as a derogation to the principle that the concept of 'public' should have a similar construction in copyright and related rights, *SCF* establishes a distinction between these two fields. This case established that the 'public' does not include patients in a waiting room of a dental practice. To explain the exclusion, the Court states rather opaquely that those patients,

98. CJEU, *Murphy*, paras 187–188: ' … given the requirements of unity of the European Union legal order and its coherence, the concepts used by that body of directives must have the same meaning, unless the European Union legislature has, in a specific legislative context, expressed a different intention'.
99. CJEU, *Mediakabel*, para. 30, CJEU, *Lagárdere*, para. 31 *SGAE*, para. 38, CJEU, *SCF*, para. 84; CJEU, *ITV Broadcasting*, para. 32; CJEU, *OSA*, para. 27; CJEU, *SBS*, para. 22; CJEU, *Reha Training*, para. 41; CJEU, *GS Media*, para. 36. In applying this definition, the Court has found the concept of public to exclude 'persons who can receive the signals from the satellite only if they use professional equipment' (in *Lagardère*), and transmissions from a broadcasting organisation to specified signal distributors without potential viewers being able to access those signals (in *SBS*). Cf. CJEU, *Lagardère*, para. 31; CJEU, *SBS*, paras 22–23.
100. CJEU, *SCF*, para. 84; CJEU, *Reha Training*, para. 43.
101. CJEU, *SGAE*, para. 39; CJEU, *PPI*, para. 35, CJEU, *ITV Broadcasting*, para. 33; CJEU, *OSA*, para. 28; CJEU, *Reha Training*, para. 44.
102. *See infra* 4.4.3.1, for the definition of 'private use'. *See also* CJEU, *SCF*, para. 86, and CJEU, *Reha Training*, para. 42, excluding from the concept communications of works to 'specific individuals belonging to a private group'.
103. CJEU, *Murphy*, paras 200, 203. CJEU, *Circul Globus*, paras 36, 37, 40.
104. CJEU, *SCF*, para. 91; CJEU, *PPI*, para. 37. *But see Opinion AG in Reha Training*, paras 66–68, giving less weight to this aspect.

albeit forming 'a very consistent group of persons and thus … a determinate circle of potential recipients', are in reality a 'very limited' or 'insignificant' number of persons; as such, they do not meet the standard of 'persons in general' required to qualify as a 'public'.[105]

As explained below, this conclusion must be understood in light of the 'profit-making nature' criterion and the type of right it applies to: a non-exclusive right of equitable remuneration. This much is confirmed in *OSA*, where the Court justifies the different treatment of related rights on the nature of the right.[106] For some authors, this pronouncement is both a blessing and a curse. A blessing, because it limits the effects of the questionable interpretation in *SCF*. A curse, as it leads to unequal treatment of related rights holders.[107]

Having explained the definition of 'public', the CJEU then adds two alternative sub-criteria to define whether there is a communication to the public.[108] According to the first sub-criterion, the right applies if the communication of a work is made through separate or different technical means as compared to the original communication.[109] Alternatively, the right applies if the work is communicated to a 'new public'.[110]

Both sub-criteria are relevant for the application of the exclusive right in the online environment, and therefore deserve further scrutiny. However, it is worth noting in advance the remarkable fact that neither sub-criterion has a clear basis in international or EU copyright law. Instead, they are creations of the Court.[111]

4.3.2.1.3 Specific Technical Means

According to the CJEU, an act of communication to the public is restricted under the exclusive right if it is made through a 'specific technical means'. In essence, this criterion is meant to safeguard situations where the act of communication of works to the public is made through different technologies, regardless of whether it reaches a new public.

For example, where a primary communication of a work occurs through satellite broadcasting and the secondary communication over the Internet, the targeted public may be the same but the technical means not. Conversely, 'on the internet all potential and different forms of communication appear to

105. CJEU, *SCF*, paras 84–85, 95–96. It is possible that the Court here is making a reference to the *de minimis* threshold of the concept of 'public'.
106. CJEU, *OSA*, paras 34–35. *See also* CJEU, *SCF*, para 74. *See infra* 4.3.2.1.3.
107. Leistner, 2015, pp. 633–637.
108. *See* CJEU, *GS Media*, para. 37 and case law cited.
109. CJEU, *ITV Broadcasting*, para. 39.
110. CJEU, *SGAE*, paras 37–38, 40, 42.
111. Cf. ALAI, 2014, arguing that both criteria are contrary to international law, and Velze, 2015, pp. 71–72, concluding similarly vis-à-vis the 'new public' criterion.

constitute the same technical means in the opinion of the CJEU.'[112] The criterion first appears in *ITV Broadcasting* and is restated in *SBS*.

The first judgment concerned the distribution of television broadcasts over the Internet, substantially in real time. TV Catch-up offered a service allowing users to receive through the Internet 'live' streams of free-to-air television broadcasts, including those transmitted by ITV. However, users could only access content which they were legally entitled to watch under a UK television licence.[113]

The Court first determined the Internet retransmission to be an 'act of communication' because TV Catch-up's service amounts to a separate act of transmission or retransmission of a work through a specific technical means. TV Catch-up's intervention went beyond the provision of a mere technical means to ensure or improve reception of the original transmission in its catchment area.[114]

Second, this communication is to a 'public', understood as an indeterminate number of potential recipients, implying a fairly large number of persons, considering the number of persons who have simultaneous and successive access to the same work.[115] TV Catch-up's Internet retransmissions were aimed at all UK residents with an Internet connection and valid television licences. As these users could simultaneously access the live streaming of television programmes online, the Court considered there was a communication to the public.[116]

Because the Internet retransmission was a separate act requiring an independent authorisation – due to specific technical conditions, means and intended public –, it was not necessary to examine the new public requirement.[117] It was also not necessary, for the qualification of the act, to analyse other complementary *non-essential* elements, such as the profit-making nature of the activity or the level of competition between the third party and the original broadcaster.[118] *SBS* later confirmed this interpretation when stating that 'every transmission or retransmission of a work which uses a specific technical means must, as a rule, be individually authorised by the author of the work in question.'[119]

---

112. Leistner, 2015, p. 634, citing CJEU, *Svensson*, para. 24. This view is consistent with the later ruling CJEU, *GS Media*, para. 42.
113. CJEU, *ITV Broadcasting*, paras 9–13.
114. *Ibid.*, paras 28–30.
115. *Ibid.*, paras 32, 34: *SGAE*, paras 37–39 (and case law cited therein).
116. CJEU, *ITV Broadcasting*, para. 35.
117. *Ibid.*, para. 39. On this requirement see: CJEU, *SGAE*, para. 40; CJEU, *Murphy*, para. 197; CJEU, *Airfield*, para. 72. On the latter case, *see* Vousden, 2012.
118. CJEU, *ITV Broadcasting*, paras 43–46. *But see* Klafkowska-Wasniowska, 2013, pp. 756–757, arguing that the profit making nature of the act may be determinative of its qualification under the communication to the public right of related rights holders.
119. CJEU, *SBS*, para. 17, citing CJEU, *ITV Broadcasting*, para. 24.

The Court in *ITV Broadcasting* and *SBS* took an economic approach and developed the 'specific technical means' requirement to interpret the exclusive right in light of the 'existence and degree of several interdependent criteria with regard to the person of the user (potential infringer) and the targeted public'.[120] The function of this approach is to safeguard, for rights holders, new technological avenues of exploitation with economic significance.[121]

4.3.2.1.4 New Public and Online Use

Even if a communication does not meet the specific technical means criterion, it may still be restricted under the exclusive right if it is to a 'new public', i.e., a public not taken into account by the copyright holder when they authorised the initial communication to the public. The concept was first used in *SGAE* and is now a staple of the CJEU's judgments on the interpretation of the right of communication to the public.[122]

In *SGAE*, the Court traced the criterion back to Article 11*bis*(1)(ii) BC and the 1987 Guide to the Berne Convention.[123] Curiously, the Guide referred to that criterion in relation to Article 11*bis*(1)(iii) BC, which raises doubts as to the validity of the Court's analysis on this point. This is because subparagraph (ii) of the BC provision relies instead on the criterion of an 'organisation other than the original one', i.e., a *new communicator* rather than a *new public*.[124]

Regardless, from the application in the offline world to acts of communication in public places (*Murphy*), hotels rooms (*SGAE*), spa establishments (*OSA*), rehabilitation centres (*Reha Training*), and in the context of satellite broadcasting (*Airfield*), the new public criterion has gained extraordinary relevance for the interpretation of Article 3(1) InfoSoc Directive in the online environment. This relevance is due especially to its use in hyperlinking cases, starting with *Svensson*.[125] Hence, the criterion is of particular importance for the study of ACS.

120. Leistner, 2014, pp. 569–570, commenting on *ITV Broadcasting*.
121. Leistner, 2014, pp. 569–572.
122. CJEU, *SGAE*, paras 37–38, 40, 42; CJEU, *Murphy*, para. 197; CJEU, *Organismos Sillogikis*, para. 38; CJEU, *Airfield*, para. 76; CJEU, *Svensson*, paras 21, 24; CJEU, *OSA*, para. 32; CJEU, *Reha Training*, para. 45, CJEU, *GS Media*, para. 37. For criticism of this criterion, *see* Hugenholtz & Velze, 2016. *See also* ALAI, 2014, concluding that the criterion is in conflict with international law.
123. CJEU, *SGAE*, para. 41.
124. Velze, 2015, pp. 36–37.
125. The preliminary reference in *Svensson* and its aftermath polarised European copyright scholarship See, e.g., ALAI, 2013, 2014, 2015a, European Copyright Society, 2013, 2014a. For commentary on the debate, *see* Ginsburg, 2014c; Lucie Guibault & Quintais, 2014; Savola, 2014; Tsoutsanis, 2014.

4.3.2.1.4.1 Initial Application in Svensson

Svensson involved a Swedish company (Retriever Sverige AB) operating a website that provided clients with links to articles published on other websites. The applicants in the main proceedings (all journalists, among them Mr Svensson) claimed compensation from Retriever for harm suffered as a result of the inclusion on its website of hyperlinks redirecting users to freely accessible press articles in which the former hold copyright. The main question before the Court was whether the provision on a website of links to protected works 'freely accessible' on another website constitutes a restricted act of communication to the public under the InfoSoc Directive.

First, the CJEU considered that the provision of direct access to the works via a link from one website to another constitutes an act of 'making available' and, therefore, 'communication to the public'.[126] Second, because the link is aimed at all potential users of the website (an 'indeterminate and fairly large number of recipients') works are indeed communicated to a public.[127] However, for such a communication to trigger Article 3(1) InfoSoc Directive it 'must also be directed at a new public', meaning a 'public … not taken into account by the copyright holders when they authorised the initial communication to the public'.[128]

In this case, there was no communication to a new public. The initial communication targeted all potential visitors to the website in question, consisting of 'all internet users', as access to the works was not subject to 'restrictive measures'. Accordingly, Retriever's website users were part of the public taken into account by the applicants when they first authorised the making available of their works.[129]

Therefore, even if there is an 'act of communication' to the 'public', no authorisation is required because it is not to a 'new public'. The conclusion remains valid even if the link causes the work to appear 'in such a way as to give the impression that it is appearing on the site on which that link is found, whereas in fact that work comes from another site'.[130]

The focus of the analysis is therefore on whether a work is 'freely accessible' online and not on the linking technique. This approach was confirmed later in *BestWater*. In that case, the Court considered that hyperlinking through 'framing' of a YouTube video did not constitute a communication to a new public because the link pointed to a work freely available online.[131] Crucially, the Court in *BestWater* did not rule on whether

126. CJEU, *Svensson*, paras 19-20.
127. *Ibid.*, para. 25.
128. *Ibid.*, para. 24.
129. *Ibid.*, paras 27–28.
130. *Ibid.*, para. 29.
131. CJEU, *BestWater* paras 16–19, citing CJEU, *Svensson*, paras 29–30.

it is relevant for the assessment of the right that the video is question was uploaded *with or without the consent* of the copyright holders.[132]

A different conclusion applies if a link allows users to circumvent restrictions put in place by the linked website in order to limit access to subscribers of the same. The circumventing link 'constitutes an intervention without which those users would not be able to access the works transmitted'; in such cases, those users are considered a new public (not targeted by the initial communication) and authorisation from the copyright owner is required.[133]

At this stage, it is important to point out an issue with the CJEU case law. Following *Svensson*, it could be said that no new public is reached if a hyperlink is made to a work freely accessible online without access restrictions. In this scenario, there would be no communication to a new public. The act would therefore not qualify as a copyright-relevant communication to the public, as it would fail to meet a cumulative criterion. In other words, this type of hyperlinking would essentially be copyright-free.

However, the later judgment of *Soulier and Doke* challenges this interpretation. The relevant passage reads:

> Thus, in a case in which it was questioned about the concept of a 'new public', the Court held that, in a situation in which an author had given prior, explicit and unreserved authorisation to the publication of his articles on the website of a newspaper publisher, without making use of technological measures restricting access to those works from other websites, that author could be regarded, in essence, as having authorised the communication of those works to the general internet public (see, to that effect, judgment of 13 February 2014, Svensson and Others, C 466/12, EU:C:2014:76, paragraphs 25 to 28 and 31).[134]

In the context of this judgment, which does not discuss application of the exclusive right to hyperlinking, it becomes clear that the Court accepts that hyperlinking to a freely accessible work without technical restrictions could be admissible under a doctrine of 'implicit consent'.[135] If that is true, the types of hyperlinks in question are not outside the realm of copyright protection, but rather subject to national doctrines of implied consent, which will ultimately determine their legal status. This interpretation has great potential for legal uncertainty and for extending copyright protection to acts that were apparently outside its scope. (As explained below, after *GS Media*, where the posting of a hyperlink to digital consent is not subject to express

132. Mezei, 2016, p. 783.
133. CJEU, *Svensson*, para. 31. On the different interpretative approach of AG Wathelet in his opinion in *GS Media*, see *infra* 4.3.2.3.
134. CJEU, *Soulier and Doke*, para. 36.
135. *Ibid.*, paras 35–36.

or implied consent, end-users may still under certain conditions benefit from what amounts to an innocent infringement defence.)

4.3.2.1.4.2 The Issue of Unauthorised Sources and GS Media

The controversial issue of the legal status of hyperlinking to unauthorised sources was addressed by the CJEU in *GS Media*. This case concerns the posting of hyperlinks on a popular Dutch website (GeenStijl.nl) operated by the company GS Media. The hyperlinks directed users to other websites hosting photos of a Dutch starlet (Ms Dekker) taken by the photographer Mr C. Hermès. The photos were destined for publication in the Dutch *Playboy* magazine, owned by the publisher Sanoma.[136]

Without the authorisation of Sanoma, the GeenStijl website initially posted links to files containing the photos on the third party website Filefactory.com. The photos were eventually removed from that website following notice by Sanoma. However, neither the links nor the articles referring to the photos on the GeenStijl website were removed, despite Sanoma's request to that effect. Instead, the GeenStijl website published additional articles containing links to other third party websites hosting the photos at issue. All of these articles and links where posted online between October and November 2011, prior to the scheduled publication of the photos in the *Playboy* issue of December 2011.[137]

Interpreting the CJEU case law post-*Svensson*, the Supreme Court of the Netherlands was of the opinion that it was not sufficiently clear whether there is a communication to the public under Article 3(1) InfoSoc Directive 'if a work has been previously published, but without the consent of the copyright holder'. It considered particularly relevant the question of whether there is a new public if the work is already posted online in a website before a link to it is created, even if the link greatly facilitated access to the work. Furthermore, the Dutch court noted, it will be extremely difficult for the operator of a website to check, prior to posting a link, whether the rights holder has consented to the early availability of that work.[138]

Before the CJEU judgment was delivered, scholars were divided on the topic. Some believed that any hyperlinks to unauthorised uploaded copies of a work should always qualify as an act of communication to a new public.[139] Others limited this conclusion to instances where the linker had knowledge of the unauthorised nature of the source.[140] Others still considered preferable to judge infringement on the basis of secondary (rather than strict) liability,

136. CJEU, *GS Media*, paras 2, 6–7.
137. *Ibid.*, paras 8–16.
138. *Ibid.*, paras 21–22.
139. Headdon, 2014, p. 665, relying on Art. 3 and recital 29 InfoSoc Directive. Cf. also Leistner, 2015, p. 636.
140. Velze, 2015, p. 42, reporting on the position of Visser.

an area of law familiar with concepts of awareness and knowledge.[141] In the latter's view, the existence of a framework for notice-and-takedown measures, in line with the E-Commerce Directive, sufficiently enabled removal of the unlawful upload copy and automatic 'breaking' of the link pointing to it.[142] A more radical proposal was to consider the new public criterion independently from the status of the upload copy. In this proposal, the unrestricted appearance of a work online meant that the internet public had 'already been reached', and that any subsequent hyperlinks would not target a new public or 'amount to a secondary act of communication to the public'.[143]

Some scholars even persuasively suggest abandoning the new public criterion altogether. In this line, Hugenholtz and van Velze propose to determine the scope of the exclusive right through a method of economic interpretation, consistent with the normative concept of communication to the public.[144] The method focuses on protecting the economic exploitation of the right against unauthorised use that affects that exploitation, rather than granting protection for technically defined acts of communication.[145] Following this method, online acts of communication that configure an 'independent economic exploitation [*of works*] for financial profit' should be restricted by copyright.[146] By focusing on the notion of an act of communication requiring an 'indispensable intervention', these authors exclude ordinary hyperlinks from the right's scope. Differently, if a hyperlink has the effect of providing direct access works, for example by circumventing access restrictions, it amounts to an active intervention and therefore triggers the exclusive right. The authors further argue that other contentious forms of hyperlinking (such as to unauthorised sources) ought to be dealt with in the context of unfair competition law.[147]

It is possible to recognise some of these views in AG Wathelet's Opinion in *GS Media*. As noted, the primary focus of the AG was on the criterion of 'act of communication', rather than the 'new public.'[148] In his opinion, hyperlinking to unauthorised sources that are 'freely accessible' does not constitute an act of communication to the public because the link is not an indispensable intervention to make the work available to Internet

141. Arezzo, 2014, p. 545 ff; Computer & Communications Industry Association, 2016; Savola, 2014, pp. 282–284; Velze, 2015, p. 42.
142. Computer & Communications Industry Association, 2016.
143. *Ibid.*
144. Hugenholtz & Velze, 2016.
145. Depreeuw, 2014, pp. 510–537; Velze, 2015, pp. 81–93.
146. Hugenholtz & Velze, 2016 ('What should be decisive is whether the service *exploits* the work by extracting substantive economic value from the use of the work'). The authors propose determining the scope of the right based on three criteria: act of communication; public; and that the 'intervention' is 'done by a party other than the original communicating party'. *Ibid.*, pp. 812–813.
147. *Ibid.*
148. *See supra* 4.3.2.1.1.

users. Rather, the actual making available results from the 'initial' communication, which is the infringing act.[149] If there is no act of communication, then a cumulative requirement for application of the exclusive right is not met. Consequently, the linker's motivation, knowledge, or awareness of the unauthorised nature of the source are irrelevant.[150]

In the alternative, the AG continues, the criterion of a new public 'is applicable only where the copyright holder has authorised the initial communication to the public', which is not the case if a link points to unauthorised sources.[151] As the criterion is not applicable, the authorisation of rights holders is not required to link to such websites.[152] Even if the criterion was applicable, there is only a communication to the new public if the linker's intervention is 'indispensable' to reach that public. That is not the case where the works linked to were freely accessible, even if the link 'facilitates or simplifies users' access to the work in question'.[153] There will be a communication to the public only if the link allows Internet users to circumvent restrictions on third party websites that limit access to protected works, such as TPMs under Article 6 InfoSoc Directive.[154]

In essence, the AG believes that the scope of Article 3 InfoSoc Directive does not 'cover the posting of hyperlinks to protected works freely accessible on another website', a result that could only be achieved through 'action to be taken by the European legislature.'[155] Crucial to this position is the view that any other interpretation of that provision would 'significantly impair the functioning of the Internet', undermine the InfoSoc Directive's main objective of 'the development of the information society in Europe' (recital 2), and distort the directive's fair balance aim (recital 31).[156] From the normative perspective, the AG adds that:

> as a general rule, internet users are not aware and do not have the means to check whether the initial communication to the public of a protected work freely accessible on the internet was effected with or without the copyright holder's consent. If users were at risk of proceedings for infringement of copyright under Article 3(1) of Directive 2001/29 whenever they post a hyperlink to works freely accessible on another website, they would be much more reticent to post them, which would

---

149. *Opinion AG in GS Media*, paras 48–64.
150. *Ibid.*, para. 63.
151. *Ibid.*, para. 67.
152. *Ibid.*, para. 68 (citing CJEU, *Svensson*, paras 28, 30).
153. *Ibid.*, paras 69–70, 74 (citing CJEU, *Svensson*, para. 27). N.B. this reasoning appears to conflate the two cumulative criteria of this right.
154. *Ibid.*, para. 73 (fn. 43 referring to Art. 6 InfoSoc Directive; citing CJEU, *Svensson*, para. 31).
155. *Ibid.*, paras 75–79 (cit. para. 79), citing the 'ceiling' imposed on the right in CJEU, *Svensson*, para. 41. *See infra* 4.3.2.1.
156. *Ibid.*, para. 77.

> be to the detriment of the proper functioning and the very architecture of the internet, and to the development of the information society.[157]

This passage echoes a fundamental rights argument in support of delimiting the scope of Article 3 InfoSoc Directive made prior to *Svensson* by the European Copyright Society. For this group of experts, to the extent hyperlinks are essential to the operation of the Internet, including access and exchange of a vast trove of information available in the network, they are crucial for exercising the fundamental freedom of expression and information online.[158] This freedom is protected by Article 11 Charter and must be balanced with copyright protection, as recognised in recital 3 InfoSoc Directive.[159]

The AG further notes that his interpretation does not preclude other remedies available to rights holders to protect and enforce their copyright. As he points out, it remains possible to bring proceedings for direct infringement against the initial uploader, and to obtain injunctions against website operators hosting the unauthorised upload copies – as they qualify as 'intermediaries' for the purposes of Article 8(3) InfoSoc Directive and Article 11 Enforcement Directive.[160] These injunctions are in his view 'a direct and appropriate remedy' for the initial infringing communication to the public.[161] It is also possible, at a national level and in certain circumstances, for the intermediary to be liable for the storage of the unauthorised works, namely if it fails to comply with the strict requirements of the E-Commerce Directive's safe harbours.[162]

Despite the AG's sensible Opinion, the CJEU chose not to follow it. In its typical redrafting of questions referred by national Courts, the Court summarised the issue in *GS Media* as follows:

> whether, and in what possible circumstances, the fact of posting, on a website, a hyperlink to protected works, freely available on another website without the consent of the copyright holder, constitutes a 'communication to the public' within the meaning of Article 3(1) of [*the InfoSoc*] Directive … [163]

The Court starts its analysis by noting that the exclusive right is preventive in nature (i.e., a right to prohibit), which meaning and scope must be determined in light of the objectives of the directive. These include, on the one hand, establishing a high level of protection for authors that enables an

---

157. *Ibid.*, para. 78.
158. European Copyright Society, 2013.
159. *See supra* 5.3.3.6.1
160. *Opinion AG in GS Media*, paras 80–83, referring also to recital 50 InfoSoc Directive and Art. 14 E-Commerce Directive.
161. *Ibid.*, para. 84.
162. *Ibid.*, paras 85–87, making reference to the interpretation of Art. 14 E-Commerce Directive in CJEU, *L'Oréal v. eBay*, para. 119.
163. *Ibid.*, para. 25.

appropriate reward for use of their works (Recitals 9 and 10). On the other hand, they include striking a fair balance between the rights of copyright holders (safeguarded by Article 17(2) Charter), and the fundamental rights of users, namely freedom of expression and information in Article 11 Charter (*see* Recitals 3 and 31).[164]

The Court then requalifies its position in *Svensson* and *BestWater* by stating that posting hyperlinks to works on another website does not constitute a communication to the public only if those works are freely accessible *with the consent (i.e., authorisation) of the rights holder*. As noted above, this requirement of consent was not clear from previous case law, especially *Svensson* and *BestWater*. The result is that hyperlinking to works freely accessible online *without the consent* of the copyright holder *is not an act excluded* from the concept of communication to the public.[165]

Does that mean that such act is restricted by copyright? In answering this question, the Court makes two preliminary remarks. First, it notes the importance of the Internet in general for freedom of expression and information, and of hyperlinks in particular for 'its sound operation as well as to the exchange of opinions and information in that network characterised by the availability of immense amounts of information'.[166] Second, it considers the extreme difficulty of individuals posting hyperlinks to ascertain the legal status of the linked-to works at the time of posting or subsequently.[167]

From here, the Court's analysis is not absolutely clear, but can be summarised as follows. If the linker 'knew or ought to have known that the hyperlink he posted provides access to a work illegally placed on the internet' (e.g., if 'he was notified thereof by the copyright holders'), the provision of the link amounts to a 'communication to the public' under Article 3 InfoSoc Directive.[168] This is because the linker intervened in full knowledge of the consequences of his conduct in order to give customers access to a work illegally posted on the internet. The Court views this 'deliberate intervention' as akin to that of posting a hyperlink that circumvents access restrictions (discussed in *Svensson*).[169] Conversely, if the linker did not know or ought to have known of that fact, then the posting of the link is not restricted. In other words, the end-user may benefit from an innocent infringement defence. In this analysis, *knowledge* becomes crucial element to establish the legal status of the act.

To determine knowledge, the Court distinguishes whether the person posting the link pursues a profit or not. If the posting of hyperlinks is carried

164. *Ibid.*, paras 28–31 and case law cited therein.
165. *Ibid.*, paras 40–43.
166. *Ibid.*, para. 45.
167. *Ibid.*, para. 46.
168. *Ibid.*, para. 49.
169. *Ibid.*, paras 48–50.

out for profit, there is a rebuttable presumption that the linker had full knowledge of the legal status of the work, as he would carry 'out the necessary checks' for that purpose. If the presumption is not rebutted, the act of hyperlinking communicates the work to a new public, and therefore falls within Article 3(1) InfoSoc Directive.[170]

Differently, if the linker does not pursue profit, knowledge cannot be presumed. This scenario seems to apply individuals using the internet for non-commercial purposes, for who it would be too cumbersome to check the legal status of the linked-to works.

Thus, in contrast with previous judgments, the Court seems to incorporate the criterion of the 'profit making nature of the communication' into the new public analysis, as a means to establish a presumption of knowledge. However, the judgment does not clarify what exactly constitutes 'posting of hyperlinks carried out for profit'.

This conceptual move by the Court is justified on the need to provide a high level of protection to copyright holders in the InfoSoc Directive. These should be entitled to 'act not only against the initial publication of their work on a website', but also 'any person posting for profit a hyperlink to the work illegally published on that website', as well as any persons posting hyperlinks that circumvent access restrictions.[171]

In addition, copyright holders may act against any linker that does not pursue financial gain but has knowledge of the 'illegal nature of the publication' and fails to remove the link. These persons, the Court notes, 'may not rely upon one of the exceptions listed in Article 5(3)', which could otherwise provide a legal permission to post the hyperlink.[172]

Applying this analysis to the particular case, the Court noted that: (1) GS Media operated the GeenStijl website, which provided the hyperlinks to the photos for profit; (2) Sanoma did not authorise the publication of photos on the Internet; (3) GS Media was aware of Sanoma's lack of consent for publication, and thus cannot rebut the presumption of knowledge. Consequently, the posting of the hyperlinks in question constitutes a restricted communication to the public within the meaning of Article 3(1) InfoSoc Directive.[173]

It remains to be seen how *GS Media* influences future cases involving acts of hyperlinking and the interpretation of the exclusive right of communication to the public in the *acquis*. In *Filmspeler*, a preliminary reference involving the provision of a multimedia player with software and add-ons containing hyperlinks to unauthorised digital content, AG Campos Sánchez-Bordona took an expansive view. The AG relied on *GS Media* not

170. *Ibid.*, paras 47–52.
171. *Ibid.*, para 53.
172. *Ibid.* N.B. the only limitation mentioned by the Court (at para. 5) in its 'legal context' section is Art. 5(3) InfoSoc Directive on reporting of current events.
173. *Ibid.*, paras 54–55.

only to reject the qualification of the multimedia player as a mere 'physical facility' for the purposes of recital 27 InfoSoc Directive, but also to conclude that the sale of such of the player constitutes a communication to a new public of the content made available without authorisation.[174]

4.3.2.1.5 *Profit-Making Nature of the Communication*

Finally, the CJEU has sometimes resorted to a third separate criterion to determine if there is a copyright relevant communication to the public: whether the communication is of 'a profit-making nature'.[175]

In relation to this criterion, as with the notion of 'public', the Court has to this point mostly drawn a distinction between copyright and related rights.[176] For communications to the public of copyright-protected works, the Court considers this factor to be relevant but not a 'necessary' or 'essential' 'condition for the existence of a communication to the public'.[177] Hence, the criterion does not appear to be determinative of the exclusive right in Article 3(1) InfoSoc Directive.[178]

A different conclusion may be reached in relation to communication to the public of subject matter protected by related rights. This is clearly seen in *SCF* and *PPI*, which deal with the *remuneration right* in Article 8(2) Rental Right Directive, as well as in the subsequent judgment in *Reha Training*.[179] The Court states that this provision 'requires an individual interpretation of the concept of communication to the public' as the right in question 'is essentially financial in nature'.[180] To make this individual assessment of the remuneration right, the Court considers it relevant to examine the profit-making nature of a communication.[181] This criterion, it seems, is used to qualify the intervention that communicates the work to the

174. *Opinion AG in Filmspeler*, paras 35–60.
175. CJEU, *SGAE*, para. 44; CJEU, *Murphy*, para. 204, CJEU, *ITV Broadcasting*, paras 42–43; CJEU, *SCF*, paras 79, 88, 97; CJEU, *Reha Training*, para. 49; CJEU, *GS Media*, para. 38.
176. Nérisson, 2015b, p. 390, noting that the bifurcated approach is justified on the different nature of the rights in question (exclusive v. remuneration) and that it may rely on the sectorial nature of the Rental Right Directive, as opposed to the 'copyright common law' status of the InfoSoc Directive.
177. CJEU, *SGAE*, para. 44; CJEU, *Murphy*, para. 204, CJEU, *ITV Broadcasting*, paras 42–43; CJEU, *Reha Training*, para. 49.
178. CJEU, *OSA*, para. 35. Cf. also the reported position of Judge Malenovský in Favale, 2016.
179. CJEU, *Reha Training*, para. 49, where it is stated that the profit-making nature of the communication is relevant for the qualification of a transmission as a communication to the public 'in particular, for the purpose of determining any remuneration due in respect of that transmission'.
180. CJEU, *SCF*, paras 76–78.
181. *Ibid.*, paras 79, 88, 89. *See also* CJEU, *PPI*, para. 36.

public and, in particular, whether the same aims to attract additional customers and revenue.[182]

In *SCF*, which dealt with the communication to the public of phonograms broadcast by radio in a dental practice, the Court concluded that the activity in question could not be reasonably expected to 'have an impact on the income of that dentist'.[183] That conclusion was reinforced by the fact that the dentist's clients are not receptive to the communication nor have an active choice in the same.[184] As a result, the activity in question is not a communication to the public within Article 8(2) Rental Right Directive.

Conversely, the *PPI* Court considered that 'the guests of a hotel may be described as 'targeted' and 'receptive'.'[185] By allowing its customers access to the broadcast works, the hotel provided 'an additional service which has an influence on the hotel's standing and, therefore, on the price of rooms'.[186] Consequently, the hotel operator's broadcasting of phonograms is of a profit-making nature, leading to the conclusion that the operator makes a communication to the public pursuant to Article 8(2) Rental Right Directive.[187] A similar line of reasoning was followed by the Court in *Reha Training*, which considered that the broadcasting of television programmes by the operator of a rehabilitation centre 'has a profit-making nature, capable of being taken into account in order to determine the amount of remuneration due, where appropriate, for such a broadcast'.[188]

The above analysis suggests the 'profit-making' is of greater relevance the determination of the existence of a communication to the public in relation to the right of equitable remuneration in Article 8(2) Rental Right Directive.[189] However, after *GS Media*, one could argue that this criterion plays a greater role than before in the assessment of Article 3(1) InfoSoc Directive, as it is not only incorporated in the new public analysis, but also key to establish a presumption of knowledge in scenarios of hyperlinking to unauthorised content. Whether such conceptual move is advisable or contributes to resolving legal uncertainty in this field is questionable.

4.3.2.2 Application to Activities of Internet Users

How does the analysis of the legal framework of the right of communication to the public apply to the previously defined types of online use? To answer

182. CJEU, *SCF*, para. 90, citing CJEU, *SGAE*, para. 44, and CJEU, *Murphy*, para. 205. *See also* CJEU, *Reha Training*, paras 48–51.
183. CJEU, *SCF*, para. 97.
184. *Ibid.*, paras 98–100.
185. CJEU, *PPI*, para. 43.
186. *Ibid.*, para. 44.
187. *Ibid.*, paras 45–46.
188. CJEU, *Reha Training*, para. 64.
189. *Opinion AG in Reha Training*, paras 55, 68. Cf. also Leistner, 2015, p. 633, and position of Judge Malenovský reported in Favale, 2016.

the question, this paragraph analyses linear uses (live streaming) and interactive uses (on-demand streaming, uploading and hyperlinking) involving the right of communication to the public.

The case of live streaming appears straightforward. If a user makes a non-commercial Internet retransmission of broadcasts, they are communicating the work to the public through a new 'specific technical means', in the sense of *ITV Broadcasting*.[190] Therefore, unauthorised retransmissions of this type qualify as copyright infringement.

The conclusion is valid for online (re)transmissions of works through different communication means. It might not apply to Internet retransmissions of an existing online transmission, due to the fact that the communication does not use a novel and separate 'technical means'.[191] As many live Internet transmissions which rights holders wish to exploit commercially are subject to technological restrictions of some kind, it is probable that an online retransmission of the same by end-users constitutes a new technical act of communication or reaches a new public beyond that initially authorised by the rights holder. If it does, it will trigger the right of communication to the public and subject unauthorised users to liability for copyright infringement.

Interactive uses – on demand streaming, uploading and hyperlinking – require a more nuanced analysis. On the one hand, certain uses may not reach a 'public', notably in the context of uploading. In general, making an upstream copy to a cloud locker (and possibly to online personal video recorders) that is only accessible to the user making it, or to a close circle of family and friends, does not make the work accessible to the public. The act constitutes instead a reproduction and should be dealt with in the context of that exclusive right.[192]

Similarly, the provision and use of cloud services that merely allow individual users (or a close circle of family and friends) to make upstream copies of works on hosting servers and subsequently download or stream their material for private or personal use do not appear to trigger the making available right.[193]

Less clear are uploads of works on social networking sites. These are intermediate cases with respect to the target audience. In these cases, the content is only available to a specific group of Internet users – consisting of a variable circle of family, friends and acquaintances – but not to the general Internet public.[194] Is such a group of users a 'public', or even a 'new public'?

190. The fact that the use is non-commercial does not affect this conclusion, especially in light of the lesser relevance of the 'profit-making nature' criterion in the field of copyright. *See supra* 4.3.2.1.3.
191. Arezzo, 2014, pp. 535–536; Klafkowska-Wasniowska, 2013, p. 756; Savola, 2014, pp. 279–288.
192. Depreeuw & Hubin, 2014, pp. 70–71, noting cases where national courts did not find a 'public' to exist in these technologies that allow for a more 'individualised approach'.
193. Triaille et al., 2013, pp. 45, 119.
194. Senftleben, 2013a, p. 88, raising the issue.

The answer is unclear as it depends on the concrete definition of the *de minimis* threshold of public in specific cases.[195] Furthermore, the question may be pre-empted by the finding that the platform itself is making the work available to the public (if not simultaneously, at least in succession), thereby exempting the end-user from the requirement of authorisation.

A different situation arises when the upload file is made accessible to a wide number of people, for instance through a P2P network or on a publicly accessible website. Here, the work is made available on demand to other Internet users. In such cases, the relationship between the rights of reproduction and making available is not clear and has led to divergent case law in national courts. These cases either consider the 'upload copy' to be consumed by the right of making available or qualify it simultaneously as an act of reproduction and making available, thereby calling into question both rights.[196] Regardless, placing the work on the Internet in such a way as to allow individualised on demand access to the same qualifies as a communication to the 'public'.[197]

The same conclusion should apply where P2P protocols (e.g., BitTorrent) cause the uploaded file to be split into several parts during the transfer process in such a way that one specific peer only effectively 'transmits' part of the work to be downloaded by subsequent users. Despite the technical differences, the situation is functionally identical to standard uploads. Given that the decisive activity of offering access to a protected work on a network for (individual) access has effectively occurred, the legal status of the uploading act in these systems should not change.[198]

If this was the entire story, the legal qualification of acts of uploading would be only relatively challenging. However, we might wonder how the criteria used by the CJEU to determine the existence of a communication to the public of works online – 'specific technical means' (in *ITV Broadcasting*) or 'new public' (from *Svensson* to *GS Media*) – influence this qualification.

In the simplest scenario, the 'upload copy' refers to a work not previously available over the Internet. Here, there is a communication to the public via a different technological means (i.e., the Internet), subject to the consent of rights holders.

But what if the 'upload copy' is of a work already accessible online? This scenario invalidates the application of the 'specific technical means'

---

195. Velze, 2015, p. 85, applies an economic interpretation method to note that '[a]n example of the de minimis rule on the Internet is if a work is communicated within the internal network of a company, only made available to a small number of employees'.
196. Depreeuw & Hubin, 2014, p. 43. *See also* Eechoud et al., 2009, p. 91, on the challenges of distinguishing the making available right from that of broadcasting in the *acquis*. The authors stress the relevance of the distinction for related rights owners, which do not have a right to prohibit the broadcast of works but a mere remuneration claim.
197. Eechoud et al., 2009, pp. 92–93.
198. Huygen et al., 2009, fig. 52; Quintais, 2012, fig. I.3.a)-I.3.b).

criterion and appears to push the analysis towards the 'new public' test. Following *Svensson*, hyperlinks pointing to 'freely accessible' content do not broaden the audience initially targeted. Therefore, they do not aim at a new public and do not constitute a communication to the public in the sense of Article 3 InfoSoc Directive.[199] (Alternatively, following *Soulier and Doke*, the hyperlinks in question would benefit from the 'implicit consent' of the rights holder.[200]) Is the same conclusion applicable to the upload copy, potentially implying exhaustion of the right of communication to the public online?[201]

To answer the question, we need to take a step back and look at the first cumulative requirement of the exclusive right. Namely, what type of act of communication is at stake here and does it justify the analogy to hyperlinking?

From the technical standpoint, uploading is different from hyperlinking insofar as it involves a prior reproduction of a digital copy of the work for purposes of subsequent accessibility and transmission to third parties over the Internet (which acts involve a series of ephemeral and possibly permanent reproductions). This is the quintessential case of interactive transmission meant to be covered by the right of making available.[202]

In hyperlinking, the deliberate intervention of the user is of a different nature. It is a reference or pointer to a file and does not involve previous storage of the same by person posting the link for the purposes of making available the work.[203] As Arezzo puts it:

> an act of linking is, by definition, not an 'uploading' of content but the provision of a set of technical information about how such content may be reached, it goes without saying that linking always presupposes that the linked content already be made available on the net by someone else: this latter person being the actual infringer if the first act of uploading took place without the rightholder's consent.[204]

This characterisation clarifies that uploading involves a preliminary reproduction step and an *independent act* of communication to the public.

199. Moir, Montagnon & Newton, 2014, p. 400. N.B. this might not prevent the possibility that injured parties avail themselves of unfair competition type of protection.
200. *See supra* 4.3.2.1.2.
201. *See* Hugenholtz & Velze, 2016, discussing the issue of exhaustion on the Internet in connection with the application of the new public criterion after *Svensson*.
202. Arezzo, 2014, p. 549.
203. CJEU, *Svensson*, para. 31.
204. Arezzo, 2014, p. 551. Arezzo goes on to suggest that the right of making available could be clarified so as to comprise also the preliminary act of 'technical act of storing copies for the purpose of making them available', leading to the conclusion that linking would not qualify as a 'form of communication of a work to the public'. Cf. Arezzo, 2014, p. 552.

The hyperlink to the upload copy would be a subsequent and separate act.[205] Because the act is different, and the exclusive right is not subject to exhaustion online, as a rule the uploading of works over the Internet should be subject to authorisation by the rights holder.[206]

Of course, if the upload copy was previously 'freely accessible' online, the act of uploading (together with the ancillary reproduction) could be authorised by contract (including via collective licensing), a copyright limitation, or national doctrines of implied licence/consent.[207] However, for the most part end-users will remain uncertain whether the work originates from an authorised source, a key aspect (after *GS Media*) to determine the legal status of their activities.

Interactive stream provision is similar to uploading and the same conclusions apply. Where an end-user provides unrestricted access to a work for download or through a stream over the Internet at a time and place chosen by the recipient, they are communicating the work to the public.[208]

The legal qualification of hyperlinking and its interpretation by the CJEU are perhaps the most complex aspects in the current law, and a boon for legal uncertainty vis à-vis the qualification of daily practices of Internet users and intermediaries. Such uncertainty is attested both by the significant case law on this topic and the steady stream of preliminary references.[209]

The Court's current understanding is that hyperlinking constitutes a restricted communication to the public if it provides access to works not previously 'freely accessible' online with the consent of the rights holder. These hyperlinks are restricted because they broaden the original website's audience to a new public, either through circumvention of access restrictions, or by pointing to a work made available online without the consent of the rights holder.

---

205. This distinction between the initial act of making available and subsequent hyperlinks to that upload copy is used by AG Wathelet to conclude that linking to freely accessible unlawful sources is not an act of communication to the public. *See Opinion AG GS Media*, para. 54.
206. In this respect, the act of uploading could possibly be authorised under doctrines of implied consent, but not because of the new public criterion.
207. *See* ALAI, 2015a, discussing these options for hyperlinking. On implied consent in the case law of the Court, *see* CJEU, *Soulier and Doke*, paras 35–36. Influential applications of doctrines of implied consent are those of the Federal Court of Justice in: BGH, 29.04.2010, I ZR 69/08 ('Vorschaubilder'), on implied consent to use of freely accessible thumbnails by search engines; and BGH, 19.10.2011, I ZR 140/10 ('Vorschaubilder II') on implied consent to use of images made available without authorisation of the rights holder by search engines. *See* Geiger & Schönherr, 2014b, pp. 458–459; Peukert, 2015, pp. 380–381. On implied licence and linking, *see* Pihlajarinne, 2012.
208. Depreeuw & Hubin, 2014, p. 29.
209. At time of writing, these included CJEU, Reference for Preliminary Ruling, Case C-527/15, *Filmspeler*, and CJEU, Reference for Preliminary Ruling, Case C-610/15, *Stichting Brein v. Ziggo*. On the first case, *see Opinion AG in Filmspeler*.

In principle, no authorisation from the rights holder is required if a link points to a work freely accessible online and does not circumvent access restrictions. In this context, a work is 'freely accessible' on the Internet if it was made available with the express or implied consent of the rights holder and without access restrictions or 'restrictive measures'.[210] The use of these terms and the related term 'circumvention' indicates that the restrictions in question are technological, a view endorsed in *Soulier and Doke*.[211]

Thus, if a link provides access to content that is subject to access control measures, like subscription pay-walls or 'session IDs', it is infringing. For instance, current geo-blocking measures used by broadcasters and service providers in the audio-visual sector would qualify as technical restrictions. Infringement would result from the fact that the content is not freely accessible and the link circumvents access requirements, resulting in a communication to a new public.[212] This would apply to content made available on demand, as well as to content originally streamed over the Internet (if subject to technical restrictions).

In a different scenario, where a link provides access to an unauthorised source, it will be infringing if the person posting the link has knowledge of the nature of the source (i.e., if he is not an innocent infringer). To establish knowledge the Court introduced a rebuttable presumption, linked to the 'for profit condition'. As noted, the concept of knowledge is not only alien to the InfoSoc Directive, but also a hotbed for legal uncertainty. The Court itself recognises this when stating that it is extremely difficult for users to ascertain the legal status of works in advance of linking.[213] To make matters worse, the 'for profit' condition is poorly defined.

The facts of *GS Media* point in the direction that the condition 'refers to the overall operations of the website owner and not a specific link.'[214] However, what this condition means beyond that is unclear. Does it apply to the operator of a user upload platform where the end-users themselves post hyperlinks? Or to the operator of a for-profit platform where links are generated automatically by algorithmic agents? Or to freely accessible news websites financed through adverting models posting links to newsworthy content unauthorised by the copyright holder? Or to individual users posting links on blogs that generate a very modest amount of revenue through

210. CJEU, *Svensson*, paras 18, 26, 31; CJEU, *GS Media*, para. 42; CJEU, *Soulier and Doke*, paras 35–36.
211. CJEU, *Soulier and* Doke, para. 36. *See also* Opinion *AG in GS Media*, para. 73 (fn. 43 referring to Art. 6 InfoSoc Directive; citing CJEU, *Svensson*, para. 31), and Mezei, 2016, p. 782 arguing that the by 'restrictions' the CJEU means not only effective TPMs 'but also paywalls, registration pages or 'robot.txt.'files'.
212. Headdon, 2014, p. 655; Moir et al., 2014, p. 400; Tsoutsanis, 2014, p. 507.
213. CJEU, *GS Media*, para. 46.
214. Tomasz Targosz, 2016.

services like Google AdSense?[215] None of these questions have a clear answer and may have implications in the qualification of hyperlinking by end-users and online platforms. (Among the implications may be a blurring of the lines between primary and secondary liability.)

Also problematic is the possibility of subsequent unavailability of a work which was initially freely accessible with consent of the rights holder. In *Svensson*, the Court identifies such a scenario as one in which a link communicates the work to a new public:

> This is the case, in particular, where the work is no longer available to the public on the site on which it was initially communicated or where it is henceforth available on that site only to a restricted public, while being accessible on another Internet site without the copyright holders' authorisation.[216]

For some commentators, this rationale implies a 'duty to monitor' the freely accessible nature of the work by 'linkers'.[217] After *GS Media*, this conclusion has to be qualified in light of the rebuttable presumption of knowledge. If an end-user had knowledge of the subsequent unauthorised nature of the source, his link thereto is infringing. Failing that knowledge, the link is either copyright irrelevant (under the initial interpretation of *Svensson*) or allowed under a doctrine of 'implicit consent' (following *Soulier and Doke*). To establish knowledge, we need to apply the aforementioned rebuttable presumption. Depending on whether the for-profit condition applies to the blog or website where the link was posted, the same may qualify as infringing. If the condition is met and the presumption applies, the user may still rebut the presumption; how she may do that is not clear.

The complexity of this analysis for such a simple everyday online activity is mind boggling. The potential for chilling effects on freedom of expression and information online is undeniable. Also clear is the legal uncertainty surrounding the legal status of hyperlinking, which extends to the effect of imposing technical restrictions on originally freely accessible content.[218] Therefore, this remains a volatile legal area, where end-users are subject to non-negligible infringement risks.

Table 4.2 provides an overview of the online uses covered by the exclusive right and the related issues of legal certainty. The significant scope of the right and the areas of uncertainty for the non-commercial activities of Internet users highlight the need for a legal solution that, like an ACS,

215. *See* Google AdSense, https://www.google.com/adsense/start/?hl=en&sourceid=aso&subid=ww-ww-et-op_adshp_ads_bt#?modal_active=none (accessed 31.01.2017).
216. CJEU, *Svensson*, para. 31.
217. Arezzo, 2014, pp. 545–546; Headdon, 2014, p. 665.
218. Debating this issue, *see* Arezzo, 2014, pp. 545–547.

enhances legal certainty and promotes breathing space for acts of personal enjoyment and expression online.

Table 4.2 Scope of Online Right of Communication to the Public and Legal Certainty Issues

Type of Online Use	*Right of Communication to the Public*	*Legal Certainty Issues*
Upload or Upstream streaming of work to restricted group (e.g., within a group on social sharing website)	?	Definition of public
Upload of freely accessible work from lawful source on publicly accessible server (no express authorisation)	Yes	Potential application of doctrines of implied consent
Upload of freely accessible work from unauthorised source on publicly accessible server (no express authorisation)	Yes	—
Upstream streaming (transmission or retransmission) of freely accessible work from lawful source (no express authorisation)	Yes	Potential application of doctrines of implied consent
Upstreaming of work (transmission or retransmission) in circumvention of access restrictions	Yes	Potential application by analogy of new public criterion
Upstreaming (transmission or retransmission) of work originating from unauthorised source	Yes	Potential application of doctrines of implied consent if unlawful source irrelevant
Hyperlinking to freely accessible work from authorised source	?	– Act is outside the scope of exclusive right (initial interpretation of *Svensson*) or – Act triggers the right but is authorised under doctrine of implied consent (*Soulier and Doke*)

Type of Online Use	*Right of Communication to the Public*	*Legal Certainty Issues*
Hyperlinking to freely accessible work from unauthorised source	Yes (*GS Media*)	– Application of rebuttable presumption of knowledge linked to for-profit condition (*GS Media*) – Possible application of Article 5(2)(d) InfoSoc Directive[219]
Hyperlinking to work in circumvention of access restrictions	Yes	Potential overlap between infringement of the exclusive right and the prohibition of circumvention of TPMs (Articles 3 and 6 InfoSoc Directive)

4.4 WHAT LIMITATIONS APPLY TO USES COVERED BY EXCLUSIVE RIGHTS?

4.4.1 General Framework, Objectives and Interpretation of Copyright Limitations

4.4.1.1 General Framework

The terms 'limitations' and 'exceptions' have multiple meanings and apply to a variety of legal mechanisms.[220] In a broad sense, they include the concept of 'negative rights',[221] exemptions from protected subject matter, conditions or limits on the scope and duration of protection, limitations and exceptions in the traditional sense, the minor exceptions doctrine, the three-step test, compulsory licences, and the doctrine of exhaustion (or first sale).[222]

From a conceptual standpoint, the terms can be understood in many possible ways. On the one hand, an 'exception' can refer to a permitted use that is unremunerated, a rule that provides immunity from liability, or a carve-out from the scope of an exclusive right. On the other hand, a 'limitation' can mean a remunerated permitted use, a category of content excluded from copyright protection, or a boundary to exclusivity.[223]

219. *See* ALAI, 2015a, pp. 7–8, discussing the application of the quotation limitation to hyperlinking.
220. See, e.g., Hugenholtz, 1997.
221. Art. 17 BC.
222. Lucie Guibault, 2002, p. 17, discussing possible meanings.
223. Christie & Wright, 2014, pp. 420–421, with a survey of influential literature. For terminology, *see also* Kur, 2008, pp. 5–8.

From a different perspective, 'exceptions' can be seen as deviations from a broad principle of copyright exclusivity, which would otherwise apply without restriction. 'Limitations', in contrast, are limits to the exclusive right, which concern 'the *definition* of the substance of the provision as such', i.e., the scope of protection of the exclusive right.[224] In this way, using the evocative metaphor of Geiger, the exclusive right is akin to 'an island of exclusivity in a sea of freedom (freedom of expression and competition)'.[225]

As shown in this section 4.4.1, although the EU legislature adopts a compromise between different legal traditions and uses both terms in the title of Article 5 InfoSoc Directive, systematic interpretation of the *acquis* in light of fundamental rights leans in favour of considering 'exceptions and limitations' as 'limitations'. It is submitted that this meaning is both descriptively – from the legal-technical standpoint – and normatively preferable to 'exceptions'.[226] For that reason, the term 'limitations' is preferentially used in this book to mean the use permissions in Article 5.

Article 5 InfoSoc Directive contains the primary regulation for limitations at EU level. It applies to all copyright subject matter, except software and databases.[227] Its first paragraph contains the directive's sole mandatory limitation, applying to transient or incidental copies, the purpose of which is to facilitate the activities of ISPs or certain lawful uses.[228] Articles 5(2)–(4) contain an exhaustive list of twenty optional limitations, applying to the otherwise exclusive rights of reproduction, communication to the public, and distribution.[229] Where Member States choose to implement these, some are conditional upon the grant of fair compensation.[230] For the others, Member States may nevertheless demand compensation in their national laws.[231]

224. Dreier, 2015, pp. 139, 146.
225. Geiger, 2010, p. 521. *See also* Geiger & Schönherr, 2014a, p. 112 (n. 6). For an early reference to this conceptual distinction, *see* Hugenholtz, 1997, pp. 4–5.
226. Cf. Dreier, 2015, pp. 139–140. *See* Hugenholtz, 1997, pp. 4–5, arguing similarly in relation to the legal nature of limitations in international law. *See also* Kur, 2008, p. 6, noting that both terminological choices are acceptable. The author further draws a distinction with 'exclusions', a term meant to identify provisions that *ab initio* exclude from protection certain subject matter.
227. Janssens, 2009, p. 328.
228. Hugenholtz et al., 2006, pp. 68–69.
229. On the exhaustive nature of the list in Art. 5, *see* recital 32 InfoSoc Directive. The list contains four optional limitations for reproduction in Art. 5(2), 15 optional limitations for reproduction and/or public communication in Art. 5(3), and the possibility to extend the previous limitations (applying to reproduction) to the right of distribution in Art. 5(4). N.B. Art. 5(3)(o) contains a deviation from the exhaustive nature of the list by including a 'grandfathering clause' for pre-existing analogue uses of minor importance (*de minimis*).
230. Namely, those in Art. 5(2)(a), (b) and (e) InfoSoc Directive.
231. Cf. recital 36 InfoSoc Directive.

Article 5(5) contains the directive's version of the three-step test, which Chapter 5 discusses in depth.[232]

Elsewhere in the *acquis*, the Rental Right Directive contains a list of optional limitations to related rights and allows Member States to apply in respect thereto limitations identical to those applicable to authors.[233] Despite the overlap between the lists in both instruments, it is commonly accepted that Article 5 InfoSoc Directive also regulates related rights.[234]

As noted, the InfoSoc Directive's limitations do not apply to software or databases, meaning that reproduction or communication to the public thereof are restricted.[235] Authorisation to perform these acts is required unless they are covered by the *lex specialis* limitations in the 'vertical' Software and Database Directives.[236]

The Software Directive exempts acts necessary by the 'lawful acquirer', the making of a back-up copy, use of the program to 'observe, study or test' its functioning, and decompilation of the program for purposes of interoperability.[237] The Database Directive contains a list of mandatory and optional limitations regarding copyright protected databases (Article 6) and those protected by the sui generis right (Article 9). For copyright protected databases, a mandatory limitation allows a 'lawful user' to perform acts required 'for the purposes of access to the contents of the databases and normal use of the contents'; furthermore, Member States may extend other copyright limitations to those databases.[238]

The relationship of limitations to contract law is in essence one between public choice or policy and private ordering.[239] Although this relationship is generally unregulated by the InfoSoc Directive, commentators by and large accept that the instrument allows contractual disposition of the limitations in Article 5(2)–(4). This understanding relies on Article 9 being without prejudice to provisions concerning contract law, and recital 45 admitting contracts on fair compensation.[240] In addition, this interpretation is

232. Chapter 5 provides a detailed analysis of this test, which is also incorporated (inconsistently) in the Software, Rental Rights and Database Directives.
233. *See* Art. 10(1) and (2) Rental Right Directive and the very similar Art. 15 RC. On the later, *see supra* 2.4.3.
234. Bechtold, 2006, p. 370; Janssens, 2009, p. 325 & fn. 40; Triaille et al., 2013, p. 247.
235. This results from the application of Art. 1(2)(a) InfoSoc Directive. *See* recital 50 InfoSoc Directive, *in fine*. *See also* Bechtold, 2006, p. 370.
236. Triaille et al., 2013, p. 246.
237. See, respectively, Art. 5(1), (2) and (3), and Art. 6 Software Directive.
238. *See* Art. 6(1) and 2(d) Database Directive. See, in this sense, Triaille et al., 2013, p. 247. N.B. Art. 9 Database Directive does not allow analogous application of copyright limitations to the sui generis database right.
239. Dreier, 2015, pp. 142–144.
240. Bechtold, 2006, pp. 370–371; Janssens, 2009, pp. 341–342; von Lewinski & Walter, 2010, pp. 1022–1023, 1062. *But see* Lucie Guibault, 2009, pp. 529–530, 2010, p. 59, describing scholarship that holds an opposite view, relying on the letter of recital 45 InfoSoc Directive: 'Whether the requirement that a contractual agreement must have the

systematically consistent with Article 6(4), fourth subparagraph of the directive, which allows contractual override of limitations where works are made available online with TPMs and on agreed contractual terms. From this perspective, the InfoSoc Directive indicates a predominance of private ordering over public policy.

However, contractual disposition may be prohibited in certain cases. These result from the definition of limitations as imperative in national law (e.g., in Portuguese and Belgian law[241]), and the application of imperative provisions protecting end-users (e.g., consumer protection rules on adhesion contracts).[242] Following a different approach, the Software and Database Directives afford absolute status to some of their limitations by explicitly prohibiting their contractual override and qualifying potential derogation clauses as 'null and void'.[243]

4.4.1.2 Relationship with Technological Protection Measures

The term Digital Rights Management (DRM) encompasses both TPMs (e.g., access and copy control measures) and electronic rights management information, such as fingerprinting or watermarking, also known as 'social DRM'.[244] The directive's regulation of the relationship between limitations and TPMs has been subject to significant criticism.[245] The tension between both regimes cannot be understated: while limitations strive to ensure access to, and dissemination of, works, TPMs increase protection of exclusivity and restrict that access and dissemination, sometimes protecting non-copyrightable content.[246] Article 6(4) InfoSoc Directive regulates that tension through a formulation that mostly allows TPMs to override limitations.[247] In doing so, it adds complexity to the balance of interests in copyright law.

goal to secure the fair compensation of right holders means that contractual agreements with the purpose to override legitimate uses are impermissible is, according to these authors, questionable'.

241. *See* Lucie Guibault, 2009, pp. 537–541; Triaille et al., 2013, p. 255 (n. 548), 472, noting that the Danish legislation is not clear on this aspect despite some commentators arguing that it includes such a rule. On the Belgian law, *see* Geiger, 2015a, p. 22.
242. Bechtold, 2006, pp. 370–371; Lucie Guibault, 2009, pp. 534–536; von Lewinski & Walter, 2010, pp. 1022–1023, 1062.
243. Art. 9 InfoSoc Directive, Arts 5(2)–(3) 6, and 8 Software Directive, and Arts 6(1), 8 and Art. 15 Database Directive.
244. Poort & Quintais, 2013. For a different classification of TPMs, *see* Efroni, 2011, pp. 195–196.
245. Janssens, 2009, pp. 333–334.
246. Bechtold, 2006, p. 390.
247. Janssens, 2009, p. 334.

Article 6 InfoSoc Directive implements and goes beyond Articles 11 WCT and 18 WPPT.[248] It instructs Member States to provide adequate legal protection against the circumvention of effective TPMs, i.e., devices or components aimed at restricting unauthorised access to or use of works. 'Access controls' are measures for protection of a work, such as encryption, scrambling or other transformation. 'Use controls' refer to mechanisms that prevent, for example, the making of copies of works. The legal regime of TPMs includes protection against circumvention and preparatory acts.[249]

Article 6(4) InfoSoc Directive entrusts rights holders (not legislators) with the role of providing the beneficiaries of certain limitations with the means of exercising the limitation through 'voluntary measures'.[250] If rights holders do not provide voluntary measures, Member States can step in to ensure exercise of the limitations and impose 'appropriate' (i.e., mandatory) measures.[251] Voluntary and mandatory measures are only required if the beneficiary has 'legal access' to the work and to the extent necessary to exercise the limitation.[252] The application of either type of measure does not prejudice the legal protection of TPMs.[253]

Such legal protection is limited to the prevention of acts not authorised by the rights holder with respect for the principle of proportionality. Therefore, the application of TPMs must be suitable to achieve that objective and cannot 'go beyond what is necessary for this purpose.'[254]

---

248. Arts 11 and 12 WCT prohibit the circumvention of TPMs, the removal or alteration of electronic rights management information, and the distribution (or other forms of marketing or use) of works or copies where that information has been removed or altered. These provisions are implemented in the EU through Arts 6 and 7 InfoSoc Directive. *See also* the corresponding Arts 18–19 WPPT. On the articulation of Art. 6 InfoSoc Directive with other anti-circumvention measures in EU law, notably on the Software Directive (Art. 7(1)(c)) and the Conditional Access Directive, *see* Bechtold, 2006, pp. 384–385. For an historical note and commentary, *see* von Lewinski & Walter, 2010, pp. 1065–1075.
249. Art. 6(1)–(3) InfoSoc Directive. On the meaning of 'effective' TPMs, *see* CJEU, *Nintendo*, paras 27–28.
250. Janssens, 2009, p. 334 criticising this as a 'remarkable policy reversal'.
251. Recital 52 clarifies the InfoSoc Directive's preference for the adoption of voluntary measures. Where these are not taken, Member States should impose them on rights holders, under the terms described above. There is little guidance on how and when to impose such measures. However, recital 51 InfoSoc Directive requires that Member States wait for a 'reasonable period of time' before imposing appropriate measures.
252. Art. 6(4), first subparagraph InfoSoc Directive. In this sense, *see* von Lewinski & Walter, 2010, p. 1073, providing examples of legal access (buying, renting, borrowing a legal copy or otherwise obtaining it with the consent of the rightholder) and illegal access ('illegal peer-to-peer network'). N.B. the Court in *ACI Adam*, when deciding that copies from unlawful sources do not fall within the scope of the private copying limitation, failed to clarify the concept of 'lawful source'. *See* Quintais, 2015b.
253. Art. 6(4), third subparagraph InfoSoc Directive.
254. CJEU, *Nintendo*, paras 29–31 (cit. ¶31), relying on Art. 6(2) and recital 48 InfoSoc Directive.

The benefit of voluntary or mandatory measures is not available to all limitations in Article 5 InfoSoc Directive. Instead, these rules apply obligatorily to certain limitations and, optionally (at the discretion of the Member State), to private copying. Some commentators are critical of this hierarchy, noting that the private use limitation, because it 'is also justified by privacy and freedom of information', should be listed as a 'privileged' limitation.[255]

The regime also applies by analogy to limitations in the Rental Right and Database Directives.[256] Member States cannot impose any measures of this type in relation to the remaining limitations, which can be fully overridden by the application of TPMs.[257]

The privileged limitations that must benefit from such voluntary or mandatory measures are those in Article 5(2)(a), (2)(c), (2)(d), (2)(e), (3)(a), (3)(b) and (3)(e) InfoSoc Directive. None of these limitations is susceptible of applying to acts licensed in an ACS.[258] Therefore, even if a limitation covers an online use, end-users may not benefit from it if the work is subject to TPMs, as that would require violating the prohibition against circumvention of technological measures.

Article 6(4), second subparagraph InfoSoc Directive, allows for the possible application of mandatory measures in relation to the private copying limitation in Article 5(2)(b), subject to additional conditions. Thus, no measures can be imposed by Member States: (1) if rights holders have adopted voluntary measures to enable private copying; or (2) vis-à-vis *copy control* TPMs that limit the number of reproductions made by users in accordance with such provisions.[259] In addition, any measures must respect rights holders' entitlement to use TPMs, the condition of fair compensation, and the three-step test.[260]

The logic of these provisions is as follows: TPMs can restrict acts of digital reproduction and subject them to additional payment, even where those acts would otherwise be privileged private copying. That would make payments through a levy system unwarranted, because there would be no

255. Geiger & Schönherr, 2014b, p. 469.
256. Art. 6(4), fifth subparagraph InfoSoc Directive. *See* von Lewinski & Walter, 2010, p. 1075.
257. These are the limitations in Arts 5(1), 5(2)(c), (d) and (f)–(o) InfoSoc Directive.
258. N.B. not even the mandatory limitation in Art. 5(1) InfoSoc Directive can benefit from 'appropriate' mandatory measures. *See* Bechtold, 2006, p. 392.
259. Art. 6(4), first and second subparagraphs InfoSoc Directive. *See* von Lewinski & Walter, 2010, p. 1073, considering the first point redundant and the second a mere clarification.
260. Recitals 39 and 52 InfoSoc Directive. Recital 39 addresses the articulation of TPMs and digital private copying and remuneration schemes, urging Member States to take into consideration 'technological and economic developments' when applying this exception and limitation, noting that the latter 'should not inhibit the use of technological measures or their enforcement against circumvention'.

unauthorised copying or harm to compensate. Consequently, some commentators contend that the *application* of effective TPMs could lead to 'phasing-out' of levies in the digital environment.[261] In this line, a recent economic study for the EU Commission concludes that, due to 'changes in the consumption of content', the best policy option in this field would be that of 'entirely removing levies'.[262]

The little space available for limitations to apply where TPMs are used is further reduced by a special rule on licensed interactive on demand services.[263] This rule prohibits Member States from implementing any measures limiting the effect of TPMs if the work in question is made available online for interactive on-demand transmission on agreed contractual terms.[264] This includes rights holders making available works online (under Article 3 InfoSoc Directive) for streaming or downloading on-demand. Thus, in such a 'technology plus contract' scenario, all limitations can be set aside.[265]

To sum up, the application of TPMs overrides the possibility for end-users to exercise most limitations potentially applicable to online sharing, and leaves little space for the digital private copying limitation.[266] This prioritising of TPMs over limitations regarding use over the Internet is also apparent in the CJEU's case law on hyperlinks. Following *Svensson*, the choice by rights holders to impose technical access restrictions on a work will determine whether linking to that work (in circumvention of those restrictions) qualifies as a restricted act of communication to the public.[267]

---

261. See: Helberger & Hugenholtz, 2007; Hugenholtz, Guibault & van Geffen, 2003; and Eechoud et al., 2009, p. 118, raising the possibility that, for cases where the application of TPMs makes private copying activities impossible or near impossible (e.g., copy controls on DVDs), no compensation should be claimed as it would be unjustified. *Contra* the argument that the InfoSoc Directive provides for automatic phasing out of levies, *see* von Lewinski & Walter, 2010, p. 1034. For a critical analysis of the 'phasing-out provision', *see* Dusollier & Ker, 2009
262. Boulanger et al., 2014, p. 103.
263. Art. 6(4), fourth subparagraph, and recital 53 InfoSoc Directive.
264. 'Agreed contractual terms' in this context seems to have a broad construction and likely applies also to standard form contracts such as typical online end-user licence agreements. See von Lewinski & Walter, 2010, p. 1074 (n. 482). For a more restrictive view, arguing for the application of the provision solely to negotiated and agreed terms, *see* Lucie Guibault et al., 2007b, p. 112 ('the exception to the main rule of article 6(4) of the Directive could be interpreted as applying only in respect of the supply of online services for which the contracting parties have negotiated the terms of use...').
265. Art. 6(4), fourth subparagraph, and recital 53 InfoSoc Directive, excluding from the scope of the provision non-interactive Internet transmissions. *See also* Poort & Quintais, 2013, p. 209.
266. Janssens, 2009, p. 334.
267. *See supra* 4.3.2.1.2. *See* the discussion in Dreier, 2015, pp. 144–145.

4.4.1.3 Objectives

The InfoSoc Directive aims at creating a 'general and flexible legal framework... to foster the development of the Information Society in Europe'.[268] The directive is based *inter alia* on the objectives of increasing legal certainty, providing a high level of protection for copyright and related rights, and ensuring the smooth functioning of the internal market.[269] Subject to the principle of subsidiarity, the harmonisation of copyright and limitations are considered necessary to achieve those objectives.[270]

Harmonisation must comply with fundamental principles of law, such as property in copyright, freedom of expression, and the public interest.[271] Limitations serve such public interest goals, including the promotion of culture and dissemination of knowledge, by enabling use outside exclusivity for purposes related to private use, educational teaching, scientific learning and research, news reporting, quotation, use by people with disabilities, public security use, and use in administrative and judicial proceedings.[272]

The CJEU has recognised that certain limitations have fundamental rights justifications underlying these purposes, such as freedom of expression and information.[273] Therefore, where rooted in public interest justifications and in fundamental rights, analysis of the existence and scope of limitations cannot be confined to market failure arguments.[274]

Against this framework, limitations function as internal tools to strike a balance between competing interests in copyright. Recital 31 InfoSoc Directive clarifies this function, as well as the need for harmonisation of limitations, especially in the digital networked environment, and in light of the cross-border exploitation of works, subject to the directive's overall internal market objective.

The list of limitations in Article 5 InfoSoc Directive attempts to achieve this balance by simultaneously taking 'due account of different legal traditions of Member States' and 'aiming to ensure a functioning internal market'.[275] A further manifestation of the balancing principle is the need for

---

268. Recital 2 InfoSoc Directive.
269. On the objectives of EU copyright law, *see supra* 1.3 and *infra* 5.5.3.
270. On the directive's general goal of harmonisation of copyright law in the EU, *see* recitals 1, 4, 6, 7, 9, 23, and 31 InfoSoc Directive. Recitals 31 and 32 refer in particular to the goal of harmonising limitations. *See also* Triaille et al., 2013, p. 250.
271. Recital 3 InfoSoc Directive.
272. Recitals 14, 34, 39 InfoSoc Directive.
273. *See infra* 4.4.1.4.
274. Triaille et al., 2013, p. 256, noting that '[b]oth the European lawmaker and the international one refer to public interest as a key justification of copyright exceptions'.
275. Recital 33 InfoSoc Directive.

Member States to consider the 'increased economic impact' of limitations in the 'new electronic environment'.[276]

Following Dreier, it is important to dispel the notion that the often-touted objective of providing a 'high level of protection' for copyright (in recitals 4 and 9 InfoSoc Directive) is synonymous with an infinitely excludable scope of protection. Instead, from the economic perspective, '"excessive protection" can have a negative impact on creativity and innovation'. Therefore, where broad exclusive rights are recognised in the *acquis* – as results from the analysis in 4.3 – the function of limitations is to 'reduce and confine the excessive protection afforded by the exclusive right to the optimal scope of protection'.[277]

In sum, limitations are an essential component of copyright, as they promote access to, and dissemination of, culture, education and knowledge. In doing so, they stimulate the creation goal of copyright, by fostering access to and use of pre-existing works.[278] Their essential role in pursuing the InfoSoc Directive's objectives and balancing copyright exclusivity with the public interest and fundamental rights has been steadily recognised by the CJEU.

4.4.1.4 The Court's Case Law: From Strict Interpretation to Restricted Flexibility

The CJEU has interpreted the InfoSoc Directive's system of limitations on multiple occasions.[279] Its rulings shape Member States' margin of discretion in implementing limitations and national courts' leeway in interpreting them.

In general terms, the CJEU's activity centres around the objectives highlighted above: fair balance, high level of protection for copyright holders, adequate compensation, circulation of culture, resolving legal uncertainty, technological development, fair competition, and harmonisation of copyright law to achieve a functioning internal market. Although recognising Member States' margin of discretion in implementing limitations, the Court has held that this margin is to be exercised within the limits

276. Recital 44 InfoSoc Directive refers to the conditions of the three-step test. For a restrictive application of this rationale, *see* CJEU, *ACI Adam*, paras 25–27. *See infra* 4.4.3.6.
277. Dreier, 2015, p. 140.
278. Geiger & Schönherr, 2014a, p. 110.
279. CJEU, *Laserdisken II*, CJEU, *LSG*, CJEU, *Infopaq I*, CJEU, *Murphy*, CJEU, *Padawan*, CJEU, *Stichting de Thuiskopie*, CJEU, *Painer*, CJEU, *Luksan*, CJEU, *Infopaq II*, CJEU, *DR and TV 2 Danmark*, CJEU, *VG Wort*, CJEU, *Amazon*.com, CJEU, *ACI Adam*, CJEU, *Copydan*, CJEU, *Ulmer*, CJEU, *Deckmyn*, CJEU, *OSA*, CJEU, *Meltwater*, CJEU, *Reprobel*.

of EU law, and in line with the aforementioned objectives and the principle of proportionality.[280]

The CJEU has primarily interpreted limitations according to the doctrine or principle of strict interpretation. The first case to do so in the copyright field was *Infopaq I*, which examined the mandatory exemption for transient copies in Article 5(1) InfoSoc Directive. In simple terms, the doctrine considers exclusivity the baseline for copyright protection; any deviation thereto is exceptional and, thus, must be interpreted strictly. The principle is drawn from previous case law on derogations to general principles and is further supported by a restrictive reading of the three-step test, from which the Court infers a requirement to interpret limitations stringently.[281]

The doctrine is a staple of CJEU decisions on limitations. Of particular relevance to the ACS debate is the application of the doctrine in *ACI Adam*, where the Court discussed whether the scope of the private copying limitation covers reproductions from unauthorised sources.[282] In this judgment, the Court relied heavily on the letter of recital 44 InfoSoc Directive, which allows the reduction of the limitation's scope in connection with 'certain new uses' of works. In contrast, it was noted, nothing in the InfoSoc Directive mentions the possibility of extending that scope.[283] Therefore, despite the directive's silence on this controversial issue, limitations should be interpreted strictly.[284] As a result, the Court ultimately concluded that Article 5(2)(b) cannot cover private copies made from unlawful sources.[285] This reasoning was later upheld in *Copydan* and *Reprobel*.[286]

The CJEU's adherence to the strict interpretation doctrine is consistent with what Leistner labels an essentially 'economic' (rather than flexible) approach to the interpretation of exploitation rights in the InfoSoc Directive. This interpretation attempts to ensure appropriate remuneration for any independent act of exploitation by users, primarily through the expansion of exclusive rights, namely reproduction.[287]

280. Triaille et al., 2013, pp. 251–252. See: CJEU, *Infopaq I*, para. 62; CJEU, *Stichting de Thuiskopie*, para. 23; CJEU, *Padawan*, paras 35–36; CJEU, *Painer*, paras 103–105, 107; CJEU, *DR and TV2 Danmark*, para. 36. Listing the objectives of EU law, *see supra* 1.3 and *infra* 5.5.3.
281. CJEU, *Infopaq I*, paras 56–57; CJEU, *Painer*, paras 109, 133; CJEU, *Murphy*, para. 162; CJEU, *Meltwater*, para. 23. *See also* Janssens, 2009, p. 323 (considering the doctrine of strict interpretation a common view point in international norms), and Senftleben, 2013b, p. 93.
282. On which *see* Quintais, 2015b.
283. CJEU, *ACI Adam*, paras 25–27.
284. *Ibid.*, paras 22, 29–30. *See also* CJEU, *Infopaq I*, para. 56, and case law cited therein.
285. CJEU, *ACI Adam*, para. 41.
286. CJEU, *Copydan*, paras 74–79; CJEU, *Reprobel*, paras 57–64.
287. Leistner, 2014, p. 569- *See also* Senftleben, 2013b, p. 93, using the expression 'dogma of strict interpretation'.

Still, post *Infopaq I* – and with the notable exception of *ACI Adam* and its progeny –, this doctrine has been tempered. In fact, it is possible to observe a gradual shift towards a more nuanced interpretation of limitations designed to secure their effectiveness in view of their objective and purpose, as well as the principle of proportionality.[288] This shift is coherent with the goal of striking a fair balance in copyright law, which is central to the InfoSoc Directive.[289] The goal, for its part, if not in direct contradiction with the strict interpretation doctrine, at least severely limits its application.[290] As noted in *Painer* and *Murphy*, the interpretation of the conditions for the application of limitations must:

> enable the effectiveness of the exception thereby established to be safeguarded and its purpose to be observed[291] … as resulting in particular from recital 31 in the preamble to the Copyright Directive and from Common Position (EC) No 48/2000 adopted by the Council on 28 September 2000 with a view to adopting that directive[292]

By referencing recital 31 and Common Position (EC) No. 48/2000, the Court clarifies that, in fulfilling the requirements of effectiveness and purpose-bound interpretation, it is essential to balance the interests of authors and rights holders, on the one hand, with those of users, on the other.[293] Recital 31 is a key element for interpretation of the InfoSoc Directive in light of international and EU copyright law and the external constraints imposed by fundamental rights in the digital networked environment.[294]

In that light, *Murphy* and *Meltwater* – when discussing the mandatory limitation for transient copies – qualify this balancing exercise as vital towards achieving the goal of development and operation of new technologies. *Murphy* states:

> In accordance with its objective, that exception must allow and ensure the development and operation of new technologies and safeguard a fair balance between the rights and interests of right holders, on the one

288. Recital 31 InfoSoc Directive. *See* inter alia: CJEU, *Deckmyn*, paras 19–23; CJEU, *Murphy*, para. 163; CJEU, *Painer*, para. 105; CJEU, *Ulmer*, paras 27, 31. Emphasising this point in legal scholarship, *see* European Copyright Society, 2014b; Leistner, 2014, p. 585; Triaille et al., 2013, pp. 487–489. *See also* Senftleben, 2013a, p. 93 calling this development a flexible interpretation of the dogma of strict interpretation.
289. CJEU, *Padawan*, para. 43; CJEU, *Murphy*, paras 163ff.; CJEU, *Painer*, para. 132; CJEU, *Deckmyn*, para. 26; CJEU, *Ulmer*, para. 43.
290. European Copyright Society, 2014b, p. 5.
291. CJEU, *Painer*, para. 133; CJEU, *Murphy*, para. 163.
292. CJEU, *Murphy*, para. 163.
293. CJEU, *Murphy*, paras 163ff.; CJEU, *Painer*, paras 132ff.; CJEU, *Deckmyn*, para. 27; CJEU, *UPC Telekabel*, para. 46; CJEU, *Bonnier Audio*, para. 56; CJEU, *Netlog*, para. 51; CJEU, *Scarlett Extended*, para. 53; CJEU, *Tele2*, para. 28; CJEU, *Promusicae*, para. 68; CJEU, *Meltwater*, para. 24.
294. Chapter 5 elaborates on this point. *See infra* 5.2.1.4 and 5.3.3.6.

> hand, and of users of protected works who wish to avail themselves of those new technologies, on the other.[295]

This understanding allows for teleological interpretation of the limitation to ensure its effectiveness and achieve its objectives, thereby mitigating the operation of the doctrine of strict interpretation.[296]

Further to the balancing component, CJEU case law explicitly recognises the impact of fundamental rights in the interpretation of limitations.[297] In *Painer*, it is noted that the quotation limitation in Article 5(3)(d) InfoSoc Directive:

> is intended to strike a fair balance between the right to freedom of expression of users of a work or other protected subject-matter and the reproduction right conferred on authors.[298]

In *Deckmyn*, it is said that the parody limitation is justified by the fundamental right of freedom of expression and that it:

> must strike a fair balance between, on the one hand, the interests and rights of persons referred to in Articles 2 and 3 of that directive, and, on the other, the freedom of expression of the user of a protected work who is relying on the exception for parody, within the meaning of Article 5(3)(k).[299]

From the aforementioned case law, it is possible to draw important conclusions regarding the influence of fundamental rights on a more flexible definition and interpretation of limitations. From an internal perspective, fundamental rights provide a justification for limitations, which is then considered when examining their purpose. At an external level, fundamental rights affect the balance of interests, functioning as rights of users (and third parties with legitimate interests) to be balanced against those of copyright owners.[300]

The latter point merits elaboration. Neither the fundamental right of intellectual property as applied to copyright (Article 17(2) Charter) nor that of freedom of expression (Article 11 Charter) are absolute. Rather, copyright is a functional right. Like other fundamental rights, its application can only impose narrow constraints on freedom of expression. In that light, the design and interpretation of a system of copyright limitations should strike a 'fair

---

295. CJEU, *Murphy*, para. 164; CJEU, *Meltwater*, para. 24.
296. Triaille et al., 2013, p. 252.
297. Leistner, 2014, p. 585.
298. CJEU, *Painer*, para. 134.
299. CJEU, *Deckmyn*, paras 25–28 (cit. para. 27).
300. Leistner, 2014, p. 586: '… the judgment in that context implicitly acknowledges the impact of the fundamental freedoms on the interpretation of the provisions on the exceptions to copyright by fairly balancing the right of the authors with the right of the users to freedom of expression'.

balance' between competing fundamental rights, guided by the principle of proportionality.

Thus, and at least for limitations justified on the basis of fundamental rights, it does not seem consistent with EU and international law to impose a 'horizontal' doctrine of strict interpretation. Rather, in certain cases, copyright might have to cede to other fundamental rights.[301] This rationale underscores CJEU decisions finding that, where conditions for benefiting from limitations are met, the fundamental rights of users may prevail over the interests of authors.[302] This conclusion is also in line with consistent case law of the Court that provides 'shelter' to the 'protection of fundamental rights in relation to copyright users'.[303]

In this light, we can read the Court's restrictive approach in *ACI Adam* and its progeny as resulting from a failure to consider the fundamental rights justification of the private copying limitation.[304] As in the other cited cases, *ACI Adam* articulates the doctrine with the need to strike a fair balance of interests between authors and users.[305] However, unlike *Painer* and *Deckmyn*, no reference is made to the impact of fundamental rights on the interpretation of limitations.[306]

Given that the private copying limitation is intended, at least in part, to safeguard privacy interests of end-users (as is clear from the analysis in Chapter 2), that omission is open to criticism, as it would provide an essential counterweight to the strict interpretation doctrine. This argument, raised by the Dutch Government in *ACI Adam* and summarily (if unconvincingly) dismissed in the AG Opinion,[307] is ignored by the Court, with important consequences.

When implementing optional limitations, Member States are subject to the principle of proportionality and the boundaries of the three-step test. Within those confines, their margin of discretion in specifying and qualifying the conditions of applicability of limitations is further subject to the principle of autonomous interpretation.[308]

In *ACI Adam*, by overly relying on the doctrine of strict interpretation, the Court's reading of the private copying limitation in connection with the

---

301. See: European Copyright Society, 2014b, pp. 4–7, and case law cited therein; Geiger & Schönherr, 2014a, pp. 118–119. *See also Opinion AG in Deckmyn*, paras 80–85. On the application of Art. 10 ECHR to copyright, *see* ECtHR, *Ashby Donald*, and ECtHR, *The Pirate Bay*.
302. CJEU, *Painer*, paras 134ff.; CJEU, *Deckmyn*, paras 25–28, 34.
303. Favale et al., 2015, p. 60, citing CJEU, *Netlog*, CJEU, *Scarlet Extended*, CJEU, *Promusicae*, and CJEU, *Bonnier Audio*.
304. *See infra* 4.4.3.6. For a detailed analysis, *see* Quintais, 2015b.
305. CJEU, *ACI Adam*, paras 53–58. *See also*: CJEU, *Murphy*, paras 163–164; CJEU, *Painer*, para. 132; CJEU, *Deckmyn*, paras 25–28, 34.
306. Leistner, 2014, p. 585.
307. *Opinion of AG in ACI Adam*, para. 78. For criticism, *see* Consumentenbond & Bureau Brandeis, 2014, p. 3.
308. Leistner, 2014, p. 586.

three-step test apparently leaves Member States with a narrower margin of discretion for national implementation of limitations.[309] To this effect, *ACI Adam* favours the position that national laws' discretion can be used solely to restrict the scope of the limitation for 'certain new uses of copyright works and other subject-matter'.[310] (Arguably, the restrictive reading of the three-step test in *OSA* supports this approach.[311])

Still, such a position is inconsistent with the CJEU's previous understanding in *Murphy* that limitations be interpreted so as to enable the development and operation of new technologies, balancing the interests of rights holders with those of users of new technologies.[312] It is also inconsistent with the Court's approach in *Deckmyn*, where it adopts a more liberal view of limitations,[313] in line with a growing body of case law considering them akin to 'user rights'.[314]

A flexible understanding of copyright limitations can also be derived from the structure and contents of the directive's catalogue in Articles 5(2) and 5(3). Whereas the list is exhaustive, therefore proscribing implementation of additional limitations, a degree of elasticity may result from its qualification as 'categorically worded prototypes', rather than narrow 'circumscribed exceptions'.[315] Quotation is a case in point, as it applies 'for purposes *such as* criticism or review, provided that… their use is in accordance *with fair practice, and to the extent required by the specific purpose*'.[316]

It is true that, in theory, Member States could use their margin of discretion in a restrictive way. This could be done by implementing and then

309. Similarly, see Rosati, 2014, pp. 710–711.
310. CJEU, *ACI Adam*, para. 27, relying on recital 44 InfoSoc Directive.
311. CJEU, *OSA*, paras 38–41. *See* Nérisson, 2015b, p. 391, stating that in *OSA* the CJEU closes the door to analogous or extensive interpretation of limitations.
312. CJEU, *Murphy*, paras 163–164, 179. The general point is made in Leistner, 2014, p. 585.
313. Rosati, 2015b, p. 10.
314. CJEU, *Padawan*, para. 43; CJEU, *Painer*, para. 132; CJEU, *Ulmer*, para. 43; CJEU, *Deckmyn*, para. 26. *See also*: European Copyright Society, 2014b, noting that 'the idea of 'users' rights' as enforceable rights of equal value has also recently featured in Case C-314/12,UPC Telekabel[2014],[57]'; and Rosati, 2015b, p. 10. *Contra* such qualification as 'user rights', *see* von Lewinski & Walter, 2010, p. 1022.
315. Hugenholtz & Senftleben, 2011, p. 2: 'the enumerated provisions are in many cases categorically worded prototypes rather than precisely circumscribed exceptions, thus leaving the Member States broad margins of implementation'. *But see*: von Lewinski & Walter, 2010, p. 1021; Rosati, 2015b, p. 9, arguing that, following the restrictive interpretation of the CJEU in *Padawan*, *DR & TV 2 Danmark* and *ACI Adam*, in most cases the limitations in Art. 5 'would not be just categorically-worded prototypes'; and Nérisson, 2015b, p. 284, arguing that *OSA* bars such interpretation.
316. Art. 5(3)(d) InfoSoc Directive, emphasis added. The point is made *inter alia* in European Copyright Society, 2014b, p. 5; Hugenholtz & Senftleben, 2011, which mention Art. 5(3)(a) and (f) InfoSoc Directive as examples. For a broad view of the quotation limitation in international copyright law, *see* Bentley, 2016 [paper forthcoming]. *Contra*, after *OSA*, Nérisson, 2015b, p. 391.

narrowing the scope of the limitations through the imposition of additional conditions, in what has been described as a 'homing' tendency.[317]

However, this possibility is limited to the extent that the CJEU provides for autonomous interpretation of the limitation's 'prototype' or key concepts. In that line, the Court in *DR and TV2 Danmark* and *Deckmyn* denied that limitations should be implemented restrictively into national laws.[318] This is in contrast with *ACI Adam*, *Copydan*, and *Reprobel*, where it imposed a narrower margin of implementation and subsequent interpretation through the addition of the condition of 'lawfulness of the source of reproduction'.[319] (Curiously, *Copydan* leaves to Member States discretion on the regulation of the use of third party devices for private copying, allowing the scope of the limitation to broaden.[320])

In fact, the practice of independent and uniform interpretation – rooted in the need for a uniform application of EU law and the principle of equality – is justified by the InfoSoc Directive's goal of achieving a harmonious interpretation of limitations that is conducive to a proper and smooth functioning of the internal market. The goal, derived from recital 32, constitutes a manifestation of an overall objective of the directive, namely the harmonisation of EU copyright law.[321] In part due to the lack of true harmonisation of the system of copyright limitations in the InfoSoc Directive's design – i.e., the number of optional limitations, the wide margin of implementation, and lack of guidance on contractual overridability – and despite the Court's efforts to the contrary, that goal has not been achieved.[322] The result, mitigated by the CJEU's expanding case law on the field, is a smorgasbord of divergent national implementation.

4.4.1.5 Interim Conclusions

To conclude, Member States' margin of discretion in defining the conditions for applicability of limitations, and national courts' freedom of interpretation, are curtailed by two opposing constraints. From one side, the strict interpretation doctrine and the three-step test seem to impede the broadening of the scope of limitations. From the other, the prototypical nature of certain

317. Lucie Guibault, 2010, p. 64, referring to the 'tendency of the Member States' legislatures when translating provisions of the Directive into national law, preserving as much as possible the old formulations and adding further specifications'.
318. CJEU, *DR and TV2 Danmark*, para. 36; CJEU, *Deckmyn*, paras 16, 24.
319. CJEU, *ACI Adam*, paras 33–34; CJEU, *Copydan*, paras 74–79; CJEU, *Reprobel*, paras 57–64. *See* Rosati, 2014, pp. 710–711.
320. CJEU, *Copydan*, paras 86–96. *See infra* 4.4.3.7.
321. CJEU, *DR and TV2 Danmark*, paras 35–37; CJEU, *Deckmyn*, para. 15.
322. Bechtold, 2006, p. 369; European Copyright Society, 2014b, pp. 2–3; Geiger & Schönherr, 2014a, pp. 113–114; Hugenholtz, 2000, p. 501; Hugenholtz et al., 2006; Janssens, 2009; Westkamp, 2007. *But see* von Lewinski & Walter, 2010, pp. 1021–1022, labelling this criticism as 'unjustified from the outset, as Art. 5 was not aimed at complete harmonization'.

limitations, the principle of autonomous interpretation, the requirements of effectiveness and purposive interpretation, the need for a balancing of interests, and the (external and internal) operation of fundamental rights, all seem to prevent an overly narrow reading of limitations. Moreover, a strict interpretation may hinder the directive's objective of harmonising limitations, with detrimental effects on the functioning of the internal market.[323]

These considerations significantly mitigate the scope of the strict interpretation doctrine. Furthermore, less conservative readings of the three-step test are possible. In fact, both legal scholarship and some CJEU decisions lay the groundwork for a flexible construction of its conditions and consideration as an enabling clause; one which adequately balances interests, rights and limitations, while being consistent with the InfoSoc Directive's aims and the internal market objective.[324]

It follows that CJEU case law allows for a flexible and functional reading of limitations, especially as these apply to digital technologies.[325] This position is coherent with the normative role of copyright limitations, namely that of securing shared constitutional values stemming from fundamental rights and serving the public interest in the dissemination of culture and knowledge.[326] However, this is true only insofar as the system of limitations ensures a fair balance between competing interests of creators/rights holders and users, as well as 'protection of, and access to, copyright works'.[327] Hence, despite this flexible and functional approach, the scope of limitations remains constrained.

These findings have important implications for the present study. From a descriptive standpoint, the analysis so far argues for a liberal interpretation of limitations. If the activities of Internet users cannot fit within these spaces, then ACS implementation will require copyright reform to adopt legalisation schemes. This clarifies the scope of an ACS by itemising which online uses trigger exclusive rights and require clearance through voluntary or mandatory models. Where copyright reform through legal licences is required, its admissibility hinges on compliance with the three-step test. (For some legal scholars, the same conclusion applies to mandatory collective management.[328])

Here, too, this chapter's analysis is important. First, because the limitations studied herein function as prototypes for 'certain special cases' (first step). Second, because the normative considerations on flexibility and balancing of interests (including the role of fundamental rights) apply,

323. Making the point in relation to *Painer*, *see* Triaille et al., 2013, p. 489.
324. *See infra* 5.2.2.2.
325. See, making a similar point, Senftleben, 2013b, p. 93.
326. European Copyright Society, 2014b, p. 3.
327. *Ibid.*
328. *See supra* the discussion at 3.3.4.2.

mutatis mutandis, to the three-step test. Third, as any voluntary or mandatory ACS should articulate with the *acquis* and the breathing spaces it provides.[329]

In the context of this chapter, the relevant question now is whether and to what extent the limitation prototypes in Article 5 InfoSoc Directive exempt any of the end-user acts of digital content sharing that trigger exclusive rights. Examining that list against the typology of online uses, five limitations emerge as potentially relevant, and are for that reason analysed in the following paragraphs: the mandatory limitation for temporary and transient or incidental copying (4.4.2); the optional limitation for private copying (4.4.3); and the limitations susceptible of application to digital adaptations, namely quotations, incidental inclusion and parody (4.4.4).

4.4.2 Temporary and Transient Copying

Article 5(1) InfoSoc Directive contains a mandatory limitation to the right of reproduction in Article 2. Together with the exemptions for services of mere conduit, caching, and hosting in Articles 12–14 E-Commerce Directive, these rules regulate the liability of service providers for copyright-relevant acts in networked environments.[330] Thus, only if there is a copyright violation pursuant to Articles 2 and 5(1) InfoSoc Directive, will the E-Commerce Directive's safe-harbours apply to determine liability of service providers.[331]

Article 5(1) was included in the InfoSoc Directive in the wake of discussions on the scope of the reproduction right dating back to the 1996 WIPO Diplomatic Conference. Those discussions focused on whether the right should extend to temporary copies of works occurring during technological processes, such as Random Access Memory (RAM) copies in computers, web browsing, and copies resulting from the use of routers and proxy servers.[332] The limitation is relevant to this study as it applies to on-screen and cached copies made during acts of web browsing and reception of streams by end-users.

This limitation exempts from copyright protection any temporary reproductions of works and related subject matter that meet certain conditions regarding their characteristics and purpose. Similar exemptions are included in the Software and Database Directives.[333] To qualify for the limitation, a reproduction must meet four conditions:

329. For example, where a legal licence ACS overlaps with existing limitations it might prove sensible to propose reform by extending existing mechanisms and considering these for the definition of remuneration.
330. Recital 16 InfoSoc Directive.
331. Bechtold, 2006, p. 371.
332. Bechtold, 2006, p. 371; von Lewinski & Walter, 2010, pp. 1018, 1023–1024.
333. Art. 5(1) Software Directive and 6(1) Database Directive.

- it must be temporary, in the sense that it is either transient or incidental;
- it must form 'an integral and essential part of a technological process';
- it must be for the sole purpose of (1) enabling Internet transmissions *or* (2) lawful uses; and
- it must have no 'independent economic significance'.

In *Meltwater*, the 'temporary' condition was examined independently. The CJEU concluded that on-screen and cached copies made during browsing meet this condition. First, on-screen copies are 'deleted when the internet user moves away from the website viewed'; second, cached copies are usually replaced automatically by different content 'after a certain time, which depends on the capacity of the cache and on the extent and frequency of internet usage by the internet user concerned'.[334]

It is notable that commentators tend to examine 'temporary' in opposition to permanent. In that sense, the term is manifested in two alternative requirements: that a copy is 'transient', i.e., that it lasts for a short period of time, or 'incidental', meaning that it has no particular relevance for copyright purposes.[335]

Examples of transient copies are those occurring in a caching process or in the RAM, which are erased at the end of a session. Transient copies also occur during browsing. In fact, the CJEU has clarified that a temporary and transient copy 'is intended to enable the completion of a technological process of which it forms an integral and essential part'; as such, it 'must not exceed what is necessary for the proper completion of that technological process'.[336] Furthermore, the process in question 'must be automated so that it deletes that act automatically, without human intervention, once its function of enabling the completion of such a process has come to an end'.[337]

Because browsing, by definition, requires the automatic creation and deletion of copies without human intervention, it follows that on-screen copies made during browsing are transient copies, and therefore exempted.[338] The requirement of automatic deletion does not prevent the same result being achieved by human intervention. In browsing, for example, it is permissible for the Internet user to activate and terminate the session without the temporary copies losing their transient nature.[339]

334. CJEU, *Meltwater*, paras 25–27.
335. Bechtold, 2006, p. 371; von Lewinski & Walter, 2010, pp. 1024–1025. *See also* Depreeuw & Hubin, 2014, p. 46 ('The transient copy is an ephemeral act of reproduction.')
336. CJEU, *Infopaq I*, para. 61.
337. CJEU, *Infopaq I*, para. 64; CJEU, *Meltwater*, para. 40.
338. Recital 33 InfoSoc Directive, See: CJEU, *Infopaq I*, para. 63; CJEU, *Meltwater*, para. 46.
339. CJEU, *Meltwater*, paras 32, 41–42.

Temporary copies that exist for too long to qualify as transient – such as those on a proxy or cache server – may nonetheless qualify as 'incidental' to the main use. This could be the case, for example, for a use privileged under a different limitation, like digital private copying.[340] Hence, for a copy to be incidental its *existence* and *purpose* must be dependent on the technological process it integrates.[341] In this light, the CJEU has found cached copies to be incidental to the technological process of browsing.[342]

A temporary (transient or incidental) reproduction is 'integral and essential to a technological process' when it fulfils two criteria. First, it is not technically severable from and is 'carried out entirely in the context of the implementation of a technological process'; second, it is required for the proper functioning of the process.[343] The copy must be a predetermined technical necessity, as occurs in the context of Internet transmissions.[344] The CJEU considers that on-screen and cached copies meet this condition because the reproductions can be made at any stage of the process, in no small part because 'without those copies, the internet would be unable to cope with current volumes of data transmitted online.'[345]

The third condition of this limitation is that the temporary reproductions are made to enable Internet transmissions or, alternatively, to allow lawful use. *A contrario*, the limitation excludes copies made for additional or different purposes.[346]

In the wording of Article 5(1)(a) InfoSoc Directive, the first purpose is for a 'transmission in a network between third parties by an intermediary'.[347] This privilege extends to intermediaries like access and service providers that enable Internet transmissions, so long as they do not 'modify the information transmitted' or 'interfere with the lawful use of technology'.[348]

The second purpose is for a lawful use, meaning a use 'authorised by the rightholder or not restricted by law'.[349] An 'authorised' use includes both express and implied licences. Hence, when a work is made available online

---

340. Bechtold, 2006, p. 371; von Lewinski & Walter, 2010, p. 1025.
341. CJEU, *Meltwater*, para. 43.
342. *Ibid.*, paras 48–50.
343. CJEU, *Meltwater*, para. 28; CJEU, *Infopaq I*, para. 61; CJEU, *Infopaq II*, para. 30.
344. Bechtold, 2006, p. 372, arguing that this feature results in an implementation of the three-step test. *See also* von Lewinski & Walter, 2010, p. 1025.
345. CJEU, *Meltwater*, paras 28, 33–38.
346. von Lewinski & Walter, 2010, p. 1025.
347. Art. 5(1)(a) InfoSoc Directive.
348. Recital 33 InfoSoc Directive. *See also* Bechtold, 2006, p. 372; von Lewinski & Walter, 2010, p. 1025. In CJEU, *LSG*, para. 46, the Court clarified that 'access providers which merely provide users with Internet access, without offering other services such as email, FTP or file sharing services or exercising any control, whether de iure or de facto, over the services which users make use of, must be regarded as 'intermediaries' within the meaning of Art. 8(3) of Directive 2001/29'.
349. Recital 33 InfoSoc Directive. *See also*: CJEU, *Murphy*, paras 167–173; CJEU, *Infopaq II*, paras 42–43.

without restrictions on browsing, the copies made by the end-user during that process are excluded from the scope of the exclusive right.[350] A use 'not restricted by law' refers to temporary copies made in the process of enabling use permitted by the limitations in Article 5(2) and (3) InfoSoc Directive.[351]

Finally, the limitation applies solely if the temporary reproduction is devoid of 'independent economic significance'. This condition – seen by some as an application of the three-step test – allows only those reproductions having 'no separate economic value on their own', i.e., technically necessary and economically insignificant copies, which do not affect the economic potential of the reproduction right.[352]

In *Murphy*, when analysing temporary copies created within the memory of the satellite decoder and on the television screen, the CJEU clarified that, for the limitation to have meaning:

> That [economic] significance must also be independent in the sense that it goes beyond the economic advantage derived from mere reception of a broadcast containing protected works, that is to say, beyond the advantage derived from the mere picking up of the broadcast and its visual display.[353]

The CJEU considered the acts in question to constitute 'an inseparable and non-autonomous part of the process of reception of the broadcasts transmitted containing the works', which were 'performed without influence, or even awareness, on the part of the persons thereby having access to the protected works'. These acts were not capable of generating an 'additional economic advantage' and, therefore, did not have independent economic significance. This conclusion was considered consistent with the limitation's objective of ensuring 'the development and operation of new technologies'.[354]

In light of the above, it is possible to draw the following conclusions regarding downstream copies by end-users. First, 'mixed forms' of copying that are not permanent but go beyond the concept of temporary, such as music playlists available offline for the subscription period or movies made available for a period of time subject to TPMs, do not satisfy the requirements of this limitation.[355]

Second, copies created during browsing by Internet users are within the scope of the limitation. They constitute temporary and transient (or even incidental, depending on duration) copies, which are an integral and essential

350. Bechtold, 2006, p. 372; von Lewinski & Walter, 2010, p. 1026.
351. Bechtold, 2006, p. 372.
352. *See* recital 33 InfoSoc Directive, and CJEU, *Infopaq II*, paras 49–50. *See also* Bechtold, 2006, p. 373; von Lewinski & Walter, 2010, pp. 1026–1027.
353. CJEU, *Murphy*, para. 175.
354. CJEU, *Murphy*, paras 176–179 (cit. para. 176).
355. Depreeuw & Hubin, 2014, p. 77.

part of the technological process of using the Internet, whose sole purpose is a lawful use (access to works available online), and have no independent economic significance.[356]

Third, copies made during the reception of streams are likely temporary (transient or incidental), and an integral and essential part of the technological process of streaming content. However, unless authorised by the rights holder directly or indirectly (via, e.g., an online service provider like Spotify), or made in the exercise of a different limitation (such as private use), they will probably be infringing.[357] This is because outside those scenarios it is difficult to argue that the copies (1) are made for a 'lawful use' and (2) have no independent economic importance, as they affect the economic potential of the reproduction right and likely generate an additional economic advantage for users.

Admittedly, the last conclusion is normatively debatable and legally uncertain. Contrary to the *ACI Adam* decision on the application of the private copying limitation to downloads, the CJEU has not ruled on the lawfulness of the source of streams in connection with Article 5(1) InfoSoc Directive. Absent technical restrictions, an Internet user receiving a stream is accessing a website and displaying it on screen. From that perspective, there are few differences from the on-screen copies made during browsing. However, due to the CJEU's interpretation of the reproduction right, it is possible that mere reception of streams would not meet all the conditions of Article 5(1), read in light of the three-step test in Article 5(5).

In that respect, *Meltwater* emphasises that rights holders' previous authorisation of the making available of the content online is essential to the finding that their legitimate interests were not affected, and that browsing did not constitute a conflict with the normal exploitation of their works.[358] In the case of stream reception from unauthorised sources, that authorisation does not exist. *ACI Adam* and its progeny seem to go in this general direction when excluding copies of works from unauthorised sources from the scope of the private copying limitation to prevent a violation of the second and third conditions of the three-step test.[359]

If the CJEU found this requirement of source in the private copying limitation in the absence of any wording to that effect, it is not a stretch to consider it would find a similar requirement where Article 5(1) InfoSoc Directive mentions 'lawful use'. (On this point, it is noted that where the lawful use requirement is tied to the application of the private copying limitation, *ACI Adam* indirectly reduces the scope of the temporary and

356. von Lewinski & Walter, 2010, p. 1027. This conclusion is anticipated in recital 33 InfoSoc Directive.
357. Depreeuw & Hubin, 2014, p. 73, concluding similarly.
358. CJEU, *Meltwater*, paras 54–62.
359. *See infra* 4.4.3.6.

transient copying limitation.[360]) Furthermore, given the emergence of access-based online business models relying on streaming technology, it is possible to foreshadow a conflict with the normal exploitation, in violation of the second step of the test.

This is for the most part the view of AG Campos Sánchez-Bordona in *Filmspeler*. In his opinion, because the hyperlinks installed on the multimedia player device at issue in that case lead to protected works not authorised by the rights holders, then 'streaming by and end-user by means of that device is not consistent with the 'lawful use' for the purposes of Article 5(1)(b)' InfoSoc Directive.[361] Furthermore, the AG relies on *ACI Adam* to state rather broadly that none of the conditions of the three-step test are met in *Filmspeler*.[362]

On balance, a cautious interpretation suggests that the reception of streaming content is likely excluded from the scope of Article 5(1), despite the harshness of this outcome for end-users. Importantly, if an ACS for non-commercial use is put in place, any temporary *downstream copies* made in the context of browsing or stream reception will be ancillary to lawful use and have no independent economic significance (as the system entails remuneration).

Finally, Depreeuw and Hubin argue that certain upstream copies transmitted to user devices might be exempted under this limitation. This would occur if the copies are temporary and incidental to the principal act of exploitation of a work – the communication to the public of streams 'as catchup service or services of download' –, as the copies would be an essential and integral part of the technological process of transmission. Of course, this presupposes these acts are authorised by rights holders (and thus 'lawful') and that their economic significance derives from the main exploitation act of making available.[363] However, as the authors admit, that conclusion is limited to specific technology configurations; these, it is added, seldom occur for non-commercial acts by end-users.

4.4.3 Private Copying

To the extent the right of reproduction applies to downloading, stream capture and uploading, private copying is the most relevant limitation under analysis here. In fact, many legal licence ACS rely on an extended version of this limitation.[364] Article 5(2)(b) InfoSoc Directive applies to reproductions

360. Depreeuw & Hubin, 2014, p. 73.
361. *Opinion AG in Filmspeler*, para. 72. For the analysis of this point, *see ibid.*, paras 64–72.
362. *Ibid.*, paras 73–82.
363. Depreeuw & Hubin, 2014, pp. 71–72.
364. Cf. *supra* 3.3.5.2.

made on all technologies and media, whether analogue or digital.[365] It covers acts of reproduction of all subject matter, with the exclusion of software and databases.[366]

The provision is subject to a number of cumulative requirements, which have been the object of a rich body of CJEU case law in *Padawan*, *Stichting de Thuiskopie*, *Luksan*, *VG Wort*, *Amazon.com*, *ACI Adam*, *Copydan*, *Reprobel*, *Austro-Mechana*, *EGEDA II*, and *Microsoft Mobile Sales International*.[367] Due to the complexities of this case law and the importance of the limitation for the study of ACS, this section examines in detail its scope and requirements with a view to clarifying which online activities are privileged by the limitation.

4.4.3.1 Private Use[368]

First, the limitation can only apply for private use, an expression left undefined in the InfoSoc Directive. There is a consensus that 'private' requires beneficiaries of the provision to be natural persons making reproductions for their personal purposes and within their private sphere, which may include a broader or narrower circle of family and friends.[369]

This excludes wider concepts in national law, such as 'personal use' and 'own use', which may include professional and commercial use.[370] Consequently, acts carried out by natural persons on behalf of legal persons are not exempted.[371] However, copies made on behalf of individuals and/or for their private use may fall in the private use category.[372]

Less clear is the case of third party copying by a legal person acting as a commercial provider that facilitates private copying by a natural person for private purposes. Here, it seems that Member States must regulate the effect of the intervention of intermediaries and service providers in the act of

---

365. Bechtold, 2006, p. 375; Poort & Quintais, 2013, p. 207; von Lewinski & Walter, 2010, pp. 1031–1032.
366. Art. 1(2)(a) and (e) InfoSoc Directive. This is despite recital 38 solely mentioning audio, visual and audio-visual material. *See also*: Eechoud et al., 2009, p. 117; and von Lewinski & Walter, 2010, p. 1031, for an explanation of the historical background of this provision and the articulation of the recital with lit. (b). On the latter point, *see also supra* 2.3.
367. At the time of writing, the following cases are pending: CJEU, Reference for Preliminary Ruling, Case C-265/16, *VCAST Limited v. R.T.I. SpA*.
368. This paragraph relies on and develops my analysis in Poort & Quintais, 2013, pp. 207–208.
369. *See* Poort & Quintais, 2013, p. 207, and von Lewinski & Walter, 2010, p. 1032, noting that the term 'private use' is present elsewhere in the *acquis* and international copyright law, namely in Art. 15(1)(a) Rental Right Directive and Art. 6(2)(a) and 9(a) Database Directive. *See also* Depreeuw & Hubin, 2014, p. 54.
370. Poort & Quintais, 2013, pp. 207–208; von Lewinski & Walter, 2010, pp. 1032–1033.
371. Poort & Quintais, 2013, pp. 207–208; von Lewinski & Walter, 2010, p. 1033.
372. Poort & Quintais, 2013, pp. 207–208; von Lewinski & Walter, 2010, p. 1033.

reproduction.[373] Undeniably, such differences have led to divergent national implementation.[374] The CJEU tackled the issue in *Copydan*, as explained below (*see infra* 4.4.3.7).

This brief sketch suffices to highlight the legal certainty challenges facing national courts in fixing the meaning of 'private', especially in light of its potential application in the digital environment (e.g., within social networking platforms) and against a dynamic concept of 'public' in the *acquis*.[375] For instance, is uploading a copy of a work to a cloud locker accessible only to a number of close friends and family a 'private' use? How big does that group have to be before the act loses its privileged nature?

4.4.3.2 Non-commercial[376]

A second requirement to qualify under the limitation is that the reproduction must not be for directly or indirectly commercial ends. The expression is not defined by the directive and is further confused by the fact that, whilst private acts are usually non-commercial, non-commercial acts can fail to qualify as private.[377]

As noted throughout this book, the term 'commercial' includes a wide range of meanings, from 'economic' to 'for profit'. Furthermore, the scope of non-commerciality is complex to define, especially in connection with online use.[378] At the very least, it was argued, commercial should not be a synonym for economic, as a private copying limitation excluding all use with economic significance is devoid of meaning and application.[379] Such a limitation would therefore likely contravene the principle of effectiveness.

National legislators and courts have attempted to define this term by setting forth subjective and objective criteria, namely the infringing intent of the copier – meaning actual or constructive knowledge, linked to a profit-making aim – and the definition of a specific number of admissible private copies.[380] However, it is challenging to apply these criteria to define

373. Bechtold, 2006, p. 375; Poort & Quintais, 2013, pp. 207–208.
374. Karapapa, 2012, pp. 53–59, with an overview.
375. Poort & Quintais, 2013, p. 208. *See also* Karapapa, 2012, pp. 49–78, with a detailed analysis. Karapapa proposes a test for the determination of the private character of the copyright use, which aims at assessing the relationship between the copier and the audience, the perception of the latter by the rightholder vis-à-vis the commercial exploitation of the work, and the (private) nature of the place where the use is made. For the concept of 'public' in the *acquis*, *see supra* 4.3.2.1.2.
376. This paragraph relies on and develops my analysis in Poort & Quintais, 2013, p. 208.
377. Bernault & Lebois, 2005, p. 30; Karapapa, 2012, p. 80; Poort & Quintais, 2013, p. 208.
378. *See supra* 1.2 and 3.4.2. *See also* Poort & Quintais, 2013, p. 208.
379. *See supra* 3.4.2.
380. Poort & Quintais, 2013, p. 208. *See also* Karapapa, 2012, p. 91, noting that the examination of the copier's intent of commercial exploitation means that the judicial test for non-commerciality is not the exact counterpart of the definition of commerciality. N.B. Art. 6(4), second subparagraph InfoSoc Directive allows rights holders to take

indirect commerciality in digital private copying.[381] This complexity also exists in the context of ACS, as mentioned in the previous chapter.[382]

In this respect, it is difficult to clarify the commercial nature of the many types of online use that qualify as copyright reproductions. The exclusive right extends, for example, to making copies of TV broadcasts for time-shifting, cloning copies of compact discs or digital versatile/video discs for playback or to share with family and friends, making back-up copies of works, and downloading and storing works from authorised and unauthorised Internet sources, as well as making subsequent copies thereof.[383]

Furthermore, it is unclear the extent to which the intervention of online service providers (e.g., vis-à-vis online 'personal video recorders' or virtual storage space) enabling end-user copies but acting as commercial intermediaries – by charging subscription fees or generating advertisement revenues – affects the 'non-commercial' nature of the act of reproduction and, consequently, the application of the limitation.[384]

4.4.3.3 Fair Compensation

If the limitation is implemented by the Member State, it must be accompanied by fair compensation. According to recital 35 InfoSoc Directive, the 'form, detailed arrangements and possible level' of the compensation depend on the 'circumstances of each case'; one significant criterion to determine these circumstances is 'the possible harm … resulting from the act in question'. Furthermore, if rights holders have already received payment for the use (e.g., through licence fees), it is possible that no additional (or double) payment is due.[385]

Therefore, the criterion of harm forms the basis of the concept of fair compensation.[386] This is a corollary of the fact that fair compensation is a 'recompense for the harm suffered by the author' for the introduction of the limitation.[387]

As a rule, the recompense should focus on the 'actual harm' suffered. Only if that proves impossible, for example because the harm remains

'adequate measures regarding the number of reproductions in accordance with these provisions' (Arts 5(2)(b) and 5(5)).

381. Poort & Quintais, 2013, p. 208. For attempts in legal scholarship, *see* Depreeuw & Hubin, 2014, p. 55; Karapapa, 2012, p. 98.
382. *See supra* 3.4.2.
383. Poort & Quintais, 2013, p. 216.
384. Depreeuw & Hubin, 2014, p. 55. *See infra* the discussion at 4.4.3.7
385. Recital 35 InfoSoc Directive.
386. CJEU, *Padawan*, paras 38–42. *See also* Poort & Quintais, 2013, p. 208, noting the difference from the concept of equitable remuneration in Art. 8(2) Rental Right Directive. *See also supra* 2.2.4.
387. CJEU, *Padawan*, paras 40, 42; CJEU, *Stichting de Thuiskopie*, para. 24; CJEU, *Reprobel*, para. 36.

unknown at the moment the tariff is set, can the calculation use as a reference point the 'potential harm'.[388] Nevertheless, the final amount of compensation must be adjusted to reflect the actual harm (e.g., through reimbursement mechanisms), avoiding scenarios of overcompensation contrary to the objective of fair balance between rights holders and users set forth in recital 31 InfoSoc Directive.[389]

As noted, the limitation interfaces with the regulation of TPMs. Article 5(2)(b) InfoSoc Directive requires that the method for calculation of the 'level' of fair compensation takes into consideration the application of TPMs in Article 6 of the directive.[390]

In 'certain situations where the prejudice to the rightholder would be minimal', no obligation to pay fair compensation may arise.[391] Member states have a wide margin of discretion in setting the threshold for when the prejudice caused to rights holders is to be considered minimal, provided the definition of that *de minimis* threshold is consistent with, *inter alia*, the principle of equal treatment in Article 20 Charter.[392]

Fair compensation is an autonomous concept of EU law, subject to uniform interpretation in countries that have implemented the provision.[393] According to the CJEU, this qualification is required by the InfoSoc Directive's objectives of establishing a high level of protection, ensuring a functioning internal market, and balancing the rights and interests of rights holders and users.[394]

In light of these objectives and the fact that the directive imposes on Member States an obligation of result regarding the actual recovery of fair compensation, the respective right not only vests in the individual rights holder, but must also be qualified as unwaivable.[395]

Importantly, fair compensation is only due to the holders of the exclusive reproduction right in Article 2 InfoSoc Directive: authors, performers, phonogram producers, film producers, and broadcasting organisations. Only they can suffer harm requiring compensation and not subsequent exploiters, such as publishers.[396]

388. CJEU, *Reprobel*, paras 69–71, 82.
389. *Ibid.*, paras 84–88.
390. Recital 35 InfoSoc Directive.
391. *Ibid. See* Poort & Quintais, 2013, p. 208, and Bechtold, 2006, p. 374, noting that both time and space-shifting might be covered by such *de minimis* cases.
392. CJEU, *Copydan*, paras 56–62; *Opinion AG Copydan*, paras 97–101.
393. CJEU, *Padawan*, paras 32, 37. *See* Poort & Quintais, 2013, p. 209.
394. *See* recitals 31 and 32 InfoSoc Directive, and CJEU, *Padawan*, paras 34–35. Clarifying the different objectives of the directive, see: CJEU, *Murphy*, paras 186; CJEU, *DR and TV2 Danmark*, para. 35; CJEU, *Painer*, para. 132.
395. CJEU, *Luksan*, paras. 88–109. *See also*: CJEU, *Stichting de Thuiskopie*, para. 34; Leistner, 2014, pp. 587–588; Poort & Quintais, 2013, pp. 209–210.
396. CJEU, *Reprobel*, paras. 44–49.

Member States are left with some discretion regarding the determination of the compensation system, which is however limited by recitals 35 and 38 InfoSoc Directive, the three-step test, and the principle of effectiveness.[397]

4.4.3.4 Rights Holders' Authorisation[398]

One of the complex issues in determining the scope of private copying relates to the effect of the explicit or implicit authorisation of rights holders on fair compensation. On this topic, the main CJEU judgments are *VG Wort* and *Copydan*.[399]

In *VG Wort*, the Court states that if the acts of copying by end-users fall within the scope of a limitation, any authorisation of the same by rights holders is irrelevant for the application or calculation of fair compensation.[400] If Member States implement the limitation, the respective fair compensation must be based on the harm caused to rights holders by unauthorised reproductions.[401] Activities covered by the limitation are permissible regardless of rights holders' authorisation, which is 'devoid of legal effects'; therefore, that authorisation does not affect the potential harm caused by the copying activities and cannot be considered in the calculation of the compensation.[402]

When *Copydan* came around, the AG Opinion in that case departed somewhat from *VG Wort* and considered that the CJEU left open the question of whether levies are due if rights holders have made available a work online subject to payment that includes fair compensation (e.g., a licence fee for the download of a song from an authorised platform). In light of the principle of fair compensation and the directive's objective of fair balance, the AG posited that no levy should be due where the authorised content had already been subject to 'a payment or other form of fair compensation', as that would lead to an unjustified double payment by users.[403]

That conclusion echoes the recommendation of Mediator Vitorino on the topic.[404] It also opened the door for what Peukert called a 'two-tier system', where levies would be charged mostly for works lawfully made available online for no fee and unrestricted by TPMs. Interestingly, this

397. CJEU, *Stichting de Thuiskopie*, paras. 33–41 CJEU, *Padawan*, paras 7, 39–41. *See also* Leistner, 2014, p. 587.
398. This paragraph relies on and develops my analysis in Poort & Quintais, 2013, pp. 210–211; Quintais, 2015a.
399. CJEU, *VG Wort*, paras 48–50; CJEU, *Copydan*, paras 63–67.
400. CJEU, *VG Wort*, para. 40. Proposing a different interpretation *see Opinion AG in Copydan*, paras 57–68. *See also* Poort & Quintais, 2013, p. 210.
401. Poort & Quintais, 2013, p. 210.
402. CJEU, *VG Wort*, paras 34–39. On this point the Court diverges from the *Opinion AG in VG Wort*, paras 119–121. *See* Poort & Quintais, 2013, p. 210; Quintais, 2015b, p. 78.
403. *Opinion AG in Copydan*, paras 57–68. *See also* Quintais, 2015a.
404. Vitorino, 2013, pp. 6–8.

would mean a significant change of direction for CMOs in the field, who would now be responsible for fostering a 'sharing culture'.[405]

The *Copydan* judgment disagreed with the AG and re-stated the *VG Wort* doctrine, clarifying that it also applies where a work is made available subject to payment.[406] However, because the authorisation in question is devoid of legal effects, the rights holder should not be entitled to any additional remuneration for that act:

> Since, in circumstances such as those set out in paragraph 65 above, such authorisation is devoid of legal effects, it cannot, of itself, give rise to an obligation to pay remuneration of any kind in respect of the reproduction, for private use, by the user of the files concerned to the rightholder who authorised such use.[407]

The 'circumstances' mentioned in the citation relate to the optional nature of the limitation, meaning the choice by Member States to implement the limitation. The most straightforward interpretation of this statement is that Member States choosing to implement the limitation exclude from its material scope any authorisation from rights holders for acts of private copying. No 'two-tier system' is possible and the positions of Mr Vitorino and the AG are rejected. Also, one might add, the possibility of contractual disposition of the limitation outside the cases expressly allowed in the InfoSoc Directive becomes difficult to accept. This seems to be the CJEU's method of avoiding the problem of double payments.[408]

However, it is likely that rights holders will price into the purchase of content the possibility of private copies, causing consumers to pay twice for private copies. This outcome contradicts the principle of *de minimis* harm. If rights holders have already received payment for private copies they suffer no further (or only negligible) harm. Therefore, Member States should be free to exempt such use from levies.[409]

To avoid double payments, Member States could consider that, because rights holders price private copying acts into the purchase of content, paid authorised use causes only *de minimis* harm, meaning that no fair compensation is due. If properly defined, this solution would be within their margin of discretion and respect the principle of equal treatment (Article 20 Charter),

405. Quintais, 2014, pp. 6–8, 2015a, 2015b, pp. 78–79.
406. CJEU, *Copydan*, para. 65 (citing CJEU, *VG Wort*, para. 37).
407. *Ibid.*, para. 66. *See also* Quintais, 2015a.
408. Quintais, 2015a.
409. A less obvious interpretation is that it is up to national law to exclude from its material scope any authorisation from rights holders for those acts. Where it does not make this exclusion, the authorisation of rights holders is not devoid of legal effects and it is possible to set aside fair compensation, triggering a two-tier system in those countries. *See* Quintais, 2015a.

while achieving a fair balance between the interests of rights holders and users.[410]

4.4.3.5 Application of Technological Protection Measures[411]

The relationship of the private copying limitation with TPMs was introduced above.[412] The CJEU has addressed the issue in *VG Wort*, *ACI Adam*, and *Copydan*.[413] In the Court's view, TPMs allow rights holders to restrict unauthorised acts and help define the scope of the private copying limitation. The limitation is a legislative permission from Member States, who must therefore ensure its proper application. This includes preventing acts that rights holders do not authorise.[414]

Because TPMs are voluntary, even where they are available but not applied, the condition of fair compensation remains applicable.[415] However, Member States may decide that application of such measures has an impact on the level (i.e., calculation and amount) of fair compensation so that 'rightholders are encouraged to make use of them and thereby voluntarily contribute to the proper application of the private copying exception'.[416]

Here, it is important to remember that the *Nintendo* Court stated that legal protection of TPMs must respect the principle of proportionality: their application by rights holders should be suitable to achieve the goal of preventing unauthorised acts and not go beyond what is required for that purpose.[417]

The emphasis on fair compensation as a means to encourage voluntary adoption of technological measures and proper delimitation of the limitation introduces the possibility that TPM-ed works are subject to higher levies than unrestricted works. This odd outcome seems prejudicial to end-users and the InfoSoc Directive's fair balancing aim.[418]

Instead, it would be logical for application of these measures to result in lower or even no levies. This is because the possibility of engaging in private copying is reduced, making the prejudice to rights holders minimal. Here, again, application of the *de minimis* criterion may provide an escape valve to prevent unwarranted payments by consumers.[419]

---

410. *Ibid.*
411. This paragraph relies on and develops my analysis in Quintais, 2015a.
412. *See supra* 4.4.1.2.
413. CJEU, *VG Wort*, paras 52–57; CJEU, *ACI Adam*, paras 43–44; CJEU, *Copydan*, paras 68–73.
414. CJEU, *VG Wort*, paras 48–52. *See also* Quintais, 2015a.
415. CJEU, *VG Wort*, paras 48–57. *See also: Opinion AG in VG Wort*, para. 104; CJEU, *ACI Adam*, paras 43–44; Poort & Quintais, 2013, p. 211; Quintais, 2015a.
416. *Opinion AG in Copydan*, paras 69–80; CJEU, *Copydan*, paras 68–73; CJEU, *VG Wort*, para. 58. *See also* Quintais, 2015a.
417. CJEU, *Nintendo*, paras 29–31. *See also* Quintais, 2015a.
418. Quintais, 2015a.
419. *Ibid.*

4.4.3.6 Lawfulness of Source[420]

In *ACI Adam*, the CJEU ruled that the private copying limitation, when interpreted in light of the three-step test, can only privilege reproductions made from lawful sources. This interpretation was later confirmed in *Copydan* and *Reprobel*.[421]

These judgments are important because they qualify multiple daily acts of end-users – such as downloading and streaming entertainment content from unlicensed Internet sites – as clearly infringing, thereby extending the scope of the exclusive right of reproduction. Furthermore, the decisions impact the calculation of levies and interpretation of the three-step test.

A preliminary question to address here is what constitutes an unlawful source. In a survey of twenty-seven Member States prior to *ACI Adam*, a WIPO report stated that most laws prohibited reproduction from unlawful sources, which it identified as including 'peer-to-peer network, newsgroups, torrent sites and the like, where music and films have been uploaded without consent from the rights holders'.[422]

A comparison of the survey with commentaries on national laws leads to a different conclusion. In fact, only a small number of Member States' laws expressly and unequivocally excluded copies from unlawful sources from the limitation's scope. How that is made effective in practice is not clear. In all other cases, the condition is either absent or derived by certain stakeholders from ambiguous requirements, such as 'lawful publication' (which seems to be related to the right of disclosure instead).[423]

For example, in Germany, the scope of the limitation is restricted to private copies that have not 'obviously been produced or made publicly available illegally'; what exactly constitutes 'obvious' remains to be clarified by case law.[424]

Similarly, since 2006, Spanish copyright law has limited the scope of private copying to copies 'obtained from works that have been lawfully accessed', a language Xalabarder deems 'directly intended to rule out P2P downloading' but that does not entail the requirement of ownership of the copy.[425] In a 2014 amendment, the scope of the limitation was further reduced to solely cover reproductions made 'from copies of works 'acquired by commercial purchase' or received by radio or tv broadcast'.[426]

---

420. This paragraph relies on and develops the analysis in Quintais, 2015b.
421. CJEU, *ACI Adam*, paras 20–58; CJEU, *Copydan*, paras 74–79; CJEU, *Reprobel*, paras 57–64.
422. WIPO, 2014, p. 4.
423. *See* Quintais, 2015b, pp. 79–82, for a detailed analysis.
424. *See* Art. 53(1) German Copyright Act. *See also* Dreier & Specht, 2012, p. 445; WIPO, 2014, p. 63; WIPO & Stichting de Thuiskopie, 2016, p. 81.
425. *See* Xalabarder, 2012, p. 941 (n. 42), 949, 952. *See also* WIPO & Stichting de Thuiskopie, 2016, pp. 150–151.
426. *See* Xalabarder, 2014.

In France, a 2011 amendment added the requirement of lawful access to a protected work for the application of the private copying limitation ('copies ou reproductions réalisées à partir d'une source licite').[427]

Denmark and Sweden amended their copyright acts in the 2000s to the effect that the limitation does not extend to copies made 'on the basis of an unlawful representation of a work or an illegal circumvention of a technological measure', an amendment claimed to result from the three-step test.[428] The Danish Copyright Act further prohibits digital private copying 'on the basis of a copy that has been lent or hired' without the consent of the author.[429]

For its part, Italian law only allows private copying reproductions to be made by the natural person who has acquired the lawful possession of copies of the work/subject matter ('acquisito possesso legittimo di esemplari dell'opera o del materiale protetto') or had 'lawful access' to it ('accesso legittimo').[430]

In light of these different national implementations, the mechanism of preliminary reference provided the CJEU with an opportunity to offer decisive guidance on this key aspect of the limitation's scope, starting with *ACI Adam*. Examining the Court's jurisprudence in this area, it is noteworthy that unlawful sources are not defined beyond the scenario of works made available to the public without the consent of rights holders.[431] In fact, when asked to address unlawful sources 'by some other means' the *Copydan* Court found the question inadmissible because it 'failed to provide sufficient information relating to the nature of the reproductions to which the question submitted relates', thereby preventing the Court from giving a useful answer.[432]

On the issue of whether unauthorised sources are included in the scope of the limitation, both *Copydan* and *Reprobel* closely track *ACI Adam*. In the latter judgment, the CJEU's analysis departed from recital 44 InfoSoc Directive and its reference to the possibility of reducing the scope of limitations in connection with 'certain new uses' of copyright content; contrariwise, nothing in the directive mentions the possibility of extending the scope of limitations.[433] Furthermore, recital 22 InfoSoc Directive

---

427. *See* Carre, 2012, pp. 406–407, 413, 417–418, making reference to L311-1 French Intellectual Property Code and Law No. 2011-1898 of 20 December 2011 (on the private copying remuneration). For the situation prior to the 2011 amendment, including a description of contradictory case law, *see* Geiger, 2008a.
428. Rognstad, 2012, p. 858. *See also* WIPO & Stichting de Thuiskopie, 2016, pp. 152–155.
429. Art. 12(3) Danish Copyright Act (WIPO translation). *See* WIPO & Stichting de Thuiskopie, 2016, pp. 60–63.
430. Art. 71–sexies (4) Italian Copyright Act. See WIPO, 2014, pp. 77–78; WIPO & Stichting de Thuiskopie, 2016, pp. 97–102, and Sica & D'Antonio, 2012, pp. 546, 553–557.
431. CJEU, *Copydan*, paras 74, 79.
432. *Ibid.*, paras 92–95.
433. CJEU, *ACI Adam*, paras 25–27.

indicates that the objective of support for the dissemination of culture should not be achieved by 'sacrificing strict protection of rights or by tolerating illegal forms of distribution of counterfeited or pirated works'.[434]

On that basis, and despite the directive's silence on the issue, the Court applied the doctrine of strict interpretation to its reading of the three-step test. The conclusion from this analysis was that reproductions from unlawful sources may infringe the second and third steps of the test.[435]

On the second step, the Court states that allowing reproductions from unlawful sources encourages piracy, which will 'inevitably' reduce revenues from lawful sources and conflict with the normal exploitation of works.[436] Put differently, there would be a substitution effect between reproductions made from lawful *versus* unlawful sources. That assertion, which seems essential to the ruling and must rely at least partially on factual analysis, is not further explained.

Regarding the third step, the Court argues that the inclusion of unlawful sources in the scope of the limitation would force rights holders to tolerate infringements accompanying the making of private copies, thereby unreasonably prejudicing their legitimate interests.[437] There is some circularity to this argument, which relies on strict interpretation but ignores the historic role of the remuneration element (here: fair compensation) in satisfying the third step condition.[438] On this basis, it is concluded that Article 5(2)(b) InfoSoc Directive cannot cover private copies made from unlawful sources.[439]

Following that rationale, national laws that do not exclude reproductions from unlawful sources cannot ensure the proper application of the limitation. Such a conclusion, the CJEU posits, is independent of, and remains unaffected by, the non-availability of effective TPMs to prevent unauthorised reproductions.[440]

Furthermore, when interpreting the condition of fair compensation in light of previous case law and recital 31 InfoSoc Directive, a levy system which does not distinguish between the source of copies fails to respect the fair balance between the rights and interests of authors and users that the InfoSoc Directive intends to safeguard.[441] That is because under such a system the 'harm' on the basis of which fair compensation is calculated

---

434. *Ibid.*, para. 36; CJEU, *Reprobel*, para. 59.
435. CJEU, *ACI Adam*, paras 31, 38. CJEU, *Copydan*, para. 76; CJEU, *Reprobel*, para. 59.
436. CJEU, *ACI Adam*, para. 39.
437. *Ibid.*, para. 40; CJEU, *Reprobel*, para. 61.
438. On this role, *see supra* 2.3.
439. CJEU, *ACI Adam*, para. 41; CJEU, *Reprobel*, para. 57.
440. CJEU, *ACI Adam*, paras 45–46.
441. *Ibid.*, paras 47–54, 57. Recital 31 InfoSoc Directive mentions the need to adjust the degree of harmonisation of exceptions and limitations in light of cross-border exploitation of works and the new electronic environment in light of the objectives of ensuring 'the proper functioning of the internal market' and achieving a 'fair balance of rights and

includes 'an additional, non-negligible cost' for reproductions made from unlawful sources. That cost is ultimately passed on to consumers purchasing levied goods. As a result, those consumers are 'indirectly penalised', as they will contribute towards compensating for harm caused by reproductions not allowed under the directive.[442]

In sum, the joint reading of the private copying limitation and three-step test provisions led the CJEU to conclude that national laws that do not distinguish between lawful and unlawful sources for the act of reproduction are not in conformity with EU law.[443] Still, it remains unclear whether copies made from legally uncertain sources can be subject to fair compensation.[444]

4.4.3.7 Third Party Devices Used for Copying[445]

Another relevant issue relates to how the private copying limitation deals with copies made by an individual by or with the aid of a device belonging to a third party. In *Copydan*, the referring national court exemplified such use as copies made by an individual from a third party's DVD, CD, MP3 player, computer or other device. In theory, this third party can be a friend, acquaintance, or colleague, as well as a service provider. Moreover, the content in question can be acquired with or without the authorisation of the rights holder.[446]

Copydan's approach to this issue is not clear. The Court notes that Article 5(2)(b) InfoSoc Directive makes no reference to 'the legal nature of the connection, such as the right to property' between the individual that benefits from it and the device used to make copies.[447] In other words, nothing is said about use of third party devices to make copies.[448]

In that light, following the principle of strict interpretation and taking into account that the directive aims at partial harmonisation, the use of third party devices for private copying is outside the scope of the provision.[449] One could legitimately ask: is it strict interpretation when you allow third party devices for private copying, therefore extending the possibilities available for making copies?[450]

---

interests between the different categories of rightholders, as well as between the different categories of rightholders and users'.

442. CJEU, *ACI Adam*, paras 55–56; CJEU, *Copydan*, paras 77–78.
443. CJEU, *ACI Adam*, para. 58. *See also* CJEU, *Copydan*, para. 75.
444. The AG in Copydan seems to think they should not. Cf. *Opinion AG in Copydan*, paras 84–85.
445. This paragraph relies on and develops my analysis in Quintais, 2015a.
446. CJEU, *Copydan*, para. 16. For the arguments of the AG, *see Opinion AG in Copydan*, paras 86–96. *See also* Quintais, 2015a.
447. CJEU, *Copydan*, paras 80–86.
448. Quintais, 2015a.
449. CJEU, *Copydan*, paras 87–88.
450. Quintais, 2015a.

The response is that the Court argues for a different meaning for strict interpretation, interpreting *ACI Adam* and *Melzer* (a non-copyright case) by analogy, and stating that a limitation 'cannot give rise to an interpretation going beyond the cases expressly envisaged'.[451] Why the same understanding was not applied to the un/lawful nature of the source remains unclear.[452]

Consequently, says the Court, Article 5(2)(b) should not be read in light of the three-step test in Article 5(5). This is because the test 'is not intended either to affect the substantive content of provisions falling within the scope of Article 5(2) of that directive or, *inter alia*, to extend the scope of the different exceptions and limitations provided for therein'.[453] Put differently, the test does not apply to use of third party devices because that topic is outside the harmonised scope of the limitation, and it is in relation to this scope that the test operates.[454]

The result is that national legislation that imposes a levy on third party devices used for private copying is compatible with the InfoSoc Directive.[455] This is because the choice to levy these devices is outside the scope of the directive and, thus, within the margin of discretion of Member States.[456]

If a levy is applied, the use of such devices cannot be qualified as copyright infringement. This has some interesting consequences. If a user copies songs from a friend's laptop but those songs were downloaded from The Pirate Bay, the copies come from an unlawful source and are not covered by the limitation. However, the device is subject to a levy and those copies may thereby be exempted, which seems incongruous. It is up to national laws to regulate this intersection between unlawful source and copying from third party devices. In doing so, however, it is difficult to imagine that end-users will not end up paying levies for copies made from unlawful sources, i.e., for private copies they are not allowed to make.[457]

Also, *Copydan* is bound to have an effect on intermediary or secondary liability for the provision of such devices or related services. An individual setting up a service for 'do-it-yourself' copies is providing a third party device for the user to make private copies. Unless national law prohibits it, such service should not give rise to liability. However, it is easy to imagine that Member States will envisage different solutions to this problem, with potential negative effects on the internal market for the provision of these services.[458]

---

451. CJEU, *Copydan*, para. 87. N.B. *Melzer* relates to judicial co-operation in civil matters and already applies this reading by analogy to the Court's judgement in *Zuid-Chemie*.
452. Quintais, 2015a.
453. CJEU, *Copydan*, para. 90.
454. Quintais, 2015a.
455. CJEU, *Copydan*, para. 91.
456. Quintais, 2015a.
457. *Ibid.*
458. *Ibid.*

The issue is of particular complexity in relation to 'do-it-yourself' copies in the digital environment, namely cloud services that provide technical means for users to make or request their own copies, such as virtual storage spaces and online 'personal video recorders'. Member States' laws already qualify copies made by third parties differently; furthermore, the identification of the copier in the context of personal video recorder services has been subject to contrasting decisions in France and Germany.[459] In this respect, *Copydan* leaves the status quo untouched, with the above-mentioned negative effects.[460]

This uncertainty extends to the possibility of levying cloud services for making private copies (the upload copies) covered by the limitation, a topic already broached in a 2014 resolution by the European parliament.[461] If realised, the resulting regime would approximate private copying to an ACS for non-commercial digital reproductions by end-users.

4.4.3.8 Application to Activities of Internet Users

For the purposes of this book, private copying is the most relevant limitation in the InfoSoc Directive. It can apply to certain acts of downloading, (down) streaming, stream capture/ripping and uploading by end-users. Furthermore, some of its conditions are susceptible of transplant to non-voluntary ACS, namely the non-commercial purpose or character of the use and fair compensation.

However, the interpretation of the limitation by the CJEU results in a reduced space for the copying activities of Internet users. This is so because the limitation does not apply to copies made from unauthorised sources and is restricted in the context of works made available online on agreed contractual terms subject to TPMs.

Thus, digital reproductions of works made through downloading and stream capture are covered by the private copying limitation only if originating from an authorised source. That will be the case when online service providers expressly authorise the reproduction. Authorised online streaming and downloading platforms, it is noted, typically make works available subject to agreed contractual terms and TPMs, which triggers the absolute circumvention prohibition in Article 6(4) InfoSoc Directive.[462] (In

459. Depreeuw & Hubin, 2014, pp. 53–54.
460. Quintais, 2015a.
461. EP Resolution Private Copying Levies 2014, para. 30. N.B. the issue of compatibility with EU law of a compulsory licensing system for cloud services for the remote video recording of private copies of copyright works is the subject of a preliminary reference to the CJEU. *See* CJEU, Reference for Preliminary Ruling, Case C-265/16, *VCAST Limited v. R.T.I. SpA*.
462. *See* Jutte, 2015, pp. 7–11, for an analysis of terms of use and restrictions in online music stores and streaming services.

this case, there is also a high risk of double payments by end-users, which are subject to the licence fee and the levy.)

That authorisation is usually clear to a subscriber of streaming services (e.g., Spotify and Netflix) through the user interface and its technical restrictions. The same does not apply to downloading platforms (e.g., Apple's iTunes Store and Amazon Music), where the user enjoys an 'ownership' experience, but is typically subject to contractual restrictions on the subsequent use of the download copy in the form of a 'license to use'.[463] In both cases, reproduction by the end-user is limited by technology and contract, which together help define the scope of the limitation and applicable fair compensation. Copies made by that same user outside those boundaries are unauthorised and, after *ACI Adam*, appear to be outside the limitation's scope, even if that prohibition is impossible to enforce.

Outside those cases, the limitation also applies when the work is made available online without technical restrictions, for download or streaming with the express authorisation of the rights holder, for example on the author's homepage, or under a Creative Commons licence. In these cases, because the TPM regime does not apply and the source of the reproduction is lawful, it is arguable that *VG Wort* and *Copydan* leave no room for contractual restrictions on private copying, provided fair compensation is paid.[464]

However, absent express authorisation from the rights holder or their representative – or application of national doctrines of implied consent – end-users face legal uncertainty. After *ACI Adam* and its progeny, many online reproductions by Internet users probably originate from unauthorised sources, a term that may include all content not lawfully acquired, accessed or made available by the rights holder. As for the source of an act of communication to the public, it will be nearly impossible for individuals to ascertain the legal status of the same, and therefore of their acts of reproduction.[465]

Consequently, initial and subsequent reproductions (downloads) made in the context of most torrent file sharing networks, newsgroups, social networks or cyberlockers, will likely not qualify as private copies. The same holds true for many acts of stream capture, which will in addition risk violating the prohibition on circumvention of TPMs. Hence, such acts will frequently infringe the right of reproduction.[466]

---

463. *See* Jutte, 2015, pp. 4–6.
464. *See supra* 4.4.3.4. *See also* Jutte, 2015, p. 12.
465. *See supra* 4.3.2., on unauthorised sources and the right of communication to the public.
466. Depreeuw & Hubin, 2014, pp. 28–29; von Lewinski, 2005, pp. 7–8. Arguing that extending the limitation to stream-ripping would contravene the three-step test, *see* Jutte, 2015, pp. 14–18. *See also* Goldstein & Hugenholtz, 2013, pp. 370–373, questioning whether private copying levies should also compensate for unlawful use (e.g., P2P), and whether such levies and corresponding exemptions should survive in a DRM controlled digital environment.

Finally, uploading copies of works to a cloud storage locker can theoretically constitute private copying, subject to the following conditions. First, access to the locker cannot be public. Second, under the applicable law, the copier must be the individual and not the third party service provider; alternatively, that third party may be authorised to make the copy on behalf of a natural person without prejudicing the application of the limitation.[467] Third, the copy in question is from an authorised source and does not result from circumvention of TPMs.[468]

If these requirements are met, Internet users should not be infringing. It will then be incumbent upon Member States to define whether their levy systems already provide fair compensation for such copies (e.g., by levying the media/equipment used therefor) or if it is justified to levy cloud services, which does not currently happen.[469] Failing these requirements, the upload activities probably infringe the reproduction right or, if the upload copy is accessible to the public, the right of communication to the public.[470]

4.4.4 Limitations Susceptible of Application to Digital Adaptations

As noted above (at 4.2.7), digital adaptations are part of Internet users' daily online activities. Although this book does not focus on the non-harmonised right of adaptation, digital adaptations can trigger the application of certain harmonised exclusive rights and limitations in the InfoSoc Directive.[471] It is therefore important to address these acts in the context of a potential ACS, even if in practice they are not valued by Internet users as much as the remaining forms of online use examined in this chapter.[472]

Digital adaptations can involve three exclusive rights: reproduction of the pre-existing work, communication to the public of the pre-existing and

467. *See* Depreeuw & Hubin, 2014, p. 71, discussing German case law on online personal video recorders.
468. N.B. some national laws allow circumvention for purposes of private copying. *See supra* 4.4.1.2.
469. For a preliminary reference touching on issue, *see* CJEU, Reference for Preliminary Ruling, Case C-265/16, *VCAST Limited v. R.T.I. SpA*.
470. *See supra* 4.3.2.2.
471. On the exclusion from the scope of analysis of the adaptation right, *see supra* 1.3.
472. *See* Handke et al., 2015, Appendix 2, with results from a survey of a representative sample of the Dutch population on different configurations of an ACS. These results show that individuals do not value significantly the inclusion of a right to create digital adaptations in an ACS. For the perspective of creators on digital adaptations, *see* Noll et al., 2012, pp. 53–54, reporting on survey data from the Netherlands. This data shows that creators 'express little appreciation for adaptation/remixing, more appreciation for stronger copyright control', and that '30 to 60 percent of Dutch creators feels financially threatened by adaptation/remixing.'

derivative works, and adaptation per se.[473] Reproduction and adaptation are not synonyms and can be distinguished as follows:

> while reproduction concerns the copying of the particular shape of a work determined by the author, the adaptation right covers changes to the underlying corpus mysticum… to the intellectual substance of work.[474]

This distinction finds support in international law. The BC's broad and technology neutral formulation of the reproduction right does not include reproductions in a 'transformed manner' and is distinct from specific exclusive rights to make transformative uses of works. Such rights include translations in Article 8, adaptations (arrangements and other alterations) in Article 12, and cinematographic adaptations in Article 14(1).[475] These rights are in turn distinct from the protection of the translation or adaptation as a protected work.[476]

EU law does not harmonise the exclusive right of adaptation. However, all EU Member States are part of the BC, as well as WCT and TRIPS, which incorporate by reference BC provisions on adaptation. As a result, the right is part of all Member States' laws as either a standalone provision or part of the reproduction right.[477] Hence, the copyright regulation of transformative uses in the EU partly takes place at national level. This includes the definition of the exact contours of the adjacent rights of reproduction and adaptation, and the protection of independent works.[478]

The *acquis* allows some flexibility in the regulation of digital adaptations, partly resulting from legislative omission.[479] The copyright directives contain a right of translation/adaptation only in respect of computer programs and databases, although it is debatable whether the BC protects such types of work.[480] On the other hand, limitations in Article 5 InfoSoc Directive do not apply to the adaptation right but merely to reproduction and

473. Triaille et al., 2013, p. 459.
474. Hugenholtz & Senftleben, 2011, p. 26.
475. See: Hugenholtz & Okediji, 2008, pp. 14–15; von Lewinski, 2008, p. 140.
476. Dreier, 2006; von Lewinski, 2008. On translations and adaptations as protected works, *see* Art. 2(3) BC. Art. 12 BC grants authors the 'exclusive right of authorizing adaptations, arrangements and other alterations of their work'. In essence, the right covers transformative uses (excluding translations and cinematographic adaptations of works under Arts 8 and 14 BC) where the pre-existing work is perceptible, but not merely reproduced. This use goes beyond literal reproduction and influences the work's *corpus mysticum*.
477. Borgne-Bachschmidt et al., 2008, p. 188; Dreier, 2006, pp. 40, 56; Eechoud et al., 2009, pp. 83–84.
478. Dreier, 2006, p. 55; Triaille et al., 2013, p. 461; von Lewinski, 2008.
479. Hugenholtz & Senftleben, 2011, pp. 2, 26–27; Hugenholtz, 2012b, p. 55; Senftleben, 2013b, p. 90.
480. Arts 4(1)(b) Software Directive and 5(b) Database Directive. *See* Dreier, 2006, pp. 12–13, 40.

communication to the public.[481] This leads some authors to consider that the *acquis* leaves 'ample unregulated space with regard to the right of adaptation', to be shaped for example through determination of infringement criteria.[482]

Some Member States use this flexibility to enable free non-commercial online transformative uses. German law, for instance, recognises a free adaptation/use rule ('Freie Benutzung'). In the Netherlands, the 'new work' exemption provides a carve-out from the right of adaptation. Outside Europe, Canadian law has implemented a new limitation for UGC.[483] Another approach for maximising this flexibility is through a broad application of the limitations to harmonised rights susceptible of privileging adaptations, namely quotation, incidental inclusion, and parody.[484] The adoption of either approach in the *acquis*, or their combination, would probably require legal reform.[485]

In theory, a non-harmonised exclusive right of adaptation could cover all digital adaptations that effect a change to a work's *corpus mysticum*, including most types of UGC. However, there is legal uncertainty on the amplitude of such a right, due to variation in national implementation and the broad scope of the harmonised rights of reproduction and distribution, especially after *Infopaq I* and *Art & Allposters*.[486]

In *Infopaq I*, for instance, the Court considered the copying of eleven words in the title of a newspaper article to be a 'reproduction in part'.[487] This has led some authors to argue that there will always be a reproduction in part in UGC content, given the derivative works' reliance on the pre-existing

481. Eechoud et al., 2009, pp. 83–84, 100. *See infra* 4.4.4.
482. Hugenholtz & Okediji, 2008, pp. 14–15; Hugenholtz & Senftleben, 2011, pp. 2, 26. *See also* Eechoud et al., 2009, pp. 83–84, justifying this lack of harmonisation on the close connection of the issue with moral rights and the need to first harmonise the concept of work of authorship, as applied to derivative works.
483. *See* Art. 29.21 Canadian Copyright Act on 'Non-commercial User-generated Content' (introduced in 2012 through the Bill C-11 – 'Copyright Modernization Act'). For critical comments, *see* Ficsor, 2012a, arguing that such limitation is in violation of international treaty obligations under the BC (minimum right of adaptation and moral right of integrity) and the WCT (right of making available), as well as the three-step test.
484. Hugenholtz & Senftleben, 2011, pp. 26–27, making reference to Art. 24 German Copyright Act, and Arts 13 and 18b (for parody) Dutch Copyright Act. Senftleben, 2013b, p. 89, also makes reference to the exemption for 'independent new works' that result from an adaptation provided in Art. 5(2) Austrian Copyright Act. Regarding this option, the most common suggestion is the broadening of the quotation limitation to include transformative uses typical in UGC. See: in France, Lescure, 2013; in the Netherlands, Commissie Auteursrecht, 2012 (the latter a report from the Dutch Copyright Commission). Both examples are discussed in Triaille et al., 2013, pp. 522–525.
485. Triaille et al., 2013, p. 460.
486. Rosati, 2015a. The intricacy in defining the scope of an adaptation right is illustrated by the fact that this is not even typically subject to collective rights management on a voluntary basis. *See* Gervais, 2009, pp. 848–849.
487. CJEU, *Infopaq I*, paras 48, 51.

work.[488] If a reproduction is found, any subsequent unrestricted online dissemination of the derivative work will likewise trigger the right of communication to the public in respect of the reproduced part of the pre-existing work.[489] The broad interpretation of the right of distribution in *Art & Allposters* further delimits the potential scope of a right of adaptation.[490]

In short, adaptations by Internet users that are not *de minimis* or covered by contractual arrangements will constitute copyright infringement unless expressly exempted under national law or an EU level limitation susceptible of application to transformative uses, namely quotation, incidental use, or parody.[491] Therefore, the following paragraphs examine the potential application of these limitations in the InfoSoc Directive to digital adaptations.

4.4.4.1 Quotations

Article 5(3)(d) InfoSoc Directive contains a limitation to the rights of reproduction and communication to the public regarding:

> quotations for purposes such as criticism or review, provided that they relate to a work or other subject-matter which has already been lawfully made available to the public, that, unless this turns out to be impossible, the source, including the author's name, is indicated, and that their use is in accordance with fair practice, and to the extent required by the specific purpose.

The wording closely follows Article 10 BC on 'certain free uses of works', namely its paragraphs 1 (on quotations) and 3 (on indication of source and author). Limitations in the *acquis*, of course, are to be interpreted in light of the applicable rules in the BC.[492]

At national level, Member States have implemented the quotation limitation to varying degrees. While most countries accept the contractual disposition of the limitation, many only allow reproduction of relatively small parts of the pre-existing work, some require that the 'intellectual legacy' of said work is respected, while a few bar quotation for commercial purposes or where it affects the quoted work's commercial exploitation.[493]

488. Triaille et al., 2013, p. 460, following Ficsor, 2012a, p. 2.
489. Triaille et al., 2013, p. 460.
490. Rosati, 2015a.
491. Borgne-Bachschmidt et al., 2008, p. 188; Triaille et al., 2013, pp. 501–504, 522–525. N.B. the agreements mentioned are between rights holders and online platforms, and aim at filtering uploaded content within a notice-and-takedown system (e.g., YouTube's Content ID system). The agreements include revenue-sharing contracts between owners of pre-existing works and UGC platforms.
492. CJEU, *Painer*, para. 126 (and case law cited therein).
493. Triaille et al., 2013, pp. 472–473.

The directive's provision is broad in relation to its purpose: criticism, review or similar. That broad scope, indicated by the phrase 'such as', linked to a context requirement, is reduced by a series of cumulative conditions.[494]

First, the quoted work must have been 'lawfully made available to the public', i.e., with the rights holder's consent,[495] or under a legal licence.[496] This aligns with the CJEU's approach in *Painer*, where it understood the requirement as meaning the act of making that work available to the public under Article 3(2) InfoSoc Directive.[497]

Second, there must be an indication of source, including the author or performer's name, unless identification of either proves impossible.[498]

Third, the quotation must be according to 'fair practice'. This requirement is derived from Article 10(1) BC, and has prompted scholarly discussion on whether to apply the three-step test in this context.[499] In the absence of further guidance in the directive or by the CJEU, Member States have significant flexibility in the implementation of this requirement.[500]

For Dreier, fair practice in the BC does not refer to a 'prior existing practice', but rather to an objective criterion of fairness: 'the practice must be fair, in and of itself, according to an objective appreciation'. This includes quotations made in support of and having a connection with the views and ideas of the person making them, and that go beyond providing a substitute for the quoted work.[501]

Fourth, the limitation is subject to a 'context' requirement: a quotation is allowed only to the extent required by the specific purpose for which it is made, which must be criticism, review or similar.[502] It follows that the quoted work (whatever the extent of use necessary) should be ancillary to the subsequent work, and to the proposition the latter intends to illustrate or prove.[503] However, the limitation is worded as a prototype and allows quotation for purposes comparable to ('such as') criticism or review. That is to say, it enables some flexibility in national laws, including, in the view of

---

494. Hugenholtz & Senftleben, 2011, pp. 14–18; Triaille et al., 2013, p. 464.
495. Bechtold, 2006, p. 379; von Lewinski & Walter, 2010, p. 1049. Art. 3(3) BC refers to the narrower concept of 'lawfully published'.
496. Dreier, 2006, p. 44, with reference to the identical requirement in Art. 10(1) BC.
497. CJEU, *Painer*, paras 124–128.
498. *Ibid.*, paras 138–149.
499. Ricketson & Ginsburg, 2006, pp. 785–787. *Contra* application of the test in this context, *see* Bentley, 2016 [paper forthcoming].
500. von Lewinski & Walter, 2010, pp. 1049–1050. On national implementations of this requirement, *see* Hugenholtz & Senftleben, 2011, p. 7.
501. Dreier, 2006, pp. 44–45.
502. This condition is derived from the requirement in Art. 10(1) BC that the extent of the quotation does not exceed what is justified by the purpose. See: Hugenholtz & Senftleben, 2011, pp. 15–16; von Lewinski & Walter, 2010, p. 1050.
503. von Lewinski & Walter, 2010, p. 1050.

Hugenholtz and Senftleben, 'ample room for the courts to arrive at fair solutions'.[504]

How then does this limitation apply to online digital adaptations, such as UGC? Despite referring to quotation of pre-existing works in press reports, the CJEU's findings in *Painer* provide guidance.[505] The case marks the first explicit consideration of the impact of fundamental rights on the interpretation of limitations.[506] It identifies the objective of the quotation exemption as striking a fair balance between the rights holder's right of reproduction in the pre-existing work and the freedom of expression of subsequent users of the same.[507]

If the conditions for quotation are met, the fundamental right of freedom of expression can prevail over the exclusive right, irrespective of the copyright-protected nature of the 'quoting content'.[508] For digital adaptations, this means that *even if* a UGC object quoting a pre-existing work does not itself qualify as a derivative work, it can benefit from this limitation.[509]

This consideration of freedom of expression and information, coupled with the non-harmonisation of the adaptation right, could open the door for a broad understanding of quotation. Yet, it would be difficult to place within this limitation's scope the vast swathe of acts included in digital adaptation. Regardless, some authors argue that if national laws fully use the flexibility provided by the directive's prototype, this limitation could privilege a significant amount of use.[510]

The application of this conclusion to digital adaptations is debatable. First, not all digital adaptations are for purposes of criticism, review or similar. Many constitute forms of creative self-expression with different goals (e.g., artistic, entertainment, informational), which would be difficult to reconcile with the limitation.

Furthermore, the requirement that the pre-existing work has been lawfully made available to the public likely disqualifies the use of pre-existing works from unauthorised sources. This includes, for example, copying parts of a work accessed via P2P systems or unauthorised cyber-lockers, as well as works stripped of TPMs.[511]

In addition, many non-commercial digital adaptations fail to meet the requirement of indication of source. This may be rooted in ignorance of the

504. Hugenholtz & Senftleben, 2011, p. 15.
505. Triaille et al., 2013, p. 473.
506. Leistner, 2014, p. 585.
507. CJEU, *Painer*, para. 134.
508. *Ibid.*, paras 135–137.
509. Triaille et al., 2013, p. 474.
510. Hugenholtz & Senftleben, 2011, pp. 14–18, exemplifying with Art. 15a Dutch Copyright Act. For a broad interpretation of the quotation limitation in Art. 10 BC, *see* Bentley, 2016 [paper forthcoming].
511. *See supra* 4.4.3.6, on the challenges of qualifying what is an 'unlawful source' for private copying.

law by end-users, coupled with insufficient or inadequate availability and application of rights management information by rights holders.[512] Nevertheless, both the InfoSoc Directive and *Painer* clarify that only impossibility (not inconvenience) justifies the failure to meet this requirement.[513] While for some UGC indication of source and name is impossible, in other cases it is merely inopportune, in which case the limitation cannot apply.

Finally, guidance is required as to what constitutes fair practice in the context of UGC. Without a doubt, in the field of amateur creativity, many digital adaptations would struggle to comply with a high criterion of objective fairness, thereby setting aside the privilege of the limitation.

In sum, the quotation limitation to the rights of reproduction and communication to the public provides a flexible prototype to exempt certain transformative uses from authorisation. In that sense, it also functions as a limitation to the (non-harmonised) adaptation right. Flexibility is inherent to its 'context requirement', allowing acts comparable to criticism and review. After *Painer* – which recognised a fundamental rights justification for quotation – acts meeting the requirements of Article 5(3)(d) InfoSoc Directive deserve additional consideration, and should weight significantly in favour of users and against application of exclusivity. However, when transposed to the online environment, the joint application of the limitation's requirements and its inherent (limited) scope will fail to exempt a large number of digital adaptations, while creating legal uncertainty for other types of use, where doubts subsist on the meaning of each requirement.

4.4.4.2 Incidental Inclusion

Article 5(3)(i) InfoSoc Directive allows Member States to introduce a limitation to the rights of reproduction and communication to the public for the 'incidental inclusion of a work or other subject-matter in other material'. No identical parent provision exists in international treaties and the CJEU is yet to rule on the provision.[514] As with parody, this limitation is subject to the three-step test.

To qualify for the limitation, the pre-existing work must be 'included' in the subsequent work, becoming part of it.[515] The term 'incidental' refers

512. Triaillo et al., 2013, pp. 174–175.
513. CJEU, *Painer*, paras 139–148.
514. N.B. Art. 10*bis*(2) BC allows union countries to determine the conditions under which, for the purpose of reporting current events, works seen or heard in the course of said events may be reproduced and made available to the public. Hence, this provision may be used to exempt certain incidental inclusions of works. *See* Hugenholtz & Okediji, 2008, p. 52: 'the provision attempts to balance the need of reporters to provide ample coverage of current events by taking pictures or recording such events, and the interests of authors whose works may be captured incidentally by such recording'. On the conditions of application of the provision, *see* Ricketson, 2003, pp. 18–19.
515. von Lewinski & Walter, 2010, p. 1053.

to taking that is accidental or unintentional, as opposed to significant or merely in the background; this is therefore a *de minimis* limitation.[516]

To distinguish an incidental from a significant inclusion, commentators focus on factors like the portion used and the intent of the subsequent user.[517] In a recent study for the EU commission, for example, it is said that the limitation applies to:

> situations in which the purpose of the user was not to capture the sounds or the images at stake but where such capture happened at the occasion of the recording of another element which was the real subject matter of the recording/creation by the user.[518]

A typical example in the field of UGC is that of a recording and subsequent online dissemination of a private or semi-public event (e.g., birthday party, wedding) where in the background it is possible to hear a protected sound recording.[519]

In theory, this optional limitation could provide some coverage for a subset of UGC activities, as exemplified above. Yet, the absence of implementation in many Member States, and its limited implementation in others – by circumscribing it to certain types of work or purpose (e.g., reporting on current events) – leads instead to legal uncertainty for end-users and complex challenges for pan-EU solutions on this basis.[520] It would conceivably be possible to address this challenge by placing *de minimis* use, such as most incidental inclusion, outside the scope of copyright.[521] However, that was not the normative choice of the EU legislature.

4.4.4.3 Caricature, Parody and Pastiche

Article 5(3)(k) InfoSoc Directive contains a limitation to the rights of reproduction and communication to the public in respect of use 'for the purpose of caricature, parody or pastiche'. The terms are not defined in the directive, leaving Member States with some flexibility for implementation, subject to the three-step test.

The dictionary definition of these terms clarifies their ordinary meaning. A caricature is a '[g]rotesque or ludicrous representation of persons or things

516. Bechtold, 2006, p. 380; Senftleben, 2004, p. 262; Triaille et al., 2013, pp. 483–487; von Lewinski & Walter, 2010, p. 1053. von Lewinski & Walter, 2010, state that the included 'work or other subject matter must not have any compelling relation to the other material and therefore must be void of any significance for that material.'
517. Bechtold, 2006, p. 380.
518. Triaille et al., 2013, p. 482.
519. *Ibid.*, pp. 482–483.
520. *Ibid.*, pp. 483–487.
521. This is suggested by Senftleben, 2004, p. 262.

by exaggeration of their most characteristic and striking features.'[522] The key element for copyright purposes is the exaggeration of certain features of the adapted work (e.g., painting or photograph).[523] A parody refers to:

> A literary composition modelled on and imitating another work, esp. a composition in which the characteristic style and themes of a particular author or genre are satirised by being applied to inappropriate or unlikely subjects, or are otherwise exaggerated for comic effect. In later use extended to similar imitations in other artistic fields, as music, painting, film, etc.[524]

The treatment of the reproduced or adapted work or its features in an ironic, satiric or comical way is the central feature of parodies.[525] A pastiche is usually perceived as an 'imitation of style'[526] but its definition includes any work:

> incorporating several different styles, or made up of parts drawn from a variety of sources … A work, esp. of literature, created in the style of someone or something else; a work that humorously exaggerates or parodies a particular style.[527]

It is clear that some overlap exists between the definitional meanings of caricature, parody or pastiche. No international treaty contains a provision identical to Article 5(3)(k) InfoSoc Directive, although it has been argued that the use of parts of works for criticism or review purposes constitutes a form of quotation falling under Article 10(1) BC.[528] Most Member States have not expressly incorporated the limitation in their copyright legislation, although in a number of them a similar effect is achieved by application of the constitutional right of freedom of expression or general principles of law. Furthermore, in certain countries, some acts of parody are subsumed within the quotation limitation.[529]

In *Deckmyn*, the CJEU clarified important aspects of how the provision applies to cases of parody.[530] It stated that 'parody' is an autonomous concept of EU law which has two essential characteristics: evoking an 'existing work while being noticeably different from it'; and, 'to constitute an expression of

522. Oxford English Dictionary, *Caricature*, http://www.oed.com/view/Entry/27973?rskey=rPVzu8&result=1&isAdvanced=false#eid (accessed 31.01.2017).
523. von Lewinski & Walter, 2010, p. 1055.
524. Oxford English Dictionary, *Parody*, http://www.oed.com/view/Entry/138059?rskey=DnlSIH&result=2#eid (accessed 31.01.2017).
525. Similarly, von Lewinski & Walter, 2010, p. 1055.
526. von Lewinski & Walter, 2010, p. 1055.
527. Oxford English Dictionary, *Pastiche*, http://www.oed.com/view/Entry/138594?rskey=9UINNb&result=1&isAdvanced=false#eid (accessed 31.01.2017).
528. Senftleben, 2004, p. 194.
529. Triaille et al., 2013, p. 482.
530. For commentaries to the case, *see* European Copyright Society, 2014b; Rosati, 2015b.

humour or mockery'.[531] Beyond those characteristics, it does not have to possess 'original character of its own' or fulfil any additional conditions that do not derive from the usual meaning of the term or from the wording of the directive.[532]

Furthermore, the Court recognised that parody is justified on the basis of freedom of expression. As a result, application of the limitation must balance that fundamental freedom of users with the interests and rights of affected rights holders, which in this case may include legitimate interests in objecting to a discriminatory parody.[533]

As regards online use, the patchwork national landscape resulting from different implementations of the limitation is a driver for legal uncertainty. Despite the encouraging ruling in *Deckmyn*, only a subset of non-commercial UGC would likely qualify under the parody limitation (or under an extended version of the quotation limitation). Furthermore, there is a risk that many parodies made available online will constitute copyright infringement in certain Member States, even if exempted in others.

4.4.4.4 Interim Conclusions

There are three limitations to the reproduction right in the InfoSoc Directive susceptible of application to non-commercial digital adaptations: quotation, incidental inclusion, and caricature, parody and pastiche. The analysis shows these limitations to be insufficient per se to insulate Internet users from a significant number of infringement claims in the context of UGC.[534]

Even the combination of a broad interpretation of the three limitations would probably fail to exempt such activities from authorisation, or to

531. CJEU, *Deckmyn*, paras 14–17, 20. In contrast, the AG contended that the concept of parody possesses two basic features: 'structural', as the parody is a copy and a creation (i.e., a derivative work); and 'functional', as parodies have a subject (an earlier work or a different reference point), a (humorous) effect and content (which may trigger the application of fundamental rights). *See Opinion AG in Deckmyn*, paras 46–48, 65–67, 80–85.

532. CJEU, *Deckmyn*, paras 21–24, 33.

533. *Ibid.*, paras 25–27, 32–34. In light of the parody in question in the particular case, the Court noted the potential application of the principle of non-discrimination based on race, colour and ethnic origin, as confirmed, *inter alia*, by Art. 21(1) Charter, in which case copyright owners 'have, in principle, a legitimate interest in ensuring that the work protected by copyright is not associated with such a message.' CJEU, *Deckmyn*, paras 30–31.

534. For some commentators, other approaches could achieve the objective of allowing UGC. These include fundamental rights (freedom of expression and freedom to conduct a business), the proper consideration of the *ratio legis* or purpose of a limitation, and theories of implied consent and misuse/abuse of copyright. *See* Triaille et al., 2013, pp. 504–510, 522. On implied licences and tolerated use, *see* Gervais, 2009, pp. 868–870 (discussing enforcement issues in the UGC context), and Wu, 2007 (introducing the concept of 'tolerated use').

tangibly improve legal certainty in this field.[535] Instead, the more likely outcome is that users and platforms adapt their online behaviour to the most restrictive interpretation available for each limitation as a common denominator. This would lead to an overall de facto reduction of available exempted space.[536]

For some scholars, the harmonisation of the three limitations *and* their broad interpretation could cover the majority of UGC use, or at least the 'most valuable' use from the viewpoint of freedom of expression and development of culture. However, even these scholars recognise the need for legislative change to the limitations, including making them mandatory, unwaivable, and for the sole benefit of their creators.[537]

Thus, if the objective is to exempt the majority of digital adaptations, copyright reform is necessary. Absent harmonisation of the right of adaptation at EU level, Member States have some margin of discretion to recognise free uses or comparable limitations for non-commercial digital adaptations or subsets thereof.[538] Yet, that margin is narrow. This is so, first, as a result of national provisions on moral rights, namely attribution and integrity.[539] Second, a potential limitation for transformative uses would be subject to the three-step test as regards its impact on the adaptation right (at national level) and, especially, the harmonised right of reproduction.[540] The CJEU's broad

535. *But see* Triaille et al., 2013, p. 519, arguing that 'none of the exceptions taken separately could cover the great majority of UGC works; only by considering several exceptions does one cover, in our view, the majority of UGC.' In the same study, the authors conduct a detailed analysis at EU and Member State level and reach this conclusion. Cf. Triaille et al., 2013, pp. 464–510.
536. Geiger, 2015b, p. 14; Triaille et al., 2013, pp. 504–510, 522.
537. Triaille et al., 2013, pp. 524, 534–541. The authors would combine this with making the relevant limitations mandatory and at least quotation and parody unwaivable by contract, they would further make clear that only the individual creators would benefit from the limitations, as opposed to UGC platforms.
538. Borgne-Bachschmidt et al., 2008, pp. 188–189, noting that '[a]bsent harmonization of the adaptation right, Member States remain autonomous and may elect to codify exceptions or limitations to this right to permit certain non-commercial transformative uses.' *See* Hugenholtz, 2012b, p. 55: 'Member states remain free to provide for limitations and exceptions to the right of adaptation at their own discretion, subject only to the "three-step test".' *See also* Triaille et al., 2013, p. 504.
539. Borgne-Bachschmidt et al., 2008, pp. 188–189; Triaille et al., 2013, pp. 462–464. The latter study states 'that the condition of acknowledgement of the source constitutes, as a matter of fact, a uniform implementation of the right of attribution in the field of these exceptions' (illustration of teaching and scientific research, reproduction by the press, quotation, and use of political speeches).
540. Hugenholtz & Senftleben, 2011, pp. 26–28, arguing that the regulation of the right of adaptation, understood as the '*corpus mysticum* of a ... work – is left to national law making', being that the InfoSoc Directive only applies to 'literal reproduction'. *See also* Green Paper Copyright in the Knowledge Economy 2008, p. 20: 'Under the Berne convention, a transformative use would be prima facie covered by the reproduction right and the right of adaptation. An exception to these rights would have to pass the three-step test. In particular, it would have to be more precise and refer to a specific policy

interpretation of such a right (e.g., in *Infopaq I* and *Murphy*), and strict reading of limitations (e.g., in *ACI Adam* and *OSA*), further hinders that flexibility.

4.5 CONCLUSIONS

The online activities of Internet users can be categorised into different types of act: browsing, downloading, streaming, stream capture/ripping, uploading, linking, and digital adaptation. These acts are subject to the harmonised exclusive rights of reproduction and communication to the public in Articles 2 and 3 InfoSoc Directive. Digital adaptation is also subject to the non-harmonised right of adaptation, a BC minimum right, partially recognised in the Software and Database Directives.

The determination of which rights apply to which use is challenging in the online environment, largely due to the possibilities for fragmentation and overlap of rights. For example, acts of uploading may involve restricted reproduction and making available of works, whereas UGC can involve partial reproduction of the pre-existing work, its adaptation, and communication to the public. Moreover, these rights may be held by different rights holders across different territories.

The chapter focuses on harmonised rights. It shows that these rights are interpreted broadly by the CJEU, in a combination of technical and economic approaches, which safeguard for rights holders most new technological avenues of exploitation with commercial significance. A by-product of this approach is the increased risk of infringement and legal uncertainty for individuals in their online activities.

On the one hand, the prevailing understanding of the reproduction right qualifies copies in the technical sense as legally relevant. In this way, the right is extended to most digital reproductions of works, as these are technically required for online consumption, manipulation, and dissemination of content.

On the other hand, the application of the right of communication to the public to digital networks by the CJEU has seen the development of criteria – public, new public, specific technical means, profit-making nature – in a sometimes inconsistent way. The Court's case law at times extends and at times contracts the scope of the right, creating legal uncertainty in its interpretation. Moreover, the online scope of the right is influenced by the application of contractual and technical restrictions imposed by rights holder.

For example, the exclusive right does either does not cover hyperlinking if the work was previously accessible online without access restrictions (e.g.,

justification or types of justified use. It would also have to be limited to short takings (short passages, excluding particularly distinctive takings), therefore not infringing the right of adaptation'.

subscription pay-walls), or allows such type of use subject to a doctrine of 'implicit consent'.[541] However, if the work was subject to such restrictions, any type of link circumventing them is a prohibited communication to the public, as it makes the work available to a new public, irrespective of the prohibition on circumventing TPMs. This is particularly problematic for end-users where the access restriction is placed on the work after an initial period of free accessibility.

Furthermore, the CJEU clarified that linking to a freely accessible but unauthorised source is making the work available to a new public, and therefore requires prior consent. However, that assessment depends on a (judicially created) rebuttable presumption of knowledge linked to a 'for-profit' condition, the application of which is unclear. Partly due to the extension of the right to linking activities and the relevance of the communication source, a pending case before the CJEU will decide whether the activities of a website operator through a system that allows users to trace and up/download works (like The Pirate Bay) is an act of communication to the public.[542] It is also not clear whether an upload or upstream transmission of a work to a restricted group (e.g., within a group on a social sharing website) amounts to a communication to the 'public' or, instead, a non-public reproduction.

The result of this legal framework is twofold. First, due to the mixed technical and economic design of the rights, the majority of individuals' non-commercial online activities are subject to exclusive rights. The reproduction right applies theoretically to browsing, downloading, 'consumption' of streams, stream capture, certain uploads, and the making of digital adaptations. The right of communication to the public applies to the Internet transmission of streams, certain uploads, and all types of hyperlinking, with the exception of links to (copies of) works freely accessible online with the consent of the rights holder. Second, due to the inconsistent design of the rights (mainly their technological dependency and complex criteria) multiple online activities of Internet users are subject to legal uncertainty.

Where exclusive rights apply, it is possible that the non-commercial activities of users are exempted from authorisation by the application of limitations in the InfoSoc Directive. However, the directive restricts the scope of limitations and gives rise to additional uncertainty.

Limitations in the InfoSoc Directive do not apply to software and databases, and the respective sectorial directives leave little room for online use. Most limitations are optional, leading to different levels of implementation and interpretation. Only some limitations are subject to fair compensation, notably private copying. Also, although the relationship between limitations and contract law is unregulated, contractual disposition of

541. Whereas the first interpretation derives from *Svensson*, the second is advanced by the CJEU in *Soulier and Doke*.

542. *See* CJEU, Reference for Preliminary Ruling, Case C-610/15, *Stichting Brein v. Ziggo*.

limitations is generally possible. Finally, TPM application supersedes the exercise of most limitations for online use, severely hindering digital private copying.

In spite of this, examination of the directive's objectives leads to the conclusion that limitations are essential for promotion of access to and dissemination of knowledge and culture, as well as for balancing exclusivity with the public interest and fundamental rights. The CJEU recognises this normative function and its role in shaping the scope of (at least some) limitations. Two opposing forces are noticeable in this regard. On one side, the Court applies the strict interpretation doctrine and three-step test to narrow the scope of limitations. On the other, it recognises the need for flexible interpretation of limitations due to the prototypical nature of their wording, the requirements of effectiveness and purposive interpretation, the need for a balancing of interests, and the (external and internal) operation of fundamental rights. In both cases, the principle of autonomous interpretation is used to further the argument.

On balance, the analysis shows that the Court employs the highlighted arguments to mitigate the effects of strict interpretation where a limitation is justified on fundamental rights. (The most relevant deviation from this trend is found in the private copying case law.) This trend should be welcomed, as it is consistent with the InfoSoc Directive's objectives of harmonising limitations and fair balance; it is also not contrary to the directive's objective of ensuring a high level of protection, if this is understood as an 'optimal' level of protection for rights holders.

In addition, as explored in Chapter 5, this tendency is also consistent with a view that the three-step test is not primarily a restricting clause. Rather, it can be construed as an enabling provision that leaves space for a flexible and functional interpretation of limitations, especially in light of their fundamental rights' justification. Mitigation of the strict interpretation doctrine and a more flexible interpretation of the test allow limitations to strike a balance in copyright law and better achieve the internal market objective.

However, it is undeniable that the design of the directive, together with the Court's interpretation of exclusive rights and limitations – especially when focusing on strict interpretation and the 'high level of protection' mantra – skew the legal framework towards the preservation of exclusivity online and loss of legal certainty. Therefore, as a descriptive matter, limitations in the *acquis* are constrained, even if we read them in a flexible way.

The point is illustrated by the examination of how limitations in the InfoSoc Directive apply to the online activities of individuals. The mandatory limitation for temporary copies in Article 5(1) InfoSoc Directive, as interpreted by the Court, exempts browsing copies from the scope of the reproduction right. Still, its application to copies made when (down) streaming content is uncertain. It seems that absent authorisation from the rights holder, this activity fails to meet the requirements of 'lawful use' and absence of 'independent economic importance'.

The private copying limitation in Article 5(2)(b) InfoSoc Directive is susceptible of application to acts of downloading, (down) streaming, stream capture and uploading. The limitation is equally relevant because some of its conditions (non-commercial, fair compensation, and the design of levy systems) are candidates for transplant to legal licence ACS. As interpreted by the CJEU, the limitation does not privilege up/downstream copies made from unauthorised sources. Therefore, the limitation excludes or casts doubt on the legality of a large set of non-commercial online reproductions made by end-users. Uncertainty remains in relation to copies made using cloud services (including private online video recorders), and the possibility of imposing a levy on the respective providers.

Digital adaptations, including transformative uses, have an intricate regulation. On the one hand, due to legislative omission in the *acquis*, these uses may be in part covered by the non-harmonised right of adaptation at national level, separately from the right of reproduction. On the other hand, some of these uses are privileged by limitations to harmonised rights, namely quotation, incidental inclusion and parody in Article 5(3)(d), (i) and (k) InfoSoc Directive. However, these apparent flexibilities are limited in relation to non-commercial online use.

First, due to the broad interpretation of harmonised exclusive rights by the CJEU, a viable adaptation right would require that the scope of the right of reproduction is delimited to literal reproductions. Second, the scope of the applicable limitations does not necessarily encompass most digital adaptations. Even if the limitations are interpreted broadly and considered jointly, it is doubtful that they are sufficient to privilege a large portion of non-commercial digital adaptations, or seriously reduce legal uncertainty for UGC.

The quotation limitation offers a flexible prototype to privilege certain transformative uses comparable to criticism and review. After *Painer*, the fundamental rights pedigree of the privilege may broaden its scope. Still, its application to online use is constrained by the requirements of context, lawful availability of quoted work, source indication, and fairness.

The incidental inclusion limitation is either not implemented or only partially so in domestic laws. Hence, reliance thereon to exempt even a small subset of (quasi) *de minimis* digital adaptations is doubtful.

The limitation for caricature, pastiche and parody is also implemented unevenly. The CJEU has interpreted the provision in relation to parody, which *Deckmyn* qualified as an autonomous concept of EU law, justified by the fundamental right of freedom of expression. Still, only a portion of non-commercial UGC will qualify as a parody or be covered by an extended version of the quotation privilege. Furthermore, there is a risk that many online parodies are infringing in some Member States, but not others.

In sum, a significant portion of non-commercial online use is subject to exclusive rights and not privileged by limitations in the *acquis*. In many cases, there is appreciable uncertainty in the application of the right or limitation to a use. It seems, however, that the tendency is to extend exclusivity to activities of personal enjoyment and expression – irrespective of their non-commercial purpose – that would functionally not appear to be within the realm of copyright (e.g., linking). Furthermore, the legal framework affords priority to 'private choice' contractual and technological measures in shaping the scope of the exclusive right and applicable limitations.

This was already a design feature in the InfoSoc Directive of the relationship between limitations, on the one hand, and contract and TPMs, on the other. It is reinforced by the CJEU in the relevance afforded to the 'authorised source' of the online communication to the public or private copying, as well as the 'freely accessible with prior consent' / 'access restrictions' binomial inherent in the new public criterion. Countervailing forces seem to be the purposive interpretation of limitations in light of their fundamental rights justification, and the reinforced nature of the private copying limitation and fair compensation vis-à-vis contractual dispositions (absent TPM application).

From a normative perspective, at least two insights emerge from this chapter's analysis. The first is that the current system is at least partly inconsistent with key objectives of the InfoSoc Directive. These include a fair balance of the interests of rights holders and users (and the public interest), enhancing legal certainty, the smooth functioning of the internal market (through the coherent application of exclusive rights and limitations), promoting the development of the information society (and that of new technologies), and fostering the circulation of culture. As noted previously, it is also arguable whether the technically based expansion of exclusive rights and contraction of limitations, at the expense of the aforementioned objectives and without achieving an 'appropriate reward', adequately meets the goal of providing a 'high level of protection' to rights holders, understood as 'adequate' or 'optimal' protection.[543]

The second insight relates to the complexity of substantive and territorial fragmentation of overlapping exclusive rights as they apply to mass online use of copyright works. The analysis provided is a snapshot of a volatile moving target, subject to the interpretative winds of the CJEU. If legal reform through ACS is to be effective, its best hope is to rely on models capable of aggregation of rights and enhancing legal certainty. ACS relying

543. The connection between a 'high level of protection' with creative incentives and 'adequate remuneration' for rights holders is patent in recitals 9 and 10 InfoSoc Directive. For the use of 'fair balance' and 'adequate protection' by the CJEU as teleological arguments to limit a broad interpretation of rights in the copyright *acquis*, *see* Favale et al., 2015, pp. 65–68. *See also infra* 5.5.3.

on legal licences or mandatory collective management are the best options available in this regard.

If a non-voluntary ACS is the way forward, its admissibility hinges on passing the three-step test, at least for a statutory licence system. As noted in Chapter 3, it is debatable whether the test applies to mandatory collective management, which appears to affect only the *exercise* of copyright. Regardless, due to the contentious nature of the topic (especially after *Soulier and Doke*), the policy legitimacy of an ACS based on mandatory collective management would benefit from its compliance with the test. For this purpose, it is possible to use the more restrictive option of statutory licensing as an analytical proxy. That is to say, if such a licence is compliant with the test, *a maiore ad minus*, so will be the less restrictive model of mandatory collective management.[544] In this light, the following chapter examines the consistency of a legal licence ACS with EU copyright law.

544. *See supra* 3.5.

Chapter 5

Copyright Reform: Admissibility of Legalisation under the Three-Step Test and the Objectives of EU Copyright Law

5.1 INTRODUCTION

It is now clear that copyright law significantly restricts the online use of works by individuals. Strict enforcement of this use is often impossible, costly, or simply undesirable. Moreover, both enforcement and criminalisation of non-commercial use alienate end-users and contribute to diminishing the respect and legitimacy of copyright law.[1] Yet, empirical research shows that individuals are willing to participate in, and pay for, alternative models of access to and use of copyright works, like ACS. Despite facing lower legal hurdles, voluntary ACS are exposed to the risks of substantive and territorial fragmentation of copyright, and are dependent on the participation of rights holders. As a result, they will likely fail to provide a satisfactory all-encompassing legalisation scheme. Conversely, a system based on a compensated limitation and statutory licensing has the potential to enable large-scale non-commercial online use in the EU.[2]

1. *See supra* 1.1, making these points, and the analysis in Chapter 4, regarding the reach of exclusive rights to online use. *See also* Geiger, 2014c, p. 127ff.
2. As noted *supra* at 4.5 the statutory licence ACS is used here as an analytical proxy for mandatory collective management assuming, *arguendo*, that an ACS based on such a model would be subject to the three-step test.

It is therefore crucial to inquire whether such a system is admissible under EU copyright law and consistent with its objectives. This chapter is divided into two parts, each examining one of the following research questions. While the first question is predominantly doctrinal, the second is normative:

> To what extent is a statutory licence ACS for non-commercial online use of works by individuals admissible under EU copyright law, namely the three-step test?
> To what extent is a model of access and remuneration, such as an ACS, consistent with the general aims of copyright and the objectives of EU copyright law?

The first part builds on the previous analysis by assuming that a statutory licence ACS is the best model to regulate mass individual non-commercial online use. A statutory licence has the advantage of dealing with most high-level challenges associated with territorial and substantive fragmentation, representing a comparative advantage in relation to voluntary licences. However, as demonstrated in the previous chapter, exclusive rights of reproduction and communication to the public in the *acquis* cover many types of online use. Thus, a statutory licence ACS entails an expansion of existing limitations to those rights.

The main obstacle to such expansion is the three-step test, which regulates the introduction of use privileges by national laws. This chapter views the international and EU versions of the test as normative benchmarks for copyright limitations. Because EU law must be interpreted in light of international law, the international provisions in relation to the three-step test feature prominently in the analysis.

The second and more normative part of the chapter examines the consistency of a legalisation model enabling remunerated online access to and use of works with the aims of copyright (i.e., its prevailing rationales) and the objectives of the EU *acquis*. To carry out this examination, this part looks into the dominant theories of copyright in the European legal tradition – natural rights and utilitarianism –, the access and remuneration dimensions of copyright, and the objectives of copyright law, as derived from the recitals of different directives and CJEU case law.

The chapter proceeds as follows. The first part contains the doctrinal analysis of ACS under the three-step test, spanning sections 5.2–5.4. Section 5.2 develops an analytical framework for the test: it clarifies the different variants of the test in international and EU law, elucidates its addressees and functions, and maps its potential interpretations. Section 5.3 examines the three-step test to discover the space available for a limitation-based ACS. It analyses the test sequentially but considers it as a whole aimed at balancing competing interests through the principle of proportionality. The analysis is innovative in that it includes normative elements in all steps of the test, and integrates fundamental rights in the assessment of the third step. This balancing exercise identifies a potential conflict with the normal exploitation of works as the main obstacle to ACS. In that light, section 5.4 explores whether certain mechanisms advanced in legalisation proposals – embargo periods and opt-out systems – assist in overcoming such conflict in a way consistent with international law and the *acquis*. The second part of the chapter (section 5.5) examines the legalisation of non-commercial online use as a normative choice between exclusivity and remunerated access. It assesses the consistency of ACS with the rationales of copyright, its access and remuneration dimensions, and the objectives of EU copyright law. Section 5.6 offers a summary and the conclusions of the chapter.

5.2 ANALYTICAL FRAMEWORK OF THE THREE-STEP TEST

A statutory licence for non-commercial online use requires a limitation to the exclusive rights of reproduction and communication to the public. The introduction of a limitation in the *acquis* is subject to the three-step test in international law, in which light Article 5(5) InfoSoc Directive must be interpreted. That makes it important to understand the web of international rules on the test, its addressees, and possible readings. For that purpose, this section develops an analytical framework for the test, which first clarifies its different variants in international and EU law, and their relationship to each other (5.2.1). This is followed by a discussion of the spectrum of interpretations of the test (5.2.2).

5.2.1 Variants and Interpretation

The test is a set of three conditions that regulate the imposition and permissible scope of limitations to copyright. According to it, copyright limitations must:

(1) Be certain special cases,
(2) Not conflict with the normal exploitation of the work,
(3) Not unreasonably prejudice the legitimate interests of the author or rights holder.

The three-step test was originally suggested by the British delegation at the Stockholm revision conference of the BC. This origin makes it appropriate to analyse the test with reference to its English language versions found in different treaties.[3]

3. Pursuant to Art. 37(1) BC the French version prevails in the event of conflict with the English version. The only such linguistic discrepancy is found in the second step, when

In international intellectual property law, there are eight variations of the test in four conventions currently in force: Article 9(2) BC; Articles 10(1) and (2) WCT; Article 16(2) WPPT; and Articles 13, 17, 26(2) and 30 TRIPS.[4] Articles 17, 26(2) and 30 TRIPS do not refer to copyright but to trademarks, designs and patents. They differ from their copyright counterparts insofar as they expressly mention 'limited exceptions' instead of 'certain special cases' (in the first step), and the need to take into account the legitimate interests of 'third parties' (in the third step). The trademark test, furthermore, omits the second condition, making it in fact a two-step test. In the absence of an explanation in the drafting history of TRIPS, these differences should be resolved through legal interpretation.[5]

In the *acquis*, the main embodiment of the test is Article 5(5) InfoSoc Directive. However, the Software, Database and Rental Right Directives contain substantially similar (if partial) versions it.[6]

The myriad tests have different wordings with slightly varying purpose and operation.[7] Still, the copyright versions share a common structure and content in relation to the three criteria.[8] They also share an intentionally general and abstract formulation, intended to enable BC members to accommodate existing national limitations, and afford them discretion on how to give effect to the test.[9] The same lack of specificity makes the test a challenging standard for interpretation, especially in the dynamic context of new technologies.[10]

The interpretation of the international law versions of the test should be made in accordance with Articles 31–33 VCLT. As noted in Chapter 1, these rules favour a literal approach, mitigated by systematic ('context') and teleological ('object and purpose') interpretation of treaty provisions.[11] The

contrasting the English and French translation of 'unreasonable prejudice'. Still, it is possible to reconcile the meaning of both versions. *See* Peukert, 2005, pp. 29–30; Senftleben, 2004, p. 114.

4. Christie & Wright, 2014, with a comparative analysis of the three-step tests in international treaties. The test is also included in Art. 11 WIPO Beijing Treaty and Art. 11 WIPO Marrakesh Treaty.
5. Kur, 2008, pp. 19–20; Senftleben, 2006, pp. 412, 421–422. N.B. Art. 17 TRIPS does not refer to a conflict with the normal exploitation of trademarks (but rather provides an example: 'fair use of descriptive terms'), as their primary function is distinguishing goods and services in the course of trade. Cf. *EC–Trademarks I*, para. 7.664. Kur, 2008, p. 20, notes that the WTO panel reports on the different tests are to be read as not overstating the differences in formulation. For a detailed breakdown of the discrete elements of all tests, *see* Christie & Wright, 2014.
6. Art. 6(3) Software Directive; Art. 6(3) Database Directive. Application of the test in the Rental Right Directive operates by virtue of Art. 11(1)(b) InfoSoc Directive.
7. Christie & Wright, 2014.
8. Senftleben, 2004, p. 105. *Contra*, Christie & Wright, 2014.
9. Ricketson & Ginsburg, 2006, pp. 182–183.
10. Griffiths, 2009, pp. 20–21; Koelman, 2006, p. 407; Westkamp, 2008, p. 65.
11. *See supra* 1.3. On the interpretation of international copyright law, *see also* Ricketson, 2003, pp. 6–7; Senftleben, 2004, pp. 100–101; Sinclair, 1984, pp. 117–121.

'context' comprises the text of the treaty, including preamble and annexes, together with related agreements and instruments made or accepted by all the parties in relation to the treaty.[12] It only includes documents approved by all signatories to a treaty that are contemporaneous with its ratification.[13] These documents include the majority of Agreed Statements to different provisions of the WIPO Treaties.[14] The 'object and purpose' of a treaty relies on elements like preambles.[15]

In certain circumstances, Article 32 VCLT allows recourse to extrinsic elements to the treaty's text.[16] Express reference is made to preparatory works of the treaty, and the circumstances of its conclusion.[17] Admissible supplementary materials also include national court decisions, authoritative scholarship, and a wide range of materials.[18] Amongst supplementary sources, particular attention should be given to preparatory works in international conventions and reports of panels appointed in the course of procedures of the World Trade Organization (WTO) Dispute Settlement Body.[19]

Preparatory works include published documents typically identified as 'Actes', 'Documents', or 'Records' of diplomatic conferences preceding and resulting in the conclusion of a treaty or convention.[20] They should also include the 'uncontested statements' made during the course of preparatory works, which would thus not qualify as 'context'.[21] This is the case for Professor Ulmer's statements as Chairman of the Main Committee I of the

12. Art. 31(2) VCLT.
13. Iuliano, 2011, p. 473; Sinclair, 1984, p. 119. Finally, Art. 31(4) VCLT reads: 'A special meaning shall be given to a term if it is established that the parties so intended.'
14. Ficsor, 2002c, pp. 63–64; Ricketson, 2003, p. 6.
15. Ricketson, 2003, pp. 6–7; Senftleben, 2004, p. 102; Sinclair, 1984, pp. 117–118.
16. Recourse to supplementary materials is allowed to confirm the meaning resulting from the application of Art. 31 VCLT or to determine the meaning of a provision when Art. 31 leads to an interpretation that is unclear or 'manifestly absurd or unreasonable.' *See* Bouthillier, 2011, p. 843, Christie & Wright, 2014, pp. 411–416; Ricketson & Ginsburg, 2006, pp. 197–198; Senftleben, 2004, p. 103; Sinclair, 1984, p. 116.
17. 'Circumstances of the treaty's conclusion' are not particularly relevant for this study. They include the 'historical background against which the treaty was negotiated, and the individual characteristics and attitudes of the contracting parties.' *See* Ricketson, 2003, pp. 8–9; Ricketson & Ginsburg, 2006, pp. 197–208. *See also* Bouthillier, 2011, pp. 859–861.
18. Bouthillier, 2011, pp. 854, 861–863; Senftleben, 2004, p. 111.
19. Sorel & Eveno, 2011, pp. 820–821, noting that the Dispute Settlement Body refers almost automatically to the VCLT rules in the interpretation of TRIPS.
20. Ricketson, 2003, pp. 7–8.
21. Bouthillier, 2011, p. 852; Ricketson, 2003, pp. 7–8; Ricketson & Ginsburg, 2006, p. 198; Sinclair, 1984, p. 130. *See also* Sinclair, 1984, p. 130, finding this the better interpretation and stating that the importance of these elements may be enhanced 'by the authority of the person making the statement'.

Stockholm Conference, often relied upon for strict interpretation of the three-step test in Article 9(2) BC.[22]

The WTO Panel reports are relevant for the interpretation of the three-step test of Article 13 TRIPS. Despite their limited binding force, the influential nature of the reports in scholarship makes them unavoidable, even when examining Article 5(5) InfoSoc Directive.[23]

The following paragraphs examine the different versions of the copyright three-step test at international level, starting with the BC (5.2.1.1) and moving on to the WIPO Treaties (5.2.1.2) and TRIPS (5.2.1.3). Subsequently, the investigation turns to Article 5(5) InfoSoc Directive and the extent to which its interpretation should reflect the international tests (5.2.1.4).

5.2.1.1 The Berne Convention and Its Relationship to Other Treaties

There is no authoritative interpretation of Article 9(2) BC.[24] The original version of this provision was introduced in the 1967 Stockholm revision conference:[25]

> It shall be a matter for legislation in the countries of the Union to permit the reproduction of such works in certain special cases, provided that such reproduction does not conflict with a normal exploitation of the work and does not unreasonably prejudice the legitimate interests of the author.

The provision applies to the reproduction right and mentions the interests of authors. The analysis of the private copying precedent in Chapter 2 clarifies the mixed nature of the test in Article 9(2) BC. On the one hand, the test is a limiting clause, to be read in a sequential and cumulative manner.[26] On the other hand, due to the abstract nature of the criteria and its

22. Ricketson & Ginsburg, 2006, pp. 190–192, with further analysis.
23. Kur, 2008, pp. 32–33, arguing that WTO panel decisions do not qualify as definitive interpretations, subsequent agreements or practices, even after adoption by the Dispute Settlement Body. *See also* Geiger et al., 2014, pp. 600–601 (WTO Panel Reports are not binding interpretations of the TRIPS test for all members of the agreement or for future WTO panels examining the test), and Shabalala, 2010, p. 149 (WTO Panel Reports bind only the parties to the dispute and concern the debated provisions in its specific context, object and scope).
24. A definitive interpretation can only be given by the International Court of Justice (Art. 33 BC) but no case has ever been brought before this Court, as dispute resolution procedures under the BC are not deemed effective. Cf. Hugenholtz & Okediji, 2008, p. 21; Iuliano, 2011, p. 471.
25. For historical background, *see* Ficsor, 2002b, p. 115ff.; Kur, 2008, pp. 17–18; Senftleben, 2004, pp. 43–82. *See also supra* 2.3.2.
26. Ficsor, 2002b, pp. 125–127. *See supra* 2.3.2.1, referring to the reported statements of Professor Eugen Ulmer, chairman of Main Committee I at the 1967 Stockholm

compromise nature, the test is flexible enough to accommodate diverse national limitations on the right of reproduction with social, cultural and economic motivations.[27]

As copyright law evolved so did the three-step test, both within the international framework and in regional and national laws. Westkamp aptly describes the evolution as more of a 'contemporaneous compromise' than 'a rigid obstacle to creating new limitations'.[28] From a relatively moderate scope at inception, the test currently extends (with different wordings) to all rights and rights holders, by virtue of TRIPS and the WIPO Treaties.[29] In addition, as these treaties incorporate Article 9(2) BC by reference, the context of the BC provides common ground for analysis of the subsequent tests.[30]

When considering these 'interwoven contexts', it must be remembered that the object and purpose of the later treaties is more complex, especially due to their reference to notions of balance and public interest.[31] For example, the WCT Preamble introduces considerations of competing interests to those of authors and 'the need to maintain a balance between the rights of authors and the larger public interest, particularly education, research and access to information, as reflected in the Berne Convention.'[32]

The mention of the BC highlights a 'balance' dimension not immediately apparent in the text of that convention, but nevertheless unanimously recognised and adhered to by the WCT parties. Ricketson and Ginsburg find the reference meaningful and indicative of 'the need to interpret Berne

---

Conference. Cf. Records BC Stockholm 1967, 885. *But see* Geiger, Gervais & Senftleben, 2014, pp. 609–611, noting that '... one cannot derive the entire interpretation from these statements'.

27. Geiger et al., 2014, p. 616; Griffiths, 2009, p. 21; Hugenholtz & Okediji, 2008, p. 18; Senftleben, 2006, pp. 411–412, 2013c, p. 16; Westkamp, 2008, p. 5; Wright, 2009, pp. 603–604.
28. Westkamp, 2008, p. 11.
29. Arts 13 TRIPS, 10 WCT (and its Agreed Statements), and 16(2) WPPT, including the Agreed Statements to the latter treaties.
30. Senftleben, 2004, p. 106, calls this a phenomenon of 'interwoven contexts'. *See* Arts 9(1) TRIPS and 1(4) WCT. This much can be deduced from references in the preparatory works of TRIPS and the WCT. Cf. Senftleben, 2004, pp. 111–112, and supplementary sources cited therein. This approach was followed in WTO, *Canada Patent*, paras 6.14–6.15, 7.72, and WTO, *US–Copyright*, paras 6.73, 6.179, 6.181. Cf. also Ficsor, 2002b, pp. 177–179.
31. The attention to the object and purpose of the treaty is fully consistent with the rules of the VCLT. Cf. Geiger et al., 2014, p. 597 ff.
32. The preamble to the WPPT contains similar wording but omits the reference to the BC and replaces 'authors' with 'performers and producers of phonograms'. In the analysis the position is taken that the ordinary meaning of the terms 'rights' (of authors) and 'interests' (of the general public) do not translate into different hierarchical value (e.g., of rule *v.* exception), but rather their different technical nature: rights are specifically regulated, whereas the notion of interests is broader. Cf. Kur, 2008, pp. 46–47.

provisions in a qualified way'.[33] It is also consistent with the aforementioned diplomatic compromise nature of the BC.[34]

Like the BC, TRIPS affords a central role to 'balance', namely when dealing with the objectives and principles of the treaty in its preamble and Articles 7 and 8. These provisions consider intellectual property rights as functional tools for the promotion of trade, technological development, and economic and social purposes, to be balanced with competing and often rival interests of users.[35] The emphasis on public interest, some scholars argue, increases the space for limitations.[36]

This brief excursion shows that the three-step tests in TRIPS and the WIPO Treaties can be interpreted in a more flexible way than the BC test, if read in light of the object and purpose of the respective treaties.[37] The point is reinforced for online limitations, due to temporal issues on interpretation. Article 31(1) VCLT mandates that interpretation of the ordinary meaning of a provision is fixed at the date of conclusion of the treaty text.[38] In the BC, that date significantly precedes the digital age and refers to a substantially different technological and economic context, where the definition of 'primary' exploitation markets was more transparent and stable.[39] Accordingly, the more up to date tests in TRIPS and the WIPO Treaties are of greater relevance to assessment of limitations in the digital age.[40] At the very least, they warrant exploring a flexible interpretation of the test.[41]

---

33. Ricketson & Ginsburg, 2006, p. 213. The position is shared by other scholars. See, e.g., Hugenholtz & Okediji, 2008, p. 16.
34. Geiger, 2007b, p. 3; Koelman, 2006.
35. Ricketson & Ginsburg, 2006, pp. 196–197.
36. Geiger & Schönherr, 2014b, pp. 442–444 & n. 130. N.B. some authors argue that the benchmark for assessing the minimum safeguards for intellectual property rights is not a 'property-biased approach' but rather one focused on competition and the prevention of international market failure. *See* Kur, 2008, pp. 36–39, arguing for a greater interpretative relevance of Arts 7 and 8 following the Doha Declaration (2001). *See also* Geiger et al., 2014, p. 597.
37. Ricketson, 2003, p. 7; Ricketson & Ginsburg, 2006, pp. 208–209. The conclusion is not affected by the 'special agreement' nature of the WIPO Treaties under Art. 20 BC, which means they should not derogate from existing obligations under the BC and comply with the incorporated substantive provisions. It is likewise not contrary to the similar non-derogation provision in Art. 2(2) TRIPS. *But see* Ricketson & Ginsburg, 2006, pp. 210–211, with an apparently different view.
38. See, e.g., Sinclair, 1984, pp. 124–126.
39. Cf. Westkamp, 2008, pp. 7–8. For example, in the music sector, the primary market is characterised by single authors (writers, lyricists, composers) directly contracting with music publishers or the record company, whilst the secondary market is characterised by 'use of products of the primary market (for example, public performance of phonograms or DVDs, lending books or broadcasting)' for which individual management is generally not feasible. Cf. Hilty & Nérisson, 2013, p. 3.
40. *See* Ricketson & Ginsburg, 2006, p. 218, for temporal issues in interpretation of international law.
41. Kur, 2008, p. 35.

5.2.1.2 The WIPO Treaties and the Agreed Statements

The three-step test in the WCT applies only to authors, like the test in the BC. Unlike the BC version, the WCT test extends beyond the reproduction right, including limitations to all WCT-rights (paragraph 1)[42] and 'when applying the Berne Convention' (paragraph 2). The latter reference fulfils an 'additional safeguard function' regarding exclusive rights in the BC.[43] For its part, the WPPT test benefits performers and producers of phonograms.

The tests in the WIPO Treaties are accompanied by near identical Agreed Statements. The Agreed Statement on Article 10 WCT, adopted *mutatis mutandis* for Article 16 WPPT, states:

> It is understood that the provisions of Article 10 permit Contracting Parties to carry forward and appropriately extend into the digital environment limitations and exceptions in their national laws which have been considered acceptable under the Berne Convention. Similarly, these provisions should be understood to permit Contracting Parties to devise new exceptions and limitations that are appropriate in the digital network environment.
>
> It is also understood that Article 10(2) neither reduces nor extends the scope of applicability of the limitations and exceptions permitted by the Berne Convention.

This statement is between all parties to the WCT, which makes it 'context' for interpretation of the treaty.[44] That status means, first, that it ranks higher than supplementary sources (e.g., most statements in preparatory works) and, second, that it must be read in direct relation to the treaty text.[45]

One of the implications is that the Agreed Statements should be interpreted in light of the preambles of the WIPO Treaties. As noted, these preambles accentuate the need for balance between authors/rights holders and the public interest. In this way, the Agreed Statements open the door for a flexible interpretation of the test, taking into account policy considerations and relevant societal values in assessing digital limitations.[46]

---

42. Art. 10(1) WCT applies to the newly granted rights in Arts 6, 7 and 8 WCT. *See* Christie & Wright, 2014, pp. 418–419, with a view that the wording in this paragraph allows countries to go beyond 'certain special cases' based on a textual interpretation.
43. Hugenholtz & Okediji, 2008, p. 20; Senftleben, 2004, pp. 121–124. The difference of wording in the first paragraph ('may provide') and the second paragraph ('shall confine') does not seem to affect the substance of the provisions. Cf. Ficsor, 2002b, pp. 165–167.
44. Art. 31(2)(a) VCLT. *See* Ricketson & Ginsburg, 2006, p. 870.
45. Reinbothe & von Lewinski, 2002, p. 19; Senftleben, 2004, p. 106.
46. European Copyright Society, 2013; Kur, 2008, p. 46; Senftleben, 2013c, p. 17; Shabalala, 2010, p. 185. On the relevance of the WCT Preamble for interpretation of the test in the digital environment, *see* Senftleben, 2004, p. 98. *But see* Reinbothe & von Lewinski, 2002, p. 132, considering that Art. 10(2) WCT contains 'a scrutiny test', rather than an 'enabling clause'.

This interpretation is, on the one hand, supported by the drafting history of the WCT – which is populated with references to balancing concerns[47] – and, on the other hand, consistent with the test's technology neutral character, as it allows it to adjust to an evolving landscape of copyright use.[48] With a view to a good faith interpretation, the Agreed Statements and preamble could even 'retroactively infuse meaning into the norms of the BC as incorporated into TRIPS and the three-step test'.[49]

Without a doubt, the Agreed Statements are difficult to reconcile with rigid sequential interpretation of the test that prevents extension of limitations to the digital environment.[50] A more defensible interpretation views them as guidelines for: (1) the adaptation and extension of existing limitations to BC rights to the digital environment, including reproduction and certain forms of communication to the public; and (2) the creation of new limitations for digital use, which go beyond the scope of those already in existence, such as making available online.[51] This is relevant for a statutory licence ACS, which partially relies on pre-WCT limitations extended to the digital environment and, at least regarding the making available right, on a new limitation.

5.2.1.3 The Agreement on Trade-Related Aspects of Intellectual Property Law

The three-step test in TRIPS is a compromise 'grandfathering-clause'.[52] The inclusion of the test in TRIPS gave rise to fears that a norm of international copyright law would be transformed into a norm of international trade law, degrading its normative content and further hindering the balance between access and exclusivity.[53] This version of the test replaces 'authors' with 'the right holder', broadening the scope of the provision to derivative rights holders.[54] It also extends the test to new rights provided for in TRIPS.[55]

---

47. Geiger et al., 2014, pp. 589–591; Senftleben, 2013c, pp. 17–18, referring to the basic proposal for the WCT and the Minutes of Main Committee I, which clearly reflect the different balancing concerns of national delegations.
48. Ficsor, 2012, p. 6, emphasising the technology-neutral nature of the test.
49. Hugenholtz & Okediji, 2008, p. 25.
50. Geiger et al., 2014, p. 610.
51. *Ibid.*, pp. 591, 617, 625–626; Senftleben, 2013c, pp. 17–19. *See also* Christie & Wright, 2014, pp. 418–419, arguing on the basis of the wording of Art. 10(1) WCT and the Agreed Statement that member states are not restricted to implementing exceptions in the digital environment only in certain special cases or in those permitted in the BC.
52. Hugenholtz & Okediji, 2008, p. 18.
53. *Ibid.*, p. 17.
54. It is noteworthy that TRIPS contains slightly different versions of the test in the fields of trademarks (Art. 17), designs and models (Art. 26(2)) and patents (Art. 30).
55. This includes rental of computer programs and cinematographic works. *See* Art. 11 TRIPS.

WTO Panels interpreted the TRIPS tests on four occasions: *US–Copyright* (in 2000); *Canada–Patent* (in 2000); and *EC–Trademarks I* and *II* (in 2005).[56] Only *US–Copyright* interprets Article 13 TRIPS, making its findings of greater importance to this book. As supplementary means of interpretation[57] these panel reports may assist in defining the scope of the TRIPS and BC tests and, to an indirect extent, the WCT test.[58] Their importance is qualified by the fact that they are taken in the context of international trade, not copyright. This makes them less sensitive to public interest arguments, despite the objectives of TRIPS requiring such interests to be balanced in the protection and enforcement of intellectual property rights.[59] The main value of the reports lies in the provision of a roadmap to apply the test.[60] It is in this capacity they are used in the following analysis, without forgetting the significant criticism to which they have been subject.[61]

Finally, it is noted that the panel reports have less weight than the aforementioned Agreed Statements in the interpretation of the three-step tests in the WIPO Treaties and the InfoSoc Directive. As previously mentioned the directive implements the WIPO Treaties and should be read in their light.[62] This is important because strict readings of the three-step test often rely primarily on *US–Copyright*, to the detriment of the Agreed Statements.[63]

5.2.1.4 EU Copyright Law and Its Relationship to International Law

The drafting history of Article 5(5) InfoSoc Directive shows the inception of a restrictive view of the three-step test in EU law.[64] The directive's version

56. Because the trademark reports concern parallel complaints with identical texts, the following analysis makes reference only to the most comprehensive report, namely WTO, *EC–Trademarks I*. Cf. Senftleben, 2006, p. 407 & n. 3.
57. Pursuant to Art. 32 VCLT. *See supra* 5.2.1. Cf. Ricketson & Ginsburg, 2006, pp. 200–201.
58. Senftleben, 2004, pp. 107–110.
59. Hugenholtz & Okediji, 2008, pp. 22, 39–40, emphasising Art. 7 TRIPS.
60. Kur, 2008, p. 17-, with further references. The author criticises the excessive length of the reports, their repetitive reasoning and little substance, as well as the political nature of the surrounding process. *See also* Hugenholtz & Okediji, 2008, pp. 21–22.
61. For persuasive criticism of the panel reports, *see* Geiger et al., 2014, pp. 592–611; Griffiths, 2009, p. 10; Hugenholtz & Okediji, 2008, p. 21; Iuliano, 2011, pp. 489–490; M. Kennedy, 2014; Kur, 2008, pp. 30–31; Shabalala, 2010. However, it is undeniable that the absence of new panel reports on Art. 13 TRIPS has permitted *US–Copyright* 'to become the de facto yardstick against which proposals to further restrict copyright protection have been made', especially in legal scholarship. Cf. Shabalala, 2010, p. 188.
62. N.B. no CJEU decision on limitations mentions the WTO Panel Reports, although WTO, *US–Copyright* is mentioned in *Opinion AG in VG Wort*, para. 9, and *Opinion AG in ACI Adam*, para. 55.
63. *See infra* 5.2.2, 5.3.1.2 and 5.3.2.1. See, e.g., the criticism of Iuliano, 2011, p. 468, to the analysis of Peukert, 2005.
64. Senftleben, 2013c, pp. 14–15.

of the test originates from the 1995 Green Paper on Copyright and Related Rights in the Information Society. The document is critical of Article 9(2) BC for being detrimental to the effectiveness of the reproduction right and causing divergent national limitations for reprography and private copying.[65]

The criticism is again patent in a 1996 follow-up paper, where the Commission adopts a 'rights-holder centric' approach to what it views as an 'economic prejudice test'.[66] However, with the adoption of the WIPO Treaties in 1996 (which the EU later joined as a member), the Commission was forced to adjust its view. This adjustment is patent in the 1997 proposal for a new directive.[67]

The InfoSoc Directive's explanatory memorandum expresses the Commission's concern that obligations arising from the WIPO Treaties' tests could cause different interpretations, thereby posing a risk to the establishment of an internal market for online services.[68] The memorandum stresses the need to interpret those provisions in light of the *acquis*, namely the similar tests in the Software and Database Directives.[69] It therefore advances a draft wording closer to that of existing directives than that of international treaties.[70] During the legislative process, the wording was tweaked and the possibility of an open-norm rejected. Ultimately, even the desire to follow the *acquis* was abandoned by the Council Working Group, which realigned the draft provision with its international counterparts.[71]

Against this background, Article 5(5) InfoSoc Directive states that the limitations provided in the same article:

> shall only be applied in certain special cases which do not conflict with a normal exploitation of the work or other subject-matter and do not unreasonably prejudice the legitimate interests of the rightholder.[72]

This test became the 'benchmark for all copyright limitations' in the EU.[73] The wording is similar to that of international treaties and provides the reference point for the subsequent analysis in this chapter. The main function of this test is to control the application of limitations to the directive's

65. Green Paper on Copyright and Related Rights in the Information Society 1995, pp. 50–51.
66. *See* Senftleben, 2004, pp. 246–247, and Follow-up to Green Paper 1996.
67. Proposal InfoSoc Directive, COM(97) 628 final – 97/0359 (COD).
68. *Ibid.*, pp. 16, 19, 20–21, 23, 28–29.
69. *Ibid.*, pp. 28–29. Cf. Senftleben, 2004, p. 247.
70. For example, by switching the last two criteria (mentioning certain 'specific' cases and conflict with 'the' normal exploitation) and assessing a limitation with reference to its 'interpretation'.
71. Senftleben, 2004, p. 250, describing the adoption process. *See also* Common Position (EC) No. 48/2000, reflecting the new text.
72. Art. 5(5) InfoSoc Directive.
73. Green Paper Copyright in the Knowledge Economy 2008, p. 5.

exclusive rights. For national legislators, this means that limitations must comply with the conditions set forth in the exhaustive list of Article 5(1) to (4) and the three-step test in paragraph (5). This design means the EU test has a similar additional safeguard function to Article 10(2) WCT.

The EU test deviates from its international predecessors by stating that limitations 'shall only be applied in certain special cases'. The references to the modal verb 'shall' and to *application* in the article (and also in recital 44 InfoSoc Directive) raise the question of whether the test doubles as a substantive norm for national judges to decide on specific instances of liability.[74]

The topic is debated in scholarship and has not been settled by the CJEU. Whereas the Court does not consider the test to affect the substantive content of limitations, it likewise holds that where certain acts of a defendant fall within their scope, the requirements of Article 5(5) must be met.[75] In addition, the Court has stated on several occasions that limitations must be construed *in light* of Article 5(5).[76] On this basis, some authors and AGs consider that the test is also addressed to national courts.[77]

Beyond this aspect, the relationship of Article 5(5) with the aims of the InfoSoc Directive and international obligations is often at the centre of interpretations on the scope and flexibility of the test. As noted in the previous chapter, among the main objectives of the directive are increased legal certainty, a high level of protection, and a functioning internal market; to achieve them it is crucial to harmonise copyright and its limitations, while giving respect to fundamental rights.[78] The harmonisation goal intersects with the adaptation of EU law to international standards, in particular the WIPO Treaties, as expressly stated in recital 15.[79] Furthermore, recital 44 states that limitations 'should be exercised in accordance with international obligations'. The EU, of course, is a member of TRIPS and the WIPO

---

74. Geiger, 2007b, pp. 13–17; Griffiths, 2009, pp. 3–4; Janssens, 2009, pp. 328–329; Koelman, 2006, pp. 407–408. For a general discussion of the issue, *see* Arnold & Rosati, 2015; Senftleben, 2004, pp. 278–281.
75. CJEU, *Murphy*, para. 181; CJEU, *Meltwater*, para. 53; CJEU, *ACI Adam*, paras 25–26; CJEU, *Copydan*, para. 90; CJEU, *Ulmer*, para. 56.
76. CJEU, *Infopaq I*, para. 58; CJEU, *OSA*, para. 40; CJEU, *Ulmer*, para. 47. *See also* CJEU, *PPI*, paras 75–76, in connection with Art. 10(3) Rental Right Directive. Cf. Arnold & Rosati, 2015, pp. 8–9.
77. See: Arnold & Rosati, 2015; *Opinion AG in Stichting de Thuiskopie*, para. 42 (' … though being primarily a norm addressed to the legislature, the three-step test must also be applied by the national courts in order to ensure that the practical application of the exception to Article. 2 of Directive 2001/29 provided by national legislation remains within the limits allowed by Article 5 of that drective' [sic]); *Opinion AG in ACI Adam*, para. 48.
78. *See supra* 4.4.1.3.
79. Senftleben, 2004, pp. 253–254.

Treaties, making the treaties binding on its institutions and Member States.[80]

For some authors, the reference to 'international obligations' in the InfoSoc Directive relates specifically to Article 10 WCT and its Agreed Statement.[81] Thus, if the EU three-step test is interpreted in light of this set of WCT materials (including its Preamble), these authors argue, it should be interpreted as a flexible norm that allows for the adaptation or creation of limitations in the digital environment.[82] Although this interpretation is persuasive, it should be noted that different readings are possible. For example, recital 44 InfoSoc Directive offers support for the view that the scope of future limitations for online use of works ought to be reduced due to their potential for 'increased economic impact' on the revenues of rights holders.[83]

5.2.2 Spectrum of Readings

The analytical framework presented influences the range of potential readings of the test, demarcated by two opposing views: strict versus flexible interpretation. The following paragraphs explain both views, providing background for the subsequent analysis of a limitation-based ACS.

5.2.2.1 Strict Interpretation

On one side of the spectrum, the three-step test can be interpreted as a restricting clause. This understanding derives from the doctrine of strict interpretation, which departs from the principle of exclusivity and construes derogations thereto as exceptional.[84] It posits that the test can only have a narrow sphere of operation, imposing 'limits on limitations'.[85]

80. Cf. Art. 216 TFEU. On the need to interpret the *acquis* in light of international law, *see supra* 1.3. *See also* Geiger & Schönherr, 2014a, p. 135 & n. 102, 2014b, p. 443, citing CJEU jurisprudence in support of this principle regarding 'mixed agreements', such as TRIPS and the WCT. N.B. the WIPO Treaties were approved on behalf of the European Community by Council Decision 2000/278/EC.
81. Geiger & Schönherr, 2014a, p. 121 & n. 41; Senftleben, 2013c, pp. 15–17. *See also* Senftleben, 2004, p. 256.
82. Geiger & Schönherr, 2014a, p. 121.
83. The final sentences of recital 44 InfoSoc Directive mention the possibility that limitations may have an increased economic impact in the digital environment. Hence, their scope 'may have to be even more limited when it comes to certain new uses of copyright works and other subject-matter'. The recital anchors a restrictive interpretation of limitations in *ACI Adam*. On its basis the Court argues that the scope of limitations can only be reduced but not extended, as such a possibility is not expressly envisaged in the InfoSoc Directive. *See* CJEU, *ACI Adam*, para. 27; *Opinion AG in ACI Adam*, para. 49. For criticism, *see* Quintais, 2015b.
84. *See supra* 4.4.1.4 and 4.4.3.6.
85. Cf. Senftleben, 2006, p. 413, describing the WTO Panel approaches to the test.

The approach can be synthesised as follows. The three conditions have a conjunctive structure: they are cumulative and successive 'steps' instead of factors.[86] The initial steps have priority. Analysis starts from the first condition and works its way up. If along the way a condition is not met, the limitation fails the test.

The first and second conditions are designed to impose quantitative thresholds and economic standards that restrict the qualification of what constitutes a 'certain special case', and broaden the concept of 'normal exploitation'. The reference point for the first condition is reduced to a subset of exclusive rights instead of the area of exclusivity affected by the limitation. The second condition is deemed to include not only current but also *potential new forms of exploitation of works* in relation to *each type of right affected*, the foreseeability of which is not necessarily required. Through this approach, the strict interpretation doctrine eschews normative considerations that could temper the quantitative elements.

The result is an analytical framework in which most limitations for online use, even if narrow in scope, likely conflict with a broad notion of normal exploitation. Moreover, this method disallows the introduction of equitable remuneration to cure potential conflicts in the second step, while only admitting a balancing of rights and interests in the third step.

It is possible to find this approach at international, regional and national levels. First, the strict interpretation method is pervasive in the WTO panel reports on different TRIPS tests.[87] In the influential *US–Copyright*, for instance, the panel posits that Article 13 TRIPS can only have a narrow or limited operation, and that the conditions are to be applied cumulatively and successively, in a hierarchy of analysis.[88] The remaining tests are similarly understood as allowing only a 'small diminution of the rights'.[89] Although all panel reports recognise elements of flexibility in the test, usually by identifying normative considerations in each condition, the strict interpretation lens favours a restrictive economic reading over policy considerations.

At EU level, both the AGs and the CJEU have followed this doctrine in a number of cases, including the method of cumulative and successive reading.[90] Likewise, it is possible to identify interpretations of the test as a restrictive standard by national courts across Europe.[91]

86. See, e.g., He, 2009, pp. 277–278; Rietjens, 2006, p. 326.
87. Cf. Kur, 2008, p. 22.
88. WTO, *US–Copyright*, para. 6.97. Cf. Ginsburg, 2001, pp. 39–41. *See also* Peukert, 2005, p. 30.
89. WTO, *Canada–Patents*, para. 7.30; WTO, *EC–Trademarks I*, para. 7.650.
90. CJEU, *Infopaq I*, paras 56–58, 75; CJEU, *Stichting de Thuiskopie*, paras 21–23, 31; CJEU, *Meltwater*, para. 23; CJEU, *Murphy*, para. 162; CJEU, *ACI Adam*, paras 22–23, 26 (test 'is not intended either to affect the substantive content of ... or, inter alia, to extend the scope of the different exceptions and limitations ... '); CJEU, *Deckmyn*, paras 22; CJEU, *Copydan*, para. 90; CJEU, *Ulmer*, para. 47; CJEU, *Painer*, para. 109; CJEU, *OSA*,

The strict interpretation method is problematic because the initial conditions of the three-step test exclude flexibility and a balancing exercise, facilitating the rejection of limitations at an early stage. This pre-empts normative analysis and transforms the test into a tool to perpetuate exclusivity, solely (or predominantly) allowing copyright limitations for *de minimis* use of works.[92] From this perspective, the focal point of the test is to safeguard the normal exploitation of works, relegating the consideration of prejudice to the legitimate interests of the authors to a secondary role. This interpretation is in no small part inspired by a historical approach, as it closely follows Ulmer's position reported in the BC preparatory works.[93]

5.2.2.2 Flexible Interpretation

In contrast, more flexible constructions are advocated which tend to see the test as an enabling clause, allowing consideration of different interests at national level and the adequate balancing of rights and limitations.[94]

To achieve a flexible reading, scholars have advanced different (and often conceptually overlapping) approaches. First, inspired by the US fair use doctrine, it is suggested that the different steps are not cumulative or successive conditions. Rather, the provision is a multi-factor test subject to a 'comprehensive overall assessment' and teleological interpretation, balancing competing interests on equal grounds.[95] A different approach is to read

---

paras 37–40; *Opinion AG in OSA*, para. 35; *Opinion AG in Infopaq I*, paras 134–143; *Opinion AG in VG Wort*, paras 67–68.

91. Griffiths, 2009, pp. 4–7. See, for influential cases: French Supreme Court, 28.02.2006, Perquin and UFC Que Choisir v. SA Films Alain Sarde, Ste Universal Pictures video France et al. ('Mulholland Drive'); District Court of The Hague, 2.03.2005, Case No. 192880, LJN: AS 8778 ('Press copies in ministries'); District Court of The Hague, 25.06.2008, Case No. 246698, LJN BD5690 ('Private Copying from Illegal Sources'); Court of First Instance of Brussels, 13.02.2007, 2007 WL 1623283 (RB (Brussels)), [2007] ECDR 5 (Google Inc v. Copiepresse SCRL).
92. *See* Rietjens, 2006, p. 332, reaching this conclusion when examining a potential P2P licence.
93. Records BC Stockholm 1967, p. 885. *See* Ricketson & Ginsburg, 2006, pp. 190–192, qualifying the statements of Professor Ulmer (then chairman of the Main Committee I of the Stockholm Conference) on Art. 9(2) BC as an 'uncontested interpretation' that is 'context' to interpretation of the treaty, i.e., a *primary* means of interpretation). As noted *supra* in 5.2.1, these statements should rather be viewed as *supplementary* means of interpretation.
94. Geiger, 2007b; Geiger et al., 2014; Geiger & Schönherr, 2012, 2014a; Gervais, 2005; He, 2009; Hugenholtz & Okediji, 2008, p. 25; Hugenholtz & Senftleben, 2011; Koelman, 2006; Kur, 2008; Senftleben, 2006; Westkamp, 2008; Wright, 2009. Notable efforts by groups of academics in this regard include the MPI Declaration and the Wittem Code. *See* Geiger, Hilty & Griffiths, 2008; Wittem Group, 2010.
95. See, e.g., Geiger et al., 2014, p. 607, 2008; Koelman, 2006, pp. 411–412; Kur, 2008; Senftleben, 2010. *Contra* Lucas, 2010, p. 281, arguing that such an interpretation is contrary to the wording of the text, as clarified by BC preparatory works. *See also*

the test in reverse, incorporating normative considerations at the beginning of the analysis.[96] A third method emphasises fair balance and proportionality, either suggesting their consideration at the second step or by favouring the third step, where balancing traditionally takes place.[97] Yet another suggestion is to take into account compensation in the analysis of the second step as a means to counteract conflicts with the normal exploitation.[98] Finally, some authors advocate a narrow definition of 'normal exploitation' of works, either by rejecting a purely economic view of the concept and focusing on the justification of limitations, or by not taking into account the potential harm dimension of the concept advanced in *US–Copyright*.[99]

In this line, Hugenholtz and Senftleben examine the *acquis* and argue that the InfoSoc Directive's exhaustive list of limitations consists in many cases of 'categorically worded prototypes rather than precisely circumscribed exceptions, thus leaving the Member States broad margins of implementation'. In combination with the three-step test, this interpretation 'would effectively lead to a semi-open norm almost as flexible as the fair use rule of the United States'.[100]

The authors, along with other scholars, support their position on a systematic reading of the InfoSoc Directive, noting the link in recitals 15 and 44 to compliance with international obligations. Recognising the historic compromise nature of the provision and the inherent flexibility required by the WCT, they interpret the directive's test in light of international law as an enabling clause for digital limitations.[101]

This position has parallels with a recent shift in CJEU case law towards a more balanced view of the test – what Chapter 4 terms 'restricted flexibility'. The key feature in this shift lies with the normative justifications of a limitation. The Court attempts to secure the effectiveness of limitations by interpreting them in light of their objective and purpose, the principle of

---

Westkamp, 2008, pp. 42–43, arguing for a more liberal balancing of interests, modelled on the US fair use clause. Regarding Art. 30 TRIPS, *see* a similar position in Lamping, 2014, pp. 688–689, 693.

96. See, e.g., Gervais, 2005, proposing a reverse reading of the test based on the US fair use doctrine, which would transform it into an 'effects based norm'. *See also* Geiger, 2007b; Hugenholtz & Okediji, 2008, p. 21.
97. See, e.g., Geiger, 2007b; Geiger et al., 2010; Hugenholtz & Okediji, 2008, pp. 21, 25, Kur, 2008; Senftleben, 2006.
98. Geiger et al., 2008, p. 711.
99. Geiger, 2007b; Senftleben, 2006. *See also* He, 2009, proposing an 'adapted fair use test' for this effect.
100. Hugenholtz & Senftleben, 2011, p. 2. It is noted that the possibility that such a reading would support interpretation of the test to create new limitations to Arts 2 and 3 is denied by the Court in *OSA*, in line with the exhaustive nature of the list of limitations in Art. 5. *See* CJEU, *OSA*, paras 37–41. Cf. the position of Nérisson, 2015a.
101. Hugenholtz & Senftleben, 2011. *See also* Geiger et al., 2014, p. 582; Geiger & Schonherr, 2012, p. 145.

proportionality, and the overall objectives of the InfoSoc Directive. The result seems to be greater flexibility in the interpretation of limitations that are justified on fundamental rights or that facilitate the development and operation of new technologies.[102] An illustration of this approach is visible in *Meltwater* and *Ulmer*, where the Court reads the test in a non-sequential manner to achieve a balanced interpretation.[103] In synch with this shift by the Court, a growing body of national decisions recognises the three-step test as a flexible and enabling standard.[104]

Of course, different interpretations of the test lead to its inconsistent application. For some authors, the distance between the strict and flexible views is symptomatic of the test's inadequacy for regulation of competing interests.[105] While it is possible to view the test in a restrictive way, it is submitted that its conditions can and in certain cases *should* be read as 'open-ended factors' enabling the 'introduction and broadening of limitations' in light of their objective and purpose.[106] This is especially true for limitations justified on fundamental rights and freedoms. Any restriction imposed on these by the competing fundamental right of copyright (in Article 17(2) Charter) must strike a fair balance and be proportional, necessary and, under certain circumstances, exceptional.[107] Due to the challenges and costs of imposing exclusivity for non-commercial online use, it is justifiable to explore whether a flexible interpretation of the test leaves space for a limitation-based ACS.

---

102. Cf. *supra* 4.4.1.4. *See* CJEU, *Deckmyn*, paras 19–23; CJEU, *Murphy*, paras 162–164; CJEU, *Meltwater*, para. 24; CJEU, *Painer*, paras 132–134. *See also* European Copyright Society, 2014b, pp. 4–5.
103. CJEU, *Meltwater*, paras 55–63; CJEU, *Ulmer*, paras 47–48.
104. Prior to transposition of the InfoSoc Directive, see: BGH, 25.02.1999, I ZR 118/96 ('Re Supply of Photocopies of Newspaper Articles by a Public Library'); BGH, 11.07. 2002, I ZR 255/00 ('In House Press Clippings Archive – Electronischer Pressespiegel'). After transposition of the InfoSoc Directive, see: Supreme Court Switzerland, 26.06.2007, Case No. 4C.73/2007 (*ProLitteris v. Aargauer Zeitung AG*, et al., 'Electronic Press Review – Elektronischer Pressespiegel'); Supreme Court Spain, 3.04.2012, Case No. 172/2012, *Megakini.com v. Google Spain*. For commentary on these cases, *see* Geiger et al., 2014, pp. 618–625; Geiger & Schönherr, 2014a, p. 123 & n. 52; Griffiths, 2009, pp. 7–10; Senftleben, 2010, p. 75, 2013c, pp. 20–23; Westkamp, 2008, p. 40; Xalabarder, 2015.
105. Griffiths, 2009.
106. Geiger & Schönherr, 2014b, p. 444, concluding similarly. *Contra*, Nérisson, 2015b, p. 391, basing her position on *OSA*, paras 37–41 (although the author recognises the CJEU's broad purposive interpretation of limitations in some cases).
107. Art. 52(1) Charter. Cf. Geiger & Schönherr, 2014b, pp. 450–454, which highlight the consideration of copyright as a derogation to the principle of freedom of expression in ECtHR, *Ashby Donald*. *See supra* 4.4.1.4, 4.4.4.1, and 4.4.4.3, discussing the shift away from strict interpretation of limitations justified by fundamental rights in CJEU jurisprudence. *See also* Senftleben, 2013c, pp. 23–24.

5.3 THE SPACE FOR AN ALTERNATIVE COMPENSATION SYSTEM IN THE THREE-STEP TEST

This section examines the three-step test in the InfoSoc Directive to assess whether it allows for a limitation-based statutory licence ACS. CJEU judgments on the test are sparse. For that reason and the need to interpret EU law in light of international law, legal scholars often rely on the analysis of *US–Copyright* as a baseline. Consequently, and despite its shortcomings, this section pays particular attention to that WTO panel report.

To prevent redundancy and provide a structured analysis, this section adopts a sequential study of the test, considering each step separately.[108] However, it is noted that the steps overlap and are not separate tests in themselves. Rather, the three-step test is 'one single analytical whole and serves the ultimate goal to strike an appropriate balance',[109] requiring a multi-factor approach to ensure consideration of the social policy benefits of a limitation.[110] This section first looks at what requirements a limitation-based ACS must meet to qualify as a certain special case (5.3.1). It then examines whether such an ACS conflicts with the normal exploitation of works (5.3.2), and if it causes unreasonable prejudice to the legitimate interests of rights holders (5.3.3). The section concludes with a summary of findings for each step and an assessment of the margin the test allows for the legalisation of non-commercial online use in the *acquis* through a statutory licence (5.3.4).

5.3.1 Certain Special Cases

The CJEU provides little guidance on the first step of the test. Its jurisprudence suggests that the step is met if an act falls clearly within the scope of a limitation.[111] For that reason, it is assumed that all limitations in Article 5 InfoSoc Directive constitute a certain special case.[112] Against this background, the following paragraphs analyse in sequence the meaning of 'certain' cases (5.3.1.1) and 'special' cases (5.3.1.2).

108. WTO, *Canada–Patent*, para. 7.21. *See* Griffiths, 2009, cautioning against redundancy in the analysis of the test.
109. Geiger et al., 2014, pp. 585, 610–611.
110. Wright, 2009, pp. 609, 617.
111. Arnold & Rosati, 2015, p. 8; Geiger & Schönherr, 2014a, p. 122 & nn. 47, 135; Senftleben, 2013c, p. 14. Cf. *Opinion AG in ACI Adam*, paras 50–51. *See also* CJEU, *Infopaq II*, paras 55–57, CJEU, *Murphy*, para. 181, concluding that where an act falls under the scope of Art. 5(1) it must be held that it complies with the remaining steps of the test.
112. Geiger & Schönherr, 2014a, pp. 122, 135. *See Opinion AG in ACI Adam*, paras 51–53.

5.3.1.1 Certain Cases

A 'case' is an occurrence, circumstance, event or fact. In relation to copyright limitations, a case can have different meanings. *US–Copyright* described it 'in terms of beneficiaries of the exceptions, equipment used, types of works or by other factors'.[113] To be a 'certain' case, it added, domestic limitations must be 'clearly defined', which does not require privileged uses to be listed or enumerated, but merely that the provision's scope is 'known and particularized', thereby assuring 'a sufficient degree of legal certainty'.[114]

Not all scholars share this view. Some argue that in the BC preparatory works 'certain' refers to 'some' and not to 'clearly specified' cases.[115] Others note that the 'less strict and rigid' analysis in *Canada–Patent* does not contain a requirement of legal certainty at this stage.[116] Whichever the view, a good faith interpretation of the first step seems to imply that a certain case entails a foreseeability requirement, aimed at forbidding unspecified and indeterminate limitations.[117]

The legislative technique of Article 5 InfoSoc Directive – an exhaustive list of limitations – seems more aligned with a foreseeability condition than open-ended norms.[118] If that is true, a limitation that approximates the *acquis* model should be more consistent with the test than, for example, the US fair use clause, even considering the extensive case law applying it. Nevertheless, the latter is not only internationally accepted, but also considered compliant with the first step requirement of certainty by a majority of scholars.[119] Hence, if the scope of a statutory licence ACS is sufficiently concrete as regards subject matter, permitted uses and remaining criteria, it is likely to comply with the first step, even if this is subject to a strict interpretation.[120]

5.3.1.2 Special Cases: Qualitative and Quantitative Considerations

A certain case can be 'special' from the quantitative and qualitative viewpoints. The first viewpoint refers to quantifiable restrictions on allowed

113. WTO, *US–Copyright*, para. 6.110.
114. *Ibid.*, para. 6.108.
115. Griffiths, 2009, p. 16; Ficsor, 2012, p. 3; Senftleben, 2004, p. 134. N.B. a foreseeability requirement is proposed by Geiger et al., 2008, p. 711. For a more in depth criticism, *see* Shabalala, 2010, p. 170.
116. Senftleben, 2006, p. 418.
117. Iuliano, 2011, p. 476; Reinbothe & von Lewinski, 2002, p. 124.
118. Geiger, 2007a, pp. 4–5.
119. Geiger, 2007b, pp. 5–6; Geiger et al., 2014, pp. 612–616; Hugenholtz & Okediji, 2008, pp. 25–26; Iuliano, 2011, p. 477; Kur, 2008, pp. 9–10, 23; Ficsor, 2012, p. 5; Senftleben, 2004, p. 135, 162ff. For an argument that fair use results in greater legal certainty than the EU system of closed exceptions coupled with a restrictive three-step test, *see* Cook, 2012, p. 244; Senftleben, 2010, 2013c. *But see* Lucas, 2010, pp. 278–279, questioning whether fair use complies with the test.
120. Rietjens, 2006, p. 327.

uses.[121] The second viewpoint pertains to the function of a limitation, namely its justification and public interest dimension.[122]

US–Copyright exemplifies a predominantly quantitative approach. It initially recognises both viewpoints by stating that to be a 'special' case a limitation should have 'an individual or limited application or purpose', 'be narrow in quantitative as well as a qualitative sense', and have an 'exceptional or distinctive objective' (as opposed to 'normal').[123] In essence, an exception must be narrow in 'scope and reach'.[124]

Narrowness refers to the types of exempted use (a subset of exclusive rights), categories of works,[125] and the number of *potential* beneficiaries (users).[126] The benchmark for examination of this scope is the state of technology at the time of assessment.[127]

One issue with this approach is that it does not follow from a limitation being 'limited in its field of application' that it must be qualitatively and quantitatively narrow.[128] Other approaches are conceivable. For example, the quantitative reference point in *Canada–Patent* and *EC–Trademarks I* was not the impact of the limitation on specific rights or subsets thereof but rather on broader exclusive rights granted in relation to patented inventions and trademarks.[129]

But the analysis in *US–Copyright* poses another problem. Despite drawing the distinction between quantitative and qualitative, the report eschews the qualitative assessment. Based on previous Appellate Body decisions, the report states that the first step does not require assessment of the 'subjective aim or objective pursued by national legislation'.[130] This results from a strict interpretation method, motivated by a desire to analyse each step separately and deal with policy considerations at a later stage. The

---

121. The qualitative viewpoint does not require an analysis of the economic impact of the limitation, which typically takes place in the second step. *See* Senftleben, 2006, p. 417, describing the approach of the WTO panels.
122. Ficsor, 2002b; Geiger, 2007b; Senftleben, 2004.
123. WTO, *US–Copyright*, para. 6.109.
124. *Ibid.*, paras 6.112, 6.159.
125. *Ibid.*, paras 6.102–6.153. See, critically, Senftleben, 2006, pp. 416–417, arguing for the possibility of using broader reference points, 'such as the field of public performances or broadcasts'.
126. WTO, *US–Copyright*, paras 6.127, 6.143. *But see* WTO, *EC–Trademarks I*, para. 7.654, for a less stringent approach regarding third party beneficiaries.
127. WTO, *US–Copyright*, paras 6.137, 6.150, 6.153. *See* Ginsburg, 2001, p. 17. This approach marks a difference from the panel's analysis of 'normal exploitation', which considers potential markets.
128. Gervais, 2005, p. 15. Regarding the patent test, Lamping, 2014, p. 687, states that an exception is 'limited' if it 'is reasonably proportionate to its objective and purpose' and adequately fulfils a 'legitimate purpose'.
129. Senftleben, 2006, p. 419.
130. WTO, *US–Copyright*, paras 6.111–6.112. Critically, *see* Ficsor, 2002b, pp. 223–229. *See also* Gervais, 2005, p. 15, noting that following this position Member States would not have a burden of proof regarding the limitation's justification.

main risk, noted before, is the rejection of limitations without assessing their policy underpinnings.[131]

Rietjens' analysis of broadband levies is a good illustration of the dangers of this approach vis-à-vis ACS. The author compares the number of broadband users with the total number of households in the Netherlands, and concludes that the number of potential beneficiaries of the limitation does not qualify as quantitatively narrow. He further argues that a P2P licence would be broader (as it relates to works covered) than the home-style exception rejected in *US–Copyright* and, therefore, would not pass the quantitative first step.[132]

In response, one could point out the importance of examining factors delimiting the licence's scope, which may lead to a different conclusion. These factors include subject matter exclusions, articulation with other limitations, the non-commercial purpose of use, the exclusion of legal persons as beneficiaries, or the application to works after first publication or making available.

Furthermore, a purely quantitative interpretation conflates the scope of a limitation with its effect on the exploitation of the right,[133] while rejecting its justifications. Indeed, full adoption of a cumulative approach could turn the test into a 'one-step inquiry', invalidating even existing limitations in the InfoSoc Directive, such as digital private copying.[134] Of course, this would not be a satisfactory outcome.

Consequently, it is important to consider the qualitative viewpoint, pursuant to which a case is 'special' if it serves an objective of public policy, cultural interests or 'some other exceptional circumstance'.[135] In fact, considering these elements is consistent with the context and history of the BC.[136]

For Gervais, for example, the first condition of the test was historically designed as a last filter to the two subsequent 'operational' conditions. In that

131. Kur, 2008, pp. 23–24, identifying this undesirable outcome regarding the stockpiling exception in *Canada–Patent*. *See also* Iuliano, 2011, pp. 477–478, noting critically that a shifting qualitative standard without a policy rationale check opens the possibility for the inadmissible outcome that legislatures 'frame categories in order to pass laws that would otherwise be invalid'.
132. Rietjens, 2006, pp. 327–329.
133. Peukert, 2005, p. 32. *See also*: WTO, *Canada–Patent*, para. 7.49, stating that the first step 'is neither designed nor intended to address the issue of economic impact directly'; and Senftleben, 2006, p. 436, noting that 'quantitative considerations … should not be overestimated' and arguing for a conceptual approach to this step, where the same would confine limitations solely to a 'specific kind of use'.
134. Rietjens, 2006, p. 329. *See also* Iuliano, 2011, pp. 479–480, making the general argument for the importance of incorporating public policy into the first step.
135. Ficsor, 2002b, pp. 129–133; Koelman, 2006, p. 409; Ricketson, 1987, p. 482. *See also* Senftleben, 2004, pp. 145–152, requiring the existence of a 'rational justificatory basis' for a limitation to qualify as a certain special case.
136. Iuliano, 2011, p. 477; Ricketson, 1987, p. 482; Senftleben, 2004, p. 139.

sense, it is of little relevance beyond the recognition that the term 'special' requires limitations to have a 'sound policy justification'.[137] Besides, the qualitative lens enables respect for international and EU law, as it ensures consideration of a limitation's function, a key aspect when the same derives from fundamental rights recognised in legal instruments to which states are bound.[138] Such a view aligns with the CJEU's interpretation of fundamental rights-based limitations, the aims of the test, and the more general goals of the InfoSoc Directive, interpreted in light of international law.[139]

However, we must be cautious when taking into account quantitative and qualitative connotations. Considered cumulatively, they turn a special case into a 'maximum requirement of narrowness' precluding most limitations from application online.[140] Conversely, meshing both viewpoints avoids a mechanical sequential analysis and allows subsequent consideration of the wider social benefits of a limitation.[141]

In sum, a 'special' case ought to be a mixed quantitative and qualitative standard. This standard should clarify the limitation's justification and scope, while setting the stage for the analysis of the remaining steps to answer the decisive question of 'whether the exception is *limited enough* in view of its purpose and potential impact'.[142] Quantitatively, 'special' requires an assessment of the extent to which a limitation curtails exclusive rights.[143] Quantitative restrictions should be considered as delimiting the limitation's scope, but are not determinative, as they merely offer a 'rough estimate' of the threshold beyond which the viability of the exclusive right is affected – i.e., whether the scope of the limitation is reasonably foreseeable.[144] Qualitatively, the limitation should have a policy justification that operates as a check and balance to prevent overly restrictive quantitative standards. In that role, it would avert the premature rejection or phasing out of online

---

137. Gervais, 2005, pp. 15–16, citing the Records BC Stockholm 1967, p. 1145. *See also Opinion AG Infopaq I*, para. 135 (' … limitations must be clearly defined and must be based on specified particular objectives').
138. Geiger, 2007b, p. 5.
139. On which, *see supra* 1.3, 4.4.1.3, and 4.4.1.4.
140. Eckersley, 2004, p. 157; Senftleben, 2006, p. 418. The restrictive outcome seems to be the suggested approach of Ficsor, 2002b, pp. 227–229.
141. Senftleben, 2006, pp. 418–419, identifying this as the approach in *Canada–Patent*. *See also* Wright, 2009, pp. 617–618.
142. Kur, 2008, p. 24. The proposed approach attempts to merge the common principles derived from the WTO panel reports on the test, enunciated for example in Senftleben, 2006, pp. 420–421.
143. *See* He, 2009, p. 290, although the author distinguishes his point of reference from that of the 'overall commercialization of works'. *See infra* 5.3.2.3, on the point of reference for analysis of the second step.
144. Geiger et al., 2008, p. 711; He, 2009, p. 290. Examples of quantitative restrictions are those 'on specific technical equipment, a specific administrative process or specific forms of use'. *See* Senftleben, 2006, p. 420.

limitations that serve fundamental social welfare aims on grounds of potential (or actual) technological control of uses.[145]

5.3.2 Conflict with the Normal Exploitation of Works

This subsection discusses the second step of the test and whether a statutory licence ACS poses a conflict with the normal exploitation of works. This step is usually considered the most restrictive of the three and the major challenge to the adoption of a legalisation system.[146] The concept of 'normal exploitation' of works is a legal fiction with no clear meaning and undeniable circularity: exploitation occurs in markets to which exclusive rights extend, whereas privileged uses are by definition outside those markets. Hence, the analysis should avoid turning the step into a 'self-validating' mechanism for limitations, while rejecting a construction of the concept so broad that it prevents all but *de minimis* use.[147] Within this range lies the appropriate definition of normal exploitation.

The examination starts by considering the traditional view of normal exploitation, rooted in *US–Copyright*, and its application to ACS (5.3.2.1). It then raises some objections to the traditional view, which justify a more flexible interpretation (5.3.2.2). For that reason, the subsequent analysis proposes a flexible reading of the concept to assess whether an ACS complies with the second step of the test (5.3.2.3).

5.3.2.1 The Traditional View of Normal Exploitation

'Exploitation' refers to the economic value extracted from rights through the commercialisation of works.[148] An ACS privileges use by individuals that is 'non-commercial'. It does not cover use of works that is of a profit-making nature or in direct competition with the commercial exploitation of works. As a result, the effects of an ACS on the normal (commercial) exploitation of works are mostly *indirect*. That is to say, they refer to unintended side-effects on commercial channels caused by the legal permission of non-commercial use.

The definition of 'normal' in relation to exploitation is challenging. To address the challenge legal scholars commonly seek guidance from the WTO

145. He, 2009, pp. 291–292.

146. On the restrictive nature of the step, *see* Geiger, 2007b, p. 6; Koelman, 2006; Kur, 2008, pp. 25–27; Senftleben, 2014. Regarding its application to ACS, *see* Colin, 2011a, pp. 51–55; Dusollier & Colin, 2011, p. 829; Eckersley, 2004, pp. 155–156; Geiger, 2007b, p. 9; Geiger & Schönherr, 2014a, p. 135; Peukert, 2005, pp. 32, 43; Rietjens, 2006.

147. Kur, 2008, p. 25; Rietjens, 2006, p. 329. The 'circular reasoning' critique of the step originates from Goldstein, 2001.

148. Gervais, 2005, p. 16; Ficsor, 2012, p. 3. See: WTO, *Canada–Patent*, para. 7.53; WTO, *US–Copyright*, para. 6.165.

panel reports on the test.[149] The broadest – and likely most influential – view of 'normal' exploitation is contained in *US–Copyright*. Most commentators that reject the legal admissibility of statutory licence ACS proposals rely to some extent on this report. Accordingly, we should reflect on its reasoning and potential application, together with the remaining panel reports.

'Normal' exploitation has empirical and normative dimensions, the contours of which are sometimes unclear. The first dimension reflects the degree of market displacement caused by a limitation as measured by different standards, including lost profits, reasonably expected licensing fees, or actual and potential effects.[150] There is some confusion as to the normative dimension, which is ascribed different meanings, ranging from the effect of a limitation on potential markets (in *US–Copyright*) to the policy justifications of exclusive rights (in the remaining WTO panel reports).[151]

In *US–Copyright*, normal exploitation involves the assessment of the *actual* and *potential* impact on the market of a limitation. The actual or 'empirical' aspect reflects the effect of the limitation on forms of exploitation that 'currently generate significant or tangible revenue'.[152] This effect is measured in relation to markets that rights holders would expect to exploit if not for the limitation, and the reference point for analysis is the exclusive right or category of right affected.[153] If this were the sole test, normal exploitation would exclude uses for which there is no expectation of compensation.[154]

In contrast, the potential or 'normative' aspect in *US–Copyright* relates to forms of exploitation that 'with a certain degree of likelihood and plausibility, could acquire considerable economic or practical importance'.[155] In other words, the emphasis is on the potential effect of a limitation on the market.[156]

To give meaning to this normative dimension, the copyright panel relied on the Swedish/BIRPI Study Group report of 1964.[157] According to this, 'normal' includes current and future forms of exploiting a work of

149. Kur, 2008, pp. 16–17.
150. Peukert, 2005, p. 33.
151. Hugenholtz & Okediji, 2008, p. 24.
152. WTO, *US–Copyright*, para. 6.180.
153. *Ibid.*, paras 6.172–173. The report adds that a rights holder is entitled 'to exploit each of the rights for which a treaty, and the national legislation implementing that treaty, provides.' *Ibid.*, para. 6.175. *See also* Kur, 2008, p. 25.
154. WTO, *US–Copyright*, paras 6.177–6.178. Cf. Senftleben, 2006, p. 425.
155. WTO, *US–Copyright*, para. 6.180.
156. *Ibid.*, paras 6.184–6.185.
157. *See* BIRPI, 1965, discussed *supra* at 2.3.2.1. This study group was composed of representatives of the Swedish Government and the United International Bureaux for the Protection of Intellectual Property (BIRPI), which was set up to prepare for the 1967 Stockholm revision conference. The report in question was adopted in 1965.

'considerable economic or practical importance in potential future markets'.[158] The reliance on this document, without scrutinising its status, has been qualified as a 'significant misapplication of normal practice under the Vienna Convention'.[159]

The consequences are far-reaching. Infused with this meaning, 'normal' exploitation includes 'potential, permissible or desirable' forms of exploitation, including new technological modes of exploitation not presently 'common or normal in an empirical sense'.[160] It covers potential sources of income for every individual right, irrespective of their importance in the overall commercialisation of works.[161]

Because the potential impact is based on unknown and uncertain factors, the reference point for analysis is the current and 'near future' commercial and technological conditions.[162] Yet, the copyright panel rejects treating the non-exercise of rights as indicative that a use is outside normal exploitation.[163] Hence, it does not exclude from the concept of normal exploitation uses for which rights holders are unwilling or unable to exercise their rights. Read in this way, the second step is an economic test deprived of policy considerations.[164]

Thus, according to this view, a conflict with the normal exploitation of works arises when newly exempted uses enter into 'economic competition with the ways that right holders normally extract economic value' from the exclusive right affected, depriving them of 'significant or tangible commercial gains.'[165] As the hypothetical economic loss caused by the limitation is compared to the *actual and potential* full exploitation of the right, most limitations whose scope goes beyond *de minimis* use are outlawed.[166]

It is possible to find this type of strict interpretation in CJEU case law. In *ACI Adam*, for example, the Court states that allowing reproductions from unlawful sources encourages piracy, 'inevitably' reducing revenues from lawful sources and conflicting with the normal exploitation of works.[167] That

158. WTO, *US–Copyright*, para. 179.
159. Shabalala, 2010, pp. 173, 174.
160. Gervais, 2005, p. 16.
161. WTO, *US–Copyright*, paras 6.166, 6.178, 6.180ff. *See* Kur, 2008, p. 25.
162. WTO, *US–Copyright*, para. 6.187.
163. *Ibid.*, para. 6.188. The examples provided are those of 'current licensing practices' and cases 'where, due to lack of effective or affordable means of enforcement, right holders may not find it worthwhile or practical to exercise their rights'.
164. Kur, 2008, pp. 26–27. *See also* Wright, 2009, pp. 612–613.
165. WTO, *US–Copyright*, para. 6.183 and, for the analysis, paras 6.176–6.183. *See also* Shabalala, 2010, p. 174.
166. Kur, 2008, pp. 26–27; Senftleben, 2006, pp. 426, 429. *See also* Kur, 2008, p. 26 & n. 98, noting that the lack of reference to reasonableness in Art. 13 TRIPS enables black-letter interpretations to bar limitations under the second step.
167. CJEU, *ACI Adam*, para. 39. *See also*: CJEU, *Copydan*, paras 74–79; *Opinion AG in Copydan*, paras 81–85.

is to say, the Court believes there is a substitution effect between reproductions made from lawful sources and those made from unlawful sources. Still, the judgment does not provide evidence for this claim or address the limitation's justification, anchored on the fundamental right of privacy.[168] As noted in the previous chapter, this interpretation was restated in *Copydan* and *Reprobel*.[169]

In reaching this conclusion, the CJEU and the AG in *ACI Adam* rejected an alternative reading. During oral observations, several stakeholders made the argument that a literal, systematic and teleological interpretation of the InfoSoc Directive would not exclude from the scope of the private copying limitation copies made from unlawful sources. Because such copies could not be prevented by technological means, the private copying levy was the sole means to effectively deal with mass unauthorised use, and should therefore qualify as a normal exploitation of works for the type of use in question.[170]

The application of the traditional view of normal exploitation, supported in *US–Copyright* or *ACI Adam* and its progeny, probably prevents the adoption of a statutory licence ACS. The basic argument for rejecting such a legalisation proposal could be structured as follows. A limitation for non-commercial online use of works by individuals privileges acts of downloading, streaming, uploading, and other forms of online dissemination of copyright works. It is irrelevant whether such use is susceptible of monetisation or enforcement; what matters is that it enters into economic competition with current and potential forms of exploitation of works. The limitation-based ACS has a negative impact on offline sales of protected content (e.g., CDs), and legal access channels online, including business models such as pay-per-use, pay-per-download, subscription, content streaming and content renting.[171] It results in a substitution effect for existing paid channels for the dissemination of the same content, and has a detrimental effect on potential markets. Both actual and potential markets are included in the concept of 'normal exploitation', with which the statutory licence conflicts. Because this condition is cumulative, the ACS does not comply with the three-step test.[172]

168. For a critical assessment, *see* Quintais, 2015b.
169. *See supra* 4.4.3.6.
170. *See Opinion AG in ACI Adam*, paras 35–36, 72–79, and Quintais, 2015b, p. 73.
171. Examples of business models are taken from Samartzi, 2012, p. 67.
172. Peukert, 2005, p. 34; Rietjens, 2006, pp. 331–332. Both authors anchor their analysis on the reasoning of *US–Copyright* and reject a normative approach to normal exploitation. *See also* Colin, 2011a, p. 58, 2011b, p. 4, arguing that a non-voluntary licence removes the possibility of exclusive control of exploitation and is probably 'in direct competition with the offers of legal downloads'.

5.3.2.2 Objections to the Traditional View of Normal Exploitation

The legal analysis of the second step in *US–Copyright* and the traditional view of normal exploitation are not without problems.[173] Beyond adhering to a strict interpretation doctrine, the report seems to rely on an 'idealized' notion of normal exploitation, which includes unlicensed, non-monetised and unenforced uses.[174]

In the digital environment, the traditional view risks limitations being crystallised in time. For existing privileges, it disallows uses included in its spirit but not apparent from its letter.[175] For new limitations, the mere *possibility* that technological development creates new avenues of exploitation for previously uncontrollable uses will raise an insurmountable legal obstacle. At the extreme, if an online use is *susceptible* of technological control it will form part of the normal exploitation of works.[176] The result, as noted by Westkamp, is a chilling effect on domestic legislative freedom in the field of online copyright limitations and, more generally, communication and information law.[177]

A statutory licence ACS is aimed at restricted uses that are largely insusceptible of control or monetisation. For those uses, the conflict with normal exploitation does not result from the imposition of a limitation, but rather from difficulties with licensing or enforcement.[178] The conflict is a by-product of the fragmentation of exclusive rights.

In this scenario, normal exploitation should not correspond to the use covered by the limitation if (fictionally) controlled by rights holders. Rather, the conflict should refer to the extent to which a limitation 'crowds out the normal markets controlled by copyright owners',[179] taking into consideration the relative positions of individual creators (authors and performers) and 'exploiters', i.e., corporate, subsequent or derivative rights holders, mainly legal persons.[180]

In that light, as with other compensated limitations and mandatory collective management, if an ACS includes a mandatory compensation claim

173. Shabalala, 2010, p. 174, calling this the 'the weakest part of a generally weak legal analysis'.
174. Bernault & Lebois, 2005, p. 34; Ginsburg, 2001, pp. 19–25, 49–53; Griffiths, 2009, p. 10; Kur, 2008, p. 31.
175. Geiger et al., 2014, p. 594.
176. Geiger, 2007b, p. 6; Geiger et al., 2014, pp. 594–595; Griffiths, 2009, pp. 10–11; Senftleben, 2014, p. 9.
177. Westkamp, 2008, pp. 9–10, calling this proposition unacceptable.
178. Dusollier & Colin, 2011, p. 829; Rydning, 2010, p. 60.
179. Dusollier & Colin, 2011, pp. 829–830.
180. Geiger et al., 2008, pp. 708–710, 712. This is a conceptual simplification; under some national laws and for certain categories of works it is possible that a legal person technically qualifies as the 'original' rights holder. Also, a producer may be an individual person and an original rights holder.

for creators, it might improve their position as compared to the existing or prospective market exploitation in an exclusive rights regime.[181] If that is true, an ACS can contribute to achieving a fair balance of interests by enabling rights holders, especially creators, to obtain fair remuneration in the digital environment.

Critics of the traditional view also object to its disregard for the policy underpinnings of limitations.[182] As noted, a strict reading of the test is sequential and isolates policy considerations in the third step.[183] If we follow that interpretation, few limitations survive to the second step. The result is to foreclose analysis of the public interest dimension of limitations that should ultimately justify the restriction on the exclusive right.[184]

For its proponents, the advantage of normative analysis of the second step is to allow consideration of the social function of copyright and technological developments.[185] The approach, which has historical pedigree, is not as radical as it may seem. Indeed, the BC recognises not only several public interest limitations but also the grandfathering of existing domestic exceptions.[186] For Ricketson, the 'omnibus' nature of Article 9(2) BC and the wider context of the convention lead to the 'logical' conclusion that the three-step test includes 'non-economic normative considerations', namely whether a 'particular kind of use is one that the copyright owner *should* control'.[187]

Canada–Patent follows a similar reasoning, considering a form of exploitation to be normal if it is 'essential to the achievement of the goals of patent policy'.[188] Some commentators believe this interpretation is due solely to the policy-infused wording of Article 30 TRIPS, which mentions an 'unreasonable' conflict.[189] However, influential scholarship considers variation in the wording of Articles 13 and 30 TRIPS to be insufficient to justify

181. This point is typically analysed when considering different legitimate interests in the third step. *See infra* 5.3.3.3.
182. He, 2009, p. 284; Kur, 2008, pp. 27, 30–31; Lucas, 2010, p. 279; Ricketson, 2003, p. 25; Shabalala, 2010, pp. 172–175.
183. An alleged benefit of *US–Copyright*'s approach is to avoid redundancy in the examination of different steps. *See* Griffiths, 2009, p. 16; Ricketson & Ginsburg, 2006, pp. 767–773.
184. Shabalala, 2010, p. 156, citing Hugenholtz & Okediji, 2008.
185. Koelman, 2006, pp. 408–409. *See also* Geiger, 2007b, pp. 6–7.
186. Ricketson & Ginsburg, 2006, pp. 771–773; Senftleben, 2004, pp. 182–183. *Contra* Lucas, 2010, p. 280.
187. Ricketson, 2003, p. 25. *See also* Dusollier, 2007, p. 447. He, 2009, pp. 284–285, argues that the normative element is implicitly recognised in the report of the Swedish/BIRPI group on which *US–Copyright* relies for its strict interpretation.
188. WTO, *Canada–Patent*, paras 751–759.
189. Geiger et al., 2014, p. 600.

different treatment between intellectual property regimes, and deems it desirable to extend a similar approach to copyright law.[190]

If we accept this last interpretation, the question arises as to how to infuse normative content into the second step? One possibility is to make normal exploitation responsive to social norms in the online environment, for example by allowing limitations for private digital use and non-commercial transformative use.[191] Other approaches include approximating the second step to the fourth factor of the US fair use test,[192] taking into account reasonableness and proportionality in the analysis,[193] requiring that the application of exclusive rights to exempted forms of use be justified on policy grounds,[194] or incorporating competing considerations within the definition of normal exploitation.[195]

The common theme of these approaches seems to be the consideration of a limitation's motivations in the balancing exercise. The motivations can be economic or non-economic. In the context of the InfoSoc Directive, where contractual and technical restrictions appear to predominate over limitations, economic market failure motivations for a limitation are inherently weaker.[196] As a result, to justify a restriction on exclusivity, a limitation-based statutory licence ACS should also be motivated by non-economic arguments.[197]

As noted, beyond addressing a failure of the market in the regulation of non-commercial online use of works by individuals, an ACS aims at providing legal certainty for end-users, improving access to works and the circulation of culture over the Internet, promoting technological

---

190. *Ibid. See also*; Kur, 2008, p. 27; Ricketson, 2003, p. 26; Ricketson & Ginsburg, 2006, p. 773. Supporting the application of the *Canada–Patent* approach, *see* Hugenholtz & Okediji, 2008, p. 24; Senftleben, 2006, p. 426. For an argument that the second conditions in Arts 13 and 30 TRIPS are substantially similar, *see* Ficsor, 2002b, p. 181.
191. Gervais, 2005, p. 37ff.
192. The fourth factor of the fair use doctrine, listed in s. 107 US Copyright Act, is 'the effect of the use upon the potential market for or value of the copyrighted work'. *See* Koelman, 2006, pp. 411–412, and He, 2009, pp. 285–286, 294–300 (proposing an 'adapted fair use test').
193. Koelman, 2006, pp. 411–412.
194. Senftleben, 2006.
195. Geiger, 2007b; Geiger et al., 2008. See, similarly, He, 2009, pp. 294–300; Hugenholtz & Okediji, 2008, p. 21, who emphasise a proportionality assessment at this stage. The consideration of competing justifications in this step and in the context of its normative connotation is consistent with a balanced and comprehensive interpretation of the test, as suggested in Geiger et al., 2008. *But see* Griffiths, 2009, p. 16 & n. 114 (on the uncertainty risk of this approach), and Lucas, 2010, pp. 279–280 (against the consideration of non-economic motivations at this stage).
196. *See supra* 4.4.1, on the prevalence of contractual and technical restrictions over limitations in the InfoSoc Directive.
197. Ginsburg, 2001, pp. 51–53. In this line, Peukert argues that some widely accepted limitations, like criticism or parody, only survive the second step in the digital environment due to their normative underpinnings. *See* Peukert, 2005, p. 34.

development, ensuring fair remuneration of creators, and facilitating the respect for fundamental rights.

If international and EU copyright law indeed aim at striking a fair balance between competing rights and interests, the policy justifications for a limitation can be considered at either the second or third step. The crucial aspect is that they are considered *before* making a decision on the admissibility of a limitation under, in this case, EU copyright law. To avoid redundancy and for clarity reasons, this chapter conducts such a balancing exercise in the third step.

In sum, the combination of objections against the traditional view of the second step suggests that a more flexible interpretation of what constitutes a conflict with the normal exploitation deserves exploration. The remainder of this section takes up that challenge and applies a flexible lens to assess the legal admissibility of an ACS.

5.3.2.3 A Flexible Interpretation of Normal Exploitation

In a flexible reading of the second step, the reference point to measure conflicts with the normal exploitation is the effect of a limitation on the overall commercialisation of works, including the associated bundle of exclusive rights.[198] The range of actual and potential forms of exploitation is limited to typical major sources of rights revenue from the commercialisation of works. As a result, a conflict only arises when the proposed limitation causes substantial market impairment to those revenue sources.[199]

This flexible approach entails economic analysis for different types of work in order to estimate the impact of the limitation in areas where authors extract the most royalties.[200] The focus is on the economic core of copyright, rather than the imperfect legal construction of exclusive rights, which reflects the technical characterisation of digital use of works.[201]

There is a conflict with the normal exploitation if a limitation demonstrably deprives rights holders of substantive, reasonably expected and foreseeable sources of income under normal commercial circumstances.[202] These circumstances include the licensing of commercial or end-users for the use of works, ranging from making the content available, to pay-per-use,

198. *See* WTO, *US–Copyright*, para. 6.173, and Peukert, 2005, p. 33, arguing for a separate right analysis. *Contra*, Senftleben, 2004, pp. 177–194.
199. Senftleben, 2004, p. 177–194, 2006, pp. 427–429, 435–437. This seems to be the approach followed in *Opinion AG Infopaq I*, paras 137–138, which focuses on the effect of the limitation on a specific market (here, the newspaper market).
200. This argument is based on Senftleben, 2004, pp. 184–193.
201. Parts of this argument derive from Depreeuw, 2014; Senftleben, 2004, pp. 184–193.
202. Severine Dusollier, 2005, p. 220; Geiger et al., 2014, pp. 603–604; Gervais, 2005; Griffiths, 2009, p. 457; Lucas, 2010, p. 277. *See also* Hugenholtz & Okediji, 2008, pp. 23–24, stating that this is the correct reading of *US–Copyright* in light of historic elements. The authors conclude: 'there is a conflict with the second step if the exempted use would rob the right holder of a real or potential source of income that is substantive'.

pay-per-download, subscription, content streaming and content renting. Streaming revenues are of particular importance, as this technology appears to be replacing digital downloads as the new model of normal exploitation. This shift is initially occurring in the online music sector but will presumably extend to other sectors.[203]

The following paragraphs assess, from a legal perspective, the effect of an ACS on the normal online markets controlled by rights holders. An attempt is made to couch the arguments with empirical research, especially the studies mentioned in Chapter 1 on the economic potential of ACS and users' willingness to pay for such systems.[204] However, because an ACS is an 'unknown quantity' with no directly comparable mechanisms in the market, such studies should be treated with caution. On the one hand, we should not put too much stock in empirical research that is not based on real life experiments. On the other hand, we should not assume that a limitation-based ACS has negative effects based on incomplete or non-existent evidence.

5.3.2.3.1 Normal Exploitation and Non-commercial Use of Works

A statutory licence ACS privileges non-commercial online use of works by individuals. It targets activities that mirror the personal enjoyment of works over digital network platforms, which since the advent of the Internet have become part of the everyday life of users. Examples are the non-commercial sharing of images, as well as the accidental or transformative use of works on those platforms. Regarding the latter, Dreier makes the case for a new limitation clearly:

> The sociological function of image-sharing in particular is more like a gesture of pointing at an image made by another, which as such was always unrestricted under copyright law. The fact that such a gesture of pointing is not performed physically in the age of Facebook, WhatsApp, tablets and smartphones, but requires more or less accidental reproduction processes devoid of any independent commercial value, should not play a role where aspects of copyright are considered in a purposeful manner.[205]

Of course, as the same author points out, where the commercial threshold for the exploitation of works is passed, the situation changes and the use should not be privileged. An example is where the use of another's image generates a share of the advertising revenues of the platform provider for the user making it available online.[206]

---

203. IFPI, 2015; Karp, 2014; Vallbé et al., 2015, p. 3.
204. *See supra* 1.1.
205. Dreier, 2015, p. 8.
206. *Ibid.*

In this respect, the statutory licence ACS does not privilege online use of works against profit and direct financial consideration, or use by institutions or legal persons (even if non-commercial). Compared to commercial platforms, the direct licensing of non-commercial use by individuals does not seem to be a major form of exploitation of works online that generates significant rights revenue.

Instead, an ACS aims to license and monetise a significant share of non-commercial online use of works that is currently uncompensated. In many cases, these online activities are unenforceable or too costly to enforce. In other instances, copyright owners choose not exercise their rights for this type of use, due for example to licensing practices or strategic choices, overlap between exclusive rights, and legal uncertainty on the status of the use. In an additional set of cases, the non-commercial use may be subject to gratis open access-type licences.

In this context, it is legitimate to ask: if a use is not susceptible of exercise or monetisation, or it is not foreseeable that it will in future constitute a major source of revenue, should it be considered part of the normal exploitation of works? In this scenario and for this type of use, exclusivity does not seem the only (or best) means to yield remuneration.[207] A system of remunerated access, on the other hand, could provide a more efficient legalisation and monetisation mechanism. If this is the case, what prevents the consideration of an ACS as a normal form of exploitation for a subset of non-commercial online use?[208]

This approach is not a radical departure from the EU copyright tradition. A compensated limitation coupled with a legal licence already constitutes a normal exploitation of works for certain types of use in the *acquis*, most of which non-commercial. Relevant examples are the payment of fair compensation for digital private copying for non-commercial purposes, reprography, specific acts of reproduction by social institutions, and certain permitted uses of orphan works, like digitisation and making available (provided the rights holder triggers that mechanism).[209] In the case of private copying, the privileged acts are similar to those in an ACS (but

207. *See* Geiger & Schönherr, 2014b, pp. 475–476.

208. Roßnagel et al., 2009, p. 25, arguing that there is no conflict with normal exploitation due the high cost or impossibility of enforcing these uses. *See also* Eckersley, 2004, p. 156, arguing that the pervasiveness of P2P file sharing, the ineffectiveness of TPMs, and the paucity of legal offers might qualify a blanket licence as a 'normal exploitation' of the work. On this point, *see* Geiger & Schönherr, 2014a, p. 136, and Geiger, 2015b, p. 16 ('… it could be argued that the 'normal' exploitation in some cases can also be achieved by limitation-based remuneration rights … ').

209. The private copying limitation in Art. 5(2)(b) InfoSoc Directive is limited to use for non-commercial purposes. The limitation for permitted use of orphan works is restricted to public interest aims of the beneficiary organisations, which are allowed to generate revenue in relation thereto 'for the exclusive purpose of covering their costs of digitising orphan works and making them available to the public'. *See* Art. 6(2) Orphan Works Directive.

limited to the right of reproduction) insofar as they solely benefit end-users and cover non-commercial digital use.

If an ACS ensures compensation for non-commercial online uses that are not exercised or monetised, it is difficult to argue that it causes a direct conflict with the normal exploitation of works. This is because no major foreseeable source of income is affected; instead, the ACS creates new rights revenue.[210] A different conclusion would imply that the test prevents a profitable market from replacing an inefficient one, which appears unreasonable and inconsistent with the objective of protecting and remunerating rights holders.

5.3.2.3.2 Indirect Effect on Commercial Exploitation

The main problem with a statutory licence ACS relates to its potential adverse side-effects on commercial exploitation models on the Internet. The system would allow end-users to make and distribute perfect copies of digital works to other users. In doing so, it may incidentally affect existing models of online content dissemination by depreciating their value for rights holders. In other words, by regulating a 'secondary' form of exploitation – non-commercial use by individuals – an ACS may affect the 'primary' markets reserved to exclusivity.[211]

A similar concern was expressed by the CJEU in *ACI Adam*, *Copydan* and *Reprobel*, eventually leading to the exclusion of reproductions from unauthorised sources from the scope of the private copying limitation. In the Court's view, allowing these reproductions would force copyright holders 'to tolerate infringements of their rights which may accompany the making of copies for private use'.[212] Hence, permitting such copies would be tantamount to indirectly enabling the mass distribution of works through unlawful sources.[213]

The Court was concerned with the effects on the market of indirectly fostering online dissemination of works. *Reprobel* makes the point clearly:

> to accept that such reproductions may be made from an unlawful source would encourage the circulation of counterfeited or pirated works, thus inevitably reducing the volume of sales or of other lawful transactions

210. Bernault & Lebois, 2005, p. 35; Ricketson, 1999, p. 70. *See also* Gervais, 2005, p. 37ff., placing cases where users cannot obtain the content 'through a normal commercial transaction' outside normal exploitation.
211. Ricolfi, 2007, p. 304 & n. 53.
212. CJEU, *ACI Adam*, para. 31; CJEU, *Copydan*, para. 76; CJEU, *Reprobel*, para. 58.
213. CJEU, *ACI Adam*, paras 36, 39; *Opinion AG in ACI Adam*, paras 72, 75, 83; CJEU, *Reprobel*, para. 59. Expressing a similar concern regarding a different limitation, *see Opinion AG in Ulmer*, para. 57 ('The danger of large-scale unlawful distribution, which is present in the case of digital copies, does not exist either.').

relating to the protected works, with the result that a normal exploitation of those works would be adversely affected.[214]

Those risks are naturally greater in a statutory licence ACS, which also covers acts of communication to the public by end-users. One possible consequence is that certain online platforms enabling mass use of works benefit from the system and escape liability, namely by virtue of the exemptions for intermediaries in the E-Commerce Directive. This is a valid concern with *empirical* and *legal dimensions*. The first dimension relates to whether such a substitution effect will occur in practice. The second dimension links to the legal effects of the ACS on the liability of Internet intermediaries.

In theory, an ACS can cause the negative effects described. Yet, in practice, whether such effects occur is an empirical question with no certain answer, leaving room only for educated speculation. A good starting point is research on the effect of unauthorised use on authorised platforms, and on the supply of copyright works. This research, it is noted, is not consistent on the negative effect of unauthorised copying through file sharing on the revenues of rights holders.[215] Most evidence suggests that file sharing has a relatively small effect on media sales, far from a 'one-to-one displacement of sales by illegal copies'.[216]

As noted in Chapter 1, existing studies do not support the claim that unauthorised online use has long-term negative effects on social welfare or the creation and supply of works.[217] In fact, some studies report a positive effect, especially in the networked environment where costs of distribution are near zero.[218] Positive effects leading to increased demand for works include the possibility of users 'sampling' different works, and 'purchasing related products or services, such as concerts or merchandise'.[219] In a similar fashion, studies on competing legal offers show that free streaming or advertisement based channels have a reduced impact on the revenues of paid services.[220] What to make of this?

The combination of results suggests that unauthorised or free (legal) use – the closest proxy we have for a statutory licence ACS – does not destroy the rights revenues generated by the online commercial market for the same type of use. Data showing an annual increase in the digital revenues of rights holders reinforces this conclusion.[221]

214. CJEU, *Reprobel*, para. 60 (citing CJEU, *ACI Adam*, para. 36).
215. Poort & Weda, 2015, pp. 65–66. *See also* Handke, 2011, 2012, reporting on a survey of empirical studies.
216. Poort & Weda, 2015, p. 65.
217. Cammaerts & Meng, 2011; Grassmuck, 2010b; Handke, 2012; Huygen et al., 2009; Watson, Zizzo & Fleming, 2014. *See supra* 1.1.
218. Eijk et al., 2010; Grassmuck, 2010b; Huygen et al., 2009; Karaganis & Renkema, 2013.
219. Poort & Weda, 2015, p. 65.
220. Aguiar & Martens, 2013; Papies, Eggers & Wlomert, 2010; Vallbé et al., 2015, p. 3.
221. *See supra* 1.1, with further citations.

Thus, the evidence points towards the possibility that an ACS can co-exist with commercial exploitation, as many users remain willing to pay for commercial offers that are sufficiently appealing in terms of price, convenience, branding, aggregation, usability, quality, fairness, or simply due to lack of awareness of alternatives.[222]

On the other hand, despite the deployment of enforcement measures and the growth of legal alternatives, unauthorised services continue to exist and develop. At this point, it is difficult to believe that the market provides the sole solution to the territorial and substantive fragmentation issues faced by EU copyright law in the digital environment.[223] In this context, legal offerings will likely remain unable to cater to consumers' expectations and demands for cultural access channels.[224]

If unauthorised and authorised services can co-exist online while preserving the digital revenues of rights holders through online platforms, it is legitimate to ask whether an ACS for non-commercial use of works that is not exercised, enforceable, or remunerated will significantly hinder reasonably foreseeable major sources of rights revenue online.

The answer seems to hinge on the above-mentioned legal dimension. Would a statutory licence ACS allow copyright owners to enforce their exclusive rights of reproduction and communication to the public against unauthorised websites and platforms that profit from the availability of works?

The answer to this question depends on the design of the system and the copyright limitation underlying it. To be clear, websites or platforms that host and make available copyright works without rights holders' consent (e.g., unauthorised cyberlockers), take an active role in their online availability, and make a direct or indirect commercial use of said content will mostly remain infringing despite the proposed legalisation scheme. In fact, the services provided by these websites/platforms frequently go beyond the mere (neutral) storage of information provided by the individual recipient of the service. Therefore, it is difficult to envision that they would be completely exempt from liability as a result of the hosting 'safe-harbour' in Article 14 E-Commerce Directive.[225] Rather, many of these hybrid websites and platforms appear to make a genuine own use of copyright works, at least from the perspective of the right of communication to the public.

However, the ACS may potentially benefit decentralised P2P systems using BitTorrent software. If end-users in such a system have a legal authorisation to copy and disseminate works online, it is less clear whether

222. Iuliano, 2011, pp. 485–486.
223. Ricolfi, 2007, p. 300, making a similar argument.
224. Kantar Media, 2012; Poort & Leenheer, 2012; Vallbé et al., 2015. *See also supra* 1.1.
225. On the legal regime of Art. 14 E-Commerce Directive, *see* Angelopoulos, 2016, pp. 51–61. N.B. 'the safe harbours apply to the relevant activities, not to service providers *per se*.' *Ibid.*, p. 46.

the provider of the software or platform is directly infringing.[226] Assuming the legalisation of this type of P2P system has a greater potential to substitute for significant parts of the current online market, the likelihood that they escape any type of liability is problematic for the admissibility of a statutory licence ACS under the second step of the test.

In part, it is possible to solve this problem through the definition of 'non-commercial' use under the licence. The scope of the permitted 'non-commercial' use could for example exclude P2P exchanges by the operator (individual, group of individuals or legal person[227]) of a platform that generates advertising or sponsorship receipts or any type of financial consideration in connection with the works exchanged.[228] Such a definition would preserve the economic core of the right of communication to the public in Article 3 InfoSoc Directive and allow copyright owners to enforce their rights against unauthorised websites or platforms deriving commercial benefit from the use of works.

Another solution relates directly to the definition of the scope of the right of communication to the public in EU law, and is very much an open issue not only in light of the Court's ruling in *GS Media*, but also due to pending preliminary references in *Filmspeler* and *Stichting Brein v. Ziggo*.[229]

After *GS Media*, and in line with previous national court judgments, the posting of hyperlinks to unauthorised but freely accessible sources constitutes a restricted act of communication to the public.[230] If hyperlinking to an unauthorised freely accessible source is a restricted act of communication to the public, what prevents the qualification of the services provided by the operators of platforms such as The Pirate Bay or Popcorn Time as acts of communication to the public?

The Pirate Bay, for example, provides a system containing search engine functionalities by means of which metadata on protected works is present on the users' computers and indexed and categorised for users, so that they can trace and upload and download the protected works on the basis thereof. This type of reference to cryptographic metadata information of

226. Quintais, 2012. Outside copyright, it is possible to argue that the operation of such sites may be prevented on grounds such as unfair competition (in most EU jurisdictions) or passing-off (e.g., in the UK). *See* Guibault & Quintais, 2014, p. 21, discussing hyperlinking.
227. N.B. in respect to certain operators, such as The Pirate Bay and Popcorn Time, whether they 'actually exist de jure as natural or legal persons is doubtful. More likely, these actors are merely 'brands' that are used by fluid groups of loosely organized individuals'. *See* Hugenholtz & Quintais, 2017 (forthcoming).
228. In this respect, *see* the specifications for the definition of commercial uses made by the French CMO SACEM in the context of a pilot project reported by Metzger & Heinemann, 2015, p. 16. *See also* the definition of 'non-commercial' in the CC Non-Commercial 4.0 International Public License.
229. *See supra* 4.3.2.1.
230. *See supra* 4.3.2.1.4 and 4.3.2.2 In Germany, *see* BGH, 9.07.2015, I ZR 46/12 ('Die Realitaet II'), with commentary by J.B. Nordemann, 2016.

copyright works is also called a 'magnet link'.[231] The label appears adequate, as such referencing is functionally and visually similar to the provision of standard hyperlinks and in that sense could be argued to make works available for subsequent up/download.[232]

Many (if not most) works accessed through P2P platforms are made available online through those means without the prior consent of rights holders. It is also the case that these platforms operate on a for-profit basis. If it is accepted that the platform's provision of a reference to files is analogous to hyperlinking, then it is arguable that the *GS Media* presumption of knowledge applies to the operator of the platform. If the presumption applies, it will be extremely difficult for the operator to rebut it. In this scenario, the activities of P2P platforms would amount to own use of works and direct copyright infringement. Even if the presumption does not apply, it is conceivable that a notification by the rights holder and failure to remove the infringing work (or prevent access thereto) will trigger primary liability for the platform operator.

The first scenario (application of the presumption) would be in line with the Opinion of the AG in *Filmspeler*.[233] As noted, the case deals with the provision of a multimedia player with software and add-ons containing hyperlinks to *inter alia* digital content made available without the authorisation of rights holders. The AG Opinion rejects the qualification of the multimedia player as a mere 'physical facility' (under recital 27 InfoSoc Directive), and qualifies the sale of such a player as a communication to a new public of the content made available without authorisation, pursuant to Article 3(1) InfoSoc Directive.[234]

In this light, if CJEU case law leads to an interpretation of the exclusive right that prohibits hyperlinks (and other online acts of communication) to unauthorised sources and qualifies the unauthorised acts of operators of decentralised P2P systems as direct infringement, then a statutory licence ACS would have a limited effect on the lawful commercial exploitation of works. It would only afford a defence against infringement for end-users sharing works on a non-commercial basis, as well as to a limited set of online

231. Koolen, 2016, p. 593.
232. This issue is at the heart of CJEU, Reference for Preliminary Ruling, Case C-610/15, *Stichting Brein v. Ziggo*.
233. *Opinion AG in Filmspeler*, para. 51: 'I believe that there is no significant difference between posting hyperlinks to protected works on a website and, as in the present case, installing hyperlinks in a multimedia device designed specifically for use with the internet (in particular, so that, through it, users are able to access straightforwardly, directly and immediately, digital content made available without the consent of the authors). The provision of links to that protected content, the making available of that content to the public, is a feature common to both types of conduct, and its apparently incidental or ancillary nature cannot conceal the fact that the activities concerned are aimed at ensuring that anyone may, merely by clicking on the hyperlink, enjoy the protected works'.
234. *Ibid.*, paras 52–60.

intermediaries, namely those that enable or facilitate the licensed use but whose activities do not qualify as an *own use* of works. Online platforms whose intermediary activities fail to cross the 'non-neutral' threshold and whose activities qualify for the liability exemptions in Articles 12–14 E-Commerce Directive should continue to benefit from those provisions, where applicable. However, the exemptions will not apply to other activities/services by platforms that fall outside that limited scope and consist of own use of copyright works.[235]

A potential grey area is that of hybrid content sharing platforms, such as YouTube. The primary or intermediary liability of these platforms rests on the qualification of their activities as own use or mere intermediary use, a distinction which is increasingly unclear after the introduction of a knowledge test in *GS Media*. Ultimately, it should be for legislators to more clearly define the scope of exclusive rights and intermediary liability, as well as their application to hybrid platforms. There are already different proposals to subject certain types of platforms to collective licensing schemes (some of which non-voluntary) or even to exclude content sharing platforms from the liability exemption for hosting providers in Article 14 E-Commerce Directive.[236] Whatever the approach followed, an ACS can and should be calibrated to account for such adjustments.

In sum, the limitation-based statutory licence would not privilege for-profit acts of making available online by individuals or platforms, or the activities of operators of P2P platforms, which would typically not qualify as 'non-commercial' or 'individual use of works by natural persons'. Rights holders could avail themselves of remedies against these individuals and platforms, most notably proceedings for direct infringement of the exclusive right and injunctions.[237]

If these scenarios play out, the situation for rights holders under a statutory licence ACS would not be worse than the current status quo in terms of enforcement measures available against unauthorised platforms. If they do not play out, the limitation could be designed to include requirements that achieve a similar effect while allowing true intermediary services to benefit from applicable liability exemptions. Then, the relevant differences introduced by the ACS would be that end-users have a legal authorisation for non-commercial use, and the copyright owners receive remuneration for that use.

235. On the complex question of the 'neutrality' of intermediary service providers in the E-Commerce Directive and CJEU case law, *see* Angelopoulos, 2016, pp. 46–48.
236. *See*, e.g., Kreutzer et al., 2016 (discussing a system of monetary compensation and limitation of liability), and French High Council for Literary and Artistic Property, 2016 (proposing the exclusion from the hosting liability exemption of 'information society service providers that give access to the public to copyright works and/or subject-matter'). *See also* Leistner, 2016.
237. On this point, *see supra* 4.3.2.3, and the argument of AG Wathelet in *Opinion AG in GS Media*, paras 75–79.

Furthermore, copyright owners and online intermediaries would continue to be able to pursue self-regulation through voluntary agreements for online copyright enforcement against unauthorised third party websites, possibly focusing on the 'follow the money' approach endorsed by the Commission.[238] In those agreements, parties could define the scope of allowed 'non-commercial' use in the terms described above (and in line with future interpretation of the concept by the CJEU) thereby ensuring the preservation of the core of the exclusive right for commercial exploitation and genuine use of works.

5.3.2.3.3 Normal Exploitation and Compensation

Most interpretations of the second step hold that a conflict with the normal exploitation entails a level of economic loss to the rights holder. However – and therein lies the contradiction – that conflict may not be cured by the provision of compensation to rights holders. Rather, compensation operates only to make the prejudice to rights holders *reasonable* under the third step.[239] Although the CJEU is typically agnostic on this point, it has on occasion uncritically endorsed the approach.[240]

This position does not result from the ordinary meaning of the test but from the preparatory works of Article 9(2) BC and the consideration of equitable remuneration in the system of the test.[241] It is debatable whether such elements are determinative for the EU test. In principle, the rules of legal interpretation would not preclude considering compensation in the second step. In fact, some high-level national court decisions have done so and there have been increasing calls to that effect in academia.[242]

---

238. See, endorsing this approach: Communication Digital Single Market 2015, pp. 6–8; SWD Digital Single Market Strategy 2015, p. 30; Communication on Modern European Copyright Framework 2015, pp. 10–11. ALAI, 2015b. *See also*: Hugenholtz, 2010, describing the emergence of 'self-regulation' as a mode of extra-judicial copyright enforcement online, with the participation of ISPs and other online intermediaries; and Pérez, 2015, for a recent example of a Memorandum of Understanding aimed at protecting copyright and related rights online'. *But see infra* 5.3.3.6., noting the potential conflict of these measures with fundamental rights.

239. Geiger, 2007b, p. 7; Ginsburg, 2001, pp. 44–47; Koelman, 2006, p. 409; Peukert, 2005, pp. 32–33.

240. CJEU, *Padawan*, para. 30; CJEU, *Stichting de Thuiskopie*, paras 21–22. Cf. *Opinion AG in ACI Adam*, para. 54. *But see Opinion AG in Stichting de Thuiskopie*, para. 60, expressly considering fair compensation in the analysis of the second step.

241. Records BC Stockholm 1967, pp. 1145–1146; WTO, *US–Copyright*, paras 6.73–6.74; Ficsor, 2002b, pp. 125–127; Senftleben, 2004, pp. 129–130. *See also supra* 2.3.2.1.

242. On national case-law, *see* e.g. Geiger, 2007b, pp. 7–8 citing: BGH, 25.02.1999, I ZR 118/96 ('Re Supply of Photocopies of Newspaper Articles by a Public Library'), and BGH, 11.07. 2002, I ZR 255/00 ('In House Press Clippings Archive – Electronischer Pressespiegel'). For academic arguments, see: Geiger et al., 2008; Geiger, 2007b, pp. 7–8; He, 2009, p. 300, including adequate remuneration on the fourth factor of his

An influential example is the MPI Declaration, which states that limitations do not conflict with the normal exploitation where they reflect significant competing concerns, including of a normative nature, particularly if 'adequate compensation is ensured', for example through a legal licence.[243] This aspect is important mainly where a traditional view of the test would foreclose analysis of a limitation based on a conflict with the normal exploitation, without considering the possibility that the same can fully compensate rights holders for the use allowed.

As noted in Chapter 1, an empirical study in the Netherlands concluded that a statutory licence ACS for the online rights of reproduction and communication to the public applying to recorded music has the potential to compensate rights holders fully. In concrete terms, a EUR 1.74 surcharge on the ISP subscription for all households with Internet connection in that country would equal the entire revenue of the Dutch physical and digital market for recorded music in 2012, including all conventional purchases of recorded music of approximately EUR 144 million.[244] As users are willing to pay a monthly amount well above that price point, this system would be welfare increasing, even after correcting the results for overestimation.[245]

If similar results apply to other content types and countries in the EU, a limitation-based statutory licence ACS would provide sufficient compensation to cure any conflict with the normal exploitation of works. Again, there is no certainty that the results hold across the board, as they merely reflect a snapshot of the moving target that is the online market for one type of content in one Member State. However, together with the uncertain negative effects of an ACS on online copyright markets, the study gives pause to question whether such a legalisation proposal would conflict with the normal exploitation of works.

5.3.3 Unreasonable Prejudice to Legitimate Interests

The third step of the test requires that limitations do not cause 'unreasonable prejudice' to 'legitimate interests' of authors or rights holders. Scholars read both expressions in quotation marks as opening the door for public interest

adapted fair use test, used to examine the normal exploitation condition; Geiger & Schönherr, 2014a, pp. 135–136. *Contra*, *see* Lucas, 2010, p. 278.

243. Geiger et al., 2008, p. 711. Similarly, *see* Geiger, 2010, pp. 546–547.

244. Revenues are calculated resorting to industry statistics, such as IFPI, 2013, which estimates rights holders revenues in the Dutch recorded music market at EUR 143.6 million. The focus is on revenues rather than profits due to the lack of reliable information on costs. Data on private copying levies collected in the Netherlands was taken from WIPO, 2013. The results assume the unlikely scenario that an ACS substitutes all current sales of recorded music (perfect substitution) and provides no cost savings. *See* Handke et al., 2015.

245. *See supra* 1.1. *See also* Handke et al., 2015.

considerations when assessing limitations.[246] This allows a balancing exercise between the interests of copyright owners in retaining exclusivity and the larger public interest in benefiting from a limitation.[247]

Striking a fair balance of rights and interests between the different categories of rights holders, as well as between them and users of works, is a central objective of the InfoSoc Directive.[248] To achieve that objective and resolve conflicts between fundamental rights the CJEU uses the principle of proportionality.[249] Proportionality is a general EU law principle that guides substantive interpretation of rights and calibration of remedies in the *acquis*.[250] Through the objective of fair balance, this principle is afforded additional relevance for the interpretation of limitations.[251]

For some scholars, the principle of proportionality should apply to the three-step test as a whole.[252] However, as previously argued, in the context of a flexible analysis, the third step seems a suitable place for the final examination of competing interests.[253] In this setting, a proportionality analysis involves an evaluation of the appropriateness of a limitation for achieving its purpose, the relevance of its policy justifications, and its impact on the interests of rights holders and the public.[254] Hence, this section carries

246. Cf. Hugenholtz & Okediji, 2008, pp. 24–25; Wright, 2009, p. 610.
247. *See* R. Hilty & Nérisson, 2012, and *supra* 5.2.1.
248. Recital 31 InfoSoc Directive.
249. Angelopoulos, 2015, pp. 77–81. On the consideration of copyright as a fundamental right, see: Art. 1 of Protocol No. 1 to the ECHR; Art. 17(2) Charter; recital 9 InfoSoc Directive; recital 32 Enforcement Directive.
250. Arts 5(4) TEU and 52(1) Charter. Concerning remedies in the *acquis*, *see* Arts 8(1) InfoSoc Directive and 3(2) Enforcement Directive. Regarding intellectual property case-law, see, e.g., CJEU, *Promusicae*, paras 68, 70; CJEU, *L'Oréal v. eBay*, paras 143–144; CJEU, *Bonnier Audio*; CJEU, *Scarlet Extended*; CJEU, *Netlog*; CJEU, *UPC Telekabel*, para. 46. In general, regarding EU law, see: CJEU, *Lindqvist*, para. 87; CJEU, *Ordre des barreaux francophones and germanophone and Others*, para. 28. At the institutional level, *see* Council of Europe Recommendation CM/Rec(2008)6. For an overview of the concept of proportionality in EU copyright law, *see* Fischman Afori, 2014.
251. See *supra* 4.4.1.3 and 4.4.1.4. Cf. CJEU, *Deckmyn*, paras 19–23; CJEU, *Murphy*, paras 162–164; *Opinion AG in Ulmer*, para. 38. *See also* Arnold & Rosati, 2015, pp. 13–14. At the international level, TRIPS requires observance of the principle of proportionality (in Arts XX GATT and XIV GATS), which is an inherent feature of the WTO system. *See* Grosse Ruse-Khan, 2008; Kur, 2008, pp. 1, 38–40.
252. Kur, 2008, p. 40, noting the adequacy of proportionality to interpret 'gradual' criteria, like 'certain special cases' and 'normal exploitation'.
253. Colin, 2011a, p. 57; Geiger, 2007b, p. 18, 2010, p. 549; Geiger et al., 2014, pp. 604–605; Griffiths, 2009, p. 17; Lamping, 2014, pp. 687–688; Ficsor, 2012, p. 4; Roßnagel et al., 2009, pp. 25–26; Senftleben, 2004, pp. 210–212, 226–227, 274, 2010, p. 78. *See also* Geiger et al., 2014, pp. 599, 604–605, suggesting that proportionality is examined through a methodology akin to that employed when settling conflicts between fundamental rights.
254. The analysis of this paragraph draws on Kur, 2008, pp. 39–40. *See also*: Roßnagel et al., 2009, p. 26; Fischman Afori, 2014, pp. 895–896, calling proportionality a new 'mega

out a balancing exercise between the conflicting legitimate interests and the reasonableness of the prejudice caused by a statutory licence ACS.

First, an examination is made of the meaning of the expressions 'unreasonable prejudice' (5.3.3.1) and 'legitimate interests' (5.3.3.2). This is followed by the balancing exercise proper, which scrutinises the interests of rights holders as a group and the issue of fair compensation (5.3.3.3), as well as the conflicting interests of creators and exploiters (5.3.3.4). The subsequent analysis follows an innovative approach to the third step by taking into consideration the public interest in an ACS. This includes first an examination of the interests derived from the promotion of creativity and dissemination of works (5.3.3.5) and, second, a consideration of the public interest in the respect and protection of fundamental rights of end-users and intermediaries (5.3.3.6).

5.3.3.1 Unreasonable Prejudice

The term 'prejudice' means 'damage, harm or injury'.[255] By requiring that prejudice to copyright owners is 'not unreasonable' the third step is setting a threshold 'slightly stricter' than reasonable.[256] Hence, a limitation may impose a certain amount of prejudice up to the point where it 'causes or has the potential to cause an unreasonable loss of income to the copyright owner.'[257]

As a result, the prejudice can be substantial without being unreasonable if copyright owners do not 'bear costs that are out of proportion to the benefits derived by the public'.[258] Only then should measures be put in place to countenance it, like the payment of compensation.[259] Logically, where the prejudice is minimal, it is possible that no compensation is required.[260]

To make this assessment it is necessary to quantify the 'legitimate interests' at stake. *US–Copyright* does so with reference to the economic

standard' in European copyright law and identifying a four-factor test for proportionality in European law where the last factor – 'balancing' – is often known as 'proportionality *stricto sensu*'; and Angelopoulos, 2015, pp. 78–79, noting that the CJEU approach in fundamental rights cases is to parse down proportionality to a balancing exercise.

255. WTO, *US–Copyright*, para. 6.225.
256. *Ibid.*, para. 6.225. *See also* Records Stockholm 1967, p. 1145. This book adopts the position that the potential linguistic conflict between the originally proposed English language expression 'unreasonable prejudice' and its French translation '*préjudice unjustifié*' do not alter the interpretation of the third step. For an analysis of the linguistic issue with reference to Stockholm records, *see* Ficsor, 2002b, pp. 141–147; Geiger et al., 2014, pp. 584–585.
257. WTO, *US–Copyright*, para. 6.229. *See also* Iuliano, 2011, pp. 487–488.
258. Iuliano, 2011, p. 487.
259. Senftleben, 2006, p. 436.
260. Ginsburg, 2001, p. 53.

value of exercising different exclusive rights, measured for example through licensing.[261] Based on the BC preparatory works, the copyright panel states that the prejudice is restored to tolerable levels if compensation is provided, such as via 'a system of compulsory licensing with equitable remuneration'.[262] Compensation therefore plays a central role in the third step.

This position, however, is rather 'arithmetic', as it foregoes policy considerations.[263] Beyond remuneration, the third step contains several flexibility tools, namely the legitimacy and unreasonableness filters.[264] For that reason, the third step ought to account for the conflicting interests invoked by exploiters and creators against each other and 'against the reasons justifying the use privilege', like fundamental rights.[265] Similarly, it should assess reasonableness in light of a limitation's non-economic motivations, which mirror the legitimate public interest.[266] This is relevant because a strong public interest motivation may provide sufficient justification for a limitation, even if the same causes loss of revenue to rights holders.[267]

5.3.3.2 Legitimate Interests of Rights Holders and the Public Interest

The third step considers *interests* of rights holders taken together (creators and exploiters) that qualify as *legitimate*.[268] An interest is the economic basis

261. WTO, *US–Copyright*, paras 6.227–6.228.
262. *Ibid.*, para. 6.229 (& n. 205), citing the WIPO Guide to the Berne Convention, authored by Claude Masouyé (then-Director of WIPO's copyright division). Cf. Senftleben, 2004, pp. 235–241. Professor Ulmer first suggested the approach in the 1967 Stockholm revision conference in his capacity as Chairman of Main Committee I, inspired by the then-recent German Copyright Act of 1965. *See* Records Stockholm 1967, pp. 1145–1146. This statement should be qualified as a supplementary means of interpretation. Cf. *supra* 5.2.1.
263. Kur, 2008, p. 29 & n. 108, noting the similarity of this approach with the second step analysis in *US–Copyright*. Kur also observes that the legislative motives behind the US 'home-style' and 'business' exemptions discussed in *US–Copyright* strengthened the position of rights holders.
264. Senftleben, 2014, p. 8.
265. Geiger et al., 2014, pp. 595, 605, 626; Senftleben, 2014, p. 8.
266. Ginsburg, 2001, p. 57; Lucas, 2010, pp. 277–278. *See also* Iuliano, 2011, p. 486; Senftleben, 2006, p. 436. At EU level, *see Opinion AG in Infopaq I*, para. 139, recognising the normative element (the 'qualitative nature of the effect') but failing to properly consider it in the analysis.
267. Gervais, 2005, p. 19. *See also* WTO, *Canada–Patent*, para. 7.69.
268. Christie & Wright, 2014, pp. 428–429; Geiger et al., 2008; Senftleben, 2006, p. 436; R. Wright, 2009, p. 610. *See also*: Geiger et al., 2014, p. 595, arguing that legitimacy is 'context-dependent'; and Senftleben, 2004, pp. 216–219, on the inclusion of licensees as holders of legitimate economic interests to be considered in the third step.

of the substantive right, meant to reflect the value of exclusive rights as measured by their possibilities of exercise.[269]

Normatively, an interest is legitimate if 'justifiable in the light of the objectives that underlie the protection of exclusive rights'[270] or if 'supported by relevant public policies or other social norms'.[271] This view presupposes a balancing act and consideration of a limitation's justification.[272] Therefore, interests are legitimate if lawful and justifiable on normative grounds.[273]

If this understanding is correct, it is necessary to identify the parties whose interests are legitimate because they reflect the public interest.[274] In this respect, the industrial property three-step tests in TRIPS provide more clarity than the copyright tests, as they mention 'third party interests'. This phrase denotes interests in the derogation of exclusive rights 'in certain situations to encourage wider social access to and use of knowledge, information and cultural products'.[275] 'Third parties', then, are those adverse in interest to the rights holder in the sense they are excluded from using works but for the limitation. They are the direct and indirect beneficiaries of a limitation.[276]

Although the copyright tests only mention 'authors' or 'rights holders', some influential scholarship posits that the balancing aims of international and EU copyright law require in addition a consideration of the public interest in the final step.[277] Limitations serve the public interest by advancing the objectives of the copyright system and enabling its co-existence and coherence with fundamental rights or freedoms, allowing copyright to fulfil its social function.[278]

As argued in the previous chapter, the public interest drives the function of copyright limitations as essential instruments to define the scope of

---

269. WTO, *US–Copyright*, para. 6.227, following this approach. *See also* Senftleben, 2004, pp. 215–219, 273.
270. WTO, *US–Copyright*, para. 6.224.
271. WTO, *Canada–Patent*, para. 7.69; WTO, *EC–Trademarks I*, para. 7.663.
272. Gervais, 2005, p. 18.
273. Cf. Christie & Wright, 2014, p. 429; Iuliano, 2011, pp. 486–487; Senftleben, 2004, pp. 213–216.
274. Geiger et al., 2014, p. 587.
275. Wright, 2009, p. 600.
276. Cf. Kur, 2008, p. 30. *See* WTO, *Canada–Patent*, para. 4.14 (argument of Canada) and WTO, *EC–Trademarks I*, paras 7.676–7.678. The latter report explains the concept of 'third party' and states that it includes the interests of users of protected geographical indications.
277. Geiger et al., 2008; Kur, 2008, p. 41. For a broad view of interests involved in the TRIPS patent test, *see* Lamping, 2014, pp. 687–688, 694.
278. Geiger, 2014d, pp. 15–17, 19–21; Shaheed, 2014, pp. 13–16. On the relevance of 'values that underpin fundamental rights', *see* Geiger et al., 2008, p. 710. On the objectives of the InfoSoc Directive, *see supra* 1.3 and 4.4.1.3, and *infra* 5.5.3. Noting the connection between the concept of 'social function' and the terms 'general' or 'public interest' in EU legislation, *see* Sganga, 2015, pp. 16–17.

copyright protection.[279] Nowhere is that stated clearer than in *Luksan*, where in connection with a film director's claim for fair compensation the CJEU interpreted Article 17 Charter as follows:[280]

> Finally, it should be pointed out that, under Article 17(1) of the Charter of Fundamental Rights of the European Union, everyone has the right to own, use, dispose of and bequeath his or her lawfully acquired possessions. No one may be deprived of his or her possessions, *except in the public interest and in the cases and under the conditions provided for by law, subject to fair compensation* being paid in good time for their loss. The *use of property may be regulated by law in so far as is necessary for the general interest*. Article 17(2) provides that intellectual property is to be protected.

The CJEU sets aside the notion that the recognition of copyright as property and as a fundamental right implies its absolute protection in the form of an exclusive right. Instead, the Court states that exclusive rights may be replaced by a right to fair compensation 'in the public interest and in the cases and under the conditions provided for by law'.

Because the introduction of limitations in the *acquis* is regulated by the three-step test, and the balancing of competing interests – including the grant of fair compensation – usually occurs in the third step, it seems that this is the place to take into consideration the public interest.

A statutory licence ACS legalises large-scale non-commercial online use of works by individuals, in relation to which the exercise of exclusive rights is costly, impossible or undesirable. Beyond the market failure argument explained throughout this study, the public interest in regulating this use potentially falls under two headings, recognised as expressions of such interest in the MPI Declaration.[281]

The first relates to the promotion of creativity and dissemination of works that comes with the statutory licence ACS and the ensuing legal certainty for end-users. In the MPI Declaration, this corresponds to the category of public interest based on 'scientific progress and cultural, social, or economic development', which would include the interest of users and certain stakeholders in access to information and works, education and research.[282]

---

279. In this sense, *see supra* 4.4.1.1 and 4.4.1.3. *See also* Dreier, 2015.
280. CJEU, *Luksan*, para. 68.
281. Geiger et al., 2008, p. 712. The MPI Declaration also refers to a third category: interests in competition. As noted in Chapter 2, competition law may justify restrictions to abusive or collusive use of exclusive rights, as well as motivate the adoption of limitations or compulsory licences. See, e.g., *supra* 2.4.2.2, on the justification for the broadcasting compulsory licence. *See also* Guibault, 2002, pp. 56–68.
282. In this respect, *see* Wittem Group, 2010, p. 127 & n. 34, emphasising the legitimate interests of members of the public 'in improving the access to the work.'

The second category relates to the respect of fundamental rights and freedoms of individuals and intermediaries affected by the enforcement of their non-commercial use. These rights include the protection of users' personal data and privacy in telecommunications, their freedom of information and expression online, and intermediaries' freedom to conduct a business.[283] As a fundamental right, copyright is interpreted in light of its social function. This may result in restrictions to its scope for reasons of public interest in order to strike a fair balance with countervailing fundamental rights.[284] As a result, and in line with *Luksan*, copyright has a relative character.[285] Furthermore, the CJEU recognises that fundamental rights can operate as justifications for limitations. As noted in Chapter 4, by virtue of the principle of effectiveness and the objective of legal certainty, consideration of fundamental rights prevents a restrictive interpretation of certain limitations and may warrant a widening of their scope.[286]

5.3.3.3 The Interests of Rights Holders and Fair Compensation

The legitimate interests of rights holders are primarily economic. Exclusive rights are the traditional tools to protect them.[287] As a group, rights holders have a legitimate interest in the commercial exploitation of works through digital platforms.

If an ACS causes prejudice to copyright owners, it is possible to return that prejudice to reasonable levels by providing remuneration or compensation through a statutory licence.[288] Where an ACS provides an adequate, efficient and fair means to remunerate *different groups of affected rights*

---

283. Similarly, *see* Roßnagel et al., 2009, p. 16.
284. Griffiths, 2013; Griffiths & McDonagh, 2013; Ramalho, 2014, pp. 87–92, with further development on the requirements of proportionality. See, *inter alia*: CJEU, *Germany v. Council*, para. 78 (and cited case law); CJEU, *Schmidberger*, para. 80; CJEU, *Kadi*, para. 360. For a list of case law, *see* Geiger & Izyumenko, 2014, p. 322 & nn. 27, 331; Sganga, 2015, p. 8ff. *See also infra* 5.5.2.
285. CJEU, *Promusicae*, paras 61–68; CJEU, *Painer*, para. 113; CJEU, *Bonnier Audio*, paras 49–60; CJEU, *Scarlet Extended*, paras 43–46; CJEU, *Netlog*, 41; CJEU, *UPC Telekabel*, para. 61; and, by implication, CJEU, *Luksan*, para. 68. Cf. Angelopoulos, 2015, pp. 72–73; European Copyright Society, 2014b, pp. 6–7; Geiger & Izyumenko, 2014, p. 334.
286. *See supra* 4.4.1.4. For CJEU case law, *see* in particular CJEU, *Murphy*, paras 163–164, and CJEU, *Painer*, para. 133. *See also* Sganga, 2015, p. 19.
287. Senftleben, 2004, pp. 216–219. But some authors view the third step as opening the door for consideration of non-economic interests, such as moral rights. *See* Ginsburg, 2001, p. 27; Ricketson & Ginsburg, 2006, p. 774. Because the *acquis* does not harmonise moral rights, the InfoSoc Directive test refers solely to legitimate economic interests. Cf. Senftleben, 2004, p. 273, and recital 19 InfoSoc Directive.
288. Dusollier & Colin, 2011, p. 830.

holders, it should not cause an unreasonable prejudice to their legitimate interests.[289]

But how to define and calculate compensation in an ACS? As a principle, compensation should be fair and adequate to remunerate rights holders for the non-commercial online use of works by individuals.[290] Because the statutory licence ACS examined here assumes the adoption of a compensated limitation in the *acquis*, it makes sense that it adopts the template of the existing and comparable autonomous EU law concepts of 'fair compensation' or 'equitable remuneration'. Of these concepts, fair compensation provides the sounder approach: not only because it attaches to the InfoSoc Directive's limitations (and thus to the rights licensed in a future ACS), but also for the reason that recital 36 of the directive favours this concept for future compensated limitations on the directive's exclusive rights.[291]

Chapter 4 deals with fair compensation in some detail. That analysis shows that the right of fair compensation is unwaivable and its calculation based on the harm caused to copyright owners by the introduction of a limitation. That calculation takes into consideration different mitigating factors: the *de minimis* nature of the use, whether the use was authorised (for free or against payment), and the application of TPMs.[292]

The resulting harm corresponds to the 'prejudice' mentioned in the third step of the test. Analysis of step two clarified that the potential prejudice to copyright owners from a statutory licence ACS includes its direct and indirect effects on normal modes of commercial exploitation online. As noted, it is unclear whether the licence will have direct negative effects on that commercial exploitation if the non-commercial use it covers is too difficult to enforce, exercise or monetise. The statutory licence will remunerate this use, generating a novel revenue stream for copyright owners, thus improving their situation from a financial standpoint.[293]

However, it was also stated that such a legalisation scheme may have the unintended adverse effect of removing liability from unauthorised for-profit websites or platforms, who either make works available over the Internet on a large-scale or, depending on the legal status of their activities,

289. Bernault & Lebois, 2005, p. 36; Eckersley, 2004, p. 156; Peukert, 2005, pp. 42–43.
290. The term 'adequate compensation' is used in the *MPI Declaration*. *See* Geiger et al., 2008. For a different approach, *see* Art. 5.7 Wittem Code mentioning 'fair and adequate remuneration', which seems an attempt to avoid tension between the concepts of equitable remuneration and fair compensation in the *acquis*. Cf. Geiger & Schonherr, 2012, p. 165; Wittem Group, 2010.
291. Art. 5(2) (a), (b) and (e), and recital 36 InfoSoc Directive. The Orphan Works Directive follows a similar approach in Art. 6(5) and recital 18. For an outline of this concept and relevant case law, *see supra* 4.4.3.3.
292. *See supra* 4.4.3.3, 4.4.3.4, and 4.4.3.5. For the factors mentioned, *see* recital 35 InfoSoc Directive. The standard for equitable remuneration is the 'economic value of the use in trade'. *See supra* 2.2.4.
293. See, e.g., Geiger, 2014a, p. 21; Roßnagel et al., 2009, p. 14.

facilitate that availability for economic benefit (e.g., The Pirate Bay and Popcorn Time). If this occurs, legalisation may conflict with the normal exploitation of works and cause economic harm to rights holders. For that reason, different approaches were outlined that allow rights holders to retain effective remedies against unauthorised websites/platforms despite the adoption of an ACS. If those remedies remain at the disposal of rights holders, no significant prejudice should arise from the activities of those websites *as a legal consequence of an ACS, or that is attributable to its adoption.*[294] Rather, the only prejudice that should be examined in the context of the three-step test here is the economic harm caused by the licensed non-commercial acts of individual users on existing authorised commercial offerings (e.g., on the revenues of streaming services such as Spotify or Netflix).[295]

Now, it is not possible to quantify this harm with certainty. In part, this is because harm is measured against the effects of the limitation on the market, which are difficult to assess for non-commercial online use.[296] A statutory licence ACS would apply to public goods or goods not yet released on the market,[297] and to forms of use for which there is no clear market due to lack of exercise or monetisation. Moreover, certain types of use licensed by an ACS are *de minimis* or already compensated through contractual means (i.e., priced into the purchase or licence of digital content); in these cases, fair compensation may be unwarranted due to the lack of harm to copyright owners.[298]

One approach to calculate harm for non-commercial use is to determine its value to end-users benefiting from the ACS. This value would correspond to the prejudice suffered by copyright owners due to the inability to exercise and enforce their rights for that use. To pass the third step of the test, then, an ACS would have to return that prejudice to reasonable levels, taking into account the aforementioned harm-mitigating factors.

If this approach is accepted, the value of the licensed non-commercial use with no clear market can be determined by gauging users' willingness to pay through a method of contingent valuation.[299] This method was applied in

294. *See* the analysis *supra* at 5.3.2.3.
295. It is noted that by applying a limitation to acts of end-users an ACS would likely induce savings on administrative and enforcement costs. *See* Lescure, 2013, p. 31.
296. Geiger et al., 2008, pp. 708–710, suggesting that adequate compensation may be set at or below market rate.
297. Handke et al., 2015.
298. Similar arguments are made in the context of private copying. *See supra* 4.4.3, and Quintais, 2015a.
299. Handke et al., 2015, adopting this approach to ACS through conjoint analysis and flagging the challenges of applying this method to a licence that is an unfamiliar and complex quasi-public good. In this way, the ACS would address a major criticism of legalisation proposals and, in general, compulsory licences: that calculation of an overall amount of compensation outside market conditions is inefficient. *See* Stan Liebowitz, 2003; Stan J. Liebowitz & Watt, 2006; Merges, 2004a.

the ACS research in the Netherlands mentioned in Chapter 1 and in the analysis of the second step of the test.[300] The findings of that study suggest that a statutory licence system can provide sufficient revenue to supplant the direct and indirect losses caused by the legalisation of the types of use in question.[301]

If these results remain valid for other types of work and across the territory of the EU, and in addition copyright owners are able to enforce their exclusive rights against unauthorised websites or platforms that enter into competition with authorised commercial channels over the Internet, the provision of fair compensation in the terms described above should reduce the actual or potential harm to reasonable levels. It may even afford fair compensation the character of an appropriate reward to promote creativity, which some authors believe to be required by the aims of the InfoSoc Directive.[302]

5.3.3.4 The Conflicting Interests of Creators and Exploiters

Rights holders are not a homogenous group with aligned interests. For the purposes of the third step, it is important to distinguish individual creators from exploiters.[303] This distinction, as one author puts it, 'is one of the characteristics of modern copyright'.[304]

The distinction finds legal basis in EU law, international law (the BC and WCT solely protect authors and do not consider the interests of exploiters), and even the fundamental rights framework, where authors are the sole beneficiaries of the human right to protection of authorship.[305]

The *acquis*, for its part, differentiates between categories of rights holders in their legal entitlements, and for the purpose of striking a fair balance.[306] The particular place of authors is recognised by the CJEU for example in *Luksan* and *Reprobel*, from where it is clear that the economic rights granted in EU law – including exclusive, remuneration or fair compensation rights – are originally owned by authors and rights holders expressly identified in the law and not subsequent or related rights holders, such as publishers.[307]

300. *See supra* 1.1 and 5.3.2.3 (on normal exploitation and compensation).
301. Handke et al., 2015; Vallbé et al., 2015.
302. *See Opinion AG in Padawan*, paras 79–80, relying on the wording of recital 10 InfoSoc Directive ('appropriate reward'). Cf. Geiger & Schönherr, 2014a, pp. 132–133. *See also infra* 5.5.2 (on the remuneration aspect of copyright), and 5.5.3 (on adequate compensation as an objective of EU law).
303. Geiger et al., 2008, pp. 708–710, 712. This is a conceptual simplification, as under some national laws and for certain categories of works it is possible that a legal person technically qualifies as the 'original' rights holder.
304. Kur, 2008, pp. 12–13 & n. 45.
305. Kur, 2008, p. 44; Shaheed, 2014, pp. 9–11, 13, 15, 2015.
306. Cf. e.g. recital 31 and Arts 1(1), 2 and 3(2) InfoSoc Directive.
307. CJEU, *Luksan*, para. 67; CJEU, *Reprobel*, paras 44–49.

Implicit in the distinction is the recognition of different sets of legitimate interests. Such interests can be *concurrent*, for example regarding the prevention of unauthorised use, or *conflicting*. An example of conflict is the case of compensated limitations, often viewed as beneficial to the material interests of creators but prejudicial to the ability of exploiters to maximise profits.[308] This tension is central to the debate on legalisation proposals.

If a statutory licence is coupled with an unwaivable right to fair compensation, creators are likely to receive more remuneration for the licensed use than they would otherwise receive through the exploitation of assignable exclusive rights. Also, a statutory licence better protects creators from inequality in legal expertise and imbalance in bargaining power vis-à-vis third parties.[309] This is especially true as emerging online access-based models of exploitation come in for criticism for their lack of transparency and failure to ensure fair remuneration to creators.[310]

The benefits of compensated limitations, recognised by commentators and courts, are particularly salient when contrasted with the preference given by exploiters to addressing unauthorised use through enforcement measures that disregard remuneration.[311] In light of these benefits, some scholars argue that a compensated limitation is a three-step test-compliant solution to conflicts between creators and exploiters.[312] Underlying this position is the view that the prejudice to rights holders *as a whole* can be reduced to reasonable levels if the benefit to creators from a statutory licence offsets the harm caused to exploiters by the imposition of a copyright limitation on a use previously covered by an exclusive right.

308. Christie & Wright, 2014, pp. 429–430, referring also to conflicting interests in relation to moral rights and licensing scenarios.
309. *See supra* 4.4.3.3, on the nature of the right of fair compensation in the *acquis*. *See also* Europe Economics, Guibault, Salamanca & Gompel, 2015, pp. 120–121; Geiger, 2010, pp. 528, 532; Geiger & Schonherr, 2012, pp. 166–167; Griffiths, 2009, p. 9; Shaheed, 2014, p. 20; Westkamp, 2008, p. 38. At the institutional level, *see* SWD Digital Single Market Strategy 2015, pp. 30–31.
310. Consumentenbond & Bureau Brandeis, 2014, p. 3; Europe Economics et al., 2015. On streaming, see: Chalis, 2015; IFPI, 2015; Vallbé et al., 2015.
311. *See supra* 1.1. *See also* Geiger, 2007b, pp. 7–9, 2014c, pp. 138–139, Kur, 2008, p. 12, citing: BGH, 11.07. 2002, I ZR 255/00 ('In House Press Clippings Archive – Electronischer Pressespiegel'); Supreme Court Switzerland, 26.06.2007, Case No. 4C.73/2007 (*ProLitteris v. Aargauer Zeitung AG*, et al., 'Electronic Press Review – Elektronischer Pressespiegel').
312. Geiger & Schönherr, 2014a, p. 135 (n. 102). *See also*: Westkamp, 2008, pp. 58–59, following a similar approach under national constitutional law but noting that TPM protection makes the argument less persuasive vis-à-vis the InfoSoc Directive; and Hugenholtz & Okediji, 2008, p. 24, pointing out that the reference to 'authors' in the BC and WCT leaves more ample space for a far-reaching compensated limitation than the reference to 'rights holders' in TRIPS.

5.3.3.5 Public Interest in the Promotion of Creativity and Circulation of Works

Copyright serves the public interest through the promotion of creativity, and dissemination of culture and knowledge.[313] Access to cultural works – and thus information, knowledge and culture – is not only a goal of copyright law,[314] but also has a human rights dimension, derived from the right to take part in cultural life and to enjoy the benefits of scientific progress, in itself a manifestation of the human right to science and culture.[315]

The InfoSoc Directive establishes a link between intended creativity, remuneration, and the scope of copyright protection through exclusive rights and limitations. Recital 9 views the harmonisation of rights through a 'high level of protection' of copyright and related rights as crucial to intellectual creation. This protection, it continues, 'helps to ensure the maintenance and development of creativity in the interests of authors, performers, producers, consumers, culture, industry and the public at large'. Recital 10 adds that if creators 'are to continue their creative and artistic work, they have to receive an appropriate reward for the use of their work, as must producers in order to be able to finance this work.'

As argued in the previous chapter, a high level of protection cannot mean endorsing infinitely extendable protection. Doing so would contradict 'the finding that overly strong exclusivity in the sense of 'excessive protection' can have a negative impact on creativity and innovation'.[316] Therefore, a high level of protection should be interpreted as an 'adequate' or 'optimal' level of protection, aimed at providing remuneration for use of works that is in turn sufficient to incentivise creation, while maintaining a fair balance between private and public interest.[317]

Infinite extension of protection would not only prejudice rights holders, but also the public interest. Limitations thus become essential tools to calibrate broadly interpreted exclusive rights and define an ideal scope of protection.[318] A limitation-based statutory licence ACS for non-commercial use may promote creativity and access to works by providing remuneration for that use, improving legal certainty, and fostering the circulation of

313. Sganga, 2015, p. 7, arguing that the promotion of creativity is a utilitarian function ascribed to copyright in the InfoSoc Directive, as demonstrated by recital 9 thereof. *See also* EP Resolution Implementation InfoSoc Directive 2015, para. 25.
314. Geiger & Schönherr, 2014a, p. 141. On the circulation of culture as a goal of EU copyright law in the jurisprudence of the CJEU, *see* Favale et al., 2015, pp. 33, 66–67. *See also supra* 1.3 and *infra* 5.5.3.
315. *See* Art. 27 UDHR and Art. 15(1) ICESCR. *See also* Shaheed, 2014, pp. 3–5. On the access aspect of copyright and its role as an objective of the *acquis*, *see infra* 5.5.2–5.5.3.
316. Dreier, 2015, p. 2.
317. *See supra* 4.4.1.3 and 4.4.1.4.
318. Dreier, 2015, pp. 2–3.

culture – all declared objectives of EU copyright law, often expressly identified as such by the CJEU.[319]

Remuneration is central to intellectual creation. If an ACS provides an unwaivable right to fair compensation, creators gain a new rights revenue and an 'appropriate reward for the use of their work', consistent with recital 10 InfoSoc Directive. All the more so when, as argued before, exclusive rights and strict enforcement fail to provide that reward for mass non-commercial online use.[320] A statutory licence system could improve the status quo in this respect, and in this way provide a boon to intellectual creation. Furthermore, it is not obvious that this system would result in an unreasonable prejudice to exploiters, since it would provide fair compensation to all categories of rights holders in the InfoSoc Directive, precisely those whose legitimate interests are protected by Article 5(5).[321]

From a different perspective, a statutory licence system may enhance legal certainty and foster the circulation of works. Improvement at this level results from the licence authorising users to reproduce and communicate works to the public over the Internet in the EU territory, thereby releasing individuals from liability for these online activities. Individuals would benefit from a clearer and simplified set of rules governing their online use of works, in line with the InfoSoc Directive's objectives, including the harmonisation of copyright law through the coherent application of limitations.[322]

This clarified legal framework naturally helps the dissemination of culture and should have the added benefit of improving the legitimacy of copyright law, by approximating it to prevailing online social norms, and mitigating the costly social conflict arising from litigation.[323] In this line, the additional legal certainty that a statutory licence brings to the regulation of the activities of end-users online would also contribute to the efficient administration of justice, especially as it relates to costs associated with copyright litigation against these users.

Finally, gains in legal certainty further contribute to intellectual creation by allowing authors to learn from, and build on, pre-existing knowledge and materials.[324] Authors benefit from the availability of such materials through

319. Favale et al., 2015, pp. 33, 66–67
320. From a human rights perspective, the right to protection of authorship 'does not imply perfect authorial control over creative works' and ought to be interpreted as requiring fair remuneration. *See* Shaheed, 2014, pp. 9–11, 13, 15, 20, 2015.
321. CJEU, *Reprobel*, paras 44–49, on the attribution of fair compensation to these rights holders.
322. Cf. recitals 4 and 32 InfoSoc Directive, and Favale et al., 2015, pp. 33, 66–67. See, generally, European Copyright Society, 2014b, pp. 2–3.
323. Grassmuck, 2012, on the social 'turn' towards a sharing norm.
324. Geiger, 2010; Geiger & Schönherr, 2014a, pp. 110, 114; Hugenholtz & Okediji, 2008, pp. 10–11.

limitations,[325] which operate as access mechanisms to 'empower new creativity'.[326]

5.3.3.6 Public Interest in the Respect of Fundamental Rights and Freedoms

A main assumption of this book is that strict enforcement of exclusive rights against individuals for non-commercial file sharing is problematic. This results in part from the potential conflict between enforcement measures and fundamental rights. If a statutory licence ACS can mitigate this conflict, it will serve the public interest, providing a counterbalance to the prejudice caused to rights holders by the imposition of a copyright limitation for non-commercial online use. This section therefore examines whether certain fundamental rights and freedoms of individuals and intermediaries – freedom of expression and information, respect for privacy and protection of personal data, and freedom to conduct a business – can justify the adoption of an ACS.

5.3.3.6.1 Freedom of Expression and Information

The right to freedom of expression and information is recognised at international, European, and national levels.[327] In the copyright *acquis*, recital 3 InfoSoc Directive identifies it as on a par with intellectual property and the public interest:

> The proposed harmonisation will help to implement the four freedoms of the internal market and relates to compliance with the fundamental principles of law and especially of property, including intellectual property, and freedom of expression and the public interest.

Copyright promotes freedom of expression by fostering and incentivising independent intellectual creation.[328] However, freedom of expression imposes restrictions on the scope and enforcement of the exclusive right. In fact, States have a positive obligation to protect this fundamental freedom from interference by private parties, such as in the exercise of copyright.[329] The risk of conflict between these rights is particularly visible in the digital environment.

On the one hand, the Internet has become an essential medium for the enjoyment and effective exercise of freedom of expression and

325. Geiger, 2010, p. 532; Hugenholtz & Okediji, 2008, p. 10.

326. Shaheed, 2014, p. 13. *See also* Westkamp, 2008, p. 4 & n. 7. N.B. if these uses cross the commerciality threshold they are outside the scope of the ACS. This design helps preserve the economic core of the exclusive right.

327. *See* Art. 19 UDHR, Art. 19 International Covenant on Civil and Political Rights, Art. 11 Charter, and Art. 10 ECHR.

328. Lee, 2015, p. 12.

329. Article 19, 2013, p. 7; Geiger & Izyumenko, 2014.

information.[330] This freedom includes the possibility to impart, seek and receive information and ideas online.[331] It extends to the individuals' enjoyment of digital cultural goods, including activities like reading, listening, viewing, browsing, hyperlinking, and sharing works online.[332]

On the other hand, many digital cultural and information artefacts qualify for copyright protection.[333] However, through broad interpretation of exclusive rights and strict interpretation of limitations, EU copyright law restricts the space available for non-commercial use of works that would potential qualify as a legitimate exercise of freedom of expression and information. The result is a conflict between fundamental rights.[334] If a statutory licence ACS assists in resolving the conflict, it may find a policy justification in this fundamental freedom.

To understand the operation of freedom of expression as a limit on the scope of copyright protection it is instructive to briefly examine judgments from the ECtHR and CJEU.[335] In ECtHR case law, exceptions to freedom of expression, including those imposed by copyright, are subject to strict interpretation.[336] A decision or sanction for copyright infringement that restricts a person or organisation's freedom of expression must not only refer to an unauthorised and unprivileged use, but also 'be pertinently motivated as being necessary in a democratic society, apart from being prescribed by law and pursuing a legitimate aim'.[337]

In *Ashby Donald* and *The Pirate Bay*, the ECtHR interprets freedom of expression and information as an external limit to copyright capable of justifying infringing uses of works, even on a for-profit basis.[338] This consideration implies a reversal in the traditional analysis of restrictions to copyright as derogations to a general principle of exclusivity. In the ECHR

330. Article 19, 2013, p. 7. Cf. ECtHR, *Yildirim v. Turkey*, ¶54.
331. Article 19, 2013, p. 13.
332. European Copyright Society, 2013; Lee, 2015, pp. 16–17.
333. Favale, 2012, pp. 14–16; Lee, 2015, pp. 12–13.
334. *See supra* 4.4.1.4, 4.4.4.1, and 4.4.4.3. On freedom of expression and UGC, see, e.g., Lee, 2015, p. 16.
335. As noted in Chapter 1, the EU fundamental rights framework includes principles derived from the ECHR, some of which are codified in the Charter, thus justifying the reference to it and to ECtHR judgments. *See supra* 1.3.
336. European Copyright Society, 2014b, p. 6, with further references. *See also* Article 19, 2013, p. 9.
337. Voorhoof & Høedt-Rasmussen, 2013. *See also* Geiger, 2014c, pp. 135–136; Geiger & Schönherr, 2014a, pp. 118–119, citing the ECtHR in *Pirate Bay* and *Ashby Donald* ('copyright law *as a derogation of the principle of freedom of expression* … needs to be prescribed by law and be necessary'). Cf. also Fischman Afori, 2014, p. 903.
338. N.B. in those judgments the infringing uses were *not* considered justified by freedom of expression.

framework, the exclusive right is perceived as 'an exception to a broader principle of freedom of use', which is the 'point of departure' of analysis.[339]

Ashby Donald offers further insight. It clarifies that the additional protection provided by Article 10 ECHR only attaches to 'expression and content contributing to an issue of public debate or a debate of general interest for society' and not to commercial speech, i.e., '[s]peech, messages, pictures and content which are merely money driven'.[340] Although the ECtHR is not clear on the 'commerciality' criterion, it is at least apparent that expressions of a non-commercial character will fare better on a balancing test as justified restrictions on copyright.[341] Thus, it is arguable that some (certainly not all) instances of non-commercial online use of works may benefit from added-value protection provided by this fundamental freedom against copyright.

Based on ECtHR case law, some scholars argue that in conflicts between copyright and freedom of expression, the rights holder should bear the onus of showing that the restrictions operated by copyright are proportionate.[342] In this light, freedom of expression and information functions as a justification to redefine the boundaries of exclusivity.[343]

The interpretation of Article 11 Charter by the CJEU has significant parallels with that of the ECtHR. On an external level, the CJEU finds that freedom of expression and information imposes limits on remedies for copyright infringement, as illustrated by the restrictions on enforcement measures like filtering and blocking injunctions in *Scarlet Extended*, *Netlog*, and *UPC Telekabel*.[344] It is noteworthy in this respect that an increasing number of national courts interpret this fundamental freedom as a limit on exclusive rights.[345]

On an internal level, freedom of expression and information functions as a justification to broaden the scope of certain limitations, which would otherwise be inconsistent with this fundamental right and, by derivation, the objectives of the InfoSoc Directive. Chapter 4 explains and exemplifies this approach, patent in the CJEU's interpretation of the limitations of parody and quotation in *Deckmyn* and *Painer*.[346]

---

339. Geiger & Izyumenko, 2014, pp. 318–325, with analysis of the cases mentioned. *But see* Angelopoulos, 2015, p. 85, noting that neither case involved Internet users' rights.
340. Voorhoof & Høedt-Rasmussen, 2013.
341. Geiger & Izyumenko, 2014, pp. 322–323, 325–330.
342. The proportionality requirement would derive from the standard of 'necessary in a democratic society' in Art. 10(2) of the ECHR. *See* Angelopoulos, 2015, p. 82; Lee, 2015, p. 22, with further references.
343. Geiger & Izyumenko, 2014, p. 333.
344. CJEU, *Scarlet Extended*, paras 43, 50, 52–53; CJEU, *Netlog*, paras 41–43, 48, 50–51; CJEU, *UPC Telekabel*, paras 46–47, 55–57.
345. Favale, 2012, p. 15; Geiger & Izyumenko, 2014, p. 324; Lee, 2015 with further references.
346. *See* the discussion *supra* at 4.4.1.4, 4.4.4.1, and 4.4.4.3. *See also* European Copyright Society, 2014b, pp. 4–7.

For the purposes of this book, the core fundamental rights tension susceptible of offering a justification for a statutory licence ACS concerns the application of enforcement measures to non-commercial file sharing.[347] To illustrate this tension and the risk of disproportionate restrictions to freedom of expression and information, two remedies may be singled out: disconnection of access to the Internet, and filtering or blocking injunctions.

Disconnection from access to the Internet is usually discussed in the context of graduated response systems, although it may also be imposed through injunctions based on Article 8(3) InfoSoc Directive.[348] In either scenario, the measure has the potential to impose disproportionate restrictions on freedom of expression.[349]

The issue first came up in France. In a 2009 decision, the French Constitutional Council used freedom of expression and information to qualify Internet access as a fundamental right and reject the first iteration of the so-called HADOPI law, which allowed for individual subscribers to be disconnected from the Internet without prior judicial review.[350] The French Constitutional Council stated that:

> in the current state of online means of communications and in light of the importance that these services have acquired for participation in democratic life and the expression of ideas and opinions, the right of freedom of expression implies the freedom of access to these services.[351]

As a result, in 2013 France passed a law prohibiting Internet disconnection as a sanction for copyright infringement.[352] The reasoning of the French court captures the importance of free access to Internet services in

---

347. Article 19, 2013, pp. 15–18; Mazziotti, 2013, p. 133; Shaheed, 2014, p. 11.
348. Husovec & Peguera, 2015.
349. Article 19, 2013, p. 15.
350. French Constitutional Council, 10.06.2009, Decision 2009-580DC, J.O. 9675 ('Loi favorisant la diffusion et la protection de la création sur internet'), referring to Law No. 2009-669 of 12 June 2009, promoting the Dissemination and Protection of Creation on the Internet, which set up the *Haute Autorité pour la Diffusion des œuvres et la Protection des droits d'auteur sur Internet* (HADOPI). The legal basis for the decision was the embodiment of the right of freedom of expression in Art. 11 of the French Declaration of Human Rights of 1789. For the second iteration of the HADOPI law, *see* Law No. 2009-1311 of 28 October 2009. On the topic, *see* Geiger, 2011, p. 466–ff. *See also* Lucchi, 2011, with an analysis of the HADOPI decision and legislative changes in light of the constitutional concept of freedom of speech, including Internet access.
351. French Constitutional Council, 10.06.2009, Decision 2009-580DC, J.O. 9675 ('Loi favorisant la diffusion et la protection de la création sur internet'), para. 12 (WIPO Translation). Cf. Geiger, 2014a, pp. 8–9 & n. 38. *See also* Geiger, 2014c, pp. 136–137, noting that the French Constitutional Council rejected a purely administrative solution and required judicial intervention sanctioning any penalty of Internet disconnection.
352. Geiger, 2014c, p. 137, referring to Decree No. 2013-596 of 8 July 2013, removing the Complementary Penalty of Suspending Access to an On-Line Public Communication Service and relating to the Information Transmission Methods provided for in Art. L331-21 of the French Intellectual Property Code.

light of this fundamental right. It also seems to imply a value judgment favouring the preservation of freedom for online exchange of content embodying ideas and opinions.

The European Parliament supported an identical view in a 2010 resolution, adopted in the context of the Anti-Counterfeiting Trade Agreement (ACTA) negotiations. The resolution stated the need for judicial examination prior to any termination of users' access to the Internet 'in order to respect fundamental rights, such as the right to freedom of expression and privacy'.[353]

Article 1(3)(a) Framework Directive endorses this view in EU law. It imposes an obligation on Member States implementing measures that may restrict access and use by end-users of electronic communications networks, for example through a graduated response system. The obligation is to 'guarantee to the affected parties a prior, fair and impartial procedure and an effective and timely judicial review'[354] in conformity with the ECHR, fundamental freedoms and general principles of Community law.[355]

Similar arguments apply when considering Article 8(3) InfoSoc Directive as a valid ground for injunctions to order ISPs to disconnect allegedly infringing providers from Internet access. As argued by Husovec and Peguera, injunctions of this type raise issues of compatibility with the Charter and the ECHR, even when their effectiveness is low due to the possibility that users switch providers or obtain online access from a public space. Thus, the authors conclude, 'it seems unlikely that this form of relief may end up being an attractive and effective tool to curb online infringement.'[356]

Serious freedom of expression concerns may also arise from a different type of injunction, notably filtering and blocking. Critics of these measures state that they lack effectiveness and pose serious risks, such as general monitoring and over-blocking. For example, blocking access to content or imposing a filtering system may hinder users' right to receive information, and interfere with website operators or targeted ISPs' freedom of expression.[357]

In *UPC Telekabel*, the CJEU showed openness to blocking injunctions that allow intermediaries to choose which measure to apply so long as the ISP *itself* strikes a fair balance between competing fundamental rights. The

353. EP Resolution on ACTA Negotiations 2010, para. 11.
354. Mazziotti, 2013, pp. 134–135.
355. Art. 1(3) Framework Directive, as amended by Directive 2009/140/EC during the 2009 revision of the Telecoms Package. *See also* Husovec & Peguera, 2015, pp. 30–31.
356. Husovec & Peguera, 2015, p. 36.
357. Council Guidelines on Freedom of Expression 2014, 18. Cf. Article 19, 2013, pp. 15–18; Husovec & Peguera, 2015, pp. 31–32, 35; Lee, 2015, pp. 17–20; Mazziotti, 2013, pp. 133–136. *See also* Angelopoulos, 2015, pp. 88–90, noting that filtering systems are likely to fail the fair balance test due to their propensity to involve general monitoring of uses, as well as the risks of over-blocking.

Court stated that in the implementation of an injunction the ISP must 'ensure compliance with the fundamental right of internet users to freedom of information', *inter alia* by adopting strictly targeted measures and subjecting them to immediate judicial review.[358] To strike a fair balance, the ISP must meet two conditions. First, Internet users cannot be deprived unnecessarily of the 'possibility of accessing the information available'.[359] Second, the measures must have the effect of preventing unauthorised access to copyright works 'or, at least, of making it difficult to achieve and of seriously discouraging internet users' from accessing such works through the provider's services.[360]

As noted by Angelopoulos, this case and its effects would 'not easily be reproduced' outside its native jurisdiction of Austria, due to the idiosyncratic nature of the injunctive order at stake. Still, the case illustrates the ease with which the CJEU shifted the responsibility of striking a fair balance from the national courts to intermediaries. The result is further legal uncertainty, opening the door for potential violation of the fundamental freedom of information of Internet users.[361]

The link drawn between the right to Internet access and freedom of expression and information of individuals online is reminiscent of Fisher's main justification for an ACS, namely its potential to advance 'semiotic democracy'.[362] This concept relates to the ability to 'use and manipulate cultural artifacts … playfully or critically'[363] or the 'power to make cultural meanings'.[364] By extending this power to a more generalised group that includes end-users, the Internet generated a qualitative and quantitative improvement in semiotic democracy.[365] From this perspective, access to the Internet and the ability to engage with copyright works outside the market sphere are essential to democratic culture and free speech.

In sum, a statutory licence ACS may facilitate freedom of expression and information online, preventing some of the negative effects of the strict enforcement measures. In a best-case scenario, it will foster follow-on creativity, the personal enjoyment of cultural goods, semiotic democracy, and

358. CJEU, *UPC Telekabel*, paras 55–57.
359. *Ibid.*, paras 62–64.
360. *Ibid. See also* CJEU, *Mc Fadden*, para. 95, making a similar point while discussing a measure consisting in password protecting an Internet connection.
361. Angelopoulos, 2015, pp. 76, 88. An adjustment to this approach was suggested by AG – in his Opinion in *Mc Fadden*, according to which even for 'outcome' injunctions national Courts should first ensure the existence of appropriate measures to achieve the objective of the injunction in compliance with EU law. *See Opinion AG in Mc Fadden*, paras 119–124. However, the Court's ruling in *Mc Fadden* does not support such an adjustment in the same terms as the AG Opinion.
362. Fisher, 2004, pp. 28–31, 245.
363. Benkler, 2006, p. 275.
364. Fisher, 2004, p. 30; Fiske, 1987. *See also* Balkin, 2004; Elkin-Koren, 1996.
365. Benkler, 2006, p. 276.

the circulation of culture, information, ideas and opinions.[366] If it achieves these benefits and provides sufficient compensation to mitigate the financial harm caused to rights holders, an ACS will reflect a legitimate public interest based on freedom of expression and information, in a way that justifies the potential prejudice imposed on rights holders.[367]

5.3.3.6.2 Protection of Privacy and Personal Data

The fundamental rights to privacy and protection of personal data are guaranteed in the Charter and the ECHR.[368] CJEU case law on conflicts between these rights and copyright mostly relates to requests for injunctions by rights holders against ISPs pursuant to Article 8(3) InfoSoc Directive and Article 8 Enforcement Directive.[369] In general, these injunctions require gathering of evidence through the monitoring (e.g., via filtering systems) of electronic communications of allegedly infringing Internet users, and the collection and processing of their IP addresses.[370]

The right of information in Article 8 Enforcement Directive allows rights holders, following a justified and proportionate request, to obtain a judicial order directed at infringers or intermediaries to disclose 'information on the origin and distribution networks' of infringing goods and services. For the provision to apply, those goods of services must be provided on a 'commercial scale'. This requirement presents interpretative challenges, giving rise to distinct national implementations and judicial rulings.[371] For example, it is not clear whether commercial-scale includes mass non-commercial online use of works by individuals, such as high-volume uploads in a decentralised P2P network.[372]

One of the issues at stake on the intersection between copyright enforcement and the protection of privacy and personal data is that the injunction in question is aimed at IP addresses. Because these addresses qualify as personal data, the right of information in Article 8 Enforcement Directive must be applied without the prejudice of data protection rules on collection and processing in the Data Protection and E-Privacy Directives.

The CJEU tackled this issue in two very similar cases: *Promusicae* and *LSG*. The first case involved unauthorised P2P exchanges of works by ISP

366. Lee, 2015, pp. 16–17, discussing freedom of expression and file sharing.
367. Favale, 2012, p. 16, subscribing to the principle 'in dubio, pro libertate' postulated by Hoeren, 2006, pp. 26–27.
368. Arts 7 and 8 Charter, and Art. 8 ECHR.
369. See, e.g., CJEU, *Promusicae*, CJEU, *Scarlet Extended*, CJEU, *Netlog*, and CJEU, *Bonnier Audio*. The earliest CJEU decision on injunctions against intermediaries and enunciating the 'fair balance' principle was CJEU, *L'Oréal v. eBay*, concerning trademarks.
370. Mazziotti, 2013, pp. 138–139. *See* CJEU, *Scarlet Extended*, para. 51, classifying IP addresses as personal data because they allow for the precise identification of users.
371. Iglezakis, 2012; Mazziotti, 2013, p. 142.
372. Mazziotti, 2013, p. 140, suggests the provision would apply in this case.

subscribers. In it, the CMO Promusicae requested that an ISP disclose its clients' personal data on grounds of copyright infringement. The Court ruled that Member States may choose not to impose on ISPs an obligation to disclose their subscribers' personal data in the context of civil copyright cases, thus restricting the right of property in copyright in light of the right of privacy in electronic communications.[373] The CJEU further stated that where national legislators decide to implement such an obligation, the same should be proportionate and strike the required balance between property and the rights of privacy and personal data.[374] This means that any national procedures for effective enforcement must respect data protection rights of individual users of electronic communication services.[375] In essence, *LSG* reiterates this interpretation.[376]

In *Scarlet Extended* and *Netlog*, the CJEU examined the imposition through an injunction of filtering systems on, respectively, an Internet access provider and a hosting provider. The broad filtering injunctions requested were aimed at identifying works exchanged on the providers' networks for their subsequent blocking. As with *L'Oréal v. eBay* before, the Court confirmed that the general monitoring prohibition in Article 15 E-Commerce Directive does not permit active monitoring of all customer data from a provider.[377] Because filtering systems tend to require general monitoring of use, they likely violate the rights of privacy and personal data of a provider's customers, and as a result fail the fair balance test.[378]

Importantly, the CJEU follows the fair balance test whenever a conflict arises between copyright and privacy, even where the specific litigation does not touch upon the prohibition of general monitoring.[379] The Court's case law on this topic highlights the privacy risk of copyright enforcement, namely that available remedies become tools to monitor personal data and intrude on the privacy of telecommunications. That risk, it seems, lies primarily with measures going beyond the bounds of the legitimate purpose that justifies the treatment of personal data, without respect for the tests of proportionality and fair balance.

373. *See* CJEU, *Promusicae*, para. 53, deriving such right from Art. 15(1) E-Privacy Directive and Art. 13(1) Data Protection Directive.
374. CJEU, *Promusicae*, para. 53. *See also* Iglezakis, 2012.
375. Iglezakis, 2012.
376. For a description of *LSG*, *see* Frabboni, 2010, pp. 130–133.
377. Angelopoulos, 2013, 2015, pp. 74–76.
378. Angelopoulos, 2015, pp. 88–89.
379. CJEU, *Promusicae*, para. 68; CJEU, *LSG*, paras 28–29; CJEU, *Scarlet Extended*, paras 43, 45; CJEU, *Netlog*, paras 41, 43; CJEU, *UPC Telekabel*, paras 46–47. *See*, however CJEU, *Bonnier Audio*, paras 55–57, reaching a different 'fair balance' between privacy and copyright. For criticism, *see* Sganga, 2015, p. 13. N.B. in France, the issue of incompatibility of HADOPI's graduated response system with the right of privacy was a central topic of discussion. Cf. Geiger, 2014c, p. 135 & n. 94, making a connection with the CJEU's consideration of the right of privacy in *Promusicae*.

The examination of existing judgments suggests that the main areas of concern are over broad filtering injunctions and, in the opinion of some authors, graduated response systems that require the processing of IP addresses to deal with infringing users.[380] In this light, the question arises whether the potential encroachment on an individual's private sphere is fair, adequate and suitable in relation to the non-commercial use of works to be licensed through an ACS.

It is difficult to respond in the affirmative. The privacy risks involved in strict enforcement measures seem high vis-à-vis non-commercial use, and perhaps unjustified if an alternative model has the potential to ensure remuneration for the same activities. Of course, for this trade-off to make sense, the design of the statutory licence system ought to respect the privacy of users in electronic communications and prohibit any processing of personal data outside a legitimate purpose. For example, such a system should guarantee that monitoring of online exchanges is anonymous, with the sole purpose of enabling collection and distribution of rights revenue.[381] The system should also prevent that end-users are allowed to pay with personal data as a counter-performance or consideration for the authorisation to use works, a method of payment recognised in the proposed Digital Content Directive.[382] If these requirements are met, an ACS could cater to the public interest in a way similar to that of private copying since its inception – by providing an alternative to strict enforcement for acts in relation to which individuals have a legitimate interest in the respect of privacy and personal data.[383]

5.3.3.6.3 Intermediaries and Freedom to Conduct a Business

Limitations have economic value to certain businesses, which rely on privileged uses to generate revenue. This is true even for compensated limitations, due to savings in search, negotiation and litigation costs.[384] Online intermediaries may therefore benefit indirectly from the limitation for non-commercial use introduced by a statutory licence ACS. However, at least ISPs may suffer prejudice from such a system if they are designated intermediate debtors of the broadband levy. It is therefore important to consider their legitimate interests in the balancing exercise of the third step.

380. Mazziotti, 2013, p. 139. Whether targeted monitoring constitutes an acceptable measure must be assessed on a case-by-case basis.
381. *See supra* 3.4.4, on ACS proposals emphasising the importance of a privacy respecting design.
382. *See* Arts 3 and 13 of the Proposal for a Directive of the European Parliament and the Council on certain aspects concerning contracts for the supply of digital content, COM/2015/0634 final – 2015/0287 (COD).
383. *See supra* 2.3, on the privacy underpinning of private copying.
384. Geiger, 2010, p. 526, noting that these businesses are sometimes called 'added-value services'.

From a fundamental rights perspective, the obvious basis for such consideration is Article 16 Charter. The provision recognises the fundamental freedom to conduct a business 'in accordance with Union law and national laws and practices', in light of its social function.[385] The CJEU defines this freedom as 'the right of any business to be able to freely use, within the limits of its liability for its own acts, the economic, technical and financial resources available to it'.[386] In its jurisprudence on the InfoSoc Directive, the Court further identifies this freedom as a limit on copyright, giving rise to the need to strike a fair balance between the rights of economic agents – broadcasting organisations, ISPs, hosting service providers – and the proprietary interests of rights holders.[387]

In *UPC Telekabel*, the CJEU stated that an injunction violates the freedom to conduct a business if it restricts the free use of the resources at the disposal of an ISP by obliging it to take measures representing a 'significant cost', having a 'considerable impact on the organisation of his activities', or requiring 'difficult and complex technical solutions'.[388] This begs the question of whether, in relation to the non commercial online use of works, a statutory licence ACS translates into a less costly and complex measure for online intermediaries than copyright enforcement through injunctions or graduated response systems.

In this respect, the Opinion of AG Szpunar in *Mc Fadden*, a case involving an operator of a Wi-Fi network, is instructive, especially as it concerns the scope of permissible injunctions.[389] The Opinion states that, when issuing an injunction against an intermediary service provider, national courts must ensure three requirements are met. First, the measures in question must comply with Article 3 Enforcement Directive; in particular, they should be effective, proportionate and dissuasive. Second, in accordance with Articles 12(3) and 15(1) E-Commerce Directive, these measures must be 'aimed at bringing a specific infringement to an end or preventing a specific infringement and … not entail a general obligation to monitor'. Third, 'that the application of the provisions mentioned, and of other detailed procedures laid down in national law', must achieve 'a fair balance between the relevant fundamental rights', namely freedom of expression and

385. Hins, 2014, pp. 669–670.
386. CJEU, *UPC Telekabel*, para. 49.
387. CJEU, *DR and TV2 Danmark*, para. 57, CJEU, *Scarlet Extended*, paras 45–46, 49; CJEU, *Netlog*, paras 44, 47, 51; CJEU, *UPC Telekabel*, paras 47–49. For an analysis of this fundamental right in relation to the so-called 'right to short reporting' in Art. 15(6) AVMS Directive, *see* the commentary of Hins, 2014, to CJEU, *Sky Österreich*. At the time of writing, the relevant pending case on this issue is CJEU, Reference for Preliminary Ruling, Case C-484/14, *Mc Fadden*, on which *see Opinion AG in Mc Fadden*.
388. CJEU, *UPC Telekabel*, para. 50.
389. *Opinion AG in Mc Fadden*, paras 105–150.

information, freedom to conduct a business, and copyright as property (Articles 11, 16 and 17(2) Charter).[390]

Applying these requirements, the AG found that none of the measures at stake in *Mc Fadden* were consistent with EU law, including (with relevance here) injunctions requiring Internet disconnection or broad filtering obligations.[391] The termination of Internet connection was found to be incompatible with the requirement of fair balance, 'since it compromises the essence of the freedom to conduct business of persons who, if only in ancillary fashion, pursue the economic activity of providing Internet access'. That measure is likewise inconsistent with Article 3 Enforcement Directive, as it creates a barrier to legitimate trade.[392] Furthermore, the examination of all communications passing through that Internet connection was considered to amount to a general monitoring obligation, and therefore be incompatible with Article 15(1) E-Commerce Directive.[393]

It is true that the CJEU in *Mc Fadden* ultimately ruled on the admissibility of an injunction consisting in password-protecting an Internet connection and requiring users reveal their identity in order to obtain the required password. However, the Court agreed with the AG in considering inadmissible measures consisting in monitoring all of the information transmitted through an Internet connection, as well as terminating that connection.[394]

In light of the above, broad copyright injunctions aimed at preventing mass online use of works may be inconsistent with the fundamental freedom to conduct a business, mainly due to the costs imposed on the activities of Internet intermediaries. In contrast, it can be argued that an ACS would bring benefits to intermediaries, both in enforcement savings and by opening up 'legal' space for provision of services aimed at facilitating lawful non-commercial use. Hence, and in the abstract, an ACS imposes lesser restrictions on the economic, technical and financial resources of intermediaries, as compared to strict enforcement measures, such as Internet disconnection and filtering injunctions.

Of course, this is not the whole story. Most legalisation proposals require the imposition of a levy on the Internet access subscription fee of households and include ISPs in the system. Therefore, at least for ISPs, an ACS imposes costs and, one might argue, a hindrance to their freedom to conduct a business.

De lege lata, ISPs do not engage in restricted acts and are not liable for the practices of end-users, despite being subject to injunctions. This makes

390. *Ibid.*, para. 115.

391. *Ibid.*, paras 125–130. On the issue of the password-protection of the Internet connection, *see ibid.*, paras 134–150.

392. *Ibid.*, para. 131.

393. *Ibid.*, para. 132.

394. CJEU, *Mc Fadden*, paras 86–101.

their voluntary participation in an ACS unlikely. However, that participation is crucial to ensure effectiveness of the system, and would likely be required, *de lege ferenda*.[395]

ISP involvement in an ACS makes sense because it would be economically efficient. Not only does a (flat or metered) surcharge on the Internet subscription payment for households raise the least transaction costs among users, but it also facilitates the provision of adequate compensation to rights holders.[396] It is improbable that the ISP business model would suffer, as a reasonably priced subscription fee (i.e., a broadband levy lower than end-users' estimated willingness-to-pay) will probably not have strong adverse effects on demand for these services.[397]

From a fairness perspective, ISPs derive value from non-commercial exchanges of works, which significantly increase their traffic and demand for their services. ISPs can choose to pass on (at least part of) the levy or absorb it – while bundling it with other products – thereby having a competitive advantage to increase their subscription base; competition at this level benefits end-users.[398]

Through their inclusion in the system, ISPs should be involved in shaping it into a fair and efficient mechanism, together with CMOs and user representatives, under government and/or judicial supervision.[399] For example, these negotiations could define the fraction of the levy that ISPs may retain to cover their administrative costs.[400] If these costs are covered, participation of ISPs in an ACS should not impair their freedom to conduct a business, in the sense of *UPC Telekabel*.

Whether this is a better option than the status quo in light of ISPs' freedom to conduct a business is unclear. A correct answer would likely require empirical research into the costs of ISP participation in the system. However, it is important to note that the current policy orientation of EU institutions and industry stakeholders is towards increasing the role and collaboration of online intermediaries in enforcement measures, such as filtering and blocking, which entail costs and additional liability exposure for these intermediaries.[401] If such a future scenario materialises, ISPs may come to view ACS as a benign proposition.

---

395. Dusollier & Colin, 2011, p. 832, arguing that the most feasible contractual model is one 'in which P2P users contract with and pay fees to the CMOs'.
396. Handke et al., 2015, analysing the recorded music market in the Netherlands.
397. *Ibid.*
398. The possibility to pass on the levy is a feature of the private copying system. Cf. CJEU, *Padawan*, paras 46, 48. *See supra* 2.3.4, 3.4.6, and 4.4.3.
399. Colin, 2011a, pp. 78–91, 2011b, pp. 6, 11–12; Dusollier & Colin, 2011, p. 823.
400. Aigrain, 2008.
401. At institutional level, see: Communication E-Commerce and Online Services 2011, 13, p. 15; Communication IPR Strategy 2011, pp. 22–23; SWD E-Commerce Action Plan 2012–2015 – State of play 2013, pp. 17–18; Communication Digital Single Market 2015, pp. 7–8 (discussing a novel 'duty of care' on intermediaries), 11–12; SWD Digital

5.3.4 Summary: Application of the Three-Step Test

This paragraph summarises the main findings of each step's analysis and highlights the space available for a limitation-based statutory licence ACS in the *acquis* under the three-step test. A limitation is a certain special case if generally determinable, not overly broad, with a reasonably foreseeable scope of application, and justified on a sound policy basis. The first step should not be so strict as to foreclose a comprehensive overall assessment of a limitation pursuant to the subsequent steps.[402]

The scope of an ACS is delimited by several exclusions. The system only benefits natural persons, usually excludes different categories of works (at least software, videogames and databases[403]), commercial use of works, and non-commercial use already covered by existing limitations, like private copying, quotation, parody, and incidental inclusion.

Furthermore, an ACS has economic and non-economic motivations relevant for copyright policy. The economic motivations reflect a market failure argument stemming from the high transaction costs of imposing full exclusivity, individual management and enforcement on the non-commercial online use of works. The non-economic motivations concern the public interest dimension of an ACS. They range from the promotion of creativity and dissemination of knowledge, to the protection of the fundamental rights and freedoms of individuals (access to science and culture, privacy, personal data, and freedom of expression and information) and online service providers (freedom to conduct a business). The analysis of step three looks in detail at these motivations.

In sum, the above characteristics may be sufficient for a potential ACS to constitute a qualitative and quantitative 'certain special case' and meet the first condition of the test. However, doubts remain as to whether the exception is overly broad as it pertains to types of work and subject matter covered.

The traditional interpretation of the second step views 'normal exploitation' as an economic competition standard to judge the actual and potential impact of a limitation on the market. This standard compares the hypothetical

---

Single Market Strategy 2015, pp. 55–57; EP Resolution Implementation InfoSoc Directive 2015, para. 66 ('stresses the need to adjust the definition of the status of intermediary in the current digital environment'); Communication on Modern European Copyright Framework 2015, pp. 10–11. *See also* Giblin, 2014b, pp. 58–59, describing the enforcement strategy of the content industries since 2007 against online intermediaries.

402. Geiger, 2007b, p. 4; Geiger et al., 2008, p. 711; Hugenholtz & Okediji, 2008. *See also* Bernault & Lebois, 2005, p. 33, regarding the need to consider normative justifications, such as 'freedom of speech, information of the public, teaching and research. *But see* Griffiths, 2009, p. 20', doubting whether the test incorporates a standard of foreseeability.

403. *See supra* 3.4.1, identifying the subject matter scope of selected ACS proposals.

losses caused by a limitation to an idealised full exploitation of exclusive rights.

In a strict and sequential reading of the test, this traditional view prevents most online limitations from passing the second step. The result is to reject limitations irrespective of their policy rationales, remunerative potential, or consistency with the objectives of copyright. This interpretation likely precludes a limitation such as that envisioned here. However, by ignoring policy rationales, the traditional view may prevent a fair balance between the interests of copyright owners and the public interest. If this balance is one of the principal objectives of EU copyright law and the three-step test, it is worth exploring a flexible interpretation of the second step.

The flexible interpretation redefines normal exploitation and recognises the need to conduct a balancing exercise in the third step – the place to consider the non-economic motivations of a limitation – *regardless* of the results of the analysis in step two. This interpretation focuses on the effect of a limitation on the overall commercialisation of works. From this perspective, a conflict with the normal exploitation arises if a limitation deprives creators and exploiters of major and foreseeable sources of income under regular commercial circumstances. These sources of revenue include the online licensing of the exclusive rights of reproduction and communication to the public to commercial and end-users through digital download and streaming platforms. Excluded are uses already privileged in the *acquis* and *de minimis* uses.

A statutory licence ACS is aimed at non-commercial online use by individuals, which for the most part does not generate remuneration or is not exercised by copyright owners. In relation to this type of use, a statutory licence would create new rights revenue and constitute a normal form of exploitation, like other compensated limitations in EU copyright law. Regardless, relevant legal and empirical doubts subsist in relation to the compliance of an ACS with the second step. One main concern is with the (unknown) unintended adverse effects of such a system on the overall commercial exploitation of works. Another relates to the enforceability of exclusive rights against unauthorised for-profit commercial websites or platforms capable of impinging on the normal exploitation of works.

Empirically, the issue is whether legalisation causes users to abandon lawful channels. The magnitude of such a substitution effect is unknown. The best available proxy is the effect of unauthorised use on the market; on this, empirical research suggests that the long-term effect is uncertain. In addition, unauthorised websites/platforms subsist despite the steady growth of digital revenues and available enforcement measures. The result is that authorised and unauthorised channels already co-exist in the online environment. The implication is that an ACS will not replace the commercial market, but rather offer consumers an alternative means to access and use works beyond the constraints of territorial and substantive fragmentation of copyright.

However, if compliance with the second step hinges on the statutory licence preserving the economic core of the commercial exploitation of works, it should allow rights holders to enforce their copyright against unauthorised for-profit websites or platforms. This is especially true if those websites or platforms escape liability as a result of the adoption of a statutory licence.

The challenge, then, is to devise a system that preserves these enforcement avenues but still provides the legal authorisation for non-commercial acts by end-users and remuneration for copyright owners. One possible way to do so is to define the allowed non-commercial use strictly, expressly excluding online exchanges by platform operators against – or linked to – financial consideration. Another option, flowing from CJEU case law (especially after *GS Media* and relying on its knowledge test) is to define the scope of the right of communication to the public so as to include unauthorised acts of for-profit communication to the public by profit-making online platforms. This would cause the non-neutral and non-intermediary activities of such platforms to qualify as own use of copyright works, thereby excluding them from the benefit of the limitation.[404] A supplementary approach could be the institutional endorsement of self-regulation (of copyright owners and online intermediaries) aimed at enforcement against unauthorised for-profit third party websites or platforms.

If these scenarios are actualised, the scope of the statutory licence will only benefit end-users and a limited set of online intermediaries, namely those that enable or facilitate the licensed use but do not cross the 'non-neutral' Rubicon to own use territory. The licence would thus not affect the legal status of those mostly 'neutral' intermediaries and the possibility that they benefit from the E-Commerce Directive's liability exemptions in relation to their specific activities covered by those provisions. Other online intermediaries (or intermediary services) are outside the scope of the legalisation scheme. Thus, for-profit online platforms that make available works without the authorisation of rights holders (e.g., The Pirate Bay and Popcorn Time) will remain liable for copyright infringement and subject to strict enforcement measures. Of course, existing authorised commercial online service providers (e.g., Spotify and Netflix) will continue to require authorisation from rights holders to offer their services. The situation of content sharing and other hybrid platforms (e.g. YouTube) will depend on the legal status of their activities (own versus intermediary use), to be defined at

404. In this respect, *see also* the pending preliminary references: CJEU, Reference for Preliminary Ruling, Case C-527/15, *Filmspeler*; CJEU, Reference for Preliminary Ruling, Case C-610/15, *Stichting Brein v. Ziggo*. On the first case, *see Opinion AG in Filmspeler*.

judicial or legislative level.[405] An ACS can and should be calibrated to account for such adjustments.

De lege lata, only the circumscribed scope outlined here appears to enable a statutory licence ACS to avoid a conflict with the normal exploitation of works, even under a flexible reading of the second step.

The third step prevents limitations that cause an unreasonable prejudice to legitimate interests. This assessment requires a multi-level balancing exercise guided by the principle of proportionality. The exercise takes into account the reasonableness of the prejudice caused and attempts to strike a fair balance between interests viewed as lawful and justifiable on normative grounds.

It is necessary to assess the concurrent and opposing interests of creators and exploiters, on the one hand, and the individual and collective public interest – as manifested in the interests of third parties that are beneficiaries of the limitation – on the other. Although disputed, the consideration of third party interests seems aligned with the objectives of copyright law, and a corollary of the principle of fair balance in the InfoSoc Directive. In relation to a limitation-based statutory licence ACS, relevant public interests stem from the promotion of creativity and dissemination of works, and the protection of fundamental rights.

A limitation causes unreasonable prejudice if the harm suffered by rights holders from its introduction is out of proportion to the benefits derived by the public. The potential harm caused by an ACS refers primarily to its unintended adverse effects on the normal forms of exploitation of works online. Payment of fair compensation through a statutory licence is an acceptable means to reduce that harm to reasonable levels. The empirical research cited suggests that an ACS may provide sufficient revenue to compensate affected rights holders for non-commercial online use of works. However, the existing research has its limitations, making it crucial to examine the different policy arguments that justify the prejudice caused.

Creators and exploiters have conflicting interests. The main concern of creators is fair remuneration. Because remuneration is elusive in the digital environment, an unwaivable fair compensation right could be more favourable to creators than an assignable exclusive right. Conversely, exploiters typically have a bias against legalisation proposals; they prefer to maintain their exclusive rights and promote enforcement measures to reign in infringement.

In safeguarding the material interests and bargaining power of creators, a statutory licence system favours their interests over those of other rights holders in exclusivity and enforcement. This choice makes sense in the

405. *See*, in this respect, the different proposals by Kreutzer et al., 2016, French High Council for Literary and Artistic Property, 2016, and Leistner, 2016.

system of the test if the benefit to creators offsets the harm to exploiters, thereby reducing the prejudice to rights holders *as a whole* to tolerable levels.

Beyond the legitimate interests of creators in fair remuneration, the main justification for an ACS lies in its public interest dimension. Further to addressing a market failure in the regulation of mass-scale non-commercial use of copyright over the Internet, an ACS promises improvement over the status quo in the promotion of creativity and access to works, and thus the circulation of culture and knowledge online.

In addition, a well-designed statutory licence seems preferable to strict enforcement measures (filtering, blocking and Internet disconnection) in relation to the fundamental rights of Internet users to privacy in telecommunications, and freedom of expression and information online. It is also arguable that subjecting online intermediaries to injunctions and intermediary liability for their customers' non-commercial use may interfere with the fundamental freedom to conduct a business. In the specific case of ISPs, it is not clear if an ACS is a superior alternative to the status quo, as the system requires their participation in the system as intermediary debtors. However, if the system allows ISPs to recover their administrative costs and pass on the broadband levy to users, it should interfere less with this fundamental freedom than broad injunctions and participation in graduated response systems.

In conclusion, there are valid arguments to suggest that a fairly compensated limitation for non-commercial online use of works and the accompanying statutory licensing system are compliant with EU copyright law.[406] The option for an ACS rests on a fair balancing of interests that emphasises the public interest and fair compensation over exclusivity, and rests partly on the internal effect of fundamental rights in shaping the scope of copyright protection.

However, doubts linger as to whether such a system can overcome potential conflicts with the normal exploitation of works, even following a flexible reading of normal exploitation and the test as a whole. In other words, the proposed flexible reading is controversial, especially in light of some CJEU case law that posits a strict interpretation of limitations. Therefore, it is important to explore whether certain legal mechanisms can be combined with a statutory licence ACS to ensure that it overcomes potential conflicts with normal exploitation, thereby providing a more viable model of copyright reform.

---

406. For a number of authors, provided the fair compensation paid to rights holders covers their losses, the public interest motivation of an ACS-type limitation justifies restricting exclusivity under this step. *See* Bernault & Lebois, 2005, pp. 36–41; Geiger & Schönherr, 2014a, pp. 136–137; Peukert, 2005, p. 43.

5.4 OVERCOMING CONFLICTS WITH THE NORMAL EXPLOITATION OF WORKS

The main obstacle to the adoption of a limitation-based ACS in the *acquis* is step two of the test. The risk is that copyright owners' major sources of revenue suffer by the migration of users from online commercial channels to the new system. In this scenario, to ensure compliance with the three-step test, an ACS could contain rules to avoid a conflict with the normal exploitation of works. The taxonomy of ACS in Chapter 3 identifies mechanisms providing additional flexibility to legalisation schemes. Particularly promising are embargo periods and opt-out rules.[407] This section examines these mechanisms as supplements to a statutory licence ACS and their compliance with international and EU law in order to assess whether they may help overcoming potential conflicts with normal exploitation.

5.4.1 Embargo Periods

Embargo periods are rules that subject the availability of works to a temporal condition. For example, in the field of academic publishing, an embargo period refers to a situation where an article is first available for paid online subscription and only later on open access. In that contractual context, this period of embargo corresponds to the amount of time required for journals to 'deliver value to subscribing customers before a manuscript becomes available for free to the public'; the period 'begins from the date the article is formally published online in its final and fully citable form (i.e., online publication date).'[408]

An example of an embargo period in copyright law is found in Article 38(4) of the German Copyright Act. This provision allows authors of scientific contributions resulting from 'a research activity publicly funded by at least fifty percent' previously published in some types of periodic publication, 'to make the contribution available to the public in the accepted manuscript version upon expiry of 12 months after first publication'. The subsequent open access publication cannot be for a commercial purpose and must indicate the source of the first publication.[409]

In relation to copyright limitations, an embargo period is a legal rule that causes a limitation to come into effect after a period of time has elapsed from the first lawful publication or making available of the work.[410] Thus, an

407. *See supra* 3.3.3 and 3.4.1. *See also* Senftleben, 2014, pp. 10–18, for an analysis of embargo periods and 'opt-out formalities' in the context of the test.

408. Elsevier, *Journals*, *Poetics*, *Open access options*, *Embargo Period*, https://www.elsevier.com/journals/poetics/0304-422X/open-access-options#fee (accessed 31.01.2017).

409. Peukert, 2015, p. 383.

410. Senftleben, 2014, p. 10.

'embargoed limitation' functions as a procrastinated statutory licence (*see* Figure 5.1). Ideally, the limitation comes into force after a grace period corresponding to the normal exploitation of works, thereby avoiding conflicts with the second step of the test.[411]

Figure 5.1 Embargo Period Alternative Compensation System

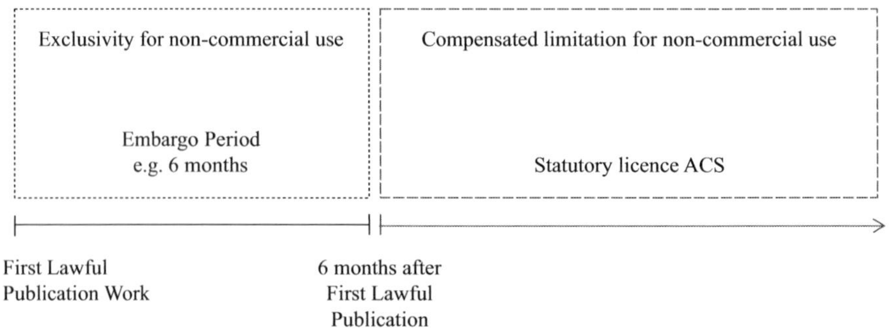

For example, if an ACS has an embargo period of six months, end-users are only free to exchange a film online six months after its release date. Downloading or making the work available before that date amounts to copyright infringement.

A rule of this nature could assist in overcoming conflicts with the normal exploitation by preventing or significantly reducing harm to rights holders during the period in which they extract the most rights revenues from the online exploitation of works. With a properly defined period, the risk of a limitation conflicting with significant online sources of revenue is low. In the example above, if a film makes most of its revenue in the months following release, the embargo period ensures that during those months the work benefits from full exclusivity, even for non-commercial online use.

Is such a rule consistent with international and EU law?

The preparatory works of the BC do not mention embargo periods, so there is no historical argument that prevents their consideration as a means to overcome conflicts in step two of the test.[412] In addition, normal exploitation refers to significant or tangible rights revenue for use of considerable economic significance. If the major sources of revenue from exploitation are reaped in the months following commercial release, a rule that preserves their integrity should be legally acceptable.[413]

There are no clear-cut examples of embargo period rules in the EU *acquis*. However, Senftleben sees the outline of such a rule attached to the

411. *Ibid.*
412. As noted above, such an argument is often made in relation to equitable remuneration. *See supra* 5.3.2.3 and 5.3.3.1.
413. Senftleben, 2014, pp. 10–11.

limitation that permits certain uses of orphan works by qualified institutions on the condition that the rights holder is not found after a diligent search.[414] In his opinion, the orphaned status of a work, the failure to find the rights holder, and the application of the limitation, are all unlikely to occur during the period of normal exploitation.[415] Furthermore, the rights holder can choose to put an end to the orphan work status and receive fair compensation for the privileged uses.[416] Drawing on the mechanism in the Orphan Works Directive, Senftleben considers embargo periods as flexible tools to allow digital use in compliance with the three-step test. To that effect, he recommends their adoption for mass digitisation projects and UGC.[417]

The literature on legalisation systems contains proposals for embargo periods on audio-visual works.[418] These proposals build on existing practices in the EU to organise film exploitation chronologically in a system of release windows. Applied to a limitation-based ACS, the embargo period could correspond to an EU-wide release window permitting online non-commercial use of works after their first commercial release or online availability. The system could extend to one or more types of work, depending on the potential impact of the limitation on their normal exploitation. The specifics ought to be subject to periodically reviewed stakeholder agreements. In particular, the duration of the embargo should allow for the preservation of the core exploitation of a work following its release on the market affected by the limitation. In this way, the ACS would prevent cannibalisation of major revenue sources and aspire to monetise the long tail of works.[419]

A rule of this type may have additional (and unintended) benefits. One is to incentivise clearance of rights for multi-territorial commercial exploitation of works in the EU, which would be advantageous to rights holders and consumers.[420] Another is that coupling a statutory licence with such a rule could offer partial relief to the access problems created by the excessive term of protection, at least for end-users.[421]

However, despite the potential benefits, an embargo period rule is not without its problems. On the one hand, it is probably too simplistic to assume that a 'one-size-fits-all' embargo rule makes sense for all types of work

414. *Ibid.*, p. 11, referring to Arts 3 and 6 Orphan Works Directive.
415. *Ibid.*
416. Art. 6(5) Orphan Works Directive.
417. Senftleben, 2014, p. 12.
418. *See, e.g.*, Creation-public-internet, 2011; L'ALLIANCE public.artistes, 2006b, 2006c.
419. With similar proposals, *see* Kamina, 2012; L'ALLIANCE public.artistes, 2005; Modot et al., 2011, p. 14.
420. Mazziotti, 2013, pp. 59–67, discussing several policy options to create a digital single market for audio-visual content.
421. *See* Peukert, 2005, p. 56, making a similar argument in favour of his bipolar copyright system. *See also* Senftleben, 2014, p. 11.

covered by an ACS. Assuming that differentiated embargo rules per category of work are more suitable, it may be difficult to implement a system that is comprehensible for end-users across different EU Member States, even assuming they are aware of it (many will probably not be). For example, it will already be difficult for users to identify the release or making available date of a sound recording for the purposes of calculating when an embargo period elapses; asking them in addition to calculate different embargo periods for music, films, and e-books is likely too cumbersome. The legal certainty issues here are problematic.

On the other hand, it is fair to wonder whether end-users are willing to accept and pay for an ACS with embargo periods. A statutory licence of this type hopes to solve *inter alia* the problem of large-scale copyright infringement, a substantial amount of which seems to refer to newly released works. Would users accept an embargo rule preventing them from access to these works? Or, assuming awareness of the rule, would they disregard it, continuing to unlawfully download and share these works?

Perhaps surprisingly, at least one study shows consumers are willing to accept a licence including some sort of temporal restrictions on access to catalogues of at least recorded music and audio-visual content, if the price is right.[422] However, without further empirical research on specific designs for an embargo period rule and its EU-wide application, it is not possible to be certain on this point. In particular, it is unclear whether such a rule would in fact contribute to the decline of unauthorised file sharing for the period of its duration. Unless that is the case, the addition of such a rule to a statutory licence will fail to prevent an existing conflict with the normal exploitation of works.

5.4.2 Opt-Out Rules

In an ACS with an opt-out rule, the non-commercial use of works is subject to a statutory licence and the copyright owner is entitled to opt out of a regime where the same use is subject to exclusivity. The opt-out allows rights holders to switch from a liability rule to a property rule for the type of use in question. The choice of rule, through action or omission, makes the ACS optional for rights holders.[423]

422. Handke et al., 2015. The specific length of the temporal restriction was not defined, with participants instead being informed through a tooltip that 'some rights holders prefer to wait with the online release of their works till they have broken even through other channels. A certain time after their release, all works will be available in the system, but using them before that is illegal'. (Translated from Dutch.)

423. Proposals of this type include Eckersley, 2004; Fisher, 2004; Gratz, 2004; Litman, 2004; Partido Comunista Português (Grupo Parlamentar), 2012; Peukert, 2005.

5.4.2.1 Opt-Out Rules and Alternative Compensation Systems

An opt-out rule allows rights holders to render a limitation inapplicable to their works through a reservation of rights. The textbook example in international copyright law is Article 10*bis*(1) BC, which allows legislators to impose an uncompensated exception for reproduction, broadcasting and communication to the public of certain articles and broadcast works. These uses correspond to normal forms of exploitation of the works in question. The BC provision allows copyright owners to reserve their rights in relation to the initial exploitation period, applying to 'the use of fresh articles with news value'. This can be done, for example, through a statement in a published article similar to 'all rights reserved', as prescribed for in German copyright law.[424] By allowing a reservation of rights during the period of normal exploitation, the rule mitigates the potential for conflict under the second step of the test.[425]

The limitation in Article 10*bis*(1) BC is justified on the freedom of the press, and has a strong public interest dimension. That justification has allowed the rule to survive challenges during the 1967 revision conference in Stockholm and to this day.[426] The TRIPS and the WCT incorporate the BC provision and subject it to the respective three-step tests. At no time during the negotiation of those treaties was the consistency of Article 10*bis*(1) BC with the second step challenged, a fact some authors attribute specifically to the reservation of rights rule.[427]

In light of this international framework, Senftleben proposes the adoption of opt-out rules for new online limitations applicable to search engine services and UGC. In his view, these rules would make the limitations legally admissible and provide the policy benefit of examining rights holders' perception of the effects of the exemption on the normal exploitation of works.[428]

In the realm of ACS, proposals containing opt-out rules vary in the detail they offer. Most leave the design of the rule to further legislative action or administrative acts of a central agency, the mandated CMO, or stakeholder agreement.[429] Eckersley suggests an opt-out right for creators in his 'virtual market system' as a solution to overcoming potential vulnerabilities related

424. Peukert, 2005, p. 66.
425. Senftleben, 2014, pp. 12–14, with a historical background of Art. 10*bis*(1) BC.
426. Ricketson & Ginsburg, 2006, pp. 796–799.
427. Senftleben, 2014, p. 14.
428. *Ibid.*, pp. 14–15, proposing that search engines are allowed to provide image searches of copyright works by default, while preserving the possibility to use technical tools to exclude the work *a posteriori*. For an argument against the admissibility of opt-out to make a limitation compliant with the test, also in light of BC's no formalities proviso, *see* Ginsburg, 2013, pp. 1604–1611.
429. See, e.g., Beltrandi et al., 2008, 2007; Dimita, 2010; Partido Comunista Português (Grupo Parlamentar), 2012; Rocha, 2010.

to government dependence for income.[430] Fisher's 'tax-and-reward system' allows rights holders to opt out by releasing a work solely with TPMs, which retain legal protection.[431] Rights holders are allowed a 'digital reservation of rights' for adaptations, by excluding the right to prepare derivative works when registering works in the system.[432] In Baker's system, the opt-out rule requires that beneficiaries can only exit after a certain amount of time from the last payment of compensation.[433]

One of the most detailed schemes is advanced by Litman. Her notice based opt-out mechanism requires the work to be in a specific DRM format, as well as 'affirmative but relatively modest steps' from the rights holder to exclude it from the system and inform consumers of the status change through electronic rights management information. Works only made available online 'under the copyright owners' authority' with that '*.drm' digital file format would be 'ineligible for sharing or compensation'; to opt back into the system, owners would need only to release the work again without such a format.[434] Works already released are subject to a 'presumption of shareability' in favour of users. Furthermore, to remove incentives to opt out, the process of withdrawing a work from the licence is purposefully burdensome.[435]

Figure 5.2 illustrates the basic workings of an opt-out rule in a statutory licence ACS where the liability rule is the default regulation for non-commercial use, including the necessary grace period between opt-out and its effectiveness.

430. Eckersley, 2004, pp. 164–165.
431. Fisher, 2004, pp. 247–248. Fisher's expectation is that his tax and reward system generates greater revenues and thus convinces rights holders to release works without technical protection.
432. *Ibid.*, p. 242: 'By checking a box on the registration form, registrants could retain the entitlements they currently enjoy to control the preparation of derivative works (entitlements qualified, of course, by the fair-use doctrine).'
433. Baker, 2003.
434. Litman, 2004, pp. 45–47.
435. *Ibid.*, p. 48. The process would require consensus from all owners, involve recalling the work in non-'*.drm' format, a 24 month grace period to produce legal effects and, at the infringement level, the burden of proof that consumers had knowledge of the withdrawal. *See also* Gratz, 2004, pp. 421–423.

Figure 5.2 Opt-Out Rule in Statutory Licence Alternative Compensation System

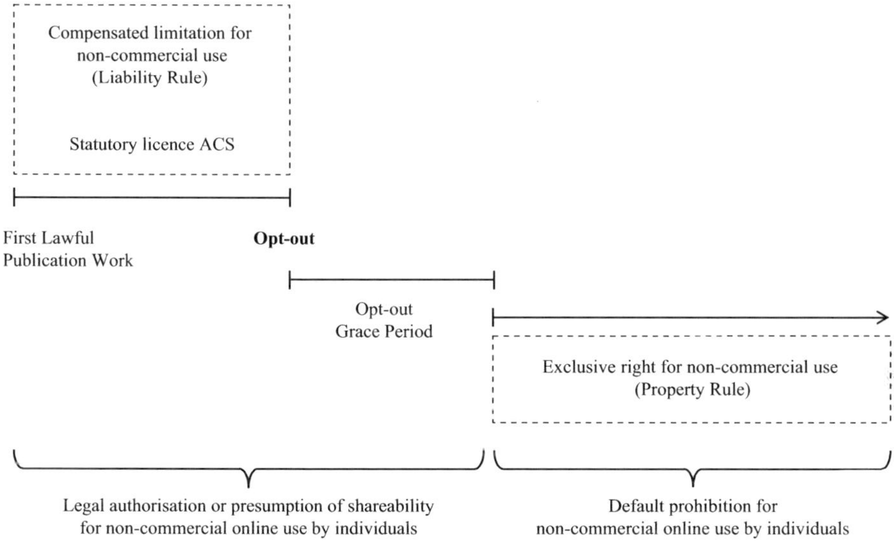

From the perspective of normal exploitation, the possibility of opting out restores legal exclusivity, either at the time of online availability of the work or later. As Sprigman puts it, even if the liability rule is set up as the default, the requirement for 'authors to opt out to preserve their ability to exploit the property rule' means that 'the system – unlike the usual system of compulsory licenses – is still voluntary' because it merely extends the rights holder's options for exploitation.[436] By placing rights holders in an identical situation to the status quo as from the effective date of withdrawal, the opt-out rule mitigates the risk of violating step two of the test.

Nevertheless, the opt-out variant of ACS is not immune to criticism. If the legal default is a liability rule as from the first lawful publication of a work, the ACS will regulate non-commercial use of works during the initial – typically more profitable – period of exploitation. To prevent potential economic harm, rights holders may opt out of the system. However, it may be impossible to avoid a conflict with the normal exploitation if the opt-out process is too cumbersome, or if the grace period between withdrawal and its effectiveness is too long.[437]

One solution is to implement a streamlined and relatively short grace period, making the opt-out as simple as possible for rights holders. To that effect, the rule could follow the best practices from the field of ECL and the

436. Sprigman, 2004, p. 557.
437. For works made available online before the licence is implemented, it would be necessary to recognise a legislative transitional period where rights holders can opt out before the limitation comes into force.

on-going national implementation of Article 5 Orphan Works Directive.[438] Ideally, an opt-out rule should deal efficiently with challenges related to fragmented ownership of copyright, especially in the film and music sectors.

The downside of an effective opt-out is that it provides a strong incentive for rights holders to exercise it, diminishing the attractiveness of the ACS for end-users. In addition, users would be subject to legal uncertainty and increased exposure to liability, as it would be difficult to identify works withdrawn from the system.

Different measures could mitigate these problems. First, the system could ensure that information on works, and names and contact details of the rights holder opting out is recorded in a publicly accessible database.[439] Rights holders could be required to give constructive notice of withdrawal through a simplified one-time declaration effective in all Member States, registered on publicly accessible databases (either by rights holders or the responsible CMO), and possibly signal their choice through DRM on digital copies of works.[440]

In particular, incentivising the accessibility of opt-out information in a publicly accessible online registry contributes to the effectiveness and fairness of the system, by ensuring that reference is made to the work itself (instead of a specific copy thereof), and that users are informed.[441]

To protect good faith end-users, the system should recognise a reasonable grace period between the moment of opt-out and effective exclusion of a work from the ACS.[442] Users would not be liable for use prior to the effective date of opt-out, as the same is covered by a statutory licence and subject to fair compensation (*see* Figure 5.2).

Even then, the solution may remain unattractive to users if a great number of rights holders choose to withdraw their most popular works from the system. To curtail this risk, it is possible to introduce embargo periods that disincentivise early opt-out from the ACS. However, such a solution

438. Senftleben, 2014, pp. 15–16. On the desirability that prospective formalities be simple, universally applicable and affordable, *see* van Gompel, 2011, pp. 297–298. *See also* Carroll, 2013, p. 1523, arguing that in a dynamic interpretation of BC a formality that is easy to comply with in the digital environment – e.g. a mandatory notice or registration formality – is not prohibited.

439. *See* Eechoud et al., 2009, p. 280 & n. 859, making the suggestion in relation to ECL in general. In this respect, any limitations applicable to making the personal data of authors and copyright owners accessible to the public, for example by privacy regulations, must be respected. *See* van Gompel, 2013, p. 1429.

440. Litman, 2004, pp. 48–49 & n. 177, arguing that, under Art. 5(2) BC, 'it should be possible to establish an optional registry of withdrawn works, and provide that listing of a work on the registry for 24 months would allow the copyright owner to show constructive notice of withdrawal.' Failing that, the author suggests 'copyright owners suing for infringement of withdrawn works would need to prove actual notice.'

441. In this way the system would address the criticism levied at the proposals of Lessig and Sprigman by Dusollier, 2011, pp. 88–89.

442. Colin, 2011a, p. 96.

would introduce additional complexity to the management of the system, and suffer from the same problems raised above vis-à-vis embargo periods.[443]

5.4.2.2 Are Opt-Out Rules Prohibited Formalities?

In his objection to the opt-out variant of an ACS, Peukert ties the examination of normal exploitation to that of formalities, concluding that a violation of the test results from the qualification of opt-out rules as prohibited formalities.[444] It is worth exploring this critique, as it may prevent the adoption of an opt-out rule altogether.

Formalities aim at filtering protected from unprotected subject matter, clarifying subject matter and scope of protection, identifying subject matter and informing users of its existence, establishing a link between owners and protected works, and providing information on works, ownership and rights to third parties.[445] There are different types of formality, spanning registration of works, recordal of transfers of copyright ownership, notice requirements, and deposit of works.[446]

Article 5(2) BC prohibits formalities that affect the 'enjoyment' or 'exercise' of protected rights in relation to non-domestic works. The prohibition is not absolute.[447] The *enjoyment* dimension relates to author's rights coming into existence and being recognised absent any formality. Enjoyment therefore means 'existence', including the coming into being and continuation of copyright.[448] The *exercise* dimension links to the possibility of enforcing rights.[449]

The term 'exercise' was introduced in the 1908 Berlin revision conference with the objective of clarifying that the prohibition extended beyond constitutive formalities to those that 'are prerequisites to sue', i.e., to initiate an enforcement action.[450] Hence, exercise is meant to preserve the 'process by which a liability finding is made' but not 'what follows from such a finding', namely the 'means of redress'.[451]

This meaning is different from the broader use of the term 'exercise' in this book, which also includes the transfer and management of copyright. Unsurprisingly, the term has given rise to problems of interpretation.[452] It is submitted that, *in the context of Article 5(2) BC*, prohibited formalities as to

443. *See supra* 5.4.1.
444. Peukert, 2005, pp. 58–75. Similarly, *see* Ginsburg, 2013, pp. 1604–1611.
445. van Gompel, 2011, pp. 31–52, 286–287, identifying the following functions of formalities: filtering, demarcation, signalling and publicity, evidentiary, and information.
446. van Gompel, 2011, pp. 15–27.
447. Gervais, 2010, pp. 22–27.
448. Ricketson & Ginsburg, 2006, pp. 323–325; van Gompel, 2011, p. 195.
449. Gervais, 2010; Ginsburg, 2013; Ricketson & Ginsburg, 2006; von Lewinski, 2008.
450. Dusollier, 2011, p. 92; Gervais, 2010, pp. 22–26; Ginsburg, 2013, pp. 1587, 1590; Ricketson & Ginsburg, 2006, pp. 323–326; van Gompel, 2011, pp. 200–201.
451. Sprigman, 2013, pp. 1570–1571.
452. Dusollier, 2011, pp. 87–93; van Gompel, 2011, p. 201.

'exercise' of rights refer solely to formal requirements on the initiation of enforcement of copyright.[453]

Consequently, banned formalities are those that relate to the 'coming into existence, the maintenance and enforcement of copyright', but not those that merely affect its options of exercise.[454] The prohibition includes mechanisms that prevent acquisition of protection or entail its loss 'during the existence of copyright'; in essence, the prohibition rules out constitutive and maintenance formalities in respect of works of non-domestic origin, as well as those that function as 'conditions to sue for infringement'.[455] Conversely, certain declaratory formalities are allowed, for example if they present only evidentiary or procedural advantages, operating as incentives rather than obligations.[456]

In ACS proposals, the possibility to opt out is typically exercised through so-called new-style formalities. These are 'legal tools that establish a link between works, their creators, and/or the current copyright owners', including 'metadata-tagging of digital works, the storage of rights management information in digital repositories', and other digital tools.[457]

One possibility consists of a reservation of rights attached to the digital copy of the work through electronic rights management information. Another consists of a simple declaration with the CMO in charge of the system, similar to the current operation of the mechanism in ECL. The declaration is then reflected on a publicly accessible database, signalling the status of works to users.[458]

These mechanisms do not impose conditions for the enjoyment or enforcement of copyright, but merely enable its exercise through collective management under the statutory default, or individual exercise (following opt-out).[459] They therefore allow for the efficiency benefits of collective licensing, while offering copyright owners the option to regain full exercise

453. van Gompel, 2011, pp. 200–212.

454. *Ibid.*, pp. 179–193, 212. *See also* Bernault & Lebois, 2005, pp. 55–56; Gervais, 2010, pp. 24–25; Senftleben, 2014, p. 15.

455. van Gompel, 2013, p. 1439. *See also* Ricketson & Ginsburg, 2006, pp. 325–327.

456. Ginsburg, 2013, pp. 1592–1600; van Gompel, 2013, p. 1439.

457. van Gompel, 2013, p. 1435. *See also* Sprigman, 2004, 2013, mentioning new-style formalities.

458. *See supra* 5.4.2.1., for a brief description of opt-out through new-style formalities. Gervais, 2010, pp. 25–27, suggested that the opt-out declaration can be as simple as an email. The author further notes that Art. 5(2) BC does not include 'all civic and judicial formalities' concerned with the exploitation of works, neither does it include formalities that are not government related, as would occur with those imposed by CMOs, which are mostly private entities. Therefore, the prohibition does not extend to the ECL opt-out feature.

459. Gervais, 2010, pp. 22–27, supporting his arguments on the basis of a thorough analysis of the drafting history of Art. 5(2) BC. *See also* Koskinen-Olsson, 2010, pp. 303–304, discussing the legislation in Denmark and arguing that the opt-out mechanism exists to ensure conformity with international treaties and EU directives.

and individual management of their rights.[460] In this sense, they constitute an additional Berne-compliant legal tool for the exploitation of copyright.[461]

However, not all opt-out rules have the same effect, making it necessary to draw a distinction between different types of ACS. In legalisation proposals that rely on ECL, the opt-out mechanism does not restore exclusivity. Instead, it offers copyright owners a choice between two models for exploitation of exclusive rights: collective versus individual. Thus, the opt-out regulates the extent of protection.[462]

The opt-out mechanism in a statutory licence ACS is different – the choice to exclude the work restores exclusivity (*see* Figure 5.2 above, signalling a switch from a liability to a property rule). For some authors, opt-out is only admissible where the limitation otherwise meets the conditions of the three-step test.[463] According to this school of thought, because the international system – and in particular the BC – is built to preserve exclusivity, the purpose of the test is only met if the exclusive right is 'the statutory default rule'.[464]

In this line, new-style formalities, such as opting-out through a DRM notice or requiring copyright owners to register works, relate to the 'genesis' and enforcement of the right. As a result, they are formalities 'for the enjoyment of minimum exclusive rights'.[465]

This position promotes exclusivity to a totemic status, mandating its default imposition even if detrimental to the interests of authors.[466] In doing so, such interpretation appears to conflate the tests applicable to formalities (Article 5(2) BC) and copyright limitations (Article 9(2) BC). Indeed, if a limitation passes the test, the discussion of opt-out becomes 'redundant' vis-à-vis its effects on exclusivity.[467] Only where the opt-out is the key feature that makes the limitation compliant with the test is the issue relevant.

From the conceptual standpoint, an opt-out is an internal condition akin to a method of exercising rights.[468] For statutory licences, it eases compliance with the three-step test by allowing owners to regain exclusivity, mitigating the effects of the limitation.[469] Article 10*bis*(1) BC provides a strong indicator that an opt-out right is an admissible means to make a

460. Colin, 2011a, pp. 56–63, 2011b, p. 4, referring to ECL.
461. van Gompel, 2011, p. 209, debating ECL.
462. Colin, 2011a, p. 62; Dusollier & Colin, 2011, p. 832; van Gompel, 2011, p. 190.
463. Ginsburg, 2013, p. 1606; Peukert, 2005, p. 65.
464. Peukert, 2005, pp. 61, 65–67.
465. *Ibid.*, pp. 65–67, concluding that both Litman and Fisher's opt-out models with default legal licences would violate Art. 5(2) BC. It is on this basis that Peukert proposes his opt in 'bipolar copyright system'. *See* Peukert, 2005, p. 69. *See also* Dusollier, 2011, p. 91, tentatively agreeing with Peukert, without however considering the possibility that such a limitation would be compliant with the three-step test.
466. Sprigman, 2004, pp. 558–560.
467. van Gompel, 2011, pp. 210–211.
468. Dusollier & Colin, 2011, pp. 831–832.
469. Senftleben, 2014; van Gompel, 2011, p. 211.

limitation compliant with the test, where otherwise it would not be. Both the opt-out right and the no formalities rule aim to protect authors and their ability to exploit works. If they share this rationale, adoption of an opt-out should not violate the prohibition on formalities.[470] Article 5(2) BC should therefore not impede a rule that allows authors to switch from a liability to a property rule.[471]

In sum, the BC prohibition on formalities does not prevent the adoption of an opt-out rule in a statutory licence system.[472] Such a rule is therefore consistent with international copyright law and may, in theory, help an ACS overcome conflicts with the normal exploitation of works. It is even conceivable that through a combination of CMO expertise, electronic rights management information, and publicly accessible databases, the system could be efficient, while providing legal certainty for copyright owners and users. However, the question that remains is whether the availability of such a tool would incentivise mass opt-out by rights holders, thereby reducing the ACS repertoire and, by extension, its value for end-users.[473]

5.5 THE NORMATIVE CHOICE BETWEEN EXCLUSIVITY AND REMUNERATED ACCESS

A choice between exclusivity and remuneration implies a normative reference point or benchmark. This book has argued that the current system falls short of meeting the objectives of EU copyright law as it concerns the regulation of non-commercial online use by individuals. The question therefore is how to rethink the *acquis* to adapt its rules to reflect those objectives.

The present section contains the second – and markedly normative – part of this chapter, which builds on the previous compliance analysis. It addresses the question of whether and to what extent a model of access and remuneration, such as an ACS, is consistent with the general aims of copyright and the objectives of EU copyright law. To answer the question, this section draws on and recasts the findings of this book to present a normative argument for a right of access and remuneration in relation to non-commercial online use of works in EU copyright law. The argument proceeds in three stages. The first stage takes a step back from the *acquis* and examines whether such a right is consistent with the dominant theories or rationales of copyright law; as Strowel puts it, 'in situations of uncertainty,

470. Senftleben, 2014, pp. 15–16. *Contra* Ginsburg, 2013, pp. 1604–1611.

471. Sprigman, 2004; van Gompel, 2011, p. 211.

472. Colin, 2011a, pp. 59–63, 2011b, p. 4; Dusollier & Colin, 2011, p. 832; Gervais, 2010. *See also* Sprigman, 2004, p. 568, referring to his proposal for new-style formalities.

473. *See supra* 3.3.3.2, pointing out this issue in relation to ACS proposals based on ECL.

there is a need to refer to the basic philosophy of copyright.'[474] The analysis pays particular attention to the natural rights and utilitarian arguments that form part of the European legal tradition, in order to present an argument about what the law should be (5.5.1). The second stage discusses why and how normative considerations support a right for access and remuneration for mass non-commercial use (5.5.2). The third stage assesses whether such a right is consistent with the objectives of EU copyright law (5.5.3).

5.5.1 Copyright Theories, Exclusivity and Remuneration

The literature on the foundations of copyright is vast and a proper review of the same is beyond the scope of this book. The objective of this section is to provide a brief overview of such theories and consider their value in determining the role of exclusivity, access, and remuneration in copyright protection. As the main research question of the book concerns EU copyright law, the focus is on the natural rights and utilitarian theories, which have the greatest relevance in the European legal tradition.

Theoretical attempts to justify copyright are derivations of more general theories of intellectual property, and property rights in general. These can be classified in four categories or clusters: utilitarianism or welfare, labour or fairness, personality or personhood, and culture or social planning.[475] This last theory, it is noted, is comparatively recent and is by far the least influential, especially in Europe. In their application to copyright, these theories provide both the rationale for protection and the meta-objectives of the copyright system.

All theories have a philosophical basis, sometimes dating back to the seventeenth century; the application of these theories to intellectual property and copyright, however, is much more recent.[476] The works of Bentham, Mill and Pigou influence utilitarianism.[477] Locke's theory of property in his 'Second Treatise of Civil Government' is the touchstone of the labour or

474. Strowel, 1994, p. 240.
475. Fisher, 2001. More recently, the same author has renamed these categories as welfare (previously utilitarianism), fairness (previously labour theory), personhood (previously personality theory), and culture (previously social planning). Cf. William Fisher, *Maps of Intellectual Property, Theories of IP*, http://cyber.law.harvard.edu/people/tfisher/IP/IPTheory.swf (accessed 31.01.2017).
476. See, e.g.: Fisher, 2001, Hughes, 1988 (on the Lockean and Hegelian theories), van Gompel, 2011, pp. 215–284 (on the fairness and personality theories), Goldstein & Hugenholtz, 2013, pp. 17–21 (briefly exploring the philosophical arguments underpinning the common law and civil law copyright traditions).
477. The reference works in this respect are Bentham's 'A Manual of Political Economy' (1800), Mill's 'Principles of Political Economy' (1848), and Pigou's 'The Economics of Welfare' (1920).

fairness theory.[478] The works of Kant, Fitche, and Hegel are the main inspiration for the personality theory.[479]

The utilitarian or welfare theory combines utilitarianism and economic analysis of law to make the general argument that copyright protection should have as a central objective the promotion of the social good through the creation and supply of works.[480]

The fairness theory contends that individuals are entitled to the fruits of their intellectual labour. In essence, this is a manifestation of a broader equity argument with ample support in Western culture, according to which individuals deserve 'a share of the fruits of a collective project proportionate to the magnitude of his or her contribution to the venture'.[481]

The personality theory understands intellectual creations as manifestations or even extensions of the creator's personality. In this conception, 'property provides a unique or especially suitable mechanism for self-actualisation, for personal expression, and for dignity and recognition as an individual person.'[482] Therefore, the approach of the fairness theory is oriented towards the object, whereas that of the personality theory is oriented to the subject.[483]

Both fairness and personality arguments are commonly placed under the umbrella of natural rights arguments for copyright protection, providing arguments for the protection of material and moral interests of creators respectively.[484] From a natural rights perspective, then, the law does not create a (positive) right but is rather a formal act of recognition of an existing (natural) right.[485]

The culture theory 'is rooted in the proposition that … intellectual-property rights … can and should be shaped so as to help foster the achievement of a just and attractive culture'.[486] This theory would likely support the adoption of an ACS for non-commercial online use of works.

---

478. Locke, 1988. Locke's reference work in this area dates from 1690. The most relevant part of his Second Treatise of Civil Government for our purposes is Chapter 5 ('Of property').
479. The reference works in this respect are Kant's 'On the Injustice of Reprinting Books' (1785), Fitche's 'Proof of the Illegality of Reprinting' (1793), and Hegel's 'Elements of the Philosophy of Rights' (1821).
480. Some authors distinguish these two arguments in their analysis. See, e.g., Guibault, 2002, pp. 10–15, treating separately the utilitarian and economic arguments.
481. William Fisher, *CopyrightX: Lecture 2.2, Fairness and Personality Theories: Fairness*, *https://www.youtube.com/watch?v=HYJuhPf9s5k&feature=youtu.be* (accessed 31.01.2017), referring to the modified form of the Equity Theory.
482. Hughes, 1988, p. 330. *See also* Geller, 1994, pp. 168–169, on Kant's general theory of authorship of norms.
483. van Gompel, 2011, p. 218.
484. Guibault, 2002, p. 8, refers to the 'personality rights' and 'reward' elements of the natural rights argument.
485. Ginsburg, 1994; van Gompel, 2011.
486. Fisher, 2001, p. 172.

Indeed, two scholars whose works are identified within this theory, William Fisher and Neil Netanel, are also early and influential proponents of ACS.[487] However, it is undeniable that the culture theory is of little application, influence or acceptance in European copyright law, policy or scholarship. Even in its native US, the application of this theory to copyright and its conceptual development are at an early stage. Therefore, it is not possible to classify it as a 'dominant' or 'influential' theory from which to derive rationales to assess an ACS, especially if the ultimate aim of the legalisation model is reform of EU copyright law.[488] This section will therefore not further examine the culture theory.

As we shall see, there is no *one true theory* that provides a full justification for intellectual property rights. Instead, it is common for law-making in this field to combine multiple theories, sometimes inconsistently. Yet, existing theories tend to compartmentalise core themes of intellectual property – 'fairness, incentives, culture-shaping' – that are frequently perceived by legislators and policy makers as interrelated and complementary, with obvious detrimental effects to their usefulness.[489]

This conceptual severability can perhaps be traced back to academic theorisation according to political and legal science axioms (e.g., the parallels drawn with property in general), where the above-mentioned theories are perceived as canonical 'rival perspectives'.[490] The effects of such severability are twofold. First, these theories are inconsistent insofar as they denote 'gaps, conflicts and ambiguities'.[491] Second and consequently, their value as interpretative guidelines for the legislative and judicial powers is hampered, limiting their practical use.[492]

Despite their indeterminacy, these theories have significant normative value, especially in informing doctrinal discussions, legislation and policy making in the field of intellectual property.[493] As such, they provide a valid platform for discussions on the optimal design of copyright law when faced with new technological and social paradigms.

In the area of copyright proper, the underlying rationales for its grant are customarily divided between principles of natural right (integrating

487. *Ibid.*, pp. 192–194.
488. For a selection of sources that argue for the application of this theory to intellectual property rights, *see* William Fisher, *Maps of Intellectual Property*, *Theories of IP*, http://cyber.law.harvard.edu/people/tfisher/IP/IPTheory.swf (accessed 31.01.2017). ('Culture', 'Sources', *maxime* 'Law').
489. Fisher, 2001, pp. 176–178.
490. *Ibid.*
491. *Ibid.*
492. *Ibid.*, pp. 195–196, arguing that the value of intellectual property theories is not so much to 'provide comprehensive prescriptions concerning the ideal shape of intellectual property law' but to assist in the identification of 'nonobvious attractive resolutions of particular problems' and 'foster valuable conversations among the various participants in the lawmaking process'.
493. *Ibid.*, pp. 194–199.

fairness and personality arguments), traditional to civil law jurisdictions, and principles of utilitarianism, followed by common law countries.[494]

While in civil law countries the natural rights approach conceives the 'authorial entitlement … as a juridical recognition of rights inherent in the act of authorship as such', common law countries regard copyright 'as a policy instrument designed to serve the public interest in the production and dissemination of works of authorship'.[495] Hence, the distinction between 'author's rights' (or *droit d'auteur*) and 'copyright'.[496] The former term follows a 'deontic' approach, focusing on the link between creator and expression. The latter term is 'instrumental', emphasising the effect of copyright on creativity.[497]

These distinctions are important for understanding substantive legal differences between the copyright systems of countries belonging to each tradition. However, they should not be overstated, for several reasons. First, because even representative copyright systems of different theoretical currents such as the French and US laws have, since inception, had far closer principles and goals than generally acknowledged.[498] Second, because international harmonisation of copyright law, initiated with the BC, has led to the convergence of legal theories and traditions.[499] On this point, some authors view copyright law as 'a product of nineteenth-century Western culture', which found its modern identity 'with the conclusion of the Berne Convention, in 1886'.[500] Third, as Goldstein and Hugenholtz observe, because the evolution of copyright law is predominantly shaped by economic forces. In that process, the main role of philosophical theories is to provide arguments for the creation of new rights or the imposition of limits thereto.[501]

Beyond providing philosophical foundations for copyright protection, the legitimacy of these theories in the field of copyright stems from references made in the legislative texts, such as preambles, and judicial

494. Goldstein & Hugenholtz, 2013, p. 6.
495. Drassinower, 2012, p. 108. *See also* Ginsburg, 1994.
496. Drassinower, 2012, p. 108. On the distinction between these legal traditions, see, e.g., Strowel, 1994.
497. Balganesh, 2012, p. 1678, exemplifying with the works of Landes and Posner.
498. Ginsburg, 1994; Goldstein & Hugenholtz, 2013, pp. 14–15; Grosheide, 1994, pp. 207–208.
499. Goldstein & Hugenholtz, 2013, pp. 14–15; Grosheide, 1994, pp. 207–208.
500. Grosheide, 1994, pp. 206–207, considering that the different normative considerations of copyright stem from the different legal traditions brought together in international copyright law, with their diverse philosophical underpinnings. A similar point is made by Strowel, 1994, p. 249: 'the differences between *droit d'auteur* and copyright can be explained not by positive or natural law conceptions but by more fundamental divergences between civil law and common law: differences which are located at the level of the drafting and interpretation of legislative and judicial texts'.
501. Goldstein & Hugenholtz, 2013, pp. 8, 15.

decisions, which often rely on teleological interpretation.[502] Herein as well lies a basis for this book's focus on the objectives of EU law as a normative reference point to evaluate a statutory licence ACS.

It is possible to find manifestations of utilitarian arguments, for example in recital 4 InfoSoc Directive, where it indicates that harmonisation of EU copyright law:

> will foster substantial investment in creativity and innovation, including network infrastructure, and lead in turn to growth and increased competitiveness of European industry, both in the area of content provision and information technology and more generally across a wide range of industrial and cultural sectors. This will safeguard employment and encourage new job creation.

Conversely, recitals 10 and 11 InfoSoc Directive emphasise the material interests of creators, echoing natural rights arguments. This is apparent from references to the 'high level of protection' mantra (also featured in recital 4) in connection with incentives for creativity and the material interests of (*inter alia*) creators, especially to 'receive an appropriate reward for the use of their work'.

These recitals, it is noted, also mention the interests of 'producers, consumers, culture, industry and the public at large', thereby incorporating investment protection and the public interest as motivation for adequate copyright protection, which again brings a utilitarian flavour to this mix. Investment protection, it is noted, is usually considered in the EU to be the main justification for affording protection to producers and broadcasters through related rights.[503] The situation is different for performers, whose protection is considered justified on similar fairness and personality arguments to authors, and whose skills have been compared to creative authors of derivative works.[504] From this perspective as well, then, there are grounds to draw a distinction between the legitimate interests of creators and exploiters, as previously done in this chapter.[505]

In the end, both utilitarian and natural rights theories are reflected in the goals of the *acquis* and provide justification for copyright protection in the EU, as they do in copyright regimes of the *droit d'auteur* and common law copyright tradition.[506] It is up to the lawmaker and interpreter to bring coherence to the copyright system by striking a fair balance between different interests. In this respect, the predominance of utilitarian or natural law

502. Fisher, 2001, pp. 172–173.
503. Eechoud et al., 2009, pp. 190–193.
504. See, e.g., the discussion in Eechoud et al., 2009, pp. 186–190.
505. *See* the distinction drawn in the analysis of the three-step test *supra* at 5.3.3.4 and *infra* at 6.1.5.
506. *See*, regarding the latter point, Strowel, 1994, p. 248.

principles in a legal regime may provide 'an indication as to where the balance rests between conflicting interests of the rights holders and the public'.[507]

This realisation, together with the recognition of the importance of both arguments in the European legal tradition, justifies exploring further the normative considerations of natural rights and utilitarianism. The analysis of both theories demonstrates how the public interest can shape copyright protection and justify restrictions to the exclusive right in favour of a right of access and remuneration for non-commercial online use of works.

5.5.1.1 Natural Rights

As noted, it is possible to ascribe to the natural rights theory 'fairness' and 'personality' dimensions. These reflect a more individualistic approach to copyright protection than in utilitarianism. The fairness dimension reflects the material interests of authors in copyright protection for the commercial exploitation of works. The personality dimension applies to the non-material interests of authors, reflected strongly in the protection of their moral rights most common in countries of the *droit d'auteur* tradition.[508]

As the *acquis* does not harmonise moral rights and an ACS does not aim at such harmonisation, the Lockean fairness theory is more relevant for this book than the Hegelian personality theory.[509] However, fairness and personality arguments are compatible. Insofar as they provide support for the material and moral interests of authors in their creative works, their combination supplies a capable natural rights justification for copyright protection.[510]

The traditional Lockean desert-for-labour argument posits that an individual who labours on resources that are free of ownership or held in common has a natural right of property on the results of that effort, i.e., the fruits of their labour, which right should be recognised and enforced by the state.[511]

This natural right is largely justified in the negative by two conditions or caveats, commonly known as 'provisos'. The provisos operate as delimitations on the scope of protection, and 'are designed to reconcile the

507. Guibault, 2002, p. 7.
508. *Ibid.*, p. 8; Hughes, 1988, pp. 350–351.
509. On the Hegelian justification of intellectual property rights, *see* Hughes, 1988, pp. 330–365; Radin, 1982. More generally on the personality rights theory of copyright, including references to the influences of Kant, Fichte & Hegel, *see* van Gompel, 2011, pp. 247–268.
510. Hughes, 1988, pp. 365–366; Strowel, 1994, p. 239; van Gompel, 2011, p. 218.
511. Locke's argument for a natural right to physical property is contained in Chapter V (ss 25–51), of his 'Second Treatise of Government'.

rights of individual creators with the larger claims of society in general',[512] i.e., the public interest.[513]

The first is known as the 'sufficiency' proviso or 'enough and as good condition'. According to this, a property right in the results of one's labour is admissible '...at least where there is enough, and as good, left in common for others'.[514]

The second, referred to as the 'spoilage' proviso or 'non-waste condition', 'prohibits the accumulation of so much property that some is destroyed without being used.'[515] Where such spoilage does not occur, the right is justified. With the introduction of the money economy as a means to prevent waste (e.g., by selling the surplus production), this condition assumes less relevance. In the field of copyright, due to the quasi-public good nature of intellectual works, this proviso is for the most part irrelevant.[516]

At the outset, it is not obvious that Locke's theory of property applies to intellectual property. Fisher, for example, considers such application to depend on 'which aspects of his original theory are considered dominant.'[517] Yet, legal scholarship generally accepts the extension of the fairness argument to intellectual property.[518]

To be sure, ideas (unlike physical property) are non-rivalrous and non-excludable.[519] At first glance, these characteristics raise doubts as to the extension of Locke's theory to copyright. But such doubts are dissipated by looking deeper into Locke's notion of 'common', and recognising that it implies an inexhaustibility condition, which is better satisfied by ideas than by physical goods held in common ownership.[520]

In the words of Becker: 'if it is the case that people can 'deserve' property in the (unowned) *tangible* objects they improve with their labor, then surely the case is no weaker for their deserving property in the

---

512. Merges, 2009, p. 104.
513. See, e.g., Fisher, 2001, pp. 187–189, and Gordon, 1992, identifying the Lockean proviso as a potential source of public interest restrictions on the scope of intellectual property rights. Both Gordon and Fisher recognise a 'duty of charity' as a third proviso, mostly implicit in Locke's work.
514. *See* Locke, 1988, pp. 287–288. (Second Treatise of Government, Chapter V, s. 27). Cf. Guibault, 2002, p. 9.
515. Hughes, 1988, p. 298. *See* Locke, 1988, pp. 294–295 (Second Treatise of Government, Chapter V, s. 37).
516. Hughes, 1988, pp. 325–329, noting that '[i]n intellectual property systems, manifestations of a non-waste condition are few and far between'. *But see* Damstedt, 2003, and van Gompel, 2011, p. 222 (noting the possible justification of a limited term of protection in this proviso).
517. Fisher, 2001, pp. 184–185; Shiffrin, 2001. *See also* van Gompel, 2011, p. 220 (n. 18) (and references cited therein), on doubts that the Lockean theory applies to intellectual property.
518. See, e.g., Guibault, 2002, p. 9; Hughes, 1988, pp. 296–297; Senftleben, 2004, pp. 10–12; van Gompel, 2011, p. 220.
519. On the meaning of these terms, *see infra* 5.5.1.2.
520. Hughes, 1988, p. 315.

intellectual objects they create.'[521] The intuitive appeal of using Locke's theory to 'propertize' ideas is made clear by Hughes:

> We can justify propertizing ideas under Locke's approach with three propositions: first, that the production of ideas requires a person's labor; second, that these ideas are appropriated from a 'common' which is not significantly devalued by the idea's removal; and third, that ideas can be made property without breaching the non-waste condition.[522]

As it relates to copyright, the raw materials that provide the material input for the creative labour are ideas, facts or concepts. The labour of the creator in relation to these materials 'held in common' would contribute to the value of the finished product – the expressive work – and be rewarded through a proprietary entitlement over that expression.[523]

The expression, as the reflection of the executed labour (rather than the idea or fact), is the object of copyright protection.[524] That protection comprises the elements of prohibition (exclusivity) and reward (remuneration or compensation) inherent in exploitation rights.[525] However, this protection can be limited.

The sufficiency proviso, for example, limits the grant of copyright insofar as it constrains the scope of 'common'. The application of the proviso to copyright would then entail a series of restrictions on the scope of protection, including the exclusion of protection for ideas per se, concepts, and algorithms. The proviso would also justify the adoption of copyright limitations, such as parodies, and durational limits on protection.[526]

The sufficiency proviso embodies public interest concerns that may operate to limit the scope of copyright, including its power to exclude. However, in the context of the fairness theory, limitations on the right and its exclusive element in the public interest seem to derive more clearly from the social and political contract that accompanies a transition from the state of nature to a civil and political society.[527] In contrast with what occurs in the state of nature, 'Locke emphasizes that in the civil society, a representative

521. Becker, 1992, p. 610.
522. Hughes, 1988, p. 300.
523. *Ibid.*, pp. 296–297, explaining that different interpretation of the theory view of reward as a condition for labour ('we *must* provide rewards to get labor') or, from a normative standpoint, as recompense ('labor *should* be rewarded'). For an in depth discussion on the different possible interpretations of this theory, *see* Hughes, 1988, pp. 296–330. *See also* Gordon, 1992, arguing that Locke's theory has multiple strands and that a natural rights dimension can only be extracted from a 'no-harm principle' as a 'fundamental law of nature'.
524. Hughes, 1988, p. 314.
525. van Gompel, 2011, p. 218.
526. Hughes, 1988, pp. 315–323.
527. van Gompel, 2011, pp. 222–225.

government may always restrict the enjoyment and exercise of property by positive law, if the public interest so requires.'[528]

In the context of a civil and political society, then, the public interest (or 'common good') functions as both rationale and limit for restrictions operated by positive law on property rights.[529] To accommodate the public interest, that restriction operates on the prohibition element of the right, while retaining the reward element as an essential safeguard of the author's material interests.

As shown earlier in the analysis of the three-step test, such an approach would be consistent with a balanced consideration of legitimate manifestations of the public interest within copyright law.[530] The analysis of precedents in Chapter 2 provides two clear illustrations – private copying in Germany and the broadcasting compulsory licence in the BC – where protection was extended to a use based on natural rights arguments, and consequently limited to a right of access and remuneration due to public interest concerns.

This is also the approach followed in the ECHR and the Charter when considering the possibility of public interest limitations to copyright as part of the fundamental right of property, possibly subject to payment of fair compensation, as highlighted by the CJEU in *Luksan*.[531]

Therefore, from a natural rights fairness perspective, the main justifications for a model of remunerated access over exclusivity are twofold. First, the concept of desert or reward for (intellectual) labour requires compensation or remuneration for the use of creative works, but not necessarily absolute protection in the form of exclusive rights.[532] Second and related, the definition of copyright protection around the reward element and to the detriment of the power to exclude is justified on the public interest. In this light, to the extent we can apply the Lockean theory to copyright, this theory ought to accommodate a statutory licence for non-commercial use of copyright works.[533]

---

528. *Ibid.*, pp. 219, 225.
529. *Ibid.*, p. 227: '… from a Lockean viewpoint, copyright can always be statutorily restricted if that would be in the public interest'.
530. *See supra* 5.3.3 and 6.1.5.
531. *See supra* 5.3.3 and 6.1.5, and *infra* 5.5.2. In the CJEU's jurisprudence, perhaps the best example of this is *Luksan*, para. 68.
532. See: Becker, 1992; Gordon, 1992 (noting that a compulsory licence, as a liability rule mechanism, 'could offer the laborer some reward while preserving for the public its liberty to use the common.'); William Fisher, *CopyrightX: Lecture 2.2, Fairness and Personality Theories: Fairness*, https://www.youtube.com/watch?v=HYJuhPf9s5k&feature=youtu.be (accessed 31.01.2017) (discussing this issue from minute 29 onwards). *Contra* Merges, 2011, arguing that monetary compensation for authors is insufficient under the fairness theory, and that affording them a property right must entail the power to exclude.
533. To be sure, the Lockean theory includes too many ambiguities to provide more than a general answer to the types of problem faced by contemporary copyright law in the

In fact, if the mechanism of the exclusive right fails to provide the creators with financial reward for their labour, a model of remunerated access and use appears better suited to safeguard their material interests in a fair and proportionate manner. The restriction of the authors' power to exclude is justified not only because the same is ineffective in the digital environment, but primarily on public interest grounds, namely the respect of fundamental rights and freedoms, and the promotion of creation and dissemination of works over digital networks.[534] That restriction is further justified as it applies to non-commercial online use of works, and is less susceptible of affecting the material interests of authors, as results from the previous three-step test analysis.[535]

5.5.1.2 Utilitarianism

The utilitarian theory provides a framework for the traditional economic view of copyright. According to this theory, the attribution of temporary copyright protection to creators has the purpose of providing incentives for creativity and dissemination of works.[536]

The utilitarian argument fundamentally diverges from its natural rights counterpart. On the one hand, as regards its orientation, it does not provide a *retrospective* reward for intellectual labour, but rather focuses on *prospective* incentives for the creation and dissemination of works. On the other hand, the utilitarian theory has a *collective* focus on societal welfare, which differs from the more *individualistic* approach of the natural rights argument.[537]

This theory does not understand copyright as a derivation of natural law but as a positive right granted to further societal goals, which can and should be balanced with public interest policy concerns to shape the scope of protection.[538] The utilitarian theory thus approximates the Benthamite goal of 'the greatest good for the greatest number', setting as the purpose of copyright the stimulation of 'production of the widest possible variety of creative goods at the lowest possible price.'[539]

---

digital environment. *See* William Fisher, *CopyrightX: Lecture 2.2, Fairness and Personality Theories: Fairness*, https://www.youtube.com/watch?v=HYJuhPf9s5k&feature=youtu.be (accessed 31.01.2017).

534. *See* the discussion *supra* in 5.3.3 and 6.1.5.
535. *See supra* 5.3 and 6.1.5.
536. Eckersley, 2012, p. 23; Gordon & Bone, 1999; Kur & Schovsbo, 2011, p. 2; Landes & Posner, 1989.
537. William Fisher, *CopyrightX: Lecture 4.1, Welfare Theory: The Utilitarian Framework*, https://www.youtube.com/watch?v=3ISstJYsCWs&feature=youtu.be (accessed 31.01.2017).
538. Guibault, 2002, pp. 11–12. In this conception, copyright is sometimes described in the common law tradition as a legal monopoly. *See* Strowel, 1994, pp. 236–237.
539. Goldstein & Hugenholtz, 2013, p. 14. *See also* Guibault, 2002, pp. 10–11.

In this framework, the exclusive right is a legal device to solve a public goods or free-rider problem in the production and dissemination of information goods, enabling its transfer to the 'highest valued use' through efficient market transactions.[540] 'Public goods' are defined as non-rivalrous (or inexhaustible) and non-excludable. A good is non-rivalrous if the benefit each individual derives from it is not affected or diminished when others simultaneously access it. A good is non-excludable when upon its creation and public availability it becomes difficult or impossible to prevent others from accessing or using it.[541]

Copyright shares some characteristics of public goods.[542] Although fluid and difficult to recognise in physical embodiments of traditional copyright subject matter (e.g., books, paintings, CDs), it is undeniable that the acts involved in their creation – such as authorship and composition – possess a substantial amount of both the non-rivalrous and non-excludable characteristics. Therefore, such acts are categorised and economically modelled as either quasi-or full-fledged public goods.[543] The case is clearer still for works manifested in digital embodiments (copies) and made available online.[544]

The non-excludability feature implies that third parties can freely access and use works without payment to the creator or rights holder, meaning that the price of their use would fall below the price of creation. Hence, non-excludability would prevent private market actors from charging prices allowing a return on investment and, as a consequence, from providing these goods.[545]

This scenario entails a risk of under-supply or underproduction, as the price creators must charge for recouping their costs would be higher than the market price for the use of a copy of the work.[546] The problem is clear in the case of digital recordings of music or films. The low marginal cost associated with their reproduction and dissemination (e.g., through file sharing) exacerbates the public goods problem and creates a risk that copies of works are spread without compensation to creators, affecting their incentives for creating works in the first place.

A major assumption of this model is that creators are motivated by the prospect of economic reward which is only achievable through the making available of the work. In that configuration, a good to which access cannot be excluded is susceptible of lacking the incentives required for its

540. Cohen, Loren, Okediji & O'Rourke, 2010, pp. 6–7, Gordon & Bone, 1999, p. 190.
541. Cohen et al., 2010, p. 6.
542. Gordon & Bone, 1999, p. 190, Landes & Posner, 1989.
543. Eckersley, 2012, p. 23. *See also* Gordon & Bone, 1999, pp. 192–194.
544. Eckersley, 2012, pp. 23–24.
545. Landes & Posner, 1989. *See also* Drexl, 2010, pp. 159–161, using the alternative terms 'public', 'common' and 'collective' goods to categorise copyright from an economic perspective.
546. Gordon & Bone, 1999, p. 192.

creation.[547] However, this assumption is subject to criticism in copyright scholarship on the basis that there are alternative motivations for creation.[548] This is particularly true in the online environment in the context of what Peukert calls an 'access culture', which is for the most part 'fed by non-commercially motivated contributions', both public and private.[549]

Hence, it is more accurate to argue that the promise of a reward is but one of different motivating factors; 'without it, some works would not be produced, and some authors might not create at all'.[550] Alternative motivations for creation – especially non-monetary incentives – are important because they mitigate the public goods problem, thereby weakening the utilitarian argument for legal protection.[551]

To solve the problem of non-excludability efficiently, copyright law uses as a default the legal mechanism of exclusivity.[552] The expectation is that by recognising a property-like enforceable right to prohibit use absent authorisation (or at least payment) the free-rider problem is eliminated in a way that is compatible with a Coasean market model.[553]

Through the exclusive right, copyright owners get a legal monopoly allowing them to suppress competition in the creation and distribution of (copies of) works, and to charge prices for the use of the same that are sufficiently high to offset and recoup the costs of creation (so-called 'costs of expression'). In theory, this legal entitlement allows price discrimination by copyright owners in the commercialisation of their works well above their costs of expression, leading to profit maximisation. (In practice, only imperfect price discrimination is available to copyright owners.) The social welfare beneficial result of this legal design would be to induce future creative activities and maximise the output of works, which would otherwise not occur.[554]

---

547. *Ibid.*
548. William Fisher, *Economic Analysis of Law*, http://cyber.law.harvard.edu/people/tfisher/IP/EAL.swf (accessed 31.01.2017), identifies the following 'alternative motivations for production' in the broader context of intellectual property: passion, prestige, tenor, norms of science, advertising, and collaborative voluntary creation. Regarding the latter, Benkler, for example, argues that in models of peer-production the organisational framework of certain projects triggers non-monetary social-psychological rewards securing sufficient individual participation. *See* Benkler, 2002, pp. 378–380, 2004.
549. Peukert, 2015, p. 369.
550. Cohen et al., 2010, p. 7.
551. William Fisher, *CopyrightX: Lecture 4.1, Welfare Theory: The Utilitarian Framework*, https://www.youtube.com/watch?v=3ISstJYsCWs&feature=youtu.be (accessed 31.01.2017), identifying in addition the following mitigating circumstances: lead time for first movers, custom or extra-legal norms that protect first movers, self-help through technological measures and/or contract, and philanthropy.
552. Drexl, 2010, pp. 159–161; Gordon & Bone, 1999, pp. 192–193.
553. Gordon & Bone, 1999.
554. William Fisher, *CopyrightX: Lecture 4.2, Welfare Theory: The Incentive Theory of Copyright*, https://www.youtube.com/watch?v=t9wqQNCC-Vs&feature=youtu.be (accessed 31.01.2017). NB 'consumer surplus' is the difference between the maximum

In essence, the legal recognition of exclusivity is an artificial imposition of scarcity grounded on a concern to secure and incentivise the creation and supply of works. In a world where these are mostly or partially embodied in physical objects such a construct is difficult to achieve, but arguably possible. However, when the same logic is applied to digital use over the networked information environment, the complexities of legally imposed digital scarcity grow exponentially.[555]

The question that then arises is whether the benefits of property rights protection and exclusivity outweigh its costs, especially as regards the regulation of mass non-commercial online use of works by individuals. From a different perspective, it is possible to consider the costs as disadvantages of exclusive rights in relation to alternative legal solutions.[556]

To make this assessment, we must identify the costs introduced by the grant of property rights, especially when their scope is too broad. Gordon and Boone group these costs into four categories: monopoly pricing, chilling effects on follow-on creativity, transaction costs, and administration and enforcement costs.[557] Some of these costs or disadvantages justify restrictions on the exclusive right.

The first category of costs – monopoly pricing – is characterised by the deadweight losses (i.e., foregone consumer surplus or allocative inefficiency) derived from the impossibility of perfect price discrimination, amplified by the non-rivalrous nature of intangible copyright goods.[558] In other words, because copyright owners use the exclusive right to set a price for their works well above marginal cost, a significant group of potential consumers will be priced out of the market.

The second category of costs refers to chilling effects on future creativity. It is linked to the cumulative nature of information goods, particularly salient for online use. Creative expression builds on pre-existing materials, many of which are subject to copyright protection. By establishing a property interest in creative goods, copyright imposes a cost on subsequent

---

price a consumer is willing and able to pay for a work as a good or service (indicated by the demand curve) and the actual market price they in fact pay for that good or service.

555. Eckersley, 2012, p. 24.
556. William Fisher, *CopyrightX. Lecture 4.3, Welfare Theory: Applications and Assessment*, https://www.youtube.com/watch?v=_xHEcRFlLok&feature=youtu.be (accessed 31.01.2017).
557. Gordon & Bone, 1999, p. 194–ff. Some of these costs are mentioned also in Cohen et al., 2010, p. 7.
558. *See* Wikipedia, *Deadweight loss*, https://en.wikipedia.org/wiki/Deadweight_loss (accessed 31.01.2017): 'In economics, a deadweight loss (also known as excess burden or allocative inefficiency) is a loss of economic efficiency that can occur when equilibrium for a good or service is not achieved or is not achievable. Causes of deadweight loss can include monopoly pricing (in the case of artificial scarcity), externalities, taxes or subsidies, and binding price ceilings or floors (including minimum wages).'

creators that require pre-existing works as input for their own expressive works.[559]

To limit the reach of this cumulative effect and the related social cost of exclusivity, copyright law employs devices such as the delimitation of its subject matter scope (e.g., the idea/expression distinction), and the adoption of limitations, which can be unremunerated (free uses) or remunerated. Remunerated limitations, such as in a statutory licence ACS, translate into liability rules. This economic argument for copyright limitations is echoed somewhat in normative considerations related to promotion of access and dissemination of works, and freedom of expression and information online, used in this study as normative justifications for the adoption of an ACS.[560]

The third category relates to transaction costs of licensing, namely those associated with negotiations. These costs are usually mitigated by the clear definition of rights, consolidation of ownership interests and, if individual licensing is too costly, by the intervention of CMOs or the adoption of liability rules.[561]

The fourth category is administration and enforcement costs. Whereas administration costs are dependent on the existing regulatory infrastructure for their management and operation, enforcement costs are calculated with reference to the frequency of copyright infringement and the relative cost of enforcement in each instance thereof.[562] That is to say, the proper functioning of the incentive mechanism for copyright depends on the existence of reasonably effective enforcement measures. As noted throughout this book, this condition is not satisfied in relation to unauthorised file sharing (or, generally, non-commercial use by individuals) over digital networks, and the legislative fortification of enforcement measures has failed to change that situation.[563]

The third and fourth categories of costs are usually at the centre of market failure justifications for the adoption of limitations or collective rights management of copyright. They likewise provide the core economic motivation for an ACS for non-commercial online use by individuals, as used throughout this book.[564]

In essence, the above-described costs of exclusive rights provide admissible justifications for deviations from the principle of exclusivity in light of the utilitarian goal of incentivising the creation and supply of works. These costs also reflect public interest considerations that may dictate

559. Gordon & Bone, 1999.

560. *See supra* 5.3.3.5 and 5.3.3.6.

561. Gordon & Bone, 1999, p. 196, providing the example of fair use in US copyright law.

562. *Ibid.*

563. Cf. *supra* 1.1 and 5.3. *See also* William Fisher, *CopyrightX: Lecture 4.3, Welfare Theory: Applications and Assessment*, https://www.youtube.com/watch?v=_xHEcRFlLok&feature=youtu.be (accessed 31.01.2017).

564. On market failure as justification for an ACS, *see supra* 2.5, 3.3.4.1, 3.3.5.1, 4.4.1.3, 5.3.2.2, 5.3.4, 5.5.1., and *infra* 6.1.5.

whether social welfare is better served by an adjustment of the incentive element to achieve the utilitarian goal of copyright.[565]

In the case of mass online use by individuals carried out for non-commercial purposes, where direct licensing and enforcement are socially costly and/or ineffective, a legal alternative to exclusivity in the form of a right of access and remuneration appears consistent with the utilitarian rationale of copyright.[566]

In purely economic terms, whether an ACS does in fact provide such a solution will then depend on empirical research that assesses its relative costs and benefits as compared to the status quo for the copyright regulation of the use in question. As noted throughout this book, although further research is required, there are indicators that such a system may increase social welfare.[567] Therefore, as with the natural rights theory, utilitarianism seems to leave policy makers an eminently normative choice between retaining the status quo of exclusivity or, as suggested here, promoting reform through an access and remuneration model for non-commercial online use.

5.5.2 The Access and Remuneration Dimensions of Copyright

In Europe, different philosophical approaches translate into a plethora of theories on the legal nature of copyright.[568] As noted, especially in continental Europe, copyright laws are predominantly of an authors' rights tradition and follow a natural rights legal conceptual approach. At its core, this approach is guided by the objective of guaranteeing a just reward for creators, using the grant of an exclusive right as the principal legal instrument for that purpose.[569]

565. Guibault, 2002, p. 11.
566. William Fisher, *Maps of Intellectual Property, Theories of IP*, http://cyber.law.harvard.edu/people/tfisher/IP/IPTheory.swf (accessed 31.01.2017), identifying his ACS proposal as a possible mandatory solution in copyright to a public goods problem ('Incentive Theory', 'Possible Solutions', 'Solution #3: Government Issues Prizes to Successful Private Producers',) N.B. the mention of 'prizes' in this context better applies to what the taxonomy in Chapter 3 refers to as 'State Systems', but the argument would apply also to ACS based on legal licences and mandatory collective management.
567. *See supra* 5.3.2.3, 5.3.3.3, 5.3.3.4, and *infra* 6.1.1 and 6.1.5.
568. These include, to name a few, the intellectual property theory of Poulliet, Drone and Klosterman, the personality rights theory of Gierke, the *doppelrecht* theory of Kohler, the exclusive rights theory of Piccard, the monopoly theory of Roguin, Roubier's clientele rights theory (later developed by Desbois), the immaterial rights theory of Greco, the dualist theories of Plaisant, De Sanctis and Le Tarnec, Savatier's concept of 'parallel rights', De Boor and Ulmer's monism (and its openness to Hubman's *geistiges Eigentum*), and Recht's property-creation theory. *See* Pereira, 2008, pp. 83–168, for a discussion of these theories.
569. See, e.g., Goldstein & Hugenholtz, 2013, pp. 7, 14, 19–21.

Since the mid-twentieth century, authors (but not exploiters) have enjoyed the human right to benefit from the moral and material interests that result from their works, pursuant to Article 27(2) UDHR and, later, Article 15(1)(c) International Covenant on Economic, Social and Cultural Rights (ICESCR).[570] Furthermore, the fundamental rights protection of copyright as property in Europe is well established.[571] It derives from the 'property clause' in Article 1 Protocol No. 1 ECHR,[572] from the express mention in Article 17(2) Charter that 'intellectual property shall be protected' (as part of the general guarantee of property in paragraph 1 of that provision), from references in recitals 9 InfoSoc Directive and 32 Enforcement Directive, and from various CJEU judgments.[573]

This approximation to the right of property suggests that copyright requires a power of exclusion of third parties from access and use of works absent authorisation, i.e., a right of prohibition. Yet, such a contention is at odds with the existence of legal structures within copyright law that allow restrictions to the exclusive right.

Beyond the realisation that utilitarian and fairness arguments admit public interest limitations to copyright (*see* 5.5.1), this book contains multiple examples of admissible restrictions on the exercise and nature of copyright. They include voluntary and mandatory models of collective rights management, statutory and compulsory licences, and even uncompensated limitations to copyright, all of which are consistent with EU copyright law.[574]

Furthermore, the legal framework contains a normative filter for the future inclusion of limitations to exclusive rights: the three-step test. The very existence of such a norm suggests that it is possible to ensure copyright protection outside the template of the exclusive right. In that line, this book

570. This level of protection of material and moral interests appears to mirror the fairness and personality prongs of the natural rights theory, as well as the traditional distinction between economic and moral rights in copyright. See, e.g., Gervais, 2015, p. 19. On Art. 15(1)(c) ICESCR, *see* G. W. Austin & Zavidow, 2015, pp. 313–321, 331.

571. *See* Goldstein & Hugenholtz, 2013, pp. 23–26, with examples of how different Member States' laws protect copyright as a fundamental right. On the consideration of copyright as a human right see, generally, P. L. C. Torremans, 2015.

572. Art. 1 Protocol No. 1 ECHR ('Protection of property') states: 'Every natural or legal person is entitled to the peaceful enjoyment of his possessions. No one shall be deprived of his possessions except in the public interest and subject to the conditions provided for by law and by the general principles of international law. The preceding provisions shall not, however, in any way impair the right of a State to enforce such laws as it deems necessary to control the use of property in accordance with the general interest or to secure the payment of taxes or other contributions or penalties.' On ECtHR jurisprudence applying this provision to copyright, see: ECtHR, *Melnychuck v. Ukraine*; ECtHR, *Balan v. Moldova*; ECtHR, *Ashby Donald*; ECtHR, *The Pirate Bay*.

573. CJEU, *Laserdisken*, paras 64–65; CJEU, *Promusicae*, para. 62; CJEU, *Scarlet Extended*, paras 43–44; CJEU, *Deckmyn*, paras 27–32.

574. Examples of such restrictions are the non-voluntary licences discussed in Chapter 2, the different types of collective rights management described in Chapter 3, and the copyright limitations explained in Chapter 4. *See also infra* 6.1.2–6.1.4.

argues that a flexible interpretation of the test admits a properly delimited statutory licence ACS.[575]

The possibility of imposing restrictions on the exclusive right while retaining the core of copyright protection as a fundamental right is consistent with calls to rethink copyright as an access right, rather than a prohibition right. To do so, according to Geiger, requires adapting the rules of copyright:

> to its initially dual character: 1) of a right to secure and organize cultural participation to creative aspects (access aspect); and 2) of a guarantee that the creator participates fairly in the fruit of the commercial exploitation of his works (protection aspect).[576]

This proposition bridges the utilitarian and natural rights justifications for copyright, and recasts them in a fundamental rights framework. It emphasises not only the social dimension of copyright but also 'the inclusive rather than the exclusive nature of copyright protection.'[577]

The positive definition of an 'access right' as focusing on the availability of works and cultural participation is in stark contrast with the more traditional definition of copyright in the online environment as a 'negative' right. That is to say, a legal entitlement to prohibit the access and subsequent use of copyright works, achieved through exclusivity with legal protection of TPMs and the prohibition of their circumvention.[578]

As is apparent, the positive meaning of the access right is consistent with the privilege afforded to end-users in an ACS. Borrowing the terminology of Peukert with a twist, a statutory licence ACS would adapt copyright law to foster an online 'access culture', rather than an 'exclusivity culture'.[579]

In Geiger's proposal, an access right is justified by a combination of the social function of copyright with the public interest. This social function stems from the notion that the law requires a measure of balance in order to regulate private and private-public relationships within society. If that is accepted, then a right cannot be absolute, as it is constrained by competing interests within a set community. The result, then, is that subjective rights are 'limited in social terms'[580] and, regarding copyright, that the scope of

575. *See supra* Chapter 5 and *infra* 6.1.5.
576. Geiger, 2015a, p. 4.
577. *Ibid.*, pp. 2, 4–5.
578. *Ibid.*, p. 4 (n. 9).
579. Peukert discusses the use of copyright to foster access or exclusivity as two cultures of online communication. The twist here is that Peukert's proposal, in line with his earlier bipolar copyright system, is for a system that allows rights holders to choose between obtaining remuneration for online use of their works either through 'individual license fees (exclusivity culture) or by statutory levy (access culture). The levy would be reserved exclusively for subject matter that is available without technical barriers on the internet.' *See* Peukert, 2015, p. 393.
580. Geiger, 2015a, pp. 5–7. *See also* Austin & Zavidow, 2015, p. 320, mentioning the social function of copyright in the context of Art. 15(1) ICESCR.

protection – including the objectives and conditions of its exercise – is drawn in light of the public interest.[581]

The argument set forth in this chapter is that the best approach to define the public interest as a limit on the exclusive or prohibition element of copyright is through the identification of its collective and individual manifestations, qualified as legitimate interests in the third condition of the three-step test. This approach allows consideration of such interests within a balancing framework designed to assess restrictions on copyright protection.[582]

However, it is also possible to consider the public interest from an *external* perspective, identifying foundations for a right of access in the international human or fundamental rights framework and domestic constitutional law.

In the first place, these foundations derive from the recognition in Articles 27(1) UDHR and 15(1) ICESCR of a universal right to culture and science.[583] Such rights, as noted before, provide strong public interest arguments in favour of a right of access as an element of an ACS, related to the promotion of creativity and circulation of works, and freedom of expression.[584] In this respect, Gervais notes that:

> the UDHR in particular would allow exceptions that demonstrably augment access where such access (enjoyment) is not commercially reasonable or possible, and the right to reuse and thereby participate in the cultural life of the community. This seems to justify both consumptive use exceptions where commercial access is undesirable or impracticable … and exceptions for transformative uses.[585]

In the second place, the elevation of copyright to human or fundamental rights status as a property right implies restrictions based on the social function of the right and the application of competing fundamental rights. Both sets of restrictions play a role in justifying a right of access and remuneration.

---

581. *See supra* 5.5.1. *See also* Geiger, 2015a, pp. 7–8, referring to 'the interest of society and the common interest'.
582. *See supra* 5.3.3. *See also* Gervais, 2015, p. 21, arguing that human rights principles can 'inform the determination of the proper scope of exceptions' under the third step of the test.
583. Art. 27(1) UDHR states: 'Everyone has the right freely to participate in the cultural life of the community, to enjoy the arts and to share in scientific advancement and its benefits.' Art. 15(1) ICESCR states: '1. The States Parties to the present Covenant recognize the right of everyone: (a) To take part in cultural life; (b) To enjoy the benefits of scientific progress and its applications; (c) To benefit from the protection of the moral and material interests resulting from any scientific, literary or artistic production of which he is the author.'
584. *See supra* 5.3.3.5 and 5.3.3.6.1.
585. Gervais, 2015, p. 21.

Regarding copyright's social function as a justification for a right of access,[586] Article 1 Protocol No. 1 ECHR, for example, in its first paragraph allows natural or legal persons to be deprived of their property 'in the public interest and subject to the conditions provided for by law and by the general principles of international law.' It further allows States to enforce laws 'necessary to control the use of property in accordance with the general interest'.

In the same line, we must note the social limits identified in the general property clause of Article 17(1) Charter, which restricts the regulation of property to what is 'necessary for the general interest'. This reference, as noted in the preparatory works of the Charter, applies to the protection of intellectual property in Article 17(2) Charter, considered a manifestation of the general property right. In this way, the non-absolute character of intellectual property rights is apparent.[587]

In addition to the social function dimension, the operation of competing human or fundamental rights as external limits to copyright protection provides justification for an access right. In this respect, the present book illustrated several instances where the balancing of conflicting fundamental rights resulted in the exclusive right having to cede in the interests of privacy, protection of personal data, freedom of expression and information, and freedom to conduct a business.[588]

In the context of the three-step test analysis, this chapter has derived from these *external* limits *internal fundamental rights-based justifications* for a right of access and remuneration for non-commercial online use of works, which are coherent with the CJEU's teleological interpretation of existing *acquis* limitations, illustrated in *Painer* and *Deckmyn*.[589]

The CJEU elucidates the point in *Luksan*. In that judgment, the Court accepts the property qualification of copyright, but recognises the possibility of restrictions 'in the public interest and in the cases and under the conditions provided for by law, subject to fair compensation being paid in good time for their loss'. The Court further notes, '[t]he use of property may be regulated by law in so far as is necessary for the general interest'.[590] In this light, the public interest and respect for fundamental rights are admissible grounds to

586. Geiger, 2013a, p. 15.
587. *Ibid.*, pp. 16–17, with further references. *See also supra* 5.3.3.6.
588. *See supra* 4.4.1.4, 4.4.1.5, 4.4.4.1, 4.4.4.3, and 5.3.3.6. On ECtHR jurisprudence and the possibility of imposing limitations on the grounds of freedom of expression (Art. 10 ECHR), *see* ECtHR, *Ashby Donald*, and ECtHR, *The Pirate Bay*. On CJEU jurisprudence in this respect, see: CJEU, *Promusicae*, paras 65–68; CJEU, *LSG*, paras 28–29; CJEU, *Bonnier Audio*, para. 56; CJEU, *Painer*, paras 105, 132; CJEU, *Scarlet Extended*, para. 53; CJEU, *Netlog*, para. 51; CJEU, *UPC Telekabel*, para. 46; CJEU, *Deckmyn*, paras 26–27.
589. *See supra* 4.4.1.4, 4.4.1.5, 4.4.4.1, 4.4.4.3, and 5.3.3.6.
590. CJEU, *Luksan*, para. 68.

justify a restriction on the nature of the exclusive right in favour of a right of access and fair compensation.[591]

That restriction, if effectuated through a statutory licence, may in fact serve the creative incentive goal of copyright and further the circulation of culture online. As noted, statutory licences have a productive function, due to their ability to foster creative use by securing access to existing works and, thus, afford a degree of freedom to authors in their creative processes. As is apparent, from this perspective, such a licence would have a basis in freedom of (artistic) expression in Articles 10 ECHR and 11 Charter.[592]

The contention of this book is that these non-economic motivations, when considered in the normative framework of the three-step test, support the adoption of a model of remunerated access for non-commercial online use of works, in the form of a statutory licence ACS. This has implications for the access and remuneration aspects of copyright in the *acquis*.

From the access perspective, the question arises as to whether such motivations, especially those related to fundamental rights, are sufficient to qualify the privilege of end-users as a *positive user right* of equal value to the exclusive right. This would entail, for example, the ACS-limitation being mandatory and privileged, i.e., not subject to contractual disposition or pre-emption by technological measures.[593]

As described in Chapter 4, the InfoSoc Directive mostly opens the door for contractual disposition of limitations by end-users and affords priority to TPMs over limitations. The possibility of contractual disposition can be set aside by the definition of limitations as imperative (e.g., as occurs in Portugal and Belgium), or by the application of imperative rules protecting end-users (e.g., consumer law). In relation to some limitations, Article 6(4) InfoSoc Directive mandates Member States to put in place appropriate measures to ensure exercise of limitations despite application of TPMs. However, that possibility is not available for works made available online on agreed contractual terms.[594]

This priority of contract and especially TPMs over limitations is not required by the international law provisions (in the WIPO Treaties) that Article 6 InfoSoc Directive implements. It is therefore a choice by the EU legislature. In that light, the different public interest manifestations of the access dimension of copyright discussed to this point (namely those arising

591. Geiger, 2015a, p. 20.

592. Cf. *supra* 5.3.3.5 and 5.3.3.6.1. *See also* Geiger, 2015b, pp. 9–20, proposing a statutory licence for creative reuses of derivative works.

593. Geiger, 2015a, pp. 21–22, and references cited.

594. *See supra* 4.4.1.2, and 4.4.3.5. For an analysis of the impact of digital technology on the position of consumers of licensed digital content from the perspective of EU law on copyright, contract and consumer protection, *see* Guibault, 2016.

from fundamental rights), together with the lack of efficiency of TPMs, the lack of proportionality of their application to non-commercial online acts, and the requirement of effectiveness of limitations, all justify a different approach for a limitation-based ACS.

One possible approach could be to build on the 'appropriate measures' language of the directive and the general proposal of Article 5.8 Wittem Code. Rather than an outright prohibition on these measures, rights holders would be allowed to apply TPMs, subject to an obligation to make available means of benefiting from the ACS-limitation. That obligation would in turn be subject to the condition that those means are necessary to fully exercise the limitation.[595] If the rights holder fails to meet such obligations, end-users or their representatives (including consumer associations or state entities) could judicially enforce this right to exercise the statutory limitation. Whether such a set-up creates a 'subjective right' to the ACS-limitation is up for discussion; however, this approach appears to be consistent with the normative considerations that inform the access dimension of copyright under EU copyright law.[596]

However, the promotion of the access dimension of copyright for the regulation of non-commercial online use through a limitation, at the expense of the exclusive nature of the right, does not necessarily entail transforming prohibited uses into free uses. In fact, the CJEU in *Luksan* accepts a restriction on the exclusive dimension of copyright 'in the public interest and in the cases and under the conditions provided for by law, *subject to fair compensation* being paid in good time for their loss'.[597] In requiring that the enhancement of access be accompanied by a remuneration condition, the Court emphasises the central role of that condition in securing the material interests of rights holders in general, and creators in particular.

This approach is coherent, first, with the role of remuneration in both utilitarian and natural rights theories, as either creative incentive or a fairness reward for intellectual creations.[598] Second, it mirrors the focus on the material interests of creators in the human and fundamental rights framework of copyright, especially in the UDHR and ICESCR, which do not require copyright protection to include a power to exclude users. That is to say, under these instruments, the material and moral interests of creators can be secured

595. *See* Wittem Group, 2010 (Art. 5.8).
596. Geiger, 2015a, p. 22, suggesting the possibility of enforcing limitations as a 'subjective right'. In EU law, further support for the consideration of user rights as enforceable rights of equal value to the rights of copyright owners could arguably derive from CJEU, *Ulmer*, para. 43, CJEU, *Deckmyn*, para. 26, CJEU *UPC Telekabel*, para. 57, CJEU *Painer*, para. 132. *See also* European Copyright Society, 2014b; Geiger, 2015a, pp. 22–23.
597. CJEU, *Luksan*, para. 68 (emphasis added).
598. *See supra* 5.5.1.

through a right of access and remuneration, rather than a pure exclusive right.[599]

To this effect, the present book has argued that a statutory licensing system for non-commercial use would likely provide better protection to creators than a non-enforceable exclusive right for the same use. The reasons are essentially twofold. First, the exclusive right in this scenario will generate little rights revenue and, where it does, the same will accrue mostly to exploiters to whom creators have transferred the right. Second, the remuneration or compensation right attached to the statutory licence system is typically (in the EU at least) unwaivable and distributed on fair terms in the institutional setting of a CMO, ensuring that the rights revenue generated in the system finds its way to creators.[600]

On this point, the fact that similar results can in theory be achieved through improvements in contract law should be considered as a *supplement*, rather than an *alternative*, to the deployment of statutory licences as tools to improve the position of creators in enjoying the benefits of the digital exploitation of works.[601]

Affording special attention to creators is fully justified not only by their role – especially that of authors – in the international and EU legal frameworks, but also on philosophical grounds. From a natural rights perspective, it is the creator (not the exploiter) that has a direct moral and material link to his intellectual creations. From a utilitarian perspective, 'if one wants to reach an optimal promotion of creativity, it is absolutely consistent to allocate a special role to the person who performs the social added value, i.e., the creator.'[602]

The CJEU's wording in *Luksan* points towards qualifying the remuneration element within the system of EU copyright law as a right of fair compensation, rather than a right of equitable remuneration. Following an analysis of the *acquis*, this book makes a similar suggestion when defining the element of compensation attached to a prospective limitation for non-commercial use of works in a statutory licence ACS.[603]

Furthermore, after *Luksan* and *Reprobel*, it appears that the fair compensation element of such an access right belongs only to the rights holders of the restricted exclusive right, i.e., the rights of reproduction and communication to the public in the InfoSoc Directive. This means that the right of fair compensation for non-commercial use attributed *ab origine* to creators is unwaivable and not transferable to exploiters. In this fashion, the right ensures an adequate or appropriate level of compensation,

599. Austin & Zavidow, 2015, pp. 316–321, 329–330; Geiger, 2015a, pp. 33–34; Shaheed, 2014.

600. *See supra* 5.3.2.3.3, 5.3.3.3, 5.3.3.4, and 5.3.4 (and references cited). *See also* Austin & Zavidow, 2015, p. 330; Geiger, 2015b, pp. 5–7.

601. Geiger, 2015a, pp. 33–34, making a similar point.

602. Geiger, 2015b, p. 5.

603. *See supra* 5.3.3.3 and 5.3.4.

remuneration, or reward required to incentivise creation, in line with the objectives of the InfoSoc Directive.[604]

5.5.3 NORMATIVE CONSISTENCY WITH EU COPYRIGHT LAW

It is not an easy task to identify a clear set of objectives for EU copyright law. The view expressed throughout the book is that the best way to do so is by extracting those objectives from the *acquis*, namely the existing copyright directives and their interpretation by the CJEU in over forty cases.[605]

The Court often relies on the recitals of directives for teleological interpretation and identification of normative arguments that elucidate its objectives. Such arguments are informed by several concerns, including different philosophical justifications (utilitarianism *v.* natural rights), distinct legal traditions (civil law *v.* common law), respect for fundamental economic freedoms in EU law, and respect for fundamental rights and freedoms in the Charter.[606]

The InfoSoc Directive is of particular importance in this respect, as it is based on principles and rules already laid down in the directives in force in the area of intellectual property.[607] For the present purposes, it is doubly important because it harmonises the exclusive rights and limitations within which framework an ACS would integrate.

In this light, it makes sense to rely on the empirical research on the CJEU's copyright jurisprudence by Favale, Kretschmer and Torremans (mentioned in Chapter 1), which identifies a range of interpretative or rhetorical arguments followed by the Court that mirror objectives of the *acquis*. The arguments/objectives identified by the authors are listed here in a different order:[608]

(1) Fair balance between the rights and interests of authors and the rights of users.

---

604. *See supra* 4.4.3.3 (on fair compensation), 5.3.3.1–5.3.3.4, and *infra* 5.5.3. On the use of the compensation or remuneration terminology *see Opinion AG in Padawan*, paras 79–80, and Geiger, 2015b, pp. 7–9 (endorsing the term 'limitation-based remuneration rights' or 'claims' instead of 'levies' or 'statutory licences')
605. *See supra* 1.1 and 4.4.1. *See also* Favale et al., 2015, pp. 38–39.
606. Hugenholtz & Quintais, 2017 (forthcoming). *See supra* 1.1, 4.4.1, 5.5.1 and 5.5.2. *See also* recital 3 InfoSoc Directive, stating that the '[t]he proposed harmonisation will help to implement the four freedoms of the internal market'.
607. *See* recital 20 InfoSoc Directive, and CJEU, *Murphy*, para. 187 (and caselaw cited).
608. Favale et al., 2015, pp. 33, 66–67. This list omits the objective of 'fair competition' listed by the authors, as the same is not called into question by the adoption of an ACS. The authors note also the Court's preference for the teleological method and that these arguments, while possibly rhetorical, may provide an indication of whether the outcome of a case is favourable to rights holders or users. *See also* Guibault et al., 2007a, pp. 4–6, for the use of recitals as a means to identify the objectives of the InfoSoc Directive.

(2) High level of protection for copyright holders.
(3) Adequate compensation or appropriate reward.
(4) Circulation of culture.
(5) Resolution of legal uncertainty.
(6) Technological development (including the promotion of the information society), and
(7) Harmonisation of copyright law to achieve a functioning internal market.

To be sure, these objectives operate at different levels of concreteness, may overlap, and at times seem contradictory. For example, it is not always apparent how to reconcile the aims of technological development and circulation of culture with a high level of protection, while safeguarding the 'independence and dignity of artistic creators and performers.' Thus, it is difficult to derive from this list of objectives or the preamble of the InfoSoc Directive a unitary and coherent benchmark from which to assess a reform proposal.[609]

Regardless, if a statutory licence ACS is to be normatively consistent with EU copyright law, it should generally conform to these objectives. The remainder of this section briefly examines whether that is the case, recasting the main findings of this study in light of each objective.

Objective 1: Fair Balance

The different dimensions and applications of the concept of fair balance (objective 1) are sufficiently explained in this and the previous chapter.[610] Extant legal rules subject non-commercial online use of works to exclusive rights, TPMs and strict enforcement measures. Such rules do not sufficiently consider the interests of creators and the public interest. On the one hand, they fail to secure remuneration for creators. On the other, they create legal uncertainty, fail to promote the circulation of creative works online, and subject end-users to liability for online activities of personal enjoyment and expression. This comes at a high social cost, illustrated by the decreasing legitimacy of copyright law in the eyes of the public, and the erosion of the rule of law in this area.

This chapter carried out a balancing exercise of the legitimate interests at stake in an ACS in the context of the three-step test. The analysis suggests that such a system could contribute to restoring the balance in the *acquis* regarding the regulation of non-commercial online use. The introduction of a properly delimited right of access and fair compensation would not significantly harm rights holders, should add a revenue stream (by

609. Hugenholtz & Quintais, 2017 (forthcoming). Contrast recitals 4, 9–11 InfoSoc Directive.
610. Recitals 3 and 31 InfoSoc Directive. *See supra* 4.4.1.4, 4.4.1.5, 4.5, 5.1, 5.2.2, 5.3.3, and 5.3.4.

monetising hitherto uncompensated uses), and would likely improve the position of creators. Furthermore, a statutory licence ACS would better serve the public interest by improving legal certainty for end-users, reducing their liability exposure, facilitating the circulation of works online, and respecting individuals' fundamental rights and freedoms, namely privacy in telecommunications, personal data, and freedom of expression and information. (Regarding intermediaries' freedom to conduct business, the impact of such a reform appears to be at worst neutral.)

Objectives 2 and 3: High Level of Protection and Adequate Compensation or Appropriate Reward

Perhaps the objective of EU law that is most difficult to reconcile with a legalisation scheme is that of a high level of protection for copyright holders (objective 2).[611] It is on this basis that the CJEU interprets exclusive rights broadly and limitations strictly. Still, this book argues throughout that it is a misconception to equate the objective with an 'absolute' level of protection. Such interpretation is harmful to rights holders and contrary to the public interest, as it supports broadening of exclusive rights *ad infinitum* irrespective of the possibility and desirability of individual management and enforcement of copyright.

Rather, a systematic and teleological interpretation of the preamble of the InfoSoc Directive shows that what is meant is a level of copyright protection that ensures adequate compensation or an appropriate reward for rights holders (objective 3),[612] while allowing space for the fulfilment of the remaining objectives of EU copyright law, including the aforementioned fair balance of interests. This articulation between protection and remuneration, patent in recitals 9 and 10 of the directive, is crucial in designing an optimal scope of protection for copyright aimed at fostering creativity and the dissemination of works.

A statutory licence ACS in this mould will not directly affect the exclusive rights of creators for commercial use of works. The system focuses on non-commercial online use by individuals in relation to which exclusivity is ill suited for monetisation and/or too costly to enforce (at economic and social levels). Hence, a statutory licence system affords a level of protection that better serves the material interests of creators.

611. Objective supported by recitals 4, 9, and arguably 11 (referring to '[a] rigorous, effective system for the protection of copyright and related rights') InfoSoc Directive. *See also* recital 16 Rental Right Directive.

612. Objective supported by recitals 10 (appropriate reward) and 35 (adequate compensation) InfoSoc Directive. Note that Favale et al., 2015, p. 33, mention solely 'adequate compensation'. In this respect, *see* the *Opinion AG in Padawan*, paras 79–80, relying on the wording of recital 10 InfoSoc Directive ('appropriate reward'). Cf. Geiger & Schönherr, 2014a, pp. 132–133.

It is debatable whether other rights holders will see their financial situation improve. That will largely depend on whether the new rights revenue received under the ACS supplants the potential harm caused by its adoption on online commercial channels. On this point, existing research shows the potential of a statutory licence to generate sufficient revenue to offset any losses. Furthermore, a proper definition of the scope of the limitation could mitigate potential negative (indirect) effects on the normal exploitation of works.

Objective 4: Circulation of Culture

If we accept that a carefully designed limitation for non-commercial online use will not negatively affect incentives for creation, then it is difficult to argue that it will not improve the circulation of culture online (objective 4).[613] A statutory licence ACS will provide users with breathing space for lawful acts of enjoyment of cultural works online in a non-market sphere; it will also provide creators with novel rights revenue, which may incentivise further creation and dissemination of works. Those same activities of end-users were previously prohibited (or shrouded in legal uncertainty) and generated no remuneration.

It is true that in some private copying judgments the CJEU considered it 'apparent from recital 22 in the preamble to Directive 2001/29 that the objective of proper support for the dissemination of culture must not be achieved by sacrificing strict protection of rights or by tolerating illegal forms of distribution of counterfeited or pirated works'.[614] However, this statement and the consequent interpretation of recital 22 need to be qualified.

First, the reference to 'strict protection of rights' is uncannily similar to the absolutist view of a 'high level of protection' rejected above. Where we interpret this phrase to mean *adequate protection to generate appropriate remuneration*, it becomes clear that a statutory licence for non-commercial online use – under the terms discussed here – is not a measure that unjustifiably sacrifices copyright protection.

Second, the effect of an ACS is not to tolerate 'illegal forms of distribution of counterfeited or pirated works'. Rather, it is to promote the access and remuneration aspects of copyright protection, while safeguarding

613. Objective supported by recitals 14 and 22 InfoSoc Directive. The link between creativity and culture was from an early stage recognised in the Green Paper on Copyright and the Challenge of Technology 1988, p. 6 (para. 1.4.4): 'Intellectual and artistic creativity is a precious asset, the source of Europe's cultural identity and of that of each individual State. It is a vital source of economic wealth and of European influence throughout the world. This creativity needs to be protected; it needs to be given a higher status and it needs to be stimulated'. *See also* Art. 167(1) TFEU, containing the so-called 'culture clause'.

614. CJEU, *Reprobel*, para. 59; CJEU, *ACI Adam*, para. 36. For criticism on the use of the Court's interpretation of this recital in the context of its private copying jurisprudence, *see supra* 4.4.3.6.

exclusivity and enforcement against for-profit unauthorised uses. This distinction between individuals' non-commercial use of works (privileged in a limitation-based ACS) and their unauthorised commercial use thereof (subject to the exclusive right) is an important part of the system and one of the reasons why it can comply with the three-step test.[615]

Objective 5: Resolution of Legal Uncertainty

It is also clear from the analysis so far that the adoption of a statutory licence ACS would contribute to resolving legal uncertainty in EU copyright law (objective 5).[616] It is true that the flexible interpretation of the *acquis* and especially the three-step test, proposed in this book, may be detrimental to legal certainty. But this risk is easily offset by the advantages the system would bring. As amply demonstrated in Chapter 4, rules in the *acquis* give rise to considerable uncertainty regarding the application of exclusive rights and limitations to individuals' online use of copyright, for example in the cases of reproduction from unauthorised sources and hyperlinking.[617] In this context, a limitation clearly covering some of these uses would remove uncertainty in the online application of copyright.

Objective 6: Technological Development (Including the Promotion of the Information Society)

An important objective of EU copyright law is to foster technological development, including the promotion of the information society through a flexible interpretation of the legal framework (objective 6).[618] This objective is a clear manifestation of the InfoSoc Directive's *raison d'être*: to adapt EU copyright law to the digital networked environment and the information society. It also has a clear public interest component, as the future development of a technological society, such as ours, is undeniably served by a well-functioning Internet.[619]

In this light, the interpretation of copyright ought to provide stimulus for the development of digital technologies within a 'general and flexible legal framework at Community level', in line with recital 2 InfoSoc Directive. This would seem to require, for example, a technology neutral and functional approach to the interpretation of exclusive rights, thus responding

615. *See supra* 5.3.2 and 6.1.5.
616. Objective supported by recitals 4, 6, 7, 21, and 25 InfoSoc Directive.
617. *See supra* 4.3.1.2, 4.3.2.3, and 4.4.3.6.
618. Objective supported inter alia by recitals 2, 5, 6, 7, 20, and 38 InfoSoc Directive; recitals 2 and 5, in particular, emphasise the need for a flexible legal framework in respect of this objective.
619. Peukert, 2015, p. 380, citing BGH, 17.07.2003, I ZR 259/00 ('Paperboy'), which identifies search engines and hyperlinking as essential components to secure the proper functioning of the Internet.

'adequately to economic realities such as new forms of exploitation' (recital 5).[620]

However, the *acquis* falls short of this objective. As shown in Chapter 4, exclusive rights are mostly interpreted broadly and, to a significant extent, in a technical way. The result is that they extend to a substantial array of forms of online use by individuals, many of which are instrumental to the online enjoyment of works, and do not constitute forms of commercial exploitation. Furthermore, the priority of contract and technological measures in defining the scope of protection, and the use of opaque concepts (e.g., 'unauthorised source'), further hinder the space available for online use.[621]

Perhaps the best example of how this approach can be harmful to the development of the Internet is the application of the right of communication to the public to hyperlinking.[622] As noted by the European Copyright Society in its opinion prior to the *Svensson* judgment:

> Although hyperlinking takes many forms and has multiple functions, there can be no doubt that it is the single most important feature that differentiates the Internet from other forms of cultural production and dissemination. Hyperlinking is intimately bound to the conception of the Internet as a network, and hyperlinks constitute paths leading users from one location to another. As the Supreme Court of Canada has stated '[h]yperlinks … are an indispensable part of [the Internet's] operation.
>
> The legal regulation of hyperlinking thus carries with it enormous capacity to interfere with the operation of the Internet, and therefore with access to information, freedom of expression, freedom to conduct business, as well – of course – with business ventures that depend on these types of linkages. Europe has developed a significant sector of SMEs, many of whose web operations depend on the use and provision of links. The Court must not under-estimate the importance of its ruling in this case.[623]

Unfortunately, the Court's judgment in *Svensson* and its application of the new public criterion not only failed to recognise the importance of placing standard hyperlinks completely outside the scope of copyright, but also added further uncertainty. This uncertainty led to further preliminary references, including the question of whether linking to an unauthorised source is a restricted act. In his Opinion in *GS Media*, AG Wathelet made clear the technological development issues of the question, including potential chilling effects, when he mentioned that:

620. *See* Velze, 2015, pp. 74–75, making a similar point regarding the right of communication to the public.
621. *See supra* 4.3.1.2, 4.3.2.3, and 4.5.
622. This issue is analysed *supra* at 4.3.2.
623. European Copyright Society, 2013, p. 1 (paras 3–4) (footnotes omitted).

as a general rule, internet users are not aware and do not have the means to check whether the initial communication to the public of a protected work freely accessible on the internet was effected with or without the copyright holder's consent. If users were at risk of proceedings for infringement of copyright under Article 3(1) of Directive 2001/29 whenever they post a hyperlink to works freely accessible on another website, they would be much more reticent to post them, which would be to the detriment of the proper functioning and the very architecture of the internet, and to the development of the information society.[624]

Although the Court recognised these very points in its *GS Media* ruling, it nevertheless chose to balance the different competing interests at stake through a rebuttable presumption of knowledge linked to a for-profit condition, the application of which is unclear. As a result, a significant amount of hyperlinking acts is either restricted by copyright, or subject to legal uncertainty.[625]

By placing these and other types of non-commercial use of works under a statutory licence system, the ACS will curtail some of the negative effects arising from the overbroad and technologically determined interpretation of online rights. From this perspective, the system will preserve the functioning of the Internet and foster its development.

Another way in which an ACS may promote this objective is by eliminating the risk of intermediary liability of (certain) intermediaries whose services enable end-users to exercise the limitation. This argument, it merits pointing out, is reminiscent of one rationale underlying the creation of the private copying system in Germany.[626] As it now stands, intermediaries may be subject to enforcement measures in relation to their clients' use of their services, which impose significant burdens on their operation, e.g., filtering or blocking injunctions. The increased focus of EU institutions and rights holders on bolstering the role of intermediaries in copyright enforcement will likely add to the strain, with negative implications for their ability to innovate.[627]

The mere threat of enforcement likely has a chilling effect on the development of new online technologies that may involve the reproduction and communication to the public of works by end-users, even in a context where the intermediary's activity is not considered a normal form of exploitation of works. The ACS may provide breathing space to such technology providers, while retaining the possibility of enforcement of the exclusive right against unauthorised for-profit online platforms.

---

624. *Opinion AG in GS Media*, para. 78. (This passage is cited *supra* at 4.3.2.3).
625. *See supra* 4.3.2.1.4 and 4.3.2.2.
626. *See supra* 2.3.
627. *See supra* 1.1 and 5.3.3.6.3. *See also* Hugenholtz & Quintais, 2017 (forthcoming).

Objective 7: Harmonisation of Copyright Law to Achieve a Functioning Internal Market

Finally, an overall objective of the directive is the harmonisation of copyright and related rights as a means to achieve an internal market (objective 7).[628] In recent communications, the Commission refers to this ultimate target as the 'digital single market'.[629]

Harmonisation refers to the co-ordination or approximation 'of different legal solutions through the elimination of major differences and the creation of minimum requirements or standards'.[630] The EU path to harmonisation of copyright and related rights is briefly described in Chapter 1. Nothing in this study indicates that the adoption of a statutory licence ACS is detrimental to the existing level of harmonisation in copyright law or the digital single market goal.

If anything, the experience of the patchwork design and national implementation of limitations in the InfoSoc Directive suggests that a new limitation for non-commercial online use would better promote these goals, especially if such a limitation is defined as mandatory. This would ensure that the limitation is implemented in all Member States, therefore guaranteeing a higher level of harmonisation than if the limitation is qualified as optional. However, even in this latter case, it is difficult to argue that an ACS would hinder the current level of harmonisation, as the vast majority of existing limitations in the *acquis* are facultative.

In addition to the objectives discussed thus far, it is important to consider briefly the *requirement* that an ACS complies with international copyright law, as this plays a role in the Court's interpretation of the *acquis*.[631] On this point, the analysis in the first part of this Chapter argues that a flexible interpretation of the three-step test is more consistent with international law (and in particular with Article 10 WCT and its Agreed Statement) than the strict interpretation sometimes followed by the CJEU. That flexible interpretation allows a statutory licence ACS to comply with the three-step test and informs the design of all elements of the corresponding limitation.[632] Therefore, if such a flexible interpretation is accepted, the statutory licence ought to be consistent with international copyright law.

In conclusion, the foregoing analysis shows that a limitation-based ACS for non-commercial online use of works is consistent with the normative

628. Other than in the title of the directive, the harmonisation objective is mentioned in recitals 3, 4, 6, 7, 9, 23, 25, 31, 32, 47, and 56 InfoSoc Directive. Recitals 31 and 32 refer in particular to the goal of harmonising limitations (on which *see supra* 4.4.1.3).

629. See, e.g., Communication on a Digital Single Market 2015, and Communication on Modern European Copyright Framework 2015.

630. Angelopoulos, 2016, p. 8.

631. Guibault et al., 2007a, pp. 4–6. On compliance with international law, *see* recitals 15 and 44 InfoSoc Directive. *See also supra* 1.1 and 5.2.1.4.

632. *See supra* 5.3 and *infra* 6.2, and 5.5.2. On the proposed design for an ACS, *see infra* 6.2.

objectives of EU copyright law. This conclusion results from a flexible reading of the law in light of the public interest and the concept of fair balance. Other, stricter, readings are certainly possible, and could lead to a different conclusion. As with the legal interpretation of positive EU copyright law, the final position on the admissibility of an ACS may depend on one's normative preferences and view of how copyright law should look in the future.

5.6 CONCLUSIONS

This chapter examines two related questions at the heart of this book. First, it looks at whether and to what extent a limitation-based statutory licence ACS for non-commercial online use of works by individuals is admissible under EU copyright law, namely the three-step test. Second, it examines whether and how such a legalisation model is consistent with the general aims of copyright and the objectives of EU copyright law.

From a compliance perspective, the main legal challenge to an ACS-limitation is the three-step test. The chapter proposes a framework for the interpretation of the test in light of international copyright law, which considers the different versions of the test – with an emphasis on Article 10 WCT and its Agreed Statement – and spectrum of interpretations. The analysis concludes that a flexible interpretation of the test and its conditions is more consistent with the aims of copyright law, as it enables consideration of the public interest and the fair balance of competing claims. Using that flexible lens, this chapter examines a statutory licence ACS against each step of the test, with a view to its comprehensive overall assessment.

Under the first step, a potential limitation must constitute a qualitative and quantitative 'certain special case'. Its scope of application should be reasonably foreseeable and not overly broad. Furthermore, the limitation should be justified on a sound policy basis.

The aim of a statutory licence ACS is to privilege use for personal enjoyment and expression online. Its scope is restricted to natural persons, certain types of work, and non-commercial acts of reproduction and communication to the public over the Internet (not already exempted by existing limitations). Compliance with this step is contentious as regards the subject matter scope, which may require exclusion of categories of work beyond software, databases, and videogames.

On the qualitative side, the limitation is soundly justified not only by the failure of exclusive rights to regulate non-commercial online use of works, but also on non-economic public interest grounds. These include the promotion of creativity and circulation of culture, and the respect for the fundamental rights and freedoms of individuals – freedom of expression and information, privacy, and personal data – and, to a lesser extent, intermediaries' freedom to conduct a business.

The main obstacle to a statutory licence ACS lies with the second step of the test, and more specifically with the traditional view of normal exploitation of works, anchored on the principle of strict interpretation. After exploring this view, it is argued that the same is not only overly restrictive, but also foregoes consideration of policy rationales, remunerative potential and the consistency of a limitation with the policy objectives of copyright. On that basis, in accordance with the principle of fair balance, it seems preferable to adopt a flexible understanding of the second step.

In this reading, there is a conflict with the normal exploitation if a limitation deprives creators and exploiters of major and foreseeable sources of income under normal commercial circumstances. These sources include revenue generated through online commercialisation of the exclusive rights of reproduction and communication to the public to commercial and end-users via digital network platforms.

An ACS targets non-commercial online use by individuals, which is in many cases not exercised or monetised by rights holders, and in other instances can be classified as *de minimis*. The introduction of a statutory licence to regulate this type of use has the potential to create new rights revenue, and to constitute a normal form of exploitation thereof. On the other hand, it is possible that the licence has unintended adverse effects on downloading and streaming channels. However, the scale of these negative side-effects is unknown and can only be speculated at. Based on empirical research on the effect of unauthorised use on the market, it is conjectured that a properly designed system could co-exist with authorised commercial channels. (This conjecture, naturally, requires empirical testing.)

An adequate system, in any case, requires that exclusive rights are enforceable against unauthorised for-profit websites or platforms capable of impinging on the normal exploitation and the commercial core of copyright. One avenue to achieve this is through the strict definition of what constitutes an authorised non-commercial use in an ACS, and the corresponding exclusion from the scope of the licence of online exchanges by for-profit unauthorised platforms. Another option, in line with a current trend in CJEU case law (and the *GS Media* knowledge test), is to include in the scope of the right of communication to the public acts of linking to unauthorised sources, as well as unauthorised profit-making acts of communication to the public of copyright works by online platforms.[633]

If it is possible to delimit the scope of the statutory licence in this way, the ACS will only legalise the activities of end-users and a limited number

633. See, in this respect, the pending preliminary references: CJEU, Reference for Preliminary Ruling, Case C-527/15, *Filmspeler*; CJEU, Reference for Preliminary Ruling, Case C-610/15, *Stichting Brein v. Ziggo*. (On the first case, *see Opinion AG in Filmspeler*.) A supplement to both options discussed in the text could be the promotion at EU level (e.g., through a Commission communication or Memorandum of Understanding) of self-regulation measures between rights holders and online intermediaries aimed at curtailing the activities of unauthorised for-profit platforms.

of online intermediaries, such as those enabling or facilitating the licensed use but not directly reproducing or communicating the works to the public, i.e. not making an own use of works. The licence would not affect those mostly 'neutral' intermediaries that benefit from the E-Commerce Directive's safe-harbours, in relation to their activities that are exempt from liability under those provisions. *De lege lata*, only this circumscribed scope would seem to enable a statutory licence ACS to avoid conflicting with the normal exploitation of works, even under a flexible reading of the second step. Of course, to the extent that such a legalisation scheme is limited vis-à-vis online intermediaries and platforms, it raises the (different) question of whether this is a desirable or satisfactory system *de lege ferenda* from the perspective of end-users.

Examination of the third step involves a multi-level balancing exercise guided by the principle of proportionality, which considers the reasonableness of the prejudice caused and conflicting legitimate interests. These include, on the one hand, the concurrent and opposing interests of creators and exploiters. On the other hand, and in line with the principle of fair balance, they include the individual and collective public interest of users stemming from the promotion of creativity and dissemination of works, and the respect of fundamental rights.

A limitation causes unreasonable prejudice if the harm suffered by rights holders from its introduction – mainly its indirect effect on the overall exploitation of works online – is out of proportion to the benefits derived by the public.

Payment of fair compensation through a statutory licence is an acceptable means of reducing that harm to reasonable levels, and there is research suggesting this is feasible. Following such research, it is proposed that compensation is calculated based on harm (including the mitigating factors described in the InfoSoc Directive) but pursuant to a contingent valuation method that approaches the notion of appropriate reward for creativity. However, the shortcomings of empirical research and the rapid evolution of the market warrant caution and emphasise the need to examine the policy motivations of the ACS, expressed in different legitimate interests.

The main concern of creators is fair remuneration for online use, whereas exploiters favour assignable exclusive rights and stricter enforcement measures. By imposing an unwaivable fair compensation right, an ACS would support the material interests of creators. However, because it also creates a novel revenue stream for exploiters, it would potentially not prejudice their financial interests. In any case, this trade-off should be acceptable if the benefit to creators offsets the harm to exploiters.

On the normative level, an ACS promises to serve the public interest by promoting access to culture and knowledge in the digital environment, and ensuring an operational non-market sphere of personal enjoyment and expression for end-users. In the regulation of non-commercial use, it is further argued that a well-designed ACS is more respectful of the fundamental rights of Internet users – especially privacy in telecommunications and freedom of expression and information online – than strict enforcement measures, such as filtering, blocking and Internet disconnection.

From the perspective of the fundamental freedom to conduct a business, the advantages of a statutory licence ACS over enforcement are apparent for Internet intermediaries otherwise subject to injunctions. However, for ISPs such advantages may not offset the costs resulting from their qualification as intermediary debtors of the broadband levy. Nevertheless, if the system allows recovery of administrative costs and the levy to be passed on to users, it could be worth experimenting with, especially in light of the institutional thrust towards increasing the role of online intermediaries and platforms in enforcement measures. (Here, again, further research is required.)

On balance, there is space available for a statutory licence ACS compliant with EU copyright law. However, doubts remain as to whether the system can overcome potential conflicts with the normal exploitation of works, even following a flexible interpretation. Thus, the chapter explores two flexibility mechanisms to overcome these potential conflicts: embargo periods and opt-out rules.

Embargo periods allow exclusivity to remain the default rule for a period of time coinciding with the most intense commercial exploitation of works. After that period, the ACS would regulate non-commercial use. An opt-out rule allows rights holders to restore exclusivity as their preferred model of exploitation of non-commercial online use of works.

The analysis shows that both models are legally feasible but there is insufficient information on their hidden complexities and costs of adoption, which require additional empirical study. The main challenges lie with the difficulty of implementation across different categories of works, and the fact that they reduce the value for users of an all-encompassing legalisation scheme. A combination of an opt-out rule with an embargo period would ensure that all works eventually return to the ACS, a promising long-term solution. Yet, it will come at the high cost of additional complexity for the management of the system in the interim, making it a difficult policy proposition.

In sum, reform of EU copyright law via a statutory licence ACS is feasible in a limited fashion. However, its adoption rests on a set of binary normative choices for policy makers as to how to regulate non-commercial use: flexible versus strict interpretation of limitations, remunerated access versus exclusivity with strict enforcement, and public versus private ordering. The public interest choice for access, furthermore, requires that we recognise the internal effect of fundamental rights in shaping the scope of copyright protection. Neither choice is wrong per se. Rather, the choices hinge on a normative view of copyright and of where to strike a fair balance of interests.

The second part of the chapter therefore looks deeper into this normative dimension. It asks whether and to what extent a model of access and remuneration – a statutory licence ACS – is consistent with the general aims of copyright and the objectives of EU copyright law. This part begins by examining whether a right of access and remuneration for the non-commercial online use of works can be reconciled with the dominant rationales for copyright protection in the European legal tradition, namely natural rights (including the fairness and personality theories) and utilitarianism. Both theories, beyond their influence in *droit d'auteur* and common law countries, are reflected in the objectives of the copyright *acquis* and provide justification for copyright protection in EU law. Consequently, they play a role in the balancing of competing interests that underlies the determination of the scope of protection, including the imposition of restrictions on the exclusive right.

From the perspective of natural rights, a statutory licence ACS impacts the material interests of authors in the commercial exploitation of copyright. Therefore, it mainly calls into question the fairness justification for copyright protection, developed from the Lockean desert-for-labour argument. Assuming *arguendo* that Locke's theory applies to copyright and provides an acceptable rationale for granting a property right over the expressive results of creative labour, the fairness theory does not impose absolute protection for the right, but allows restrictions thereto. Those restrictions result not only from the sufficiency proviso, but more clearly from the consideration of the public interest when transitioning from the state of nature to a civil and political society. In actualising the public interest, the prohibition element (exclusivity) of copyright protection can be curtailed, while retaining its reward element (remuneration), thereby safeguarding the material interests of authors.

A statutory licence ACS can therefore be accommodated by the fairness theory, insofar as it ensures remuneration for the use of works (arguably on more favourable terms than an exclusive right) and is justified not only by market failure but also by the public interest in both the protection of fundamental rights and freedoms of users, and the promotion of creation and dissemination of works.

The utilitarian theory justifies copyright protection on the basis of the prospective incentives it provides for the creation and dissemination of works. It views copyright as a positive right granted to further the public interest, and the exclusive right as a device to solve a public goods problem in the production and dissemination of works. According to this theory, the recognition of a property-like enforceable right to prohibit use without authorisation or remuneration would address the free-rider problems arising from the non-excludable character of copyright goods, allowing a functioning market for their production and supply. The exclusive right would enable copyright owners to charge prices sufficiently high to recoup their costs of creation, inducing as a result future creative activities and maximising the production of works.

The artificial imposition of exclusivity is justified if its benefits outweigh its costs. With regard to an ACS, the question is whether regulating non-commercial online use of works through an exclusive right imposes costs that validate restrictions to that right. The analysis suggests that certain costs of exclusivity – chilling effects on follow-on creativity, transaction costs, and administration and enforcement costs – may justify the adoption of a liability rule in the form of a limitation-based statutory licence.

Hence, imposing a restriction on the exclusive right through a right of access and remuneration for non-commercial online use is in principle consistent with the utilitarian rationale of copyright. In practice, whether this switch from a property to a liability rule is desirable rests on empirical research on the costs and benefits of the new system as compared to the status quo. On this point, there are indicators that such a switch would increase social welfare.

Building on these theories, the chapter then examines the human and fundamental rights characterisation of copyright in different legal instruments (UDHR, ICESCR, ECHR, and the Charter), including its qualification as a property right. It follows from this examination that copyright protection is not absolute and has at its core access and remuneration dimensions, characterised by the availability of works and cultural participation, and respect for the material interests of rights holders (especially creators). The possibility of restricting the prohibition element of copyright and modulating the options for its exercise is illustrated throughout this book in mechanisms that include voluntary and mandatory models of collective rights management, and statutory licences.

This conceptual turn towards an access and remuneration right is justified by the social function of copyright. The argument here is that the scope of protection is not absolute. Rather, it should be drawn in light of the public interest. One method for introducing this social function into the determination of the scope of copyright is by incorporating the public interest within the three-step test analysis of a limitation, through identifying the legitimate interests of third parties and considering them in the fair balancing exercise. (This method was followed in the first part of the chapter.)

Another method is to consider the public interest from an external perspective, as a fundamental (or constitutional) rights' foundation for a right of access and remuneration and a limit on absolute copyright protection. From this perspective, it is possible on the one hand to find support for such a right in the universal right to culture and science in the ICESCR and UDHR. On the other hand, the fundamental rights qualification of copyright implies restrictions on its scope based not only on the public interest (*see* Article 1 Protocol No. 1 ECHR and Article 17 Charter) but also on the application of conflicting fundamental rights and freedoms, sometimes subject to the payment of fair compensation (see, e.g., *Luksan*).

The result of the application of these normative considerations to the regulation of mass non-commercial online use of works by individuals, is that a limitation-based statutory licence ACS is an admissible alternative to the exclusive right. There are also strong normative arguments to qualify the underlying fair compensation right as unwaivable and potentially mandatory, as well as to afford it some level of protection against disposition by contract or technological measures.

Finally, the last section of the chapter explores the consistency of a statutory licence ACS with the objectives of EU copyright law, as derived from the recitals of the copyright directives (with an emphasis on the InfoSoc Directive) and CJEU jurisprudence. The objectives are the following: (1) Fair balance between the rights and interests of authors and the rights of users; (2) High level of protection for copyright holders; (3) Adequate compensation or appropriate reward; (4) Circulation of culture; (5) Resolution of legal uncertainty; (6) Technological development (including the promotion of the information society); and (7) Harmonisation of copyright law to achieve a functioning internal market.

On balance, the analysis shows that a properly delimited ACS is consistent with these objectives, in most cases more so than the current regime. This conclusion relies on a nuanced consideration of what should constitute a desirable 'high level of protection' for non-commercial online use of works – viewed as an *optimal level of protection that ensures adequate compensation for rights holders* – and its articulation with the aim of circulation of culture online. The conclusion also emphasises the importance of ACS to resolve legal uncertainty for end-users in their online activities, as well as the potential beneficial effects of a legalisation scheme for technological development in the information society.

To conclude, the narrative arch of this chapter (and indeed the whole book) provides a credible glimpse into the future shape of copyright regulation for non-commercial online use. The analysis allows us to make an informed choice between private versus public ordering, strict versus flexible interpretation, and exclusivity versus remunerated access. The current regime, which tends towards an online culture of exclusivity, embodies the first set of choices. A statutory licence ACS, which emphasises access and remuneration for non-commercial use, represents the second set of choices. This chapter develops a normative argument for why a 'public choice' approach is consistent with the rationales and objectives of the *acquis*. On balance, the analysis suggests that EU copyright law can and should be adapted to include a right of access and remuneration for this type of online use by individuals. In light of these findings, the following and concluding chapter summarises the findings of this book and provides a blueprint for reform through a statutory licence ACS.

Chapter 6

Summary and Conclusions: Towards Access and Remuneration

This book explores the flexibility of EU copyright law for the regulation of mass online use of copyright works in light of the public interest. Its main research questions are as follows: Are ACS for non-commercial online use of works by individuals admissible under EU copyright law and consistent with its objectives and, if so, to what extent? How can and should EU copyright law incorporate an ACS?

These questions have been for the most part answered in the previous chapters. The first part of this concluding chapter summarises that analysis and its findings (6.1). This summary clarifies whether and to what extent an ACS is admissible in the legal framework of the copyright *acquis*, and consistent with its objectives. The analysis shows that the most promising model to solve the problem identified in this book is a limitation-based statutory licence for non-commercial online use of works by individuals.

Building on these findings, the second part of this chapter proposes a model for such a legalisation scheme, thereby answering the question of how EU copyright law should incorporate an ACS (6.2). The proposed model is presented as a blueprint for copyright reform in the EU. Following the pragmatic approach of the research, such a blueprint is susceptible of adaptation for lower impact reform, for example relying on voluntary types of collective rights management and soft law approaches, like recommendations. The hope is that the outcome of this examination has a realistic chance of adoption, or at least offers a basis for future consideration of models of access and remuneration (rather than exclusivity and strict enforcement) for online use as viable options to modernise EU copyright law.

Chapter 6

6.1 SUMMARY

This section summarises the main findings of the previous five chapters. The narrative arch of the study starts with making the case for reform of EU copyright law (6.1.1). It then moves on to extract the lessons of copyright past for compensation systems (6.1.2), before designing a taxonomy of legalisation proposals that assist in the definition of their scope, limits, and effects on the exclusive right (6.1.3). This is followed by an exploration of the space available for an ACS in the *acquis*, which sheds light on the intersection between exclusive rights and limitations for online use of works by individuals (6.1.4). Having concluded that the best legal solution to address the fragmentation challenges of copyright law is a limitation-based statutory licence ACS, an examination is made of whether and to what extent such a licence for non-commercial online use: is admissible under EU copyright law, namely the three-step test; and is consistent with the general aims of copyright and the objectives of EU copyright law (6.1.5).

6.1.1 The Case for Reform of EU Copyright Law

Technological development allows the exploitation and use of works in different and innovative forms, influencing the social norms that regulate the online conduct of users. This cycle involving copyright, technology, and social norms, has shaped the evolution of the law since its inception.

Copyright law was originally aimed at regulating the commercial use of works between professionals. In that context, the central role of the exclusive right in the legal regime was mostly justified. However, throughout history, the landscape in which copyright operated has gradually transformed by virtue of technology, social norms, and the market. These forces influenced and shaped the exploitation of copyright and the use of works.

In general, the response of legislators was to extend the subject matter and substantive rights scope of copyright, which currently includes all manner of digital content and different types of online use. This expansion is visible in international and EU copyright law in the multiple revisions to the BC, the adoption of TRIPS, and the WIPO Internet Treaties, which adapted the international framework to the digital network environment. It is likewise clear from the multiple copyright directives, with a particular emphasis on the InfoSoc Directive – which implemented the WIPO treaties into EU law beyond their minimum standards –, and its interpretation by the CJEU.

With the evolution of technology, it became increasingly possible for individuals to access and use works for non-commercial purposes ubiquitously and at a low cost. But the extension of copyright's scope also meant that such use, largely for enjoyment and personal expression, may be restricted. In this way, copyright law shifted from mainly regulating professional relationships to also cover activities of individual users in the private or non-commercial sphere.[1] The default application of such a legal regime to mass online use of works created a powerful disconnect between the law and technology-influenced social norms.[2] This mismatch leads to a costly social conflict, which negatively affects the legitimacy of copyright law and pre-empts exploration of alternative legal solutions to remunerate this online use.

Advocates of the current system and stronger protection argue that strict enforcement is an effective deterrent to unauthorised file sharing, which they consider to not only be the main cause of the content industry's losses, but also to jeopardise creative incentives. But there is reason to doubt such arguments.

Most empirical research does not consider file sharing to be a direct substitute for paid sales or services in digital platforms, and some authors even identify positive effects from these practices on the demand for content and ancillary products. Also, it is noteworthy that in a content market in transition – from physical to digital, and from ownership to access-based models – global digital rights revenues have steadily increased. The problem, however, is that creators have not seen a corresponding benefit from that increase, especially in the context of emerging streaming channels.

Furthermore, enforcement is of limited effectiveness in deterring file sharing. This much is clear from the experience of copyright litigation since the early 2000s. Despite the strengthening of exclusive rights, the recognition of legal protection of TPMs, the growing array of available enforcement measures, and institutional backing of rights holders, strict enforcement has not resulted in the elimination of file sharing. Legal, technological and social factors all play a part in this outcome.

From the legal perspective, uncertainty arises from the application of a territorial and substantively fragmented copyright regime to the online use of works. In addition, the jurisprudence of national courts and the CJEU has highlighted the significant legal risks of enforcement. Perhaps the main peril is the potential hindrance to fundamental rights and freedoms, which have emerged as external limits to copyright protection, de facto preventing (for the time being) some of the severest enforcement measures, like broad filtering injunctions and graduated response systems.

From the technological and social standpoints, the possibilities afforded by digital technologies shape consumer expectations and habits, and allow users to meet those expectations where the law and market fail to do so. Despite the evolution of legal offerings and its potential to fulfil unmet demand, the level of fragmentation of EU copyright law all but ensures a perennial mismatch between what end-users expect and what the market can provide.

1. Gervais, 2009, pp. 845–857, 869–870.
2. Hugenholtz, 2013b, p. 26.

In this light, it is reasonable to conclude that a model of exclusive rights and strict enforcement will remain inadequate to address that mismatch, while imposing significant social cost. In tandem, the current legal regime is incapable of generating remuneration for the mass online use of works, and risks creating conflicts between copyright and other fundamental rights.

To address this problem, the present book examines reform proposals that focus on models of remunerated access to copyright works in the online environment, rather than full exclusivity. These models are defined under the umbrella term 'ACS'. ACS replace the need for direct authorisation for the online use of works by individuals (e.g., downloading and uploading), resulting from the application of exclusive rights, with a licensing scheme authorising such use and ensuring remuneration to rights holders or at least creators. In other words, an ACS restricts the nature or exercise of copyright to replace the current regime for non-commercial online use of works by individuals with a 'permitted-but-paid' model.

Empirical research provides a boon for the study of ACS, as it shows these models to be not only acceptable to end-users but also economically promising for rights holders. On the one hand, there is evidence of public support for such legalisation schemes, especially among users that already consume culture online, including high intensity file-sharers. The support is strongest for schemes that provide holistic access to works, with few use restrictions, and at a reasonable price (e.g., a surcharge on the monthly rate of Internet access, within the price range of existing premium streaming services). On the other hand, despite the limitations of existing research, at least one recent study in the Netherlands suggests that a statutory licence system for online recorded music can be welfare increasing and generate superior rights revenue. If nothing else, that study highlights the potential cost of exclusivity over a model of access and remuneration for copyright-protected works online.

The possible benefits of a welfare increasing ACS are many. Rights holders would not only see increased revenues but also savings in enforcement costs. Creators could benefit too if the system includes a mandatory claim to fair compensation, which would mitigate the problems with fair remuneration they suffer due to contractual imbalances in the digital exploitation of exclusive rights. End-users would face a lower risk of infringement, increased legal certainty for their online activities, and experience better online access to works. In the long term, an ACS could promote the circulation of culture and technological development in the information society. In all, a legalisation model that ensures remuneration for non-commercial use of works promises to strike a fair balance between the interests of rights holders and users. These are all good arguments to explore the legal and normative admissibility of an ACS within EU copyright law.

6.1.2 Lessons from the Past

The legal inquiry proper into legalisation systems begins with a trip to the past. If an ACS constitutes a deviation from the principle of exclusivity, it is sensible to investigate instructive precedents in the history of copyright law. Such analysis could assist in identifying legal regimes that ensure remuneration while restricting exclusivity and striking a fair balance between the public interest and the interest of rights holders. It would also allow an understanding of the underlying policy justifications for the adoption of precedents.

Precedents are rules or schemes that address similar problems and share core characteristics to ACS. They are copyright regimes that regulate large-scale use of works through compensated non-voluntary licences. Precedents aim to solve problems relating to the inability of the law to regulate the large-scale use of works made possible by technological developments, manifested in market failures, and in the difficulty or undesirability (practical, legal, or political) of enforcing exclusive rights.

The analysis focuses on two precedents that have inspired multiple legalisation proposals: statutory licences for private copying, and compulsory licences for broadcasting and communication to the public, regimes which are often combined with obligatory collective management.

The origins of private copying can be traced back to the 1950s in Germany. A series of landmark decisions by the BGH extended the right of reproduction to acts of home taping by individuals, simultaneously imposing contributory liability on the providers of copying technology. In response, the German legislator adopted a statutory licence system subjecting such use to a remunerated legal authorisation. The remuneration was paid through a levy imposed on the technology providers, who had a right to pass it on to the final user. This solution provided a workable system for the payment of remuneration (managed by CMOs), ensured a link between the actual use and the payment, respected the privacy of users, and imposed a proportionate burden on intermediaries that benefited indirectly from the legal permission, in exchange for immunity from liability. The technological neutrality of the legal formula ensured the expansion of the levy across a range of tangible media and devices (as levy targets), as well as types of content.

Internationally, references to private copying are found in the preparatory works of different copyright treaties. In the BC's Stockholm revision conference (1967), the German system was pivotal in shaping the three-step test and equitable remuneration as a flexibility tool to accommodate public interest restrictions to the exclusive right. The debates leading to the WIPO Treaties (1996), on the other hand, addressed the possibility of phasing out levies due to developments in TPMs, but recognised the privacy underpinning of the limitation.

Private copying eventually made it to the *acquis* as an optional limitation in Article 5(2)(b) InfoSoc Directive, which extends to digital private use and is combined with a right to fair compensation. The provision remains relevant to this day despite the legal protection of technological measures and the possibility of contractual disposition of limitations. This relevance, it is submitted, results not only from its market failure justification, but also – and predominantly – from its fundamental rights pedigree.

The BC compulsory licence exempts broadcasters from authorisation for acts of communication to the public of works, subject to equitable remuneration – a largely undefined concept beyond its ordinary meaning of a fair and just amount, linked to market value and actual use. The licence was introduced in the Rome Act of 1928 in response to the development of radio broadcasting, and amended in the Brussels Act of 1948, allowing *inter alia* its extension to different modalities of wireless diffusion (television broadcasting, satellite broadcasting, rebroadcasting), and wire transmissions (e.g., Internet retransmissions).

Despite proposals to abolish it, the licence survives to this day, most notably through the Agreed Statement to Article 8 WCT, interpreted by some academics as allowing the application of this regime to the online right of communication to the public. In the *acquis*, such an interpretation appears to be pre-empted by Article 3 InfoSoc Directive, which would subject a compulsory licence to the three-step test.

The BC licence further provided inspiration for similar regimes in the field of related rights (in the RC, TRIPS, and WPPT), which have survived in the *acquis* due to the limited scope of Article 3(2) InfoSoc Directive. Also noteworthy is the presence, in the SatCab Directive, of a special regime of mandatory collective management, functionally similar to compulsory licencing.

The two precedents studied illustrate the tendency of copyright law to expand its scope to novel technologies that allow exploitation and use of works outside the exclusive control of rights holders. Although it was initially unclear whether either use should be subject to protection, the response of courts and legislatures was in both cases to extend the exclusive right to such uses. This was done essentially out of a concern that failure to thus extend copyright protection would harm the economic interest of authors and preclude future avenues of commercial exploitation. For private copying, the main justification for this extension was the author's right to a just pecuniary reward. For broadcasting, the motivation offered was fairness to authors, due to the fact that broadcasting programs were essentially comprised of copyright works.

However, the widening of the exclusive right gave rise to a conflict with the public interest. In private copying, the conflict was prompted by the intrusion of copyright in the private sphere, causing a clash between copyright and consumer rights, the fundamental right of privacy, and the ability of technology providers to carry out their activities. In broadcasting, the conflict resulted from interference with a new means of communication of profound social and democratic value (for the circulation of culture, education, and free speech), and from risks to competition caused by the potential refusal by CMOs to license broadcasters.

Both precedents, therefore, share similar public interest dynamics. On the one hand, the extension of protection is justified by an essential financial consideration: the preservation for authors (and later other rights holders) of benefits arising from the commercial exploitation and use of their works through new technologies. On the other hand, allowing authors to appropriate those exploitation possibilities through the grant of exclusive rights was deemed problematic. First, because it could give rise to market failures; and second, because it conflicted with the public interest in accessing and dissemination of knowledge, protection of privacy, technological development, and competition.

At the intersection of these competing claims, the legal alternative that emerged was to restrict the nature or exercise of the exclusive right, promoting in its stead non-voluntary models of remunerated access and use of works. These models allowed authors to retain the core element of copyright protection – remuneration for the use of works – while preserving and respecting the public interest.

This is the essential lesson from the study of precedents: exclusivity is not totemic, but rather a legal tool for copyright protection, subject to the public interest. Where a conflict emerges between the exclusive right and legitimate manifestations of the public interest, models of remunerated access and use – including those based on copyright limitations – offer a legal solution to reconcile and balance competing interests. From this perspective, remuneration becomes more central to copyright protection than exclusivity.

Another important lesson from the analysis concerns the power of rhetoric in copyright policy. It is nothing short of remarkable how much the copyright discussions of yore resemble today's debates on file sharing and other online activities, especially in relation to the arguments advanced in defence of stronger protection and stricter enforcement. Time has not only revealed these arguments to be inaccurate, but also shown balanced solutions, such as that devised in Germany for private copying, to be more sensible. This should give pause to reflect on whether the current policy direction at EU level – towards exclusivity, priority of technological measures, and stringent enforcement – is the most adequate, in particular vis-à-vis individual non-commercial online uses that are at their core activities of personal enjoyment and expression.

6.1.3 A Taxonomy of Alternative Compensation Systems

Having examined historical precedents, the book turns to the conceptual understanding and definition of ACS. For that purpose, a taxonomy is developed to systematise a representative sample of legalisation proposals. The taxonomy incorporates different models and attributes, characterises their legal nature and effects on copyright in light of international and EU copyright law, and assists in defining the scope of ACS.

The first level of the taxonomy identifies five rights acquisition schemes for the wholesale legalisation of online use: voluntary collective licensing, ECL, mandatory collective management, legal licences (including statutory and compulsory licences), and State Systems. Excluded from the taxonomy are proposals that rely solely on private ordering, that fail to ensure remuneration, or that favour the abolishment of copyright protection.

Voluntary collective management and ECL with the possibility of opt-out for rights holders only operate restrictions on the exercise of copyright. From the purely legal standpoint, these voluntary models would be the most feasible and least impactful legalisation options for rights holders. However, the analysis raises concern as to their ability to facilitate the broad blanket multi-territorial licence required by an ACS. This is for two reasons.

The first reason concerns the hurdles imposed on a voluntary licensing scheme by the substantive rights and territorial fragmentation of copyright in the EU. For example, for an EU-wide licence to cover online music it would require aggregation of multiple rights in each sound recording (often from different owners) across the twenty-eight Member States of the EU.

The second reason relates to potential problems with securing the initial and continued participation of rights holders in different sectors. For either model to work, rights holders would have to, in the first place, adhere to collective management in large enough numbers to make the system worthwhile for users (in voluntary collective licensing), or to meet a representativeness threshold sufficient to trigger the extension effect (in ECL). The challenge is particularly great in sectors (such as the audio-visual) that do not have an established practice of collective rights management of online rights. However, even if the challenge is met, the possibility of opting out is a constant threat to the viability of either system. This is especially true as the value of a legalisation system to end-users is linked to the breadth of the repertoire and consequent licence, especially regarding the most popular works. If major rights holders decide to withhold or hoard these works, an ACS offers little value to its users.

For these reasons, legalisation schemes based on non-voluntary licences yield greater promise. In this book, the term refers to models such as legal licences, mandatory collective management and so-called 'compulsory' ECL (i.e., not allowing rights holders to opt out). Such regimes solve the problems of participation and fragmentation, while ensuring fair remuneration. Furthermore, at least in the music sector, they could leverage the infrastructure and know-how of the existing CMO system in the EU. Of course, State Systems could also, theoretically, address some of the problems identified. However, for pragmatic reasons, proposals of this type imply replacing copyright protection for non-commercial use of works with a public funded system *external* to copyright. This would require a major overhaul of EU copyright law, to an extent that is not politically realistic or legally feasible. Therefore, State Systems are discarded as a valid policy option for an ACS.

The meaning of 'non-voluntary licence' is ambiguous in copyright scholarship. Here, the term is used broadly to mean legal regimes that impose on the rights holder a certain model for exercising copyright, but do not necessarily entail a change to the exclusive nature of the right. In other words, the effect of a non-voluntary licence is not necessarily to transform an exclusive right into a right of remuneration or compensation. Of course, this is a controversial line to walk in legal scholarship, and carries significant consequences for the legal qualification of legalisation proposals of this type. While it is clear that the application of a statutory licence to an exclusive right leads to its conversion into a remuneration right for the licensed use, it is less obvious whether that is so for mandatory collective management (and compulsory ECL), despite the functional similarities between the models.

After analysing the legal arguments for both sides of the debate, this book takes the view that, from the conceptual and legal-technical standpoints, mandatory collective management affects the options for exercise of copyright, not its nature or existence. Thus, it should not be considered a copyright limitation. The upshot is that mandatory collective management of exclusive rights for non-commercial online use of works (e.g., for the licences mentioned in Article 5(3) CRM Directive) could be explored as a model for ACS, subject to the rigorous requirements of this type of collective management, but not the three-step test.

Nevertheless, the contentious nature of this interpretation raises obstacles to its adoption as a policy option at EU level, especially after the CJEU judgment in *Soulier and Doke*. Hence, from the pragmatic and legitimacy standpoints, it is advisable to inquire whether such a model would comply with the three-step test. That same test would apply to a legalisation proposal based on statutory licensing, as the same would require the adoption of a copyright limitation to the exclusive rights affected by the licence.

In addition to characterising different rights acquisition schemes, their key attributes are examined: subject matter scope, substantive rights scope, compensation type, management system, compensation target, and burden of compensation. These attributes help delimit the scope and contours of an ACS, providing a roadmap to design a legalisation scheme consistent with EU copyright law (*see infra* 6.2).

In sum, this detailed conceptual analysis provides an in depth understanding of the nature, scope and effects of an ACS, as well as the major legal and practical obstacles to its implementation. These are all essential aspects for the study of the admissibility and consistency of such systems with EU copyright law. The analysis also confirms and adds to the findings of the study of precedents, by demonstrating that legalisation proposals are not radical departures from the status quo. Instead, they are extensions and adaptations of existing copyright regimes. Inspiration is taken predominantly from examples of collective rights management and legal licences, with the objective of enabling a model of access and remuneration in the online environment. This realisation should allow us to view the ACS taxonomy as a toolbox of interoperable models and attributes to explore the flexibility of EU copyright law in search of viable reform options.

6.1.4 The Legal Space for Non-commercial Online Use of Works in EU Copyright Law

The following stage of the analysis is to assess *what the law is* in the *acquis* for the regulation of online use of works by individuals. This requires an explanation of how exclusive rights and limitations apply to those uses *de lege lata*, including areas of legal uncertainty. It is only with this knowledge at hand that we can assess the need and scope for legal reform through an ACS.

Individuals' online use can be classified in different categories: browsing, downloading, streaming, stream capture or ripping, uploading, hyperlinking, and digital adaptation. These activities trigger application of the harmonised exclusive rights of reproduction and communication to the public in Articles 2 and 3 InfoSoc Directive. Digital adaptations may also be subject to the right of adaptation, which although not harmonised in EU law, is a minimum right in the BC.

In the EU, territorial and substantive fragmentation of copyright makes the adjudication of online uses challenging. The challenge increases due to the CJEU's complex case law, often a boon for legal uncertainty. In general, the Court interprets exclusive rights broadly, combining technical and economic methods of interpretation to safeguard new modes of exploitation and use of works for rights holders.

The right of reproduction includes most reproductions made over digital networks, applying to browsing, downloading, (down) streaming, stream capture, certain uploads, and the making of digital adaptations. The scope of the online right of communication to the public is less stable in the CJEU's case law, mostly due to the inconsistent application of different criteria, and the fact that such scope may be influenced by the application of contractual and technical restrictions by rights holders (e.g., in the case of hyperlinking). Regardless, it is reasonable to conclude that this right applies broadly to online use of copyright works by individuals, including Internet transmission of streams, certain uploads, and most types of hyperlinking, with the only clear exception being links to works made 'freely accessible' with the prior consent of rights holders. (Even in the latter case, however, the Court's case law can be interpreted as subjecting such acts to copyright protection while allowing them under a doctrine of 'implicit consent'.)

The outcome of the analysis is that harmonised exclusive rights restrict a broad swath of online activities of end-users. The Court's fickle case law and technical definition of rights leave other types of online use in a legal grey area. This is the case for example for hyperlinking to unauthorised sources where application of the *GS Media* presumption of knowledge is not straightforward, the legal qualification of the acts of certain platforms under the right of communication to the public (e.g., The Pirate Bay), and uploading copies of works to a restricted group on a social sharing platform. This uncertainty may have a chilling effect on the online activities of providers and end-users, incentivising them to avoid activities that may turn out to be lawful.

Where an exclusive right restricts a use, a copyright limitation in the InfoSoc Directive may nevertheless permit it. The directive's limitations are mostly optional, do not apply to software and databases, can (in principle) be set aside by contract, and for the most part are superseded by the application of TPMs. However, a teleological interpretation of limitations sees them as crucial for striking a fair balance between the interest of rights holders in exclusivity and the public interest in circulation of culture and the respect of fundamental rights.

Study of the CJEU's case law highlights the tensions inherent to this balancing exercise. On the one hand, the Court adopts a doctrine of strict interpretation of limitations, using the three-step test as a tool to narrow the scope of limitations. On the other hand, in some of its most well-crafted judgments,[3] it uses the teleological method to interpret the prototypical wording of some limitations flexibly, in light of their purpose and with respect for the principle of effectiveness. Where a fundamental right provides a motivation for a limitation, the latter's scope is reinforced in the balancing of interests, to the detriment of the exclusive right.

Therefore, fundamental rights assume an *internal* function in the determination of the scope of protection. This function is in addition to their operation as external limits to copyright in situations of conflict between fundamental rights. Through this method, the CJEU mitigates the doctrine of strict interpretation in a way consistent with the InfoSoc Directive's objectives of harmonisation of limitations and fair balance. Arguably, such an approach is also coherent with the goal of achieving a high level of protection, if we take it to mean an 'optimal' rather than absolute level of protection.

This approach likewise allows the contemplation of the three-step test as a tool for a flexible and functional interpretation of limitations, a perspective adopted in this study when examining the legal admissibility of a statutory licence ACS (*see infra* 6.1.5). Yet, even recognising the CJEU's emergent jurisprudence on fundamental rights-based limitations, it is undeniable that the scope of existing limitations in the *acquis* is relatively narrow.

3. This book is critical of the CJEU's failure to recognise a fundamental rights motivation for the private copying limitation, which may have mitigated the effect of strict interpretation of the Court's case law on Art. 5(2)(b) InfoSoc Directive.

This is clear from the analysis of the limitations potentially applicable to the types of online use by individuals identified above.

The mandatory limitation for transient and temporary copies in Article 5(1) InfoSoc Directive privileges acts of browsing, but does not clearly exclude from the scope of the reproduction right copies made during (down) streaming of content. The private copying limitation in Article 5(2)(b) InfoSoc Directive could privilege acts of download, (down) streaming, stream capture, and uploading. However, after *ACI Adam*, the limitation does not cover up/downstream copies made from unauthorised sources, raising doubts as to the lawful character of many common online non-commercial reproductions made by end-users. It is likewise unclear whether upload copies made to cloud servers are within the scope of the limitation and, thus, subject to the payment of fair compensation through levies.

Due to a legislative omission in the *acquis*, digital adaptations may be subject to the right of reproduction *and* non-harmonised national rights of adaptation. Where they are covered by an exclusive right, certain adaptations may be exempted by the optional limitations for quotation, incidental inclusions, and parody in Article 5(3)(d), (i) and (k) InfoSoc Directive.

The analysis shows that despite some flexibility in this respect, the legal space for unrestricted digital adaptations is limited. First, regulating digital adaptations through a national right of adaptation that allows breathing room for non-commercial use would require narrowing the scope of the reproduction right to literal reproductions. This is a difficult proposition in light of the current CJEU interpretation of the reproduction right. Second, the scope of the aforementioned limitations is too narrow to privilege a significant number of digital adaptations, or decisively reduce legal uncertainty in this field. This conclusion holds true even for fundamental rights-based limitations subject to broad purposive interpretation, such as quotation (after *Painer*) and parody (after *Deckmyn*).

The conclusion of the analysis is that a substantial part of individuals' online non-commercial activity is restricted by an exclusive right, or at least tainted by legal uncertainty. Looking forward, the trend is to reinforce the status quo and extend exclusivity to acts that, in the offline world, would be unencumbered by copyright. An example of this trend in the online environment is the legal status of certain types of hyperlinking by Internet users. In no small part, the current state of affairs is due to the priority afforded to exclusivity, contract and technological measures in the determination of the scope of protection.

The priority of 'private choice' over 'public choice' stems from the legal design of the InfoSoc Directive and is reinforced by some CJEU judgments. Illustrations include the interpretation of concepts like 'authorised source' (in hyperlinking and private copying), or whether the content is 'freely accessible' or subject to 'restrictions' (in defining the 'new public' criterion online). In contrast, 'public choice' concerns emerge in the purposive reading of limitations and the impossibility of contractual disposition of fair compensation and of the private copying limitation (provided TPMs are not applied).

This tension between public and private choice at the intersection of rights and limitations leads to a normative insight: the current legal framework, as interpreted by the CJEU, is partly inconsistent with the objectives of EU copyright law, as extrapolated from the InfoSoc Directive and the Court's interpretation.[4] As it applies to non-commercial online use of works by individuals, the *acquis* arguably does not ensure adequate compensation, promote the circulation of culture online, enhance legal certainty, strike a fair balance between the rights and interests of authors and the rights of users, or secure a coherent application of limitations that contributes to their harmonisation. Furthermore, a regime that focuses on strict enforcement online poses barriers to technological development in the information society.

The main objective that might be served by the current system is to secure a 'high level of protection for copyright holders'. Still, as noted, this phrase should not be interpreted as a synonym for absolute protection, as that may be detrimental to rights holders. Instead, it should refer to an adequate or optimal level of protection, to be assessed in relation to the ability to generate an appropriate reward for rights holders, as well as its coherent application with the remaining objectives of copyright and the public interest.

If the current regulation of non-commercial online use by individuals is inconsistent with the *acquis*, reform through ACS should strive for a better alignment of the legal rules with those objectives. As noted in the development of different ACS proposals (*see* 6.1.3), the main obstacles to the wholesale legalisation of the mass online use of works relate to the territorial and substantive fragmentation of copyright, and to difficulties in ensuring the participation of rights holders in voluntary models of collective rights management, especially in sectors (like the audio-visual) where that practice is uncommon. Furthermore, the analysis of the current legal framework, summarised in this section, highlights the significant uncertainty shrouding the legal status of the online use of works by individuals.

To overcome these obstacles, a future ACS must rely on a legalisation model that ensures aggregation of rights across the EU territory and legal certainty for the types of online use covered. *De lege ferenda*, the best legal solution to achieve these aims is a limitation-based statutory licence applying to non-commercial online acts of reproduction and communication to the public by individuals. The admissibility of such a licence rests on its ability to comply with the three-step test. *A maiore ad minus*, if a statutory licence of this type meets the conditions of the test, so should a legalisation model based on mandatory collective management, as it would arguably impose a lower level of restriction on the affected exclusive rights.

4. On the objectives of EU copyright law, *see supra* 1.3, 4.4.1.3, and 5.5.3.

6.1.5 The Admissibility of a Limitation-Based Statutory Licence for Non-commercial Online Use under the Three-Step Test and Its Consistency with the Objectives of EU Copyright Law

An ACS based on a compensated limitation and statutory licensing provides the best option for wholesale legalisation of non-commercial online use of works. The admissibility of such a model in EU copyright law depends on it passing the three-step test, viewed as a normative tool to strike a fair balance of interests in copyright.

This book develops a framework to interpret the test in light of international law, namely Article 10 WCT and its Agreed Statement, as required by the InfoSoc Directive. After exploring this framework and the spectrum of possible interpretations of the test, it concludes that a flexible interpretation is more in line with the objectives of copyright law, as it enables the consideration of the public interest in the context of a fair balancing exercise. This flexible reading anchors the subsequent overall assessment of a limitation-based ACS in the system of the test and each of its steps or conditions.

The first step ('certain special cases') requires that an ACS has a sound policy justification, and its scope is both reasonably foreseeable and not overly broad. An ACS is motivated on economic grounds – market failure of exclusivity and enforcement regarding large-scale online use of works by individuals – and by non-economic factors, including the promotion of creativity, circulation of culture, and the protection of fundamental rights and freedoms of end-users (freedom of expression and information, privacy, personal data) and intermediaries (freedom to conduct a business).

From the quantitative perspective, the scope of the ACS is restricted to natural persons and non-commercial online acts of reproduction and communication to the public that are not already exempted by existing limitations to those rights. In relation to the subject matter covered by the licence, it is argued that it should at least exclude software, sui generis databases, and videogames. These exclusions would mirror or go beyond some existing limitations in the InfoSoc Directive, such as private copying. Nevertheless, it is open for debate whether the licence ought to exclude additional subject matter to meet the quantitative first condition of the test. A definitive answer to this question would likely require empirical research into the effects of the licence on the normal exploitation of the categories of works affected, which analysis should occur in the second step.

The second step of the test ('no conflict with the normal exploitation of works') is the main obstacle to a limitation-based ACS. The study finds that the traditional strict interpretation of this step probably prevents the adoption of a legalisation scheme. However, such an interpretation is arguably inconsistent with the objectives of international and EU copyright law, as it removes from the balancing exercise consideration of the public interest and other normative concerns, as well as the remunerative potential of a limitation. This realisation favours a flexible reading of the second step.

Hence, an ACS conflicts with the normal exploitation if it denies creators and exploiters major and foreseeable sources of rights revenue under normal commercial circumstances. In this context, such sources comprise the online commercial channels for exploitation of the exclusive rights affected by the limitation.

On the one hand, a statutory licence ACS is aimed at non-commercial online use of works by individuals. In relation to this type of use, copyright is often not exercised or monetised by rights holders. Moreover, in many circumstances, the use in question only causes minimal harm. The new limitation and accompanying statutory licence will therefore allow the monetisation of this type of use, in what could be qualified *de lege ferenda* as a normal form of exploitation.

Still, a statutory licence ACS with the proposed scope may have unintended adverse effects on authorised downloading and streaming platforms, for which there is a licensing market. The scale of such negative effects is unknown and is therefore only subject to speculation. The best available proxy to make that calculation comes from empirical research on the effect of unauthorised file sharing. Based on existing research, this study conjectures (but cannot state with certainty) that a properly delimited statutory licence can co-exist with authorised commercial offerings. (On this empirical question, further research is necessary, including experiments.)

For this finding to hold, however, the statutory licence should ensure that exclusive rights are enforceable against unauthorised for-profit websites capable of having a significant negative effect on the normal exploitation of copyright online, e.g., through existing authorised commercial channels. Different legal approaches in the design of the limitation or interpretation of exclusive rights may assist in achieving this objective. One is to clearly define what constitutes a permitted non-commercial use by individuals in the ACS, excluding from that scope (and the benefit of the limitation) unauthorised online acts of communication to the public by for-profit websites or platforms. Another option, which more clearly addresses the definition of the exclusive right rather than the limitation, is to include within the scope of the right of communication to the public acts of linking to unauthorised sources and unauthorized profit-making acts of communication to the public by online platforms. The combination of an ACS-limitation with this interpretation of the exclusive right would in effect exclude such unauthorised for-profit platforms from the benefit of the licence. This last option, it is noted, may materialise (at least partly) as a result of the CJEU's on-going interpretation of the right of communication to the public to different hyperlinking scenarios. These options could be supplemented by self-regulation, endorsed at EU level, aimed at targeting unauthorised bad-faith for-profit platforms, but not end-users.

Assuming it is possible to delimit the scope of the ACS along these contours, the system will legalise online use by end-users, eliminating primary liability for their actions, and a limited set of online intermediaries. Among the intermediaries indirectly benefiting from this legalisation effect will be those providers that enable or facilitate permitted acts by individuals under the licence, but whose activities do not qualify as reproduction or communication to the public of works, i.e. own use of copyright works. The ACS should also not affect the application of liability exemptions in the E-Commerce Directive to the activities of predominantly 'neutral' intermediaries that fall within the scope of those provisions. Outside that limited scope, the legal status of the activities of intermediaries or platforms will be assessed on the above terms. As a rule, the delimited scope of the statutory licence will mean that unauthorised online platforms providing access to works on a for-profit and non-neutral basis will not benefit from the legalisation scheme.

As noted before, even on a flexible interpretation of the second step, only by delimiting the scope of the statutory licence in this manner is it possible to argue that it does not conflict with the normal exploitation of works. However, it is legitimate to ask, *de lege ferenda*, whether this limited legalisation effect on online intermediaries is the most satisfactory from a normative perspective.

The third step ('unreasonable prejudice to legitimate interests') warrants a balancing exercise pursuant to the principle of proportionality. This exercise takes into account the reasonableness of the prejudice imposed by the limitation, together with a consideration of the legitimate interests of rights holders (i.e., the creators and exploiters of exclusive rights identified in the InfoSoc Directive) and the collective and individual manifestations of the public interest. The legitimate interests of rights holders include the concurrent and opposing interests of creators and exploiters; a major tension between creators and exploiters relates to the focus of the former on fair remuneration and the preference of the latter for assignable exclusive rights and stricter enforcement. On the other side of the spectrum, the public interest should include the legitimate interests of users and intermediaries in the protection of their fundamental rights and freedoms, as well as in the promotion of creativity and circulation of works.

A limitation leads to unreasonable prejudice if it causes harm to rights holders in a way that is disproportionate to the benefits it brings to the public interest. The main prejudice caused by an ACS for rights holders relates to the aforementioned indirect effects on the commercialisation of works through authorised online channels.

One method to reduce harm to reasonable levels is through the provision of fair compensation. Existing research suggests that a statutory licence ACS is able to generate sufficient rights revenue to operate such a reduction. In light of this research, it is suggested that fair compensation in an ACS is calculated on the basis of harm, observing the mitigating factors identified in the InfoSoc Directive, but following a method of contingent valuation. This method would maintain the required link between harm and privileged use, while approximating fair compensation to the notion of 'appropriate reward' to incentivise creativity, thereby fulfilling a declared objective of EU copyright law.

Still, in light of the limitations of existing research and the volatile nature of business models in digital networks, the study stresses the need to examine the policy motivations of an ACS, extracted from the analysis of different legitimate interests of creators, exploiters, and the users.

A limitation-based statutory licence ACS coupled with an unwaivable fair compensation right would favour the interests of creators in fair remuneration for online use of their works. It would, it is true, run counter to the declared preference of some (perhaps most) exploiters for preserving assignable exclusive rights in the online environment and for stronger enforcement measures. However, the system simultaneously ensures rights holders of the affected exclusive rights a share of the fair compensation collected, which amounts to a new rights revenue stream from previously uncompensated use.

The prejudice caused by the ACS should be considered reasonable if the fair compensation provided to creators and exploiters as a whole offsets the harm caused by the limitation. Because this calculus relies to a significant extent on empirical questions for which there is no definitive answer, the fate of the limitation ought to rest on the balancing of normative considerations. In other words, the public interest should be the final arbiter of whether it is justified and proportionate to adjust the scope of protection of the exclusive rights of online reproduction and communication to the public in EU law to accommodate an ACS-limitation.

On a balance of interests, this book finds that a statutory licence ACS serves the public interest better than the status quo on two important levels, which relate to goals of EU copyright law. First, it is a superior scheme to promote access and dissemination of knowledge, and therefore the circulation of culture over digital networks, as it concerns non-commercial individual online use of works. Second, for the regulation of such types of use, a properly designed statutory licence provides superior protection for the fundamental rights and freedoms of Internet users as compared to strict enforcement measures (e.g., filtering, blocking, and Internet disconnection). This is true for the right of privacy in telecommunications, the protection of personal data, and freedom of information and expression.

Analysis of the fundamental right to conduct a business is inconclusive in this respect. Some intermediaries will benefit from the ACS, as the risk of intermediary liability arising from the online activities of their users will diminish. For ISPs, however, these benefits may be offset by the requirement that they participate in the system as intermediary debtors of a broadband levy. Allowing ISPs to pass on the levy to their non-professional subscribers and to recover administrative costs imposed by the system will reduce most of the burden; this option may even be preferable to a future scenario where these intermediaries are subject to additional liability and responsibilities in the application of enforcement measures.

The net result of the balancing exercise is that it is legally admissible to adopt a limitation-based statutory licence in compliance with EU copyright law. This possibility, however, hinges on careful delimitation of the scope of the limitation and a flexible reading of the concept of 'normal exploitation of works', which turns on complex legal and empirical questions. Whereas this book addresses the legal issues, resolution of the crucial empirical questions is outside its scope.

In this light, the book resorts to the toolbox developed in the ACS taxonomy to explore two flexibility mechanisms that have the potential to assist in overcoming conflicts with the normal exploitation of works: embargo periods and opt-out rules. Although embedding either model in an ACS is legally feasible, it concludes that they add complexity and impose costs that are difficult to quantify. Therefore, their adoption warrants caution. Notably, it appears extremely challenging to implement either mechanism across different categories of works and content sectors. Consequently, managing such a differentiated system could translate into a costly logistical challenge, detrimental to its consideration as a policy option. Furthermore, adoption of either mechanism would hinder the value of the system to end-users by reducing the subject matter scope of the licence, and significantly decreasing legal certainty for Internet users. The balance of arguments suggests that, absent compelling evidence to that effect, the coupling of an embargo period or opt-out rule to a statutory licence ACS would not be decisive in overcoming a conflict with the normal exploitation of works.

The analysis concludes for the tentative admissibility under EU copyright law of an ACS for mass non-commercial online use of works by individuals based on a statutory licence and compensated limitation to the exclusive rights of reproduction and communication to the public. That admissibility, however, rests on fundamental normative choices for policy makers on the regulation of non-commercial use of works. A choice for such a legalisation model is a choice for flexible over strict interpretation, for access and remuneration over exclusivity and enforcement, for public over private ordering. Furthermore, a public ordering approach requires recognition of the *internal* effect of fundamental rights in determining the scope of copyright protection. As noted before, both choices are possible and have their merits and drawbacks. Whether we favour one over the other will in essence turn on our normative view of EU copyright law and where its fair balance should be struck in the regulation of this type of use.

The remainder of the analysis therefore assesses whether a public ordering choice for a model of access and remuneration for non-commercial online use through a statutory licence ACS is consistent with the rationales for copyright, various normative considerations, and the objectives of EU copyright law.

In the first instance, an examination is made as to whether the dominant theories of copyright in the European legal tradition – natural rights (encompassing the fairness and personality theories) and utilitarianism – can accommodate a right of access and remuneration. Manifestations of these theories, it is noted, serve both as justifications for the grant of protection and objectives of EU copyright law. Therefore, they play a role in determining the scope of protection, including in justifying restrictions on exclusivity.

From the perspective of the natural rights theory, a statutory licence ACS impacts the material interests of authors in the online exploitation of their works. Therefore, the main challenge it poses is to Locke's fairness theory. The application of the theory and its desert-for-labour argument to copyright is not undisputed. However, assuming that its application provides a sound rationale for copyright protection through a property right in creative works, the fairness theory does not mandate the absolute nature of that right. Instead, it allows restrictions thereto. For the present purposes, the most relevant restrictions result from the operation of the sufficiency proviso and, even more prominently, from the public interest. In particular, Locke's theory envisages that the transition from the state of nature to a civil and political society can be accompanied by restrictions on rights based on public interest considerations. Among the acceptable restrictions is the contraction of the prohibition element of copyright (exclusivity), provided its reward element (remuneration) is secured. In this way, the material interests of authors, central to copyright protection, are safeguarded.

The result of the analysis is that there is space in the fairness theory to accommodate an ACS for non-commercial use, subject to certain conditions. First, that it ensures remuneration for the permitted use. Second, that it is justified on the public interest, arguably beyond market failure. For the reasons detailed above in the examination of the three-step test analysis, it is submitted that both conditions are met by statutory licence ACS.

From the viewpoint of the utilitarian theory, copyright protection is justified in the public interest, with the aim of incentivising the creation and dissemination of works. Copyright works share some of the characteristics of public goods, meaning that they are non-rivalrous and non excludable. Consequently, they also share some of its problems, namely that third parties can freely access and use works without payment to the creator or rights holder, preventing private market actors from charging prices that allow a return on investment and ultimately endangering the provision of such goods. The exclusive right (a property rule) is viewed as an efficient solution to the problem of non-excludability, as it allows copyright owners to recover their costs of creation in a market setting, fostering the production and supply of works.

In the context of the utilitarian theory, the grant of exclusive rights is justified if the benefits it creates offset the costs it imposes. Conversely, if the costs outweigh the benefits, it is justifiable to impose restrictions on the exclusive nature of the right. For the regulation of non-commercial online use by individuals, the application of the exclusive right imposes different types of cost: chilling effects on follow-on creativity, transaction costs, and administration and enforcement costs. It is argued that these costs could justify regulating this type of use through a liability rule, such as a limitation-based statutory licence ACS. Therefore, and in theory, such a legalisation model is consistent with the utilitarian theory. Still, whether its adoption is desirable ultimately depends on empirical research on the associated costs and benefits, as compared to the current regime. In this respect, although further evidence is required, existing research cited throughout the book suggests that a properly designed ACS could be welfare increasing.

After establishing that it is possible to accommodate a model of access and remuneration in the natural rights and utilitarian theories, the analysis focuses on whether such a model is coherent with the human and fundamental rights characterisation of copyright, including its property right status in certain legal instruments, such as the ECHR (Article 1 Protocol No. 1) and the Charter (Article 17). It is clear from this study that copyright protection is not absolute, and by extension neither is the exclusive dimension of the right. Rather, copyright protection has at its core dimensions of access (the availability of works and cultural participation), and remuneration (securing the material interests of authors).

It is suggested that restrictions to the scope of copyright protection are a result of its social function, which requires an adequate balance of interests in the definition of that scope. Hence, the contours of the right, including the objectives and conditions of its exercise, should consider not only the position of rights holders, but be drawn in light of the public interest.

There are different methods to incorporate the social function and public interest in the calibration of the scope of protection. From an *internal* perspective, it is possible to consider individual and collective manifestations of the public interest in the three-step test and its balancing exercise, thereby providing a justification for the introduction of a copyright limitation. (An example of this approach is found in Chapter 5 of this book).

From an *external* perspective, we can envisage two different angles. From one angle, certain fundamental (or constitutional) rights provide a justification for a positive right of access and remuneration. This is the case for the universal right to culture and science in Articles 27(1) UDHR and 15(1) ICESCR. From another angle, the property right protection of copyright allows restrictions on its scope resulting from the public interest in the relevant provisions of the ECHR and Charter, and imposes limits on protection by virtue of the application of conflicting fundamental rights and freedoms; in some cases, like in *Luksan*, those limits are admissible subject to the payment of fair compensation.

These normative considerations lead to the conclusion that it is admissible to modulate the nature and options for exercise of copyright in light of the public interest. This is evidenced throughout this book in mechanisms that include voluntary and mandatory models of collective rights management, as well as statutory and compulsory licences. Translating these considerations into the regulation of mass non-commercial online use of works by individuals, there are strong normative arguments to accept the replacement of the exclusive right with a limitation-based statutory licence ACS. In addition, the analysis supports the qualification of the underlying fair compensation right as unwaivable, and denotes a preference for its mandatory imposition, together with some level of protection against disposition by contract or technological measures.

The last stage of the normative analysis explores whether and to what extent the proposed legalisation model is consistent with objectives of EU copyright law. These objectives are taken from the recitals of the copyright directives – especially the InfoSoc Directive – and the vast jurisprudence of the CJEU on copyright. The seven objectives identified are: fair balance between the rights and interests of authors and the rights of users; high level of protection for copyright holders; adequate compensation or appropriate reward; circulation of culture; resolution of legal uncertainty; technological development, including the promotion of the information society; and harmonisation of copyright law to achieve a functioning internal market.

The analysis concludes that a statutory licence ACS for non-commercial online use by individuals, subject to the delimitations arising out of the three-step test analysis, is more consistent with these objectives than the current regime. A touchstone of this analysis, derived from the previous normative considerations, is the view that a 'high level of protection' does not mean an 'absolute' level of protection. Rather, it means an optimal level of protection to ensure adequate compensation for copyright owners, with an emphasis on creators. Furthermore, this level of protection is not determined in a normative vacuum. It must be articulated with the remaining objectives. That is to say, the level of copyright protection – and with it the scope of the right – can and should be modulated in order to achieve the remaining objectives of the law, such as the circulation of culture, the improvement of legal certainty for users in the online environment, and the removal of obstacles to technological development in the information society.

Ultimately, where there once was a wall, this book hopes to open a policy window for lawmakers in the copyright field regarding the regulation of non-commercial online use. The view from that window shows a possible alternative to a legal regime that favours private ordering, strict interpretation, exclusive rights, and technological measures. It shows a system based on public ordering, a flexible and technology neutral reading of copyright law, and an online culture of access and fair remuneration. That system, as demonstrated here, can be reconciled with the justificatory theories of copyright and the particular objectives of EU copyright law, arguably better than the current regime. As a result, it is concluded that the *acquis* can and should be reformed to include a limitation-based statutory licence ACS. The following section draws the contours of such a system, offering a blueprint for copyright reform.

6.2 A BLUEPRINT FOR REFORM: A LIMITATION-BASED STATUTORY LICENCE FOR NON-COMMERCIAL ONLINE USE OF WORKS BY INDIVIDUALS

Until this point, the present book has developed a normative argument for reform of EU copyright law to accommodate a right of access and remuneration for non-commercial online use of works by individuals. This section concludes the analysis and provides the last piece to answer the book's research questions by setting out a workable structure for such a right. In other words, this section provides a legal blueprint for a limitation-based statutory licence ACS that is consistent with a flexible view of EU copyright law. The objective is to supply policy-makers with a modest proposal to inspire legal reform. The following paragraphs set forth the scope and essential elements of that ACS.

6.2.1 Beneficiaries (and Intermediaries)

The ACS authorises acts by Internet users that are natural persons. Legal persons and institutions are not direct beneficiaries of the system. Nevertheless, a limited number of online intermediaries may benefit indirectly from the statutory licence, to the extent they were subject to intermediary liability for acts of their users that are now exempt from authorisation. As noted above, this legalisation effect will benefit providers that enable or facilitate permitted acts of individuals under the licence, but whose activities do not qualify as acts of reproduction or communication to the public of works. In other words, it will not benefit the acts of online platforms considered own use of copyright works.

It is difficult to make an exact determination of the number and type of intermediaries exempted. Although the arguments outlined in this book should allow a coherent articulation the proposed limitation with the E-Commerce Directive, some fine tuning will be required. This is for two main reasons. First, intermediary liability is not harmonized in EU law beyond the liability exemptions in the E-Commerce Directive. Much will depend on whether and to what extent such harmonisation occurs. Second, the introduction of a knowledge presumption in *GS Media* has blurred the lines between primary and secondary liability. It is not always clear what constitutes genuine own use of works, especially as regards the activities of hybrid content sharing platforms (e.g. YouTube).

A properly scoped licence should exclude unauthorised commercial or profit-making acts of communication to the public of works by online platforms. This exclusion could result from the careful definition of non-commercial use authorised under the ACS and/or follow from the application of the knowledge test in *GS Media* to the online activities of non-neutral profit-making online platforms, such as The Pirate Bay or Popcorn Time. In addition, as also argued, online platforms whose intermediary activities fail to cross the 'non-neutral' threshold and qualify for the exemptions in Articles 12–14 E-Commerce Directive should continue to benefit from that regime. *A contrario*, if the activities/services of platforms fall outside the scope of those exemptions and qualify as genuine own use of works, they should give rise to primary liability. The situation of content sharing and other hybrid platforms will depend on how their activities are qualified within this spectrum, a qualification which may ultimately result from targeted legislative intervention or broader harmonisation of 'European intermediary accessory liability'.[5] Whereas an ACS can and should be calibrated to account for such adjustments, it is submitted that the legislator should strive to keep in place robust liability exemptions for intermediaries, especially hosting providers.

As with other compensated limitations in the *acquis*, pragmatic considerations should make it possible to identify an intermediary as the primary debtor of fair compensation, with a right to pass on the levy to end-users.[6] For efficiency reasons, ISPs are the preferred levy targets. However, as discussed below at 6.2.6, other intermediaries may be targeted, namely online service providers that indirectly benefit from the limitation. While that is a possibility, the analysis in this book and existing empirical research suggest that it is sufficient to levy solely ISPs and household connections.[7] Therefore, the extension of the levy base to other goods or services should be justified by evidence, as it may unforeseen adverse effects and/or needlessly interfere with the affected intermediaries' freedom to conduct a business.

6.2.2 Subject Matter Scope

In theory, the ACS can apply to all types of work capable of digital expression and online sharing. This is one of the advantages of the system: that it presumptively includes all works made available online, both domestic

5. For targeted reform proposals regarding hybrid content sharing platforms, *see*, e.g., Kreutzer et al., 2016, French High Council for Literary and Artistic Property, 2016, and Leistner, 2016. For detailed arguments and proposals for a future 'European intermediary accessory liability' in copyright, *see* Angelopoulos 2016.
6. See, in the context of private copying, CJEU, *Padawan*, paras 46, 48; CJEU, *Reprobel*, para. 70.
7. *See supra* 5.3.3.6.3. *See also* Handke et al., 2015.

and foreign to an EU Member State.[8] An ACS in this form would amount to a 'global' as opposed to sector-specific legalisation scheme.

However, a global licence extending to all conceivable categories of work and subject matter may not be compliant with the three-step test for failing to be a certain special case.[9] Thus, in line with other legalisation proposals, it is important to consider subject matter exclusions to the licence.[10]

If the ACS-limitation applies to the exclusive rights regulated in the InfoSoc Directive, logic dictates the exclusion from its scope of software and databases.[11] These types of work or subject matter have idiosyncratic justifications and legal regimes, set out in the 'vertical' Software and Database Directives, which are difficult to articulate in a single system with other types of work. Moreover, the software and database sectors do not suffer to the same extent from the problem of mass-scale infringement, and operate according to specific logics.[12]

Similar arguments apply to videogames. These complex works of authorship include and combine different types of copyright subject matter that may be individually protected (e.g., film, music, text, databases, photographs, and maps) and involve an element of human interaction 'while executing the game with a computer program on specific hardware.'[13] The majority of video games contain as core elements an audio-visual component and the software on which they run, there being significant controversy as to their legal qualification as multimedia works, audio-visual works, or software.[14] The CJEU seems to embrace a multi-layered protection approach in *Nintendo*, when it states that videogames:

> constitute complex matter comprising not only a computer program but also graphic and sound elements, which, although encrypted in computer language, have a unique creative value which cannot be reduced to that encryption. In so far as the parts of a videogame, in this case, the graphic and sound elements, are part of its originality, they are protected,

---

8. N.B. solutions based on collective rights management can only include foreign works if mandated by law or based on representation agreements with foreign CMOs.
9. *See supra* 5.3.1, 5.3.4, and 6.1.5.
10. *See supra* 3.4.1.
11. *See supra* 4.4.1, on the legal framework of limitations in the InfoSoc Directive.
12. See, regarding software, Kantar Media, 2015.
13. Ramos et al., 2013, pp. 7–9. *See also* Grosheide, Roerdink & Thomas, 2013.
14. Grosheide et al., 2013, pp. 9–11; Ramos et al., 2013, pp. 7, 10–11. In distinguishing videogames from audio-visual works, the element of control/interaction in the former seems to be crucial. Cf. Grosheide et al., 2013, p. 11: 'So it may be said that control is the defining keyword that discerns video games from movies. Stated differently: when a film runs, it performs the same work every time, whereas when an interactive game is played it follows the instructions by its user.'

together with the entire work, by copyright in the context of the system established by Directive 2001/29.[15]

The complex legal nature of videogames, their proximity to software, the specificities and norms of the sector, and the absence of infringement and enforcement issues that justify an ACS, all argue for their exclusion from the system.[16]

It may also be sensible to exclude categories of work linked to particular purposes and sectors which are alien to the rationale of an ACS. One possibility is to exclude scientific publications which are used primarily for research purposes, rather than self-expression or personal enjoyment. Currently, online access to these works in the EU results from a combination of paid subscription and open access models, with much debate on the best model going forward. The objective of an ACS is not to solve this problem. Furthermore, the InfoSoc Directive already contains a limitation for 'teaching or scientific research', as well as 'research or private study'.[17]

The main policy choice on the table is whether to extend the ACS to all or most types of work covered by the InfoSoc Directive, carving out specific categories where justified, or build the system on a sectorial approach, as occurs in ECL systems.[18] Sectorial approaches – like a statutory licence for online music, audio-visual works, photos or literary works – may be easier to implement and justify with recourse to empirical research. For example, a licence specifically tailored to the audio-visual sector can better take into consideration the territorial segmentation practices in that area than a 'one-size-fits-all' scheme.

A sectorial or category-based approach would also have the practical advantage of building on existing infrastructures of collective rights management. For example, these infrastructures are already in place in the music and literature sectors, but are far less developed or even non-existent in other sectors. This reality should inform policy makers and may steer them

15. CJEU, *Nintendo*, para. 23.
16. *See* e.g.: Katzenbach, Herweg & Roessel, 2016, finding imitation is accepted as a common practice in at least a sector of the videogame industry, despite copyright law; Ramos et al., 2013, pp. 7–11, 93–96, on the legal qualification of video games, concluding that the 'majority of jurisdictions tend to protect these works of authorship as software', but noting that it is a common practice in the industry to share part of the source code between different developers; and Grosheide et al., 2013, p. 13, noting that 'in the EU generally and in the Netherlands particularly, proceedings about infringing intellectual property rights in video games seldom take place'. On the relatively low volume of online infringement of videogames, *see*, e.g., Kantar Media, 2015. On the intersection between the legal protection of videogames and TPMs in EU law, *see* Rendas, 2015.
17. Art. 5(3)(a) and (n) InfoSoc Directive. Another example, less relevant for mass online use, is sheet music. Sheet music is already excluded from the scope of the reprography and private copying limitations. *See* CJEU, *Reprobel*, paras 50–56.
18. N.B. ECL is typically adopted in a sectorial logic. Cf. Colin, 2011a, p. 115.

towards the more pragmatic approach of considering an ACS for more traditional categories of protected works and related subject matter.[19]

In addition, from the perspective of evidence-based reform, it is wise to experiment with the system in discrete fields based on research on the inadequacy of the market to fulfil user expectations. A limitation of this fashion is not foreign to EU copyright tradition, and subject matter-specific privileges can be found for example in the InfoSoc Directive.[20]

The disadvantage is obvious: end-users will have only a limited licence for one type of content. The resulting system may be unattractive to users desiring access to other types of content for non-commercial purposes. For the excluded categories, the issue of large-scale unauthorised use may persist. What is more, the value of an ACS to users resides in the universal nature of the licence. It turns out that the sum of all parts (a global licence) is more valuable than each part in isolation (a sector-specific licence). For that reason, research shows that the relative revenue generated by a sectorial licence may be lower than its value *within a global licence*.[21]

In the end, there is an inextricable link between the subject matter and substantive rights scope of an ACS. If it is possible to delimit the permissible non-commercial online use so as to prevent conflicts with the commercial exploitation of the same category of works, the policy benefits of an ACS point towards its extension to the same subject matter covered by the InfoSoc Directive, with additional discrete exclusions (e.g., videogames and scientific publications). On a balance of arguments, this appears to be the preferable design choice. Still, if this approach proves too challenging, policy-makers could alternatively delimit the scope of the statutory licence to the types of content for which the risk of conflict with major sources of rights revenue is minor, and for which the payment of fair compensation reduces the potential harm to tolerable levels.

Furthermore, the scope of the ACS should only include works or subject matter lawfully published or made available online. That is to say, a work is only available for non-commercial online use after rights holders authorise its first public disclosure offline or over the Internet.[22] This condition does not require the lawfulness of the source of the copy of a work for its subsequent online use by individuals. As argued before when discussing private copying post-*ACI Adam* and hyperlinking post-*Svensson*, such a

19. *See* Hugenholtz & Quintais, 2017 (forthcoming), exemplifying with music, text, visual, and video.
20. See, e.g., Art. 5(3) (c), (f), (h), and (m) InfoSoc Directive.
21. *See* the results reported in Vallbé et al., 2015 and the results reported in Handke et al., 2015 (Appendix 2, Table 5, 'Subject matter').
22. *See* ALAI, 2012, on the determination of the country of origin when a work is first publicly disclosed over the Internet.

requirement would be impractical and detrimental to an ACS-limitation's effectiveness, rendering it devoid of meaning.[23]

Instead, it makes sense to require the authorisation of rights holders for use of a commercial nature, allowing them to enforce their copyright against unauthorised for-profit websites. This set-up allows the preservation of enforcement avenues against dissemination of works through unauthorised sources that may cause economic harm to copyright owners, without subjecting end-users to liability for infringement or high transaction costs to use works online.[24]

6.2.3 Substantive Rights Scope: Authorised Non-commercial Online Use of Works

The limitation-based statutory licence ACS applies to non-commercial online acts of reproduction and communication to the public by individuals. For that type of use, the aforementioned exclusive rights in the InfoSoc Directive are recast as rights of fair compensation. Hence, the limitation covers the *online* rights required by end-users to engage in non-commercial exchanges of digital works over the Internet, 'including other interconnected wired or wireless networks.'[25]

As a matter of legislative design, the application of the statutory licence ACS to at least two exclusive rights can give rise to one or more copyright limitations. For example, Article 5(2) InfoSoc Directive lists cases allowing for a limitation to the reproduction right, whereas Article 5(3) InfoSoc Directive and the Orphan Works Directive prescribe limitations to the rights of reproduction *and* communication to the public.

The scope of the limitation or limitations does not need to encompass types of use of works already covered in the directive by other limitations, discussed in Chapter 4. These include temporary and transient copying, private copying, quotation, incidental inclusion and caricature, parody and pastiche. However, the possibility of overlap with existing limitations cannot be discounted. This is not problematic per se, as overlap of this type already exists in the InfoSoc Directive, for example between the reprography and private copying limitations,[26] and should not be detrimental to the adoption

23. *See* the discussion *supra* at 4.3.2.2, 4.3.2.3, 4.4.3.6, 4.4.3.8, 5.3.2.3, 5.3.4, 5.5, 6.1.4, and 5.5.3. *See also* the criticism in Poort & Quintais, 2013; Quintais, 2015a, 2015b.
24. With respect to the enforcement avenues available to rights holders in the context of an ACS *see supra* 5.3.2.3. *See also Opinion AG in GS Media*, paras 80–87, regarding enforcement measures available even if copyright protection did not extend to hyperlinking from unauthorised sources (discussed *supra* at 4.3.2.1.4 and 4.3.2.2).
25. Hugenholtz & Quintais, 2017 (forthcoming). The 'online' portion of the definition should not be problematic as it mirrors an existing reference in the *acquis*, namely that of 'online rights in musical works' in Art. 3(n) CRM Directive.
26. For an example of this overlap, *see* CJEU, *Reprobel*, paras 32–43. *See also* von Lewinski & Walter, 2010, pp. 1027–1028.

of an ACS. Rather, this possibility ought to inform the design of the system and the calculation of fair compensation (*see infra* 6.2.4).

A central characteristic of the proposed limitation is that it privileges 'non-commercial' use. This book argues that the term should be understood as a legal standard and an autonomous concept of EU law.[27] In the context of a statutory licence ACS, the concept covers online use of works by individuals that is not in direct commercial competition with parallel use by rights holders. Using the language of the private copying limitation in Article 5(2)(b) InfoSoc Directive, the use in question is 'for ends that are neither directly or indirectly commercial'.

The main issue lies with drawing a precise line between *direct* and *indirect* commercial ends, acts or types of use. In the field of private copying, national legislators and courts struggle with the application of subjective and objective tests to draw this line and define the scope of the limitation.[28] For an ACS, it is likewise possible to define non-commercial use with recourse to objective or subjective criteria.

A *subjective* criterion focuses on the intention of the user. It suggests knowledge as to the state of mind of the individual in relation to their online use of works. This intent-based approach is followed for example in the creative commons licences, which define non-commercial use as 'not primarily intended for or directed towards commercial advantage or monetary compensation.'[29]

In contrast, an *objective* criterion emphasises the commercial nature or character of the use itself (rather than the intention of the user) and attempts to identify indicators of the same. In the field of private copying, for instance, examples of this objective approach include the number of permissible copies per person or the number of persons included in the private sphere of the copier. Another notable use of this criterion is the concept of 'commercial scale' in Article 61 TRIPS. This concept has been interpreted to mean 'counterfeiting or piracy carried on at the magnitude and extent of typical or usual commercial activity with respect to a given product in a given market'.[30]

Infringements on a commercial-scale are the focus of efforts by the Commission to modernise enforcement of intellectual property rights with the objective of achieving better access to digital content and a functioning

27. *See supra* 1.2 and 5.1.
28. *See supra* 4.4.3.2. *See also* Karapapa, 2012, pp. 82, 91.
29. *See* Creative Commons, *NonCommercial interpretation*, https://wiki.creativecommons.org/wiki/NonCommercial_interpretation (accessed 31.01.2017): 'The definition is intent-based and intentionally flexible in recognition of the many possible factual situations and business models that may exist now or develop later.' *See also* Creative Commons, 2009, for an in depth study of the user understanding of the term 'non-commercial'.
30. WTO, *China–Intellectual Property Rights*, para 7.577.

Digital Single Market.[31] In this respect, it is informative to remember the European Parliament's criticism of the use of the 'commercial-scale' concept in relation to criminalisation of copyright infringement by end-users in the proposed (and rejected) directive on criminal measures. Indeed, the European Parliament requested that commercial-scale expressly exclude acts 'carried out by private users for personal and not-for-profit purposes'.[32] This exclusion introduces subjective criteria to delimit an objective concept.

If we consider the non-commercial concept to be a standard, it makes sense to accept a combination of subjective and objective factors to assess the purpose or nature of the use. The concept should focus on online activities carried out by individuals for personal consumption and enjoyment of works (not necessarily in the private sphere) and outside the market sphere. Hence, 'non-commercial' should exclude online use of works for profit, within a commercial context (e.g., a business activity of an individual), or otherwise directed at commercial advantage or monetary compensation.

In principle, end-users should not derive profit or monetary consideration from the use. An illustration is the use of works 'in combination with ads, publicity actions or any other similar activity intended to generate income for the user', or for the user and a third party.[33] The third parties here are online platforms, like Google, whose main business model is online advertisement.[34] As noted, this definition would prevent individual operators of P2P and other platforms that generate advertising or sponsorship or other financial consideration in connection with the usage of works from being exempt from liability *as a result* of the adoption of the statutory licence.[35]

31. Communication Digital Single Market 2015, pp. 6–8; SWD Digital Single Market Strategy 2015, p. 30; Communication on Modern European Copyright Framework 2015, pp. 10–11. Both Communications endorse a 'follow the money' approach. *See also* EP Resolution Implementation InfoSoc Directive 2015, p. 15.
32. Position of the European Parliament adopted at first reading on 25 April 2007 with a view to the adoption of Directive 2007/.../EC of the European Parliament and of the Council on criminal measures aimed at ensuring the enforcement of intellectual property rights (EP-PE_TC1-COD(2005)0127), p. 7. On which, *see* Geiger, 2014c, pp. 118–122.
33. *See* Metzger & Heinemann, 2015, p. 13, reporting on a pilot project in the Netherlands developed by the CMO Buma/Stemra, which defined 'commercial' as including use made against any 'financial compensation', such as 'the use of the work in combination with ads, publicity actions or any other similar activity intended to generate income for the user or a third party'. In my proposal, differently from the Dutch pilot project, an online act by an individual user would only qualify as 'commercial' if it generates compensation/ income for him, whether or not that compensation is shared with a third party. That is to say, end-user acts that only indirectly generate revenue for a third party are not qualified as 'commercial' use by the individual.
34. Eijk et al., 2015, pp. 12–13.
35. *See* the discussion *supra* at 5.1 and 5.3.2.3.2, with reference to Metzger & Heinemann, 2015, p. 16. *See also supra* 6.1.5 and 6.2.1. As noted, this should not prevent certain predominantly neutral good faith online platforms from qualifying for exemptions of liability under Arts 12–14 E-Commerce Directive, subject to the conditions thereof.

However, this definition should not prevent individual Internet users from benefiting from the ACS where their use is for enjoyment of cultural works online. Hence, it must be clear that the non-commercial scope of the limitation leaves space for acts of end-users that, although not carried out with a profit-making intention, nonetheless bear economic significance. To define the concept otherwise – i.e., to exclude from its scope any type of use or works with economic value – would deprive the ACS-limitation of any useful scope and effect, limiting it to *de minimis* use. The example that comes to mind is that of cost savings for users that would be willing to pay for access to the work outside the ACS. The payment of fair compensation is designed to address such potential harm to rights holders (and return it to tolerable levels), provided the permitted use does not conflict with major sources of right revenues of copyright owners.

In the few instances where end-users' online activities fall in the grey area between commercial and non-commercial use, it will be up to the courts – and ultimately to the CJEU in the interpretation of this autonomous concept – to qualify the use. Regardless, whatever indirect financial consideration end-users receive in grey-area cases, it is unlikely to cause substantial harm to rights holders, and should therefore be susceptible of compensation in the context of a statutory licence ACS.

6.2.4 Fair Compensation

An ACS should provide 'fair compensation' to rights holders.[36] To be consistent with EU law, the limitation for non-commercial use should be aligned with this autonomous concept, as interpreted by the CJEU in a number of judgments on the private copying and reprography limitations.[37]

The right to fair compensation is unwaivable, and vests solely in the authors and related rights holders that in EU law are granted the exclusive rights affected by a limitation. As a result, the grant of a right of fair compensation ensures, first, that creators receive a share of the amounts collected under the statutory licence system and, second, that they are not forced to transfer that share to exploiters (e.g., publishers).[38] Therefore, as argued previously, this design contributes to the objective of adequate compensation or appropriate reward to authors, in line with the remuneration aspect of copyright and its philosophical mandate to protect the material interests of authors, which are instrumental to incentivising creation.[39]

---

36. *See supra* 5.3.3.3, 5.5.2, 5.5.3, and 6.1.5.
37. On private copying, see *supra* 2.3 and 4.4.3. On potential solutions to structure collection and distribution of rights revenue, *see supra* 3.4.4–3.4.6.
38. CJEU, *Reprobel*, paras 44–49. *See also* European Copyright Society, 2015.
39. Cf. *supra* 5.5.

Fair compensation should reflect the harm suffered by creators and other rights holders of the affected exclusive rights.[40] As suggested in Chapter 5, the potential harm caused by the introduction of an ACS-limitation should be considered in terms of the prejudice suffered by copyright owners due to their inability to exercise their copyright for the non-commercial online use of works. Because there is no market to accurately determine the price for the type of use in question, harm should be calculated on the basis of a different reference point. It could be determined, for instance, by measuring users' willingness to pay through a method of contingent valuation.[41] In addition, the calculation of fair compensation ought to account for the mitigating factors mentioned in the InfoSoc Directive. These include the *de minimis* nature of use, prior payments for the same use, and the application of TPMs.[42] Each factor deserves further explanation.

First, following recital 35 InfoSoc Directive, if fair compensation reflects harm, its calculation should exclude use of works causing only minimal prejudice to rights holders. This approach is consistent with a method of contingent valuation, as it is unlikely that individuals place any value on minor online use of works.

Second, calculation of fair compensation and the respective broadband levy should take into account whether rights holders include in the licence fee or purchase price of digital content an additional amount to compensate for the types of use privileged by an ACS. If this occurs, the principle of *de minimis* harm and the fair balance aim of the InfoSoc Directive may warrant that 'no specific or separate payment' is due.[43]

However, there are obstacles to reduction of the levy on this account. On the one hand, after *VG Wort*, it seems that use of works allowed by the private copying limitation is permissible regardless of authorisation by copyright owners. If the same rationale is valid for the non-commercial use permitted by an ACS, any authorisation by rights holders for that use is devoid of legal effect. Consequently, such authorisation should not influence the calculation of harm.[44]

On the other hand, it is challenging for rights holders to price into their online transactions the utility to end-users of a licence for non-commercial use. Like with private copying from unauthorised sources, rights holders will struggle to indirectly appropriate that utility.[45] Because the marginal costs of copying and sharing files online are constant and near zero, and the size of

40. CJEU, *Padawan*, paras 40 – 42; CJEU, *Reprobel*, paras 36, 48–49.
41. *See supra* 5.3.3.3 and 6.1.5.
42. *See supra* 4.4.1.1, 4.4.3.3–4.4.3.5. Cf. CJEU, *VG Wort*, paras 73, 77; CJEU, *Reprobel*, paras 37–38 (mentioning recital 32 of the directive).
43. Recital 35 InfoSoc Directive. *See also* Quintais, 2015a.
44. *See supra* 4.4.3.3 and 4.4.3.4.
45. Indirect appropriability refers to the 'economic mechanism according to which, under certain conditions, the demand for originals will reflect the value that consumers place

the user group is not fixed, rights holders are not able to price discriminate to an extent that makes indirect appropriability feasible.[46] Hence, reducing the levy on this account may be unjustified.

In addition, calculation of the broadband levy should avoid overlap between the ACS-limitation and other compensated limitations, namely private copying. Users should not pay two levies for the same use. If private copying does not apply to copies from unauthorised sources, as is the case after *ACI Adam*, the ACS could focus on compensating the harm caused by that use in relation to the right of reproduction. In practice, one method to achieve a harmonious system is to select distinct levy targets for each limitation. Thus, the levy in the statutory licence ACS should target household Internet subscriptions but not goods or services covered by the private copying levy.[47]

The third mitigating factor that influences the level of fair compensation is the degree of use of TPMs. In the current regime, fair compensation remains applicable irrespective of the availability or application of technological measures.[48] However, Member States may decide that application of these measures affects the calculation and amount of fair compensation.[49] Largely, this calibration will depend on how policy-makers choose to regulate the interface between TPMs and the ACS, namely whether and to what extent users have a right to exercise the statutory limitation.

If the level of TPM adoption is high and the means to exercise the limitation ineffective, the scope of the privilege will be constrained. In this scenario, the harm to rights holders is lower, and so should be the amount of fair compensation. In theory, compensation could even be eliminated if TPMs reduce that harm to *de minimis* levels, although that scenario seems unrealistic in light of the relatively low level of adoption of these measures and their reduced effectiveness in preventing many types of unauthorised online use by individuals. If the adoption of TPMs is low and users are able to enjoy the statutory limitation effectively, the level of fair compensation should not be reduced significantly. These considerations suggest that it is possible to adopt an ACS without interfering with the legal protection of TPMs in the current legal framework. This, despite the strong normative arguments in favour of affording individual users some level of protection against technological measures regarding the permitted use in an ACS.[50]

To conclude, a right of fair compensation modelled along the lines described above ought to provide sufficient recompense to rights holders for

---

both on originals and subsequent copies they make.' *See* Poort & Quintais, 2013, p. 216; Quintais, 2015b, pp. 85–86, on indirect appropriability and private copying.

46. Quintais, 2015b, pp. 85–86.
47. Bernault & Lebois, 2005, p. 40.
48. *See supra* 4.4.1.2 and 4.4.3.5.
49. *Opinion AG in Copydan*, paras 69–80; CJEU, *Copydan*, paras 68–73. *See also* CJEU, *VG Wort*, paras 52–57; CJEU, *ACI Adam*, paras 43–44.
50. *See supra* 5.5.2 and 6.1.5.

the harm suffered by the adoption of an ACS, in line with CJEU interpretation of the concept of fair compensation, and the objectives of EU law.[51]

6.2.5 Agreed Contractual Terms

The general scheme of the InfoSoc Directive opens the door to contractual disposition of limitations. As noted, there are various cases where a prohibition on contractual disposition is justified, spanning from the definition of limitations as imperative in national law, to instances of consumer law protection, or to cases where a limitation is subject to fair compensation. In addition, the Software and Database Directives expressly prohibit contractual disposition of limitations.[52]

After *VG Wort*, there is increased support for the view that limitations take precedence over freedom of contract in relation to the privileged use, at least with respect to the reproduction right. Accordingly, an authorisation for acts covered by a limitation is not valid and does not affect the right to fair compensation.[53] However, where TPMs are applied, Article 6(4)(4) InfoSoc Directive excludes priority for limitations regarding works or other subject matter made available to the public on agreed contractual terms.

De lege ferenda, two options are available for an ACS to address this issue in EU copyright law. The first option is to favour private ordering and allow contractual disposition of the ACS-limitation, letting the market influence the scope of the limitation. If this option is followed, the priority of contract over the limitation would have to be taken into account in the calculation of fair compensation, as an additional factor susceptible of mitigating the harm caused to rights holders. The second option is to follow a 'public policy' approach and prohibit contractual disposition of the limitation.[54] This can be done in different ways. One method is to distinguish between individual contracts, allowing contractual waiver of a limitation in the exercise of private autonomy, but prohibiting such waiver in standard terms and conditions. Another method is to distinguish the purpose of limitations and prohibit waivers on agreed contractual terms for limitations motivated strongly by the public interest.[55]

Several arguments support the adoption of a public policy approach through either of the suggested methods in the context of a statutory licence ACS. First, the strong public interest foundation of the ACS limitation,

51. See, e.g., CJEU, *Padawan*, paras 40–42; CJEU, *Reprobel*, para 36. On adequate compensation as an objective of EU law, *see supra* 5.5.3.
52. *See supra* 4.4.1, 4.4.3.4, 4.5, 6.1.4, and 5.5.2.
53. Dreier, 2015, pp. 5–6, referring to *VG Wort* and the following national cases: BGH, 06.12.2007, I ZR 94/05 ('Drucker und Plotter'), and BGH, 21.07.2011, I ZR 28/11 ('Drucker und Plotter II').
54. Dreier, 2015, p. 6.
55. *Ibid. See also* Guibault, 2002, pp. 302–304.

namely the respect for users' fundamental rights, and the promotion of creativity and dissemination of works.[56] Second, the application of the principle of effectiveness to the limitation, which would be hindered if contracts were allowed priority over limitations.[57] Third, the consideration that this legalisation proposal privileges non-commercial use by individual users, who as a rule require protection from a structural disadvantage in contractual negotiations.[58]

To preserve a measure of differentiation, the system could allow contractual terms to prevail in individually negotiated agreements. However, outside those cases, the ACS-limitation should have absolute protection against contractual stipulations.

6.2.6 Basic Operation

Finally, it is possible to identify some high level features of the basic operation of a statutory licence ACS. Figure 6.1 provides a simplified representation of these features and a window into how the system could operate at EU and national level.

56. *See supra* 5.3.3.5, 5.3.3.6, and 6.1.5.
57. In this respect, *see* EP Resolution Implementation InfoSoc Directive 2015, paras 61–62, stressing that effective exercise of limitations 'should not be waived by contract or contractual terms' and calling on 'distributors to publish all available information concerning the technological measures necessary to ensure interoperability of their content'.
58. Dreier, 2015, pp. 6–7.

Figure 6.1 Simplified Design for Alternative Compensation System

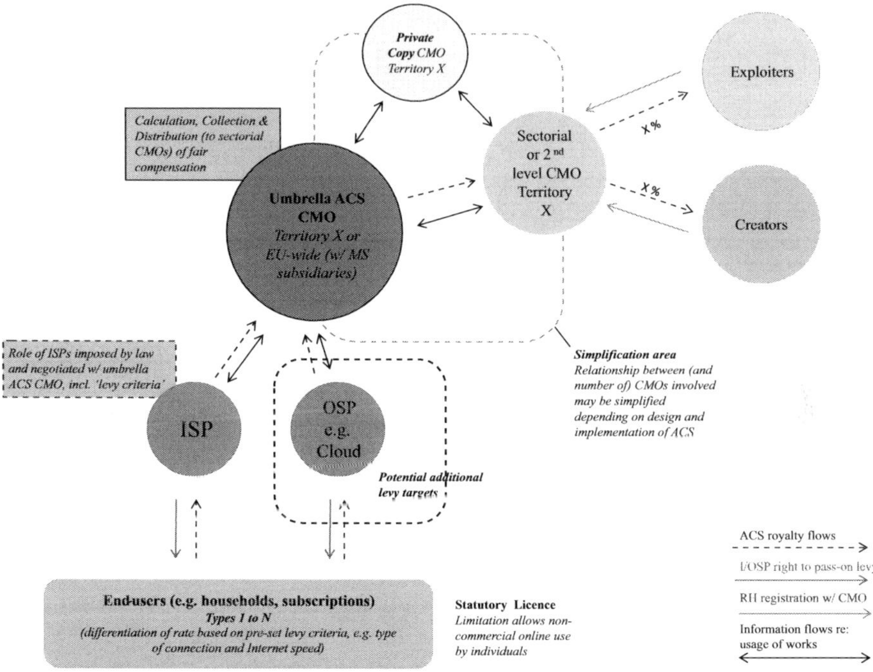

First, as regards the determination of the total amount of fair compensation generated by the ACS, the calculation should follow the method outlined above in 6.2.4. The European tradition on collective rights management and statutory licensing highlights different possibilities for how to implement such a method. These include setting the applicable rates by law or regulation, with the intervention of a government agency and/or stakeholder negotiations, subject to judicial or administrative review. It is also possible to allocate this task to an independent authority or an arbitration board. The process should include stakeholder participation, involving rights holders (and their CMOs), intermediary debtors, and representatives of end-users subject to the levy.[59]

As shown in Figure 6.1, CMOs play a central role in this system. This makes sense due to the long-standing and well-developed infrastructure of collective rights management in the EU.[60] In an ACS, CMOs are involved not only in the process of determination of fair compensation, but also in different facets of management of the system, namely the collection and

59. *See supra* 3.4.4, on possible variations of an ACS management system.
60. See *supra* 3.4.3–3.4.6, on potential solutions to structure collection and distribution of rights revenue.

distribution of rights revenue. All aspects related to the functioning of CMOs in the system are regulated in the CRM Directive.[61]

The statutory licence ACS will be tied to obligatory collective management of the fair compensation right. In this system, CMOs 'play a role in centralizing and monitoring information as well as in granting fair and efficient distribution (not neglecting the defence of creators' interests against the copyright-based industries)'.[62] Subject to the rules of the CRM Directive, cross-border articulation of CMOs could rely on a network of representation agreements of national members to manage and enforce the fair compensation right. It is also conceivable that an EU-wide umbrella CMO centralises certain aspects of the system, including data processing, information on uses, and distribution of rights revenue, to the benefit of second-level national CMOs (or subsidiaries) and other stakeholders (*see* Figure 6.1).[63]

A crucial aspect that will affect the management of the system and the number of CMOs involved is the scope of the limitation. Thus, it is necessary to decide whether the ACS is embodied in one limitation covering two exclusive rights (reproduction and communication to the public), or two limitations, each covering one exclusive right. The most efficient design seems the 'one limitation' option.

The system must also address issues of overlap between limitations, namely whether it will incorporate existing compensated limitations, most prominently private copying. In this respect, there are strong legal arguments against the merger of limitations, beyond the political challenges inherent to such legislative engineering. They include the difference in substantive rights covered (as private copying only applies to the reproduction right), the distinction between types of use covered regarding acts of reproduction (e.g., copies from unauthorised sources in the case of ACS), and the different levy targets. This does not prevent, from an operational standpoint, the same CMOs that manage the private copying system extending their mandate to manage the ACS, leveraging their expertise and infrastructure to reduce complexity. (*See* Figure 6.1 and the reference to a 'simplification area').

Collection of the rights revenue should be carried out by the competent national CMO directly from the intermediary debtor. As regards distribution

---

61. On which, *see supra* 3.3.1–3.3.2.
62. Hilty & Nérisson, 2013, p. 13, discussing the prospective role of CMOs in the digital environment. The authors suggest CMOs 'could develop tools to enhance non-commercial uses of protected works thanks to micropayments and blanket licences', thus enabling 'compensation of creative people' and allowing 'end-users sufficient access to copyrighted works'. In this respect, they add, '[e]xtending cases in which copyrights were to be statutorily collectively managed would help'.
63. *See* SWD CRM Directive 2012, pp. 46–47, discussing and rejecting the option of a centralised portal for the EU-wide collective administration of online music *on a voluntary basis*. It does not seem that the centralised portal option in the context of an ACS-limitation would give rise to the same competition issues that lead to its rejection by the Commission as a model for multi-territorial licensing of musical works.

of fair compensation, the beneficiaries of the compensation are the rights holders of the exclusive rights of reproduction and communication to the public identified in the *acquis*. Furthermore, because the right of fair compensation is unwaivable and non-transferable, creators are entitled to a fair share of the distributable rights revenue, with the remaining amount going to exploiters, as shown in Figure 6.1.[64]

The specific distribution key for these amounts is determined by law or stakeholder negotiation, as already occurs with existing compensated limitations in the *acquis*. If an objective of EU law is to provide adequate compensation to incentivise creation and safeguard the 'independence and dignity of artistic creators and performers' (recital 11 InfoSoc Directive), it is submitted that creators should be apportioned at least half of the rights revenue collected.

The subsequent distribution of revenue among individual rights holders within a category should be dealt with by the second-level CMOs representing each category, following the general rules of the CRM Directive.[65] This book suggests using contingent valuation methods to ascribe a value to the prejudice suffered by rights holders and, to approximate the notion of harm, using techniques such as the measurement of use through electronic rights management information, sampling, and strictly anonymous monitoring with the assistance of ISPs. The combination of these methods should allow a fair distribution of revenue to rights holders.[66]

For practical reasons, the preferred compensation target or payment mechanism is a surcharge on the Internet subscription of individual households. The burden of compensation lies primarily with the intermediary debtors, i.e., the ISPs, and ultimately with the end-users benefiting from the limitation. To make this system effective, ISPs are allowed to pass on the levy to end-users in the price of their household (but not professional) subscriptions. As a matter of transparency, this surcharge should be visible to end-users. This set-up is similar to that of private copying systems, and should therefore be familiar to stakeholders.[67]

As discussed above in 6.2.1, it is possible to extend the pool of levy targets to include online service providers. (For the sake of argument, this possibility is reflected in Figure 6.1 with a reference to 'OSP'.) However, this possibility does not currently seem justified on existing empirical research and, as such, is not recommended. A similar argument can be made in relation to targeting mobile Internet connections, a possibility envisaged by

64. *See supra* 6.2.4.
65. On which, *see supra* 3.3.1 and 3.4.4 (making reference to this topic as part of an ACS attribute).
66. *See supra* 5.3.2.3.3 and 5.3.3.3, on the use of contingent valuation to determine the total amount of fair compensation.
67. As with certain debtors of the private copying levy, ISPs may choose to compete on price by absorbing the broadband levy. *See* Roßnagel et al., 2009, p. 22.

some legalisation proposals, but one which does not seem empirically justified at this time.[68]

Not all end-users engage in file sharing or consume digital culture online to the same extent. For example, a recent study in the Netherlands shows that 49% of Dutch consumers, including those without Internet access, do not access digital channels to consume music, audio-visual content or books.[69] Therefore, in a logic similar to the payment of utilities (e.g., gas, electricity and water), it is sensible for the system to differentiate between users and targeted households, while retaining the link between harm and end-user.

If we use the cited study as an indicator, a statutory licence ACS in the Netherlands could include exemptions or reductions to the broadband levy for categories of households. Candidates would be households whose residents are above a certain age or below a pre-defined income level; it is also rational to reduce the levy for slower types of Internet connection (*see* Figure 6.1 and the box referring to 'End-users'). Once the system matures, it will be advisable to contemplate further variations, linked to the number of residents per household, and the possibility of users choosing between fixed or metered surcharges (dependent on Internet speed and usage).[70] This differentiation allows for a more equitable system that better reflects the concepts of fair compensation and harm, whilst leveraging consumers' willingness to participate in and pay for an ACS.[71]

6.2.7 Scaling Down Reform: Adaptability of the Proposal to Collective Licensing

What is normatively desirable and what is imminently doable are not always the same thing. While the present book shows that copyright reform through a right of access and remuneration for non-commercial online use of works is consistent with EU law, this by no means guarantees its adoption in the short or even medium term.

In a political climate where limitations for worthy purposes such as freedom of panorama or text-and-data mining for research are controversial, the proposal for a limitation-based statutory licence ACS will surely meet

68. For legalisation proposals mentioning this possibility, *see supra* 3.4.5.
69. Vallbé et al., 2015, attributing this result to holdout groups, characterised by older less educated people that predominantly use TV and radio ('non-consumers'), and older educated people who prefer books ('bookworms'). The non-consumers amount to ca. 29%, whereas 'bookworms' amount to 20%.
70. This general approach is foreseen by multiple ACS proposals. *See supra* 3.4.4. See, e.g., Colin, 2011a, p. 99.
71. Vallbé et al., 2015. *See also* Handke et al., 2015, regarding recorded music.

with fierce opposition.[72] Therefore, and following the book's pragmatic approach advocated in Chapter 1,[73] this section briefly outlines how the reform blueprint set out above can be scaled down to a more feasible legal solution. In this way, some of the core aspects of an ACS can be actualised in the shorter term.

One approach to scale down reform is to narrow the scope of the statutory licence ACS with regard to subject matter. Section 6.2.2. addresses this possibility, as well as its potential advantages and drawbacks.

Another option is to forego the application of a statutory licence and adapt the ACS blueprint to a model of pure collective rights management. Chapter 3 discusses the basic features of voluntary, extended and mandatory collective management, as well as some of their potential drawbacks, including issues of substantive and territorial fragmentation, and participation.[74] Whatever the model adopted, CMOs could frame the substantive rights scope of the licence in Article 5(3) CRM Directive, according to which '[r]ightholders shall have the right to grant licences for non-commercial uses of any rights, categories of rights or types of works and other subject-matter that they may choose.'

Voluntary and extended collective licences require that rights holders entrust CMOs with their exclusive online rights of reproduction and communication to the public for the non-commercial online use of works. Assuming for the sake of argument that mandatory collective management only affects the exercise of copyright,[75] this model would require a legal mandate for CMOs to manage exclusive rights for non-commercial online use. In either scenario, the substantive rights scope of a 'collective management ACS' could be identical to that suggested above, as could many of the features of the reform blueprint.

One important difference would of course be the nature of the remuneration, as a collective licence for exclusive rights cannot rely solely on a concept of fair compensation, designed in EU law for limitations. Instead, such a licence would more clearly follow the concept of 'appropriate remuneration' in Article 16(3) CRM Directive, pursuant to which tariffs for exclusive or remuneration rights must be:

> reasonable in relation to, inter alia, the economic value of the use of the rights in trade, taking into account the nature and scope of the use of the work and other subject-matter, as well as in relation to the economic

72. *See* Julia Reda, *EU copyright evaluation report – full current text*, https://juliareda.eu/copyright-evaluation report/full/ (accessed 31.01.2017), on the drafting history of the recent EP Resolution Implementation InfoSoc Directive 2015.
73. *See supra* 1.3.
74. These issues are also addressed in the other chapters and inform this study's preference for a statutory licensing model. *See supra* 4.5, 5.1, 5.5, 6.1.4, and 6.1.5.
75. This issue is debated *supra* at 3.3.4 and 4.5. *See also supra* 6.1.3–6.1.5.

value of the service provided by the collective management organisation.

However, due to the non-commercial nature of the licensed use and the difficulty in defining its economic value in trade, this concept of 'appropriate remuneration' offers little guidance beyond a criterion of reasonableness. Thus, it seems that the approach outlined above in 6.2.4 for a right of fair compensation does not contravene the spirit of the law, especially because a contingent valuation method offers a proxy for the market value of the licensed use.

An obvious distinction between the models of collective management mentioned is the level of legislative change to the *acquis* required by each of them. Mandatory collective management, for example, would probably necessitate an intervention at the level of secondary EU law, similar to the special regime for cable retransmission in Articles 9–12 SatCab Directive.[76]

It is not clear that the same is true for ECL or voluntary collective management. First, because Article 5(3) CRM Directive provides a legal basis for a voluntary licence. Second, because the CRM Directive significantly harmonises the functioning of CMOs in the EU, containing most of the rules needed to establish a voluntary ACS through a network of representation agreements.[77] Still, at least regarding a legalisation scheme based on ECL, there are good arguments for adopting in the *acquis* a basic framework for the grant of non-commercial licences for the online rights of reproduction and communication to the public. Such a framework could include, for example, a country of origin rule to enable cross-border effect for the national licences, clarify the operation of an opt-out mechanism, and set out other key aspects of the system.[78]

However, if the necessary rules are already in place in EU law, a more politically feasible short-term solution is to promote a voluntary EU-wide system through a 'soft law' instrument that nudges CMOs to grant such non-commercial licences. The obvious candidate in this respect is a recommendation by the Commission under Article 288 TFEU.

Recommendations are non-binding legislative instruments directed primarily at Member States, and possibly also at other economic operators (e.g., CMOs).[79] In the area of copyright, the Commission has issued recommendations in, for example, the fields of online music, digitisation and

---

76. On which, *see supra* 2.4.4 and 3.3.4.1.
77. This view is not consensual. Some authors believe the adoption of an ECL at EU level would require commensurate legislative recognition. *See* the discussion *supra* at 3.3.3.2, where one of the objections levied against legalisation schemes based on ECL is precisely that they would require legal changes to the *acquis*.
78. *See supra* 3.3.3.2.
79. For exceptions to this non-binding nature of recommendations in the area of economic and monetary policy, *see* Bradley, 2014, p. 102.

digital preservation, as well as access to and preservation of scientific information.[80]

For the present purposes, it is suggested that a recommendation incorporates and develops the key elements of the ACS blueprint above, and elucidates its articulation with the rules of the InfoSoc and CRM Directives. To increase its effectiveness, the recommendation could be addressed not only at the Member States but also at 'all economic operators which are involved in the management of copyright and related rights' in the EU.[81] This would clarify the application of the instrument to CMOs and 'independent management entities' (Article 3(b) CRM Directive), reinforcing its persuasive character despite the lack of binding force.

In relation to the content of the recommendation, this instrument should:

- Recommend a subject matter and substantive rights scope for the licence in line with the proposal above in 6.2.2–6.2.3.
- Provide interpretative guidelines on the concept of 'non-commercial uses' in Article 5(3) CRM Directive, in line with the CJEU definition of the autonomous concept, and the principles outlined above at 6.2.3. In particular, said definition should exclude from the scope of the concept any use by unauthorised platforms that derive financial consideration from the online exchange of works.[82]
- Endorse a methodological approach for the calculation of 'appropriate remuneration' that uses the combination of techniques identified in 6.2.4, especially contingent valuation and anonymous measurement of uses.
- Clarify the articulation of the ACS with the private copying limitation and the concept of fair compensation (on which *see supra* 6.2.4 and 6.2.6).
- Include suggestions on ensuring that monitoring of online exchanges in the system is anonymous, with the sole purpose of enabling collection and distribution of rights revenue, and on preventing that end-users are allowed to pay with personal data as a counter-performance or consideration for the authorisation to use works.[83]
- Provide guidance on the basic operation of the system as regards collection and distribution of amounts, including reserving a fair share of rights revenue to creators (on which *see above* 6.2.6).
- Support the negotiation of licences between CMOs or independent management entities, on the one hand, and ISPs and online service

80. Online Music Recommendation 2005; Recommendation on Digitisation, Online Accessibility and Digital Preservation 2006; Recommendation on Access to and Preservation of Scientific Information 2012.
81. Online Music Recommendation 2005, para. 19.
82. *See supra* 5.3.2.3.2.
83. *See supra* 5.3.3.6.2.

providers, on the other hand. These intermediaries would then extend the benefit of the licence to their subscribers (natural persons) against payment of an additional fee or bundled in the services provided (*see supra* 6.2.6).

It is true that recommendations are not always successful, as illustrated by the much-criticised 2005 Online Music Recommendation.[84] However, in light of the problem of mass unauthorised online use of works and the need to actualise Article 5(3) CRM Directive, a properly designed recommendation could provide a valuable low-impact contribution to improve the regulation of this type of copyright use in the *acquis*. Thus, failing legal reform through statutory licensing or mandatory collective management, this possibility should be explored as a softer version of a system of online access and remuneration in EU copyright law. If the mitigated version proves successful, it will increase the policy space available for a limitation-based statutory licence ACS.

6.3 A WAY FORWARD

The contours of copyright protection are shaped by the public interest, and rightly so. It is in the public interest for creators to receive fair remuneration for the online use of their works, thereby rewarding and incentivising creation. It is also in the public interest for end-users to retain a personal sphere of enjoyment and expression in the online environment, for which it is essential they can interact with copyright works without restriction in a non-commercial context, with legal certainty, and without fear of liability.

The current EU copyright regime does not achieve these goals. Rather, it promotes a culture of online exclusivity at the expense of cultural access and fair remuneration. It is therefore necessary to rethink how copyright can and should apply to large-scale individual use of works over the Internet.

This book advances a reform proposal that recasts copyright as a right of access and remuneration for non-commercial online use. This alternative compensation system (or ACS), if properly designed, is consistent with the normative aims of EU copyright law, and would improve the regulation of this type of online use. Where that model is judged too bold, the analysis offers alternative legal solutions to 'scale down' reform, so as to increase its political feasibility.

In the end, copyright reform through a model of remunerated access is a matter of normative choice or preference. It is neither a utopian nor, depending on one's perspective, a dystopian proposition. Rather, it is a legally viable policy option worthy of further exploration and empirical research as to the details and nuances of the system.

---

84. On which, *see* Guibault & van Gompel, 2010, pp. 155–158.

The main argument of this book is that we can and should reform EU copyright law to foster a culture of online access that is respectful of the material interests of creators, the fundamental rights of end-users, and the general interests of society. Whether policymakers take on the mantle will depend on their vision of how the copyright law of the future should look, and to what extent it should reflect the public interest.

Bibliography

Abramowicz, M. B. (2003). Perfecting Patent Prizes. *Vanderbilt Law Review*, *56*, 115–236.

Aguiar, L., & Martens, B. (2013). *Digital Music Consumption on the Internet: Evidence from Clickstream Data* (No. 2013/04).

Aigrain, P. (2008). *Internet & création: comment reconnaître les échanges hors-marché sur internet en finançant et rémunérant la création? Libro Veritas, Cergy-Pontoise*, In Libro Veritas.

Aigrain, P. (2012). *Sharing: Culture and the Economy in the Digital Age*. Amsterdam University Press.

ALAI. (1983). *Public Lending Right. Reports of an ALAI-Sumposium and Additional Materials*. (H. C. Jehoram, ed.). Amsterdam: Kluwer Law and Taxation Publishers.

ALAI. (1987). Rapport sur le 56è congrès de l' ALAI tenu sous le patronage du Conseil Fédéral du 8-12 septembre 1986 á Berne. In *Report on the 56th ALAI-congress under the Patronage of the Swiss Government*. Berne: Association Suisse pour la protection du droit d'auteur et les auterus.

ALAI. (2006). *ALAI Resolution 'Affirmation Droit Exclusif'* Adopted: 14 January 2006.

ALAI. (2012). *Determination of Country of Origin When a Work Is First Publicly Disclosed Over the Internet. Report by the Country of Origin Study Group of the International Literary and Artistic Association (ALAI)* .Adopted: 14 January 2012 (Paris).

ALAI. (2013). *REPORT and OPINION on the making available and communication to the public in the internet environment – focus on linking techniques on the Internet*. Adopted: 16 September 2013.

ALAI. (2014). *ALAI Opinion on the criterion 'New Public', developed by the Court of Justice of the European Union (CJEU), put in the context of making available and communication to the public*. Adopted: 17 September 2014.

ALAI. (2015a). *ALAI Report and Opinion on a Berne-compatible reconciliation of hyperlinking and the communication to the public right on the internet*. Adopted: 17 June 2015.

ALAI. (2015b). *ALAI Resolution Bonn 2015*. Bonn: ALAI. Adopted: 17 June 2015.

Allen, D. W. (2000). Transaction Costs. In B. Bouckaert & G. De Geest (eds), *Encyclopedia of Law and Economics, Volume I. The History and Methodology of Law and Economics* (pp. 893–925). Cheltenham: Edward Elgar.

Anderson, J. (2011). Stream Capture: Returning Control of Digital Music to Users. *Harvard Journal of Law & Technology*, *25*(1), 159–177.

Angelopoulos, C. (2009). Filtering the Internet for Copyright Content in Europe. *IRIS-Plus*, *4*, 1–12.

Angelopoulos, C. (2013). Beyond the Safe Harbours: Harmonising Substantive Intermediary Liability For Copyright Infringement in Europe. *Intellectual Property Quarterly*, *3*, 253–274.

Angelopoulos, C. (2014). Are Blocking Injunctions Against ISPs Allowed in Europe? Copyright Enforcement in the Post-Telekabel EU Legal Landscape. *Journal of Intellectual Property Law & Practice*, *9*(10), 812–821. http://doi.org/10.1093/jiplp/jpu136.

Angelopoulos, C. (2015). Sketching the Outline of a Ghost: The Fair Balance Between Copyright and Fundamental Rights in Intermediary Third Party Liability. *info, 17*(6), 72-96, 8.

Angelopoulos, C. (2016). *European Intermediary Liability in Copyright: A Tort-Based Analysis*. University of Amsterdam (PhD Dissertation).

Arezzo, E. (2014). Hyperlinks and Making Available Right in the European Union – What Future for the Internet after Svensson? *IIC*, *45*(5), 524–555.

Arnold, R., & Rosati, E. (2015). Are National Courts the Addressees of the Infosoc Three-Step Test? *Journal of Intellectual Property Law & Practice*, *10*(10): 741-749.

Arrow, K. J. (1962). Economic Welfare and the Allocation of Resources for Invention. In *The Rate and Direction of Inventive Activity: Economic and Social Factors* (pp. 609–626). National Bureau of Economic Research.

Article 19. (2013). *The Right to Share: Principles on Freedom of Expression and Copyright in the Digital Age*. International Standards Series.

Astier, H. (1986). Private Copying. *Revue Internationale Du Droit d'Auteur*, *128*(4), 112–145.

Attali, J. (2008). *Rapport de la Commission pour la libération de la croissance française*. XO Editions : La Documentation française.

Austin, G. (2012). Radio: Early Battles over the Public Performance Right. In B. Sherman & L. Wiseman (eds), *Copyright and the Challenge of the New* (pp. 115–140). Alphen aan den Rijn: Kluwer Law International.

Austin, G. W., & Zavidow, A. G. (2015). Copyright Law Reform Through a Human Rights Lens. In P.L.C. Torremans (ed.), *Intellectual Property Law and Human Rights* (pp. 303–333). Alphen aan den Rijn: Kluwer Law International.

Australian Copyright Council. (2001). *Remuneration for Private Copying in Australia: A Discussion Paper.*

Axhamn, J., & Guibault, L. (2012). Cross-Border Extended Collective Licensing: A Solution to Online Dissemination of Europe's Cultural Heritage. *Amsterdam Law School Research Paper No. 2012-22.*

Baker, D. (2003). *The Artistic Freedom Voucher: An Internet Age Alternative to Copyrights.* Washington D.C.: CEPR – Center for Economic and Policy Research.

Balganesh, S. (2012). The Obligatory Structure of Copyright Law: Unbundling the Wrong of Copying. *Harvard Law Review*, *125*, 1664–1690.

Balkin, J. (2004). Digital Speech and Democratic Culture: A Theory of Freedom of Expression for the Information Society. *New York University Law Review*, *79*, 1–55.

Basso, M. (2000). *O Direito internacional da propriedade intellectual.* Porto Alegre: Livraria do Advogado.

Bechtold, S. (2006). Information Society Directive. In T. Dreier & P. B. Hugenholtz (eds), *Concise European Copyright Law* (pp. 343–403). Alphen aan den Rijn: Kluwer Law International.

Becker, L. C. (1992). Deserving to Own Intellectual Property. *Chicago-Kent Law Review*, *68*(2), 609–629.

Beltrandi, Bernardini, Zamparutti, Coscioni, F., Turco, M., & Mecacci. (2008). CAMERA DEI DEPUTATI N. 187. PROPOSTA DI LEGGE – Modifiche alla legge 22 aprile 1941, n. 633, in materia di comunicazione di opere al pubblico da parte di persone fisiche che scambiano archivi attraverso reti digitali per fini personali e senza scopo di lu.

Beltrandi, D'Elia, Turco, Mellano, & Poretti (2007). CAMERA DEI DEPUTATI N. 2963. PROPOSTA DI LEGGE – Modifiche alla legge 22 aprile 1941, n. 633, in materia di comunicazione di opere al pubblico da parte di persone fisiche che scambiano archivi attraverso reti digitali per fini personali e senza scopo di l.

Benkler, Y. (2002). Coase's Penguin, or, Linux and 'The Nature of the Firm.' *Yale Law Journal*, *112*, 371–446.

Benkler, Y. (2004). Sharing Nicely: On Shareable Goods and the Emergence of Sharing as a Modality of Economic Production. *Yale Law Journal*, 273–358.

Benkler, Y. (2006). *The Wealth of Networks: How Social production Transforms Markets and Freedom.* Yale University Press.

Benkler, Y. (2012). Open Wireless vs. Licensed Spectrum: Evidence from Market Adoption. *Harvard Journal of Law & Technology*, *26*(1), 69–163.

Benkler, Y., Roberts, H., Faris, R., Solow-Niederman, A., & Etling, B. (2013). Social Mobilization and the Networked Public Sphere: Mapping the SOPA-PIPA Debate. *SSRN Electronic Journal*. http://doi.org/10.2139/ssrn.2295953.

Bentley, L. (2016). Article 10(1) of the Berne Convention: Global, Mandatory Fair Use? Presentation at the Institute for Information Law (IViR), University of Amsterdam. (8 April 2016).

Bernault, C., & Lebois, A. (2005). *Peer-to-Peer File Sharing and Literary and Artistic Property A Feasibility Study Regarding a System of Compensation for the Exchange of Works via the Internet*. Institute for Research on Private Law, University of Nantes (Translated from the French by Leigh Smith and Cédric Palazzetti).

BIRPI. (1965). *General Report of the Swedish/BIRPI Study Group Established at July 1, 1964 – Committee of Governmental Experts (1965)*. Geneva.

Blázquez, F. J. C. (2011). Private Copying Levies at the Crossroads. *IrisPlus* (4), 7–22.

Boorstin, D. J. (1941). Tradition and Method in Legal History. *Harvard Law Review*, *54*, 424–436.

Borgne-Bachschmidt, F. Le, Girieud, S., Leiba, M., Munck, S. de, Limonard, S., Poel, M., … Swart, E. (2008). *User-Created-Content*: *Supporting a Participative Information Society Understanding the Digital World, Final Report 2008*. Amsterdam Law School Research Paper No. 2012-32.

Boulanger, J., Carbonnel, A., Coninck, R. De, & Langus, G. (2014). *Assessing the Economic Impacts of Adapting Certain Limitations and Exceptions to Copyright and Related Rights in the EU. Analysis of Specific Policy Options*. Study prepared for DG MARKT, European Commission. London.

Bouthillier, Y. le. (2011). Art. 32 of the 1969 Vienna Convention. In O. Corten & P. Klein (eds), *The Vienna Conventions on the Law of Treaties*: *A Commentary* (pp. 841–861). Oxford: OUP.

Boyle, J. (2003). The Second Enclosure Movement and the Construction of the Public Domain. *Law and Contemporary Problems*, *66*, 33–74.

Boytha, G. (1993). The Intellectual Property Status of Sound Recordings. *IIC*, *24*(3), 295–306.

Bradley, K. S. C. (2014). Legislating in the European Union. In C. Barnard & S. Peers (eds), *European Union Law* (pp. 97–139). Oxford: OUP.

Bridy, A. (2009). Why Pirates (Still) Won't Behave: Regulating p2p in the Decade after Napster. *Rutgers Law Journal*, *40*, 565–611.

Brison, F. (2006). WIPO Performances and Phonograms Treaty. In T. Dreier & B. Hugenholtz (eds), *Concise European Copyright Law* (pp. 165–194). Alphen aan den Rijn: Kluwer Law International.

Burger, P. F. (1988a). The New Photocopy Remuneration Provisions in the Federal Republic of Germany and Their Application to Foreign Authors under International Copyright Law – Part One. *IIC*, 319–336.

Burger, P. F. (1988b). The New Photocopy Remuneration Provisions in the Federal Republic of Germany and Their Application to Foreign Authors under International Copyright Law – Part Two. *IIC*, 488–514.

Calabresi, G., & Melamed, A. D. (1972). Property Rules, Liability Rules, and Inalienability: One View of the Cathedral. *Harvard Law Review*, *85*(6), 1089–1128.

Cammaerts, B., & Meng, B. (2011). *Creative Destruction and Copyright Protection: Regulatory Responses to File-Sharing*. London: Department of Media and Communications, London School of Economics and Political Science.

Carre, S. (2012). France. In R. Hilty & S. Nerisson (eds), *Balancing Copyright – A Survey of National Approaches*. Springer.

Carroll, M. W. (2013). A Realist Approach to Copyright Law's Formalities. *Berkeley Technology Law Journal*, *28*, 1511–1535.

Chalis, B. (2015). The 1709 Blog: Spotify Leak Puts Streaming Royalties in Focus. Retrieved 12 October 2015, *1709 Blog*, http://the1709blog.blogspot.co.uk/2015/05/spotify-leak-puts-streaming-royalties.html.

Christie, A. F., & Wright, R. (2014). A Comparative Analysis of the Three-Step Tests in International Treaties. *IIC*, *45*(4), 409–433.

Ciurcina, M., Martin, J. C. De, Margoni, T., Morando, F., & Ricolfi, M. (2009). *Remunerating Creativity, Freeing Knowledge: File-Sharing and Extended Collective Licenses*, NEXA Center for Internet and Society Politecnico di Torino.

Cohen, J. E., Loren, L. P., Okediji, R. L., & O'Rourke, M. A. (2010). *Copyright in A Global Information Economy* (Third). Wolters Kluwer.

Colin, C. (2011a) (sous la supervision et avec la participation de la Prof. Séverine Dusollier). *Etude the Faisabilite de Systemes de Licences pour les Echanges d'Oeuvres sur internet*. Rapport pour la SACD/SCAM – Belgique. Centre de Recherche Information, Droit et Société (CRIDS) Facultés Universitaires Notre-Dame de la Paix – Namur.

Colin, C. (2011b) (under the supervision and with the participation of Prof. Séverine Dusollier). *Feasibility Study of Licensing Systems for The Peer-To-Peer Exchange of Works on the Internet – Executive Summary*. Report for the SACD/SCAM – Belgium. Research Centre Information, Law and Society (CRIDS) University of Namur.

Collopy, D. P., & Bahanovich, D. (2012). Music Experience and Behaviour in Young People: Winter 2012–2013 [2011 National Survey]. International Association of Music Business Research.

Collová, T. (1966). Copyright, Closely Related Rights and the Utilization of Intellectual Works Trough Tape-Recorders. *Revue Internationale Du Droit d'Auteur*, *50*(7), 61–178.

Collová, T. (1991). A propos de la remuneration pour copie privée. *Revue Internationale Du Droit d'Auteur*, *149*, 35–149.

Commissie Auteursrech. (2012). *Advies 'Een flexibele regeling voor user-generated content'. Deel 1: Een flexibele regeling voor user-generated content*, https://www.rijksoverheid.nl/documenten/rapporten/2012/10/30/advies-een-flexibele-regeling-voor-user-generated-content.

Computer & Communications Industry Association. (2016). *CCIA Comments on the GS Media Case (C-160/15)*, http://www.ccianet.org/library/resource-library/briefs-and-filings/.

Consumentenbond, & Bureau Brandeis. (2014). Letter to the ECJ 'Re: Opinion of Advocate-General Cruz Villalón Regarding Downloading from Illegal Sources.' Amsterdam.

Cook, T. (2012). Exceptions and Limitations in European Union Copyright Law. *Journal of Intellectual Property Rights*, *17*, 243–245.

Cornish, W. R. (1993). Sound Recordings and Copyright. *IIC*, 306–313.

Cornish, W. R. (1995). Copyright Across the Quarter-Century. *IIC*, 801–812.

Correa, C. M. (2007). *Trade Related Aspects of Intellectual Property Rights: A Commentary on the TRIPS Agreement*. Oxford: OUP.

Creation-public-internet. (2011). The Proposals of Création-Public-Internet. Available at http://creationpublicinternet.fr/blog/index.php?post/2011/06/28/The-proposals-of-Cr?ation-Public-Internet.

Creative Commons. (2009). *Defining 'Noncommercial' A Study of How the Online Population Understands 'Noncommercial Use.'*

Damstedt, B. G. (2003). Limiting Locke: A Natural Law Justification for the Fair Use Doctrine. *Yale Law Journal*, *112*, 1179–1221.

Daum, F. (2010). Copyright, European Competition Law, and Free Movement of Goods and Services. In M. Walter & S. von Lewinski (eds), *European Copyright Law. A Commentary*. Oxford: OUP.

Depreeuw, S. (2014). *The Variable Scope of the Exclusive Economic Rights in Copyright*. Kluwer Law International.

Depreeuw, S., & Hubin, J.-B. (2014). *Study on the Making Available Right and Its Relationship with the Reproduction Right in Cross-Border Digital Transmissions*. DOI: 10.2780/20538.

Dietz, A. (1986). L'enrégistrement privé et la reprographie en Allemagne (RFA). Rapport complémentaire. In *Report on the 56th ALAI-congress under the patronage of the swiss government* (pp. 254–286). Berne: Association Suisse pour la protection du droit d'auteur et les auterus.

Dimita, G. (2010). *Copyright and Shared Networking Technologies*. Queen May, University of London. (PhD Dissertation).

DLA Piper. (2009). *EU Study on the Legal Analysis of a Single Market for the Information Society*. Study commissioned by the European Commission's Information Society and Media Directorate-General.

Doctorow, C. (2009). Streaming Will Never Stop Downloading The Guardian *The Guardian*. Date: 8 December 2009. Available at https://www.theguardian.com/technology/2009/dec/08/music-streaming-cory-doctorow.

Dougherty, M. (2006). Voluntary Collective Licensing: The Solution to thee Music Industry's File Sharing Crisis? (Note). *Journal of Intellectual Property Law, 13*, 405–434.

Drassinower, A. (2012). Copyright Is Not about Copying. *Harvard Law Review*, *3*(2003), 108–119.

Dreier, T. (2006). Berne Convention. In T. Dreier & P. B. Hugenholtz (eds), *Concise European Copyright Law* (pp. 7–86). Alphen aan den Rijn: Kluwer Law International.

Dreier, T. (2010). Satellite and Cable Directive. In M. Walter & S. von Lewinski (eds), *European Copyright Law: A Commentary*. Oxford: OUP.

Dreier, T. (2015). Thoughts on Revising the Limitations on Copyright under Directive 2001/29. *Journal of Intellectual Property Law & Practice, 11*(2), 138–146.

Dreier, T., & Hugenholtz, P. B. (2006). Agreement on Trade-Related Aspects of Intellectual Property (Arts. 9–14). In T. Dreier & P. B. Hugenholtz (eds), *Concise European Copyright Law* (pp. 195–209). Alphen aan den Rijn: Kluwer Law International.

Dreier, T., & Specht, E. (2012). Germany. In R. Hilty & S. Nerisson (eds), *Balancing Copyright – A Survey of National Approaches* (pp. 431–445). Springer.

Drexl, J. (2010). Comment: in Favor of a Multi-track Copyright System. In R. C. Dreyfuss, D. L. Zimmerman, & H. First (eds), *Working Within the Boundaries of Intellectual Property – Innovation Policy for the Knowledge Society* (pp. 157–175). Oxford: OUP.

Dusollier, S. (2005). L'encadrement des exceptions au droit d'auteur par le test des trois étapes. *I.R.D.I.*, 213–223.

Dusollier, S. (2007). *Droit d'auteur et protection des œuvres dans l'univers numérique: Droits et exceptions à la lumière des dispositifs de verrouillage des œuvres*. 2e Edition. Larcier.

Dusollier, S. (2011). (Re)Introducing Formalities in Copyright as a Strategy for the Public Domain. In L. Guibault & C. Angelopoulos (eds), *Open Content Licensing: From Theory to Practice* (pp. 75–105). Amsterdam: Amsterdam University Press.

Dusollier, S., & Colin, C. (2011). Peer-to-Peer File Sharing and Copyright: What Could Be the Role of Collective Management? *Columbia Journal of Law & the Arts*, *34*, 809–835.

Dusollier, S., & Ker, C. (2009). Private Copy Levies and Technical Protection of Copyright: The Uneasy Accommodation of Two Conflicting Logics. In E. Derclaye (ed.), *Research Handbook on the Future of EU Copyright* (p. 349-372). Edward Elgar.

Earp, M., & McDiarmid, A. (2008). *An Investigation of Voluntary Collective Licensing for Music File-Sharing at UC Berkeley*. UC Berkeley.

Eckersley, P. (2004). Virtual Markets for Virtual Goods: The Mirror Image of Digital Copyright? *Harvard Journal of Law & Technology*, *18*(1), 85–166.

Eckersley, P. (2012). *Digital Copyright & The Alternatives. An Interdisciplinary Inquiry*. University of Melbourne (PhD Dissertation).

Edstrom, J., & Nilsson, H. (2009). The Pirate Bay Verdict – Predictable, and Yet... *European Intellectual Property Review* (9), 483–487.

Eechoud, M. Van. (2012). Along the Road to Uniformity – Diverse Readings of the Court of Justice Judgments on Copyright Work. *Journal of Intellectual Property, Information Technology and Electronic Commerce Law*, *3*, 60–80.

Eechoud, M. van, Hugenholtz, P. B., Gompel, S. van, Guibault, L., & Helberger, N. (2009). *Harmonizing European Copyright Law. The Challenges of Better Lawmaking*. Kluwer Law International.

Efroni, Z. (2011). *Access-Right – The Future of Digital Copyright Law*. Oxford, New York: OUP.

Eijk, N. van, Fahy, R., Til, H. van, Nooren, P., Stokking, H., & Gelevert, H. (2015). *Digital Platforms: An Analytical Framework for Identifying and Evaluating Policy Options*. TNO 2015 R11271: Final report. The Hague.

Eijk, N. Van, Poort, J., & Rutten, P. (2010). Legal, Economic and Cultural Aspects of File Sharing. *Communications & Strategies*, *77*(1st Q.), 35–54.

Elkin-Koren, N. (1996). Cyberlaw and Social Change: A Democratic Approach to Copyright Law in Cyberspace. *Cardozo Arts & Entertainment Law Journal*, *14*.

Esmeijer, J., Nieuwenhuis, O., Mijs, C., & Versloot, C. (2012). *Making User Created News Work*. TNO 2012 R11277: Final Report. Delft.

Europe Economics, Guibault, L., Salamanca, O., & Gompel, S. van. (2015). *Remuneration of Authors and Performers for the Use of Their Works and the Fixations of Their Performances: Final Report*. Study prepared for the European Commission, DG Communications Networks, Content & Technology. Brussels.

European Commission. (2013). *Public Consultation on the Review of the EU Copyright Rules Contents Introduction Context of the consultation*. Available at http://ec.europa.eu/internal_market/consultations/2013/copyright-rules/docs/consultation-document_en.pdf.

European Commission. (2014). Report on the Responses to the Public Consultation on the Review of the EU Copyright Rules (July), 1–101. Directorate General Internal Market and Services Directorate D – Intellectual property, D1 – Copyright. Retrived from http://ec.europa.eu/internal_market/consultations/2013/copyright-rules/docs/contributions/consultation-report_en.pdf.

European Copyright Society. (2013). *The Reference to the CJEU in Case C-466/12 Svensson*. Available at https://europeancopyrightsociety.org/how-the-ecs-works/ecs-opinions/.

European Copyright Society. (2014a). *European Copyright Society Answer to the EC Consultation on the Review of the EU Copyright Rules*. Available at https://europeancopyrightsociety.org/how-the-ecs-works/ecs-opinions/.

European Copyright Society. (2014b). *Limitations and Exceptions as Key Elements of the Legal Framework for Copyright in the European Union Opinion on The Judgment of the CJEU in Case C – 201/13 Deckmyn*. Available at https://europeancopyrightsociety.org/how-the-ecs-works/ecs-opinions/.

European Copyright Society. (2015). *ECS Opinion in Case C572_13 HP Belgium Reprobel 2015*. Available at https://europeancopyrightsociety.org/how-the-ecs-works/ecs-opinions/.

Eurostat. (2015). Information Society Statistics – Households and Individuals – Statistics Explained. In *Europe in Figures – Eurostat Yearbook*. Eurostat.

Favale, M. (2012). The Right of Access in Digital Copyright: Right of the Owner or Right of the User? *The Journal of World Intellectual Property*, *15*(1), 1–25.

Favale, M. (2016). The Quest for Balance in CJEU Copyright Jurisprudence, as explained by Judge Malenovský. Available at from http://www.create.ac.uk/blog/2016/01/18/the-quest-for-balance-in-cjeu-copyright-jurisprudence-as-explained-by-judge-malenovsky/.

Favale, M., Kretschmer, M., & Torremans, P.L.C. (2015). Is There a EU Copyright Jurisprudence? An Empirical Analysis of the Workings of the European Court of Justice. *Modern Law Review*, *79*(1), 31–75.

Ficsor, M. (2002a). *Colective Management of Copyright and Related Rights*. Geneva: World Intellectual Property Organization (WIPO Publication No. 855(E)).

Ficsor, M. (2002b). How Much of What? Three-Step Test and Its Application in Recent WTO Dispute Settlement Cases. *Revue Internationale Du Droit d'Auteur*, *192*(4), 110–251.

Ficsor, M. (2002c). *The Law of Copyright and the Internet: The 1996 WIPO Treaties, Their Interpretation and Implementation*. Oxford: OUP.

Ficsor, M. (2003a). Collective Management of Copyright and Related Rights at a Triple Crossroads: Should It Remain Voluntary or May It Be 'Extended' or Made Mandatory? *UNESCO E-Copyright Bulletin* (October), 1–10.

Ficsor, M. (2003b). *Guide to the Copyright and Related Rights Treaties Administered by WIPO and Glossary of Copyright and Related Rights Terms*. Geneva: World Intellectual Property Organization.

Ficsor, M. (2012a). *Comments on the UGC Provisions of the Canadian Bill C-32:: Potential Dangers for Unintended Consequences in the Light of the International Norms on Copyright and Related Rights.*

Ficsor, M. (2012b). The Three-Step Test under the TRIPS Agreement and the Specific Exceptions or Limiations Permitted by the Berne Convention – Its Role under the WCT and the Draft Instrument/Treaty on Exceptions or Limitations for the Visually Impaired.

Ficsor, M. (2016). Collective Rights Management from the Viewpoint of International Treaties, with Special Attention to the EU Ácquis'. In D. Gervais (ed.), *Collective Management of Copyright in Europe* (pp. 31–79). Alphen aan den Rijn: Kluwer Law International.

Ficsor, M., & Chatalbashev, M. (2016). Collective Management in Central and Eastern Europe. In D. Gervais (ed.), *Collective Management of Copyright and Related Rights* (Third, pp. 111–138). Alphen aan den Rijn: Kluwer Law International.

Fischman Afori, O. (2014). Proportionality – A New Mega Standard in European Copyright Law. *IIC*, *45*(8), 889–914.

Fisher, W. W. (2001). Theories of Intellectual Property. In S. R. Munzer (ed.), *New Essays in the Legal and Political Theory of Property* (pp. 168–200). Cambridge: CUP.

Fisher, W. W. (2004). *Promises to Keep: Technology, Law, and the Future of Entertainment*. Stanford University Press.

Fisher, W. W. (2010). The Implications for Law of User Innovation. *Minnesota Law Review*, *94*(5), 1417–1477.

Fiske, J. (1987). *Television Culture*. Routledge.

Flowers, A. (2015). Maybe Spotify Isn't Killing the Music Industry After All. *FiveThirtyEight*. Date: 2 November 2015. Available at https://fivethirtyeight.com/features/maybe-spotify-isnt-killing-the-music-industry-after-all/.

Frabboni, M. M. (2010). File-Sharing and the Role of Intermediaries in the Marketplace: National, European Union and International Developments. In I. Stamatoudi (ed.), *Copyright Enforcement and the Internet* (pp. 119–146). Alphen aan den Rijn: Kluwer Law Intermational.

Françon, A. (1986). The Future of Copyright. General Report. In *Report on the 56th ALAI-Congress under the Patronage of the Swiss Government* (pp. 199–222). Berne: Association Suisse pour la protection du droit d'auteur et les auterus.

French High Council for Literary and Artistic Property (2016). Mission to Link Directives 2000/31 and 2001/29 – Report and Proposals, Journal *of Intellectual Property, Information Technology and Electronic Commerce Law*, *7*(2), 88–95.

Frosio, G. F. (2011). *COMMUNIA Final Report*. Deliverable D1.11: Final Report, Ref ECP-2006-PSI-610001, Available at http://COMMUNIA---project.eu/.

Geiger, C. (2007a). From Berne to National law, via the Copyright Directive: The Dangerous Mutations of the Three-Step Test. *European Intellectual Property Review*. *29*(12), 486-491.

Geiger, C. (2007b). The Role of The Three-Step Test in the Adaptation of Copyright Law to the Information Society. *UNESCO E-Copyright Bulletin* (January-March), 1–21.

Geiger, C. (2008a). Legal or Illegal? That Is the Question! Private Copying and Downloading on the Internet. *IIC*, *39*, 597–603.

Geiger, C. (2008b). The Implementation of the Directive of 22 May 2001 on Copyright in the Information Society in France: A Promising Debate for a Disappointing Result. *AMI*: *Tijdschrift Voor Auteurs-, Media- & Informatierecht*, *1*, 1–7.

Geiger, C. (2010). Promoting Creativity Through Copyright Limitations: Reflections on the Concept of Exclusivity in Copyright Law. *Vanderbilt Journal of Entertainment & Technology Law*, *12*(3), 515–548.

Geiger, C. (2011). Honourable Attempt but (ultimately) Disproportionately Offensive against Peer-to-peer on the Internet (HADOPI) – A Critical Analysis of the Recent Anti-File-Sharing Legislation in France. *IIC*, *42*(4), 457–472.

Geiger, C. (2014a). Challenges for the Enforcement of Copyright in the Online World: Time for a New Approach. *Max Planck Institute for Innovation and Competition Research Papers* (14), 1–23.

Geiger, C. (2014b). Legalize It? Quelques réflexions sur la mise en oeuvre du droit d'auteur dans la contexte de l'utilisation non autosisée des oeuvres sur internet. In C. Geiger (ed.), *Le Droit de la Proprieté Intellectuelle dans un Monde Globalisé. intellectual Property law in a Globalized World – Mélanges en L'honneur du professeur Joanna Schmidt-Slzalewski* (pp. 167–185). Strasbourg: CEIPI.

Geiger, C. (2014c). The Rise of Criminal Enforcement of Intellectual Property Rights... and Its Failure in the Context of Copyright Infringements on the Internet. In S. Frankel & D. Gervais (eds), *The Evolution and Equilibrium of Copyright in the Digital Age* (pp. 113–142). Cambridge: Cambridge University Press.

Geiger, C. (2014d). The Social Function of Intellectual Property Rights, Or How Ethics Can Influence the Shape and Use of IP law. In G. B. Dinwoodie (ed.), *Intellectual Property Law: Methods and Perspectives*. Cheltenham, UK / Northampton, MA, Edward Elgar.

Geiger, C. (2015a). Copyright as an Access Right, Securing Cultural Participation Through the Protection of Creators' Interests. *Max Planck Institute for Innovation & Competition Research Paper No. 15-07*.

Geiger, C. (2015b). Statutory Licenses as Enabler of Creative Uses. *Max Planck Institute for Innovation & Competition Research Paper No. 15-14*.

Geiger, C., Gervais, D., & Senftleben, M. (2014). The Three-Step-Test Revisited: How to Use the Test's Flexibility in National Copyright Law. *American University International Law Review*, *29*(3), 581–626.

Geiger, C., Hilty, R., & Griffiths, J. (2008). Declaration A Balanced Interpretation of the 'Three-Step Test' in Copyright Law. *IIC*, *6*, 707–713.

Geiger, C., Hilty, R., Griffiths, J., & Suthersanen, U. (2010). Declaration A Balanced Interpretation Of The 'Three-Step Test' In Copyright Law. *Journal of Intellectual Property, Information Technology and Electronic Commerce Law*, *1*(2), 119–122.

Geiger, C., & Izyumenko, E. (2014). Copyright on the Human Rights' Trial: Redefining the Boundaries of Exclusivity Through Freedom of Expression. *IIC*, *45*(3), 316–342.

Geiger, C., & Schonherr, F. (2012). Defining the Scope of Protecion of Copyright in the EU: The Need to Reconsider the Acquis Regarding Limitations and Exceptions. In T.-E. Synodinou (ed.), *Codification of European Copyright Law. Challenges and Pespectives* (pp. 133–168). Kluwer Law International.

Geiger, C., & Schönherr, F. (2012). Defining the Scope of Protection of Copyright in the EU: The Need to Consider the Acquis Regarding Limitations and Exceptions. In T.-E. Synodiou (ed.), *Codification of European Copyright Law. Challenges and Perspectives* (pp. 133–167). Alphen aan den Rijn: Kluwer Law International.

Geiger, C., & Schönherr, F. (2014a). Limitations to Copyright in the Digital Age. In *Research Handbook on EU Internet Law* (pp. 110–142). Edward Elgar.

Geiger, C., & Schönherr, F. (2014b). The Information Society Directive (Articles 5 and 6(4)). In I. Stamatoudi & P. Torremans (eds), *EU Copyright Law. A Commentary*. Cheltenham: Edward Elgar Publishing.

Geller, P. E. (1991). Reprography and Other Processes of Mass Use. *Journal of the Copyright Society of the U.S.A.*, *38*(21), 21–40.

Geller, P. E. (1994). Must Copyright Be for Ever Caught Between Marketplace and Authorsip Norms. In B. Sherman & A. Strowel (eds), *Of Authors and Origins*: *Essays on Copyright Law* (pp. 159–201). Oxford: Clarendon Press.

Gera, M. (2016). Extended Collective Licensing under the New Slovak Copyright Act. *Journal of Intellectual Property Law & Practice*, *11*(3), 170–171.

Gervais, D. (2001). *Collective Management of Copyright and Neighbouring Rights in Canada*: *an International Perspective*. Canadian Heritage. Available at http://works.bepress.com/daniel_gervais/28/.

Gervais, D. (2003). *Application of an Extended Collective Licensing Regime in Canada*: *Principles and Issues Related to Implementation*. Vanderbilt Public Law Research Paper No. 11-26.

Gervais, D. (2004). The Price of Social Norms: Towards a Liability Regime for File-Sharing. *Journal of Intellectual Property Law, 12*(December), 39–73.
Gervais, D. (2005). Towards A New Core International Copyright Norm: The Reverse Three-Step Test. *Marquette Intellectual Property Law Review, 9*, 1–35.
Gervais, D. (2008). *The TRIPS Agreement. Drafting History and Analysis* (Third Edition). London: Sweet & Maxwell.
Gervais, D. (2009). The Tangled Web of UGC: Making Copyright Sense of User-Generated Content. *Vanderbilt Journal of Entertainment and Technology Law, 11*, 841–870.
Gervais, D. (2010). Collective Management of Copyright: Theory and Practice in the Digital Age. In D. Gervais (ed.), *Collective Management of Copyright and Related Rights* (2nd ed., pp. 1–28). Alphen aan den Rijn: Kluwer Law International.
Gervais, D. (2011). Keynote: The Landscape of Collective Management Schemes. *Columbia Journal of Law & the Arts, 34*(4), 423–449.
Gervais, D. (2015). How Intellectual Property and Human Rights Can Live Together: An Updated Perspective. In P.L.C. Torremans (ed.), *Intellectual Property and Human Rights* (Third Edition, pp. 3–26). Alphen aan den Rijn: Kluwer Law International.
Gervais, D. (2016). Collective Management of Copyright: Theory and Practice in the Digital Age. In D. Gervais (ed.), *Collective Management of Copyright and Related Rights* (Third Edition, pp. 3–30). Alphen aan den Rijn: Kluwer Law International.
Gerven, W. (2008). Politics, Ethics & the Law, Legal Practice & Scholarship. *LSE law, society and economy working papers, 19-2008*. Department of Law, London School of Economics and Political Science, London, UK.
Giblin, R. (2011). *Code Wars: 10 Years of P2P Software Litigation*. Edward Elgar Publishing.
Giblin, R. (2012). P2P Physical World Assumptions and Software World Realities (and Why There Are More P2P Software Providers than Ever Before). *Columbia Journal of Law & the Arts, 35*(1), 57–118.
Giblin, R. (2014a). Beyond Graduated Response. In S. Frankel & D. Gervais (eds), *The Evolution and Equilibrium of Copyright in the Digital Age* (pp. 81–112). Cambridge: Cambridge University Press.
Giblin, R. (2014b). Evaluating Graduated Response. *Columbia Journal of Law & the Arts, 37*(2), 147–210.
Ginsburg, J. (1994). A Tale of Two Copyrights: Literary Property in Revolutionary France and America. In B. Sherman & A. Strowel (eds), *Of Authors and Origins: Essays on Copyright Law* (pp. 131–158). Oxford: Clarendon Press.
Ginsburg, J. (2001). Toward Supranational Copyright Law? The WTO Panel Decision and the 'Three-Step Test' for Copyright Exceptions. *Revue Internationale Du Droit d'Auteur, 187*(1), 3–65.

Ginsburg, J. (2013). 'With Untired Spirits and Formal Constancy': Berne Compatibility of Formal Declaratory Measures to Enhance Copyright Title-Searching. *Berkeley Technology Law Journal*, *28*(3), 1583–1622.

Ginsburg, J. (2014a). Comments of Professor Jane C. Ginsburg – Study on the Right of Making Available Docket No. 2014–2. New York. Date: 7 April 2014. Available at https://copyright.gov/docs/making_available/comments/docket2014_2/Jane_Ginsburg.pdf.

Ginsburg, J. (2014b). Fair Use for Free or Permitted-But-Paid? *Berkeley Technology Law Journal*, *28*, 1383–1446.

Ginsburg, J. (2014c). Hyperlinking and 'Making Available.' *European Intellectual Property Review*, *36*(3), 147–148.

Goldstein, P. (2001). *International Copyright. Principles, Law, and Practice*. New York: OUP.

Goldstein, P., & Hugenholtz, P. B. (2013). *International Copyright. Principles, Law, and Practice* (Third Edit). New York: OUP.

Gordon, W. J. (1992). Property Right in Self-Expression: Equality and Individualism in the Natural Law of Intellectual Property, A. *Yale Law Journal*, *102*(7), 1533-1609.

Gordon, W. J., & Bone, R. G. (1999). 1610: Copyright. In B. Bouckaert & G. De Geest (eds), *Encyclopedia of Law & Economics* (pp. 189–215). Edward Elgar; University of Ghent.

Grassmuck, V. (2008). State of the Culture Flat-Rate. Available at http://waste.informatik.hu-berlin.de/grassmuck/Texts/08-03_state-of-flatrate.html.

Grassmuck, V. (2009). The World is Going Flat (-Rate): A Study Showing Copyright Exception for Legalising File-Sharing Feasible, as a Cease-Fire in the "War on Copying" Emerges. *Intellectual Property Watch*, 1–30. Date: 11 May 2009,

Grassmuck, V. (2010a). A Copyright Exception for Monetizing File-Sharing: A Proposal for Balancing User Freedom and Author Remuneration in the Brazilian Copyright Law Reform. In *Rethink Music: A Briefing Book* (pp. 41–56). Cambridge, MA: The Berkman Center for Internet & Society At Harvard University.

Grassmuck, V. (2010b)., Academic Studies on the Effect of File-Sharing on the Recorded Music Industry: A Literature Review. *Report for Acesso a bens educacionais e culturais no Brasil; Projeto de Pesquisa de Grupo de Pesquisa em Política Pública para o Acesso à Informação Escola de Artes, Ciências e Humanidades Universidade de São Paulo*. Available at https://ssrn.com/abstract=1749579.

Grassmuck, V. (2012). The Sharing Turn: Why We Are Generally Nice and Have a Good Chance to Cooperate Our Way Out of the Mess We Have Gotten Ourselves Into. In W. Sützl, F. Stalder, R. Maier & T. Hug (eds), *Cultures and Ethics of Sharing / Kulturen und Ethiken des Teilens* (pp. 17–34). Innsbruck University Press.

Grassmuck, V. (2013). Sharing Licence Library (last updated 13.04.2013). Available at http://www.vgrass.de/?p=1048.

Grassmuck, V., & Stalder, F. (2003). *Models for Alternative Compensation for Entertainment Content: A Critical Review* (written for the workshop on Alternative Compensation Schemes, Berkman Center for Internet & Society, 5.12.2003).

Gratz, J. (2004). Reform in The 'Brave Kingdom': Alternative Compensation Systems For Peer-To-Peer File Sharing. *Minnesota Journal of Law, Science & Technology*, *6*(1), 399–430.

Grece, C., Lange, A., Schneeberger, A., & Valais, S. (2015). *The Development of the European Market for On-Demand Audiovisual Services: Digital Agenda for Europe*. Report prepared by the European Audiovisual Observatory for DG Connect. European Audiovisual Observatory-.Griffiths, J. (2009). The 'Three-Step Test in European Copyright Law – Problems and Solutions. *Intellectual Property Quarterly*, 4, 428–457.

Griffiths, J. (2013). Constitutionalising or Harmonising? The Court of Justice, the Right to Property and European Copyright Law. *European Law Review*, *38*(1), 65–78.

Griffiths, J., & McDonagh, L. (2013). Fundamental Rights and European IP Law: The Case of Art 17(2) of the EU Charter. In C. Geiger (ed.), *Contructing European Intellectual Property. Achievements and New Perspectives* (pp. 75–117). Cheltenham: Edward Elgar.

Grosheide, F. W. (1994). Paradigms in Copyrigth Law. In B. Sherman & A. Strowel (eds), *Of Authors and Origins: Essays on Copyright Law* (pp. 204–223). Oxford: Clarendon Press.

Grosheide, F. W., Roerdink, H., & Thomas, K. (2013, December 30). Intellectual Property Protection for Video Games – A View from the European Union. *Journal of International Commercial Law and Technology*, *9*(1), 1–13.

Grosse Ruse-Khan, H. (2008). Proportionality and Balancing within the Objectives of Intellectual Property Protection, In P. Torremanns (Ed.), *Intellectual Property and Human Rights. Enhanced Edition of Copyright and Human Rights* (pp. 161-194). Austin: Wolters Kluwer Law & Business.

Guibault, L. (2002). *Copyright Limitations and Contracts, An Analysis of the Contractual Overridability of Limitations on Copyright*. London; The Hague; Boston: Kluwer Law International.

Guibault, L. (2009). Relationship Between Copyright and Contract Law. In Estelle Derclaye (ed.), *Research Handbook on the Future of EU Copyright* (pp. 517–542). Cheltenham: Edward Elgar.

Guibault, L. (2010). Why Cherry-Picking Never Leads to Harmonisation: The Case of the Limitations on Copyright under Directive 2001/29/EC. *Journal of Intellectual Property, Information Technology and Electronic Commerce Law*, *1*(2).

Guibault, L. (2014). Collective Rights Management Directive. In I. Stamatoudi & P. Torremans (eds), *EU Copyright Law. A Commentary* (pp. 696–798). Cheltenham: Edward Elgar Publishing.

Guibault, L. (2015). Cultural Heritage Online? Settle It in the Country of Origin of the Work. *Journal of Intellectual Property, Information Technology and Electronic Commerce Law* (6), 173–191.

Guibault, L. (2016). Individual Licensing Models and Consumer Protection. In R. M. Hilty & K.-C. Liu (eds), *Exploring Sensible Ways for Paying Copyright Owners?* Berlin; Heidelberg: Springer.

Guibault, L., & Gompel, S. Van. (2016). Collective Management in the European Union. In D. Gervais (ed.), *Collective Management of Copyright and Related Rights* (Third, pp. 139–174). Alphen aan den Rijn: Kluwer Law International.

Guibault, L., & Quintais, J. P. (2014). Copyright, Technology and the Exploitation of Audiovisual Works in the EU. *IRIS-Plus*, *4*, 7–22.

Guibault, L., & van Gompel, S. (2010). Collective Management in the European Union. In D. Gervais (ed.), *Collective Management of Copyright and Related Rights* (2nd ed., pp. 135–168). Alphen aan den Rijn: Kluwer Law International.

Guibault, L., Westkamp, G., Rieber-Mohn, T., Hugenholtz, P. B., Eechoud, M. van, Helberger, N., … Bohn, P. (2007a). *Study on the Implementation and Effect in Member States' Laws of Directive 2001/29/EC on the Harmonisation of Certain Aspects of Copyright and Related Rights in the Information Society (Executive Summary of final report)*. Amsterdam.

Guibault, L., Westkamp, G., Rieber-Mohn, T., Hugenholtz, P. B., Eechoud, M. van, Helberger, N., … Bohn, P. (2007b). *Study on the Implementation and Effect in Member States' Laws of Directive 2001/29/EC on the Harmonisation of Certain Aspects of Copyright and Related Rights in the Information Society (Final Report)*. Amsterdam.

HADOPI DREV – Département Recherche Etudes et Veille. (2013). *Accès aux œuvres sur Internet*, 1–14 Available at https://hadopi.fr/actualites/actualites/acces-aux-oeuvres-sur-internet-l-hadopi-engage-l-analyse-d-un-systeme-de-remun.

Handke, C. (2011). *Economic Effects of Copyright: The Empirical Evidence So Far*. Commissioned paper prepared for: The Committee on the Impact of Copyright Policy on Innovation in the Digital Era. Rotterdam.

Handke, C. (2012). A Taxonomy of Empirical Research on Copyright – How Do We Inform Policy? *Review of Economic Research on Copyright Issues*, *9*(1), 47–92.

Handke, C., Bodó, B., & Vallbé, J.-J. (2015). Going Means Trouble and Staying Makes It Double: The Value of Licensing Recorded Music Online. *Journal of Cultural Economics*. http://doi.org/10.1007/s10824-015-9251-8.

Handke, C., Quintais, J. P., & Bodó, B. (2013). *The Economics of Copyright Compensation Systems for Digital Use*. Paper presented at the SERCI Annual Congress 2013 (Paris), 8 and 9 July 2013.

Handler, P. (2013). Legal History. In D. Watkins & M. Burton (eds), *Research Methods in Law* (pp. 85–99). Routledge.

Harris, D. P. (2012). The New Prohibition: A Look at the Copyright Wars Through the Lens of Alcohol Prohibition. *Tennessee Law Review*, *80*, 101–166.

Hayward, J. O. (2008). Grokster Unplugged: It's Time to Legalize P2P File Sharing. *Intellectual Property Law Bulletin*, *12*(1), 1–18.

He, H. (2009). Seeking a Balanced Interpretation of the Three-Step Test – An Adjusted Structure in View of Divergent Approaches. *IIC*, 274–308.

Headdon, T. (2014). An Epilogue to Svensson: The Same Old New Public and the Worms That Didn ' t Turn. *Journal of Intellectual Property Law & Practice & Practice*, *9*(8), 662–668.

Heijden, J. van der. (2014). Selecting Cases and Inferential Types in Comparative Public Policy Research. In I. Engeli & C. R. Allison (eds), *Comparative Policy Studies: Conceptual and Methodological Challenges* (pp. 35–56). Hampshire: Palgrave Macmillan Ltd.

Helberger, N., & Hugenholtz, P. B. (2007). No Place Like Home for Making a Copy: Private Copying in European Copyright Law and Consumer Law. *Berkeley Technology Law Journal*, *22*, 1061–1098.

Hellings, B., & Piryns, F. (2010). Proposition de loi visant à adapter la perception du droit d'auteur à l'évolution technologique tout en préservant le droit à la vie privée des usagers d'Internet.

Hilty, R., & Nérisson, S. (2012). Overview of National Reports about 'Balancing Copyright.' In *Balancing Copyright – A Survey of National Approaches* (pp. 1–78). Springer.

Hilty, R., & Nérisson, S. (2013). Collective Copyright Management and Digitization: The European Experience. In R. Towse & C. Handke (eds), *Handbook of the Digital Creative Economy*. Edward Elgar.

Hins, W. (2014). The Freedom to Conduct a Business and the Right to Receive Information for Free: Sky Osterreich. *Common Market Law Review*, *51*(2), 665–677.

Hoeren, T. (2006). Access Right as a Postmorden Symbol of Copyright Deconstruction? In *Direito da Sociedade da Informação. Vol. VI* (pp. 9–27). Coimbra: Coimbra Editora.

Hugenholtz, P. B. (1997). Fierce Creatures. Copyright Exemptions: Towards Extinction? In *Rights, Limitations and Exceptions: Striking a Proper Balance IFLA/IMPRIMATUR Conference* (p. 14). Amsterdam: IViR.

Hugenholtz, P. B. (2000). Why the Copyright Directive is Unimportant, and Possibly Invalid. *European Intellectual Property Review*, *11*, 501–502.

Hugenholtz, P. B. (2006). Satellite and Cable Dir. In T. Dreier & P. B. Hugenholtz (eds), *Concise European Copyright Law*. Alphen aan den Rijn: Kluwer Law International.

Hugenholtz, P. B. (2009a). Copyright without Frontiers: The Problem of Territoriality in European Copyright Law. In E. Derclaye (ed.), *Research*

Handbook on the Future of Copyright (pp. 12–26). Edward Elgar Publishing.

Hugenholtz, P. B. (2009b). SatCab Revisited: The Past, Present and Future of the Satellite and Cable Directive. *IrisPlus* (8), 7–19.

Hugenholtz, P.B. (2010). Codes of Conduct and Copyright Enforcement in Cyberspace. In I. Stamatoudi (ed.), *Copyright Enforcement and the Internet* (pp. 303–320). Alphen aan den Rijn: Kluwer Law International.

Hugenholtz, P. B. (2012a). The Story of the Tape Recorder and the History of Copyright Levies. In B. Sherman & L. Wiseman (eds), *Copyright and the Challenge of the New* (pp. 179–196). Alphen aan den Rijn: Kluwer Law International.

Hugenholtz, P.B. (2012b). The Dutch Case for flexibility. In I. Hargreaves & P. Hofheinz (eds), *Intellectual Property and Innovation: a framework for 21st Century Growth and Jobs*. Lisbon Council.

Hugenholtz, P. B. (2013a). Copyright in Europe: Twenty Years Ago, Today and What the Future Holds. *Fordham Intellectual Property, Media & Entertainment Law Journal, 23*(2), 503–524.

Hugenholtz, P. B. (2013b). Fair Use in Europe. *Communications of the ACM, 56*(5), 26–28. Hugenholtz, P. B., Eechoud, M. Van, Gompel, S. Van, Guibault, L., Helberger, N., Rossini, M., … Bohn, P. (2006). *The Recasting of Copyright & Related Rights for the Knowledge Economy (Executive Summary of final report)*. Amsterdam: Institute for Information Law.

Hugenholtz, P. B., Gompel, S. van, Guibault, L., & Obradović, R. (2014). *Extended Collective Licensing: panacee voor massadigitalisering? Onderzoek in opdracht van het Ministerie van OCW*. Amsterdam: Institute for Information Law.

Hugenholtz, P. B., Guibault, L., & van Geffen, S. (2003). *The Future of Levies in a Digital Environment*. Amsterdam: Institute for Information Law.

Hugenholtz, P. B., & Okediji, R. L. (2008). *Conceiving an International Instrument on Limitations and Exceptions to Copyright: Final Report*. Study commissioned by the Open Society Institute (OSI). Institute for Information Law (University of Amsterdam) and University of Minnesota Law School.

Hugenholtz, P. B., & Quintais, J. P. (2017). *Towards a Universal Remuneration Right*. Amsterdam. Paper developed in the context of the project 'Reconstructing Rights: Rethinking copyright's economic rights in a time of highly dynamic technological and economic change'. Forthcoming Kluwer Information Law Series 2017.

Hugenholtz, P. B., & Senftleben, M. (2011). *Fair Use in Europe. In Search of Flexibilities*. Amsterdam: Institute for Information Law (University of Amsterdam) and VU Centre for Law and Governance (VU University Amsterdam).

Hugenholtz, P.B. & Velze, S. C. van. (2016). Communication to a New Public? Three Reasons Why EU Copyright Law Can Do Without a 'New Public.' *IIC – International Review of Intellectual Property and Competition Law*, *47*, 797–816.

Hughes, J. (1988). The Philosophy of Intellectual Property. *Georgetown Law Journal*, *77*, 287–366.

Husovec, M. (2013). Injunctions Against Innocent Third Parties: The Case of Website Blocking. *Journal of Intellectual Property, Information Technology and Electronic Commerce Law*, *4*(2), 116–129.

Husovec, M., & Gera, M. (2016). Slovakia Adopts a New Copyright Act: It's a Mixed Bag – Part II – Kluwer Copyright Blog. Retrieved 15 March 2016, from http://kluwercopyrightblog.com/2016/03/10/slovakia-adopts-a-new-copyright-act-its-a-mixed-bag-part-ii/.

Husovec, M., & Peguera, M. (2015). Much Ado about Little – Privately Litigated Internet Disconnection Injunctions. *IIC*, *46*(1), 10–37.

Huygen, A., Rutten, P., Huveneers, S., Limonard, S., Poort, J., Leenheer, J., … Helberger, N. (2009). *Ups and downs. Economic and Cultural Effects of File Sharing on Music, Film and Games*, TNO Report. Delft.

Ibbetson, D. (2005). Historical Research in Law. In M. Tushnet & P. Cane (eds), *Oxford Handbook of Legal Studies* (pp. 863–879). Oxford: OUP.

IFPI. (2013). *IFPI Digital Music Report 2013. Engine of a Digital World.*

IFPI. (2015). *IFPI Digital Music Report 2015. Charting the Path to Sustainable Growth.*

Iglezakis, I. (2012). The Legal Struggle in the EU Against Online Piracy. In T.-E. Synodinou (ed.), *Codification of European Copyright Law. Challenges and Pespectives* (pp. 283–304). Alphen aan den Rijn: Kluwer Law International.

Institute for Information Law. (2012). 'Information Law: Expanding Horizons' – IViR Research Program 2012–2016. Amsterdam: Institute for Information Law.

International Bureau of WIPO. (2000). International Protection of Copyright and Related Rights, WIPO/CR/GE/00/2. World Intellectual Property Organization.

International Confederation of Music Publishers. (2015). The Value Gap. Retrieved 3 November 2015, from http://www.icmp-ciem.org/node/574.

Iuliano, J. (2011). Is Legal File Sharing Legal? An Analysis of the Berne Three Step Test. *Virginia Journal of Law & Technology*, *16*(4), 464–501.

Janssens, M.-C. (2009). The Issue of Exceptions: Reshaping the Keys to the Gates in the Terrtory of Literary, Musical and Artistic Creation. In E. Derclaye (ed.), *Research Handbook on the Future of EU Copyright* (pp. 317–348). Cheltenham: Edward Elgar.

Jutte, B. J. (2015). Coexisting Digital Exploitation for Creative Content and the Private Use Exception. *International Journal of Law and Information Technology*, *24*(1), 1–21.

Kamina, P. (2012). Author's Right as Property: Old and New Theories. *Journal of the Copyright Society of the U.S.A.*, *48*, 383–448.
Kamina, P. (2015). Agreement on Trade-Related Aspects of Intellectual Property (Arts 9–14). In T. Cottier & P. Véron (eds), *Concise International and European IP Law* (pp. 37–53). Alphen aan den Rijn: Kluwer Law International.
Kantar Media. (2012). *OCI Tracker Benchmark Study Q3 2012. Technical Report.*
Kantar Media. (2015). *Online Copyright Infringement Tracker. Wave 5 (Covering Period Mar 15 – May 15). Overview and Key Findings.* Newport.
Karaganis, J., & Renkema, L. (2013). *Copy Culture in the US and Germany.* The American Assembly.
Karapapa, S. (2012). *Private Copying*. Routlege.
Karp, H. (2014). Apple iTunes Sees Big Drop in Music Sales. *The Wall Street Journal*. Date: 24 October 2014.
Katzenbach, C., Herweg, S., & Roessel, L. van. (2016). Copies, Clones, and Genre Building: Discourses on Imitation and Innovation in Digital Games. *International Journal of Communication, 10*(2016), 838–859.
Kennedy, D. (1997). *A Critique of Adjudication: fin de siécle*. Harvard University Press.
Kennedy, M. (2014). The 'Three-Step Test' and the Burden of Proof in Disputes Under the TRIPS Agreement. *IIC*, *45*(2), 161–177.
Klafkowska-Wasniowska, K. (2013). Public Communication Right: Towards the Full Harmonisation? *European Intellectual Property Review*, *35*(12), 751–758.
Koelman, K. J. (2006). Fixing the Three-Step Test. *European Intellectual Property Review*, *8*, 407–412.
Koolen, C. (2016). The Use of Hyperlinks in an Online Environment: Putting Links in Chains? *Journal of Intellectual Property Law & Practice*, *11*(8), 585–598.
Koskinen-Olsson, T. (2010). Collective Management in the Nordic Countries. In D. Gervais (ed.), *Collective Management of Copyright and Related Rights* (2nd ed., pp. 283–306). Alphen aan den Rijn: Kluwer Law International.
Koskinen-Olsson, T., & Sigurdardottir, V. (2016). Collective Management in the Nordic Countries. In D. Gervais (ed.), *Collective Management of Copyright and Related Rights* (Third, pp. 243–262). Alphen aan den Rijn: Kluwer Law International.
Kreutzer et al. (2016), The Berlin Gedankenexperiment on the restructuring of Copyright Law and Author's Rights, *Journal of Intellectual Property, Information Technology and Electronic Commerce Law*, *7*(2), 76–87.
Ku, R. S. (2002). The Creative Destruction of Copyright: Napster and the New Economics of Digital Technology. *The University of Chicago Law Review*, *69*(1), 263–324.

Kur, A. (2008). Of Oceans, Islands, and Inland Water – How Much Room for Exceptions and Limitations Under the Three-Step Test? *SSRN Electronic Journal*. http://doi.org/10.2139/ssrn.1317707.

Kur, A., & Schovsbo, J. (2011). Expropriation or Fair Game for All? The Gradual Dismantling of the IP Exclusivity Paradigm. In A. Kur & M. Levin (eds), *Intellectual Property in a Fair World Trade System. Proposals for Reform of TRIPS* (pp. 408-451). Edward Elgar Publishing.

L'ALLIANCE public.artistes. (2005). PRESS KIT. Downloading and sharing files on the Internet. An alliance against legal proceedings. An alliance for a global licence.

L'ALLIANCE public.artistes. (2006a). FAQ. Available at http://www.lalliance.org/pages/4_1.html.

L'ALLIANCE public.artistes. (2006b). Pourquoi une licence globale? Available at http://www.lalliance.org/pages/3_1.html.

L'ALLIANCE public.artistes. (2006c). Qu'est-ce que la licence globale? Available at http://www.lalliance.org/pages/2_1.html.

La Quadrature du Net, & Aigrain, P. (2013). Elements for the Reform of Copyright and Related Cultural Policies.

Lamping, M. (2014). Declaration on Patent Protection. *IIC*, *45*(6), 679–698.

Landes, W. M., & Posner, R. A. (1989). An Economic Analysis of Copyright Law. *The Journal of Legal Studies*, *18*(2), 325–363.

Lee, Y. H. (2015). *Copyright and Freedom of Expression: A Literature Review* (CREATe Working Paper Series No. 4). Glasgow.

Leeuw, F.L. (2015). Emprirical Legal Research: The Gap between Facts and Values and Legal Academic Training. *Utrecht Law Review*, *11*(2), 19–33.

Leistner, M. (2014). Europe's Copyright Law Decade: Recent Case Law of the European Court of Justice and Policy Perspectives. *Common Market Law Review*, *51*(2014), 559–600.

Leistner, M. (2015). Copyright at the Interface Between EU Law and National Law: Definition of 'Work' and 'Right of Communication to the Public.' *Journal of Intellectual Property Law & Practice*, *10*(8), 626–637. http://doi.org/10.1093/jiplp/jpv086.

Leistner, M. (2016). Reformbedarf im materiellen Urheberrecht: Online-Plattformen und Aggregatoren, *ZUM*, 580–594.

Lemley, M. A. (2012). Contracting Around Liability Rules. *California Law Review*, *100*, 463–486.

Lescure, P. (2013). *Mission 'Acte II de l'exception culturelle': contribution aux politiques culturelles à l'ère numérique*. Direction de l'information légale et administrative.

Lessig, L. (2001). *The Future of Ideas: The Fate of the Commons in a Connected World*. Random House.

Lessig, L. (2004). *Free Culture: The Nature and Future of Creativity*. Penguin.

Lessig, L. (2008). *Remix: Making Art and Commerce Thrive in the Hybrid Economy*. Penguin.

Liebowitz, S. J. (2003). *Alternative Copyright Systems: The Problems with a Compulsory License*. Paper Based upon a talked delivered at a conference sponsored by the Progress and Freedom Foundation on June 10, 2003. Retrived from http://www.utdallas.edu/~liebowit/intprop/complpff.pdf

Liebowitz, S. J. (2005). MP3s and Copyright Collectives: A Cure Worse than the Disease? In *Developments in the Economics of Copyright: Research and Analysis* (pp. 37–59). Cheltenham: Edward Elgar Publishing.

Liebowitz, S. J., & Watt, R. (2006). How to Best Ensure Remuneration for Creators in the Market For Music? Copyright and Its Alternatives. *Journal of Economics Surveys*, *20*(4), 513–545.

Lincoff, B. (2002). *A Full, Fair And Feasible Solution to The Dilemma of Online Music Licensing*. Available at http://www.bennettlincoff.com/music.pdf

Lincoff, B. (2008). Common Sense, Accommodation and Sound Policy for the Digital Music Marketplace. *Journal of International Media & Entertainement Law*, *2*(1), 1–64.

Linklater, E. (2014). UsedSoft and the Big Bang Theory: Is the e-Exhaustion Meteor about to Strike? *Journal of Intellectual Property, Information Technology and Electronic Commerce Law*, *5*(1), 12–22.

Litman, J. (2004). Sharing and Stealing. *Hastings Communications & Entertainment Law Journal*, *27*(1), 1–50.

Liu, J. P. (2001). Owning Digital Copies: Copyright Law and the Incidents of Copy Ownership. *William and Mary Law Review*, *42*(4), 1245–1366.

Locke, J. (1988). *Two Treatises of Government*. (P. Laslett, ed.). Cambridge: CUP.

Lohmann, F. Von. (2004). Voluntary Collective Licensing for Music File Sharing. *Communications of the ACM*, *47*(10), 21–24.

Lohmann, F. Von. (2008). A Better Way Forward: Voluntary Collective Licensing of Music File Sharing (Version 2.1.). *"Let the Music Play" Whitepaper*. Electronic Frontier Foundation.

Lohmann, F. Von. (2014). Copyright as Innovation Policy. Talk as the Information Influx Conference (2–4 July 2014, Amsterdam) Retrieved 9 October 2014, from https://www.youtube.com/watch?v=p87w0vyMTWo. Amsterdam: Institute for Information Law.

Lord Windlesham. (1980). *Broadcasting in a Free Society*. Blackwell.

Loren, L. P. (2014). The Dual Narratives in the Landscape of Music Copyrights. *Houstan Law Review*, *52*(2), 537–582.

Love, J. (2003). Artists Want to Be Paid: The Blur/Banff Proposal. Power at Play in Digital Art and Culture (11-13 April 2002) User Experience. Available at http://keionline.org/blur-banff.

Lucas, A. (2010). For a Reasonable Interpretation of the Three-Step Test. *European Intellectual Property Review*, *32*(6), 277–282.

Lucchi, N. (2011). Access to Network Services and Protection of Constitutional Rights: Recognizing the Essential Role of Internet Access for the Freedom of Expression. *Cardozo Journal of International and Comparative Law*, *19*, 645–678.

Lunney, G. S. (2001). The Death of Copyright: Digital Technology, Private Copying, and the Digital Millennium Copyright Act. *Virginia Law Review*, *87*(5), 813–920.

Lunney, G. S. (2014). Copyright on the Internet: Consumer Copying and Collectives. In Susy Frankel & D. Gervais (eds), *The Evolution and Equilibrium of Copyright in the Digital Age* (pp. 285–311). Cambridge: CUP.

Mac, D. G. (1973). Tape Recording for Home Use: The Right of Delayed Enjoyment. *Revue Internationale Du Droit d'Auteur*, *78*(10), 66–119.

Machado, J., & Ortellado, P. (2013). Legalizing File Sharing on the Internet: Solving the Conflict between Copyright Owners and Consumers of Culture [A Brazilian Perspective]. Translation by Pedro Paranaguá. Available at https://pedroparanagua.files.wordpress.com/2010/09/brazil_legalizing_p2p.pdf.

Machlup, F., & Penrose, E. (1950). The Patent Controversy in the Nineteenth Century. *The Journal of Economic History*, *X*(1), 1–29.

MacLeod, C. (1988). *Inventing the Industrial Revolution: The English Patent System, 1660–1800*. Cambridge: CUP.

Masouyé, C. (1967). Stockholm: A landmark. *Revue Internationale Du Droit d'Auteur*, *54*(10).

Masouyé, C. (1981). *Guide to the Rome Convention and the Phonograms Convention. WIPO Publication 617(E)*. Geneva: WIPO.

Masouyé, P. (2009). Copyright Is Dead... Long Life to the Right...of Users ... *Revue Internationale Du Droit d'Auteur*, *222*, 189.

Mazziotti, G. (2008). *EU Digital Copyright Law and the End-User*. Springer.

Mazziotti, G. (2013). *Copyright in the EU Digital Single Market. Report of the CEPS Digital Forum*. Brussels: Centre for European Policy Studies.

McDaniel, K. L. (2007). Accounting for Taste: An Analysis of Tax-and-Reward Alternative Compensation Schemes. *Tulane Journal of Technology & Intellectual Property*, *9*, 235–312.

McLeod, K., & DiCola, P. (2011). *Creative License: The Law and Culture of Digital Sampling*. Duke University Press.

Meale, D. (2013). A Triple Strike Against Piracy as the Music Industry Secures Three More Blocking Injunctions. *Journal of Intellectual Property Law & Practice*, *8*(8), 591–594.

Mehra, S. K. (2008). The IPod Tax: Why the Digital Copyright System of American Law Professors' Dreams Failed in Japan. *University of Colorado Law Review*, *79*, 421–465.

Menell, P. S. (2011). In Search of Copyright's Lost Ark: Interpreting the Right to Distribute in the Internet Age. *Journal of the Copyright Society of the U.S.A.*, *59*, 1–67.

Menell, P. S. (2015). Adapting Copyright to the Mashup Generation. *University of Pennsylvania Law Review*, *164*, 441–512.
Merges, R. P. (1996). Contracting into Liability Rules: Intellectual Property Rights and Collective Rights Organizations. *California Law Review*, *84*, 1293–1393.
Merges, R. P. (2004a). Compulsory Licensing vs. the Three 'Golden Oldies' Property Rights, Contracts, and Markets. *Policy Analysis* (508), 1–15.
Merges, R. P. (2004b). Compulsory Licensinig vs. the Three 'Golden Oldies' Property Rights, Contracts, and Markets. *Cato Policy Analysis*, *508*, 1–15.
Merges, R. P. (2009). Locke for the Masses: Property Rights and the Products of Collective Creativity. *36, Hofstra Law Review*, 1179–1191.
Merges, R. P. (2011). *Justifying Intellectual Property*. Harvard University Press.
Metzger, A., & Heinemann, T. (2015). The Right of the Author to Grant Licenses for Non-Commercial Use: Creative Commons Licenses and the Directive on Collective Management. *Journal of Intellectual Property, Information Technology and Electronic Commerce Law*. *6*(1), 11–22.
Mezei, P. (2016). Enter the Matrix: The Effects of CJEU Case Law on Linking and Streaming Technologies. *Journal of Intellectual Property Law & Practice*, *11*(10), 778–794.
Mihály Ficsor. (2010). Collective Management of Copyright and Related Rights form the Viewpoint of International Norms and the Acquis Communautaire. In D. Gervais (ed.), *Collective Management of Copyright and Related Rights* (2nd ed., pp. 29–74). Alphen aan den Rijn: Kluwer Law International.
Mihály Ficsor. (2012). Short Paper on the Three-Step Test for the Application of Exceptions and Limitations in the Field of Copyright. Available at http://www.copyrightseesaw.net/archive/?sw_10_item=28.
Modot, A., Fontanel, H., Garnett, N., Lambert, E., Chaubeau, A., Chung, J., & Jalladeau, P. (2011). *The 'Content Flat-Rate*: *A Solution to Illegal File-Sharing?* Brussels.
Moir, A., Montagnon, R., & Newton, H. (2014). Communication to the Public: The CJEU Finds Linking to Material Already 'Freely Available' Cannot Be Restricted by Copyright Owners: NilsSvenssonand Others v Retriever Sverige AB (C-466/12). *European Intellectual Property Review*, *36*(6), 399–400.
Momirov, A., & Naude Fourie, A. (2009). Vertical Comparative Law Methods: Tools for Conceptualising the International Rule of Law. *Erasmus Law Review*, *2*(3), 291–309.
Morael, M. J., & Piryns, F. (2010). Proposition de loi visant à adapter la perception du droit d'auteur à l'évolution technologique tout en préservant le droit à la vie privée des usagers d'Internet.

Morgan, O. (2010). The Protection of 'Related Rights' in TRIPS and the WIPO Performances and Phonograms Treaty. In C. M. Correa (ed.), *Research Handbook on the Interpretation and Enforcement of Intellectual Property under WTO Rules: Intellectual Property in the WTO* (pp. 379–407). Edward Elgar.

Motion Picture Association of America. (2015). *MPPA – 2014 Theatrical Statistics Summary*. Available at http://www.mpaa.org/wp-content/uploads/2015/03/MPAA-Theatrical-Market-Statistics-2014.pdf

Nadel, M. S. (2004). How Current Copyright Law Discourages Creative Output: The Overlooked Impact of Marketing. *Berkeley Technology Law Journal*, *19*(2), 785–856.

Nérisson, S. (2014). The Rental and Lending Rights Directive. In I. Stamatoudi & P. Torremans (eds), *EU Copyright Law. A Commentary* (pp. 149–202). Cheltenham: Edward Elgar Publishing.

Nérisson, S. (2015a). CJEU in OSA: A Victory for Right Holders Against Free Use and of CMOs Against the European Commission? *Kluwer Copyright Blog*. Retrieved 29 July 2015, from http://kluwercopyrightblog.com/2014/09/07/cjeu-in-osa-a-victory-for-right-holders-against-free-use-and-of-cmos-against-the-european-commission/.

Nérisson, S. (2015b). Last Year at Marienbad: The ECJ OSA Decision: Milestones on the Way to a European Law of Copyright and of its Management. *European Intellectual Property Review*, *37*(6), 399–405.

Netanel, N. W. (2003). Impose a Noncommercial Use Levy to Allow Free Peer-to-Peer File Sharing. *Harvard Journal of Law & Technology*, *17*(1), 1–84.

Noll, R. van der, Gompel, S. van, Guibault, L., Weda, J., Poort, J., Akker, I., & Breemen, K. (2012). *Flexible Copyright: The Law and Economics of Introducing an Open Norm in the Netherlands*. Study commissioned by the Dutch Ministry of Economic Affairs, Agriculture & Innovation. Amsterdam: Institute for Information Law and SEO Economic Research.

Nordemann, J. B. (2016). Linking to Illegal Content Unlawful under Copyright Law, According to the German BGH. *Kluwer Copyright Blog*. Retrieved 12 February 2016, from http://kluwercopyrightblog.com/2016/02/10/linking-to-illegal-content-unlawful-under-copyright-law-according-to-the-german-bgh/.

Nordemann, W. (1980). Right to Control or Merely to Payment? Towards a Logical Copyright System. *IIC 11*(1), 49–54.

Nordemann, W., Vinck, K., Hertin, P., & Meyer, G. (1990). *International Copyright and Neighboring Rights Law: Commentary with Special Emphasis on the European Community*.

OECD, Vickery, G., & Wunsch-Vincent, S. (2007). *Participative Web and User-Created Content. Web 2.0, Wikis and Social Networking*. Paris: OECD Publications.

Ohly, A. (2009). Economic Rights. In Estelle Derclaye (ed.), *Research Handbook on the Future of EU Copyright* (pp. 212–241). Cheltenham: Edward Elgar.

Okpaluba, J. (2012). The Phonogram: A Tale of Vested Interests and Seized Opportunities. In B. Sherman & L. Wiseman (eds), *Copyright and the Challenge of the New* (pp. 77–114). Alphen aan den Rijn: Kluwer Law International.

Oksanen, V., & Valimaki, M. (2005). Copyright Levies as an Alternative Compensation. *Review of Economic Research on Copyright Issues*, *2*(2), 25–39.

Oliar, D. (2012). The Copyright-Innovation Tradeoff: Property Rules, Liability Rules, and Intentional Infliction of Harm. *Stanford Law Review*, *64*, 951–1020.

Palfrey, J. G. (2010). Four Phases of Internet Regulation. *Berkman Center Research Publication No. 2010–9*.

Papies, D., Eggers, F., & Wlomert, N. (2010). Music for Free? How Free Ad-Funded Downloads Affect Consumer Choice. *Journal of the Academy of Marketing Science*, *39*(5), 777–794.

Partido Comunista Português (Grupo Parlamentar). (2012). Projeto de Lei No. 228/XII/1.a: Regime Jurídico da Partilha de Dados Informáticos.

Patry, W. (2011). *How to Fix Copyright*. Oxford: OUP.

Pereira, A. D. (2008). *Direitos de Autor e Liberdade de Informação*. Coimbra: Almedina.

Pérez, M. F. (2015). Portugal: 'Voluntary' Agreement Against Copyright Infringements. *EDRI.org*. Retrieved 3 September 2015, from https://edri.org/portugal-voluntary-agreement-against-copyright-infringements/.

Perzanowski, A., & Schultz, J. (2014). Legislating Digital Exhaustion. *Berkeley Technology Law Journal*, *29*, 1535–1557.

Peukert, A. (2005). A Bipolar Copyright System for the Digital Network Environment. *Hastings Communications & Entertainment Law Journal*, *28*, 1–80.

Peukert, A. (2015). Copyright and the Two Cultures of Online Communication. In P.L.C. Torremans (ed.), *Intellectual Property Law and Human Rights* (Third, pp. 366–395). Alphen aan den Rijn: Kluwer Law International.

Pihlajarinne, T. (2012). Setting the Limits for the Implied License in Copyright and Linking Discourse: The European Perspective. *IIC*, *43*(6), 700–710.

Polanyi, M. (1944). Patent Reform. *Review of Economic Studies*, *11*, 61–76.

Pool, I. de S. (2009). *Technologies of Freedom*. Harvard University Press.

Poort, J., & J. Leenheer. (2012). *File sharing 2@12: Downloading from Illegal Sources in the Netherlands*. Amsterdam; Tilburg.

Poort, J., Leenheer, J., van der Ham, J., & Dumitru, C. (2014). Baywatch: Two Approaches to Measure the Effects of Blocking Access to the Pirate Bay. *Telecommunications Policy*, *38*(4), 383–392.

Poort, J., & Quintais, J. P. (2013). The Levy Runs Dry: A Legal and Economic Analysis of EU Private Copying Levies. *Journal of Intellectual Property, Information Technology and Electronic Commerce Law*, 4(3), 205–224.

Poort, J., & Weda, J. (2015). Elvis Is Returning to the Building: Understanding a Decline in Unauthorized File Sharing. *Journal of Media Economics*, *28*(2), 63–83.

Quintais, J. P. (2012). *On Peers and Copyright: Why the EU Should Consider Collective Management of P2P*. Nomos.

Quintais, J. P. (2013). Proposal for a Directive on Collective Rights Management and (Some) Multi-Territorial Licensing. *European Intellectual Property Review*, *2*, 65–73.

Quintais, J. P. (2014). Legalizing File-Sharing: An Idea Whose Time Has Come Or Gone? Report from the Information Influx Conference 2014. *SSRN Electronic Journal*. http://doi.org/10.2139/ssrn.2510545. Amsterdam: Institute for Information Law.

Quintais, J. P. (2015a). Everything You Always Wanted to Know about Private Copying But were Afraid to Ask (Case C-463/12 Copydan Båndkopi v Nokia Danmark A/S). *Kluwer Copyright Blog*.

Quintais, J. P. (2015b). Private Copying and Downloading from Unlawful Sources. *IIC*, *46*(1), 66–92.

Radin, M. J. (1982). Property and Personhood. *Standford Law Review*, *34*, 957.

Rahmatian, A. (2011). Intellectual Property and the Concept of Dematerialised Property. In *Modern Studies in Property Law – Volume 6* (pp. 361–383). Oxford: Hart Publishing.

Ramalho, A. (2014). *The Competence of the European Union in Copyright Lawmaking – A Normative Perspective of EU Powers for Copyright Harmonization*. University of Amsterdam (PhD Dissertation).

Ramos, A., López, L., Rodríguez, A., Meng, T., & Abrams, S. (2013). *The Legal Status of Video Games: Comparative Analysis in National Approaches*. Geneva: WIPO.

Reinbothe, J. (1981). Compensation for Private Taping Under Sec. 53(5) of the German Copyright Act. *IIC*, *2*(1), 36–49.Reinbothe, J. (2010). The EU Enforcement Directive 2004/48/EC as a Tool for Copyright Enforcement. In I. A. Stamatoudi (ed.), *Copyright Enforcement and the Internet* (pp. 3–28). Alphen aan den Rijn: Kluwer Law International.

Reinbothe, J., & von Lewinski, S. (1993). *The E.C. Directive on Rental and Lending Rights and on Piracy*. London: Sweet & Maxwell.

Reinbothe, J., & von Lewinski, S. (2002). *The WIPO Treaties 1996*. London: Butterworths.

Rendas, T. (2015). Lex Specialis(sima): Videogames and Technological Protection Measures in EU Copyright Law. *European Intellectual Property Review, 39(1)*, 39–45.

Ricketson, S. (1987). *The Berne Convention for the Protection of Literary and Artistic Works: 1886–1986*. Kluwer.

Ricketson, S. (1999). The Boundaries of Copyright: Its Proper Limitations and Exceptions: International Conventions and Treaties. *Intellectual Property Quarterly*, 56–94.

Ricketson, S. (2003). *WIPO Study on Limitations and Exceptions of Copyright and Related Rights in the Digital Environment*. Geneva: WIPO.

Ricketson, S., & Ginsburg, J. (2006). *International Copyright and Neighbouring Rights: The Berne Convention and Beyond (Vols I and II)* (2nd Edition). Oxford: OUP.

Ricolfi, M. (2007). Individual and Collective Management of Copyright in a Digital Environment. In P. Torremans (ed.), *Copyright Law: A Handbook of Contemporary Research*. Edward Elgar.

Rietjens, B. (2006). Copyright and the Three-Step Test: Are Broadband Levies Too Good to Be True? *International Review of Law, Computers & Technology*, *20*(3), 323–336.

Riis, T., & Jens Schovsbo. (2010). Extended Collective Licenses and the Nordic Experience: It's a Hybrid But Is It a Volvo or a Lemon? *Columbia Journal of Law & the Arts*, *33*(4), 471–553.

Riis, T., & Schovsbo, J. (2012). Extended Collective Licenses in Action. *IIC*, *43*(8), 930–950.

Rocha, A. (2010). Proposal for Introduction of a New Article in Copyright Law to Legalize the Sharing of Digital Files. Letter to To the Minister in Chief of the President's Office Erenice Alves Guerra. Date: 31 August 2010. Originally Available at: http://www.compartilhamentolegal.org/ (On file with the author).

Rodrigues, R., & Druschel, P. (2010). Peer-to-Peer Systems. *Communications of the ACM*, *53*(10), 72–82.

Rognstad, O. A. (2012). Scandinavia (Norway, Denmark and Sweden). In R. Hilty & S. Nerisson (eds), *Balancing Copyright – A Survey of National Approaches*. Springer.

Rosati, E. (2014). Copyright: Private Copying Exception May Only Apply to Reproductions from Licensed Sources. *Journal of Intellectual Property Law & Practice*, *9*(9), 710–711.

Rosati, E. (2015). 2015: The Year of Blocking Injunctions? *Journal of Intellectual Property Law & Practice*, *10*(3), 147–147.

Rosati, E. (2015a). CJEU Says That Copyright Exhaustion Only Applies to the Tangible Support of a Work. *Journal of Intellectual Property Law & Practice*, *10*(5), 329–330.

Rosati, E. (2015b). Just a Matter of Laugh? Why the CJEU Decision in Deckmyn is Broader than Parody. *Common Market Law Review*, *52*(2), 511–529.

Rose, J. (2010). Studying the Past: The Nature and Development of Legal History as a Academic Discipline. *Journal of Legal History* (2001), 294–304.

Rosén, J. (2011). News from the Nordic Countries. *Revue Internationale Du Droit d'Auteur*, *227*(Janvier), 163–207.

Rósen, J. (2014). The Satellite and Cable Directive. In I. Stamatoudi & P. Torremans (eds), *EU Copyright Law. A Commentary*. Cheltenam; Northampton: Edward Elgar.

Rösler, H. (2012). Interpretation of EU Law. In J. Basedow, K. J. Hopt, & R. Zimmermann (Eds.), *The Max Planck Encyclopedia of European Private Law* (pp. 979-982). Oxford: OUP.

Roßnagel, A., Jandt, S., Schnabel, C., & Yliniva-Hoffman, A. (2009). *The Admissibility of a Culture Flat-Rate under National and European Law: Short Report*. Institute of European Media Law (EML) in collaboration with The Project Group for Constitutionally Compatible Technology Design (provet) at the University of Kassel. Saarbrücken/Kassel.

Rouart, N. (1967). The Right of Reproduction. *Revue Internationale Du Droit d'Auteur*, *54*(10), 285–317.

Rubí Puig, A. (2013). Copyright Exhaustion Rationales and Used Software: A Law and Economics Approach to Oracle v. UsedSoft. *Journal of Intellectual Property, Information Technology and Electronic Commerce Law*, *4*(3), 159–178.

Rydning, C. (2010). *Extended Collective Licences – The Compatibility of the Nordic Solution with the International Conventions and EC Law*. Oslo: Norwegian Research Center for Computers and Law.

Samartzi, V. (2012). Account-Sharing: A Legitimate Alternative to Unlawful Circumvention for the Purposes of Achieving Content Portability? *International Journal of Law and Information Technology*, *21*(1), 66–91. Samuelson, P. (2012). Book Review: Is Copyright Reform Possible? *Harvard Law Review*, *18*(2011), 740–779.

Samuelson, P. (2013). The Quest for a Sound Conception of Copyright's Derivative Work Right – Georgetown Law Journal. *Gerogetown Law Journal*, *101*(6), 1505–1564.

Samuelson, P. (2016). Extended Collective Licensing to Enable Mass Digitisation: A Critique of the US Copyright Office Proposal. *European Intellectual Property Review*, *38*(2), 75–82.

Savola, P. (2014). Blocking Injunctions and Website Operators' Liability for Copyright Infringement for User-Generated Links. *European Intellectual Property Review*, *36*(5), 279–288.

Schierholz, A. (2010). Collective Management in Europe-Practice and Legal Framework. In M. Walter & S. von Lewinski (eds), *European Copyright Law: A Commentary*. Oxford: OUP.

Schlag, P. J. (1985). Rules and Standards. *UCLA Law Review*, *33*, 379–430.

Schulman, B. M. (1999). The Song Heard 'Round the World: The Copyright Implications of Mp3s and the Future of Digital Music. *Harvard Journal of Law & Technology*, *12*(3), 559–646.

Seawright, J., & Gerring, J. (2008). Case Selection Techniques in Case Study Research: A Menu of Qualitative and Quantitative Options. *Political Research Quarterly*, *61*(2), 294–308.

Seay, J. E. (2010). Legislative Strategies for Enabling the Success of Online Music Purveyors. *UCLA Entertainement Law Review*, *17*, 163–179.

Senftleben, M. (2004). *Copyright, Limitations and the Three-Step Test. An Analysis of the Three Step Test in International and EC Copyright Law*. Amsterdam: Kluwer Law International.

Senftleben, M. (2006). Towards a Horizontal Standard for Limiting Intellectual Property Rights? – WTO Panel Reports Shed Light on the Three-Step Test in Copyright Law and Related Tests in patent and Trademark Law. *IIC*, *37*(4), 407–438.

Senftleben, M. (2010). The International Three-Step Test. A Model Provision for EC Fair Use Legislation. *Journal of Intellectual Property, Information Technology and Electronic Commerce Law*, *1*(2), 67–82.

Senftleben, M. (2013a). Breathing Space for Cloud- Based Business Models Exploring the Matrix of Copyright Limitations, Safe Harbours and Injunctions. *Journal of Intellectual Property, Information Technology and Electronic Commerce Law*, *4*(2), 17.

Senftleben, M. (2013b). Breathing Space for Cloud-Based Business Models. *Journal of Intellectual Property, Information Technology and Electronic Commerce Law*, *4*(2), 87–103.

Senftleben, M. (2013c). Comparative Approaches to Fair Use: An Important Impulse for Reforms in EU Copyright Law. In G.B. Dinwoodie (ed.), *Methods and Perspectives in Intellectual Property*, Cheltenham, UK/ Northampton, MA, Edward Elgar (2014, Forthcoming). Available at SSRN: https://ssrn.com/abstract=2241284.

Senftleben, M. (2014). How to Overcome the Normal Exploitation Obstacle: Opt-Out Formalities, Embargo Periods and the International Three-Step Test. *Berkeley Technology Law Journal Commentaries*, *1*, 1–19.

Sganga, C. (2015). EU Copyright Law Between Property and Fundamental Rights: A Proposal to Connect the Dots. In R. Caso & F. Giovanella (eds), *Balancing Copyright Law in the Digital Age* (pp. 1–26). Berlin, Heidelberg: Springer.

Shabalala, D. (2010). United States – Section 115(5) of the US Copyright Act: Summary and analysis. In C. M. Correa (ed.), *Research Handbook on the Interpretation and Enforcement of Intellectual Property under WTO Rules. Intellectual Property in the WTO Volume II* (pp. 142–190). Cheltenham: Edward Elgar.

Shaheed, F. (2014). Copyright Policy and the Right to Science and Culture. *Report of the Special Rapporteur in the Field of Cultural Rights*.

Document A/HRC/28/57. Human Rights Council, Twenty-eighth session, Agenda item 3: Promotion and protection of all human rights, civil, political, economic, social and cultural rights, including the right to development. Date: 24 December 2014.

Shaheed, F. (2015). Statement Made by the Special Rapporteur on Cultural Rights at the 28th Session of the Human Rights Council. Document A/HRC/28/57. United Nations Human Rights Office of the High Commissioner. Available at http://www.ohchr.org/EN/Issues/CulturalRights/Pages/AnnualReports.aspx.

Shavell, S., & Ypersele, T. Van. (2001). Rewards Versus Intellectual Property Rights. *The Journal of Law and Economics*, *44*, 525–547.

Sherman, B., & Wiseman, L. (2012). Copyright: When Old Technologies Were New. In B. Sherman & L. Wiseman (eds), *Copyright and the Challenge of the New* (pp. 1–10). Alphen aan den Rijn: Kluwer Law International.

Shiffrin, S. V. (2001). Lockean Arguments for Private Intellectual Property. In S. R. Munzer (ed.), *New Essays in the Legal and Political Theory of Property* (pp. 138–167). Cambridge: CUP.

Sica, V., & D'Antonio, M. (2012). Italy. In R. Hilty & S. Nerisson (eds), *Balancing Copyright – A Survey of National Approaches*. Springer.

Sinacore-Guinn, D. (1993). *Collective Administration of Copyrights and Neighboring Rights: International Practices, Procedures, and Organizations*. Little, Brown.

Sinclair, S. I. M. (1984). *The Vienna Convention on the Law of Treaties*. Manchester University Press.

Sinnreich, A. (2010). *Mashed Up: Music, Technology, and the Rise of Configurable Culture*. University of Massachusetts Press.

Slater, D., Smith, M., Bambauer, D., Gasser, U., & Palfrey, J. G. (2005). Content and Control: Assessing the Impact of Policy Choices on Potential Online Business Models in the Music and Film Industries. *Berkman Publication Series Paper No. 2005-01*.Berkman Center for Internet & Society at Harvard Law School.

Sobel, L. S. (2003). DRM as an Enabler of Business Models: ISPs as Digital Retailers. *Berkeley Technology Law Journal*, *18*, 667–695.

Songwriters Association of Canada. (2011). *The Songwriters Association of Canada's Proposal to Monetize the Non commercial Sharing of Music*. Available at http://www.songwriters.ca/proposaldetailed.aspx.

Sorel, J.-M., & Eveno, V. B. (2011). Commentary to Art.31 of the 1969 Vienna Convention. In O. Corten & P. Klein (eds), *The Vienna Conventions on the Law of Treaties: A Commentary* (pp. 804–837). Oxford: OUP.

Souza, A. R. de, Machado, J., Mendonça, L., Ortellado, P., & Schmidt, P. (2013). *Anteprojecto de lei para legalização do Compartilhamento de Arquivos Digitais 2013*. Available at http://www.forum-global.de/docs/pl_p2p.pdf.

SPEDIDAM. (2006). *La licence globale optionnelle Faire du peer-to-peer un instrument d'équilibre et de diversité*. Paris: SPEDIDAM – Société de Perception et de Distribution des Droits des Artistes- Interprètes de la Musique et de la Danse.

Sprigman, C. J. (2004). Reform(aliz)ing Copyright. *Stanford Law Review*, *57*, 485–568.

Sprigman, C. J. (2013). Berne's Vanishing Ban on Formalities. *Berkeley Technology Law Journal*, *28*, 1565–1582.

Stalla-Bourdillon, S., Rosati, E., Turk, K., Angelopoulos, C., Kuczerawy, A., Peguera, M., & Husovec, M. (2016). A Brief Exegesis of the Proposed Copyright Directive. Available at https://papers.ssrn.com/sol3/papers.cfm?abstract_id=2875296.

Stallman, R. (1993). Copywrong. *WIRED*. Date: 3 January 1983. Available at https://www.wired.com/1993/03/1-3-stallman-copyright/. Sterling, J. A. L. (2008). *The GILA System for Global Internet Licensing*. Available at www.law.qmul.ac.uk/docs/staff/ccls/sterling/121967.pdf

Sterling, J. A. L. (2009). *The Future of Copyright: Approaches. for the New Era. An address to the British Literary and Artistic Copyright Association*. Date: 12 March 2009. Available at www.blaca.org/BLACA Future of copyright 120309.doc?

Strowel, A. (1994). Droit d'auteur and Copyright: Between History and Nature. In B. Sherman & A. Strowel (eds), *Of Authors and Origins: Essays on Copyright Law* (pp. 235–253). Oxford: Clarendon Press.

Swedish Performing Rights Society (STIM). (2009). *Pirates, File-Sharers and Music Users. A Survey of the Conditions for New Music Services on the Internet*. (On file with the author).

The Department of Commerce and Internet Policy Task Force. (2013). *Green Paper on Copyright Policy, Creativity and Innovation in the Digital Economy*. USPTO. Available at https://www.uspto.gov/sites/default/files /news/publications/copyrightgreenpaper.pdf.

Tomasz Targosz. (2016). A New Chapter in the Linking Saga. *Kluwer Copyright Blog*. Date: 9 September 2016. Available at http://kluwercopy rightblog.com/2016/09/09/a-new-chapter-in-the-linking-saga-its-becom ing-a-horror/.

Torremans, P.L.C. (2015). Copyrigth (and Other Intellectual Property Rights) as a Human Right. In P. L. C. Torremans (ed.), *Intellectual Property and Human Rights* (Third, pp. 221–254). Alphen aan den Rijn: Kluwer Law International.

Triaille, J.-P., Dusollier, S., Depreeuw, S., Hubin, J.-B., Coppens, F., & Francquen, A. de. (2013). *Study on the Application of Directive 2001/29/EC on copyright and related rights in the information society*. Study for European Commission (DG MARKT). Available at http://ec .europa.eu/internal_market/copyright/studies/index_en.htm.

Tsoutsanis, A. (2014). Why Copyright and Linking Can Tango. *Journal of Intellectual Property Law & Practice*, *9*(6), 495–509.

U.S. Copyright Office. (2014). Study on the Right of Making Available; Comments and Public Roundtable. *Federal Register*, *79*(37), 10571–10573.

Ulmer, E. (1970). The Revision of the Copyright Conventions in Light of the Washington Recommendation. *IIC*, 235–254.

Ulmer, E. (1971). The Revisions of the Copyright Conventions. *IIC*, 345–371.

Ulmer, E. (1986). One Hundred Years of the Berne Convention. *IIC*, 707–715.

UNCTAD-ICTSD. (2005). *Resource Book on TRIPS and Development*. Cambridge: CUP.

Vallbé, J.-J., Bodó, B., Handke, C., & Quintais, J. P. (2015). *Knocking on Heaven's Door. User Preferences on Digital Cultural Distribution*. Amsterdam: Institute for Information Law. Available at https://papers.ssrn.com/sol3/papers.cfm?abstract_id=2630519.

van de Donk, W. B. H. J., Hancher, L., van Lieshout, P. A. H., Meurs, P. L., Pelkmans, J. L. M., Schoonenboom, I. J., … Winsemius, P. (2005). *Media Policy for the Digital Age*. The Hague; Amsterdam: WRR; Amsterdam University Press.

Van Gestel, R., Micklitz, H.-W., & Maduro, M. P. (2012). Methodology in the New Legal World. *SSRN Electronic Journal*. EUI Working Papers LAW No. 2012/13. Available at https://ssrn.com/abstract=2069872 or http://dx.doi.org/10.2139/ssrn.2069872.

van Gompel, S. (2011). *Formalities in Copyright Law: An Analysis of Their History, Rationales and Possible Future*. Alphen aan den Rijn: Kluwer Law Intermational.

van Gompel, S. (2013). Copyright Formalities in the Internet Age: Filters of Protection or Facilitators of Licensing. *Berkeley Technology Law Journal*, *3*, 1425–1458.

Van Nus, J. (1967). Stockholm: The Preparatory Work. *Revue Internationale Du Droit d'Auteur*, *54*(10).

Velze, S. C. van. (2015). *Communication to a New Public? A Critical Analysis of the CJEU's 'New Public' Criterion in European Copyright Law*. Amsterdam Institute for Information Law, University of Amsterdam (Master's Thesis).

Vermeule, A. (2007). Connecting Positive and Normative Legal Theory. *University of Pennsylvania Journal of Constitutional Law*, *10*, 387–398.

Vitorino, A. (2013). *Recommendations Resulting from the Mediation on Private Copying and Reprography Levies*. Brussels. Available at http://ec.europa.eu/internal_market/copyright/levy_reform/index_en.htm.

von Lewinski, S. (2004). Mandatory Collective Administration of Exclusive Rights – A Case Study on Its Compatibility with International and EC Copyright Law. *UNESCO E-Copyright Bulletin, January–March*, 1–14.

von Lewinski, S. (2005). Certain Legal Problems Related to the Making Available of Literary and Artistic Works and Other Protected Subject

Matter Through Digital Networks. *UNESCO E-Copyright Bulletin, January–March*, 1–16.
von Lewinski, S. (2008). *International Copyright Law and Policy*. Oxford: OUP.
von Lewinski, S., & Walter, M. M. (2010). Information Society Directive. In M. M. Walter & S. von Lewinski (eds), *European Copyright Law. A Commentary*. Oxford: OUP.
Voorhoof, D., & Høedt-Rasmussen, I. (2013). Copyright vs Freedom of Expression: ECtHR (5th section), 10 January 2013, case of Ashby Donald and others v. France, Appl. nr. 36769/08. *ECHR Blog*. Retrieved from http://echrblog.blogspot.dk/2013/01/copyright-vs-freedom-of-expression.html.
Vousden, S. (2012). Airfield, Intermediaries and the Rescue of EU Copyright Law. *I.P.Q.*, *4*, 311–325.
Watal, J. (2001). *Intellectual Property Rights in the WTO and Developing Countries*. Springer.
Watson, S. J., Zizzo, D. J., & Fleming, P. (2014). Determinants and Welfare Inplications of Unlawful File Sharing: A Scoping Review. *CREATe Working Paper 2014/05.*
Westkamp, G. (2007). *Part II: The Implementation of Directive 2001/29/ EC in the Member States*. Study for the European Commission's Internal Market Directorate-General. London: Queen Mary Intellectual Property Research Institute.
Westkamp, G. (2008). The 'Three-Step Test'and Copyright Limitations: European Copyright Law Between Approximation and National Decision Making. *Journal of the Copyright Society of the U.S.A.*, *56*, 1–65.
Wiggin, & Entertainment Media Research. (2011). *2011 Digital Entertainment Survey. Full report.*
WIPO. (1996). *Implications of the TRIPS Agreement on Treaties Administered by WIPO (WIPO Publication No 464(E))*. Geneva: WIPO.
WIPO. (2012). *International Survey on Private Copying. Law & Practice 2012*. Geneva: WIPO.
WIPO. (2013). *International Survey on Private Copying. Law & Practice 2013*. Geneva: WIPO.
WIPO. (2014). *International Survey on Private Copying. Law & Practice 2013 (WIPO Publication No. 1037E/14)*. Geneva: World Intellectual Property Organization.
WIPO, & Stichting de Thuiskopie. (2016). *International Survey on Private Copying Law & Practice 2015*. Geneva: WIPO.
Wittem Group. (2010). European Copyright Code. *Journal of Intellectual Property, Information Technology and Electronic Commerce Law*, *1*(2), 123–128.
Wizards of OS. (2004). Berlin Declaration on Collectively Managed Online Rights: Compensation without Control. Available at http://www.wizards-of-os.org/index.php?id=1699.

Wright, B. D. (1983). The Economics of Invention Incentives: Patents, Prizes, and Research Contracts. *The American Economic Review*, *73*(4), 691–707.

Wright, R. (2009). The 'Three-Step Test' and the Wider Public Interest: Towards a More Inclusive Interpretation. *The Journal of World Intellectual Property*, *12*(6), 600–621.

Wu, T. (2007). Tolerated Use. *Columbia Journal of Law & the Arts*, *31*(4). 617–635.

Wu, T. (2011). *The Master Switch: The Rise and Fall of Information Empires*. Alfred A. Knopf.

Xalabarder, R. (2012). Spain. In R. Hilty & S. Nerisson (eds), *Balancing Copyright – A Survey of National Approaches*. Springer.

Xalabarder, R. (2014). A Bill to Amend the Spanish IP Law. *Kluwer Copyright Blog*. Date: 10 July 2014. Available at http://kluwercopyrightblog.com/2014/07/10/a-bill-to-amend-the-spanish-ip-law/.

Xalabarder, R. (2015). Spanish Supreme Court Rules in Favour of Google Search Engine. *Kluwer Copyright Blog*. Date: 15 June 2012. Available at http://kluwercopyrightblog.com/2012/06/15/spanish-supreme-court-rules-in-favor-of-google-search-engine/.

Yu, P. K. (2005). P2P and the Future of Private Copying. *University of Colorado Law Review*, *76*, 653–765.

Yu, P. K. (2010). The Graduated Response. *Florida Law Review*, *62*, 1373–1430.

Zelnik, P., Toubon, J., & Cerutti, G. (2010). *Creation et internet – Rapport au ministre de la culture et de la communication*.

Zittrain, J. (2008). *The Future of the Internet – And How to Stop It*. New Haven, London: Yale University Press.

Electronic Sources

AGICOA: Association of International Collective Management of Audiovisual Works, *Frequently asked questions*, http://www.agicoa.org/english/toolsandhelp/faq.html (accessed 31.01.2017).

Creative Commons, *NonCommercial interpretation*, https://wiki.creativecommons.org/wiki/NonCommercial_interpretation (accessed 31.01.2017).

Elsevier, *Journals, Poetics, Open access options, Embargo Period*, https://www.elsevier.com/journals/poetics/0304-422X/open-access-options#fee (accessed 31.01.2017).

Eurofund, *Industrial Relations Dictionary, Acquis Communautaire*, http://www.eurofound.europa.eu/observatories/eurwork/industrial-relations-dictionary/acquis-communautaire (accessed 31.01.2017).

EUR-Lex, *Sources of European Law*, http://eur-lex.europa.eu/legal-content/EN/TXT/?uri=uriserv:l14534 (accessed 31.01.2017).

EUROPEAN COMMISSION, *The EU Single Market, Copyright and Neighbouring Rights, Private copying levies*, http://ec.europa.eu/internal_market/copyright/levy_reform/index_en.htm (accessed 31.01.2017).

EUROPEAN COMMISSION, *The EU Single Market, Copyright and Neighboring Rights, Studies*, http://ec.europa.eu/internal_market/copyright/studies/index_en.htm (accessed 31.01.2017).

FREE SOFTWARE FOUNDATION, *About, What is Free Software*, http://www.fsf.org/about/what-is-free-software (accessed 31.01.2017).

GOOGLE ADSENSE, https://www.google.com/adsense/start/?hl=en&sourceid=aso&subid=ww-ww-et-op_adshp_ads_bt#?modal_active=none (accessed 31.01.2017).

INSTITUTE FOR INFORMATION LAW (IViR), *Research, Copyright in an Age of Access: Alternatives to Copyright Enforcement*, https://www.ivir.nl/projects/copyright-in-an-age-of-access-alternatives-to-copyright-enforcement/ (accessed 31.01.2017).

JULIA REDA, *EU copyright evaluation report – full current text*, https://juliareda.eu/copyright-evaluation-report/full/ (accessed 31.01.2017).

OPEN SOURCE INITIATIVE, *History of the OSI*, https://opensource.org/history (accessed 31.01.2017).

OXFORD ENGLISH DICTIONARY, *Caricature*, http://www.oed.com/view/Entry/27973?rskey=rPVzu8&result=1&isAdvanced=false#eid (accessed 31.01.2017).

OXFORD ENGLISH DICTIONARY, *Parody*, http://www.oed.com/view/Entry/138059?rskey=DnlSIH&result=2#eid (accessed 31.01.2017).

OXFORD ENGLISH DICTIONARY, *Pastiche*, http://www.oed.com/view/Entry/138594?rskey=9UlNNb&result=1&isAdvanced=false#eid (accessed 31.01.2017).

WILLIAM FISHER, *CopyrightX: Lecture 2.2, Fairness and Personality Theories: Fairness*, https://www.youtube.com/watch?v=HYJuhPf9s5k&feature=youtu.be (accessed 31.01.2017).

WILLIAM FISHER, *CopyrightX: Lecture 4.1, Welfare Theory: The Utilitarian Framework*, https://www.youtube.com/watch?v=3ISstJYsCWs&feature=youtu.be (accessed 31.01.2017).

WILLIAM FISHER, *CopyrightX: Lecture 4.2, Welfare Theory: The Incentive Theory of Copyright*, https://www.youtube.com/watch?v=t9wqQNCC-Vs&feature=youtu.be (accessed 31.01.2017).

WILLIAM FISHER, *CopyrightX: Lecture 4.3, Welfare Theory: Applications and Assessment*, https://www.youtube.com/watch?v=_xHEcRFlLok&feature=youtu.be (accessed 31.01.2017).

WILLIAM FISHER, *Economic Analysis of Law*, http://cyber.law.harvard.edu/people/tfisher/IP/EAL.swf (accessed 31.01.2017).

WIKIPEDIA, *Crowdsourcing*, https://en.wikipedia.org/wiki/Crowdsourcing (accessed 31.01.2017).

WIKIPEDIA, *Deadweight loss*, https://en.wikipedia.org/wiki/Deadweight_loss (accessed 31.01.2017).

WIKIPEDIA, *Download*, http://en.wikipedia.org/wiki/Download#cite_note-main-1 (accessed 31.01.2017).
WIKIPEDIA, *History of Broadcasting*, https://en.wikipedia.org/wiki/History_of_broadcasting (accessed 31.01.2017).
WIKIPEDIA, *Upload*, http://en.wikipedia.org/wiki/Upload (accessed 31.01.2017).
WIKIPEDIA, *Web browser*, http://en.wikipedia.org/wiki/Web_browser (accessed 31.01.2017).

Primary Sources: Legal Texts

International Treaties and Conventions

BC: Berne Convention for the Protection of Literary and Artistic Works, of 9 September 1886 (completed at Paris on 4 May 1896, revised at Berlin on 13 November 1908, completed at Berne on 20 March 1914, revised at Rome on 2 June 1928, at Brussels on 26 June 1948, at Stockholm on 14 July 1967, and at Paris on 24 July 1971, and amended on 28 September 1979).

Doha Declaration (2001): WTO, Ministerial Conference, Fourth Session, Doha, 9 – 14 November 2001, Ministerial Declaration of 14 November 2001, WT/MIN(01)/DEC/1, 20 November 2001.

International Covenant on Civil and Political Rights, 16 December 1966, United Nations, Treaty Series, vol. 999, p. 171.

ICESCR: International Covenant on Economic, Social and Cultural Rights, 16 December 1966, United Nations, Treaty Series, vol. 993, p. 3.

RC: International Convention for the Protection of Performers, Producers of Phonograms and Broadcasting Organisations, done at Rome on 26 October 1961.

TRIPS: Agreement on Trade Related Aspects of Intellectual Property Rights, 15 April 1994, Marrakesh Agreement Establishing the World Trade Organization, Annex 1C, The Legal Texts: The Results of The Uruguay Round Of Multilateral Trade Negotiations 320 (1999), 1869 U.N.T.S. 299, 33 I.L.M. 1197 (1994).

UDHR: Universal Declaration of Human Rights, adopted in Paris on 10 December 1948.

VCLT: Vienna Convention on the Law of Treaties, 1155 U.N.T.S. 331, 8 I.L.M. 679, entered into force 27 January 1980.

WCT: WIPO Copyright Treaty, adopted in Geneva on 20 December 1996.

WPPT: WIPO Performances and Phonograms Treaty, adopted in Geneva on 20 December 1996.

WIPO Beijing Treaty: Beijing Treaty on Audiovisual Performances (adopted by the Diplomatic Conference on the Protection of Audiovisual Performances in Beijing, on 24 June 2012).

WIPO Marrakesh Treaty: Marrakesh Treaty to Facilitate Access to Published Works for Persons Who Are Blind, Visually Impaired, or Otherwise Print Disabled (adopted by the Diplomatic Conference to Conclude a Treaty to Facilitate Access to Published Works by Visually Impaired Persons and Persons with Print Disabilities in Marrakesh, on 27 June 2013).

WTO Agreement: Marrakesh Agreement Establishing the World Trade Organization, 15 April 1994, The Legal Texts: The Results of The Uruguay Round Of Multilateral Trade Negotiations 4 (1999), 1867 U.N.T.S. 154, 33 I.L.M. 1144 (1994).

Proposed International Agreements Cited

ACTA: Anti-Counterfeiting Trade Agreement (Final Text dated May 2011), available at https://www.eff.org/document/final-text-acta-agreement-may-2011 (accessed 31.01.2017).

Council of Europe

ECHR: European Convention on Human Rights, signed in Rome on 4 November 1950.

European Union: Treaties and Charter

Charter: Charter of Fundamental Rights of the European Union, OJ C 364/1, 18.12.2000.

TEU: Treaty on European Union (Consolidated Version), Treaty of Maastricht, 7 February 1992, OJ EC C 325/5; 24.12.2002.

TFEU: Consolidated Version of the Treaty on the Functioning of the European Union, 5 September 2008, 2008 O.J. (C 115) 47.

European Union: Directives

AVMS Directive: Directive 2010/13/EU of the European Parliament and of the Council of 10 March 2010 on the coordination of certain provisions laid down by law, regulation or administrative action in Member States concerning the provision of audiovisual media services (Audiovisual Media Services Directive) (Text with EEA relevance) OJ L 95, 15.04.2010, pp. 1–24.

Consumer Rights Directive: Directive 2011/83/EU of the European Parliament and of the Council of 25 October 2011 on consumer rights, amending Council Directive 93/13/EEC and Directive 1999/44/EC of the European Parliament and of the Council and repealing Council Directive 85/577/EEC and Directive 97/7/EC of the European Parliament and of the Council, OJ L 304, 22.11.2011, p. 64–88.

CRM Directive: Directive 2014/26/EU of the European Parliament and of the Council of 26 February 2014 on collective management of copyright and related rights and multi-territorial licensing of rights in musical works for online use in the internal market, OJ L 84, 20.03.2014, p. 72–98.

Database Directive: Directive 96/9/EC of the European Parliament and of the Council of 11 March 1996 on the legal protection of databases, OJ L 77/20, 27.03.1996.

Data Protection Directive: Directive 95/46/EC of the European Parliament and of the Council of 24 October 1995 on the protection of individuals with regard to the processing of personal data and on the free movement of such data, OJ L 281, 23.11.1995 P. 0031 – 0050.

Enforcement Directive: Directive 2004/48/EC of the European Parliament and of the Council of 29 April 2004 on the enforcement of intellectual property rights, OJ L 157, 30.04.2004.

E-Commerce Directive: Directive 2000/31/EC of the European Parliament and of the Council of 8 June 2000 on certain legal aspects of information society services, in particular electronic commerce, in the Internal Market, OJ L 178, 17.7.2000.

E-Privacy Directive: Directive 2002/58/EC of the European Parliament and of the Council of 12 July 2002 concerning the processing of personal data and the protection of privacy in the electronic communications sector (Directive on privacy and electronic communications), OJ L 201, 31.07.2002.

Framework Directive: Council Directive 2002/21 of 7 March 2002 on a common regulatory framework for electronic communications networks and services as amended by Directive 2009/140/EC and Regulation 544/2009.

InfoSoc Directive: Directive 2001/29/EC of 22 May 2001 on the harmonisation of certain aspects of copyright and related rights in the information society, OJ L 167/10, 22.06.2001.

Orphan Works Directive: Directive 2012/28/EU of the European Parliament and of the Council of 25 October 2012 on certain permitted uses of orphan works.

Rental Right Directive: Council Directive 92/100/EEC, of 19 November 1992 on rental right and lending right and on certain rights related to copyright in the field of intellectual property, 1992 O.J. (L 346/61) as republished and amended by Directive 2006/115/EC of the European

Parliament and of the Council of 12 December 2006 (codified version), 2006 O.J. (L 376/28).

Resale Right Directive: Directive 2001/84/EC of the European parliament and of the Council of 27 September 2001 on the resale right for the benefit of the author of an original work of art, OJ L 272/32, 13.10.2001.

SatCab Directive: Council Directive 93/83/EEC of 27 September 1993 on the coordination of certain rules concerning copyright and rights related to copyright applicable to satellite broadcasting and cable retransmission, OJ L 248/15, 06.10.1993.

Software Directive: Council Directive 91/250/EEC, of 14 May 1991 on the legal protection of computer programs, 1991 O.J. (L 122/42), as republished and amended by Directive 2009/24/EC, of the European Parliament and of the Council of 23 April 2009 (codified version), 2009 O.J. (L 111/16).

Term Directive: Directive 2006/116/EC of the European Parliament and of the Council of 12 December 2006 on the term of protection of copyright and certain related rights, 2006 O.J. (L 372/12), as amended by Directive 2011/77/EU of the European Parliament and of the Council of 27 September 2011, 2011 O.J. (L 265/1).

European Union: Proposed Legislation

Proposal for a Regulation of the European Parliament and of the Council on ensuring the cross-border portability of online content services in the internal market, COM/2015/0627 final – 2015/0284 (COD).

Proposal for a Directive of the European Parliament and of the Council on copyright in the Digital Single Market, COM(2016)593.

Proposal for a Directive of the European Parliament and the Council on certain aspects concerning contracts for the supply of digital content, COM/2015/0634 final – 2015/0287 (COD).

National Legislation

Austria

Austrian Copyright Act: Bundesgesetz über das Urheberrecht an Werken der Literatur und der Kunst und über verwandte Schutzrechte (Urheberrechtsgesetz) (zuletzt geändert durch das Bundesgesetz BGBl. I. Nr. 99/2015) [Federal Law on Copyright in Literary and Artistic Works and Related Rights (Copyright Act) (as amended up to Federal Law Gazette (BGBl) I No. 99/2015)], available at http://www.wipo.int/wipolex/en/details.jsp?id=15941 (accessed 31.01.2017).

Canada

Canadian Copyright Act: Copyright Act (R.S.C., 1985, c. C-42) (consolidated version, status as at 31 March 2015), available at http://www.wipo.int/wipolex/en/details.jsp?id=15561 (accessed 31.01.2017).

Denmark

Danish Copyright Act: Consolidated Act on Copyright 2010 (Consolidated Act No. 202 of 27 February 2010), available at http://www.wipo.int/wipolex/en/details.jsp?id=7394 (accessed 31.01.2017).

France

French Intellectual Property Code: Code de la propriété intellectuelle (version consolidée au 1er janvier 2014) [Intellectual Property Code (consolidated version of 1 January 2014)], available at http://www.wipo.int/wipolex/en/details.jsp?id=14082 (accessed 31.01.2017).

Loi No. 2009-669 du 12 juin 2009 favorisant la diffusion et la protection de la création sur internet [Law No. 2009-669 of 12 June 2009, promoting the Dissemination and Protection of Creation on the Internet], available at http://www.wipo.int/wipolex/en/details.jsp?id=5613 (accessed 31.01.2017) [HADOPI Law].

Loi No. 2009-1311 du 28 octobre 2009 [Law No. 2009-1311 of 28 October 2009] (amends the HADOPI Law), available at http://www.wipo.int/wipolex/en/details.jsp?id=14292 (accessed 31.01.2017).

Loi No. 2011-1898 du 20 décembre 2011 relative à la rémunération pour copie privée [Law No. 2011-1898 of 20 December 2011, on Private Copying Remuneration], available at http://www.wipo.int/wipolex/en/details.jsp?id=12749 (accessed 31.01.2017).

Decree No. 2013-596 of 8 July 2013, removing the Complementary Penalty of Suspending Access to an On-Line Public Communication Service and relating to the Information Transmission Methods provided for in Article L. 331-21 of the Intellectual Property Code, available at http://www.wipo.int/wipolex/en/details.jsp?id=13838 (accessed 31.01.2017).

Germany

German Copyright Act (Current): Gesetz über Urheberrecht und verwandte Schutzrechte (Urheberrechtsgesetz, geändert durch Gesetzes vom 4. April 2016) [Act on Copyright and Related Rights (Copyright Act, as amended up to Act of 4 April 2016)], available at http://www.wipo.int/wipolex/en/details.jsp?id=16047 (accessed 31.01.2017).

Italy

Italian Copyright Act: Legge 22 aprile 1941, n. 633 sulla protezione del diritto d'autore e di altri diritti connessi al suo esercizio (aggiornata con le modifiche introdotte dal decreto-legge 30 aprile 2010, n. 64) [Law No. 633 of 22 April 1941, for the Protection of Copyright and Neighbouring Rights (as amended up to Decree-law No. 64 of 30 April 2010)], available at http://www.wipo.int/wipolex/en/details.jsp?id=13133 (accessed 31.01.2017).

Netherlands

Dutch Act: Wet van 23 september 1912, houdende nieuwe regeling van het auteursrecht (Auteurswet 1912, tekst geldend op: 01-07-2015) [Act of 23 September 1912, containing New Regulation for Copyright (Copyright Act 1912, as amended up to 1 July 2015)], available at http://www.wipo.int/wipolex/en/details.jsp?id=15987 (accessed 31.01.2017).

Norway

Norwegian Copyrigth Act: Copyright Act (Act No. 2 of 12 May 1961, relating to Copyright in Literary, Scientific and Artistic Works) (consolidated version of 2015), available at http://www.wipo.int/wipolex/en/details.jsp?id=15949 (accessed 31.01.2017).

Spain

Spanish Intellectual Property Law: Ley N° 21/2014, de 4 de noviembre, por la que se modifica el texto refundido de la Ley de Propiedad Intelectual aprobado por Real Decreto Legislativo 1/1996, de 12 de abril, y la Ley 1/2000, de 7 de enero, de Enjuiciamiento Civil [Law No. 21/2014 of 4 November 2014, amending the Consolidated Text of the Law on Intellectual Property, approved by Royal Legislative Decree No. 1/1996 of April 12, 1996, and Law No. 1/2000 of 7 January 2000, on Civil Procedure], available at http://www.wipo.int/wipolex/en/details.jsp?id=15435 (accessed 31.01.2017).

Royal Decree No. 1657/2012 of 7 December 2012: Real Decreto 1657/2012 que regula el procedimiento para el pago de la compensación por copia privada con cargo a los Presupuestos Generales del Estado [Royal Decree 1657/2012 regulating the procedure for paying fair compensation in respect of private copying from the General State Budget] of 7 December 2012 (BOE No 295 of 8 December 2012, p. 84 141).

US

US Copyright Act: 17 U.S.C. §§ 101–810, available at http://www.copyright.gov/title17/ (accessed 31.01.2017).

Audio Home Recording Act of 1992, Pub.L. No. 102-563, 106 Stat. 4237 (1992) (codified as 17 U.S.C. §§ 1001 – 1010).

Proposed US Legislative Acts

Stop Online Piracy Act (SOPA): HR 3261 (2011), https://www.congress.gov/bill/112th-congress/house-bill/3261 (accessed 31.01.2017).
Senate Bill 968, PROTECT IP Act (2011), https://www.congress.gov/bill/112th-congress/senate-bill/968 (accessed 31.01.2017).

Secondary Sources

International Documents (Records of Treaties and Conventions)

Records BC 1884: *Actes de la Conférence Internationale pour la protection des droits d'auteur : réunie à Berne du 8 au 19 septembre 1884* (Berne : Imprimerie K.-J. Wyss, 1884).

Records BC Rome 1928: *Actes de la Conférence réunie a Rome du 7 Mai au 2 Juin 1928* (Berne: Bureau de l'Union Internationale pour la Protection Des Œuvres Littéraires et Artistiques, 1929).

Records BC Brussels 1948: *Documents de la Conférence réunie a Bruxelles du 5 au 26 Juin 1948* (Berne: Bureau de l'Union Internationale pour la Protection Des Œuvres Littéraires et Artistiques, 1951).

Records BC Stockholm 1967: *Actes de la Conférence de Stockholm de le propriété intellectuelle : 11 juin–14 juillet 1967 : Records of the intellectual property conference of Stockholm : June 11 to July 14*, 2 vols (Geneva: OMPI/WIPO, 1971).

Records RC 1961: Records of the Diplomatic Conference on the International Protection of Performers, Producers of Phonograms and Broadcasting Organizations, Rome 10 to 26 October 1961, WIPO publication No. 326 (E), WIPO/BIRPI: Geneva 1968 (reprint 1995).

Records WIPO Treaties 1996: Records of the Diplomatic Conference on Certain Copyright and Neighboring Rights Questions 1996, WIPO Publication 348 (WIPO: Geneva 1999).

WIPO Document BCP/CE/I/3, Committee of Experts on a Possible Protocol to the Berne Convention for the Protection of Artistic and Literary Works – Questions Concerning a Possible Protocol to the Berne Convention Part II (Draft), Memorandum Prepared by the International

Bureau, 8 October 1991, http://www.wipo.int/mdocsarchives/BCP_CE_I_1991/BCP_CE_I_3_E.pdf.

WIPO Document BCP/CE/II/1, Committee of Experts on a Possible Protocol to the Berne Convention for the Protection of Artistic and Literary Works – Draft Report submitted by the International Bureau of the World Intellectual Property Organization (WIPO), 17 February 1992, http://www.wipo.int/mdocsarchives/BCP_CE_II_1992/BCP_CE_II_1%20Prov_E.pdf.

EU: Proposals and Explanatory Memoranda

Proposal InfoSoc Directive 1997: Explanatory Memorandum to the Proposal for a European Parliament and Council Directive on Harmonisation of Certain Aspects of Copyright and Related Rights in the Information Society, COM (1997) 628 final- COD 97/0359, Brussels, 10.12.1997.

Amended Proposal InfoSoc Directive 1999: Amended proposal for a European Parliament and Council Directive on the harmonisation of certain aspects of copyright and related rights in the Information Society, COM/99/0250 final – COD 97/0359.

Proposal InfoSoc Directive, Adoption by Commission of opinion on EP amendments on 2nd reading, COM/2001/0170 final.

Commission Opinion pursuant to Article 251 (2) (c) of the EC Treaty, on the European Parliament's amendments to the Council's common position regarding the proposal for a Directive of the European Parliament and of the Council on the harmonisation of certain aspects of copyright and related rights in the information society amending the proposal of the Commission pursuant to Article 250 (2) of the EC Treaty, COM/2001/0170 final – COD 97/0359, 29.03.2001.

Explanatory Memorandum SatCab Directive: Proposal for a Council Directive on the coordination of certain rules concerning copyright and neighbouring rights applicable to satellite broadcasting and cable retransmission, COM(91) 276 final – SYN 358, 11 September 1991.

Explanatory Memorandum Rental Right Directive: Explanatory Memorandum to the Proposal for a Council Directive on rental right, lending right, and on certain rights related to copyright, COM (1990) 586 final-SYN 319, Brussels, 24.01.1991.

Amended proposal Rental Right Directive 1992: Amended proposal for a Council Directive on rental right and lending right and on certain rights related to copyright in the field of intellectual property. COM (92) 159 final, 30.04.1992.

Amended proposal for a Directive of the European Parliament and of the Council on criminal measures aimed at ensuring the enforcement of intellectual property rights, COM/2006/0168 final – COD 2005/0127. (Withdrawal published in OJ C 252, 18.09.2010, p. 7–11).

Proposal CRM Directive: Proposal for a Directive of the European Parliament and of the Council on collective management of copyright and related rights and multi-territorial licensing of rights in musical works for online uses in the internal market, COM/2012/0372 final – 2012/0180 (COD), Brussels, 11.07.2012.

Proposal for a Regulation of the European Parliament and of the Council on ensuring the cross-border portability of online content services in the internal market, COM(2015) 627 final, 2015/0284 (COD).

EU: Commission Recommendations

Online Music Recommendation 2005: Commission Recommendation 2005/737/EC of 18 October 2005 on collective cross-border management of copyright and related rights for legitimate online music services, OJ L 276/54, 21.10.2005.

Recommendation on Digitisation, Online Accessibility and Digital Preservation 2006: Commission Recommendation 2006/585/EC of 24 August 2006 on the digitisation and online accessibility of cultural material and digital preservation, OJ L 236/28, 31.08.2006.

Recommendation on Access to and Preservation of Scientific Information 2012: Commission Recommendation 2012/417/EU of 17 July 20012 on access to and preservation of scientific information, OJ L 194, 21.07.2012, p. 39–43.

EU: Public Consultations and Reports

Report on the Public Lending Right in the EU 2002: Report from the Commission to the Council, the European Parliament and the Economic and Social Committee on the Public Lending Right in the European Union, COM (2002) 502 final, Brussels, 12.09.2002.

Report SatCab Directive: Report from the European Commission on the application of Council Directive 93/83/EEC on the coordination of certain rules concerning copyright and rights related to copyright applicable to satellite broadcasting and cable retransmission, COM (2002) 430 final, Brussels, 26.07.2002.

Report Enforcement Directive 2010: Report from the Commission to the European Parliament, the Council, the European Economic and Social Committee and the Committee of the Regions Application of Directive 2004/48/EC of the European Parliament and the Council of 29 April 2004 on the enforcement of intellectual property rights, COM/2010/0779 final.

Public Consultation on the review of the EU copyright rules, launched 5 December 2013, available at http://ec.europa.eu/internal_market/consultations/2013/copyright-rules/ (accessed 31.01.2017).

Report Public Consultation on the Review of the EU Copyright Rules 2014: Report on the responses to the Public Consultation on the Review of the

EU Copyright Rules, Directorate General Internal Market and Services, Directorate D – Intellectual property, D1 – Copyright, July 2014, available at: http://ec.europa.eu/internal_market/consultations/2013/copyright-rules/docs/contributions/consultation-report_en.pdf (accessed 31.01.2017).

EU: Green Papers, White Papers, Working Papers, and Memos

Green Paper on Copyright and the Challenge of Technology 1988: European Commission, 'Copyright and the Challenge of Technology', Green Paper, COM (88) 172 final, Brussels, 07.06.1988.

Follow-up Green Paper 1990**:** Follow-up Green Paper – Working Programme of the Commission in the Field of Copyright and Neighbouring Rights, COM (90) 584 final, 17.01.1991.

Green Paper on Copyright and Related Rights in the Information Society 1995: European Commission, 'Copyright and Related Rights in the Information Society', Green Paper, COM (95) 382 final, Brussels, 19.07.1995.

Follow-up Green Paper 1996: Follow-up to the Green Paper on copyright and related rights in the Information Society, COM(96) 586 final.

Green Paper 'Television Without Frontiers'**:** European Commission, 'Television without Frontiers', Green Paper, COM (84) def, Brussels, 14.06.1984.

SWD Analysis Application Enforcement Directive 2004: Commission Staff Working Document – Analysis of the application of Directive 2004/48/EC of the European Parliament and the Council of 29 April 2004 on the enforcement of intellectual property rights in the Member States – Accompanying document to the Report from the Commission to the Council, the European Parliament and the European Social Committee on the application of Directive 2004/48/EC of the European Parliament and the Council of 29 April 2004 on the enforcement of intellectual property rights.

SWD Cross-Border Collective Management of Copyright 2005: Commission Staff Working Document, Study on a Community Initiative on the Cross-Border Collective Management of Copyright, Brussels, 07.07.2005.

Green Paper Copyright in the Knowledge Economy 2008: Green Paper Copyright in the Knowledge Economy, COM(2008) 466/3, Brussels, 16.07.2008.

Green Paper on Online Distribution of Audiovisual Works 2011: Commission Green paper on the online distribution of Audiovisual works in the European Union: opportunities and challenges towards a single digital market, Brussels, COM (2011) 427 final (13.07.2011).

SWD CRM Directive 2012: Commission Staff Working Document Impact Assessment Accompanying the document Proposal for a Directive of the

European Parliament and of the Council on collective management of copyright and related rights and multi-territorial licensing of rights in musical works for online uses in the internal market, SWD(2012) 204 final, Brussels, 11.07.2012.

SWD CRM Directive – Executive Summary 2012: Commission Staff Working Document Executive Summary of the Impact Assessment Accompanying the document Proposal for a Directive of the European Parliament and of the Council on the collective management of copyright and related rights and multi-territorial licensing of rights in musical works for online uses in the internal market, SWD(2012) 205 final, Brussels, 11.07.2012.

SWD E-commerce Action plan 2012–2015 – State of play 2013: Commission Staff Working Document E-commerce Action plan 2012–2015 – State of play 2013, SWD(2013) 153 final, 23.04.2013.

Memo CRM Directive FAQ 2014: European Commission MEMO, Directive on collective management of copyright and related rights and multi-territorial licensing – frequently asked questions, Brussels, 04.02.2014, http://europa.eu/rapid/press-release_MEMO-14-79_en.htm.

SWD Digital Single Market Strategy 2015: Commission Staff Working Document A Digital Single Market Strategy for Europe – Analysis and Evidence, SWD(2015) 100 final (06.05.2015).

Memo Digital Single Market Strategy 2015: Memo/15/4920, Q&A – DSM Strategy (Brussels, 06.05.2015).

Press release, *A Digital Single Market for Europe: Commission sets out 16 initiatives to make it happen, Brussels*, 06.05.2015 (IP/15/4919).

EU: Communications of the Commission

Communication on Creative Content Online 2008: Communication from the Commission to the European Parliament, the Council, the European Economic and Social Committee and the Committee of the Regions, on Creative Content Online in a Single Market, COM (2007) 836 final (03.01.2008).

Communication on Enforcement of IPRs 2009: Communication from the Commission to the Council, the European Parliament and the European Economic and Social Committee – Enhancing the enforcement of intellectual property rights in the internal market, COM/2009/0467 final 6.

Communication IPR Strategy 2011: Communication from the Commission to the European Parliament, the Council, the European Economic and Social Committee and the Committee of the Regions, on a Single Market for Intellectual Property Rights boosting creativity and innovation to provide economic growth, high quality jobs and first class products and services in Europe, COM(2011) 287 final (24.05.2011).

Communication on Content in the Digital Single Market 2012: Communication from the Commission on Content in the Digital Single Market, COM/2012/0789 final.
Communication on a Digital Single Market 2015: Communication from the Commission to the European Parliament, the Council, the European Economic and Social Committee and the Committee of the Regions, A Digital Single Market Strategy for Europe, COM(2015) 192 final (06.05.2015).
Communication on Modern European Copyright Framework 2015: Communication from the Commission to the European Parliament, the Council, the European Economic and Social Committee and the Committee of the Regions, Towards a modern, more European copyright framework, COM(2015) 626 final (09.12.2015).

EU: Council Decisions, Resolutions and Guidelines

Council Decision 2000/278/EC: 2000/278/EC: Council Decision of 16 March 2000 on the approval, on behalf of the European Community, of the WIPO Copyright Treaty and the WIPO Performances and Phonograms Treaty, OJ L 089, 11.04.2000 P. 0006 – 0007.
Council Resolution of 25 September 2008 on a comprehensive European anti-counterfeiting and anti-piracy plan, OJ C 253 of 04.10.2008.
Council Resolution of 1 March 2010 on the enforcement of intellectual property rights in the internal market (2010/C 56/01).

EU: European Parliament

EP Resolution Proposal InfoSoc Directive (1st reading) 1999: Legislative resolution embodying Parliament's opinion on the proposal for a European Parliament and Council Directive on the harmonisation of certain aspects of copyright and related rights in the Information Society (COM(97)0628 C4-0079/98 97/0359(COD))(Codecision procedure: first reading), OJ C 150, 28.05.1999, p. 171.
Position of the European Parliament adopted at first reading on 25 April 2007 with a view to the adoption of Directive 2007/.../EC of the European Parliament and of the Council on criminal measures aimed at ensuring the enforcement of intellectual property rights (EP-PE_TC1-COD(2005)0127).
EP Resolution on ACTA Negotiations 2010: European Parliament, Resolution of on the transparency and state of play of the ACTA negotiations, P7_TA(2010)0058, 2010.
EP Resolution IPR Enforcement 2010: European Parliament resolution of 22 September 2010 on enforcement of intellectual property rights in the internal market (2009/2178(INI)).
Castex Report 2013: Draft Report on private copying levies, 2013/2114(INI), Committee on Legal Affairs (Rapporteur: Françoise Castex).

EP Resolution on ACTA Rejection 2012: European Parliament legislative resolution of 4 July 2012 on the draft Council decision on the conclusion of the Anti-Counterfeiting Trade Agreement between the European Union and its Member States, Australia, Canada, Japan, the Republic of Korea, the United Mexican States, the Kingdom of Morocco, New Zealand, the Republic of Singapore, the Swiss Confederation and the United States of America (12195/2011 – C7-0027/2012 – 2011/0167(NLE)).

EP Resolution Private Copying Levies 2014: European Parliament resolution of 27 February 2014 on private copying levies (2013/2114(INI)).

EP Resolution Implementation InfoSoc Directive 2015: European Parliament resolution of 9 July 2015 on the implementation of Directive 2001/29/EC of the European Parliament and of the Council of 22 May 2001 on the harmonisation of certain aspects of copyright and related rights in the information society (2014/2256(INI)).

Common Positions and Common Statements

Common Position (EC) No. 48/2000: Common Position (EC) No. 48/2000 of 28 September 2000, (2000/C 344/01), OJ C 344, 01.12.2000 P. 0001 – 0022.

Common Statement by the Council and Commission at the internal market Council meeting of 18 June 1992.

Council of Europe Recommendations

Council of Europe Recommendation No. R (88) 2: Recommendation No. R (88) 2 of the Committee of Ministers to Member States on measures to combat piracy in the field of copyright and neighbouring rights (Adopted by the Committee of Ministers on 18 January 1988, at the 414th meeting of the Ministers' Deputies).

Council of Europe Recommendation CM/Rec(2008) 6: Recommendation CM/Rec(2008)6 of the Committee of Ministers to Member States on measures to promote the respect for freedom of expression and information with regard to Internet filters (Adopted by the Committee of Ministers on 26 March 2008 at the 1022nd meeting of the Ministers' Deputies).

Table of Cases

Alphabetically ordered. When available, citations refer to the European Case Law Identifier (ECLI)

European Court of Human Rights (ECtHR)

Court of Justice of the European Union (CJEU): Judgments

Court of Justice of the European Union (CJEU): References for Preliminary Ruling

Court of Justice of the European Union (CJEU): Advocate General (AG) Opinions

Commission Decisions

World Trade Organization (WTO) Panel Reports

National Cases

Belgium

France

Germany

Spain

Switzerland

The Netherlands

United Kingdom

Index

V

W

INFORMATION LAW SERIES

1. Egbert J. Dommering & P. Bernt Hugenholtz, *Protecting Works of Fact: Copyright, Freedom of Expression and Information Law,* 1991 (ISBN 90-654-4567-6).
2. Willem F. Korthals Altes, Egbert J. Dommering, P. Bernt Hugenholtz & Jan J.C. Kabel, *Information Law Towards the 21st Century,* 1992 (ISBN 90-654-4627-3).
3. Jacqueline M.B. Seignette, *Challenges to the Creator Doctrine: Authorship, Copyright Ownership and the Exploitation of Creative Works in the Netherlands, Germany and The United States,* 1994 (ISBN 90-654-4876-4).
4. P. Bernt Hugenholtz, *The Future of Copyright in a Digital Environment, Proceedings of the Royal Academy Colloquium,* 1996 (ISBN 90-411-0267-1).
5. Julius C.S. Pinckaers, *From Privacy Toward a New Intellectual Property Right in Persona,* 1996 (ISBN 90-411-0355-4).
6. Jan J.C. Kabel & Gerard J.H.M. Mom, *Intellectual Property and Information Law: Essays in Honour of Herman Cohen Jehoram,* 1998 (ISBN 90-411-9702-8).
7. Ysolde Gendreau, Axel Nordemann & Rainer Oesch, *Copyright and Photographs: An International Survey,* 1999 (ISBN 90-411-9722-2).
8. P. Bernt Hugenholtz, *Copyright and Electronic Commerce: Legal Aspects of Electronic Copyright Management,* 2000 (ISBN 90-411-9785-0).
9. Lucie M.C.R. Guibault, *Copyright Limitations and Contracts: An Analysis of the Contractual Overridability of Limitations on Copyright,* 2002 (ISBN 90-411-9867-9).
10. Lee A. Bygrave, *Data Protection Law: Approaching its Rationale, Logic and Limits,* 2002 (ISBN 90-411-9870-9).
11. Niva Elkin-Koren & Neil Weinstock Netanel, *The Commodification of Information,* 2002 (ISBN 90-411-9876-8).
12. Mireille M.M. van Eechoud, *Choice of Law in Copyright and Related Rights: Alternatives to the Lex Protectionis,* 2003 (ISBN 90-411-2071-8).
13. Martin Senftleben, *Copyright, Limitations and the Three-Step Test: An Analysis of the Three-Step Test in International and EC Copyright Law,* 2004 (ISBN 90-411-2267-2).
14. Paul L.C. Torremans, *Copyright and Human Rights: Freedom of Expression – Intellectual Property – Privacy,* 2004 (ISBN 90-411-2278-8).
15. Natali Helberger, *Controlling Access to Content: Regulating Conditional Access in Digital Broadcasting,* 2005 (ISBN 90-411-2345-8).
16. Lucie M.C.R. Guibault & P. Bernt Hugenholtz, *The Future of the Public Domain: Identifying the Commons in Information Law,* 2006 (ISBN 978-90-411-2435-7).

17. Irini Katsirea, *Public Broadcasting and European Law: A Comparative Examination of Public Service Obligations in Six Member States,* 2008 (ISBN 978-90-411-2500-2).
18. Paul L.C. Torremans, *Intellectual Property and Human Rights: Enhanced Edition of Copyright and Human Rights,* 2008 (ISBN 978-90-411-2653-5).
19. Mireille van Eechoud, P. Bernt Hugenholtz, Stef van Gompel, Lucie Guibault & Natali Helberger, *Harmonizing European Copyright Law: The Challenges of Better Lawmaking,* 2009 (ISBN 978-90-411-3130-0).
20. Ashwin van Rooijen, *The Software Interface between Copyright and Competition Law: A Legal Analysis of Interoperability in Computer Programs,* 2010 (ISBN 978-90-411-3193-5).
21. Irini A. Stamatoudi, *Copyright Enforcement and the Internet,* 2010 (ISBN 978-90-411-3346-5).
22. Wolfgang Sakulin, *Trademark Protection and Freedom of Expression: An Inquiry into the Conflict between Trademark Rights and Freedom of Expression under European Law,* 2011 (ISBN 978-90-411-3415-8).
23. Stef van Gompel, *Formalities in Copyright Law: An Analysis of their History, Rationales and Possible Future,* 2011 (ISBN 978-90-411-3418-9).
24. Nadezhda Purtova, *Property Rights in Personal Data: A European Perspective,* 2012 (ISBN 978-90-411-3802-6).
25. Brad Sherman & Leanne Wiseman, *Copyright and the Challenge of the New,* 2012 (ISBN 978-90-411-3669-5).
26. Ewa Komorek, *Media Pluralism and European Law*, 2012 (ISBN 978-90-411-3894-1).
27. Joris van Hoboken, *Search Engine Freedom: On the Implications of the Right to Freedom of Expression for the Legal Governance of Web Search Engines,* 2012 (ISBN 978-90-411-4128-6).
28. Natali Helberger, Lucie Guibault, Marco Loos, Chantal Mak, Lodewijk Pessers & Bart van der Sloot, *Digital Consumers and the Law: Towards a Cohesive European Framework*, 2012 (ISBN 978-90-411-4049-4).
29. Tatiana-Eleni Synodinou, *Codification of European Copyright Law: Challenges and Perspectives,* 2012 (ISBN 978-90-411-4145-3).
30. Heather Ann Forrest, *Protection of Geographic Names in International Law and Domain Name System Policy*, Second Edition, 2017 (ISBN 978-90-411-8839-7).
31. Sari Depreeuw, *The Variable Scope of the Exclusive Economic Rights in Copyright*, 2014 (ISBN 978-90-411-4915-2).
32. Vikrant Narayan Vasudeva, *Open Source Software and Intellectual Property Rights*, 2014 (ISBN 978-90-411-5228-2).

33. Frederik J. Zuiderveen Borgesius, *Improving Privacy Protection in the Area of Behavioural Targeting*, 2015 (ISBN 978-90-411-5990-8).
34. Paul L.C. Torremans, *Intellectual Property Law and Human Rights*, Third Edition, 2015 (ISBN 978-90-411-5836-9).
35. Irini A. Stamatoudi, *New Developments in EU and International Copyright Law*, 2016 (ISBN 978-90-411-5991-5).
36. Lodewijk W.P. Pessers, *The Inventiveness Requirement in Patent Law: An Exploration of Its Foundations and Functioning*, 2016 (ISBN 978-90-411-6731-6).
37. Susy Frankel & Daniel Gervais, *The Internet and the Emerging Importance of New Forms of Intellectual Property*, 2016 (ISBN 978-90-411-6789-7).
38. Axel M. Arnbak, *Securing Private Communications: Protecting Private Communications Security in EU Law – Fundamental Rights, Functional Value Chains, and Market Incentives*, 2016 (ISBN 978-90-411-6737-8).
39. Christina Angelopoulos, *European Intermediary Liability in Copyright: A Tort-Based Analysis*, 2017 (ISBN 978-90-411-6835-1).
40. João Pedro Quintais, *Copyright in the Age of Online Access: Alternative Compensation Systems in EU Law*, 2017 (ISBN 978-90-411-8667-6).